Health Care
and the Law

HEALTH CARE AND THE LAW

4TH NEW ZEALAND EDITION

REBECCA KEENAN
(GENERAL EDITOR)

CONTRIBUTING AUTHORS
LOUISA CLERY
KATHRYN DALZIEL
GLENYS GODLOVITCH
SUE JOHNSON
DAVID KERSLAKE
ANNE O'BRIEN
JACKIE PEARSE
ROBERT F B PERRY
AUSTIN POWELL
CLARE PRENDERGAST
TREVOR WARR

PUBLISHED BY:
Brookers Ltd
Level 1, Guardian Trust House
15 Willeston St
Wellington

© 2010 Brookers Ltd

ISBN 978-0-86472-685-8

Typeset by Brookers XBook Processor
Printed by Printlink, Wellington, New Zealand

AUTHORS

General Editor

Rebecca Keenan DipN / BN/ LLB/ MA Medical Ethics and Law

Rebecca Keenan began training as a nurse in 1984 and commenced her practice as a nurse at Wanganui Base Hospital in 1987. Since then she has practised as a nurse in several countries but it was not until her return from Saudi Arabia in 1997 that she commenced study for her Bachelor of Nursing, which she did by correspondence through Massey University. It was during this period of study that her interest in law, specifically Health law, was stimulated. In 2001 she commenced her Bachelor of Law at Canterbury University while working as a nurse at Christchurch Hospital. In 2005 she I was admitted to the High Court of New Zealand as a Barrister and Solicitor. For 2 years she worked for the NZ Nurses Organisation on their legal team dealing mainly with competency and health issues under the newly enacted Health Practitioner's Competence Assurance Act 2003. From there she went to London where she read for her Master's in Medical Ethics and Law at King's College London. Rebecca returned to New Zealand in late 2008 and since her return she has begun her own practice as a Barrister Sole specialising in Health Law.

Contributing Authors

Louisa Clery

Louisa Clery works as an employment writer for Thomson Reuters. She has spent the last 18 years editing and writing about employment law and occupational health and safety, both in the UK and New Zealand. Louisa is responsible for updating a range of publications in the Brooker's people management portfolio — most of which are available in a variety of media including hard-copy and online. She also writes news and articles for other Thomson Reuters publications, including *employment today* magazine and the Alert24 People Management daily news service.

Kathryn Dalziel LLB (Cant)

Kathryn Dalziel was admitted to the legal profession in 1989 and is an Associate with Taylor Shaw, Barristers and Solicitors, Christchurch, specialising in Civil Litigation, Employment, and Privacy. She is also a part-time law lecturer at the University of Canterbury College of Law, teaching Legal Ethics. Kathryn is a member of the NZLS Human Rights and Privacy Committee, a member of a NZLS Standards Committee (Canterbury-Westland) and a member of the NZLS (Canterbury–Westland) Ethics Committee. From 2004 until 2009, Kathryn was employed as a Crown Prosecutor in Christchurch. Kathryn is one of New Zealand's leading privacy lawyers and has been employed by the Office of the Privacy Commissioner as a seminar presenter since 1996. She has written "Privacy in schools: a guide to the Privacy Act for principals, teachers and boards of trustees" (Office of the Privacy Commissioner, 2009).

Glenys Godlovitch BA(Hons) (London), LLB, PhD (Hons) (Calgary)

Glenys Godlovitch is a practising lawyer and philosopher. She is Associate Professor of Bioethics in the Faculty of Medicine at the University of Calgary, Canada, where she is a research ethicist and teacher of medical students. Retaining close ties with New Zealand health care law and ethics, Glenys was ethicist on the Canterbury Ethics Committee from 1996 to 2002.

Sue Johnson SRN, RSCN (England and Wales), LLB (Hons) (Cant)

Sue Johnson was the general editor of the first three New Zealand editions of Health Care and the Law. She retired from this role due to her work commitments as a full time Coroner. Sue was appointed as a Coroner under the Coroners Act 2006. She is one of two Regional Coroners who currently cover the greater Christchurch area, Nelson, Marlborough, Tasman, North and South Canterbury, the West Coast and the Ross Dependency. Sue trained and worked as a nurse in the 1970's and 1980's at the Liverpool Royal Infirmary and the Royal Liverpool Childrens' Hospital in Liverpool, England. She then gained a first class honours degree in law from the University of Canterbury, and in 1993 was admitted as a barrister and solicitor of the High Court of New Zealand. She worked as a solicitor in the areas of health law, civil litigation and criminal law, lectured the Medical Law Course at the University of Canterbury, and also tutored Criminal Law and the Law of Evidence. Between 1996 and 2002 she chaired the Canterbury Ethics Committee. From 2000 up until her appointment as a Coroner, Sue was a legal advisor with the New Zealand Nurses Organisation.

David Kerslake

David is an internationally-published writer and editor, whose management and other experience spans a number of top-flight organisations. He has held writing and consulting roles with England's Health Education Authority and Department of Health. In early 2009, David completed a lengthy tenure with Brookers Ltd. He has largely since been based with capital-based consultancy Working Words, providing communications support to entities across a range of sectors and industries. David managed Brookers' HR/employment best practice publishing portfolio for a number of years and is an accomplished presenter and facilitator. Both he and his published commentary have featured on TV One's "Business is Booming" and TV3's "Campbell Live". Based with global legal publishers Lexis Nexis for the spring-time months of 2009, the new year of 2010 sees David at Brookers once again, providing publishing support to the company's Commercial and Tax portfolio.

Anne O'Brien

Anne is a barrister practicing in Christchurch. She was admitted as a Barrister and Solicitor of the High Court of New Zealand in September 1991 and went to the independent Bar in 1996. She is a qualified secondary teacher and is a member of the LEADR NZ Panel of Accredited Mediators. Anne has a strong interest in ethics and medical law. Anne represents health practitioners in the Coroners Court, the Human Rights Review Tribunal, Health Practitioners Disciplinary Tribunal, Nursing Council of New Zealand Professional Conduct Committee and Health and Disability Commissioner investigations. She also has an employment law practice and represents both employees and employers. In the course of her career as a lawyer she has acted for unions, news media organisations, insurers and private individuals and has practised in the areas of general civil litigation, family law and criminal law. Between 1996 and 2004 Anne was an Instructor at the Institute of Professional Legal Studies, while continuing to practice part-time as a barrister. She continues her teaching as a tutor in Evidence and Employment Law at the University of Canterbury School of Law.

Jackie Pearse (NZGON (Invercargill), RM, ADN (Wellington), LLB (Hons) (Otago)

Jackie Pearse was a registered nurse, registered midwife, and a lecturer in the nursing and midwifery degrees at Otago before starting a law degree. She has been the national legal advisor to the New Zealand College of Midwives since 1995. NZCOM represent 85 percent of all practising midwives, and Jackie provides full legal advice and support in all areas of health law. She appears regularly in disciplinary hearings and inquests and also frequently lectures, gives seminars, and is a guest speaker on medico-legal issues.

Robert F B Perry LLB (Cant)

Robert Perry is a Barrister who now practises in Family and Mental Health Law in Christchurch. He was formerly a partner in the leading South Island firm of Duncan Cotterill, a President of the Canterbury District Law Society and board member of both the Legal Services Board and the Legal Services Agency. He has been a District Inspector of Mental Health since 1985 and in this capacity has led two major enquiries.

Austin Powell LLM (Hons) (Cant)

Austin Powell has been in practice as a litigation lawyer for 15 years. After working with Duncan Cotterill for 10 years, the last 4 as a partner based in the firm's Nelson office, he went to the independent Bar in Nelson in 2000. He specialised in employment law for most of this time. He is now at the Crown Law Office in Wellington as a Crown Counsel in the Criminal Process Group.

Clare Prendergast LLB (Vic), Registered Nurse (Wellington)

Clare Prendergast is an investigator and legal advisor for the Nursing Council of New Zealand. Before joining the Nursing Council in 1995 she was a legal editor at Brookers from 1992, employed as Chief Editor of the Commercial Publishing Team. Clare is a registered nurse and was previously employed at Wellington Hospital from 1977 to 1992.

Trevor Warr LLB (Hons) (Cant) RCpN (Nelson)

Trevor Warr is a registered nurse, and a barrister and solicitor. For the past 15 years he has worked for the New Zealand Nurses Organisation. His most recent position was as the Professional Services Manager, a role which included working with the legal team and professional nursing advisors. He has extensive experience in employment relations and a strong interest in medico-legal issues. Trevor is now a mediator with the Employment Relations Service in Christchurch.

ACKNOWLEDGMENTS

I would like to acknowledge and thank all the contributing authors for their hard work, time and commitment to this fourth edition, especially Anne O'Brien who took responsibility for three chapters, two of those requiring major rewrites to reflect legislative changes. My particular thanks to Sue Johnson who as the previous general editor had the faith and belief to pass the editorship onto me. Her busy work schedule as Coroner meant that she could no longer continue as general editor but she has maintained her connection by rewriting Chapter 18 and providing me with guidance and support.

I also acknowledge the input of contributors to previous editions of this book whose work has assisted the authors of this fourth edition: Austin Powell, Richard McElrea, Meg Wallace and Susan Fulford.

I would like to thank Brookers staff, in particular Sarah Hunt and Claire Burnet.

Last but not least I once again thank Meg Wallace. The New Zealand editions of Health Care and The Law are adapted from Meg's first edition of Health Care and the Law, an Australian work that is now in its fourth edition. Although the original structure of Meg's work remains the framework for this book, in general, with the changes in law that have occurred since the first publication the text has been changed and rewritten.

Rebecca Keenan

FOREWORD

This fourth edition of Health Care and the Law provides once again an essential, comprehensive and useful update to and expansion of the previous editions.

The often blurred interface between Law and medicine continues to provide difficult issues. Just as those involved in the administration of justice such as Police, lawyers and Courts often need guidance on health related issues, so too those involved in health care need an up-to-date, accessible source of information about legal issues.

This text once again addresses those needs, and reflects the developments in this area since 2004, including the Coroners Act 2006 and the consequent major enhancement and improvements to this area of death investigation to name but one.

The former general editor, Sue Johnson, now one of the specialist contributors, has since the last edition become uniquely placed as a fulltime Coroner under the new Act to bring on even a wider perspective to help illuminate and explore the blurred interface referred to. The other specialist contributors have also once again contributed to the same objective.

I commend this new edition to all.

Judge Neil MacLean
Chief Coroner for New Zealand

PREFACE

This fourth New Zealand edition of Health Care and the Law seeks to build upon the endeavours of the three prior editions to describe the basic principles of law relating to health care. This edition maintains the approach established in the previous editions, using many illustrations from the area of nursing, but with the principles involved being applicable to all health practitioners.

The law has been updated where necessary, and this edition incorporates a number of legislative changes that have taken place since the last edition in 2004. In particular, these changes include the Coroners Act 2006 that has replaced and reformed the Coroners Act 1988. The new Act makes provision for 20 full time legally trained Coroners instead of part time coroners. The chapter has been written by Sue Johnson, a regional coroner based in Canterbury, providing a depth of understanding to the implication for health practitioners whose practice is scrutinised as the result of a patient's death. Though the 2004 edition was written with regard to the Health Practitioner's Competence Assurance Act 2003, this chapter has been updated and reflects the knowledge and insight that the author has from working within that regime for the last four years. There have also been changes to criminal procedure with the enactment of the Criminal Disclosure Act 2008. The law surrounding the collection, use and retaining of human tissue has been reformed and is now governed by the Human Tissue Act 2008. There have been significant changes to ACC law and employment law which have meant that both these chapters have had a major rewrite.

Many more health practitioners than in the past are now aware of their legal responsibilities and accountability. Most health practitioners want clear guidance on how the law affects their work. This book does not attempt to be a complete exposition of the law relating to health care. This book can be considered as a resource of first choice when there is a question regarding the practice of health and the law that governs it. It provides direction for health practitioners or lawyers when they require a guide to some of the basic principles and sources of the law. Health law in New Zealand is a specialised area, and law relating to health care is rapidly expanding. Some of the chapters will need to be read in the light of new developments following publication.

Responsibility as between the authors for individual chapters is indicated in the table of contents. We have attempted to present the law as accurately as possible, but cannot undertake to ensure complete accuracy. Readers should not consider that this book replaces a lawyer's advice on individual cases.

The law is stated on the information available to the authors as at November 2009. It has been possible to make a few last minute additions after that date.

Rebecca Keenan

January 2010

CONTENTS

Chapter 1

WHAT IS LAW?

SUE JOHNSON

Contents

1.1 Introduction

People obey ethical and moral rules because such rules are based on what ought to be done, according to general opinion and a person's own conscience. Breaking these rules invites a feeling of guilt, shame, or embarrassment, and the disapproval of others. The governing board of a person's profession may rule that a person is unfit to practice. People obey the demands of the law, however, because breaking the law invites more tangible consequences such as imprisonment or a Court order to pay compensation or to carry out some act.

Law is the embodiment of what is considered desirable for some social good, in rules that can be enforced. Rules may be desirable because they are considered the morally or socially "right" thing to do, or best for the good government of the country, or simply a means of benefiting some members of society. Although all laws may be considered ethically acceptable, though this is often debatable,[1] not all ethical principles are covered by law; for example, you may feel morally obliged to help an injured person that you find in the street, though you are not legally required to do so (see chapter 8).

The law may affect health practitioners in many ways, either by creating obligations or by conferring rights. Some examples follow, though this list is not exhaustive.

Checklist

Some ways in which health practitioners can be found responsible at law

- *Breach of statutory duties:* for example, under the Code of Health and Disability Services Consumers' Rights (see chapter 5) and the Health Information Privacy Code (see chapter 9).
- *Negligence:* for example, failing to report a change in a client's vital signs, or giving the wrong drug (see chapter 8).
- *Assault/battery:* for example, threatening a client or forcing a client to ambulate without their consent (see chapter 6).
- *Defamation:* for example, telling friends harmful details about a client (see chapter 9).
- *Crime:* for example, wrongly handling drugs, unlawfully causing death (see chapter 16).
- *Other offences:* for example, failure to report infectious disease (see chapter 18).
- *Other liability:* for example, mishandling of clients' property (see chapter 11), failure to carry out an employer's instructions (see chapter 13), failure to obtain registration (see chapter 15), or discrimination against clients in some cases (see chapter 5).

Some rights conferred on health practitioners by law

- The right not to be unfairly dismissed, or punished (see chapter 13).
- The right to question an employer's instructions (see chapter 13).
- The right to receive compensation for work-related accidents (see chapter 14).
- The right to a fair hearing before any adverse action is taken (see chapters 1, 13 and 16).
- The right not to be discriminated against on the grounds of race, gender, disability, age, sexuality, and other grounds (see chapter 5).

---

1   There may be great conflict between the law and what some believe to be morally acceptable, for example the law allowing abortion in certain circumstances, prohibiting euthanasia and certain drugs, and the law's lack of control of in vitro fertilisation programmes. This book does not discuss the controversies, but it does set out the law on these and other bioethical dilemmas. A topical book on the subject of bioethics for nurses is the Australian text, M-J Johnstone, *Bioethics: a nursing perspective*, Sydney, W B Saunders/Bailliere Tindall, 1989.

1.2 Understanding law

Law can be studied at two levels. In its broadest sense, it is a means of creating some order in society by the evolution of rules, mores, and customs. The study at this level considers the nature of society, of "right", "justice", "common good", and other concepts that are involved in a consideration of the nature of law. This study, involving philosophical and sociological perceptions, is called *jurisprudence*. The other level of study is that in which lawyers are mainly involved, and is the dominant concern of this book — the content of our laws (*substantive law*), and the mechanics of making and enforcing them (*procedural law*) (see the table below).

CLASSIFICATIONS OF LAW

Substantive Law		Procedural Law	
Civil Law	**Criminal Law**	**Procedural Rules**	**Rules of Court**
Administrative Law	Criminal Codes	Civil Procedure	High Court Rules
Contract Law		Criminal Procedure	District Court Rules
Commercial Law		etc	
Family Law			
Health Law			
Industrial Law			
Tort Law			
etc			
Other		**Rules of Evidence**	
eg Canon Law			
Military Law			

Straddling these two levels of study is an approach to understanding law that considers both the content and process of law in our society. It studies their effects and ability to fulfil the purposes and goals that may have been recognised at the more fundamental, jurisprudential level. What, for example, is the purpose of the law on drugs, and is it having this effect? Could it be improved? Are our goals realistic and/or appropriate, acceptable, or worthwhile? Versions of this approach to law have been variously called critical legal theory, the realist school of legal theory, and sociological legal theory.[2] This perspective is used at times in this book to evaluate the law as it applies to health practitioners, and to consider desirable change.

1.2.1 Natural law

Early jurisprudential theories, propounded by such philosophers as Aristotle and Cicero, and later developed by St Thomas Aquinas, were based on the principle of natural law. This holds that the fundamental source of law is nature, and this source is higher and more

---

2   There are some subtle differences in these approaches. A useful and very readable reference work for an understanding of legal philosophies is J W Harris, *Legal Philosophies*, London, Butterworths, 1980, chapters 2, 4, 8, and 11.

binding than any laws made by human beings. Natural law, which it states is fixed and unchangeable, can be discovered by reason and an understanding of human nature. Natural law still underlies much of the Western world's legal policy, particularly in the area of human rights.[3] Some natural law principles still underlie our law today, such as the right to be heard in one's own defence before being punished (see 1.5.1).

1.2.2   Positive law

An important development in law in Western society was its separation from religion and the subsequent predominance of "positivism", that is, the removal of legal authority from God or nature to the State. The recognised founders of this approach are Jeremy Bentham and John Austen. Law is seen, in this perspective, as being a set of commands that result in certain goals being attained or evils prevented, made by someone with the recognised authority to require compliance.[4] This then separates the "moral" from the "legal" in the expression of our obligations — something is not part of our law simply because it is morally right. Or, as Bentham saw it, a moral right only existed if it extended from a legal right. Authority for law is placed in the State. The law is what the State says it is, and in the view of a positivist one cannot claim a moral right without the existence of a legal right underpinning it.

1.3   Legal systems

There are, throughout the world, several broad legal systems. Some of the main ones are, briefly:

1.3.1   Common law

This is based on the development in England of law common to the many communal systems operating throughout the country. The system was extended to the various colonies, and is therefore the basis of the New Zealand, Australian, US, and Canadian legal systems, among others. It is explained more fully below (see 1.4.2). The term "common law" is also used to:

- Differentiate Judge-made law from statutory law (see 1.4.1); and
- Differentiate common law from equity (see 1.4.2).

Therefore, it is important to determine the context in which the term is used. The common law system is based on the adversarial approach to resolving disputes. This means that the parties involved in disputes present their cases and argue the merits before a Judge and/or jury, those bodies being unable to take an active part in instigating the acquisition of knowledge, or determining what information is put before them.

1.3.2   Civil law

This is the system of law in those European countries that inherited either the French or Roman cultural influence. It is based mainly on a code that means the law is almost entirely enshrined in statutes. The approach to dispute resolution is inquisitorial, rather than adversarial. This means the judiciary takes the initiative in seeking the facts, and is not confined to dealing only with what is put before it. The Judge's role is investigatory (the

---

3   Ibid, chapter 2.
4   Ibid, chapter 3.

role assigned in our common law system to lawyers and police).[5] The lawyer for each party plays the role of an assistant to the Judge, rather than the role of advocate for the party, which they adopt in the adversarial system. The term "civil law" may also be used in our common law system to distinguish a matter from criminal law, so the context of the term's use must be considered.

1.3.3   Socialist law

This system, originally adopted by Russia in the 1920s and still used in some other countries, is based on the ideology of socialism. This affects both the content of the laws that are enacted (substantive law), as well as rules for the conduct of legal procedures (procedural rules).

1.3.4   Islamic law and some Eastern legal systems

These systems concentrate more on internal religious beliefs and motivation, and their perceived moral superiority as the source of authority for law, than on mere external control as a means of social ordering. However, religious beliefs and values are readily enforced by the laws of the land. They are more patriarchal in nature than the laws of our society. This is reflected in laws that grant the right to political and legal participation unequally, according to status conferred by gender or religious beliefs.

1.4   Sources of New Zealand law

New Zealand law is, as previously mentioned, based on the common law system. An understanding of our law is probably best gained by considering the nature and development of our sources of law.

There are two main sources of law in New Zealand — legislation and Judge-made law (common law).

1.4.1   Laws made by a recognised authority — legislation

These are documents setting out obligations and rights, penalties, and procedures. The body that makes these laws is the New Zealand Parliament (or General Assembly). This body passes laws in the form of *statutes*, otherwise called Acts of Parliament. Statutes can delegate the right to make further legislation, such as regulations and rules, which are more detailed, to other designated bodies or people, eg a government Minister or a local authority. These are in the form of rules and regulations, and are called *delegated legislation*. Statutes, which are made by Parliament, and rules and regulations, which are made by a designated person or body, can all be equally binding on people.

The New Zealand Parliament was constituted by section 32 of the New Zealand Constitution Act 1852. Section 53 of this Act gave Parliament power to make New Zealand laws for "the peace, order and good government of New Zealand", while reserving some powers for the Imperial Parliament of England. Obviously, ties to England have been weakened since this legislation was passed.

---

5   Easton et al, *Introducing the Law* (2nd ed), Sydney, CCH, 1985.

Consequently, New Zealand, unlike Australia, has no written constitution. New Zealand has a flexible system of government, and the Courts are not within the political arena as they are in the US for example, where the appointment of Judges is political.

The Judges in New Zealand are regarded as free from interference by the New Zealand Parliament in its law-making capacity and the Government in its capacity as Executive.

Legislation is the most effective method of making law. It is clear and certain, and available to the non-lawyer. Anyone can purchase an individual Act. It is also free from the restraints that hamper Judge-made law (common law), which can only be used restrictively as it relates to specific parties in particular factual circumstances.

Legislation has general effect, and Parliament need not have reference to previous Acts. Parliament can pass an Act and repeal it the next day. Parliament is New Zealand's supreme law-making power.

Many statutes are codifications of the common law. For example, the criminal law of New Zealand was codified at the beginning of this century and it is not possible for a person to be convicted of any crime in New Zealand unless it is within the Code. There are no common law crimes, and no new crimes can be made unless the Crimes Act 1961 is amended. The advantage of codification is that members of the public are able to find out exactly what the law is. The disadvantage of it is that it is inflexible, and can only be altered by amendment to legislation.

Some statutes still in force in New Zealand are those that were originally passed in the UK, including the Magna Carta in 1297. Many statutes that were once in force in New Zealand have been repealed. Since New Zealand adopted the Statute of Westminster in 1947, it is no longer possible for the UK Parliament to legislate for New Zealand.

1.4.2 Laws developed by the Courts — common law

Common law has its historical origins in the English feudal era. Then, when someone complained of having been wronged by another, the way of dealing with this was to gather one's clan, descend upon the wrongdoer, and exact vengeance on that person and their family. Feudalism was one way of maintaining order. It was fundamentally a system of land tenure, with personal service owed by many to an overlord, who had immense powers including the exercise of customary law, based on local customs. The very completeness of its application made feudalism a potent force for law and order.

England was a rural society, and overlordship carried with it as a further principle, the right of every lord to hold a Court for his tenants. There was very little legislation, but the lord enforced obedience to an existing and settled custom when disputes were to be resolved. This custom involved settling disputes by methods such as trial by oath, trial by battle, and trial by ordeal. Where one person had caused another physical harm or loss of property, the person harmed was said to have an action in the law of "wrongs", or to use the ancient French term, which is still used today, the law of "torts".

Initially, wrongs were seen as personal disputes. However, as the central government began to grow, towns and cities developed, and the king wished to extend his power, some "wrongs" were increasingly seen as breaches of the king's peace. The "king's peace" grew and flourished with the extension and consolidation of the king's power, until it covered the whole of England at all times and for all seasons. When this had come to pass, no person committed violence without being liable to a fine at the suit of the king: a precursor of modern criminal law. However, until the time of Henry II, the enforcement of law, even penal law, remained in private hands. Today, we still have the offence of "breach of the peace", where a person who causes a serious disturbance to the peaceful activities of those around her/him may be charged.

Henry II instituted some dramatic changes. He set apart certain wrongs as matters for Crown interference. Others were peculiarly the concern of the private citizen. This was the beginning of the crime/tort dichotomy ("public/private" law). Several crimes were established, for example robbery with violence, which attracted physical punishment. However, private vengeance was sought mainly through monetary compensation. Justice became the business of the monarch, not the lords.

In order to seek the aid of royal justice, it was usual to purchase a writ from the King's Chancery. This writ was a royal command based on the king's royal authority. It specified the injury complained of, and directed that whoever had caused the harm should right the wrong, or show cause before the king's justices why they should not.

It became obvious that many actions would be comparatively similar, and so common wording was used. Writs became standard in form, adapted for the particular category of action involved, for example trespass, personal injury, robbery. Over time, each category tended to develop its own peculiarities, for example the method of proof for supporting or rebutting the claim in any particular category of case would differ from others. If the writ itself did not follow a common form, it was not incorporated in the Clerk's Register of Writs, and so no action would lie for that particular set of events.

In this way then, a common law became increasingly prevalent. This was aided particularly by a lawyer, Blackstone, who wrote a many-volumed "commentary" on the law of England, bringing together the common principles he found in the law as practised throughout the land. His book became the main authority for later decisions by the Courts.

What has all this to do with today's law? The answer lies in the fact that the authority of a law is based on the idea of acceptance of a principle, rule, or standard of behaviour, from someone considered to have more authority than, or at least as much authority as oneself. By the establishment of a "common law", then, principles derived from sources with accepted authority were set down as a guide for future decision-making to be changed only by Courts with higher authority than the original Court. This laid the foundations for one of the fundamental aspects of our legal system, stare decisis, meaning, roughly, "the decision binds". It requires that a Court is bound by legal principles established by Courts with higher standing than its own (see 1.4.4).

(1)   *Equity, a development from common law*

Common law could be very harsh, and somewhat rigid. One example of this is the old common law principle that the person whose name is on a title deed to land is the person who owns it at law. They can therefore sell it at will, and have sole rights to the sale's proceeds. This can cause hardship where someone else has made a contribution to the acquisition of the property by contributing to its purchase price, or has enhanced its value by improving or renovating it. Married or de facto couples with property, for example, are one group of people where this could happen. Many people, who had found common law remedies difficult to obtain, discovered over time a developing set of alternative approaches in some of the specialised Courts, such as the Court of Chancery, the ecclesiastical Courts, and the Court of Admiralty. These Courts were based more on principles aimed at prevention of unjust enrichment at another's expense. The principles that developed were called principles of equity. Thus, where a person in the situation described above would not be able to reap the reward of their contribution to the property at common law, in equity the fact that that person had contributed to its value could lead to a claim on its value in proportion to the contribution.

The principles of equity have been incorporated into the jurisdiction of the common law Courts. This means that the Courts can consider both the common law *and* equitable remedies for which a person may be eligible. Generally, one or the other will be applicable but where there is a conflict between the rules of equity and the common law, equity must prevail.

The term "common law" includes principles of equity, unless it is clear that the writer is drawing a distinction between common law principles, strictly speaking, and principles of equity.

1.4.3   Interrelationship between statutory law and common law

Parliament creates an enormous amount of law each year. It has the power to enact statutes on any and every facet of our lives. Obviously it is impossible to cover everything, so where there is a gap in statutory law Judges and lawyers turn to the common law, as discovered through the cases, in an attempt to find enlightenment there. Sometimes the cases referred to may be very old.

If nothing on that particular matter has been decided recently, or the matter has not been the subject of judicial decision (as well as there being no statutory law to direct the Judge), the only thing left is for the Judge to look at cases with similar fact situations, and develop, using the principles used in those cases, principles for the matter now before the Court. New law will be developed for future reference where this new situation arises again. This is how the common law adapts to a changing society.

1.4.4   Precedent

This is the word used to describe the system by which the common law is passed on to influence later decisions. Courts are arranged in a hierarchy, from the lowest Courts (District Courts), to the highest Courts (in New Zealand the Court of Appeal and then the Supreme Court).[6] This hierarchy will be considered in more detail in chapter 2. Decisions made in the higher Courts have precedence over decisions made in the lower Courts. This means that under some circumstances (see 2.1.6) when one has received a judgment of a lower Court, one can appeal to a higher Court to have the lower Court's judgment quashed, and either a different judgment made or a new hearing granted. The decision of the higher Court

---

6   The Supreme Court Act 2003 has established a Supreme Court in New Zealand to be the new Court of final appeal for proceedings brought in New Zealand Courts. The Act also ends appeals to the Judicial Committee of the Privy Council, which was the final Court of appeal above the Court of Appeal. Note that the Supreme Court cannot hear any appeals until after 1 July 2004. There are transitional provisions that allow the Privy Council to determine appeals already begun.

then applies, and it and the reasons for it are binding on all Courts lower in the same hierarchy in that jurisdiction.

It is important for lawyers to know which Court a decision comes from, for a decision is only binding on a lower Court in the same hierarchy. Decisions from a Court in another hierarchy are of *persuasive precedent* only, that is, not binding on the Court, but depending upon the status of the Court it comes from, worth considering. For example, an English Court decision is persuasive precedent in New Zealand. As its name implies, persuasive precedent is not binding on a Judge, and can only be used if no binding precedent can be found.

For practical purposes this means that when considering their judgment in a case, Judges will look to decisions of the higher Courts. A lawyer arguing before the Judge will attempt to outdo the opposing party's argument by offering a precedent from those cases that have more authority than the opponent's.

It may be that the only precedent for a particular fact situation is a fairly lowly Court decision from the last century or it could even come from an earlier case in England. In this situation the lawyers offer them as *persuasive*, rather than *binding* precedent to the Judge. This type of situation is not frequent today.

The idea, then, is to follow precedent established by earlier Courts but only those of a Court that is higher in one's hierarchy ("stare decisis", see 1.4.2). If such a precedent can be found or adduced from analogous situations, the Court is absolutely bound by that earlier decision. Thus, a sort of rigidity is established that also gives some certainty to the law, otherwise people would be subject to the whims and opinions of individual Judges. They would never know whether what we were doing was right or not. This is one of the factors that leads people to complain that the law is never flexible enough to adapt to changing times.

1.4.5 No law, nor any precedent

If there is no legislation on a particular matter, and also no precedent, then the law on that matter is uncertain. It cannot be known until the matter is taken to Court and a ruling made. Sometimes, to establish the law on an issue that is becoming a frequent matter of confusion and concern, a "test case" will be brought. When lawyers see a good opportunity, and funds are available, a case is taken to Court, not merely because the particular parties want to settle the matter but also to establish the law for future reference.

1.4.6 How does the law change?

There is some scope for change in the common law, despite stare decisis, and Parliament's ability to change statutes and bring in new ones. First, it will be recalled that the case cited by a lawyer as being applicable to a particular situation must be analogous to the case being decided. Consequently, lawyers spend considerable time in Court arguing over whether the cases really are analogous. As there are an infinite number of variations for any situation, and as times change and statutes are introduced to cover more activities, it is surprising how often apparently similar situations are eventually considered by the Judges to be different enough in the circumstances to warrant distinguishing the earlier case from the current situation under scrutiny. If one can thus distinguish the cases, then the legal principle or principles established in the earlier case do not bind the Court. This results in a gradual and slow development of the law to adapt to a changing society. There is further discussion on the way common law changes in chapter 3.

1.5 Some basic principles of our legal system

English law, which we have inherited in New Zealand, has several fundamental principles and presumptions that underlie all specific legislation and common law.

1.5.1 Natural law principles

These principles were formulated by the Greek philosophers. They sought to vest some authority beyond the State, in the very nature of our humanity, if not in a god. These principles underlie the concept of human rights. They form the basis of such documents as the United Nations Declaration of Human Rights, and subsequent conventions outlining human rights in more detail, and in procedural law in our country. There are two main principles. First, that no one may be deprived of their liberty, livelihood, or goods without being given timely notice of the reasons for so doing, and without being given the opportunity to be heard in their own defence. Secondly, that no one may sit in judgment of another who has a vested interest in the outcome of the judgment. It was later recognised that these principles should apply to all citizens, regardless of their individual characteristics (see chapter 4).

1.5.2 Rule of law

This body of principles establishes two things. First, it says a person can only be found guilty of a criminal offence that existed at the time it was allegedly committed. This means that the State cannot create an offence after it has been committed. Secondly, it states that the executive branch of the government is subject to the law in the same way as a citizen, so that the citizen is protected from arbitrary action by the public service and government bodies. Further protection from unfair or ill-considered decisions by administrative bodies has been created by administrative law (see 2.1.11).

1.5.3 Presumption of innocence

This presumption requires the law to treat any accused person as innocent until they have been proved guilty.

1.5.4 New Zealand Bill of Rights Act 1990

The New Zealand Bill of Rights Act 1990 affirms, protects, and promotes human rights and fundamental freedoms in New Zealand. It affirms New Zealand's commitment to the International Covenant on Civil and Political Rights.

Among the rights that are affirmed are the right not to be deprived of life (section 8), the right not to be subjected to torture or cruel treatment (section 9), the right not to be subjected to medical or scientific experimentation (section 10), and the right to refuse to undergo treatment (section 11).

1.5.5 Treaty of Waitangi

Obligations under a treaty of any sort, including international treaties, cannot be enforced in a Court of law in New Zealand, except insofar as they have been incorporated into law (see chapter 5). However, there are statutory provisions in various Acts that provide that the Act in question is to be administered and interpreted so as to give direct legislative force to its obligations and undertakings. In those statutes where the text of the Treaty of Waitangi has been incorporated as a Schedule to the Act, it seems to have been recited for informational purposes only so as to declare what the text of the Treaty is, rather than to explain it.

The Treaty's status is as a socio-political document and not a legal one. It has no juridical standing, and cannot be enforced in domestic Courts. However, it has been held by Sir Robin Cooke while President of the New Zealand Court of Appeal to be "the most important document in New Zealand's history". It is increasingly gaining a special status of its own, and is becoming more generally relevant to legislation.

In a number of cases the Treaty has been considered as part of the context in which a statute should be interpreted. The many statutes that make express reference to the Treaty and impose duties to have regard to and comply with the principles enshrined in it, signify that under New Zealand law the Treaty is a living instrument, to be applied to give a fair result.

The broad concept of the Treaty is that it is a reciprocal bargain, whereby "Maori ceded rights of government in exchange for guarantees of possession and control of their lands and precious possessions".[7] However, there is little provided in the Treaty by way of its application. Thus the Treaty has been seen as a starting point for providing solutions and it has been held by the Court of Appeal that central to the partnership created by the Treaty is an obligation of good faith — the obligation to work out answers in a spirit of honest cooperation.[8] This obligation of good faith extends to consultation.[9] It has led to an increasing awareness of protection, not just of the property of Maori but Maori rights also, and recognition of these with regard to health service delivery has become increasingly important.

1.6   Branches of the law

There are two main branches of law, and sub-branches of these. The first branch is substantive law, or that part of the law which tells us what we can do, must do, or must not do, as well as the interpretation of the law, setting out rights and obligations, etc. It is divided into two sub-branches — civil law and criminal law. Civil law in turn has many sub-branches such as constitutional law, commercial law, contract law, bankruptcy law, administrative law, and family law. The second branch is procedural law. This tells us how to put the law into action. It includes such sub-branches as the law of evidence and Court rules.

1.7   Further reading

J F Burrows, *Statute Law in New Zealand* (2nd ed), Wellington, Butterworths, 1999.

M McDowell and D Webb, *The New Zealand legal system: structures, processes and legal theory* (3rd ed), Wellington, LexisNexis Butterworths, 2002.

---

7   *NZ Maori Council v A-G* [1987] 1 NZLR 641; (1987) 6 NZAR 353 (CA), 702; 410.
8   Ibid, at pages 664-667; 369-373 per Cooke P; at pages 682; 389 per Richardson J; at pages 693; 401 per Somers J; at pages 704; 412 per Casey J.
9   *NZ Maori Council v A-G* [1989] 2 NZLR 142 (CA), 152 per Cooke P: "that is really clear beyond argument".

R D Mulholland, *Introduction to the New Zealand Legal System* (10th ed), Wellington, Butterworths, 2001.

Chapter 2

THE LEGAL STRUCTURE

SUE JOHNSON

Contents

2.1   The Court hierarchy

2.1.1   What is a Court?

A Court is a gathering presided over by a Judge or other person invested with judicial power, who follows the rules of procedure prescribed for that Court, and is in some cases assisted by a jury. The Judge or, where there is a jury, the Judge and jury, exercising different responsibilities as outlined in chapter 3, determine such matters as:

- Whether certain facts have been established;
- Where required, the legal obligations and rights of a party or parties;
- The interpretation of statutory provisions, the provisions of a will or of a contract;
- Whether a person is guilty or not guilty of an offence;
- Whether a person is liable or not for harming another; and
- The appropriate punishment for criminal or other offences.

2.1.2   Jurisdiction

The concept of jurisdiction is central to the Court system. It means (a) the power of a Court or Judge to entertain an action, claim, or other proceeding; and (b) the district or limits within which the Court's judgment or Court's orders can be enforced or executed.[1]

In general, a Court may take notice of events that have occurred outside the area of its jurisdiction. However, in practice a defendant must be within the Court's jurisdiction at the time a notice of proceeding is served. The exception is where leave may be granted to serve the notice of proceeding out of the jurisdiction.

Courts may exercise "original" or "appellate" jurisdiction.

(1)   *Original jurisdiction*

Original jurisdiction is exercised when a case first comes to Court, and the basic facts and legal issues are determined. It is sometimes called "first instance" jurisdiction. It is where facts are determined, and those involved found guilty or not guilty in a criminal case, or liable or not liable in a civil case. Witnesses and exhibits are used for this purpose. A decision as to the facts and the legal position of those involved is made, with any appropriate orders authorised by statute being issued by the Judge.

(2)   *Appellate jurisdiction*

If a decision by the Court in its original jurisdiction can be challenged, an appeal from that decision might be made to a higher Court. For example, the High Court may hear a criminal trial in its original jurisdiction. This would be before one Judge and jury: see the explanation of criminal procedures below. If an appeal is made it will be to the Court of Appeal with three or five Judges, and without the original Judge or jury. Appeal Courts do not hear the matter all over again. They do not re-examine the witnesses, or exhibits. The parties cannot simply have another go if they think they did not do it properly the first time. It is considered that the facts have been determined, and the appellate Court takes them as established in the lower Court. Thus, appeals can be brought only by arguing, for example, that:

---

1   *Osborn's Concise Law Dictionary* (7th ed), London, Sweet & Maxwell, 1983.

- The Judge in the trial hearing made an error of law;
- The rules of evidence were not properly followed and evidence was wrongly admitted or withheld;
- Given the facts that were established, no one could reasonably have come to the decision arrived at by the Judge or jury;
- In some cases, fresh evidence has come to light that was not available at the time of trial, and its absence has most likely caused a miscarriage of justice.

The appeal Court may order a *retrial*, for example where evidence was wrongly admitted. It may quash the verdict or finding, for example where it considers that the trial Judge erred in law and the result is thus wrong at law, or where a reasonable Judge or jury could not have come to the decision arrived at, given the facts.

(3)   *The New Zealand Court system (excluding tribunals)*

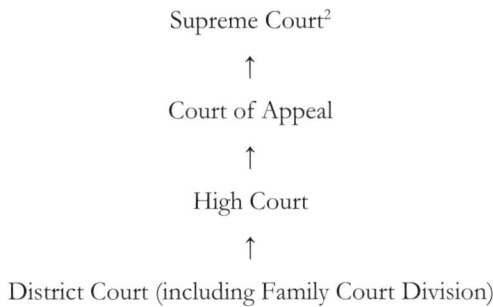

Supreme Court[2]

↑

Court of Appeal

↑

High Court

↑

District Court (including Family Court Division)

2.1.3   District Court

There are District Courts in most New Zealand towns, or city districts. The District Court has criminal and civil jurisdiction.

(1)   *Criminal jurisdiction*

There are three types of matters dealt with by this Court — summary offences, electable offences, and indictable offences.

(a)   Summary offences

These are all offences described by statute as being punishable on a summary conviction and are dealt with in "summary" proceedings. The hearing is by a presiding Judge without a jury, unless the defendant has an election to choose jury trial and has done so.

(b)   Electable offences

Where a person has been charged with a summary offence that is punishable by imprisonment for a term exceeding 3 months, or is proceeded against summarily for any offence punishable by more than 3 months' imprisonment, then the person can elect either

---

2   The Supreme Court Act 2003 has established a Supreme Court in New Zealand to be the new Court of final appeal for proceedings brought in New Zealand Courts. The Act also ends appeals to the Judicial Committee of the Privy Council, which was the final court of Appeal above the Court of Appeal. The Supreme Court cannot hear any appeals until after 1 July 2004. There are transitional provisions that allow the Privy Council to determine appeals already begun, but there is no new right of appeals against decisions made before 1 January 2004 (Supreme Court Act 2003, section 54).

trial by Judge alone, or trial by jury (which consists of 12 lay persons). Whenever trial by jury is elected, the trial takes place in the District Court under a District Court Judge with a special warrant from the Governor-General authorising him or her to conduct jury trials.

(c) Indictable offences

An indictable offence is one that must be tried by a Judge and jury, or else it is an offence, which the Crown Prosecutor chooses to charge indictably because of the serious nature of it. Under the Summary Proceedings Act 1957, the District Court has jurisdiction for many indictable offences. The Act contains a Schedule listing indictable offences that can be tried in the District Court. These include offences that almost always carry a maximum penalty of 10 years' imprisonment or less. Offences punishable by more than 10 years' imprisonment or by life imprisonment cannot be tried in the District Court. In the case of all the offences listed in the Schedule, the Crown Prosecutor has a choice to either charge the defendant indictably, in which case the trial will be by Judge and jury in the District Court, or charge the defendant summarily, in which case the trial will be by District Court Judge alone, unless the offence is electable and the defendant elects trial by jury.

There are some serious indictable offences that are not listed in the Schedule, and which are purely indictable crimes. These include sexual violation, aggravated robbery, manslaughter, murder, arson, perjury, and dealing in Classes A or B drugs. These offences can only be tried by a Judge and jury in the High Court.

(d) Preliminary hearings

A preliminary hearing was formerly one in which the evidence of an offence was laid before the Court. It was used to iron out issues and test the prosecution case and the Judge or a Justice of the Peace decided if there was enough evidence for the case to go to trial by jury. There only had to be enough evidence to show a prima facie case. However, this procedure has now changed and as of 29 June 2009 it has been replaced by a "standard committal procedure".[3]

Under this new procedure there is no hearing or consideration of the evidence; a defendant is committed to trial on the papers. The new procedure does allow for either the defence or the prosecution to apply for an oral evidence order.[4] Only if this happens and the Judge approves the order is there a hearing of the evidence pre-trial. The rationale behind this change is that it will speed up the trial process. According to this procedure the defendant should be committed for trial within 57 days of their first Court appearance and then have a date set for trial 10 days after this period. It also codifies the rules of disclosure[5] and gives a specific timeline for when disclosure should occur, depending on the nature of the proceedings.

---

3 Summary Proceedings Act 1957, section 145. Part 5 (ss 145 to 185) was substituted, as from 29 June 2009, by section 12 of the Summary Proceedings Amendment Act (No 2) 2008.

4 Summary Proceedings Act 1957, sections 178-182. Part 5 (ss 145 to 185) was substituted, as from 29 June 2009, by section 12 of the Summary Proceedings Amendment Act (No 2) 2008.

5 Criminal Disclosure Act 2008.

(2) *Civil jurisdiction*

The District Court's civil jurisdiction is found in the District Courts Act 1947. Only Judges sitting alone can hear civil cases in the District Court. There are no juries or Justices of the Peace involved.

The Court hears disputes between private parties, not usually between the Crown and a private person as is the case in the criminal jurisdiction. Civil cases may involve one or more of the following types of issue:

- *Contract:* Where there is a dispute arising out of any legally binding agreement between two or more persons.
- *Tort:* Where a civil wrong is alleged, for example negligence or trespass, independently of any contract. The District Court has jurisdiction to hear these types of cases where the money claimed, or the value of the chattels in dispute does not exceed $200,000.
- *Recovery of money:* The District Court has jurisdiction to hear cases for recovery of money payable under any statute, provided the amount does not exceed $200,000.
- *Land:* A District Court has jurisdiction over actions for recovery of land which has been leased or rented, provided the rent payable does not exceed $200,000 per year, or where the land value does not exceed $200,000.
- *Equity:* The District Court has jurisdiction to hear matters that would have previously been heard in the old Courts of equity that developed in England during the 16th and 17th centuries to ease the strict legal remedies that were available at common law. Today, all New Zealand Courts can deal with both common law and equity, as the two systems of law have been fused since the passing of the Judicature Act 1908. Equity matters that can be heard in the District Court include rights of enforcement of any charge or lien (a right to sell or use property to settle a debt); proceedings for specific performance (making the person carry out their legal obligations) or cancellation of agreements for sale and purchase of property; proceedings for recovery of a legacy; or relief against fraud or mistake.
- *Statutory jurisdiction:* Many other statutes as well as the District Courts Act 1947 confer civil jurisdiction on the District Court, for example the Fencing Act 1978 relating to fencing disputes, and some recovery of tax under the Income Tax Act 1994.

2.1.4   High Court

The High Court is a single Court, but it has offices in different centres. It has both criminal and civil jurisdiction.

(1) *Criminal jurisdiction*

There are two types of criminal jurisdiction — original jurisdiction and appellate jurisdiction, compared with the District Court which has only original jurisdiction.

(a) Original jurisdiction

This jurisdiction consists of trial by jury of persons prosecuted for indictable offences not within the District Court's jurisdiction, and the trial of persons committed for trial by jury in the District Court when a High Court Judge orders proceedings to be transferred to the High Court under section 28J of the District Courts Act 1947.

The original High Court's jurisdiction also includes jurisdiction to sentence those defendants convicted of purely indictable offences.

(b)   Appellate jurisdiction

Where a criminal charge has been dealt with summarily in the District Court, there are rights of appeal to the High Court which may be general appeals on the ground of a wrong decision on a question of law, or fact. In these appeals the High Court may exercise any of the District Court's powers. It may quash, affirm, or vary the conviction, or order a rehearing in the District Court. On appeals against sentence it may confirm, vary, increase, or decrease the sentence. Appeals may be brought by way of case stated. Either the prosecutor or the defendant may appeal against the decision on a summary hearing by way of case stated. Such an appeal can only be based on a point of law, not fact.

However, under this procedure the prosecutor can appeal against an acquittal. A special procedure must be followed under which the appellant must file, in the District Court, a written "case" setting out the facts and the grounds on which the District Court Judge decided as they did, and the questions of law on which the appeal is based. The District Court Judge must then "settle" the case, ensuring that the relevant facts found by her/him on the grounds of their decision are correctly set out. The Judge then signs it, and the document is transmitted to the High Court for the hearing of the appeal. Again the High Court may confirm, reverse, or amend the decision below, or order a re-hearing. The High Court's appellate jurisdiction is exercised by a High Court Judge, sitting alone without a jury.

(2)   *Civil jurisdiction*

The High Court has original and appellate jurisdiction.

(a)   Original jurisdiction

Since the mid-19th century the High Court has been a single superior Court of Record in New Zealand that has exercised the diverse jurisdiction of what used to be separate superior Courts in England. Consequently, the High Court has comprehensive jurisdiction in civil matters and, in contrast with the District Court, it is not limited in monetary terms.

In addition to having original jurisdiction in all the areas in which the District Court has civil jurisdiction, there are statutes governing particular areas of the law that expressly confer jurisdiction on the High Court alone. For example, bankruptcy proceedings, the enforcement of trusts and the control of trustees, and the supervision of the affairs of limited liability companies.

Part of the High Court's civil jurisdiction is the supervisory jurisdiction in relation to such matters as licensing, planning, and the conferral of benefits payable under statutory welfare schemes. Certain remedies, usually under statute, are only available in the High Court against officials or bodies exercising "public" duties. The High Court may issue certain "writs" or "orders" to achieve its object of supervision and control of the exercise of public bodies. Examples of these writs are injunctions, prohibition orders, and mandamus orders requiring a body or person to do something.

In addition to these orders, the High Court also has jurisdiction to merely declare what the legal rights of parties are. This may be done whether or not "public" duties are involved, and it is a valuable remedy when it may be unnecessary or inappropriate to order that a particular thing be done.

There is another extraordinary remedy that may be obtained only in the High Court — habeas corpus. This is an order directing that a person imprisoned be brought before the Court so that it may order their release if the detention is illegal.

(b)   Appellate jurisdiction

In civil cases, as in criminal cases, the High Court hears appeals from the District Court. However, in civil cases there is only one form of appeal — a general appeal, and no case stated.

An appeal may be on questions of law or fact, but because the High Court will not normally hear oral evidence it will be rare for the High Court to review decisions depending on an assessment of the credibility of witnesses.

2.1.5   Court of Appeal

The Court of Appeal has both criminal and civil jurisdiction.

(1)   *Criminal jurisdiction*

In appeals against conviction or indictment, any person may appeal to the Court of Appeal if found guilty by a jury in either the High Court or the District Court. This appeal is of right if based on a question of law alone, but if based on a question of fact or mixed fact and law, then leave of the trial Judge or the Court of Appeal is needed.

The Court of Appeal may allow the appeal or may quash the conviction and enter an acquittal, or it may quash the conviction and order a retrial. It may also dismiss the appeal if no error has been established.

After a jury trial a person convicted may appeal to the Court of Appeal against sentence. The Court of Appeal may affirm the sentence, or quash it and impose another sentence either more or less severe than that imposed in the High Court.

At any time during the trial the prosecutor or the defendant may request the Judge to reserve a point of law, or the Judge may do this on their own motion. After the trial the Judge must rule on the point of law, but after the verdict either party may appeal to the Court of Appeal on the question of law raised. Only in this way may the prosecutor appeal against an acquittal by a jury.

Where a case has been decided on a summary hearing in the District Court, and there has been an appeal to the High Court, either party can further appeal from the High Court to the Court of Appeal but only on a point of law, and only with leave of the High Court or special leave of the Court of Appeal.

(2)   *Civil jurisdiction*

(a)   Original jurisdiction

In some cases where there is a particular question of law arising as part of a case, one of the parties may, with or without the consent of the other party, apply to the Court of Appeal to have the case removed directly to that Court. Such a course is uncommon, and the Court of Appeal is unlikely to grant leave to consider the matter unless it involves a point of law of unusual difficulty and importance.

(b)   Appellate jurisdiction

The Court of Appeal may hear appeals against any High Court decision in any civil case. All such appeals are by way of rehearing. This means that the Court of Appeal is competent to review decisions on questions of fact, as well as law. However, as with appeals in the High Court, the Court of Appeal will rarely hear oral evidence as it will not have been able to observe the demeanour of the witnesses. If the Court of Appeal allows the appeal, it will usually substitute its own judgment for that of the High Court. However, if the trial was by jury, the Court of Appeal will usually, if it allows the appeal, order a retrial.

2.1.6   Supreme Court

(1)   *The abolition of appeals to the Privy Council*

The Supreme Court Act 2003 established a new Court of final appeal in New Zealand.[6] In doing so it ended appeals to Her Majesty in Council, the Judicial Committee of the Privy Council,[7] which sits in London and advises the monarch. One of the functions of the Privy Council is to deal with appeals from those Commonwealth countries that still retain it as their final appellate Court.

Appeals to the Privy Council were abolished in Australia in 1986. After numerous years of debate in New Zealand, from 1 January 2004 the right to appeal from New Zealand court proceedings to the Privy Council ceased. There are transitional provisions in the Supreme Court Act 2003 that allow the Privy Council to still determine appeals in certain cases, and these involve cases in which appeal proceedings have already commenced.

From 1 January 2004 there is no new right of appeal to the Privy Council against decisions made either before, or after that date. Hearings by the Supreme Court will commence after 1 July 2004. The Supreme Court is the highest Court one can appeal to, either from the High Court or from the Court of Appeal. The High Court and Court of Appeal of New Zealand will be bound by the Supreme Court's decisions.

(2)   *Criteria for leave to appeal*

Section 13 of the Supreme Court Act 2003 sets out the criteria for leave to appeal to the Supreme Court. The Supreme Court must be satisfied that it is necessary in the interests of justice to hear and determine the appeal. It will only be necessary in the interests of justice if the appeal involves a matter of general or public importance, or a substantial miscarriage of justice may have occurred or may occur if the appeal is not heard, or the appeal involves a matter of general commercial significance.[8]

Section 13(3) provides that a significant issue regarding the Treaty of Waitangi is a matter of general or public importance. In criminal cases where the section 13 leave criteria are met, there may be an appeal to the Supreme Court[9] but only also if the appeal is authorised

---

6   Supreme Court Act 2003, section 6.
7   Supreme Court Act 2003, section 42.
8   Supreme Court Act 2003, section 13.
9   Supreme Court Act 2003, section 10.

by provisions in the Crimes Act[10] or the Summary Proceedings Act[11] or the Court Martial Act.[12] In civil cases again the above leave criteria must be met and if they are, leave to appeal from:

(a)   The Court of Appeal will be granted, unless another Act prohibits it or the decision is a refusal to give leave to appeal to the Court of Appeal;[13]

(b)   The High Court where the section 13 leave criteria are met and no other enactment has prohibited the appeal or the decision involved a refusal to give leave to appeal to the High Court or Court of Appeal, or is an interlocutory one;[14]

(c)   Other Courts, but only if the section 13 leave criteria are met and another enactment provides for such an avenue of appeal.[15]

The Supreme Court will not grant leave to appeal to it unless it is satisfied that it *is necessary in the interests of justice*[16] to hear and determine the proposed appeal and except in the case of appeals from the Court of Appeal, that exceptional circumstances justify taking the proposed appeal directly to the Supreme Court.[17]

2.1.7   Specialist Courts

An example of a specialist Court is the Family Court. It deals with the dissolution of marriage, disputes over child custody, maintenance and access, and the division of matrimonial property during a marriage or after a dissolution. It can also issue injunctions, which are orders stopping someone harming or harassing a family member, or dealing with matrimonial property until appropriate arrangements can be made.

The Family Court was established by the Family Courts Act 1980 and the Family Proceedings Act 1980. It is a special Court with its own rules. It connects to the general Court hierarchy at the level of the District Court. Thus, appeals from the Family Court are to the High Court, and if not resolved, from there to the Court of Appeal.

Family law in New Zealand is based on the principle that people should be encouraged, as far as possible, to make their own decisions and to sort out their own problems. Encouragement is given to avoid lawyers and Court proceedings, and for couples to come to agreement over such issues as child custody, maintenance arrangements, and property. Its emphasis is on helping, rather than judging, and the imposition of Court orders is seen as a last resort. Importance is placed on counselling and advising, with, in some applications, the parties being required to undertake this process. Judgment by a Court is resorted to

---

10   Crimes Act 1961, section 406A, or Part 13.
11   Summary Proceedings Act 1957, section 144A.
12   Court Martial Appeals Act 1953, sections 10A or 10B(1). Sections 10A to 10C were inserted, as from 1 January 2004, by Supreme Court Act 2003 (2003 No 53), section 47. See ss 50 to 55 of that Act for the transitional and savings provisions. Section 10A was amended, as from 1 July 2009, by section 18 of the Court Martial Appeals Amendment Act 2007 (2007 No 99) by substituting "a party to an appeal to the Court of Appeal under section 10" for "the appellant in an appeal to the Court of Appeal under section 10(3) or the Chief of Defence Force". Section 10B was substituted, as from 1 July 2009, by section 19 of the Court Martial Appeals Amendment Act 2007 (2007 No 99).
13   Supreme Court Act 2003, section 7.
14   Supreme Court Act 2003, section 8.
15   Supreme Court Act 2003, section 9.
16   What is meant by *in the interests of justice* is set out in Supreme Court Act 2003, section 13.
17   Supreme Court Act 2003, section 14.

only where this is unsuccessful. Priority is given to seeking common ground between the parties and to helping them come to agreement, which the Court can then sanction, rather than the imposition of Court-generated orders. However, there are some things the Court will not countenance, such as the sanctioning of agreements that conflict with the interests of any child, and the sanctioning of any agreement that is manifestly unjust to any person. More than 80 percent of matters that arise between couples who divorce are resolved between her/him, either with the Court's help or on their own.

In keeping with its basic philosophy, the Family Court has less formal procedures than other Courts. The Judge and lawyers are not robed, and the courtrooms are more informal.[18] More importantly, in many matters the Court is given the power to make whatever orders it thinks fit, rather than orders based on strict legal requirements, or precedent. This does not mean that no consideration is given to precedent, but that, where the Judge or Judges think justice or the interests of the parties (with children given paramount consideration) requires it, precedent will not be rigidly followed.

2.1.8   Specialist tribunals

Tribunals differ from Courts in the following ways:

- They may not be permanent;
- They need not be presided over by the judiciary, but may have lay persons and specialists sitting on them;
- Tribunals, in general, do not permit legal representation, and reject formal procedure such as rules of evidence;
- Precedent is not necessarily followed by all tribunals, although most will do so for the sake of convenience and justice; and
- Tribunals' main functions are to ascertain facts, rather than to determine the law.[19]

Examples of such tribunals include:

- The Waitangi Tribunal, which investigates claims involving Treaty issues;
- The Broadcasting Standards Authority, Liquor Licensing Authority, Taxation Review Authority, and Police Complaints Authority.

The Disputes Tribunal, which deals with small claims between individuals, provides less formal procedures for parties to resolve their differences. It is designed for easier, quicker, and less costly dispute resolution. Although different rules may apply, its function is similar. It deals with claims between individuals of up to $15,000, or $20,000 with the consent of both parties. It is informal in its procedure, based on the objective of conciliation, and provides an inexpensive method of settling disputes. Lawyers are generally not involved. Decisions may or may not be enforceable, and an appeal may be available to the District Court.

Health practitioners might find themselves appearing before bodies that have the power to discipline them, and these are not tribunals of the sort just described. For example, the

---

18   However, lawyers are now more likely to appear in Court as family law legislation has become more voluminous and complex. To some extent this could be explained by the issue of property becoming more complicated and vital, with parties more likely to engage legal advice and fight cases more vigorously.

19   This is a summary of Easton et al, *Introducing the Law* (2nd ed), Sydney, CCH, 1985, para 53.

Health Practitioners' Disciplinary Tribunal has the power to discipline doctors charged with conduct unbecoming, professional misconduct or disgraceful conduct. Since September 2004, under the Health Practitioners Competence Assurance Act 2003 all health practitioners are disciplined in the one tribunal (see chapters 4 and 15).

Another tribunal, not of the sort described above, is the Human Rights Review Tribunal,[20] in which health practitioners find themselves called as a witness or, more rarely, as the defendant in a proceeding brought against them by the Director of Proceedings for a serious breach of the Health and Disability Code of Consumers Rights[21] (see chapters 4, 5, and 6.)

2.1.9   Commissions

Commissions generally have a wider mandate than tribunals. Their activities may include the carrying out of research, education programmes, conciliation and arbitration of disputes, and scrutiny of legislation and government policy.

The Human Rights Commission deals with proceedings under the Human Rights Act 1993 (see chapter 5).

(1)   *Commissioners*

The Health and Disability Commissioner deals with complaints involving breach of the Code of Health and Disability Consumers Rights (see chapters 4 and 6). The Privacy Commissioner investigates complaints of interference with privacy (see chapter 9).

2.1.10   Employment law

This is explained in more detail in chapter 13. There is an Employment Relations Authority ("the Authority") to deal with the mediation, conciliation, and arbitration of employment disputes. Appeals from the Authority are to the Employment Court.

2.1.11   Administrative law

With the rapidly increasing amount of decision-making that has been delegated to administrators[22] and those with quasi-judicial power such as nurses' registration boards,[23] there has developed a body of law by which the decisions of administrators may be regulated and subjected to the scrutiny of a Court or tribunal. The Court or tribunal may reverse the effect of abuse, misuse, or mistake in the making of decisions, which may have an enormous effect on the lives of individuals. Complaints may be that actions taken or decisions made are:

•   Contrary to law;

---

20   Previously called the Complaints Review Tribunal.
21   The Code of Health and Disability Services Consumers Rights (reproduced in Appendix 4) is in the Schedule to the Health and Disability Commissioner (Code of Health and Disability Services Consumers Rights) Regulations 1996. The Health and Disability Commissioner Act 1994 and the Health and Disability Commissioner (Code of Health and Disability Services Consumers Rights) Regulations 1996 are reviewed regularly (every 3 to 5 years). There is a present (2009) recommendation that this review occurs every 10 years. Further information can be viewed on the Health and Disability Commissioner's website at www.hdc.org.nz/act_code/review2004.html.
22   Such delegated legislation includes the Medicines Regulations 1984, which are made under the Medicines Act 1981 and are of great importance to some health practitioners: see chapter 10.

- Not in accordance with the rule of law;
- Carried out for an improper purpose, or for improperly stated reasons;
- Made on the basis of mistake of law or fact.

There are various means for the questioning of these decisions.

(1) *Judicial review*

The common law has broadened to include many types of administrative decisions that it formerly would not have dealt with. Decisions by Ministers, and price-fixing bodies, as well as individuals and bodies acting under governmental authority, have been subjected to scrutiny.

The Court cannot consider the merits of a decision itself — that is, it cannot determine whether the actual decision was right or wrong, good or bad. It can only consider whether the *process* of making the decision was correct; whether, for example, the rules of natural justice were followed, or whether an error of law was made.

(2) *The Ombudsman*

The Ombudsman is a channel for complaints by individuals about the conduct of government departments and prescribed authorities. This may involve investigating practices or decisions by individuals in those departments and authorities, and results in a report recommending appropriate action if required. The Ombudsman cannot enforce such action, but if it is not carried out, this can be the subject of an adverse report to the Minister for the department involved, or the Prime Minister.

2.2   The English Courts

The House of Lords is the ultimate English law-making body. It is presided over by Judges who are members of the House of Lords. Though it is of persuasive precedent only, New Zealand Courts will generally follow its decisions if there is no New Zealand precedent.

Another important Court in England, and one which is often quoted in our Courts, is the English Court of Appeal. This Court is directly inferior to the House of Lords. Its decisions are treated with great respect in our Courts, because of the eminent Judges who preside over it.

These Courts are mentioned because much of the law regarding health practitioners, particularly negligence law, has been developed through these two Courts. Consequently, they are quite frequently referred to in discussions of the law.

---

23   Quasi-judicial power is described as "executive powers or functions which involve the exercise of discretion and the making of a decision in a judicial manner; for example where a Minister makes an order after consideration of the findings of an inquiry which involves the hearing of evidence": *Osborn's Concise Law Dictionary* (7th ed), London, Sweet & Maxwell, 1983.

Such decisions may involve penalties, demotion, reprimand, or other disciplinary action and see chapter 15 where the disciplinary powers of the Nursing Council are discussed. Further examples of legislation granting such powers are social welfare legislation, which gives the Director-General of Social Welfare the power to make decisions regarding allocation of social welfare benefits, and for example legislation allowing licensing boards to decide on the giving or withdrawal of licences.

2.3   Judicial decisions from other countries

The Court systems of Australia and Canada are too complex to outline here, but they are a source of many decisions on health law matters. These decisions may be offered as persuasive arguments before our Courts where the matter has not been decided in New Zealand or the UK. This is especially the case with Australian decisions. US decisions are of interest, but are generally less persuasive as the US legal system is different from that in New Zealand, Australia, and Canada.

2.4   Law reporting

As precedent is so important in the legal system, accurate reporting of cases, and easy reference to them, is crucial. Official reports of appeal cases are reported by recognised bodies under the control of the New Zealand Council of Law Reporting. Reports covering each Court level in each jurisdiction are published. Cases are cited by giving the name of the case, the year of the volume (in square brackets) or the year of the decision or the year in which the case is reported (in round brackets), followed by the volume number, report series, and page number. A list of the most commonly cited series of reports is in Appendix 1.[24]

2.4.1   New Zealand

Cases from the High Court, Court of Appeal, and New Zealand appeals to the Privy Council are reported in the *New Zealand Law Reports* ("NZLR"), which have been continuous since 1886, or more recently in specialist law reports such as the *Family Reports of New Zealand* ("FRNZ") and *Employment Reports of New Zealand* ("ERNZ"). District Court cases are reported in the *District Court Reports* ("DCR"). Thus, the case of *A-G v Gilbert*, which is to be found in volume 2 of the *New Zealand Law Reports* at page 342 and was reported in the year 2002 is cited as *A-G v Gilbert* [2002] 2 NZLR 342 (CA).[25]

2.5   Further reading

P Joseph, *Constitutional and Administrative Law in New Zealand* (3rd ed), Wellington, Brookers, 2008.

M McDowell and D Webb, *The New Zealand Legal System* (4th ed), Wellington, Butterworths, 2002.

R D Mulholland, *Introduction to the New Zealand Legal System* (10th ed), Wellington, Butterworths, 2001.

---

24   An excellent tool for looking up law reports is the appendix, "Using the law library" in F K H Maher, *Derham, Maher and Waller, an introduction to law* (6th ed), Sydney, Law Book Co, 1991.

25   This case, among other things, concerned the stressful and dangerous work environment that the respondent worked in, and the appellant's failure to address the respondent's workload.

Chapter 3

THE LEGAL PROCESS

SUE JOHNSON AND REBECCA KEENAN

Contents

3.1   Introduction

The legal system, that is the operation of lawyers, Courts, and police, is concerned with two main processes. The first is that of resolving disputes, whether they are between the State and a citizen or citizens, or between two individuals. The second is concerned with establishing a person's status or rights and obligations.

3.2   Dispute resolution

3.2.1   Civil or criminal action?

Disputes at law arise when a person or body claims that another has done them a wrong. Criminal actions are instigated by the Crown (in the guise of the State, through the police or, for example, the IRD) claiming a person has committed a wrong against it by committing an offence. A civil action is instigated by an individual, who claims that another person has wronged (harmed) her/him, either physically, mentally, or economically, or is likely to cause such harm by their proposed actions.

Criminal cases are prosecuted by an agent of the State, for example serious criminal charges are prosecuted by the Crown. They are officially designated, for example, *R v Bloggs* (*Regina v Bloggs*, pronounced "The Queen and Bloggs"). If the prosecution is successful, the convicted person is punished. The Crown is not interested in compensating the victim in these cases, only in punishing the offender. However, more attention is being paid to victims, and the Victims Rights Act 2002 provides for the treatment of victims and for information to be made available to them. Victims of offences may be eligible for compensation under the Injury Prevention, Rehabilitation, and Compensation Act 2001.

Civil cases, on the other hand, are brought about mainly by:

*   One person[1] against another, claiming damage wrongfully inflicted, or a debt owing, and seeking compensation. In this type of case the first person is suing, not prosecuting, the other. The person suing is called the plaintiff, the person being sued is called the defendant.
*   A person seeking endorsement of a claim to certain rights and privileges against another. That person is called an applicant to the Court, and any person or body opposing the claim is called the respondent.

The Crown's only interest here, through the Judges, is that the contest in Court is carried out according to the established procedure and rules of evidence. It acts as a referee in both types of case (the Judges of course have the added role of interpreting the law and determining the facts). Civil cases are designated, for example, *Smith v Jones* (pronounced

---

[1]   The term "person" in law includes the plural, and refers to individuals, male or female, so long as they are born alive, and also to corporate bodies. Often the word "party" is used to refer to someone involved in a dispute.

"Smith and Jones") — the name of the plaintiff or applicant is first, followed by that of the defendant or respondent.

3.2.2 Appeals

As mentioned earlier, one can appeal from an adverse judgment, but not simply because one does not like it. It must be shown that a Judge made a legal mistake in the conduct of the case, or in the way the jury was instructed, or that the trial procedure was somehow unjust or unfair to the appellant. The case would then be designated with the appellant's name first, and the name of the defendant (who is now called the respondent) second. For example, if the defendants in the hypothetical cases cited above appealed, they would become the appellants, and the prosecutor and plaintiff respectively would become the respondents: *Bloggs v R* and *Jones v Smith*.

Court action, or litigation, is the last resort for actions other than criminal ones. The prospective expense to those concerned, as well as to the State, means that where a dispute arises those involved will attempt to resolve it before an approach to the Courts is made. Negotiations are therefore made under the shadow of the law, so to speak, with the possibility of Court action ever present. This strengthens the hand of whoever has the law clearly on their side. Where the law is unclear, those involved may feel that they are dragged into litigation because of someone else hoping to take a chance on obtaining a favourable Court judgment.

The threat of expensive litigation can be used as a bluff to frighten people into compliance, for example idle threats to sue another in defamation if they disclose certain information may prevent that person from disclosing the information out of fear of being dragged through the Courts. This response to a legitimate complaint at work, for example, of incompetence or dangerous practices by a colleague or the hospital management, or of sexual harassment by another at work, may frighten a nurse into silence (see chapter 9 for an outline of the law relating to information disclosure).

Most issues between disputants at law are resolved out of Court. No more than about 3 percent of all claims for compensation for alleged negligence end up in Court.[2] The remainder are abandoned, or settled by negotiation. This is called an "out-of-Court settlement". Insurance companies, of course, prefer to settle claims out of Court, and put great emphasis on doing so. One must also consider that many possible actions are never even started.

Most legal disputes are resolved by the parties themselves through negotiation by their lawyers, with avoidance of Court action being a high priority. Such negotiations are usually classified as "without prejudice". This means that one party to the dispute will not be able to rely on what is contained in the documents as an admission of fault by the other party if they refuse an offer to pay damages and decide to go to Court. There is always the threat of one party taking the other to Court if the matter is not resolved, and both parties have in mind the possible outcome if the matter does go to Court.

---

[2]   A comprehensive discussion and referral to authorities on this topic can be found in Luntz et al, *Torts: Cases and Commentary* (2nd ed), Sydney, Butterworths, 1985, chapter 1.

3.2.3   Cost of legal action

Legal advice costs money, and is not cheap. In New Zealand a client must pay for a lawyer's advice and other legal expenses in criminal and family law matters, whatever the outcome. The exception is where a party is eligible for, and is granted, legal aid, which is subject to a person's income and the likelihood of success. In civil matters the general principle is that the "loser" pays their own costs plus the "winner's" costs. This is a deterrent to legal action in many cases, and is a reason for the dearth of matters that go to Court. In the US and the UK some lawyers operate on the principle of the contingency fee, which means that they are only paid if they win the case. Payment is a proportion of the compensation paid to their client. An indirect result of this principle is that people are more likely to sue knowing they have nothing financially to lose.

3.2.4   Functions of the legal dramatis personae

(1)   *Solicitors and barristers*

Lawyers in New Zealand who practise law are usually barristers and solicitors of the High Court of New Zealand. They are both solicitors and barristers but must choose whether to work as a barrister or solicitor.

(2)   *Solicitors*

Some solicitors are like general practitioners, doing a variety of work. Others are specialists in a particular area of law such as conveyancing, trusts, commercial law, resource management, family law, criminal law or medical law. Some solicitors are specialists in Court work, which is in litigation, and this might be as well as being specialists in other areas. The solicitor is the person to whom one takes a problem in the first instance. The solicitor determines whether it is a problem that can be solved by the legal profession, and advises the client on what action to take. If litigation (taking the matter to Court) is advised, the solicitor may decide to undertake the litigation personally, or refer it to a litigation solicitor or to a barrister.

(3)   *Barristers*

In New Zealand a client cannot normally approach a barrister directly. The barrister must be instructed by a solicitor. Barristers specialise in Court work. Once the solicitor refers a client to a litigation solicitor or barrister, that person prepares all the arguments in favour of the client. The other party, of course, also has a litigator arguing for it. When appearing in Court these lawyers are called counsel. If one is aware that modern case law developed out of trial by battle, where the parties originally fought each other to see who would win the point, and later on paid professional fighters to fight for them, one can understand the verbal battle that takes place in our courtrooms. The decision-makers decide the winner.

Counsel on both sides may attempt to negotiate a settlement (acting under the instructions of their prospective clients), even while the matter is in Court. The parties may come to an agreement at any time in the progress of legal action, up to the Court's judgment. It may be that at a particular point in the trial counsel may consider it in their best interest to accept an offer from the other side, and will advise the client accordingly. The decision to do so, however, is up to the client.

(4)   *The jury*

Juries sit in criminal trials and in defamation hearings (chapter 9). They have the task of listening to witnesses and deciding on the facts presented to them as to what must have happened. They are guided by the Judge, who explains the law to them. For example, if a person is accused of murder, the Judge will tell the jury what constitutes murder at law (for example, what state of mind the accused must have had) and the jury then decides whether what the accused did amounts to that legal definition. The Judge also acts as a kind of referee, making sure that proper procedure is followed and that the rules of evidence are adhered to. This is to ensure that the person who is complained against has a "fair" trial as prescribed by procedural law.

(5)   *The Judge*

A Judge sitting with a jury has the task of ensuring that procedural and evidential rules are complied with. Judges rule on what evidence can be admitted and on any other legal questions that arise, including instructing the jury as to their tasks. A Judge sitting alone, which happens in most civil cases, must act as both Judge and jury. In a criminal case, where the defendant has been found guilty, the Judge determines the sentence to be imposed.

3.2.5   Proof

(1)   *The burden of proof*

A very important fact to keep in mind is that the party bringing the action usually has the burden of proving its case. This means that defendants or respondents do not have to prove their innocence. They need only raise a doubt as to the validity of the case brought by the applicant/plaintiff. Where that doubt exists, the Court must find in the defendant's favour.

(2)   *The standard of proof*

In criminal cases the prosecution has to convince the jury *beyond a reasonable doubt* that the accused is guilty. This means that unless the prosecution has left no reasonable doubt in the jury's mind as to the accused's guilt, despite the accused's attempts to create that doubt, they must acquit. In a civil case the burden on the plaintiff or applicant amounts to convincing the Court *on the balance of probabilities*. This is not as difficult as the standard of proof for a criminal case. The Court must find a defendant not liable unless the plaintiff has proved their case to that standard. The defendant does not have to prove their case, only throw doubt on the plaintiff's arguments.

3.2.6   Outline of a criminal action

The following main steps of bringing an action are necessarily sketchy and general. The main steps of a criminal action apply both to a summary and an indictable offence. They will, it is hoped, give at least a basic idea of the legal process:

Step 1:   Alleged criminal behaviour takes place.

Step 2:   The alleged behaviour is reported to the police if they are not present at the scene.

Step 3:   The police arrest the suspect (section 32 of the Crimes Act 1961 requires that where the police arrest a person without a warrant they must have reasonable and probable grounds to believe that the person committed the offence). Once arrested, the person must be charged with an offence without delay. Once charged, a person is referred to as "the accused".

Step 4:   The accused may be released on police bail, which is an agreement or "recognisance" to appear in Court when required, or they may be remanded in custody, in which case they must be brought before a Judge or Justice of the Peace as soon as practicable. The Judge or Justice of the Peace may allow police bail in the latter case. Where bail is allowed conditions may be placed on the accused to ensure that they will turn up for trial.

(1)   *Summary offence*

Summary offences are those that are defined in the legislation as such. They are generally minor offences, and are to be tried summarily, that is on the spot by a Judge without a jury.

Step 5:   The accused, now also called the defendant, appears in Court and pleads either guilty or not guilty. If the plea is guilty, sentence is passed and the matter concluded. If the plea is not guilty:

Step 6:   The prosecution presents evidence. Each witness for the prosecution is:

- Examined by the prosecution;
- Cross-examined by the defence to test their evidence;
- Re-examined by the prosecution to establish their contribution to the case.

Step 7:   The defence presents its evidence in a similar way.

Step 8:   The Judge makes a decision as to a verdict — guilty or not guilty. If not guilty, the accused is released and the matter concluded. If guilty, they are the subject of some form of penalty in the light of the maximum penalty set by law and any submissions made to the Judge on that matter by either party.

Step 9:   Either party may appeal to a higher Court.

(2)   *Indictable offence*

Indictable offences are also defined in the legislation. They are generally serious offences, and the accused is entitled to trial by Judge and jury. On 29 June 2009 there was a major change in the law as to committal proceedings.[3] Prior to this change an accused would go through a preliminary hearing stage where the judge decided if there was enough evidence on which a jury could find the defendant guilty (a prima facie case). This process has been substituted for a "standard committal procedure", where cases are set down on the papers.

Step 5:   The accused appears in the District Court and the Registrar serves the defendant notice that he/she has 42 days to file written witness statements and committal will be on the basis of these statements. The prosecution also have 42 days in which to file written witness statements.

Step 6:   Once the 42 days fall the defendant has 14 days to apply for a oral evidence hearing; the prosecution also have this opportunity. If an oral evidence hearing is not applied for, then the Registrar proceeds with a standard committal. It is not a consideration of the evidence and neither party is required to be present.

---

3   Summary Proceedings Amendment Act (No 2) 2008.

Step 7: The defendant may plead guilty before committal but this is not advisable until after full disclosure. Under the new disclosure rules[4] this would be after day 21, as initial disclosure must be within 21 days of the defendant's first appearance and full disclosure as soon as practicable once the defendant pleads either not guilty or elects trial by jury. This is to ensure that the defendant is making a decision to plead guilty on proper consideration of the facts. Prior to the change to the committal procedure, if a defendant wished to plead guilty before committal, the request had to be in writing.[5] This requirement has been repealed, and it can now be done orally.[6] If the defendant attends court for this purpose then the charge must be put to the defendant and he must be called on to either plead guilty or not guilty.[7] The standard committal procedure does not provide a formal opportunity for this and unless prompted by the defendant they will proceed automatically to a post committal hearing.

Step 8: Once through this committal process then the trial process continues as set out below.

Step 9: The accused appears before the Judge and jury for trial and pleads. If the plea is guilty, and the Judge is satisfied the defendant is genuine and mentally competent to so plead, sentence is passed and the case concluded. If the plea is one of not guilty, the case is set down for trial where both prosecution and defence cases are again presented. However, although the examination of witnesses and exhibits occurs as before, this time it occurs before a jury. The jury is guided in matters of law by a Judge and it must decide, based on the facts presented, whether the offence with which the accused is charged has been proved beyond reasonable doubt. The jury brings in its verdict of guilty or not guilty, which must be accepted by the Judge whose task then is to either release the accused if not guilty, or to pronounce sentence. Though the maximum punishment for any particular offence is set by the legislation, the Judge has some discretion within that limit to impose anything from a token punishment, for example a suspended sentence, to the maximum provided by the legislation. In making this decision the Judge considers arguments on behalf of the parties as to what the sentence should be.

Step 10: An appeal may be made to a higher Court by either party.

3.2.7 Outline of a civil action

Step 1: Harm occurs to a person (the plaintiff), or that person's property.

Step 2: The plaintiff sends the other party a letter of demand, stating the party's case and demands. If the claim is not met by the other person, or a settlement not negotiated, the plaintiff sends a letter stating that if there is not resolution within a set time, the matter will be taken to Court.

Step 3: The plaintiff issues, through the appropriate Court, a notice of proceeding (a claim to have been wronged and a command to appear in Court to answer the

---

4   Criminal Disclosure Act 2008.
5   Summary Proceedings Act 1957, (former) section 153A.
6   Summary Proceedings Act 1957, section 160.
7   Summary Proceedings Act 1957, section 161.

allegations), together with a statement of claim (a detailed list of allegations and statement of compensation claimed). The wrong must be one recognised by law and named accordingly, for example, battery and negligence: see chapters 5 and 7.

Step 4:   The person accused (the defendant) has a set period of time, for example 30 days, to lodge a statement of defence with the Court, setting out an answer to the claim. The defendant may in fact make a counterclaim, alleging that they have been harmed by the plaintiff. The plaintiff must duly answer this in a similar way.

Step 5:   Either party may seek further information through processes called "interrogatories" and "discovery", which may be required under certain circumstances to provide the other side with answers to questions and access to documents. At any stage the defendant may offer the plaintiff a settlement, which is a sum less than that demanded or of course the full amount. The matter may be resolved by the plaintiff accepting it (settlement out of Court). This option is very tempting to the plaintiff as it relieves the hardship and anxiety associated with this sort of case. As explained above, this happens in most cases.

Step 6:   If both parties intend to proceed, they notify the Court when they are ready and set a date for the hearing. Legislation has provided that juries rarely appear in civil cases, especially those concerning negligence, so that the case is usually before a Judge alone.

Step 7:   Evidence is presented in a similar way to that described for criminal trials. A decision is made, and an award of compensation is ordered if the plaintiff's case is successful.

Step 8:   A party may be ordered by the Judge to pay the other party's legal costs.

Step 9:   An appeal may be made by either party to a higher Court.

3.2.8   Applications

At common law and under some statutes, one may apply to the appropriate Court for a ruling in one's favour on particular matters. In these cases the person bringing the application is the applicant, and anyone opposing it is the respondent. Some examples of applications are:

* An application for dissolution of marriage (contrary to popular terminology, one does not sue for divorce), custody of children, property distribution on dissolution, and declaration of property interests.
* An application to appoint a guardian for certain people under the Protection of Personal and Property Rights Act 1988.[8]
* An application for an injunction from the Court in some circumstances, which is a Court order under which a party to an action is ordered either to refrain from doing an act (restrictive injunction), or to carry out an act (mandatory injunction). The Court must be satisfied that the applicant would suffer harm unjustly if the injunction is not issued, and that various rules regarding the petitioner's eligibility to apply, and the worthiness of the action are met.

---

8   Under this Act one can apply for guardianship over those who are incapable of handling their own affairs.

One can apply for a declaration in some circumstances. A declaration is:

- A formal statement by a Court intending to create, assert, preserve or testify to a person's right;
- A finding on a question of law.

An example of an application for a declaration is the case of *Auckland AHB v A-G* (see 16.5.4(8)).[9] In this case the plaintiffs applied for a declaration under the Declaratory Judgments Act 1908 that their actions in switching off a ventilator of a patient suffering from an extreme case of Guillain-Barre syndrome would not amount to an offence under sections 151 and 164 of the Crimes Act 1961 (accelerating death and homicide).

3.3 Legal reasoning

The law is handed down to us by statute or precedent. We interpret it for ourselves in everyday life. However, where there is a dispute as to the meaning of the law or how it is to be applied, the Courts use legal reasoning to come to an answer. It is important to remember that:

- Legal reasoning is not the same as common sense, although common sense is invoked as the approach to use in some circumstances.
- Legal reasoning may produce a result different from the morally just or fair. An example of this is where the Court found that a doctor who did not bother to examine a man who was desperately ill was not liable in negligence, even though the man later died of arsenic poisoning. One might think that justice would place responsibility with the doctor, but the Court found that he did not fulfil all the requirements for liability in negligence (see chapter 8).[10] One could argue, of course, that this is justice according to law.

How, then, do Courts reason? This question is addressed in examining statutory interpretation and the use of precedent separately.

3.3.1 Statutory interpretation

Statutory provisions are subject to the same problem found with all language — they are not always clear. Words may be ambiguous or vague. One provision of an Act may appear to contradict another, or, despite clear language, appear ambiguous in its overall construction.

Courts, in interpreting statutes, are guided by rules which have been developed by statute or common law. Thus, we have the Interpretation Act 1999 which sets out some rules as to how to interpret words, for example, the meaning of "month" is stated to be a calendar month and therefore not a lunar month. We also have some common law principles that apply to terms in general, or to specific terms in specific statutes.

(1)   *Rule 1 — Serve the purpose of the Act — Section 5 Interpretation Act 1999*

This important section in the Interpretation Act 1999 provides that when determining the meaning of a word within an Act or regulation, the Court must consider the text and the purpose of that Act or regulation.[11] This section is a codification of the common law

---

9   *Auckland AHB v A-G* [1993] 1 NZLR 235.
10   *Barnett v Chelsea & Kensington Hospital Management Committee* [1968] 1 All ER 1068, discussed in chapter 8.

"purpose" or "mischief" rule. The Act and every word in it are to be interpreted as widely as possible to give effect to Parliament's reason for enacting such legislation. The purpose of the Act is generally discernible from the preamble, which states what the Act is to achieve. Section 5(3) of the Interpretation Act 1999 provides some examples of what matters can be used to assist in deciding the meaning of the statute. The purpose of an Act is the reason Parliament had for legislating in that way. It is generally discernible in the Second Reading speech given by the Minister who introduces the Bill to Parliament, but may also require consideration of other sources, such as documentation of parliamentary debates, parliamentary committee reports, or Law Reform Commission reports. The Courts have a discretion to determine what materials they will use (with the proviso that they may be prohibited from consulting them).

This is not the end of the story. There may be further problems in determining the meaning of a statutory provision. Other maxims have been developed that Courts may use to help with interpretation. Though they do not have any particular order, and do not have the mandatory effect of the purposive rule, they should be considered in the light of the "purpose" rule and section 5.

(2)   Rule 2 — The literal rule

Another ancient but time-honoured rule is that words are to be given their ordinary everyday meaning, unless of course they are specific legal terms, when they must be given their legal meaning.[12] If the literal meaning is clear, the statute makes sense, and by giving that interpretation the purpose of the statute is fulfilled, one looks no further. If the purpose of the Act is not fulfilled by giving a word its ordinary and popular meaning, another meaning must be sought under the more dominant "purpose" rule. Sometimes the everyday meaning of a word may have changed since the Act was passed. The "purpose" rule and section 5 predominate, and the meaning that Parliament intended the word to have must be used, as far as is practicable, to give effect to the purpose of the Act.

An exception to this rule is where the words used are specifically defined, either in the Interpretation Act 1999, or in the specific Act itself. Most Acts have an interpretation section at the beginning, where key words are defined specifically for that Act. This, of course, is the first place to look in determining a word's meaning.

Examples of the conflict between these two rules can be seen in the cases of *Fisher v Bell*,[13] and a case described by O'Sullivan.[14] In *Fisher v Bell* the legislation provided that anyone who "sells, lends or gives" a flick-knife to another is guilty of an offence. Parliament meant to prevent the presence of flick-knives in the community. A police officer saw flick-knives in a shop window and proceeded to prosecute the shopkeeper. The Court considered the

---

11   Derived from *Heydon*'s case (1584) 3 Co Rep 7a; 76 ER 637. This ancient case has been endorsed repeatedly. It stated that the Courts should, when interpreting a statutory provision, consider (a) the common law before the Act was passed, (b) the mischief or defect for which the common law did not provide, (c) the required remedy as determined by Parliament, and (d) the "true reason" for the remedy. The Court's answer is to "suppress subtle inventions and invasions of the mischief".

12   For example, the word "negligence" has a common meaning that is much more restrictive in its legal sense (see chapter 8). The word "invitee" has a special meaning in law (see chapter 14), as does "publication" (see chapter 9).

13   *Fisher v Bell* [1961] 1 QB 394.

14   J O'Sullivan, *Law for Nurses and Allied Health Professionals in Australia*, Sydney, Law Book Co, 1983, 5.

words of the statute literally, and said that the shopkeeper did not commit an offence, as he did not actually sell them to anyone, which was required for an offence under the statute. O'sullivan describes the case of a car mechanic who was under a car and asked a colleague to turn the motor on. The colleague did, and as a result the mechanic was injured. For purposes of litigation, the Court had to decide if the colleague was a "driver". Despite the fact that the colleague was not in the driver's seat, nor did he intend to "drive" the car anywhere, the Court decided he was the driver because he was in control of the means of propulsion.

(3)   Rule 3 — The golden rule

The ordinary meaning must be given to a word, unless that would lead to absurdity or some repugnancy or inconsistency with the rest of the Act, in which case the grammatical and ordinary sense of the word may be modified to avoid absurdity and inconsistency, but no further.[15]

This rule gives the Court further leeway to alter the actual wording of an Act if it were otherwise to make the meaning of the section absurd or repugnant to common sense and justice.

(4)   Rule 4 — Statute to be read as a whole

A further basic principle is that, in determining the purport of a word or a provision, the whole statute must be considered to give meaning to its general intention. For example, a statute intended to regulate the poultry industry and devoted to the raising of and dealing in hens, ducks, and geese, which refers in one of its provisions to "eggs" (a term not otherwise defined), will probably *not* apply to the eggs of fish or birds. This principle is associated with the noscitur a sociis ("birds of a feather") rule (see 3.3.2(1)).

3.3.2   Presumptions of interpretation

There are several presumptions that Courts bring to the interpretation of statutes. The main ones are as follows.

(1)   Noscitur a sociis ("birds of a feather stick together", or "one is known by one's associates") rule

This rule is applied where a general term is interpreted according to its more restrictive neighbours. Burrows[16] gives the example of the case of *King-Ansell v Police*[17] where the New Zealand Court of Appeal held that the word "ethnic" as used in the Race Relations Act 1971, does not have a narrow technical or anthropological sense, but bears a broad meaning in the phrase in which it appears — "colour, race or ethnic or national origins".

(2)   Ejusdem generis ("of the same kind") rule

This rule is similar in its effect, but refers to things of the same class. It provides that where a general "catch all" word follows a list of specific words then the general word is construed as also being limited to that class. Burrows refers to the case of *Otley v Armstrong*[18] in which an Act regulated the wages of factory workers. "Factory" was defined as "any building,

---

15   *Grey v Pearson* (1857) 6 HLC 61, 106 per Lord Wensleydale.
16   J F Burrows, *Statute Law in New Zealand* (2nd ed), Wellington, Butterworths, 1999.
17   *King-Ansell v Police* [1979] 2 NZLR 531 (CA).

office or place in which persons were employed in handcraft". It was held that an open timber yard was not a "factory", and the word "place" had to be construed as being of the same kind as "building" and "office" thus meaning a structure of some kind.

(3)   *Expressio unius exclusio alterius ("naming one thing excludes others") rule*

If specific reference is made to a particular member of a class, then, unless it causes absurdity, injustice, or does not carry out the Act's intention, all other members of that class are excluded. For example, a statute that makes it an offence for any person to sell intoxicating liquor to a minor, or for any person to purchase intoxicating liquor intended for consumption by a minor, will catch only the seller of such liquor, not someone who gives it to a minor. In addition, it excludes the manufacturer who produces the liquor, even if it is intended for minors, so long as they do not actually sell it to a minor.

(4)   *Some statutes are to be interpreted in favour of the citizen*

When the question of the meaning of a statutory provision in, for example criminal and tax statutes, involves a decision either in favour of, or against, a citizen, and there is no reason for favouring one meaning rather than the other, Courts have adopted the approach of applying the meaning that will favour the citizen, rather than the State.

(5)   *Common law should not be altered*

As the common law is the source of human rights and the protection of liberty with the Courts being the source of the exercise of such rights, there is a presumption, all things being equal and in the absence of any clear indication otherwise, that interpretation of statutory provisions should not alter common law or limit access to the Courts.

(6)   *Statutes should not be retrospective*

In the absence of clear intention to the contrary in a statute's provisions, Courts will not construe a statute to take effect before it is passed by Parliament.

The Court's interpretation of a statute becomes common law, and is precedent for the future interpretation of that statute. The precedent only applies to the statute interpreted and to identical provisions in other statutes in the same jurisdiction. So when deciding on the meaning of a word or provision, a lawyer will look for any case law involving interpretation of the statute. There are special publications that "annotate" statutes, pointing to cases where particular provisions have been interpreted by the Courts.[19]

Checklist

Interpretation of statutes

- Is the word defined in the Act itself, or in the Interpretation Act?
- If so, use that definition.
- Has this particular provision been the subject of judicial interpretation? Is that decision binding?
- If not, what is the purpose of the Act, and what meaning would give effect to it?

---

18   *Otley v Armstrong* [1938] NZLR 328. See also *Nelson Hospital Board v Cook* [1946] NZLR 287, 291: "Medical practitioner, dentist, matron, nurse, midwife or attendant or any person employed or engaged by any board".

19   Most online legal databases will have links between statute and relevant case law.

- Is that meaning the ordinary meaning of the word or the legal meaning if it is a legal term?
- If not, is the purpose of the Act so clear as to warrant this unusual meaning of the word?
- Is the purpose of the Act clear enough to override any of the rules and presumptions mentioned above? If not, they should be applied.

3.4   Common law

Judges decide cases before them, with their primary concern being the issues as they affect the actual parties involved. Unlike statutory law, which is concerned with future behaviour and applies to all designated people for all time (until it is changed), Courts are concerned with past events and those who appear before them. As our society values fairness and stability, and this is not attainable without some degree of certainty as to how cases will be decided, Judges decide them by applying the principles of common law, as described in chapter 1.

3.4.1   Determining the reason for a decision

When declaring a decision in a case a Judge must explain the legal principle or principles applied when coming to the decision. This is part of the official reason for the decision, or "ratio decidendi" (plural "rationes decidendi"), which may be colloquially described as "the ratio". Where the Court is an appeal Court, the ratio decidendi then becomes binding on Courts that are lower in the Court hierarchy of the particular jurisdiction, or of persuasive value to Courts in other jurisdictions, that is, they are treated with respect, but following them is not mandatory. Many medical issues have been considered in Courts overseas but not in New Zealand, so the rationes from those cases are used here when such issues arise. However, they are of persuasive value only.

3.4.2   Other observations in a case

A judgment may contain more than the reason for the decision, such as observations and general comments. These are known as "obiter dicta" or "obiter" (meaning "said by the way"). They are not binding on any Court, although they may be followed anyway.

An example of the distinction between ratio decidendi and obiter dicta can be seen in a brief outline of the following case.

Case

Hedley Byrne & Co Ltd v Heller & Partners Ltd [1964] AC 465 (HL)

Advertising agents (the plaintiffs) were concerned about the creditworthiness of a client. They requested the client's bank (the defendant) to provide them with an assessment of the client's financial position. The bank responded in a letter headed "Private. For your private use and without responsibility on the part of the bank or its officials", and stated that the client was good for its ordinary business engagements, but that the enterprise mentioned was bigger than it was "accustomed to see". The advertising agency took this as a sign of approval and went ahead with the proposed deal. In fact the deal fell through when the client went bankrupt, and the advertising agency sued the bank in negligence for not giving them reasonable advice.[20]

The Court in fact relied on the law relating to the disclaimer of responsibility by the bank, and held that this protected the bank from any action, as it disclaimed any responsibility as to the validity of its comments. That was straightforward, and formed the ratio decidendi of the case. However, five of the Judges went on to consider the giving of professional advice in general, where no disclaimer is made, and set out principles of law to cover such situations. These comments were obiter dicta, the result of the Law Lords' anxiety to establish the fact that negligence could extend to cases where professional advice was badly given, although this was not such a case.[21] Although such statements were obiter dicta, as five Judges agreed on them it is generally considered they should be followed.[22] However, as they were only obiter dicta, they would not be held as laying down the "metes and bounds" of the law on negligent advice.[23]

Where more than one Judge gives judgment, there may be disagreement as to the decision which should be made. The majority decision is the one that is binding. There may be dissension, however, among these Judges as to *why* they have come to that decision. The lawyer's task is to determine whether there is any common ground among the majority Judges. This may not constitute a ratio decidendi, as there may not be a majority who have given it as the reason for their decision, as described above, but it has the same qualified authority of obiter dicta. Sometimes there may be a majority decision as to the verdict, but no common reason for it, in which event the case is said to have no ratio, and is of no use as precedent.

3.4.3   Distinguishing cases

Given that in a particular type of situation the law is established by precedent, counsel for one of the parties may argue that the facts in the previous case under consideration were significantly different from the facts in the case before the Court in this instance, and therefore the precedent cannot be applied. Suppose, for example, in *Hedley Byrne & Co Ltd v Heller & Partners Ltd* (see 3.4.2) the plaintiff's counsel pointed to a previous case where careless advice had been given, which was found to be negligent. Counsel then argued that the Court should follow that case and find that the statement given by the bank as to the client company's creditworthiness was also negligent. The defendant could argue that the waiver of responsibility in the bank's statement was a significant fact that distinguished this case from the previous one, and so the principle of law developed in the previous case should not be applied here.

The common law has inbuilt flexibility, however, in several ways:

- The facts themselves may be distinguished;
- Material (significant) facts, as opposed to the facts as a whole, may be disputed;
- The ratio decidendi of a previous case may be challenged;

---

20   The action for negligent advice is dealt with in more detail in chapter 8.

21   Easton et al, *Introducing the Law* (2nd ed), Sydney, CCH, 1985, 81.

22   In *W B Anderson & Sons Ltd v Rhodes (Liverpool) Ltd* [1967] 2 All ER 850, Cairns J commented that although the statements in *Hedley Byrne & Co Ltd v Heller & Partners Ltd* [1964] AC 465 are obiter, when five members of the House of Lords say something a single Judge in a lower Court should follow it.

23   See *Mutual Life & Citizens' Assurance Co Ltd v Evatt* [1971] AC 793, 805-809 per Lord Diplock.

- The wording of legal principles may be vague and open to various and changing interpretations, so that over time the meaning of a particular principle may be modified.

It can be seen that the process of legal reasoning is complex. The apparently simple theory of considering the facts, determining the relevant law, applying legal reasoning to them, and then declaring judgment, is not what it seems. Thus, when asked for advice on a particular issue, lawyers can, by going through the process and considering arguments for both sides, only come up with an educated opinion as to which party may have a better legal argument. No result is guaranteed, though many may be assured. See the checklist at 3.4.4(2).

3.4.4   What do Judges do where there is no legislation or precedent?

Sometimes there are situations before the Court in which the facts are so novel there is no analogous precedent case. Such a case is called "res integra", or a "case of first impression". In the absence of binding precedent, a Judge is free to choose which of three approaches to take: arguing from analogy; following persuasive precedent; or considering public policy.

(1)   *Arguing from analogy*

This involves taking binding precedent cases with similar but distinguishable facts, extracting broad principles from them, and adapting the principles to the fact situation currently before the Court.

(2)   *Following persuasive precedent*

Cases from other jurisdictions are considered and applied. Often US cases are cited in judgments on issues not previously litigated in English or New Zealand Courts.

Checklist

Applying precedent

Establish the importance of the case being applied (binding or persuasive precedent).

Analysing each case

- What seem to be the important facts in the case under consideration?
- What other cases deal with similar facts?
- In those cases what was the decision, who won, and what order was made by the Court?
- What propositions of law were relied on by the Judge(s) as essential to the decision that was reached?[24]
- What facts were essential in linking those legal propositions to the decision?[25]
- What propositions put forward in the judgment were *not* essential to the decision?[26]

Establishing any distinctions between the precedent cases

- In arriving at an overall statement on what the law is, are there any differences between the facts of the precedent cases?

---

24   The answers to this question and the one below identify the ratio of the case.
25   The answers to this question and the one above identify the ratio of the case.
26   The answer to this question identifies obiter dicta.

- Are there any important differences in the legal principles applied to the facts?

Considering a situation of your own

- Compare the facts of the situation with those of the precedent cases, noting differences and similarities.
- Are there enough similarities to apply a principle of law to your situation?
- Would you need to know more facts to reach a definite conclusion? If so, these must be established.

Case

Haynes v Harwood [1935] 1 KB 146 (Eng CA)

The defendant's employee left his horse-drawn van unattended in the street while he went about his deliveries. A child mischievously threw a stone at the horses, which panicked and bolted. A police officer nearby saw a woman and some children were endangered by the runaway horses and van, and succeeded in stopping them. He was injured, and sued the owner of the horses in negligence, as their servant had acted without due care in leaving them. The defendant appealed to the Court of Appeal from a finding of liability against it.

The Court accepted that the delivery man had acted without due care. The defendant argued that it was not liable because the police officer had voluntarily undertaken the risk of harm when he decided to stop the horses, and so this was a case of "volenti non fit injuria" (no injury is done to one who consents; freely consenting to undertake a risk, which prevents one from claiming when one is harmed by it).

In fact there was no case with similar facts to provide a precedent for the Court of Appeal. The Judges turned to US law on similar rescue scenarios. In one paragraph Lord Greer said:[27]

> "The third ground was treated as if it was a separate ground, namely, that the principle of volenti non fit injuria applied …. The effect of the American cases, although we are not bound by them, is, I think, accurately stated in Professor Goodhart's article: 'Rescue and Voluntary Assumption of Risk' (1934) 5 Cam LJ 192. In summing up the American authorities … the learned author says (at 196): 'The American rule is that the doctrine of the assumption of risk does not apply where the plaintiff has, under an exigency caused by the defendant's wrongful misconduct, consciously and deliberately faced a risk, even of death, to rescue another from imminent danger of personal injury or death, whether the person endangered is one to whom he owes a duty of protection, as a member of his family, or is a mere stranger to whom he owes no such special duty.' In my judgment, that passage not only represents the law of the United States but also of this country."

He went on to argue that a general principle from a different but similar set of facts could be applied. The cases discussed in US precedent involved rescue by passers-by:

---

27   For further discussion of the duty of care mentioned here see chapter 8.

"[The above principle] is all the more applicable to this case because the man injured was a policeman who might readily be anticipated to do the very thing which he did, whereas the intervention of a mere passer-by was not so probable."

(3)   *Considering public policy*

Judges are conscious of the fact that they are supposed to dispense justice, as recognised by the society in which they are operating, in the absence of clear legal directives. Thus public policy is a basis of legal judgments, although Judges are reluctant to be too open in applying it. Public policy serves a purpose, however. Its most famous application was in *Donoghue v Stevenson*[28] (discussed more fully at 8.4, where the facts and judgment are given). This case involved the Court's decision in the light of precedent that the Judges did not believe was fair and just. In that case Lord Atkin said:[29]

"It is said that the law of England and Scotland is that the poisoned consumer has no remedy against the negligent manufacturer. If this were the result of the authorities, I should consider the result a grave defect in the law, and so contrary to principle that I should hesitate long before following any decision to that effect which had not the authority of this House."

He went on to say that the law should not be "so remote from the ordinary needs of civilised society … as to deny a legal remedy where there is so obviously a social wrong".[30]

Policy is a nebulous thing, however, and depends very much on individual opinion. This was demonstrated by the fact that in the same case Lord Buckmaster came to the conclusion that the "poisoned consumer" should not be able to recover damages on the ground of public policy, as it would make the manufacturer liable for every bottle that issues from their works, and that they might be "called on to meet claims of damages which they could not possibly investigate or answer".[31]

In the end, the majority of the Judges adopted Lord Atkin's approach and Lord Buckmaster dissented. The majority was by a 3:2 margin, so one can see the uncertainty in relying on policy.

In a later case, *Dutton v Bognor Regis Urban District Council*, Lord Denning explained his approach to policy.

Case

Dutton v Bognor Regis Urban District Council [1972] 1 QB 373 (Eng CA)

Mrs Dutton bought a house that developed serious defects because it had been built on an old rubbish dump and had inadequate foundations. Mrs Dutton was the third owner of the house. When the house was being built the council carried out a routine inspection of the foundations and passed them as satisfactory. The Court found that the inspection was carried out negligently, but had to decide, in the absence of any precedents, whether the council should be held liable.

---

28   *Donoghue v Stevenson* [1932] AC 562.
29   *Donoghue v Stevenson* [1932] AC 562, 582.
30   *Donoghue v Stevenson* [1932] AC 562, 583.
31   *Donoghue v Stevenson* [1932] AC 562, 578.

Lord Denning was confronted with the argument that liability on the part of the council would "open the floodgates" to numerous claims which, if successful, would place an unfair burden on the ratepayers. He decided to invoke public policy and expressed the questions he should ask, in coming to a decision, in the following way:

- First, who is responsible in fact for the harm to the plaintiff? In the case before him he found that the council shared the blame with the builder, as its job was in fact to prevent the very thing that happened.
- Secondly, is there any reason in law why the council should not be held liable? He found that there was not.
- Thirdly, if the council was found liable, would this have an adverse effect on the council's work, that is, would it deter it from carrying out inspections at all, or cause it to be so cautious that inspections would be unnecessarily held up? In fact he decided that if liability were found, it would simply tend to make the council carry out the work more carefully.
- Finally, is there any economic reason why the council should not be liable? The danger of unlimited liability through frequent claims, and subsequent inability to meet the costs, is one that causes the Courts to limit the liability of potential defendants. However, Lord Denning argued that as in this particular case the council had the resources to pay, and that in nearly every expected similar case the builder would be primarily liable and would be insured, cases where a council would be expected to compensate a plaintiff would be rare.

There has been some criticism of this approach, and one can see that opinions may differ, but it is suggested that this is a good basis for reasoning in those cases where there is no clear direction from legislation or case law.

Checklist

Legal reasoning where there is no clear law

- Is there binding precedent on a different but similar fact situation, which established a broad enough principle to apply to this situation?
- If not, is there persuasive precedent on this issue?
- If not, using public policy (for example, Lord Denning's approach), what is the most just decision?

3.5 Further reading

Burrows J F, *Statute Law in New Zealand* (2nd ed), Wellington, Butterworths, 1999.

McDowell M, and D Webb, *The New Zealand Legal System* (3rd ed), Wellington, Butterworths, 2003.

Mulholland R D, *Introduction to the New Zealand Legal System* (10th ed), Wellington, Butterworths, 2002.

Todd et al, *The Law of Torts in New Zealand* (5th ed), Wellington, Brookers, 2009.

Chapter 4

ACCOUNTABILITY OF HEALTH PRACTITIONERS

ANNE O'BRIEN, SUE JOHNSON AND JACKIE PEARSE

Contents

4.1 Introduction

Health practitioners[1] in New Zealand have been the subject of international envy as they are largely protected from civil action due to a comprehensive "no fault" accident compensation scheme. While this gives considerable protection, there are still numerous other ways in that health practitioners may be held accountable for their conduct. These forums include:

- Civil law proceedings (discussed in chapter 8, and modified in New Zealand by the above-mentioned accident compensation regime discussed below).
- Disciplinary proceedings under the Health Practitioners Competence Assurance Act 2003 (see chapter 15).
- Statutory provisions, which provide for the rights of consumers, in particular, Health and Disability Commissioner Act 1994 and regulations, and the Mental Health (Compulsory Assessment and Treatment) Act 1992, which provides for the rights

---

[1]   In this book, unless the legislation specifically refers to a particular sort of practitioner (for example the ACC legislation refers to registered health professionals), all health professionals are referred to as practitioners and people receiving health and disability services are referred to where possible as consumers or clients rather than patients unless they fall within the meaning of patient in the Mental Health (Compulsory Assessment and Treatment) Act 1992 (see 7.4.1).

of patients undergoing compulsory assessment or treatment (see chapters 5, 6 and 7).

- Prosecution for breach of the criminal law (see chapter 16).
- Proceedings under the Privacy Act 1993 (see chapter 9).
- Human Rights Review Tribunal proceedings under the Human Rights Act 1993, Health and Disability Commissioner Act 1994, and the Privacy Act 1993. This tribunal has the jurisdiction to award damages up to $200,000 and to make various other orders.[2]

As well as forums that can hold a health practitioner accountable, there are other forums such as the ACC Treatment Injury and Patient Safety Branch,[3] and Coroner's inquests that can scrutinise and investigate a health practitioner's practice. Neither the ACC Treatment Injury and Patient Safety Branch, nor a Coroner has the power to impose any penalty on health practitioners. However, it is the consequences of findings in these forums that health practitioners need to be aware of. (Coroner's inquests are discussed in detail in chapter 17.) Adverse findings in these forums may lead to the health practitioner being held accountable in a different forum.

4.2 ACC

When consumers claim they have suffered personal injury caused during or due to a health procedure or treatment, they (or their family if the consumer is deceased) may make a claim to the ACC for cover and compensation. Whenever a registered health professional is involved, the claim is referred to the ACC's Treatment Injury Centre to determine if the claimant has ACC cover.

The file is allocated to a case manager, who commences an investigation. This investigator can request copies of all clinical notes and material, if not already provided with the claim, and may require reports from registered health professionals involved in the care. In practice most claimants for cover for treatment injury will be assisted by their health care provider to make their claim.

Cover will be granted only if the claimant's injury meets the requirements set out in the current ACC legislation. At the time of writing, this is the Injury Prevention Rehabilitation and Compensation Act 2001 ("the IPRCA"). The meaning of "cover" under the scheme is set out in section 8 of the IPRCA. The claimant's injury must come within the definition of personal injury in section 26 of the IPRCA, and the relevant subsection of section 20 must be met. These subsections set out the grounds for cover for personal injury. Where the relevant subsection requires that the personal injury must be the result of treatment injury (and this will usually be the case when a consumer is claiming they were injured by treatment) the definition of treatment injury[4] must also be met.[5]

---

2   The powers of the Human Rights Review Tribunal are summarised on its website www.justice.govt.nz/tribunal/human-rights-review-tribunal/about-the-tribunal/powers-of-the-tribunal.

3   Formerly the Medical Misadventure Unit (until 30 June 2005). For a detailed explanation of the medical misadventure provisions of the IPRCA in force up to 30 June 2005 see previous editions of this book and P D G Skegg and R Paterson et al, *Medical Law in New Zealand* Wellington, Thomson Brookers, 2006.

4   Injury Prevention Rehabilitation and Compensation Act 2001, section 32.

5   Injury Prevention Rehabilitation and Compensation Act 2001, sections 8 and 26.

4.2.1 Personal injury

"Personal injury" is defined in the legislation as:

- Death;
- Physical injury;
- Mental injury consequent on physical injury (mental injury is defined as "a clinically significant behavioural, cognitive or psychological dysfunction");[6] and
- Damage (but not ordinary wear and tear) to dentures or prostheses (hearing aids, spectacles and contact lens are specifically excluded).[7]

Mental injuries caused by a specific list of criminal acts (sexual assaults) are now also covered as are work-related mental injuries. These are addressed separately in the legislation.[8]

The personal injury must be occasioned by:

- Accident;
- Treatment injury;
- Treatment for a pre-existing covered injury; or
- Work-related, treatment injury-related, or treatment-related gradual process, disease, or infection.
- Personal injury does not include:[9]
- Injury caused wholly or substantially by a gradual process, disease or infection unless it is work-related, treatment injury-related, or treatment-related;
- A cardio-vascular or cerebro-vascular episode unless it is the result of treatment or is work-related;
- Injury caused wholly or substantially by the aging process; or
- Injury to teeth or dentures caused by the natural use of those teeth or dentures.
- The circumstances in which an injury occurs may restrict or even deny a person's entitlement under the ACC regime. One such circumstance may arise in clinical trials. ACC covers an injury suffered in the course of a clinical trial in one of two circumstances: where the person injured has not agreed in writing to participate in the trial[10] or where the trial has been approved by an accredited ethics committee that is satisfied the trial is not principally for the benefit of a the manufacturer or distributor of the drug or device being trialled.[11] Otherwise compensation is provided by the sponsor.[12]

---

6   Injury Prevention Rehabilitation and Compensation Act 2001, section 27.

7   Injury Prevention Rehabilitation and Compensation Act 2001, section 26(5).

8   Injury Prevention Rehabilitation and Compensation Act 2001, sections 21 and 21B respectively.

9   Injury Prevention Rehabilitation and Compensation Act 2001, section 26(2)-(4).

10   Failure to obtain the participant's informed consent in writing would be a breach of the Code of Health and Disability Consumers Rights.

11   Injury Prevention Rehabilitation and Compensation Act 2001, section 32(4)-(6). The ethics committee has to be one approved by the Health Research Council of New Zealand or the Director-General of Health.

12   Accredited ethics committees will not normally approve a clinical trial where the sponsor has not provided sufficient compensation for injured participants in accordance with the Researched Medicines Industry's guidelines ("the RMI guidelines"). Note, however, that the RMI guidelines permit cover to be excluded in certain cases including significant deviation from the protocol.

4.2.2   Treatment Injury

Following a review of the medical misadventure provisions of the IPRCA[13] the terms "medical misadventure", "medical error" and "medical mishap" were replaced with the term "treatment injury" from 1 July 2005. The focus is now on the outcome of the treatment[14] rather than — as it was under medical error — on the fault of the person who carried it out. Nor is there a requirement that the injury be serious and rare as was required under medical mishap.

This is consistent with the "no-fault" nature of the ACC scheme and the bar on proceedings for compensation where cover is available under the scheme. Registered health professionals are asked for reports of their involvement in a claimant's care where that is necessary to make a decision on the claim. Expert opinions about that care may be asked for if the case is complex. When ACC has identified a risk of harm to the public, that risk and any other relevant information, must be reported to the relevant authority responsible for patient safety (see 4.2.2(1)).

ACC is also authorised to report risks arising from claims in the nature of treatment injury but caused by persons who are not registered health professionals.[15]

(1)   *Reporting provisions for treatment injury*

Where ACC believes, as a result of information obtained to enable it to determine a claim for treatment injury, that there is a risk of harm to the public, the Corporation must report the risk, and any other relevant information, to the authority responsible for patient safety in relation to the treatment that caused the personal injury. Reporting is mandatory in these circumstances. As a matter of policy ACC will consider whether a sentinel event[16] or serious event[17] has occurred and whether this has caused a risk of public harm.

Most frequently these events are reported to the Director General of Health and MedSafe. However depending on the circumstances reporting could also be to a registration authority such as the Nursing Council or the Medical Council. Where ACC identifies a trend — whether positive or adverse — in its database the reporting provisions enable it to report this to the relevant authority without identifying the individual(s) involved. This might, for instance, relate to particular types of treatment, equipment, medical facilities or drugs.

This is a major change in the reporting regime that existed up until 1 July 2005. Previously, the Accident Compensation Corporation was required to report findings of medical error to the relevant professional body and to the Health and Disability Commissioner. These changes are consistent with the purpose and philosophy of the Health Practitioners Competence Assurance Act 2003 and were enacted with a view to:

---

13   A consultation document Review of ACC Medical Misadventure was published and 186 submissions were received. In addition a paper was commissioned by ACC from Wellington barrister, Bruce Corkhill QC, *Medical Misadventure, Development of the Statutory Concept and its place in the current medico-legal environment.*

14   Although a mere failure to achieve a desirable outcome will not amount to treatment injury.

15   Injury Prevention Rehabilitation and Compensation Act 2001, section 284.

16   An event that results in significant additional treatment, is life threatening, or has led to an unanticipated death or major loss of function not related to the patient's illness or underlying condition.

17   An event that has the potential to result in death or major loss of function, not related to the natural course of the patient's illness or underlying condition.

- Move away from the punitive system of finding fault;
- Encourage the participation of the health sector in the claims process so as to aid fairer outcomes for claimants; and
- Encourage learning initiatives when things go wrong while still protecting public safety.[18]

Claimants for cover for treatment injury are also provided with details about the Health and Disability Commissioner's role in addressing concerns about the quality of care provided to consumers. Having cover for treatment injury does not stop a consumer making a complaint to the Commissioner, or prevent the Commissioner's Office investigating that complaint.

(2) *What sort of conduct amounts to treatment injury?*

For personal injury to amount to treatment injury three requirements must be met. The first is that the injury must be one suffered by the person when they were receiving or seeking treatment from or at the direction of one or more registered health professionals or, in limited circumstances, as result of infection passed on by a person who has suffered infection from a treatment injury.[19]

Once this first requirement is satisfied then the second limb must also be met, ie the injury must have been caused by treatment.[20] For the purposes of treatment injury "treatment" is defined in section 33 and includes:

- The giving of treatment;[21]
- Diagnosis;
- A decision on the treatment to be provided or not to be provided;
- Failure to provide treatment or delay in doing so;
- Obtaining, or failing to obtain, informed consent to treatment. This includes information provided to enable a person to make an informed decision about whether or not to accept treatment;
- Providing prophylaxis;
- The failure of equipment (which includes implants and prostheses unless the failure is as a result of an intervening act or fair wear and tear) used as part of the treatment process. This applies whether the failure occurs at the time the treatment is given or subsequently;
- The application of support systems including policies, processes, practices, and administrative systems, that are used by the organisation or person providing the treatment; and directly supports the treatment.

(3) *What is specifically excluded from treatment injury?*

Just because an injury has occurred due to treatment, it does not necessarily mean there has been treatment injury. There is an express warning in section 32(3) of the IPRCA to

---

18   (5 August 2004) 619 NZPD 14695, First Reading Injury Prevention, Rehabilitation and Compensation Amendment Bill (No 3).

19   Injury Prevention Rehabilitation and Compensation Act 2001, section 32(1)(a).

20   Injury Prevention Rehabilitation and Compensation Act 2001, section 32(2).

21   Presumably as defined in section 6 and including physical rehabilitation; cognitive rehabilitation; and an examination for the purpose of providing a certificate including the provision of the certificate.

potential claimants that treatment injury does not exist solely because desired results are not achieved.

There are also statutory exceptions[22] that specifically state that treatment injury does not include personal injury that is wholly or substantially caused by a person's underlying health condition or is a result of a person unreasonably withholding or delaying their consent to undergo treatment. Nor is it treatment injury if the personal injury is solely attributable to a resource allocation decision.

This latter warning was driven in part by cases such as the *Rau Williams* case[23] where the forerunner of what is now a District Health Board had to prioritise scarce resources and refused potentially life-saving kidney dialysis to a consumer who needed such treatment. It recognises the reality that health resources are not unlimited and that can be a legitimate factor in deciding not to treat someone. Where guidelines have been properly established by a provider to prioritise resource allocation then personal injury arising from the failure to treat will not be covered by ACC as treatment injury.

Injury which is a necessary part, or ordinary consequence of treatment, taking into account all the circumstances of the treatment, including the person's underlying health condition at the time of the treatment and clinical knowledge at the time of the treatment is not treatment injury and will not be covered under the Act.[24]

(4)   *Determining a claim for treatment injury*

In order to decide whether a claim meets the criteria for treatment injury, the claim file will be referred to the Treatment Injury Centre and investigated. Once the investigator has obtained all the relevant clinical notes and reports (usually the clinical notes will be supplied by the treatment provider at the time the claim is made) a decision will be made whether or not to grant cover. If the claim is complex, and a number of claims will be, then ACC may seek clinical advice to assist it in determining the claim.[25]

For cases that are not complex a decision will usually be made within 2 months. If it is not then the claimant must be informed that an extension of time of 2 months is required to enable a decision to be made. Further extensions of time may be made with the agreement of the claimant but in any event, a decision must be made within 9 months of a claim being lodged.[26] If ACC fails to make a decision within this statutory time frame then the claimant will have cover for the personal injury claimed.[27]

If a claimant is granted cover then they may receive some compensation for the injury from ACC. This may include home help, rehabilitation, treatment, ongoing living costs or funeral expenses where the claim arises from a death. If the definition of personal injury is not met, or the claimant was not receiving treatment from or under the direction of a registered health professional, or the injury was not caused by treatment injury, the claimant will have no ACC cover and will not receive any compensation under the Act.

22   Injury Prevention Rehabilitation and Compensation Act 2001, section 32(2).
23   *Shortland v Northland Health Ltd* [1998] 1 NZLR 433; (1997) 4 HRNZ 121 (CA), and see discussion of this case in chapter 16, at 16.5.4 (8).
24   Injury Prevention Rehabilitation and Compensation Act 2001, section 32(1)(c).
25   Injury Prevention Rehabilitation and Compensation Act 2001, section 62.
26   Injury Prevention Rehabilitation and Compensation Act 2001, section 57.
27   Injury Prevention Rehabilitation and Compensation Act 2001, section 58.

(5)   *Challenging a decision regarding treatment injury*

If a claimant is unhappy with a decision made by ACC then the claimant can seek mediation or apply for a review of the decision. An application for review must be made within 3 months of the original decision. Once a review is lodged, an external organisation, Disputes Resolutions Services Ltd ("DRSL") appoints a Review Officer, and sets a review hearing date. The claimant and ACC have the right to appear and be heard at the review, either in person and/or with legal counsel. The Review Officer will consider all matters, which may include further expert evidence, and issue a finding.

Either the claimant or ACC may appeal to the District Court against the Review Officer's finding.[28] There is a limited right of appeal, on questions of law only, from the District Court to the High Court and Court of Appeal.[29]

(6)   *Case example one*

Ms Fifield was a 46 year old woman who underwent an abdominal hysterectomy. Two years previously she had been referred to an obstetrician and gynaecology consultant at a public hospital after complaining of continuous heavy bleeding and an acute episode of urinary retention. The consultant considered that she would benefit from a hysterectomy. Another O & G consultant to whom she was later referred also advised her GP that a hysterectomy was a reasonable solution to Ms Fifield's urinary retention. Both considered that an enlarging uterine fibroid was responsible for the urinary retention problem.

Subsequently Ms Fifield saw a urologist who found that her renal tracts were normal with no voiding difficulties. Nearly 18 months later the abdominal hysterectomy was performed. The operation proceeded satisfactorily and without problems. At a post-operative review 2 weeks later the surgeon reported that he was delighted with her progress. Later that week Ms Fifield suffered 2 episodes of acute urinary retention. An ultrasound of her pelvis revealed no abnormalities.

Ms Fifield continued to experience urinary retention and a cystoscopy and urethral dilation were carried out early the following year. Her urinary retention problems continued. She needed to carry out self-catheterisation up to 4 times daily. The urologist considered the symptoms were consistent with a neurogenic bladder, possibly caused by the hysterectomy operation. An MRI scan eliminated spinal cord abnormality as a cause.

Ms Fifield lodged a claim with ACC for cover of treatment injury for neurogenic bladder following hysterectomy. ACC sought clinical advice from another urologist who was provided with all the medical reports regarding Ms Fifield's medical conditions back to 2003. That urologist's opinion was that Ms Fifield had a long-standing lower urinary tract dysfunction which pre-dated the hysterectomy.

ACC then declined cover stating that as the condition pre-existed at the date of treatment, cover could not be granted. Ms Fifield applied for a review of the decision. Her father represented her and no new evidence was presented at the Review hearing. The Reviewer found that the treatment had not caused the personal injury for which cover was sought and confirmed the decision to decline cover. Ms Fifield then appealed to the District Court.

---

28   Injury Prevention Rehabilitation and Compensation Act 2001, section 150.
29   Injury Prevention Rehabilitation and Compensation Act 2001, sections 162 and 163.

In the District Court both Ms Fifield and ACC provided further opinions from the urologists who had previously provided advice. The Court reviewed all the previous clinical records and reports as well as the updated reports. Counsel for Ms Fifield argued that the urinary problem prior to surgery was due to the presence of the uterine fibroid and the neurogenic bladder was a consequence of the hysterectomy, not a pre-existing condition. Counsel for ACC did not disagree that Ms Fifield's symptoms had worsened after surgery but submitted that the symptoms did not satisfy the definition of physical injury, that there was not sufficient evidence to establish that there was a direct link between the surgery and the neurogenic bladder and even if there was, that was a normal consequence of hysterectomy.

The Court agreed with Ms Fifield.[30] It found that as a matter of fact and law neurogenic bladder was a personal injury within the meaning of the Act. Because both specialists agreed that the damage to the bladder nerves was highly likely to be a consequence of the hysterectomy, it held that Ms Fifield did suffer the injury at the time of treatment. The Court also found that it was more probable than not that the cause of the urinary problem prior to surgery was the uterine fibroids. It rejected the argument that neurogenic bladder, when it continued a year or so past surgery, was a normal consequence of hysterectomy. The Court reversed the Corporation's decision and granted Ms Fifield cover for treatment injury.

(7)   Case example two

Mr Barron started wearing contact lenses in 2002. The lenses were prescribed by a registered health practitioner. In 2005 he experienced irritation in his right eye and was subsequently diagnosed with acanthamoeba keratitis, a rare condition. The infection is very rare in people who do not wear contact lenses but there is a risk for contact lens wearers, especially where tap water is used in lens care or lenses are worn while swimming without goggles.

Mr Barron's ophthalmology consultant was of the opinion that the infection resulted from the insertion into the right eye of a contact lens carrying the parasite. Mr Barron's sight deteriorated and he eventually lost the sight in that eye. He lodged a claim for loss of the use of his eye. ACC treated the claim as a treatment injury claim. It agreed that the injury had resulted from the insertion of a contact lens carrying the acanthamoeba parasite and that the lens held the parasite against the eye for lengthy periods of time. Nevertheless it declined cover on the grounds that the claim could not be said to amount to injury suffered as a consequence of treatment. Mr Barron applied for a review of the decision.

The Reviewer reversed the decision. He considered that Mr Barron had been prescribed the contact lenses to correct visual defects so the definition of treatment was met because the parasite had been introduced to his eye and trapped there by the lens, the acanthamoeba keratitis amounted to treatment injury. ACC lodged an appeal in the District Court.

The District Court disagreed with the Reviewer. It reversed the Reviewer's decision and reinstated the decision to decline cover. Mr Barron appealed to the High Court on the question of whether he was receiving treatment at the time the injury occurred.

The High Court considered that in order to establish a right to cover Mr Barron needed to show:

---

30   *Fifield v ACC* 29/1/09, Judge Beattie, DC Auckland Decision No 8/2009.

"1)   He had suffered a personal injury;

"2)   At a time when he was receiving treatment;

"3)   From a registered health practitioner; and

"4)   The treatment caused the injury."

The Court accepted that Mr Barron had suffered a personal injury. It did not accept that at the time of the injury he was receiving treatment from or at the direction of a registered health professional. Simply having the lenses prescribed by a health professional was not enough; therefore there was no treatment injury.[31] Mr Barron's appeal failed and he was not entitled to cover.[32]

(8)   *Case example three*

Ms McCarron was diagnosed with a metabolic abnormality of fat metabolism, resulting in morbid obesity. She underwent gastric band surgery to assist her to lose weight and maintain the weight loss. She had a family history of heart disease and her sister had successfully had the same operation. Initially the banding appeared to work well but within a month there were indications that the gastric band was not working because it was leaking.

The surgeon believed there was possibly a small hole in the band from suturing that caused it to deflate and meant it was ineffective. Through her surgeon, Ms McCarron lodged a claim for treatment injury, the injury being described as "the return of metabolic syndrome and associated consequences." The claim was supported by a report from the surgeon. After obtaining further information from the surgeon ACC declined her claim. It said that she had not suffered personal injury within the meaning of the Act. Ms McCarron applied to review the decision. Her application was supported by a further letter of explanation from her surgeon.

The Reviewer ruled that the damage to the gastric band did constitute personal injury that amounted to treatment injury. He ruled that:

"(1)   The damage was not an ordinary consequence of gastric banding surgery;

"(2)   The damage had caused the stomach to revert to its normal chemistry;

"(3)   The gastric band was a prosthesis that replaced a part of the stomach; and

"(4)   It carried out the function of a bodily part to reduce the impact of food."

Therefore its failure amounted to treatment injury and Ms McCarron was entitled to cover — ACC appealed the decision.

Although Ms McCarron did not attend the hearing in the District Court, it proceeded on the basis that she was entitled to the benefit of the reviewer's decision in her favour unless ACC could establish that the decision was wrong.

The Judge ruled that Ms McCarron's claim for cover had been properly declined by ACC.[33] He said that in practical terms Ms McCarron's claim was that the failed gastric band

---

31   The Court also considered whether the contact lens was a device that had "failed" in its purpose. It held that it had not since its purpose was not to prevent infection.

32   *Barron v ACC* 9/12/08, Allan J, HC Auckland CIV-2008-485-325.

33   *ACC v McCarron* 22/9/08, Judge Beattie, DC Auckland, Decision No 236/2008.

caused her stomach to revert to its normal manner of function. The fact that the surgery had not achieved the desired result did not, of itself, constitute treatment injury. The Court accepted that the failure of the gastric band was a failure caused by treatment, since it was likely the puncture had occurred during suturing. However despite evidence from the surgeon that "the entire medical world and community considers it to be a prosthesis" the Court held the gastric band was not a prosthesis as defined in the Act and its failure could not constitute damage to a replacement part of the human body. The Reviewer's decision was quashed and ACC's initial decision to decline cover was reinstated.

4.2.3 Consequences of the accident compensation scheme for health practitioners

There are two notable consequences of the accident compensation scheme for health practitioners. First and most importantly, they generally cannot be sued in negligence at common law. In most jurisdictions, one of the most effective restraints on the conduct of professional persons is that the victims of their negligent acts or omissions may sue them. In New Zealand, if a health professional is negligent, the ACC legislation reduces their chances of being sued in Court. It does not, however, eliminate this risk completely. Chapter 8 discusses the ways in which health practitioners can still be sued; for example, it is still possible to bring a claim for exemplary damages[34] for conduct by the defendant that has resulted in personal injury.

Where a consumer suffers mental trauma (often referred to as nervous shock) as a result of treatment but has no physical injury then cover will not be available under the ACC scheme and an action for damages against a negligent practitioner will not be barred. It is also possible that someone closely affected by the result of negligent conduct to someone else suffers mental trauma. That person will have no cover under the ACC scheme and might sue the health practitioner for compensation for that mental trauma.[35]

However, negligent health practitioners and negligent health and disability services provider organisations can be the subject of a complaint and held to account by the Health and Disability Commissioner, or their professional body, and the Health Practitioners Disciplinary Tribunal. In overseas jurisdictions where many, if not most, cases are settled out of Court, the terms of such settlements are often confidential, and this has a negative effect in two ways. First, the health practitioner or hospital is often not publicly called to account for any harm done, and they can continue to practise without ongoing scrutiny. Secondly, the educative effect of an adverse finding is lost when the facts surrounding the case remain secret.

As a result of the ACC legislation, New Zealand does not have as large a body of current common law decisions that sets standards of conduct for health professionals. For example, in recent years there has been litigation in Australia, Canada, the UK, and the US on the

---

34   The purpose of exemplary damages is not to compensate the victim but to punish or deter the defendant for "high-handed disregard of the rights of a plaintiff or for acting in bad faith or for abusing a public position or behaving in some other outrageous manner": *Ellison v L* [1998] 1 NZLR 416, 419 per Blanchard J; discussed in chapter 8.

35   See for example *Van Soest v Residual Health Management Unit* [2000] 1 NZLR 179 (CA) and generally chapter 8.

issue of informed consent, and there have been helpful judicial pronouncements on appropriate standards for health professionals.[36]

This does not mean New Zealand does not have clearly expressed standards. Acts of Parliament and regulations have created codes of conduct in respect of such things as privacy, informed consent, and mental health patients' rights. These standards are contained in the Privacy Act 1993, Health Information Privacy Code 1994 (issued under section 46 of the Privacy Act 1993), Health and Disability Commissioner Act 1994, Health and Disability Commissioner (Code of Health and Disability Services Consumers' Rights) Regulations 1996, and Part 6 of the Mental Health (Compulsory Assessment and Treatment) Act 1992. Generally, the legislative standards are expressed more clearly than the corresponding judicial pronouncements in other jurisdictions. There is also a developing body of law relating to standards arising from decisions under Part 4 of the Health Practitioners Competence Assurance Act 2003.[37]

Much of this legislation affects consumer rights, and came about to address perceived power imbalances between health practitioners and consumers. A real advantage for consumers seeking redress through the Privacy Commissioner or the Health and Disability Commissioner is that this is a "free" service. The State funds each commissioner, and a lack of money is no bar to a person wanting to bring a complaint. In other jurisdictions the consumer must self-fund or be legally aided, and the complaint must reach a threshold of seriousness before it will be considered. An advantage of the New Zealand legislation is that even cases of less serious harm or breaches of professional standards, can be identified and complained about, and some remedy granted.

There have also been standards published by Standards New Zealand, which in effect are delegated legislation. In February 2002, the New Zealand Minister of Health gave notice under the Health and Disability Services (Safety) Act 2001, approving health and disability standards and mental health standards ("the standards") in the provision of hospital, residential disability, and rest home care. The approved standards of the Health and Disability Services (Safety) Act 2001 were jointly developed by the Ministry of Health and Standards New Zealand and they currently[38] include the:

- Health and Disability Sector Standards — NZS 8134:2001
- National Mental Health Sector Standards — NZS 8143:2001
- Infection Control — NZS 8142:2000
- Restraint and Minimisation and Safe Practice — NZS 8141:2001

Copies of these standards and accompanying "Audit Workbooks" are available from Standards New Zealand. They are designed as guidelines to help health organisations in the implementation of policies and protocols to ensure compliance by health and disability services provider organisations with legislation such as the Code of Health and Disability Services Consumers' Rights. They also set standards for the development of policies and

---

36   See *Bolam v Friern Hospital Management Committee* [1957] 1 WLR 582; *Sidaway v Bethlem Royal Hospital Governors* [1985] AC 871; [1985] 1 All ER 643; *Canterbury v Spence* 464 F 2d 772 (1972); *Reibl v Hughes* [1980] 2 SCR 880; (1980) 114 DLR (3d) 1; and *Rogers v Whitaker* (1992) 109 ALR 625 (HCA).

37   See for example *Martin v Director of Proceedings* 2/7/08, Courtenay J, HC Auckland CIV-2006-404-5706; *Cullen v Professional Conduct Committee of Medical Council* 14/11/08, Heath J, HC Auckland CIV-2008-404-6786.

38   As at 23 August 2009.

protocols relating to privacy, infection control, mental health services and restraint. While these standards are designed to help health agencies towards best practice, it may well be that they will be regarded as a standard against which practice is measured and that failure to follow a guideline in a standard could amount to a breach of a legal standard.[39]

There are also standards set by the various professional bodies, which are used when considering whether the test of reasonableness has been met. Standards that health professionals are measured against also include their professional and ethical standards. These include the New Zealand College of Midwives *Code of Ethics and Standards of Midwifery Practice*,[40] the Nursing Council of New Zealand *Code of Conduct for Nurses*,[41] and the Medical Council of New Zealand's *Good Medical Practice*. The New Zealand Medical Association of New Zealand has traditionally undertaken the task of providing a Code of Ethics for the medical profession.

A key development in New Zealand has been the recognition that each profession is able to determine its own standards. Ultimately, the decision of reasonableness is one for the Courts. However, the ACC, the Health and Disability Commissioner, and the Health Practitioners Disciplinary Tribunal all seek advice from relevant independent experts on the appropriate reasonable standard. It is no longer the case that all health professions are judged on a medical practitioner expert's view of what constitutes, for example, a reasonable physiotherapist, nurse, or midwife.

There continues to be important debate about the role of guidelines, protocols, policies, clinical pathways, and evidence-based care generally. Unless they clearly follow the New Zealand Standards guidelines discussed above, one of the issues is whether protocols, guidelines, and clinical pathways should be used as a measure of a reasonable standard of care. On the one hand, there is a view that guidelines, protocols, and clinical pathways are tools that must be applied without question, but on the other hand there is the view that they are only guidelines that should be interpreted by the individual practitioner as they see fit. Clearly, guidelines, protocols, and clinical pathways can only really be useful if they can be interpreted without difficulty, are practical, easy to understand, contain easily determined discriminators, and where they can be used by practitioners at every level of experience. Guidelines, protocols, and clinical pathways that are vague, ambiguous, or difficult to interpret by all practitioners should never be held up as a standard by which practice is measured.

Another frequent difficulty encountered, at least in New Zealand, is that currently many guidelines, particularly in smaller hospitals, are simply a means of enforcing the particular practice preference of a specialist. An example is a policy that all women will have continuous cardiotocography monitoring in labour. Ideally, when guidelines and protocols are formulated, they should be based on relevant, up-to-date research and evidence. They

---

39 The case of *Culverden Group Ltd v Health & Disability Commissioner* 24/4/02, CA179/01; *Culverden Group Ltd v Health & Disability Commissioner* 25/6/01, Glazebrook J, HC Auckland M1143-SD00, gives some credence to this view. See also HDC Opinion 07HDC21742 *North Shore Hospital Inquiry Report* April 2009 particularly Appendices 2-4 Expert Advice provided to the Commissioner.

40 At the time of writing the Midwifery Council is developing a Code of Conduct for Midwives but has meanwhile ratified and adopted the Code of Ethics and Standards for Midwifery Practice set out in the Midwives Handbook for Practice (2005) published by the New Zealand College of Midwives.

41 Available at www.nursingcouncil.org.nz/pub.html.

should be developed by a working group made up of those who will work with them, circulated for comment, and they should reflect actual practice. A further concern is that some guidelines are developed by one person. In one case, it was discovered that a guideline had been developed by someone on night duties, and that this had been done without any reference back to other practitioners. The guideline slipped into the policy manual and was later used against a practitioner who had not followed it, even though the practitioner had done so on the basis it did not reflect actual practice.

The use of guidelines as a standard of care can also pose difficulty when a practitioner practises under one local guideline and an expert witness from another area judges their conduct by a different guideline. If the "imported" guideline is preferred over a local version this can seem unfair to practitioners who believe they have been practising reasonably.

A final concern with protocols and guidelines is that hospitals and DHBs often believe that liability can be avoided if each clinical scenario is covered by guidelines. It is, of course, impossible to do so. In practical terms there is also a further difficulty; when policies are contained in multiple volumes or manuals, practitioners seldom take the time to read them, let alone comply with them to the letter. If the manuals are not readily available to staff, for example if they are stored in locked management offices overnight, or staff have not been notified of updates or changes, then the vicarious liability of the institution may be greater, not less.

All practitioners should regularly review the protocols and guidelines of their institution. If they are not evidence based, or do not reflect current practice, they should be changed. Guidelines and protocols should be readily available, and they should be couched in clearly understandable language. They should contain clear, easy-to-determine discriminators and also need, where necessary, to acknowledge the right of consumers to decline to be subject to them. Additionally, it should be recognised that there will be clinical situations arising when practitioners will need to deviate from guidelines for good reason. Such deviations and the reasons for them should be documented, as they may require future justification.

4.3 Disciplinary proceedings

Health professionals are regulated under the Health Practitioners Competence Assurance Act 2003 — included in the HPCAA is the power for the Health Practitioners Disciplinary Tribunal to discipline and impose sanctions on registered practitioners.[42]

The HPCAA is an ambitious and far reaching piece of legislation that attempts to recognise the concerns of both consumers and health practitioners for openness, public safety, accountability, and fairness. Its principal purpose is to "protect the health and safety of members of the public by providing the mechanisms to ensure that health practitioners are competent and fit to practise their professions."[43] The major differences between the HPCAA and previous disciplinary regimes are that:

*   All registered health professions are subject to the same disciplinary regime.
*   All disciplinary hearings are heard in public unless the Tribunal orders otherwise.
*   Disciplinary and governance functions are completely separated.

---

42   For a detailed explanation of the disciplinary regimes for registered health professionals prior to the enactment of the HPCAA see previous editions of this book.

43   Health Practitioners Competence Assurance Act 2003, section 3(1).

- An "authority" is established for each registered health profession.[44]
- Each authority is responsible for education, registration, annual practising certificates, establishing scopes of practice, restricted activities, and competence reviews. It must act on information it receives regarding the competence of practitioners. It also establishes professional conduct committees, and sets standards of clinical and cultural competence.
- A single multi-disciplinary disciplinary tribunal has replaced the various professional disciplinary bodies. The Health Practitioners Disciplinary Tribunal has the power to discipline all health practitioners. The Tribunal comprises a chairperson, up to three deputy chairpersons and a panel comprising laypersons and health practitioners. All members of the Tribunal are appointed by the Minister of Health and the chairperson and deputy chairpersons must be lawyers.
- When the Tribunal sits to hear and determine a charge it comprises five people: the Chairperson or one of the deputy chairpersons, a lay person appointed from the panel, and three health professionals appointed from the panel who are professional peers of the health practitioner who is the subject of the hearing.
- There is increased consumer access to the Human Rights Review Tribunal (see chapter 5).
- There is increased reporting of complaints between the Health and Disability Commissioner, employers, and the authorities.
- A registrar of a court in New Zealand who knows that a person convicted in the court is a health practitioner must send a notice of the conviction to the responsible authority if the conviction is for an offence punishable by imprisonment for a term of 3 months or longer[45] or one of the several specified offences.
- Emerging professions can apply to come under the HPCAA.
- The Minister of Health has increased powers of appointment, monitoring and audit, and conciliation.
- There is an extended role for the Office of the Health and Disability Commissioner.
- The quality assurance provisions that had previously only applied to medical practitioners are now extended to all professional groups that come under the HPCAA. (See chapter 15 for further discussion of the HPCAA).

4.4 Complaints against health providers and Health and Disability Commissioner Investigations

Provisions in the HPCAA enable complaints to be made against health practitioners. These provisions are interrelated with the provisions in the Health and Disability Commissioner Act 1994 (HDCA). The HDCA enables consumers to bring complaints against health service practitioners and disability service providers.[46]

---

44   As at September 2009 there were 22 registered health professions.
45   This applies regardless of whether or not a term of imprisonment is actually imposed.
46   See chapter 5. At the time of writing (August 2009) the third review of Health and Disability Commissioner Act 1994 and the Health and Disability Commissioner (Code of Health and Disability Services Consumers' Rights) Regulations 1996 had been completed. Further information can be viewed on the Health and Disability Commissioner's website at www.hdc.org.nz/publications/review-act-code-09.

The complaints procedure is simple. Any person may make a complaint against a registered health professional, either orally or in writing, directly to the Health and Disability Commissioner. A written complaint may also be made to the Registrar of the authority responsible for the practitioner, for example the Registrar of the Nursing Council of New Zealand, the Medical Council of New Zealand or the Occupational Therapy Board. If the complaint relates to matters occurring after 1 July 1996 it must be referred by the authority to the Health and Disability Commissioner.

The complaint should relate to a breach of one of the 10 rights contained in the Code.[47] Patient advocates are available to help complainants with the formulating of a complaint.

Once the Health and Disability Commissioner receives the complaint he will decide whether the complaint is frivolous or vexatious, whether it can be resolved through mediation, or whether it should be referred for investigation. At this point the Commissioner will notify the responsible authority that an investigation is under way, if that has not previously occurred. A copy of the complaint will usually be sent to the practitioner.

The HDCA process is not dissimilar to that of the ACC, where clinical notes, protocols, and reports of involved practitioners are requested. The file will also be reviewed by an expert witness in the same professional group as the practitioner whose conduct is being investigated. The Commissioner will review all the reports and evidence, and issue a provisional finding to all parties involved. This provisional finding is a critical step that promotes fairness and natural justice for the health practitioner(s) involved. Often it is not until the provisional finding that the health practitioner is fully aware of the areas of concern. He or she is then able to adduce new evidence and formulate a comprehensive response to the finding before the Commissioner finalises their opinion.

The Commissioner will then consider whether the complaint has been resolved, or whether a breach of the Code has occurred. If the latter is found, then the Commissioner may make a number of recommendations to the provider.

These may include:

- An apology to the aggrieved consumer;
- Further education or upskilling of the provider;
- Mentoring or supervision;
- Review of relevant policies or protocols; or
- Refund of fee.

The Commissioner will also consider whether the breach is sufficiently serious for the matter to be referred to the Director of Proceedings for consideration. The Director is an independent statutory officer who will review the file and determine whether a disciplinary charge should be laid before the relevant professional body, and/or whether proceedings should be initiated in the Human Rights Review Tribunal. The Director may also support the complainant in other civil proceedings against the practitioner if appropriate. (See chapter 15 for an illustration of health professionals' disciplinary proceedings; see chapter 5 for a discussion on investigations carried out by the Health and Disability Commissioner.)

---

47   See chapter 5 where these rights are discussed. Also, the Code is set out in Appendix 4.

Cases reported in *Kai Tiaki: Nursing New Zealand*, the *New Zealand Medical Journal* and on the HPDT's website[48] give an indication of the types of conduct that result in disciplinary proceedings. Examples of such conduct include:

- Sexual or inappropriate relationships with consumers;[49]
- Accepting cheques from consumers;
- Physical abuse of consumers;
- Psychological abuse of consumers;
- Indiscriminately prescribing drugs in excessive dosages;
- Dishonestly claiming financial benefits;
- Issuing prescriptions to consumers knowing that they were using false names;
- Falsifying records;
- Breaching confidences;
- Failure to obtain informed consent;
- Failure to attend in an emergency;
- Failure to adequately examine consumers;
- Failure to keep proper records;
- Inappropriate diagnosis;
- Provision of unnecessary services;
- Delay in responding to a consumer's needs;
- Public and irresponsible denigration of a colleague;
- Failure to act on, or follow up, abnormal symptoms;
- Delay in referral;
- Failure to use reasonable care;
- Practicing without a current practicing certificate;
- Theft;
- Inadequate/inappropriate supervision of staff.

A frequent criticism from New Zealand health practitioners is that one complaint may be investigated by a number of different bodies, and the practitioner may need to defend their practice in each of these.

An example of this interrelatedness is where someone dies in a hospital, perhaps a consumer in a psychiatric ward or a baby following a traumatic delivery. The hospital will immediately commence risk management procedures including, for example, a Sentinel Events Review process or some internal case investigation. There will be an internal or perinatal mortality review where the care given will be scrutinised. There may also be an independent review. The matter will be referred to the Coroner and police interviews may be required. A claim for funeral expenses may be made to ACC, and this will initiate a treatment injury referral on the basis that the apparent personal injury has occurred while under the treatment of registered health professionals. ACC will require a response. The family, or other practitioners, may make a complaint to the Health and Disability Commissioner or the

---

48   www.hpdt.org.nz.

49   For an article on this written for nurses and midwives, see F Roberts, "Learning not to cross the boundaries" *Kai Tiaki: Nursing New Zealand*, August 2003, 23.

responsible authority and this may entail interviews and the formulation of reports for the Commissioner.

If a breach of the Code is found and the practitioner is referred to the Director of Proceedings, then the practitioner has a right to be heard by the Director of Proceedings before a decision is made to take the matter further. Although this is usually something that is done "on the papers", there are occasions when an interview with the Director will be required. If the Director does lay charges, there will be a full, public disciplinary hearing. Potentially there may be a further hearing before the Human Rights Review Tribunal. If the practitioner is unhappy with the decisions of either of these two latter bodies, he or she has the right to appeal to the High Court.

Even where the Commissioner does not refer a practitioner to the Director of Proceedings the results of his investigation will be referred to the responsible authority which may decide to investigate whether there has been a breach of professional standards.[50] In some particularly serious circumstances, criminal and civil proceedings may also be initiated against the practitioner. The final forum before which a practitioner may have to appear and give evidence is generally the Coroners' Court. It can take many months, even years to move through these forums, and this can leave both consumer and practitioner psychologically battered. Neither party is able to achieve closure and move on with their lives while various proceedings are still hanging over their heads.

Although the length of time between an incident giving rise to a complaint and the final resolution in all forums has been shortened as a result of the HPCAA and the Coroners Act 2006 which came into force on 1 July 2007 practitioners can still face uncertainty about outcomes for extended periods of time.[51]

Not only are the various organisations that can scrutinise a practitioner's conduct interrelated, but evidence from one forum may also be used by another.

Mention also needs to be made of the media's role in relation to accountability. "Health professionals failed victim" (who died) is a typical press headline. This sort of reporting makes it very difficult for health practitioners who are filmed or named in the media to escape damage to their reputation. This is especially damaging where such naming and filming occurs before the health practitioners have had the opportunity to present their evidence.

The Health and Disability Commissioner has recently revised his policy on naming health providers who are investigated. Until 2006 the Commissioner published investigation

---

50   Opinion/05HDC11908 regarding the co-ordination of care of patient admitted to public hospital with acute breathlessness is an example of the progress of a complaint through the HDC following the death of a consumer. The DHB was referred to the DoP but subsequently entered into a settlement with the complainant. The event occurred in September 2004 and the HDC final report was issued on 22 March 2007 following a lengthy investigation. There was no Coronial inquest. In 2008 a Professional Conduct Committee of the Nursing Council investigated the conduct of the nurses involved despite the fact that the HDC had found that understaffing had been a major contributing factor. It was not until September 2008 following a hearing by the PCC that the nurses were assured that no further action would be taken against them.

51   See for example the facts outlined in *T v A* Human Rights Review Tribunal Decision No 19/2008; 25/07 14 August 2008. The incident giving rise to the action occurred in May 2005 and the case was finally resolved by settlement in May 2009.

reports without naming the health and disability providers involved. In 2006 the Commissioner decided to name district health boards that had breached the Code on the basis that they should be publicly accountable for the quality of care they fund or provide. A proposal to extend that policy to other group providers and, in certain limited circumstances, to individuals lead to consultation with the Health sector and the current "naming policy" dated 1 July 2008.[52] Generally naming only occurs where, as a result of an investigation, the Commissioner considers there has been a breach of the Code. The decision to name is made on a case by case basis and only where the public interest in naming outweighs the potential harm to the provider. Providers will not be named without consultation and their views are taken into account. However the Commissioner has no legal power to order name suppression, so parties to an investigation may put names in the public arena.

An inquest in the Coroners Court is usually open to the public. In a very small number of cases the Coroner may decide to hold a closed inquest. All details discussed at an inquest will be heard by anyone who attends the inquest, including the media. Unless the Coroner orders otherwise, the media may publish any information that they hear except in relation to a suicide where there are restrictions imposed by law. In these Courts, the practitioner is a witness for the Coroner to often tragic events, and witnesses rely on the Coroner to protect them from premature adverse comment.[53] The usual media practice in Coroners' Courts is to publish evidence in a piecemeal way as it emerges, instead of waiting for the full evidence to be presented. Sensationalist headlines are the norm, as is the naming of individual witnesses. This can be a problem because once the reputation of a practitioner is blackened by premature publicity in the media, the media seldom return when exonerating evidence emerges and correct, or retract the erroneous reporting. The sanctions for poor or irresponsible reporting are an inadequate deterrent to such reporting.

Many health practitioners consider this as early naming, blaming, and shaming of them through media coverage at some inquests. If it continues, or becomes more widespread, it could make it increasingly difficult for health practitioners to fully and frankly disclose adverse events. Even with the arguments about transparency of process and the public interest in knowing what is happening, the right of individuals not to be named when giving evidence about adverse events in health care at Coroners' inquests can be argued to be a reasonable limit on the freedom of the press,[54] as it is consistent with the limits to be placed on rights and freedoms.[55] There is a difference in the public *interest* in knowing what is happening and the public *desire* to know. It is a distinction which is not always made.

Accountability of individual health practitioners is important where there is an individual who deviates significantly from an accepted reasonable standard of care. However, there is a worldwide concern that errors and adverse events in health are usually the result of failings in systems, rather than the fault of an individual. Reports of the HDC already cited in this chapter are examples of this as is the Ministry of Health's National Policy for the

---

52   Available on the Health and Disability website, www.hdc.org.nz.

53   *R v West London Coroner, ex p Gray* [1987] 2 ALL ER 129, 133, cited with approval in *Louw v McClean* 12/1/88, Hardie Boys J, HC Christchurch CP445/87.

54   New Zealand Bill of Rights Act 1990, section 14.

55   As set out in New Zealand Bill of Rights Act 1990, section 5. The authors of this chapter are grateful to Jonathan Coates for sharing with them his PhD research on this issue.

Management of Healthcare Incidents.[56] Unfortunately, when the media are present at a Coroner's inquest, the immediate nature of the media coverage means that the focus is always on individuals. Few reporters do the work necessary to look beyond the obvious, to the systems failures that led to the adverse outcome.

A great deal of work has been carried out, initially in the aviation and space exploration industries, showing that an adverse event can invariably be traced to a number of latent defects and active errors within a system that has continued undetected, sometimes for many years. Professor James Reasons' "Swiss cheese theory"[57] is now being applied worldwide to improving the quality of health services.[58] His theory is that all errors are consequential on a number of conditions, which may be latent defects or active errors, all of which contribute to the error occurring. He sees a number of components or "Swiss cheeses" in any organisation. These Swiss cheeses contain holes that are the latent defects, or more recent active errors. When the holes are aligned, a trajectory of error through all the aligned holes inevitably ends in an adverse event.

From 1 July 2009, all adverse events will be reported by DHBs to the Ministry of Health's centralised events reporting function. It is hoped that establishing a national reporting function for reportable events will provide the health sector with up to date data and analysis from hospitals (and eventually other health organisations[59]) across New Zealand. The data will be anonymised and it will be the responsibility of DHBs to ensure that events are reported in such a way that individual patients or staff are not identifiable. One of the aims of the centralised events reporting function is to share the lessons learned in managing incidents, mitigating their consequences, and reducing the risk of future events.

It is likely that only when health practitioners know that an inquiry into an adverse event will look at the system as a whole and not focus solely on them, that they will be willing to engage in full and frank discussion about adverse events, errors, and near misses. It remains to be seen whether the changes to ACC regarding treatment injury and the implementation of the Ministry's National Policy for the Management of Healthcare Incidents have that effect.

---

56   The policy is presently a working draft (February 2010) to be finalised in 2010: www.moh.govt.nz/moh.nsf/indexmh/improvingquality-reportableevents-resources.

57   J Reason, *Human Error*, New York, Cambridge University Press, 1990, page 173; J Reason, *Managing the Risks of Organisational Accidents*, Aldershot, Ashgate 1997, page 126; and J Reason "Human error: Models and management" (2000) BMJ 320.

58   See for example the Report of the Bristol Royal Infirmary Inquiry at www.bristol-inquiry.org.uk.

59   The intention is to extend the policy to health providers such as disability-related service and aged care providers. Consultation during 2009/10 with these providers will seek their agreement to reporting serious and sentinel events in the same way as DHBs.

Pathways of complaints or claims showing the relationship between bodies that can hold a practitioner accountable

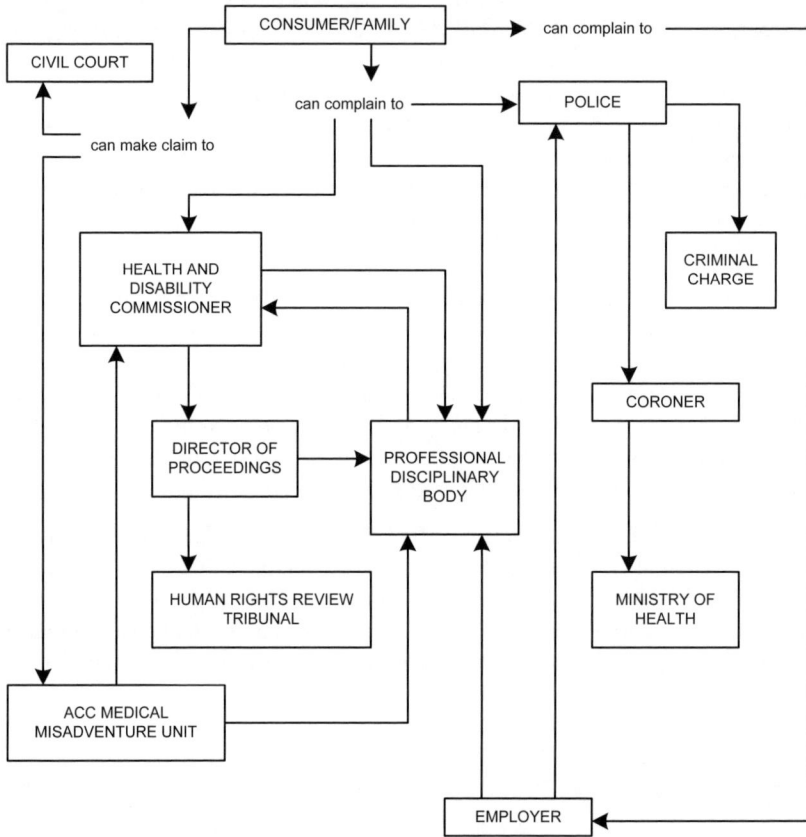

4.5 Further reading

- A A Merry and A McCall Smith, *Errors, Medicine and the Law*, Cambridge University Press, 2001.
- J Pearse, "Health professionals' standards" 2001 NZLJ 15.
- J Reason, "Human error: Models and management" (2000) BMJ 320.
- J Reason, *Human Error*, New York, Cambridge University Press, 1990, page 173.
- J Reason, *Managing the Risks of Organizational Accidents*, Aldershot, Ashgate, 1997, page 126.
- G Rossiter, "Cross disciplinary standards in health services" 2000 NZLJ 193.
- PDC Skegg and R Paterson et al, *Medical Law in New Zealand*, Wellington, Brookers, 2006.
- *The Report of the Bristol Royal Infirmary Inquiry*, www.bristol-inquiry.org.uk.
- S Todd et al, *The Law of Torts in New Zealand* (5th ed), Wellington, Brookers, 2009.

Chapter 5

RIGHTS

SUE JOHNSON

Contents

5.1 Introduction

This chapter and the following chapters will discuss consumers rights, for example the right to receive appropriate and prompt treatment; the right to make an informed choice and give informed consent to receive treatment; the right to privacy and confidentiality; the right to access health information; and so on. Every right in respect of health consumers gives rise to a correlative duty on the part of the health practitioner to give effect to that right. Breach of a duty to give effect to a patient's right can expose a health carer to a risk of accountability in the Courts or before various tribunals or commissions, or to disciplinary action by the health practitioner's own professional body.

5.2 What is a "right"?

A legal right may be defined as any advantage or benefit conferred upon a person by a rule of law. There are four distinct kinds of rights:

- Rights (true claims or demands);
- Liberties or privileges;
- Powers;
- Immunities.

There are corresponding correlatives to these rights. The four pairs or correlatives may be arranged as follows, the correlative being obtained by reading downwards.[1]

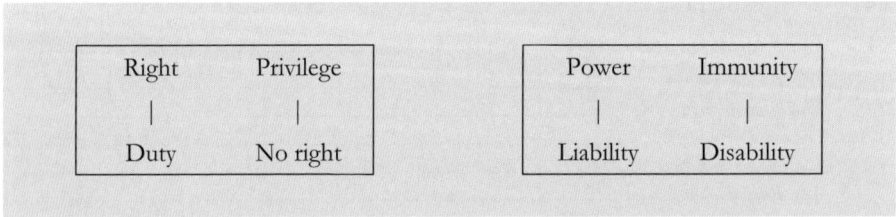

Right	Privilege		Power	Immunity
Duty	No right		Liability	Disability

Rights as true claims or demands are the benefits one derives from legal duties imposed upon others. Privileges or liberties are benefits derived from the absence of legal duties imposed upon oneself. A privilege is the right to do as one pleases, which is circumscribed by law that sets the boundaries within which it is content to leave one alone. Thus, one has the right to speak one's mind and express one's opinion but has no right to publish defamatory statements.

Another class of rights is termed "powers". For example, the power to make a will or advance directive, the power to marry or to make a complaint to a provider of health services. A power is not the same thing as a true right or a privilege. The power to make a complaint means one *can* do so; that it is legally valid to do so. A power confers upon a person the right to determine one's own, or other people's legal relations. A power can be a public one held by a person as an agent; for example a police officer is an agent of the State. The correlative of a power is a liability. It is the position of a person whose legal relation to another may be altered by the exercise of a power. For example, a person who owes money is liable to be sued because the creditor has the power to bring proceedings for recovery of the debt. A person who has killed someone may be liable to be convicted by the Courts, who have the power to do this.

---

1   The analysis of rights into the four pairs of correlatives is from Wesley Newcomb Hohfeld, *Fundamental Legal Conceptions*, published posthumously in 1923 reprinting essays first published in (1913) 23 Yale LJ 16 and (1917) 26 Yale LJ 710. The above discussion is taken from Fitzgerald P J, *Salmond on Jurisprudence* (12th ed), London, Sweet & Maxwell, 1966.

The term "right" is also used to mean immunity from having one's legal position affected by someone else's power. Salmond states that "immunity in short is no-liability".[2] The person with the power is disabled in that they cannot exercise the power.

Some legal rights are perfect rights, which correspond to perfect duties. These are not merely recognised by the law, but enforced by the law. A duty is enforceable when proceedings can be brought for a breach of it.

Some legal rights are imperfect in that while they are recognised by the law, they are unenforceable; for example a claim may still exist but be barred by lapse of time. It does not become extinct, but no action can be brought to enforce it. The right exists, but the right of the action has been severed.[3]

5.2.1 Human rights

People living in New Zealand are protected by a web of legislation and common law that confers rights on people, for example on:

- Consumers of health and disability services;
- Intellectually disabled persons;
- Patients under the Mental Health (Compulsory Assessment and Treatment) Act 1992, that is, those consumers of mental health services who are being compulsorily assessed or treated or held as special patients, and also those who are proposed patients under this Act;
- Children;
- Older persons;
- Prisoners;
- People in police custody;
- Employees;
- Tenants and boarders;
- Immigrants;
- Women;
- Consumers of goods and services;
- People who are being harassed.

Every right and power gives rise to a correlative duty or liability on the part of someone else. Many of these rights are based on an international recognition of human rights.

5.3 International law

As well as domestic (national) law, a body of international law has developed based on the recognition of human rights. Human rights apply to any person, and are based purely on their membership of the human race. They are said to be universal (applying to everyone) and immutable (they cannot be limited or qualified). The recognition of human rights at an international level takes the form of international declarations and conventions (treaties). The documents are drawn up, and nations subscribe to the principles contained in them.

---

2   Fitzgerald P J, *Salmond on Jurisprudence* (12th ed), London, Sweet & Maxwell, 1966, 231.
3   Fitzgerald P J, *Salmond on Jurisprudence* (12th ed), London, Sweet & Maxwell, 1966, 234.

The document initiating this recognition of human rights is the Universal Declaration of Human Rights, the founding document drawn up by the United Nations of what was to develop into a steady and growing commitment of nations, through further conventions and agreements, to the recognition of the rights of all people to dignity, physical security, self-fulfilment, and equal access to justice. New Zealand is a signatory to the declaration and to many of the subsequent more detailed conventions and agreements.

International law is complex, and is in many ways different from domestic law. In the following discussion it will be outlined simply, with a view to giving an understanding of the obligations of health practitioners that have resulted from our Government's involvement in the area of international human rights law.

The first and most important point to make about law between nations is that it does not consist of a set of rules that can be enforced by a Court. Nations are all sovereign entities; able to do whatever they like within their own territory. Thus, a head of State or Government of a particular country cannot be forced to change their ways, however disagreeable others may consider them. One can negotiate, attempt to persuade, or apply economic or political sanctions, and only under certain closely defined situations take up arms against another nation. The General Assembly of the United Nations can condemn a country's activities, causing widespread international moral and political disapprobation. There is also the International Court of Justice to which nations can take their grievances for a ruling against a nation's activities. Such opinions, however, cannot be the subject of forceful action. The United Nations may call on member nations to contribute to a peace-keeping armed force in its name, which can take all measures necessary to achieve peace, including enforcing sanctions and ensuring that nations who have already reached the settlement of a dispute carry out their agreed undertakings peacefully, for example, the withdrawing of an army.

5.3.1 Conventions

A convention is a treaty. An international declaration or treaty establishing human rights is not enforceable. However, nations that are signatories accept their provisions, and undertake to enact laws on human rights within their borders.[4] Signatories to conventions also undertake to make regular reports to an international committee, which is set up under the convention, on the enactment and administration of such laws. They may be asked to explain any apparent failure to act or unsatisfactory progress in the recognition of the rights involved. Failure to recognise any obligations under a convention may result in an adverse report to the General Assembly of the United Nations, and possible action by the member States (see 5.3).

The International Covenant on Civil and Political Rights has an optional protocol, signed by New Zealand, which provides that an individual can take a complaint to the United Nations Human Rights Committee. The complaint must relate to government action denying a human right to that person, and the complainant must have exhausted the avenues of complaint in their own country.

The following are the main international instruments that establish rights relevant to health care workers:

---

4   Signatories may make reservations to specific clauses of the document if they are not prepared or equipped to put them into effect.

- *International Covenant on Civil and Political Rights (art 7)*: Prohibits cruel and inhumane treatment, and medical or scientific experimentation without consent;
- *International Covenant on Social, Economic and Cultural Rights (art 12)*: Establishes the right to the highest attainable standard of physical and mental health, to be attained by, among other measures, methods to reduce stillbirth, epidemics, endemic and occupational diseases;
- *Declaration of the Rights of the Child (Principle 4)* and *United Nations Convention on the Rights of the Child (art 24)*: Bestow on children the right to special protection of, and access to, medical care;
- *Declaration on the Rights of Mentally Retarded Persons (art 2)*: Bestows the right of proper medical care and physical therapy;
- *Declaration on the Rights of Disabled Persons (art 6)*: Includes the right to medical, psychological, and functional care, rehabilitation, counselling, and vocational training;
- *Principles for the Protection of Persons with Mental Illness and for the Improvement of Mental Health Care.*

5.4 Domestic law

New Zealand is a signatory to all these instruments. It is therefore obliged to do something about them, and does so through national (domestic) law. The Human Rights Act 1993 states in its Long Title that the Act is to:

> "Consolidate and amend the Race Relations Act 1971 and the Human Rights Commission Act 1977 and to provide better protection of human rights in New Zealand in general accordance with United Nations Covenants or Conventions on Human Rights."

5.4.1 Discrimination and the law

(1) *What is discrimination?*

For legal purposes, discrimination is an act that makes distinctions between individuals or groups with the result of disadvantaging some and advantaging others. The act does not have to be done with the conscious intent of harm. This is why legislation is not punitive — it is aimed at conciliation, compensation, and education.

We discriminate all the time — some people we like and call our friends and with others we have more distant relationships. Seriously ill people are given more care and attention than those whose illness is minor. Some discrimination, then, is good or at least acceptable by the standards of our society. Other discrimination — denying recognised basic human rights — is the subject of moral approbation and, in recent times, legal prohibition.

(2) *Direct discrimination*

All New Zealand anti-discrimination law prohibits direct discrimination, that is, discrimination that treats one person less favourably than another on the basis of a characteristic appertaining to a prescribed status, for example colour, or to an attribute thought to appertain to that characteristic, for example all people of a particular race are lazy. The result is that, on this ground, the person is treated less favourably than a person who is not of that status. They are discriminated against precisely because of their status, for example in Australia a refusal to hire a woman pilot because of a company policy not to hire women for this position.[5]

(3)   Indirect discrimination

Indirect discrimination is more subtle, and hence harder to detect and remedy. It is often the result of "policies and practices which form the structures and patterns of an organisation in particular, and society as a whole".[6]

Indirect discrimination is prohibited, and the elements necessary for it are basically the same as those necessary to show that there is direct discrimination. Indirect discrimination concentrates on the results of an act, rather than the reasons for it. It occurs in the following way:

- X wants a service or a job, but is told that a certain condition is required (for example, a certain height);
- The requirement or condition is unreasonable and unnecessary (that is, a person could do the job just as well whether they fulfil the condition or not);
- X cannot fulfil the condition;
- A substantially higher proportion of persons of a different status to X, who is female, can comply with the condition (for example, men, who are on average taller).

The unnecessary and seemingly neutral condition, although innocently applied without consideration, indirectly discriminates against X and many women. It is the result of an erroneous belief that only people of a certain height can do a particular job. No conscious discrimination against women is intended, but the effect is to discriminate. Another basis of indirect discrimination is the employment of people who have similar backgrounds, education, or social status to those doing the employing, even though such attributes are irrelevant to the ability to carry out the work (recruitment in one's image).[7] This is called "homosocial reproduction".

The Human Rights Act 1993 was recently amended[8] and section 21 contains a general prohibition on discriminating on certain grounds:

- Sex (including pregnancy and childbirth);
- Marital status;
- Religious belief;
- Ethical belief;
- Colour;

---

5   *Wardley v Ansett Transport Industries (Operations) Pty Ltd* (1984) EOC 92-003. This case involved a complaint by Ms Wardley, a pilot, who was denied a position with Ansett Airlines because of its policy of not hiring women. She claimed that she was the victim of unlawful discrimination because of her sex. In evidence there was a letter from the general manager of Ansett to the Women's Electoral Lobby stating that the policy of not hiring women does not mean that women cannot be good pilots, but "we feel that an all male pilot crew is safer than one in which the sexes are mixed". Ms Wardley demonstrated her clear ability for the position, and the Sex Discrimination Board ruled that she had been unlawfully discriminated against.

6   Ronalds C, *Affirmative Action and Sex Discrimination: A Handbook on Legal Rights for Women*, Sydney, Pluto Press, 1987, page 99.

7   Wallace M, "The legal approach to sex discrimination", in M Sawer (ed), *Program for Change*, Sydney, Allen & Unwin, 1985, page 21.

8   The Human Rights Amendment Act 2001 came into force on 1 January 2002.

- Race;
- Ethnic/national origin;
- Disability (physical disability, physical illness, psychiatric illness);
- Age (16 and over);[9]
- Political opinion;
- Employment status;
- Family status;
- Sexual orientation.

There are some exceptions and these might apply in the health sector in relation to applicants for employment (see 5.4.1(8)).

Part 1A Human Rights Act 1993 introduces two standards. The New Zealand Bill of Rights standard is a guideline for discrimination by the public sector. It provides a standard that should be adhered to by the Ministry of Health, District Health Boards, and private providers who receive public funding. It does not include employment, racial and sexual harassment, and victimisation. These are contained in the Human Rights Standard.[10]

(4)   *Racial discrimination*

The Race Relations Act 1971 prohibited the discrimination against any person on the basis of race, or national or ethnic origin, in certain areas of activity. These areas of activity included employment, accommodation, delivery of goods, facilities and services, education, the disposal of land, and the administration of laws and programmes. This Act was consolidated and amended by the Human Rights Act 1993, and updated by the Human Rights Amendment Act 2001,[11] which details what constitutes racial discrimination in the context of particular activities. In particular, the Act makes the Race Relations Conciliator's office part of the Human Rights Commission. It also describes the inciting of racial disharmony and racial harassment as forms of discrimination.

Case
Proceedings Commissioner v Archer (1996) 3 HRNZ 123[12]

Archer broadcast a radio programme on whaling, which included a negative monologue about Chinese and Japanese people.

The Tribunal found that there were comments made by Archer that were insulting and threatening, likely to excite hostility, and likely to bring Chinese or Japanese into contempt on the grounds of their colour, race, and national origins. The comments were discriminatory.

---

9   It is prohibited to discriminate against children on any of the grounds, except where the child is under 16 they can lawfully be discriminated against because of their age only.

10   This standard is accompanied by guidelines produced by the Ministry of Justice.

11   This Act has had four further amendments to bring it in line with minor changes to other Acts. The most recent amendment in 2008 was in response to *Divided from Disability (United Nations Convention on the Rights of Persons with Disabilities)*. The changes relate specifically to disability and employment opportunities.

12   The Human Rights Amendment Act 2001 changed the name of the Complaints Review Tribunal to the Human Rights Review Tribunal. It makes rulings on complaints under the Human Rights Act 1993 as well as under the Health and Disability Commissioner Act 1994 and the Privacy Act 1993.

(5)   *Sex discrimination*

As a consequence of having signed the International Convention on the Elimination of All Forms of Discrimination Against Women, our legislation incorporates discrimination on the basis of sex in the Human Rights Act 1993, Employment Relations Act 2000, and Equal Pay Act 1972. It has also been recognised in section 19 New Zealand Bill of Rights Act 1990. This is in fact one of the earliest grounds of discrimination to be prohibited in New Zealand. The Human Rights Act 1993, in particular, prohibits discrimination on the grounds of sex, marital status, family status, sexual orientation, or pregnancy, in the same areas as those provided for in the context of racial discrimination. In the context of the Act, "sex" simply means the fact of being a female or a male person. To discriminate against either is a breach of the Act.

The grounds of discrimination cover not only a characteristic that appertains generally to persons on the grounds of their sex, marital status, etc, but also characteristics that are "imputed to them", for example "all women complain too much" or "pregnant women are irrational". Some overseas examples from jurisdictions with legislation similar to that in New Zealand illustrate sex discrimination.

Case
James v Eastleigh Borough Council [1990] 2 AC 751; [1990] 3 WLR 55; [1990] 2 All ER 607 (HL)
A statutory provision fixed the pensionable age for women at 60 and for men at 65. Consequently, a 61-year-old woman was admitted to a swimming pool free, but her husband of the same age was charged admission.

The Court held that the council had discriminated against the husband on the ground of his sex. The case applies the "but for their sex" test, whereby there is less favourable treatment of one sex that does not apply to the other.

Case
Dodd v Helping Hands Agency Ltd (1990) 12 CHRR D/297
The complainant required some time off work to have an abortion. Her employer suggested she should consider having the child and giving it up for adoption. She rejected this suggestion and went ahead with the abortion. She was fired following an argument with the employer.

On her complaint that she was discriminated against on the ground of sex, the British Columbia Human Rights Council held that the complaint should be allowed. Had she not become pregnant, the disagreement that led to her employment being terminated would not have occurred. In New Zealand, sex discrimination in employment is prohibited. (See the exceptions discussed in 5.4.1(8).)

Case
Trilford v Car Haulaways Ltd [1996] 2 ERNZ 351; (1997) 3 HRNZ 535; (1996) 5 NZELC 98,420 (Digest)
Trilford was employed by Car Haulaways in a relieving capacity in a transport supervision role. She applied for a permanent supervision position when it became available, but was

told that it was considered a male position and that she did not have the truck maintenance and driving experience necessary. Other male employees in that position did not have that experience either.

The Court found that Trilford had been discriminated against on the ground that she was a woman and that the discrimination was both direct and indirect.

Case

Talleys Fisheries Ltd v Caitlin Lewis 14/6/07, HC Wellington CIV-2005-485-1750

Talleys fisheries had two types of knife positions in their plant. It had a policy that only men were employed in the higher paid position of fish filleter while only women were employed in the lower paid position of fish trimmer. Ms Lewis complained that she was being discriminated against because of her sex, and that her role was the same as the men's.

The Court found that she had been discriminated against. In its judgment the Court found that the jobs were substantially similar and that Ms Lewis was receiving less money because she was a woman and allocated to the lower paying job. In the words of the Court: "Talleys did not directly pay her less because she was a woman, but discrimination need not be deliberate."[13]

(6) *Sexual harassment*

Health carers should be free from sexual harassment in the workplace. Where management does not take proper action to prevent or remedy sexual harassment in the workplace it may be found vicariously liable, as it is also for other acts of sexual discrimination.

Case

Proceedings Commissioner v S [1990] NZAR 233; (1990) 3 NZELC 97,684

The complainant worked part-time in a supermarket. She brought a complaint against her employer on the basis that he had on occasions touched her hair, stomach, or breasts, had tickled her, and so placed himself that if she wished to pass him she had to squeeze past.

The Tribunal found that the complainant had been subjected to harassment by her employer. The employer's behaviour was of a sexual nature, and the employee found it repulsive and distressing. It further found that the complainant was subjected to the advances because she was a young woman and subordinate to her employer. She would not have been subjected to this treatment, but for her sex.

Case

L v M Ltd [1994] 1 ERNZ 123; (1994) 4 NZELC 98,260 (Digest)

The male complainant received phone calls and typewritten notes by an unknown harasser because he had inadvertently been publicly identified in a company newsletter as the contact person for a workplace gay support group. Such expressions as "Dirty faggot, hope you get Aids" and "You're history poofter" were used in a letter to him.

---

13   *Talleys Fisheries Ltd v Caitlin Lewis* 14/6/07, HC Wellington CIV-2005-485-1750, para 52.

Although the employer appeared to be progressive and supportive to the group, the Tribunal nevertheless found that the employee had been constructively dismissed when he resigned. The complainant was awarded $2,000 for disruption to his life and towards resettlement (he moved to Australia), and $5,000 for the sexual harassment issue alone. The Tribunal, who considered the level of humiliation and hurt to be exceptional in this case, awarded $25,000.

The case of *Ahern v Burra Burra Hospital* is an example from South Australia under similar legislation.

Case

Ahern v Burra Burra Hospital 22/3/82, Sex Discrimination Board (South Australia)

A male student nurse was refused accommodation in the nurses' home attached to the hospital. This accommodation was available to female nurses, and was better than alternatives. The hospital claimed that it was not obliged to provide accommodation to student nurses, and that this was a benefit it could bestow at will. Ahern complained of sexual discrimination to the Board.

The Board held that although the hospital was not obliged to provide accommodation, it did so for female nurses as a matter of course. It was held that accommodation was a benefit applying to employment. The male nurse was thus denied a benefit enjoyed by other nurses, and that this was a breach of the legislation.

Clients and staff who are victims of sexual harassment can complain to the:

- Employing authority where it occurs;
- Police, where the act amounts to sexual assault;
- Appropriate professional disciplinary body governing the alleged offender;
- Provider of services under its complaints procedure;
- Human Rights Commission;
- Health and Disability Commissioner.

(7)   *Age discrimination*

Before the Human Rights Act 1993, age-related complaints had been practically confined to the employment field, where the parties contested the "contractual" rather than the "discrimination" status of what were mostly employer-imposed retirement ages. Also, older persons have the same rights as others when receiving a health or disability service. See 5.7 for a discussion on the Code of Health and Disability Services Consumers Rights. In New Zealand section 126 Health Act 1956 provides that "If any aged, infirm, incurable, or destitute person is found to be living in insanitary conditions or without proper care or attention," they may be committed to, and if necessary detained, in a hospital or institution.

In October 2004 the Old People's Homes Regulations 1987 and the Hospital Regulations 1993 were revoked by section 59 and Schedule 5 of the Health and Disability Services (Safety) Act 2001. The new standards to regulate care of the older person came into force on June 1 2009.[14] Section 40 of the Health and Disability Services (Safety) Act 2001 allows for an authorised person to inspect places that are providing heath services and to ensure

---

14   Health and Disability Services Safety Standards 8134:2008.

that the standards set are being adhered to. The standards set certain basic requirements concerning the facilities, staffing, and care — such as restraint policies — in homes providing care for the elderly.[15] In addition, the Protection of Personal and Property Rights Act 1988 provides protection for older persons who cannot fully manage their own affairs. The Act gives the Court jurisdiction to appoint welfare guardians and property managers, and make orders or recommendations for action covering such matters as the provision of living arrangements, medical advice, treatment, education, rehabilitation, and the respective services (chapter 7).

(8)   *Exceptions*

Apart from measures to achieve equality mentioned in 5.4.2, there are some exceptions to the employment provisions of the anti-discrimination law. Such exceptions are where the:

- Characteristic in question is a genuine occupational qualification, for example a male actor for a male part in a play, or a female for a wet-nurse position;
- Services offered are validly applicable to only one sex, for example counselling for women victims of sexual assault;
- Services are of an intimate nature, for example toilet attendants or where people are required or may wish to undress, such as in clothing shop dressing rooms or for medical examination.

Religious bodies, sporting bodies, charities, and voluntary bodies are excepted in some circumstances. Despite the fact that health providers provide services of an intimate nature, it is not generally considered a genuine occupational qualification that a carer is of a particular gender. Sensitive areas such as rape units in hospitals would be considered exceptions.

5.4.2   Measures to achieve equality

It is not unlawful to discriminate in favour of one of the mentioned classes of people, if that discrimination is a means of bringing about equality of access to employment, or conditions of employment, or goods and services. Measures such as training programmes for particular groups of people, such as a promotion of multi-culturalism in order to promote a greater cross-section of cultures into training institutions, and English language classes or nursing orientation classes for immigrant employees are lawful.

Exemption is also provided for discriminating where the service offered is such that it will not work effectively without it, for example female health workers for treating rape victims, or cultural gender-specific counselling. However, in most cases the employer or provider of services must apply for the exemption from the Human Rights Commission.

5.4.3   Test of discrimination for government and public sector agencies

Under the Human Rights Amendment Act 2001 all government and public sector agencies, including all District Health Boards and probably all private agencies that are publicly funded to provide health and disability services, must apply a test set out in section 19 New Zealand Bill of Rights Act 1990. This test asks:

---

15   Also includes those places that provide for health and disability services, residential services, mental health services, rest homes, and hospitals required to comply with the Health and Disability Services (Safety) Act 2001.

- Is there a differentiation on one of the prohibited grounds?
- If so, does it result in disadvantage or stigma to a person or group?

Where the answer is "yes", then the facility or organisation has to consider whether the discrimination is justified, which means reasonable in a free and democratic society. If it is, then the discrimination must be one already prescribed by law. That is, it must be linked into a readily accessible and understandable legal framework such as the New Zealand Public Health and Disability Act 2000.

The test means that a health care organisation, either a District Health Board ("DHB") or non-governmental organisation ("NGO") can be challenged if it does not have an objective and rational justification for discrimination on one of the prohibited grounds.[16]

People who believe they have experienced discrimination can complain to the Human Rights Commission. If a complaint is found to be of substance, commission mediators will try to settle the matter. If agreement is not reached, the Director of Human Rights Proceedings may decide to represent the complainant in proceedings before the Human Rights Review Tribunal. Alternatively, the Director may decide to refer the complaint back to the Commission for a further attempt at mediation, or alternatively may decide not to investigate further.

(1)   *The Human Rights Review Tribunal*

The Tribunal hearing may result from the Director of Human Rights Proceedings taking the complaint, or from the complainant doing so. Alternatively, it may result from a general inquiry into law, policy, or other matters, by the Human Rights Commission. The Tribunal's powers include conducting a hearing and deciding on a remedy. A party may appear in person, or be represented by a lawyer. Principles of natural law must be observed. Parties may be summonsed,[17] and heard on oath, although the hearing is to be as informal as possible, with no need to use the rules of evidence, or formal examination.

The Proceedings Commissioner's functions include deciding whether:

- An interim order should be made to preserve the position of the parties pending a final determination of the proceedings;
- To institute proceedings against a party to a settlement reached previously;
- To institute proceedings against the person against whom the complaint was made;
- To apply for a declaration that an act or practice is unlawful or lawful.

The Human Rights Review Tribunal can grant the following remedies:[18]

- A declaration that a person has breached the Act;
- An order restraining continuation of the breach;

---

16   The Ministry of Justice has published guidelines on the changes to the Human Rights Act entitled "The Non-Discrimination Standards for Government and the Public Sector" Available in hard copy from the Ministry of Justice or its website, www.justice.govt.nz. For other assistance the following agencies provide advice: the Human Rights Commission, PO Box 6751, Wellesley Street, Auckland, Tel 0800 496 677, www.hrc.co.nz; the Ministry of Justice Bill of Rights Team, PO Box 180, Wellington, www.justice.govt.nz; and the Crown Law Office, Human Rights Team, PO Box 5012, Wellington www.crownlaw.govt.nz.

17   Human Rights Act 1993, section 127(2).

18   Human Rights Act 1993, section 92I.

- Compensation;
- An order that a person perform an act to redress the loss or damage suffered by the complainant;
- A declaration that a contract entered into is illegal, and any relief that could be granted under the Illegal Contracts Act 1970;
- Such other relief as the Tribunal thinks fit.

Where a determination has been made, and the respondent refuses or fails to carry out any required act, either the Commission itself or the complainant can take the matter to the Courts to have the determination enforced. The Courts, if satisfied that the discrimination has occurred, can make any order they think fit. They can take the Commission's proceedings and determination into account.

5.4.4   The Human Rights Commission and discrimination in employment

The Human Rights Act 1993 provides for remedies where a person is discriminated against in employment matters. If, for instance, there were only one applicant for a job it would be unlawful for an employer to refuse to employ that person for that job if the person was qualified for that type of work. It is also unlawful to:

- Refuse, or omit, to offer the employee the same terms of employment or opportunities available to others with similar skills and experience in similar work; or
- Dismiss the employee, or take any detrimental actions when such actions would not be taken against other employees engaged by the employer in similar work.

These actions are discriminatory if they occur because of the employee's race, ethnic or national origins, sex, marital status, religious or ethical belief, or by reason of the employee's involvement in an employee organisation's activities. The grievance procedures are set out in chapter 13.

The Employment Relations Act 2000 provides for an alternative mechanism by which human rights in employment may be enforced. The Labour Relations Act 1987 made the personal grievance procedures in employment law available to claims of discrimination for the first time. The subsequent Employment Contracts Act 1991 maintained this availability and now the Employment Relations Act 2000 does so. Complainants may now choose to complain to the Human Rights Commission under the Human Rights Act 1993 or to the Employment Authority under the Employment Relations Act 2000. A complainant is not entitled to pursue both avenues.

5.4.5   Measures to achieve equality

The most important and controversial exception to discrimination in anti-discrimination legislation is the provision in section 73 Human Rights Act 1993 that measures intended to achieve equality are exempted from prohibition (see 5.4.2). It allows acts and special programmes to meet a group's specific needs, which are designed to further equality of that group with the rest of society. This provision for affirmative action gives recognition to the fact that socialisation, fewer educational opportunities, and social attitudes that have been the result of, for example race or sex discrimination in the past, have put some people at a disadvantage that no strictly equal treatment will remedy.

The Human Rights Act 1993 therefore contains exceptions to the prohibition of discrimination where that discrimination is part of measures to achieve equality for a particular group of people to put them on an equal footing with others. This is called affirmative action, and allows for the taking of positive steps to overcome the effects of past discrimination. Examples are the provision of special education facilities for people from mainly cultural groups or a particular gender, so that those who may have missed out in the past because of their race or their gender can catch up and have equal access to work.

5.5   Implications for health practitioners

The connection of international documents on human rights with domestic law means that health service providers should not be discriminated against on the grounds discussed above, and also that they should not discriminate against others in their work. They should not refuse to treat, or give any less than accepted treatment to consumers because of their age, marital status (or lack of it), or sexual orientation, or because they have a mental illness or contagious or socially stigmatised disease, such as AIDS or SARS, or because they have a drug-related illness, such as alcoholism or drug dependency. Health practitioners should maintain confidentiality and privacy, and allow clients full access to all available medical care.

Where the giving of treatment places health practitioners in danger of harm, then reasonable discriminatory activity may be acceptable, for example in nuclear medicine where special conditions may apply to pregnant women. Where practitioners find that the practice is to treat someone differently, they need to examine why this is so. Is it purely on the grounds of need (the consumer's or their own)? Common examples of discrimination in the health care area are the refusal to treat HIV-positive clients, discriminatory treatment of alcoholics or people with a mental illness, or the periodic substandard treatment of older persons.

5.6   New Zealand Bill of Rights Act

The New Zealand Bill of Rights Act 1990 aims to protect the individual freedoms of citizens. The provisions are limited to acts or omissions by the various branches of government, or public bodies and officials. The following sections apply in particular to the health profession:

- *Right not to be deprived of life (section 8):* No one shall be deprived of life, except on such grounds as are established by law and are consistent with the principles of fundamental justice.
- *Right not to be subjected to torture or cruel treatment (section 9):* Everyone has the right not to be subjected to torture or to cruel, degrading, or disproportionately severe treatment or punishment.
- *Right not to be subjected to medical or scientific experimentation (section 10):* Every person has the right not to be subjected to medical or scientific experimentation without that person's consent.
- *Right to refuse to undergo medical treatment (section 11):* Everyone has the right to refuse to undergo any medical treatment.

5.7 Code of Health and Disability Services Consumers Rights

The Code of Health and Disability Services Consumers Rights ("the Code") became law on 1 July 1996. It is in the schedule to a regulation made under the Health and Disability Commissioner Act 1994.[19] It does not override other legislation, in that it does not require people to breach other enactments to give effect to the rights in it. Thus, if another Act requires a provider to do something inconsistent with the Code, that requirement appears to prevail.[20]

The Act established a complaints process in regard to the provision of health and disability services. The purpose of the Act is "to promote and protect the rights of health consumers and disability services consumers" and to that end to facilitate the "fair, simple, speedy, and efficient resolution of complaints relating to infringements of those rights".[21]

The code confers ten rights on consumers of health and disability services in New Zealand. Providers of those services have a duty to give effect to those rights.

The duty is not absolute. Clause 3 of the Code obliges providers to take reasonable actions in the circumstances to give effect to the rights, and comply with the duties in the Code. The onus is on the provider to prove that this was done.

The term "providers" includes all individuals or organisations providing, or holding themselves out as providing, health or disability services, both public and private. It includes all health professionals (such as nurses, doctors, physiotherapists, and occupational therapists) and the places in which they work including hospitals and rest homes. The term "consumer" includes all individuals who are offered, or are receiving a health or disability service. The term "services" includes all treatments and procedures, including teaching and research.

The ten rights in the Code are:

- *Right 1:* To be treated with respect.
- *Right 2:* Freedom from discrimination, coercion, harassment, and exploitation.
- *Right 3:* Dignity and independence.
- *Right 4:* Services of an appropriate standard.
- *Right 5:* Effective communication.
- *Right 6:* To be fully informed.
- *Right 7:* To make an informed choice and give informed consent.
- *Right 8:* Support.

---

19 The Code of Health and Disability Services consumers Rights (reproduced in Appendix 4) is in the Schedule to the Health and Disability Commissioner (Code of Health and Disability Services consumers Rights) Regulations 1996. At the time of writing (early 2009) the Health and Disability Commissioner Act 1994 and the Health and Disability Commissioner (Code of Health and Disability Services Consumers' Rights) Regulations 1996 are under review. Further information can be viewed on the Health and Disability Commissioner's website at www.hdc.org.nz/files/hdc/Report-on-the-Review-of-the-Act-and-Code-2009-Easy-Read.pdf.

20 Code of Health and Disability Services Consumers Rights, clause 6. Enactments include regulations as well as Acts: Interpretation Act 1999, section 29.

21 Health and Disability Commissioner Act 1994, section 6.

- *Right 9:* In respect of teaching or research.
- *Right 10:* To complain.

Rights 5-7 and 9 are discussed in chapters 6 and 7. Right 4 may be breached if a provider is negligent (chapters 4 and 8), or commits an offence (chapter 16). Rights 1 to 3, 5, and 8 reflect the human rights laws. Right 10 confers a right to complain to the provider of the services, a health and disability advocate, or the Health and Disability Commissioner. This is an important power and consumers are now largely well aware of it.

5.7.1 Complaints

The intention of the Code and the Act is to promote resolution of complaints at the lowest appropriate level. Consumers are encouraged to deal with the provider directly so that the matter can be discussed and the consumer's concerns listened to, and hopefully resolved. Providers are obliged to inform consumers of their rights and enable them to exercise them and so should advise them of the particular complaints procedure for that provider.

If a complaint is made to a provider, the provider should listen and address it and put in place whatever changes are needed. Right 10 sets out time-frames within which providers should deal with consumers complaints. Consumers can have the support of a health and disability advocate when dealing with the provider.

Consumers also have the right to complain to the Health and Disability Commissioner. Also, anyone can make a complaint on behalf of the consumer so family, friends or staff of a health care facility can complain to the Commissioner.

Consumers can also complain to a registered health professionals' professional body, but the complaint will be referred by that body to the Health and Disability Commissioner (see chapter 15).

5.7.2 Investigation by the Health and Disability Commissioner

The Health and Disability Commissioner has to decide whether to investigate a complaint to see if there has been a breach of the Code. Any investigation is carried out independently and impartially. The Commissioner does not act on behalf of the consumer or provider.

The Commissioner has powers to gather information in the form of relevant documents, including hospital notes and oral evidence from witnesses, who can be summoned to give that evidence on oath. It is an offence to obstruct or hinder the Commissioner or any other person in the exercise of their powers under the Act. A person who does so is liable for a fine of up to $3,000.[22]. It is also an offence to give false information.

The Commissioner can consult with other agencies where necessary, for example the Privacy Commission and the Human Rights Commission.

If the Commissioner's investigation reveals a breach of the Code, the Commissioner has a number of options:

- Reporting an opinion and recommendations to the provider;
- Reporting an opinion and recommendations to the Ministry of Health;
- Complaining to a professional body;

---

22   Health and Disability Commissioner Act 1994, section 73

- Referral to the Director of Proceedings.

Recommendations might include:

- An apology from the provider;
- Implementing systems to ensure the matter will not happen again;
- Training of providers;
- Payment of complainant's costs.

5.7.3   Director of Proceedings

The Director of Proceedings decides whether to take proceedings in respect of a complaint referred by the Commissioner. The Director has discretionary powers to decide whether and what action to take. If proceedings are taken, they will be brought in either, or both, the Human Rights Review Tribunal or the health practitioner's professional body (see chapter 15 for proceedings brought before the Nursing Council and the Health Practitioners Disciplinary Tribunal).

The Human Rights Review Tribunal is established under the Human Rights Act 1993, and proceedings can be heard about matters that are alleged to infringe not only the Code of Health and Disability Services Consumers Rights, but also the Human Rights Act 1993, Privacy Act 1993, or Health Information Privacy Code.

Where the Tribunal finds that there has been a breach of the Code of Health and Disability Services Consumers Rights, there are a number of remedies available including:

- A declaration that a provider is in breach of the Code;
- An order restraining the provider from continuing or repeating the breach, or from engaging in or causing or permitting others to engage in conduct of the same kind as that constituting the breach;
- An order that the provider perform any specified acts with a view to redressing any loss or damage suffered by the consumer as a result of the breach;
- Damages up to $200,000 for pecuniary loss, expenses, loss of benefit, humiliation, or action that was a flagrant disregard for the rights of the consumer;
- Any other relief as the Tribunal thinks fit.

Damages, apart from exemplary damages, will not be awarded if injury to the consumer is covered by the Injury Prevention, Rehabilitation, and Compensation Act 2001.

A Health and Disability Sector Standard has been published by Standards New Zealand through the Ministry of Health.[23] The standard provides a framework for safe practice, and is a guideline for best practice. Adherence to the standard by health service organisations will assist the organisation in meeting its obligations under the Health and Disability Services Consumers Rights Code, as well as the Health Information Privacy Code (see chapter 9). The latest standard came into force in June 2009 and replaces standards set in 2001 that were duplicating each other. It covers all health and disability services, residential services, mental health services, rest homes, and hospitals required to comply with the Health and Disability Services (Safety) Act. The standards have thus been incorporated into law as

---

23   NZS 8134:2008; New Zealand Standard Health and Disability Sector Standards Te Awarua o Te Haurora Standards New Zealand Ministry of Health.

delegated legislation, and may be used as a measure of an organisation's adherence to its legal obligations, as well as a tool for quality control and audit.

5.8 Further reading

M Bogard, *The Legal Rights of People with Intellectual Disabilities*, Wellington, Legal Resources Trust, 1995.

J S Davidson, *Human Rights*, Birmingham, Open University Press, 1993.

J S Davidson, "Individual communication to the United Nations Human Rights Committee: A New Zealand perspective" [1997] New Zealand Law Review 375.

Human Rights Commission, Complaints Division, "Disability discrimination" (1996) 2(2) Human Rights Law and Practice 120.

Human Rights Commission, Complaints Division, "Indirect discrimination: Failure to recognise overseas qualifications" (1996) 2(1) Human Rights Law and Practice 67.

Ministry of Foreign Affairs and Trade, *Handbook on International Human Rights*, Wellington, 1998.

Redern Legal Centre, *Questions of Rights: A Guide to the Law and Rights of People with an Intellectual Disability*, Australia, Chippendale, 1992.

M N Shaw, *International Law* (3rd ed), Cambridge, Grotius Press, 1991.

Chapter 6

Consent

Sue Johnson and Rebecca Keenan

Contents

6.1   Introduction

It is part of a health practitioner's work to touch a client and to carry out procedures on that person, be it washing, or giving medication, resuscitation, or sustenance. According to the law, no such action may be taken without the client's consent to it.

Clients are termed "consumers" under the New Zealand legislation that provides for their right to consent.

The issue of consent raises at times some serious legal and ethical problems when consumer autonomy and medical paternalism conflict. Autonomy is based on the principle of the consumer's right to make decisions regarding medical treatments, no matter how unwise others may consider her/him. Paternalism is based on the desirability of allowing the health practitioner to judge what is in the consumer's interest. The trend in the past, at least in England, New Zealand, and Australia, was to allow the medical profession to decide on the balance between the two. This is no longer the case. Consent law is consumer-centred in New Zealand, and there is a statutory right for all consumers to make an informed choice and to give informed consent (see 6.5.1).

6.2   Common law

The common law has, for hundreds of years, maintained that any unwanted interference with a person's body, or creation of fear of such interference, is an actionable wrong at law. The remedy is based on the law of trespass, in this case, trespass to the person. This includes medical procedures, whether therapeutic or experimental. Thus, the hospitals' concerns are to gain consumer consent before medical procedures are undertaken. However, the action in trespass covers all actions affecting another's physical integrity, so it applies to all health practitioners, as well as the public in general. There are several actions available as trespass to the person, but assault, battery, and false imprisonment are the main ones.

6.3   Assault

The term "assault" is often used to mean the beating up of a person, and certainly that is its colloquial use in criminal law. Strictly speaking, assault is carried out simply by creating in the mind of another, the apprehension of unwanted physical contact.[1] This does not have to be harmful contact. The indication that a person is going to kiss another against their will is technically an assault. If a health practitioner, for example, threatens consumers with medication or restraint if they do not behave (unless there is a real risk of harm from their actions), this is legally an assault. The threat does not have to be explicit, it only needs to be inferred from the practitioner's words or actions. Any fear of unwanted contact placed in the mind of consumers through the practitioner's actions can therefore constitute assault. The implication that they will be treated in such a way if they do not conform, or that treatment will be given regardless of their wishes, can be considered assault.

---

1   It is, for example, an assault to advance upon a person while making an improper suggestion: *Fogden v Wade* [1945] NZLR 724.

The element of assault involves subjective interpretation of the situation. That is, the defendant need not intend to carry out the threat, it may be a joke. So long as the "victim" has reason to believe that they will be touched against their will, and the means for such touching are reasonably available, they may be able to sue in assault.[2] For example, it has been held that pointing an unloaded gun at a person who reasonably believes it is loaded is an assault.[3]

6.4 Battery

When the threat is carried out, that is the consumer or other person is touched against their will, that becomes in law, battery.

6.4.1 Damage need not be caused

While assault and battery can be considered a crime (a man has been prosecuted for kissing a female police officer on point duty), it is also the basis of a civil action, for which the aggrieved person may claim damages. An important distinction between the action in assault and battery and that in negligence is that in assault and battery the plaintiff need not show that any harm was suffered, whereas in negligence they must. The developers of the law have put such a premium on the individual's personal integrity, that a person is liable to compensate for invading it, even where they have caused no physical or mental harm to someone. The invasion itself is harm enough (see *Malette v Shulman*[4] (see 6.5.3(1)).

6.4.2 Battery may occur even where the intent is to benefit

The person who unlawfully touches another may nevertheless do so with the best intentions.

Case

Mohr v Williams 104 NW 12 (1905)

A surgeon was operating on a woman's right ear, by her consent. While she was under anaesthesia, he discovered that the left ear was much more seriously diseased. After consulting her general practitioner, who by her request was present at the operation, the surgeon proceeded to carry out an ossiculectomy on her left ear.[5]

---

2   The test of what the victim believes is not entirely subjective: it is based on what a reasonable person with the victim's characteristics would believe, or in the Court's words: "The reasonableness of the apprehension [of immediate and unlawful physical contact] may or may not be necessary … [I]f the defendant intentionally puts in fear of immediate violence an exceptionally timid person known to him to be so then the unreasonableness of the fear may not be necessary": *Macpherson v Beath* (1975) 12 SASR 174, 177 per Bray CJ. See also *Brady v Schatzel* [1911] QSR 206, 208.

3   *McLelland v Symons* [1951] VLR 157, 164; *Logden v Director of Public Prosecutions* [1976] Crim LR 121. (Such an act is a criminal as well as a civil assault.)

4   *Malette v Shulman* (1991) 2 Med LR 162; (1990) 67 DLR (4th) 321 (Ont CA).

5   Cited in J O'Sullivan, *Law for Nurses and Allied Health Professionals in Australia*, Sydney, Law Book Co, 1983, page 40. See also *Murray v McMurchy* [1949] 2 DLR 442, where a surgeon carrying out a caesarean section noted the woman had a number of fibroids that were capable of causing harm in a later pregnancy. He performed a tubal ligation. The Court held that as the harm was accidental and not imminent, his action was battery. Note the opposite result in a case where in a hernia operation the surgeon removed a diseased left testicle that posed a risk of death to the consumer from septicaemia: *Marshall v Curry* (1993) 3 DLR 260.

Even at that early date the Court was in no doubt that the operation on the woman's left ear was battery, despite the surgeon's good intentions. Given that the operation was not an emergency, the Court held that there was no justification in carrying out the operation, even though permission had been given for surgery on the right ear. Thus, the surgeon was found liable in battery for carrying out the ossiculectomy. Practitioners should keep in mind that there could be all sorts of reasons, rational or irrational, unknown by them, that might cause consumers to come to a decision they would believe improbable, impossible, or unthinkable. In that case practitioners can attempt to persuade, but they cannot, without invoking legal responsibility, impose their views on reluctant consumers.

6.4.3   The person need not be aware of battery

Battery may take place when the subject is asleep, comatose, or anaesthetised.[6] The person does not have to know that the unwanted act is taking place, nor do they have to have specifically stated an objection to it. As long as no permission for the act has taken place, and there is no necessity for the action to preserve or save the person's life or limb, then they have the right to sue the perpetrator of the act in battery. It is quite clear that any act that is not consented to and is unnecessary, is unlawful. Examples include the pelvic examination by students of anaesthetised consumers, or practice in the insertion and removal of inter-uterine devices on them.[7]

6.5   Legislation

6.5.1   Statutory right to make informed choice and give informed consent

Right 7 of the Code of Health and Disability Services Consumers' Rights confers the right on consumers to make informed choice and to give informed consent to receive health and disability services. Right 7 is one of ten rights in the Code.[8]

All ten rights are not meant to be read in isolation, and consumers are entitled to all the rights in the Code. However, this chapter focuses only on Rights 5-7. The Code is discussed generally in chapter 5, and the full-text of the Code is set out in Appendix 4.

Consent is not a single act, but a process involving communication between consumer and practitioner in which the practitioner openly and honestly provides full information in an environment, and in a manner, in which the consumer can understand it. The right to consent carries with it the right to refuse, and the right to withdraw consent. The right is a negative — a right to be left alone, the right to choose whether to agree to receive a particular

---

6   Even though no civil assault has been committed a criminal assault does not require that a threat be communicated to the victim.

7   These particular practices have been reported as occurring in Australian and New Zealand hospitals (see, for example, Johnstone M-J, *Bioethics: A Nursing Perspective*, Sydney, W B Saunders/Bailliere Tindall, 1989, page 12).

8   The Code of Health and Disability Services Consumers' Rights (reproduced in Appendix 4) is in the Schedule to the Health and Disability Commissioner (Code of Health and Disability Services Consumers' Rights) Regulations 1996. The Act and the Code are reviewed every 5 years, though there is a recommendation that this is extended to 10 years. Further information can be viewed on the Health and Disability Commissioner's website at www.hdc.org.nz.

service or whether to decline it. It is not the right to demand or have a particular procedure or treatment.

Informed consent in the Code is phrased in terms of consumers' rights. Perhaps at first sight, this gives a misleading impression that there is no unqualified duty on a practitioner to give effect to those rights. However, clause 1 of the Code provides that "consumers have rights and providers have duties" and that (cl 1(3)):

> "Every provider must take action to—
>
> "(a)   Inform consumers of their rights; and
>
> "(b)   Enable consumers to exercise their rights."

The rights in the Code are true claims with a correlative duty on the part of the provider to give effect to those claims.

It has been recognised, however, that it might be unreasonable in some situations for a provider to have to give effect to a consumer's right. In the proposed draft publication before the Act and the Code coming into force, it was stated that:[9]

> "in an ideal world providers would give effect to all the rights of all consumers. However, in reality, no provider is able to do this and unless some reasonable limits are in place, providers will constantly be in breach of the Code."

Clause 3 of the Code states that a provider will not be in breach of the Code if there is proof that all reasonable actions were taken in the circumstances to give effect to the rights and to comply with the duties in it. What is meant by "in the circumstances" includes the consumer's clinical circumstances and the provider's resource constraints. Thus, it would be reasonable to give necessary treatment in an emergency.[10]

Right 7 of the Code provides that services may be provided to a consumer only if the consumer makes an informed choice and gives informed consent, unless any other Act or regulation or the common law provides otherwise (Right 7(1)).

The Code generally does not require a provider to breach any duty or obligation imposed by any other Act or regulation. This means that if any other piece of legislation requires a provider to act in a way inconsistent with the Code, that requirement should be followed, rather than the Code. Some Acts specifically permit the provision of services without consent. For example the:

- Alcoholism and Drug Addiction Act 1966: Compulsory treatment can be provided to people with chronic alcohol or drug problems.
- Children, Young Persons, and Their Families Act 1989: Even where a parent would be the person entitled to give consent to their child receiving services, this Act permits services to be provided to children without such consent and the parent cannot refuse medical, psychiatric, or psychological treatment for their child (sections 49-53, 97, 178-181, 196, and 333).

---

9   Health and Disability Commission, *A Proposed Draft Code of Rights for Consumers of Health and Disability Services: A Resource for Public Consultation on the Proposed Draft Code*, Wellington, 28 July 1995.

10   In an emergency it is expected that only those services which are necessary to save life will be provided; anything else should be deferred until consent can be obtained.

- Care of Children Act 2004: An application can be made for a child to be placed under the guardianship of the Family Court, or High Court (section 31(a)). The Court then becomes the child's legal guardian if the application is successful, and can then order treatment be given to the child.[11] This might happen in cases where a parent refuses lifesaving treatment for their child. Applications can also be made on behalf of adults. In this situation the High Court, uses its common law power of parens patriae ("parents of the country"), to override a refusal of treatment by a competent adult or a person legally entitled to refuse on another adult's behalf.[12]

- Health Act 1956:[13] Treatment for infectious diseases can be given without consent under this Act. A person can also be isolated against their will to stop the spread of an infectious disease (see chapter 18).

- Land Transport Act 1998: Blood specimens can be compulsorily taken from a person who has failed an evidential breath test, or who has been arrested on suspicion of an offence under this Act while under the influence of alcohol or drugs (section 72). Blood can also be taken at a hospital or doctor's surgery without consent, if a person has been in an accident.

- Criminal Investigations (Bodily Samples) Act 1995: Under this Act a Court may order the taking of a blood sample without consent from a person suspected of any offence, to be used for DNA testing.[14]

- Mental Health (Compulsory Assessment and Treatment) Act 1992: Assessment and treatment for a mental disorder can be compulsorily provided. It appears that assessment of, and treatment for, only the mental disorder can be given without consent. Consent is required for the treatment of any other illness, or for the provision of any other service. Also the Act requires that consent should be sought where possible. Taking away the right to make a choice and to give consent does not take away the right of a patient under this Act to receive information about that compulsory treatment.[15]

- Tuberculosis Act 1948: Examination and treatment for tuberculosis can be compulsorily provided.

---

11   Care of Children Act 2004, section 36.

12   *P v Department of Social Welfare* (1983)1 FRNZ 117: Cooke J (as he then was) stated that there is a residual jurisdiction under the right and duty of the Crown as parens patriae to take care of those who cannot care for themselves. *Director- General of Social Welfare v B* [1995] 3 NZLR 73; (1995) 13 FRNZ 441: in this case the parents of J were Jehovah Witness's and had taken their son to hospital suffering a nose bleed. His condition deteriorated and he required a blood transfusion and possibly more in future treatment. The Court used its jurisdiction under parens patrie to give consent for the 3-year-old boy to receive a blood transfusion and placed the doctor as an agent for decision-making in terms of further blood transfusions.

13   The latest amendment to this Act was in 2007 in relation to safe drinking water.

14   At the time of writing (late 2009) there is a Bill in process that will amend this Act, which allows the police to take a DNA sample from a person "suspected" of committing a crime without prior judicial oversight. The crime will have to be either a specified offence or one that has a term of imprisonment. If the person does not consent to this sample being taken then the police can apply to the court for an order of compulsion. If convicted of the crime then the sample will be detained for a period of 10 years once the sentence of imprisonment is completed. There is criticism that this Bill breaches a person's rights under the Bill of Rights Act 1990 against unreasonable search and seizure (section 21).

15   Mental Health (Compulsory Assessment and Treatment) Act 1992, section 67 and Part 6 in general about patient rights.

(1)   *What do "informed choice" and "informed consent" mean?*

"Choice" is defined in the Code to mean a decision to receive services, or refuse services, or withdraw consent to services. The right to refuse is also enshrined in section 11 of the New Zealand Bill of Rights Act 1990, and Right 7(7) of the Code provides that "Every consumer has the right to refuse services and to withdraw consent to services".

Section 2 of the Health and Disability Commissioner Act 1994 defines informed consent as meaning:

> "in relation to a health consumer on or in respect of whom there is carried out any health care procedure, means consent to that procedure where that consent—
>
> "(a)   Is freely given, by the health consumer or, where applicable, by any person who is entitled to consent on that health consumer's behalf; and
>
> "(b)   Is obtained in accordance with such requirements as are prescribed by the Code."

It can be seen that there are a number of elements to this section of the Act. Each will be considered below.

(2)   *Consent must be freely given*

A consumer must give *voluntary* consent. Thus, even if health practitioners believe the procedure or treatment is for the consumer's own good or to save the consumer's life, they are expected never to misinterpret the nature or necessity of a procedure, or resort to any attempt to put undue pressure on a consumer to accept it. It goes without saying that threats, bribes, or other such coercion render consent involuntary.

There are also other factors that might affect the voluntariness of consent, and that may influence a consumer to give consent or to decline it. One of the factors is the consumer-provider relationship itself. Some consumers may have a desire to please the person treating them. They might feel that ongoing access to that person's care would be jeopardised by declining a particular treatment, or enhanced by acceptance. Where research is proposed, this is an important factor if the investigator is also the proposed participant's health practitioner.

Another factor, again important if research is proposed, is the pressure consumers might feel if they are aware that a particular service's survival is dependent on the outcome of the research study. Research could also sometimes mean the provision of free treatment. This might induce consumers to give consent to take part in the research where they might otherwise not have wished to do so.

Where a person is under the effects of medication, they may be unable to give voluntary consent. While the effect of the medication might affect their competence, they may still be more likely to agree with someone else's wishes.

A case at common law, *Beausoleil v La Communauté des Soeurs de la Providence*, illustrates this.

Case

Beausoleil v La Communauté des Soeurs de la Providence (1964) 53 DLR 2d 65 (CA)

> A woman asked to have a general anaesthetic rather than a spinal anaesthetic for a surgical procedure, as her mother had had serious adverse effects from a spinal anaesthetic. After she received her premedication, she was pressured into having a spinal anaesthetic by medical staff. As a result, she became a paraplegic. She sued, claiming that her apparent consent had not been valid, as it had not been voluntary.

The Court agreed that the fact that she had been given the premedication and its potential sedative effects meant that legally the plaintiff was not in a condition to agree voluntarily to the procedure. This principle indicates that any consent given after, or during, the giving of medication that might cause a person to be incapable of making a reasonable decision is suspect. However, the law does not reason that such a person cannot withdraw their consent because of their potentially confused state of mind. On the basis that it is more important not to treat an adult against their will than it is to postpone treatment, the law requires that a change of mind under these circumstances should be treated seriously. The only exceptions to this are where there is a valid Court order for treatment, or where the treatment is emergency treatment.

(3)   *Consent must be given by the consumer or, where applicable, by any person who is entitled to consent on that consumer's behalf*

The Code makes a presumption that every consumer of health and disability services is competent to make an informed choice and give informed consent, unless there are reasonable grounds for believing that the consumer is otherwise (Right 7(2)).

An English case set out a useful test for competency which has been developed in subsequent cases into a test for assessing incapacity and inability to make a choice.[16] A person is not competent if they:

*   Are unable to comprehend and retain the necessary information about the procedure or treatment; and
*   Unable to weigh the information, balancing risks and needs, and so arrive at a choice.

In some cases, the presumption may be able to be rebutted, for example where a consumer is unconscious or affected by medication. However, it is expected that incompetence is never assumed. There is no age of consent. Children, intellectually disabled consumers, the elderly, and those with a mental illness are all presumed competent. A practitioner must judge whether a particular person is competent to give informed consent to a particular procedure. While the views of parents or other caregivers may be taken into account, the practitioner is responsible for making the decision as to competence. (See chapter 7 for a discussion of the particular consent issues involved in the provision of child and youth health services.)

Even where a person is regarded as not competent to consent to a particular procedure, they still retain their other rights in the Code — including the right to receive information suitable for their age, maturity, and interest and provided in a manner that enables her/him understand it. They also retain the right to make informed choices, and to give informed consent to the extent appropriate to their level of competence.

---

16   *Re C (adult; refusal of medical treatment)* [1994] 1 All ER 819; [1994] 1 WLR 290, test developed in *MB (Adult): Medical Treatment* [1997] 2 FCR 541 and *Re B (Adult: Refusal of Medical Treatment)* [2002] 2 All ER 449.

"Consumer" is defined in clause 4 of the Code. For the purposes of Right 7, the definition includes a person entitled to give consent on behalf of that consumer. This would usually be where the consumer is not competent to do so.

Not everyone who might appear capable of consenting on behalf of an incompetent consumer can legally do so. For instance, there is no legal power for a spouse or next of kin to give legally effective consent on behalf of someone else. Parents can consent on their child's behalf, and so can any other of the child's guardians, for example a guardian appointed through a will, termed a testamentary guardian. If there is no guardian in New Zealand or no guardian can be found, or the guardian is incapable of giving consent, then consent can be given by any person who has been acting in the place of a parent. For example, if a child is temporarily under the care of an aunt or their father's girlfriend, or a babysitter or teacher, that person can validly consent on behalf of the child if no parent or other guardian can be found.

Under the Protection of Personal and Property Rights Act 1988, welfare guardians can be appointed. They might be able to give proxy consent where consumers are not competent to consent for themselves. Whether this is so depends upon the extent of the welfare guardian's powers.[17] In addition, under that Act, persons appointed under an enduring power of attorney have the power to consent on behalf of someone who is not competent to consent.[18]

A power of attorney is not the same thing as an enduring power of attorney. A power of attorney to act on behalf of someone else is only valid where that person is competent. If they become incompetent, a person with a power of attorney cannot give proxy consent. A person with an enduring power of attorney can, because the power cannot be exercised until the person becomes incompetent to make decisions for herself/himself.

(4)   *Consent must be obtained in accordance with such requirements as prescribed in the Code*

Consumers have a right to *effective* communication. This means in accordance with Rights 5 and 6, respectively, the right to effective communication and the right to full information. The information has to be communicated in a manner that enables the consumer to understand it, and providers have to discuss the matter with the consumer in an environment in which the consumer feels able to discuss concerns and ask questions. It is not up to the practitioner to decide how long a consumer should take to make up their mind, or how much discussion should take place. The test appears to be whether that particular consumer understands the information. If they do not, and it is because of ineffective communication by the provider, then there may be a breach of the Code.

"Right 5

"Right to Effective Communication

"(1)   Every consumer has the right to effective communication in a form, language, and manner that enables the consumer to understand the information

---

17   Protection of Personal and Property Rights Act 1988, sections 5, 6, 10(1)(k), 12, 18, 19, and 22.
18   Ibid, sections 94, 96, and 98.

provided. Where necessary and reasonably practicable, this includes the right to a competent interpreter.

"(2)   Every consumer has the right to an environment that enables both consumer and provider to communicate openly, honestly, and effectively."

Thus, when communicating information, practitioners are expected to use whatever method of communication is available and reasonable to use in the circumstances, including any aid to communication such as translators, computers, Braille, etc. Practitioners should take into account a consumer's culture, age, education, language, and special needs. In some cases it might be helpful to have assistance from family members or whanau, or other advisers, who can explain what these needs are. They can advise as to the effect of cultural differences and beliefs on the consumer's decision-making and understanding of the information. Non-verbal behaviour may differ from culture to culture, and might be significant especially where it expresses understanding or confusion.

The environment is also important. Wherever possible it should be private and comfortable. The consumer should not feel rushed, or unable to ask questions for fear of being overheard by others. Also, if a person is affected by medication or illness, they might take longer to understand the information, or to ask questions. Anticipating difficulties of communication will sometimes go a long way towards providing the right environment. For example, providing a glass of water to a consumer on medication that causes a dry mouth may assist that person to ask questions if they want to.

(5)   *What information should be given?*

Right 6 is the right to be *fully* informed. The important word is "fully", which emphasises that all providers are expected not to withhold information from consumers that might be relevant when deciding whether to consent to, or decline, a particular treatment. Right 6 sets out information which consumers must be made aware in order to be fully informed, and thus able to make an informed choice and to give informed consent. This right to be fully informed must, by implication, incorporate the right to waive the furnishing of information, although it would be prudent for a provider to request any waiver in writing in case of a future dispute about whether it was given.

"Right 6

"Right to be Fully Informed

"(1)   Every consumer has the right to the information that a reasonable consumer, in that consumer's circumstances, would expect to receive, including—

"(a)   An explanation of his or her condition; and

"(b)   An explanation of the options available, including an assessment of the expected risks, side effects, benefits, and costs of each option; and

"(c)   Advice of the estimated time within which the services will be provided; and

"(d)   Notification of any proposed participation in teaching or research, including whether the research requires and has received ethical approval; and "(e)   Any other information required by legal, professional, ethical, and other relevant standards; and

"(f)   The results of tests; and

"(g)   The results of procedures.

"(2)   Before making a choice or giving consent, every consumer has the right to the information that a reasonable consumer, in that consumer's circumstances, needs to make an informed choice or give informed consent.

"(3)   Every consumer has the right to honest and accurate answers to questions relating to services, including questions about—

"(a)   The identity and qualifications of the provider and

"(b)   The recommendation of the provider; and

"(c)   How to obtain an opinion from another provider; and

"(d)   The results of research.

"(4)   Every consumer has the right to receive, on request, a written summary of information provided."

Under Right 6(2) the standard of disclosure is an objective consumer standard. This reflects the shift of the legal standard for informed consent that has occurred at common law. In the past, the amount, depth, and detail of information that should be given to a consumer was measured by the medical community standard — that which an average competent doctor would reveal to a consumer. The Canadian case of *Reibl v Hughes*[19] shifted this standard to the information that a competent person would want to know to make a decision in the particular circumstances. This consumer-centred standard involves an objective test. A Court or Tribunal determines whether the standard has been met in each case by assessing consumers' wishes and needs for information in similar circumstances. The medical community standard was based on prevailing medical thought and expert medical witnesses' testimony.[20] The objective reasonable consumer standard is what is required by the Code.

When a Court, a Tribunal, or the Health and Disability Commissioner is determining whether a practitioner fell short of that standard, an assessment of the wishes and needs of consumers for information in similar circumstances will be used as a guide. Evidence from other practitioners as to what they themselves would disclose will not be used as a guide.

Right 6 defines the information that a consumer has the right to be given before any treatment or procedure. The risks and consequences and other matters set out in Right 6 are not exhaustive. It is suggested that in some cases it may be necessary and prudent for practitioners to also disclose the likely consequences of not having treatment.

Right 6 is a rigorous requirement. The legislation specifies that a consumer has a right to request a written summary of the information, which should be provided if they so request. Many consumers would certainly find information sheets helpful, but it is suggested that

---

19   *Reibl v Hughes* [1980] 2 SCR 880; (1981) 114 DLR (3d) 1.

20   The objective consumer standard and the medical community standard are not the only ones. In some jurisdictions the standard is a subjective consumer standard; what the particular consumer needs to know to make an informed choice and give informed consent.

these should not replace verbal communication because practitioners have the onus of assessing whether the consumer actually understands the information that is being given to her/him.

(6) *What sort of risks should be disclosed?*

Right 6(1)(b) provides that a consumer has the right to information, including an assessment of the *expected* risks of each option. What are expected risks? This is not clear, but the common law can be looked to for guidance. At common law there is a duty to disclose material or substantial risks.

(7) *Giving information about risks*

The law has established that there is a duty to disclose expected risks, but determination of these will depend upon the circumstances of individual cases. If the phrase "expected risks" includes what at common law are material or substantial risks, there are some conflicting common law decisions arising from similar fact situations as to the nature of material or substantial risks.[21]

Case

Sidaway v Bethlem Royal Hospital Governors [1985] AC 871; [1985] 1 All ER 643 (HL)

Mrs Sidaway was an elderly lady who underwent an operation on her cervical vertebrae. There was a 1 to 2 percent risk of paralysis occurring inherent in this operation, but she was not informed of this. Unfortunately, she did suffer some paralysis. She sued, alleging that it was the surgeon's duty to inform her of the risk.

The House of Lords rejected this claim, reaffirming the decision of *Bolam v Friern Hospital Management Committee*,[22] which gave medical staff the discretion to decide what disclosure is proper and in the consumer's interest. However, while the Court kept for itself the right to review such a decision, it would do so only where the discretion had fallen patently below what was deemed to be reasonable in the circumstances. Thus, the issue of informed consent comes under the category of negligence, rather than trespass. In the Australian case of *Battersby v Tottman*,[23] the Court strongly endorsed this approach, stating that Courts should not doubt the judgment of doctors, or refuse them the right to make decisions, unless convinced they are wrong.

The majority of the full Court of the Supreme Court held in the *Battersby* case, after basing its finding on the evidence of the medical profession, that the woman's condition was such as to render her consent unnecessary. Zelling J,[24] who dissented, held that a patient must be allowed to make their own decision, despite whether the doctor thinks her/him well

---

21 For example, in *Thake v Maurice* [1986] 1 All ER 497 the Court held that the risk of recanalisation after vasectomy should be disclosed to a consumer, whereas in *Eyre v Measday* [1986] 1 All ER 488 and *F v R* (1983) 33 SASR 189, the Australian Court of Appeal and the South Australian Court of Appeal respectively held that there was no negligence where surgeons failed to inform consumers of the remote chance of reversal of a tubal ligation.

22 *Bolam v Friern Hospital Management Committee* [1957] 1 WLR 582.

23 *Battersby v Tottman* (1985) 37 SASR 524.

24 Judges sitting in the High Court or appeal Courts are usually referred to orally as, for example, Justice Zelling, which is written as Zelling J. District Court Judges are referred to orally and in writing as Judge, for example, Judge Abbott.

enough or not, unless they are too young or mentally ill to understand the risks involved. He did not believe that Ms Battersby was too mentally ill. His was a faint voice of protest against the overwhelming tendency of the Courts to favour the opinion of doctors.

Case

Rogers v Whitaker (1992) 109 ALR 625 (HCA)

Ms Whitaker decided to have elective surgery on her right eye, which was vision-impaired from an accident that had occurred in her youth. Despite the almost total blindness resulting in the right eye, she had led a "substantially normal life", working, marrying, and raising children. However, on having a check-up, surgery was recommended on the basis that she could benefit, even cosmetically. After surgery, complications developed in the right eye, spreading to the left eye and resulting in almost total blindness. This is known as "sympathetic ophthalmia", and is a recognised risk of eye surgery. At no stage was Ms Whitaker warned of the risk of this occurring. Ms Whitaker sued in negligence on several grounds, including failure to warn her of the risk of sympathetic ophthalmia, performing an ill-advised operation, failure to follow up missed appointments, and failure to enucleate the right eye following development of symptoms of sympathetic ophthalmia in the left eye.

The defence relied on the principle enunciated in *Bolam v Friern Hospital Management Committee* (see 6.5.1(7)), stating that the case made the decision of what to tell a person one which the doctor can make, based on medical judgment. That would mean a doctor is not negligent if they act in accordance with a practice of disclosure or non-disclosure accepted at the time as proper practice by a responsible body of medical opinion, even if some doctors adopt a different practice. The defence produced evidence from a group of specialists who supported Dr Rogers' actions. They also relied on the fact that the risk of sympathetic ophthalmia was considered to be one in 14,000 and therefore too remote to mention to the consumer. The trial Judge rejected all but the first ground of complaint, ruling that the failure to warn of the risk of sympathetic ophthalmia amounted to negligence. He considered the following facts:

- Ms Whitaker had expressed a keen interest in avoiding harm to her good eye, and Dr Rogers was aware of this;
- She repeatedly asked about risks, to the point of irritating Dr Rogers;
- Dr Rogers was aware at the time of the risk, although it was remote;
- The failure to warn of the risk was not contemplated for therapeutic reasons;
- Had Ms Whitaker been advised of the risk, she would not have had the surgery.

The appeal went first to the New South Wales Court of Appeal where it was dismissed, and then to the High Court of Australia. The High Court said that the principle in *Bolam* was no longer applicable in determining whether a medical practitioner had given adequate information about a medical procedure to a consumer. Instead the Court followed the judgment of King J in *F v R*,[25] in which he stated that although the Court will consider evidence of what is considered proper medical practice, it is ultimately for the Court to determine what the appropriate standard of care is. He said that when deciding that, the paramount consideration is to be that a person is entitled to make their own decisions about

---

25   *F v R* (1983) 33 SASR 189.

their life.[26] The Court went on to say that the more drastic the proposed procedure, such as major surgery, the more necessary it is to keep the consumer informed about the risks.

The High Court drew a distinction between *diagnosis* and *treatment*, where medical judgment and proper medical practice, based on the *Bolam* test, were relevant considerations, and *informing the consumer*. Information is a right, which is not based on medical judgment, but on legal principles. It is for the Court to decide whether a person's right to be adequately informed about a procedure has been breached or not.

It would appear that the term "expected" risks could be said to include those that at common law are regarded as *material* or substantial risks. In *Rogers v Whitaker* the High Court of Australia stated that a material risk is one:

- To which a reasonable person in the consumer's condition would be likely to attach significance;
- To which the doctor knows the particular consumer will be likely to attach significance; and
- About which questions asked by the consumer reveal their concern. However, under the Code consumers are entitled to be told about material risks without having to ask questions.

In the case of *Rosenberg v Percival*[27] the High Court of Australia further clarified what "material risk" means. It indicated that it means all inherent risks in a procedure that are "real and foreseeable and within the meaning given in *Rogers v Whitaker*". The Court affirmed that risks are foreseeable if they are not far fetched or fanciful. In determining what is foreseeable, the Court noted the importance of defining the risk. Gummow J stated that the risk should be defined:[28]

> "by reference to the circumstances in which the injury can occur, the likelihood of the injury occurring and the extent or severity of the potential injury if it does occur. These factors are to be considered from the point of view of what a reasonable medical practitioner in the position of the defendant ought to have forseen at the time."

Case

Chester v Ashfar [2005] 1 AC 134

Miss Chester had consulted Mr Ashfar a neurosurgeon about surgery for a chronic back condition and underwent the surgery recommended by him. As a result of the surgery Miss Chester was left with disability[29] and pain. The injury sustained was an inherent risk of the surgery. The injury had a 1-2 percent chance of occurring but Mr Ashfar had not informed Miss Chester of this risk prior to surgery. Miss Chester sued in negligence and claimed that if she had been informed of this risk she would not have undergone the operation on that day but would have sought a second opinion before making a decision.

---

26   *F v R* (1983) 33 SASR 189.
27   *Rosenberg v Percival* (2001) 75 ALJR 734.
28   *Rosenberg v Percival* (2001) 75 ALJR 734.
29   Cauda equine syndrome, where the nerve roots become compressed cutting off sensation and movement.

This decision is important in assisting a health practitioner to determine what information should be given to a patient. The House of Lords affirmed in this case that it does not accept *Rogers v Whittaker* as the law in the United Kingdom, but they did not decide this case on normal principles of negligence. Both cases are similar fact situations, where both plaintiffs underwent surgery that resulted in injury from an inherent risk of which they were not informed.[30] They claimed that if they had been informed of this risk they would not have undergone the surgery on that day. *Chester v Ashfar* was eventually decided on policy reasons and the importance of the ability of a plaintiff/patient to make an informed choice. In coming to this decision the House of Lords considered academic literature such as Honoré[31] who promoted the proposition that the duty to warn is imposed upon the doctor because of the right of the patient to make an informed choice. This underlies the principle that it is for the patient to decide whether, and if so by whom and when to be operated on. To do this the patient must be informed of all risks, even if the inherent risk has only a 1-2 percent chance of occurring. If a doctor fails to warn of such a risk which then eventuates from the treatment performed, the doctor will more than likely be found liable.

6.5.2   Giving treatment without consent

Right 7(1) provides that the right to make an informed choice and give informed consent is subject to all other legislation and common law. This has been discussed above at 6.5.1. There are a number of instances where services may be provided without consent:

- Emergencies;
- Providing services without consent under the Code;
- Therapeutic privilege.

(1)   *Emergencies*

Practitioners need not obtain consent before providing emergency services. This would be one example of a situation where clause 3 (the reasonableness clause) would apply. This exception stems from the common law defence of necessity and therefore only necessary treatment should be provided.

(2)   *Providing services without consent under the Code*

Where a person is unable to consent for herself/himself, and no one who is entitled to consent on that person's behalf is available, services can still be provided without consent in accordance with the requirements in the Code. Right 7(4) sets out the steps that must be taken in such circumstances:

> "(4)   Where a consumer is not competent to make an informed choice and give informed consent, and no person entitled to consent on behalf of the consumer is available, the provider may provide services where—
>
> > "(a)   It is in the best interests of the consumer; and
> >
> > "(b)   Reasonable steps have been taken to ascertain the views of the consumer; and

---

30   See also *Chappel v Hart* [1998] HCA 55.

31   Honoré, "Medical non-disclosure: causation and risk: Chappel v Hart" (1999) 7 Torts LJ 1, cited in *Chester v Afshar* [2005] 1 AC 134, para 22.

"(c)   Either,—

"(i)   If the consumer's views have been ascertained, and having regard to those views, the provider believes, on reasonable grounds, that the provision of the services is consistent with the informed choice the consumer would make if he or she were competent; or

"(ii)   If the consumer's views have not been ascertained, the provider takes into account the views of other suitable persons who are interested in the welfare of the consumer and available to advise the provider."

A practitioner therefore may provide services where it is *in the best interest of the consumer*. This is an important point to note because sometimes it may be difficult to determine. For example, a person may be unconscious or mentally disordered and not competent to consent, with no one legally entitled to consent on his or her behalf. If a practitioner wants to involve that consumer in research, and if the research study is a randomised one, including a placebo arm, it may be difficult for the researcher to establish that it will be in the consumer's best interest to take part and receive the study drug. At best, the practitioner may only be able to say that the treatment would not be against the consumer's interest, or that it could be in that person's potential best interest.

A practitioner is also expected to have taken all reasonable steps to establish the consumer's views. If they cannot be ascertained from the consumer, then family members or others who are interested in the consumer's welfare must be approached to find out what they believe their view would be. Suitable persons who are interested in the welfare of the consumer might also include an ethics committee. Once these views have been ascertained, the practitioner must take them into account before deciding whether to provide services.

(3)   *Therapeutic privilege*

This concept originated in the common law defence of necessity. It allowed doctors to withhold information that would be, in the doctor's opinion, detrimental to the consumer's health, such that if it were disclosed it would hinder necessary treatment or cause severe mental trauma. It is now expected that any withholding of information on the grounds of therapeutic privilege should only occur in a situation of medical emergency, where there is an imminent danger to the consumer's life. It is also expected that once the risk to the consumer has abated, then the previously withheld information will be disclosed. It is also a concept that has stemmed from a paternalistic era of medical practice. Today with the rights of patients to self determination, which are enshrined in the Code of Health and Disability Services Consumers' Rights, it is arguable that there is no longer a place for this.

Case
Health and Disability Commissioner Inquiry / Case 04HDC04340
Anaesthetist, Dr B
Surgeon, Dr C
Otago District Health Board

The patient had tracheal stenosis and underwent laser surgery in an attempt to relieve the narrowing. Once the procedure was started it was found that the narrowing was more severe than had been anticipated and the smallest endotracheal tube used for laser surgery could not be used. It was decided to go ahead with a non-laser proof endotracheal tube. During the procedure there was an airway fire which caused full mucosal burns to the subglottis, glottis and laryngeal surface of the epiglottis, with minor burns to the tracheal mucosa, mucosa of the main bronchi and the oropharynx. The doctor had not informed the patient of this potential risk and used the reasoning of therapeutic privilege as his defence.

The Health and Disability Commissioner (the Commissioner) did not accept the doctor's submission that he could withhold information if he thought that it would cause undue anxiety and prevent the patient from undergoing a procedure that would be highly beneficial to quality of life or life expectancy. The Commissioner found that this went against patient autonomy and did not foster a true partnership between patient and doctor.

(4)   *Others matters relevant to informed consent*

Right 7 also provides that:[32]

"(5)   Every consumer may use an advance directive in accordance with the common law.

"(6)   Where informed consent to a health care procedure is required, it must be in writing if—

"(a)   The consumer is to participate in any research; or

"(b)   The procedure is experimental; or

"(c)   The consumer will be under general anaesthetic; or

"(d)   There is a significant risk of adverse effects on the consumer.

"(7)   Every consumer has the right to refuse services and to withdraw consent to services.

"(8)   Every consumer has the right to express a preference as to who will provide services and have that preference met where practicable.

"(9)   Every consumer has the right to make a decision about the return or disposal of any body parts or bodily substances removed or obtained in the course of a health care procedure.

"(10)   No body part or bodily substance removed or obtained in the course of a health care procedure may be stored, preserved, or used otherwise than —

"(a)   with the informed consent of the consumer; or

"(b)   for the purposes of research that has received the approval of an ethics committee; or

---

32   This right was changed in the 2004 HDC review and previously read "Any body parts or bodily substances removed or obtained in the course of a health care procedure may be stored, preserved, or utilised only with the informed consent of the consumer".

"(c)   for the purposes of 1 or more of the following activities, being activities that are each undertaken to assure or improve the quality of services:

"(i)   a professionally recognised quality assurance programme:

"(ii)   an external audit of services:

"(iii) an external evaluation of services."

(5)   Advance directives

Right 7(5) gives the right to consumers to use an advance directive in accordance with the common law. Practitioners are ideally placed to educate consumers about advance directives. The phrase "advance directive" is defined in clause 4 to mean:

"a written or oral directive—

"(a)   By which a consumer makes a choice about a possible future health care procedure; and

"(b)   That is intended to be effective only when he or she is not competent."

The term means that a person can make an advance choice about receiving or refusing services. In this latter sense, it is sometimes referred to as a living will. A living will is a written declaration of the treatments and procedures that a person would accept or reject if they were in danger of death and incapable of decision-making. The Code gives a right to use an advance directive "in accordance with the common law". In Canada specific legislation sets out requirements that need to be followed and met before an advance directive is legally valid. There is no equivalent legislation in this country, and the validity of an advance directive at common law is unclear in New Zealand. Involvement of family, a GP, and even a lawyer is suggested in the preparation of an advance directive because it is much more likely then to be effected. Legal advice and/or an ethics committee's opinion might be helpful on an individual case basis if a practitioner feels that the choice may be difficult, or there is strong opposition by family to the terms of the advance directive. To be regarded as valid it must be made without undue influence, by a person who is competent and fully informed about the consequences of refusing the particular future service. It must also apply to the current situation. It is most likely to be given effect if it was made fairly recently, as it could be argued that the person making it might not now hold the same views. The United Kingdom has recently included Advance Directives in their Mental Capacity Act 2005. It has a section[33] that allows an advance directive on refusing life sustaining treatment, to be found not valid if on reasonable grounds it is believed that circumstances exist which the person had not anticipated when the advance directive was written.[34] An advance directive is another extension of self-determination but there is no guarantee that once incompetent the views expressed in such a document will be held to be legally binding. This is particularly true if the next of kin or the person with enduring power of attorney

---

33   Section 25(4) (c).

34   *HE v A Hospital NHS Trust* [2003] EWHC 1017 (Fam), an advance directive refusing blood products was drawn up when the patient was a Jehovah witness. The patient's condition became life threatening but subsequent to the advance directive the patient had married and become a Muslim. Munby J found that the continuing validity of the advance directive must be proved and if there are circumstances that cast real doubt then it must give way to preservation of life.

does not support it. This is a negative right, an advance directive cannot request for certain treatment to be given.

(6)   Consent and research

Right 7(6) requires that consent must be in writing if a consumer is to participate in research, or where a procedure is experimental, or where a consumer is under general anaesthetic, or if there is a significant risk of an adverse effect. Some researchers contend that research may be difficult to conduct if written consent is needed, and that the provision for informed consent to be in writing should be removed. Noting this concern, the Health and Disability Commissioner has pointed out that under clause 3 of the Code, researchers will not be in breach of the Code if they have made reasonable efforts to give effect to its rights in the circumstances. The Commissioner has further observed that, in some cases, written consent would be culturally inappropriate. In those and similar circumstances, obtaining ethical approval for the research, and demonstrating that it has a valuable public health objective, may lead to the conclusion that the researcher acted reasonably in proceeding without written consent. The Commissioner has therefore decided that, at present, the requirement of written consent to research need not be removed because of the flexibility already provided by clause 3.[35]

So far the discussion has been restricted to therapeutic treatment, that is, treatment of someone who is ill, with the intention of effecting either cure or relief from the condition. Of course, the purpose of research is to gather information. Generally, the two approaches are considered mutually exclusive. However, it has been argued that all treatment may be considered experimental, at least to some extent as the effect of treatment on different people can never be certain. It should not be forgotten that the practitioner-consumer relationship is one of carer-consumer when treating someone. However, this relationship changes with research — it becomes researcher-subject. The practitioner's interest as treating clinician is consistent with the consumer's in the therapeutic relationship. Presumably, both want the consumer to benefit. However, the researcher's interest is not necessarily similar to the consumer-subject's. It is to gather information, although the subject's welfare is also a matter of concern.

When research is undertaken, consumers should be told this, that is, they should not believe they are undergoing procedures necessary for their welfare. Under the Code, consent must be given in writing. No research project should be undertaken unless it has been carefully scrutinised by an independent ethics committee, which considers, among other things, what information the participants will be given and how consent is to be obtained. Ethics committees in New Zealand protect the individual participants in research. Most research protocols are ethically sound, but some may be based on either lack of information or misinformation. In these cases, the committee will give careful consideration to the reasons for the research and its necessity, the risks involved, why alternative methods of seeking the information are not suitable, and the value of the research to society in general. These reasons must demonstrate clearly that the research cannot be effectively carried out in any other way, that it carries little risk, and is important and valuable enough to warrant the invasion of the physical or mental integrity of the participants, and/or the use of misinformation. Only rarely are such research protocols approved.

---

35   Health and Disability Commissioner, Review Document for Consultation, Wellington, February 1999.

This is highlighted by the findings of the Committee of Inquiry into Allegations Concerning the Treatment of Cervical Cancer at National Women's Hospital and into Other Related Matters in July 1988.[36] That committee was established to inquire into whether there had been a research programme into cervical carcinoma involving consumers. The committee found that there had been a study to find out which of two forms of treatment for cervical cancer was the best. Without their knowledge or consent, consumers were divided into two groups. One group was treated by radium and surgery, and the other group by radium and radiation. The report heightened awareness of the rights of consumers who are the subjects of research.

Section 10 of the New Zealand Bill of Rights Act 1990 declares that it is the right of every person not to be subjected to medical or scientific experimentation without their consent. This section is an enlargement of article 7 of the International Covenant on Civil and Political Rights 1966, which provides:

> "no-one shall be subjected to torture or to cruel, inhuman or degrading treatment or punishment. In particular, no-one shall be subjected without his free consent to medical or scientific experimentation."

Section 10, which is not limited to cruel or inhumane experiments, creates a general right not to be subjected to experimentation without consent. Thus, experiments on unconscious consumers and those unable to give consent themselves appear to be impossible.[37] Interpretation of the word "experimentation" is a crucial issue. The matter is legally unclear and researchers have been advised by Ministry of Health guidelines to consult legal advisers and an ethics committee.[38] Ethics committees have developed guidelines and consider each study on an individual case basis.

In 1990 the Health Research Council Act 1990 came into force. This statute established the Health Research Council, which provides for a number of research committees. The statute adopts the principles of the Declaration of Helsinki 1964, which was issued by the World Medical Association. One of the principles in that declaration is that any person taking part in medical or scientific research should have given informed consent, that is freely given consent. This consent should have been obtained, preferably in writing, after the subject had been adequately informed of the aims, methods, anticipated benefits, and potential hazards of the study and any discomfort that may ensue. Enforcement of the Declaration of Helsinki in New Zealand is through the Health Research Council, which now has economic, legal, and ethical control over health research in New Zealand.

(7)   *Consent forms*

Generally, any contact providers have with consumers will involve verbal or implied consent only. Where medical procedures are major, most providers ensure that they have written consent forms, which are signed by the consumer. These days, where people are increasingly aware of the law and more prepared to complain than in the past, a greater number of

---

36   S Coney, *The Unfortunate Experiment*, Auckland, Penguin, 1988.

37   Protection of Personal and Property Rights Act 1988, section 18(1)(f) also prevents a welfare guardian appointed under the Act from consenting to a person taking part in any medical experiment unless it is to save that person's life. See also P Pearl and D Holdaway, "Legal and ethical issues of health research with children", *Children's Issues*, Volume 2, Issue 2, 1998, page 42.

38   Ministry of Health, *Consent in Child and Youth Health Information for Practitioners*, Wellington, 1998.

situations are being covered by written consent forms. However, written consent may be verbally revoked. Health practitioners may be asked to secure a consumer's signature on a consent form, and one might question just what their responsibilities are when they are seeking to obtain a signed consent form for a procedure to be carried out by someone else.

(8)   *The legal implications of consent forms*

First, the nature of consent forms should be understood. At law, a signed document is a contemporaneous record of a person's intentions or understanding. When a person signs a contract, they are bound by its contents. However, the law has recognised that evidence of the conditions under which a person signs something may be potential evidence that credence should not be given to the document.[39] If, for example, a person is affected by drugs, whatever is said in a signed document is suspect, regardless of the signature. Similarly, a person may sign a form giving permission for others to carry out a procedure without fully understanding the nature of the procedure. The Courts would consider such consent invalid. The form is only *evidence* of consent, not consent itself. It is poor evidence of adequate knowledge on the part of a consumer if there is also no evidence of proper advice at or before the time of signing. In fact, Rozovsky[40] questions whether consent forms should be used at all, or whether it is better to adopt a more comprehensive recording procedure. This, she concludes, would involve both properly informed consent, and the adequate recording of it.[41]

Anomalies can occur where there is a focus on the signing of consent forms without sufficient appreciation of the legal implications. An extreme example of this was highlighted in the Royal Commission Report on Chelmsford where:[42]

> "consent forms were not filled in … consent forms were falsely filled in either by a signature clearly made when the patient was seriously affected by the drug regime or by a different hand, probably a doctor or a nurse, but now unidentifiable. There were times when Dr Bailey signed to authorise the treatment. There were times when the records showed treatment given even when the very record noted that the patient had expressly refused it."

Although practitioners can legally witness someone signing a consent form, they should not ask consumers to sign consent forms for treatment to be given by others if such consent relies on information. They should be wary of accepting the responsibility, for they cannot ensure the consumer knows enough about it and, as they are not going to carry out the procedure, they may lack the necessary knowledge. A Court could ignore such a document as not indicating proper consent. Practitioners should definitely not be responsible for explaining treatment that others are going to give the consumer. Legally, this is the responsibility of those others, and the form should indicate who informed the consumer. It should be borne in mind that what is said to the consumer by a health practitioner may

---

39   See, for example, the section on setting aside contracts in chapter 12.

40   F Rozovsky, *Consent to Treatment: A Practical Guide*, Boston, Little, Brown & Co, 1984, page 640.

41   However, in *Chatterton v Gerson* [1981] 1 QB 432, 443 Lord Bristow stated that "getting the patient to sign a pro forma expressing consent to undergo an operation should be a valuable reminder to everyone of the need for explanation and consent. But it would be no defence to an action in trespass to the person if no explanation had in fact been given. The consent would be expressed in form only, not in reality."

42   Parliament of New South Wales, *Report of the Royal Commission into Deep Sleep Therapy* Volume 1, Sydney, New South Wales Government Printer, 1990, pages 57-58.

influence a consent to treatment, and this influence may be misleading. It is best for practitioners to be very careful in discussing the nature and effects of treatment others are going to give. Many writers have emphasised that it is the responsibility of the practitioner who is actually going to be carrying out the treatment or procedure, not others, to do the explaining and provide the necessary information:[43]

> "The duty to disclose to the patient the nature of the treatment being undertaken and the possibility of adverse results remains squarely upon the physician. It is a duty that cannot be delegated except to another physician; it may not be delegated to the nurse."

The provider who is to carry out the treatment is the person who should witness a consumer's signature, because it is their responsibility to ensure knowledgeable consent.

Both the practitioner who neglects to undertake the responsibility of obtaining knowledgeable consent from a consumer, and the other practitioner who takes on the task of informing that consumer run legal risks. These are the risks of a finding of breach of the Health and Disability Code of Consumers' Rights — a civil action in battery or negligent misstatement, and if the consumer sustains physical injury — a finding of medical error by ACC.[44] Although it may be tempting to reassure the anxious consumer who needs information and cannot seem to get it, practitioners are advised to treat consent as not given, because clearly it was not fully *informed* consent. They should attempt to get the treating practitioner or other person concerned, back to see the consumer, or at least report the matter to superiors, who may be able to organise responsible communication with the consumer.

Consent forms should be specific to the procedures involved. "Blanket" or standard forms, signed on entry to a hospital or clinic, covering any or all treatment given there may be held to be too vague and general to be valid at law. Emergency treatment is covered by the presumption that the consumer would wish to have treatment to save life and limb, unless otherwise clearly stated by the consumer, so there is no need for general consent forms.

Checklist

Elements of a consent form

Optional items are preferred items:

- Name and full identification of consumer;
- Name of procedure agreed to;
- Name of place for carrying out of the procedure;
- (Optional) consent to specified associated treatments. These could presumably have been discussed as part of the procedure;
- (Optional) consent to or statement acknowledging possible need for emergency treatment;

---

43   I A Murchison and T Nichols, *Legal Foundations of Nursing Practice*, London, Macmillan, 1970, page 131.
44   Medical error under the Injury Prevention Rehabilitation, and Compensation Act 2001 was repealed in 2005, so a claim for personal injury from treatment did not need to be linked to medical error and as a consequence would encourage health practitioners to be more forthcoming about adverse events.

- Statement of what information had been given, for example what the procedure involves, why it is required, and why it is recommended in preference to alternatives. Further items could be added as per those in statute;
- (Optional) list of specific risks and advantages, which have been discussed;[45]
- Agreement to another person carrying out the procedure, or any other necessary procedure, if circumstances require this.

6.5.3 Issues arising

(1) *Refusal of emergency treatment*

As discussed above, where adults of apparently sound mind require emergency treatment, and are conscious, they can refuse it. Whether emergency treatment can be given in the face of a conscious adult's refusal, however, is a difficult question from a legal point of view. The conflict between principles of autonomy and the right of practitioners to carry out emergency treatment to save life has not been resolved clearly by the Courts.[46]

Case

Malette v Shulman (1991) 2 Med LR 162; (1990) 67 DLR (4th) 321 (Ont CA)

Ms Malette was seriously injured in a car accident, and taken to hospital unconscious. She was carrying a card, unsigned and unwitnessed, which stated that she was a Jehovah's Witness and that she refused any blood transfusions. She deteriorated and was bleeding profusely from severe facial injuries, a severed nose, and also internally bleeding. Dr Shulman gave her a blood transfusion. She sued him. He argued that as she had been unconscious, he had been unable to inform her properly for her "informed refusal". He was thus under a legal and ethical duty to give emergency treatment. The trial Court found in the plaintiff's favour and the doctor appealed.

The Ontario Court of Appeal dismissed the appeal, stating that the card did impose a valid restriction on treatment. The consumer did foresee this sort of situation, the Court said, which was why she was carrying the card. The Court went on to state that it recognised the doctor's dilemma. However, he would not have violated his legal duty or his professional responsibility if he respected the consumer's right to autonomy. He had no right to judge her reasonableness, provided the instructions were valid. Harmful consequences arising from her decision were her responsibility. It is important to note that Ms Malette received only nominal damages and had to pay her own legal costs. This is an indication of the legal approach to cases where a doctor may have technically breached the consumer's legal right

---

45 Some providers may wish to have additional statements to the effect that the consumer assumes all risks and acknowledges that benefits are not guaranteed or certain. This gives some protection to the professional(s) involved. Consumers should be wary of signing such conditions, and should at least insist on the above matters being included if they do.

46 The gravity of the situation would be of crucial interest to the law: for example, consideration would be given to what state the consumer was in, the urgency for action, the seriousness of the potential loss, etc. Where the consumer was lucid and determined to refuse treatment, the law would not lightly condone a lack of regard for that refusal. Certainly where time is of the essence, practitioners may be forgiven for taking action without actively seeking the consumer's consent, where to do so would be considered unreasonable, or further threaten the consumer's wellbeing. On the other hand, some adult consumers have been allowed to die as a result of refusing emergency treatment. To the author's knowledge this has not been permitted for children or young people (see chapter 7).

to autonomy, but has nevertheless acted in what is believed to be the interests of the consumer. This case is discussed more fully in *Langslow*.[47]

(2) *Can legal action be taken to authorise giving emergency treatment?*

Where there is a conflict between the practitioner and the consumer requiring emergency lifesaving treatment, staff may resolve any legal difficulties by taking the matter to the High Court, or the Family Court. The High Court has inherent jurisdiction, called "parens patriae" jurisdiction, to make any ruling affecting the well-being of any citizen who is in need. Both the High Court and the Family Court have guardianship jurisdiction over children under the age of 20.[48] Decisions can be made urgently, with consequent legal protection of medical personnel in carrying out the Court's ruling. An example of resort to the High Court is the case of *Re X (sterilisation: parental consent)*, which involved differences of opinion over whether an intellectually disabled teenager could have a hysterectomy.[49]

Most frequently, resort to the Court is used to protect the rights of minors and the mentally disabled. There are no decisions on the issue of emergency treatment to an adult in New Zealand, however see the Canadian case of *Malette v Shulman* (see 6.5.3(1)). Courts are used for this purpose on many occasions in the US and UK. Judges there have reacted with contradictory and mixed responses to cases where a consumer has refused lifesaving blood transfusions, sometimes claiming that the principle of autonomy can be overridden by the rights of other persons or bodies. In one case a woman, the mother of a 7-month-old child, refused a blood transfusion necessary to save her life. She was supported in her view by her husband, although in fact she wanted to live if that were possible without it. The hospital applied to the Court for permission to go ahead and give the transfusion. The Court granted it, saying:[50]

> "The state ... will not allow a person to abandon a child, and so it should not allow this most ultimate of voluntary abandonments. The patient had a responsibility to the community to care for her infant. Thus, the people had an interest in preserving the life of this mother."

The fact that the consumer wished to live if possible was a crucial reason for the Court making the order in this case. There was no indication what the decision would have been if she did not so wish.

Another case involved a pregnant woman who refused a blood transfusion. In that case, the Judge held that the woman could be given the transfusion because she owed a duty to the "unborn child".[51] This would be an unlikely finding in New Zealand, as the Courts do not recognise the legal rights of a foetus (see chapter 17). A UK case may also cause concern to those who believe that a woman's autonomy overrides foetal rights. It involved a woman in labour who refused to have a Caesarean section when this was considered necessary to

---

47   Langslow A, "Witness to battery?" *Australian Nurses Journal*, August 1993, pages 35-37.

48   Care of Children Act 2004, section 30, replaced the Guardianship Act 1968.

49   *Re X (sterilisation: parental consent)* (1990) 7 FRNZ 216; [1991] NZFLR 49. See also *Re a Teenager* (1989) FLC 92-006, *Re Jane* (1989) FLC 92-007, and *Re Elizabeth* (1989) FLC 92-023. See chapter 5.

50   *In the Application of Georgetown College* 331 F 2d 1000 (1964), quoted in J O'Sullivan, *Law for Nurses and Allied Health Professionals in Australia*, Sydney, Law Book Co, 1983, page 69.

51   *Raleigh Fitkin-Paul Morgan Memorial Hospital v Anderson* 201 A 2d 537 (1964), cited in J O'Sullivan, *Law for Nurses and Allied Health Professionals in Australia*, Sydney, Law Book Co, 1983, page 69.

save her own life and that of the child. The Court made a declaration that the Caesarean and any consequential treatment could be lawfully performed as it was in the interests of the mother and her unborn child, despite the mother's refusal to consent.[52] The decision was overruled on appeal, and the woman's autonomy and her right to refuse treatment was upheld.

The test for whether emergency treatment can be refused — or indeed whether any treatment can be refused — is the competency of the consumer: those who are competent to choose can decline treatment, even if it is to save their life.[53] Resort to the Court is possible; but increasingly, where a person is competent to refuse, the Courts in the UK are now upholding the principle of autonomy.[54]

(3)   *Suicide*

Where people have attempted suicide, the overwhelming practice in New Zealand has been to provide emergency treatment to preserve their lives, in the face of evidence that they do not want this. One justification used for so doing is a generalised belief that most attempted suicides are really cries for help, rather than genuine attempts to end life. No one in New Zealand has sued their "saviours" in battery to the author's knowledge, and it is doubtful whether such an action would succeed. This is because of the Court's ready acceptance of the medical opinion that although a person's behaviour is suicidal, the intention to die cannot be said with certainty to be present. The law, when in doubt, opts for life rather than no life, and treatment rather than no treatment.

(4)   *Informed consent — an analysis*

In an analysis of the nature of autonomous decision-making and informed consent, Faden and Beauchamp[55] draw a distinction between informed consent as autonomous authorisation (sense 1) and informed consent as effective consent (sense 2). They hold that informed consent in both senses does not equate with autonomous choice. However, as sense 1 it involves the crucial criteria of authorisation as well as the common features of both. These are substantial understanding, substantial absence of control by others, and intent.

(a)   Consent as authorisation

By "authorisation" Faden and Beauchamp[56] mean that the consumer takes responsibility for what has been agreed to, transferring to another the authority to implement it, with an understanding of which consequences are the consumer's and which are the doctor's or other carer's. They argue that this is the only morally acceptable sense of informed consent.

---

52   *St George's Healthcare NHS Trust v S* [1998] 3 All ER 673.

53   The UK authority for this principle is *Airedale NHS Trust v Bland* [1993] AC 789; [1993] 1 All ER 821; [1993] 2 WLR 316 (HL), if a patient of sound mind refuses, however unreasonably, to consent to treatment or care, the doctors responsible for his care must give effect to his wishes.

54   *Airedale NHS Trust v Bland* [1993] AC 789; [1993] 1 All ER 821; [1993] 2 WLR 316 (HL), and also more recently in *Re B (Adult: Refusal of Medical Treatment)* [2002] 2 All ER 449, discussed in J Manning, "Autonomy and the Competent Patient's Right to Refuse Life-prolonging Medical Treatment — Again" (2002) 10 JLM 239.

55   R Faden, and T Beauchamp, *A History and Theory of Informed Consent*, New York, Oxford University Press, 1986, page 278.

56   Ibid.

(b)   Legal consent

By contrast, informed consent in sense 2 is a consent that is effective, simply in that it fulfils requirements that constitute specific institutional policies.[57] It is not necessarily derived from the principles of autonomous authorisation, although in fulfilling the requirements for sense 2, informed consent, one may in fact autonomously authorise the treatment in question. However, Faden and Beauchamp[58] say that consent in law is delineated as a sense 2 consent. There is a preoccupation with the disclosure of facts, mainly as disclosure of risks,[59] and satisfaction of the disclosure rules virtually consumes informed consent law.

Therefore we have two types of informed consent, which arguably represent the "ideal" (sense 1) and the "legal" (sense 2) standards of consumer decision-making, with the practice in many cases falling short of either.

Despite its apparent confusion and contradictions, the law in New Zealand shows that informed consent is a process involving both practitioner and consumer. It requires a consumer-centred perspective.

6.5.4   Answering questions

Where the consumer asks specific questions, the practitioner must take even more care.

Case

Smith v Auckland Hospital Board [1965] NZLR 191 (CA)

Smith entered Green Lane Hospital, Auckland for aortography — the insertion of a catheter in the femoral artery towards the aorta and injection of dye for the purpose of x-rays. A low probability of gangrene as the result of dislodgement of arterial atheromatous material existed. However, when he asked the surgeon, "Is there any risk attached to this?" he was told, "Old chap, within a couple of days you will be back home". In fact, the risk did materialise, and Smith lost a leg through resulting gangrene.

The Court held that a doctor must use due care in answering a consumer's question where the consumer, to the doctor's knowledge, intends to place reliance on that answer in making a decision. *Rogers v Whitaker* (see 6.44) held that a "normal" consumer who asks questions which indicate a serious desire for relevant information is entitled to a careful and skilful answer, which should only omit mention of a risk if that risk is too remote, or for therapeutic reasons (see 6.2). There are two things to note about this finding:

---

57   In chapter 5, Lidz et al, *Informed Consent: A Study of Decision Making in Psychiatry*, New York, Guildford Press, 1984, point out the complex requirements established by the Pennsylvania Mental Health Procedures Act 1980, and "extensive regulations and forms issued by the Department of Public Welfare" for admission of consumers to the hospital for psychiatric care. (They also demonstrate how ineffectual these are in giving information and securing decisions.) One could include here the requirement by most institutions that there be a signed consent form (whatever form it should take).

58   R Faden, and T Beauchamp, *A History and Theory of Informed Consent*, New York, Oxford University Press, 1986, page 280.

59   In *Salgo v Leland Stanford Jr University Board of Trustees* 317 P 2d 170 (1957), the Court described informed consent as a "full disclosure of facts". Also, the US Supreme Court in *Planned Parenthood of Central Missouri v Danforth* 428 US 52 (1976) spoke in terms entirely of disclosure of facts when discussing informed consent. In the development of negligence as the means of litigation where consent is at issue, this means in practical terms disclosure of risks according to New Zealand and English Courts.

- First, it is based on *Hedley Byrne & Co Ltd v Heller & Partners Ltd*,[60] which involved advice given to the plaintiff by a bank. The Court extended that to the medical field. In *Hedley Byrne* the Court held that if any person, acting as a professional with certain skills, is asked a question and they know or ought to know that the questioner is relying on professional advice to make a decision, the professional has a duty of care to give the advice carefully and is bound by the "reasonable person" test. Thus, the giving of advice is made subject to the law of negligence.

- Secondly, it endorses the Courts' favourable approach to medical discretion, as there is no requirement to tell the consumer the truth, or all the facts. Therapeutic privilege has been rejected to a large extent under the Code, but a health carer should be aware of imparting such bad news that it could cause mental trauma or nervous shock (see chapter 7).

An instructive case as to how the Courts consider the information that should be given follows.

Case

Gover v South Australia (1985) 39 SASR 543 (SCSA)

A consumer, who suffered from thyroid eye disease, underwent blepharoplasty and canthoplasty. She had not been told what was involved in the operations, or the risks or dangers of it. She had expected only the left eye to be operated on, and so was surprised when the surgeon told her that he did not know which one it was "so we done [sic] both". These procedures involved some degree of risk of blindness, entropion, or trichiasis. In fact the consumer did develop trichiasis and entropion. The Court had to consider whether the doctor was negligent in failing to warn her of the risks.

Cox J considered first whether a duty of care was owed; he held that a doctor's duty includes "the whole of the professional relationship", including the provision of information. The next question involved what information should have been given. The Judge said that professionals should keep abreast of developments. Thus, the professional should be reasonably knowledgeable and up to date. Further, it was held that even where a risk may be small, if its effect is likely to be devastating, as blindness would be, then this should be told to the consumer. In the case of *Battersby v Tottman*,[61] Cox J quotes the Chief Justice as saying in an earlier case:[62]

> "The more drastic the proposed intervention in the patient's physical make-up, the more necessary it is to keep him fully informed as to the likely risks and likely consequences of the intervention."

However, it was stressed that the consumer's condition should be considered. It is argued that this begs the question — does that mean that if it is considered that the consumer would not be able to cope emotionally with the information, that it need not be given? The answer seems to be "yes" — the practitioner can invoke therapeutic privilege. However, as discussed above[63] it is expected that a health practitioner ought to be able to discuss the

---

60 *Hedley Byrne & Co Ltd v Heller & Partners Ltd* [1964] AC 465.
61 *Battersby v Tottman* (1985) 37 SASR 524.
62 *F v R* (1983) 33 SASR 189, 192-194.
63 See para 6.5.2 (3) therapeutic privilege.

risks in a balanced and sensitive way. The commissioner stated it thus: "A key aspect of the clinician's skill is to contextualise information about risks and provide it in a sensitive and balanced way, so that the informed patient can make her own decision about the proposed 'highly beneficial' procedure."[64] If therapeutic privilege is to be used as reasoning for withholding information, the consequence of disclosure would need to be extreme.

6.5.5 Plaintiff must prove that ignorance affected decision

Another point to be noted from the *Gover* case (see 6.5.4) is that the plaintiff was not able to convince the Court that had she been given the information, she would not have had the operation. Thus, although she should have been told of the risks, she cannot win a negligence case if she cannot show that lack of information affected her decision. There would still be a breach of the Code of Health and Disability Services Consumers' Rights in New Zealand.

6.5.6 Powers of attorney

At law, a person can make another their agent in their absence. An agent has the power to carry out legally binding actions on another's behalf, such as signing a contract. The person (principal) is bound by their agent's act as if herself/himself had carried it out. The power conferred on the agent is called a power of attorney. If a person loses their capacity to make decisions, the power of attorney lapses, as the person presumably has lost the power to decide if they want the person to act on their behalf. The Protection of Personal and Property Rights Act 1988 creates the concept of an "enduring power of attorney". This provides for an agent to continue exercising the power of attorney, even where the principal no longer has capacity to act legally.

6.6 Unlawful restraint

Allied to the action of battery, is the action of "false imprisonment". This covers situations where a person is unlawfully restrained from leaving a place against their will. This action is a relevant matter of concern to health practitioners because it covers two main types of situations:

- Refusing to allow a person to leave a premises (detention);[65]
- Placing physical, chemical, or mental restraints on a person, and thereby preventing her/him from freedom of movement (restraint).

The only time a person may be restrained against their will is where:

- There is a legal right to restrain, for example under mental health, infectious diseases, quarantine or crimes legislation where they may be subject to powers of detention;
- A person is likely to harm himself or herself or someone else, or is likely to cause damage to property.

---

64   HDC case 04HDC04340, at page 67, para 2.
65   This would include power under the mental health legislation (see chapter 7), infectious diseases legislation (see chapter 18), child welfare legislation, etc (see chapter 7).

6.6.1 Detention

Provided there is no legal justification for the detention, people are falsely imprisoned when they perceive that they are confined to a particular place and believe there is no way of escape. The confinement or absence of escape need not be fact — it is the person's own perception of the situation that is relevant. Thus, a person who is led to believe that they cannot leave a hospital until payment for care is made would be falsely imprisoned.

Case

Symes v Mahon [1922] SASR 447 (SCSA)

The defendant, a police officer in a country town, told the plaintiff that there was a warrant for his arrest for failing to maintain his child and that he should "come to town [Adelaide] to have matters cleared up". He was asked to undertake to be at the police station the next morning and responded, "I suppose I'll have to". He did turn up at the station, and accompanied the police officer in the train to Adelaide. He was not arrested at any stage, the police officer maintaining that he was "taking Mahon up for questioning". In Adelaide he was allowed to leave on two occasions, only after seeking and being granted permission to do so. It turned out that Mahon was not the person who was the subject of the warrant, but a Mr McMahon.

The Court held that although Mahon had never been in legal custody, and had at all times the freedom to leave, he submitted himself to the defendant's power, reasonably thinking that he had no way of escape which could reasonably be taken by him.

This case establishes important principles. First, allowing consumers to believe they have no alternative but to remain in a particular place or submit to the control of others is unlawful and can result in an action for false imprisonment, even though they have the physical means of leaving. A second principle is that police cannot require someone to accompany them anywhere simply for questioning, unless the law specifically allows this.

Where there is no power to detain a person, even where it is thought to be for their own good, this may be false imprisonment.

Case

Watson v Marshall (1971) 124 CLR 621 (HCA)

The defendant was a police officer who asked the plaintiff to accompany him to a psychiatric hospital. The plaintiff believed justifiably, the Court held, that if he did not go voluntarily he would be forced into going.

The Court held that it was the plaintiff's belief that he had no choice, which was relevant, not an objective assessment of the law and the situation. Thus, it is not legally acceptable to use subterfuge, or to trick a person into remaining in a particular place, or in the control of someone else, unless a person can plead a defence as outlined above.

People are also unlawfully detained when they are physically confined to a particular place, whether they are aware of this or not.

Case

Meering v Grahame-White Aviation Co Ltd (1919) 122 LT 44 (HL)

The plaintiff attended the defendant's office to give evidence relating to some stolen goods. Unbeknown to the plaintiff, three detectives were stationed outside the office to prevent his leaving.

The House of Lords held that this was false imprisonment. Lord Atkin said that "a person can be imprisoned while he is asleep … while he is unconscious, and while he is a lunatic", provided there is physical restraint in fact. It follows that the unconscious or mentally unaware consumer, who is detained in a hospital without their consent, may be the subject of false imprisonment. This was upheld in a case heard before the European Court of Human Rights, where it was held that a woman was detained in a psychiatric hospital, despite her lack of knowledge of the confinement.[66]

Case

Hart v Herron (1984) Aust Torts Reports 80-201 (NSW SC)

The plaintiff had been detained, and given treatment to which he claimed he had not consented — including electroconvulsive treatment and deep sleep therapy.

The Court held that although he had no recollection of the imprisonment, the fact did not prevent him from succeeding in his claim.

Restraint must be intentional and complete. Where there is a reasonable way out, even if it is unconventional, for example windows, there is no "imprisonment".

Case

Robinson v Balmain New Ferry Co Ltd [1910] AC 295 (PC)

A man bought a ticket for a ferry to Balmain. The sign over the wharf from which it left said that any person entering or leaving the wharf had to pay a penny, whether or not they used the ferry. Paying his penny, he entered through the turnstile and found he had missed the ferry and would have to pay another penny to leave the wharf. Employees prevented him leaving by a small opening beside the turnstile. He sued the company for false imprisonment.

The Privy Council took into account that the plaintiff had agreed to the terms of entry clearly established, that egress would cost him one penny. He had placed himself in such a position that he could not complain of a certain restraint of liberty. However, he was not being denied exit under the terms on which he had entered. Only if he had been denied exit under any circumstances would he have been imprisoned.

Case

Sayers v Harlow Urban District Council [1958] 2 All ER 342 (CA)

A tourist visited a public toilet and found that, due to a faulty lock, she was trapped in the cubicle. She failed to attract attention, and so proceeded to stand on the toilet roll holder to climb over the door. She slipped on the holder, injuring herself. Later, she brought an action against the Council in false imprisonment and negligence.

---

66   *Van de Leer v The Netherlands* (1990) 12 EHRR 567.

The Court dismissed Ms Sayers' claim of false imprisonment because there had been no intention to confine her. It upheld her claim in negligence because of the faulty lock, but reduced the damages because of her contributory negligence in standing on the toilet roll holder.

Confinement of a person to a particular place can amount to unlawful detention, regardless of awareness of such confinement. A consumer of mental health services, who is not detained under the Mental Health (Compulsory Assessment and Treatment) Act 1992, is unlawfully detained if confined behind locked doors.

It also may be unlawful detention if a consumer is being confined in an unlocked facility as a voluntary/informal "patient",[67] yet is not permitted to leave. This would be the case, whether or not the person was aware of this.[68]

A health practitioner cannot argue that it is simply for the consumer's own good that restraint be used. There should be reasonable grounds to believe in the lawfulness of such action. If a consumer wishes to leave a hospital or other place where health services are provided, and the exceptions do not apply, they should be allowed to go.

It is advisable for the health practitioner to carefully warn the consumer of the consequences of such a decision, to determine that they understand what they are doing, and to obtain (in writing if possible and witnessed by someone else), a statement signed or acknowledged by the consumer to the effect that they have been fully informed of the consequences of the decision, and are making the decision voluntarily. Under these circumstances, it is unlikely the practitioner would be liable for *not* giving the treatment.

6.6.2   Restraint

There are many situations in which it is considered necessary to restrain a consumer who is violent, disruptive, and difficult to care for, or who may be in danger of self-harm. Such restraint must be based on the principle of protection for the consumer and/or others only, and not carried out just for the convenience of providers:[69]

> "In order that justice may be achieved, nurses must assess each case individually as to the benefits and harms of physical restraint, accept the views and values of individual clients, be able to justify the use or non-application of physical restraint, and be supported by a philosophy of care in their work place that advocates justice for staff and residents."

A policy should be adopted by health service providers that clearly sets out circumstances under which restraint may be used, and those when it is not to be used. This should follow the New Zealand Standards publication, "Restraint Minimisation and Safe Practice".[70] This

---

67   The word patient is defined in the Mental Health (Compulsory Assessment and Treatment) Act at section 2 to mean a person under compulsory assessment or compulsory treatment or a special patient. It does not include a voluntary/informal patient. Not permitting a voluntary patient to leave is often referred to as a "Clayton's committal": "unless you agree to stay we will use the Act". This is unlawful.

68   *R v Bournewood Community and Mental Health NHS Trust, ex p L* [1998] 3 All ER 289; [1998] 2 WLR 107, discussed in J Dawson, "The law of emergency psychiatric detention" [1999] *New Zealand Law Review* 275, 280.

69   S Koch, "Ethical issues in restraint use", in *Nursing Law and Ethics, Meeting the Challenge of Patients' Rights: Issues for the 1990s*, Proceedings of the Conference, Faculty of Nursing, RMIT, Melbourne, November 1992, page 12.

has been published by the Ministry of Health through Standards New Zealand. It has been incorporated into legislation by notice given by the New Zealand Minister of Health under the Health and Disability Services (Safety) Act 2001. Compliance with the standard should mean the health service facility is meeting its obligations under the Health and Disability Services Code of Consumers' Rights and under the Mental Health (Compulsory Assessment and Treatment) Act 1992.

Checklist

Considerations for policy on restraint

- All providers of the consumer should be consulted to see if alternative treatment could be adopted to alleviate the consumer's need for restraint.
- Family should be consulted, as they may be able to offer assistance and ideas in relation to controlling the consumer's behaviour.
- Any restraint should be the least restrictive measure to protect the consumer. The aim should be to stop the harm, not the consumer. Materials used should be those that cause the least injury to the consumer compatible with this aim.
- Authorisation from a person with appropriate authority, (for example nursing management, the consumer's specialist doctor) should be required.
- Management should be notified of the circumstances of any restraint of a consumer.
- Family should be notified of any restraint of the consumer, if not already consulted.
- Regular assessment of the consumer and the reason for restraint should be carried out.
- Full and accurate documentation of the circumstances and type of restraint, as well as the other matters listed here, should be made in the consumer's record.

6.7 Further reading

G Annas, "When suicide prevention becomes brutality: The case of Elizabeth Bouvia", *Judging Medicine*, New Jersey, Havana Press, 1988, page 290.

B Bromberger and J Fife-Yeomans, *Deep Sleep: Harry Bailey and the Scandal of Chelmsford*, Sydney, Simon & Schuster, 1991.

D B Collins, *Medical Law in New Zealand*, Wellington, Brooker & Friend, 1992.

J Devereux, "Competency to consent to treatment: An introduction" in Ian Freckleton and Kerry Peterson (eds), *Controversies in Health Law*, Sydney, The Federation Press, 1999.

Health and Disability Commissioner, "Informed consent under the Code of Rights", presentation to the Health and Disability Commissioner Workshops, Auckland, May 1999.

I Kennedy and A Grubb, *Medical Law*, London, Butterworths, 2000.

Kerridge et al, "Advance directives" in Ian Freckleton and Kerry Peterson (eds), *Controversies in Health Law*, Sydney, The Federation Press, 1999.

---

70 NZS 8141:2001 New Zealand Standards, Ministry of Health, Wellington. This has been replaced by NZS 8141:2008, which came into force on 1 June 2009.

J Manning, "Autonomy and the Competent Patient's Right to Refuse Life-prolonging Medical Treatment — Again" (2002) 10 JLM 239.

J Manning, "Court-ordered Caesarean section: The priority of maternal autonomy" 1999 18 NZULR 546.

M Pappworth, *Human Guinea Pigs: An Experimentation on Man*, London, Routledge & Keegan Paul, 1967.

President's Commission for the Study of Ethical Problems in Medicine and Biomedical and Behavioural Research, *Making Health Care Decisions: A Report on the Ethical and Legal Implications of Informed Consent in the Patient-Practitioner Relationship*, Washington DC, Government Printing Office, 1982.

"Rogers v Whitaker reconsidered" (2001) 9 JLM — Editorial.

C Stewart, "Qumsieh's Case, civil liability and the right to refuse medical treatment" (1999-2000) 8 JLM 56.

D Sullivan, "State-sanctioned intervention on behalf of the fetus" 8 JLM 44.

R Tobin, "Standard of professional care: Rogers v Whitaker" [1994] New Zealand Law Review 34.

Todd et al, *The Law of Torts in New Zealand* (3rd ed), Wellington, Brookers, 2001.

Chapter 7

CONSENT ISSUES: CHILDREN, CONSUMERS WITH A MENTAL ILLNESS OR INTELLECTUAL DISABILITY

SUE JOHNSON, REBECCA KEENAN AND ROBERT F B PERRY

Contents

7.1 Introduction

This chapter continues the discussion of consent from chapter 6 and looks at particular consent issues that may arise when the consumer is a child or young person, or has an intellectual disability or a mental illness.[1] It also discusses the law relating to the compulsory assessment and treatment of people with a mental disorder.

7.2 Temporary incompetence

As has been discussed in chapter 6 it is the right of all competent consumers to make an informed choice and give informed consent to treatment. There is also a presumption in

---

1   The writer has, throughout this chapter, used the terms "a mental illness" and "mental illnesses" as these are the terms in common usage. It is the writer's opinion that general references to "mental illness", "the mentally ill", "mental health patients/consumers", and "mental health services" do little to reduce the stigma associated with having a mental illness. This is because such general references group together individuals with different illnesses. It is of note that people with physical illnesses are not referred to as "the physically ill" or "physical health consumers". Nor are services for them referred to as "physical health services".

Right 7(2) of the Code of Consumers' Rights that all consumers of health and disability services are competent to make an informed choice and to give informed consent. Where a consumer is temporarily unable to give permission for treatment, for example they are affected by medication or are unconscious, and the proposed treatment is not urgent, health practitioners should wait until the consumer has regained the capacity to consent. Where the consumer is not fully lucid, practitioners are legally and ethically obliged to make the effort to determine what level of understanding prevails at the particular time, or wait until the consumer is lucid. Blanket labelling of such a person as "incompetent" denies their legal and human rights.

Further consideration should be given to the effect of medicines. For example, a consumer may be asked to sign a consent form for an operation after the pre-medication is given. Any consent purportedly given in such a situation would most likely be rejected by a Court and the Health and Disability Commissioner if the patient subsequently complained.

Case

Demers v Gerety 515 P 2d 645 (1973)

The plaintiff, who spoke little English, had made it clear he did not want surgery for repair of a ventral hernia if it would affect his ileostomy. Told he could have his wish, he signed a consent form for the hernia repair only. After sedation, with no explanation and in the dark (he had to be guided as to where to sign, and could not read the form), he signed a form that happened to be a second consent form, permitting revision of the ileostomy and repair of the hydrocele.[2]

The Court rejected the argument that it was a valid consent. Obviously, several factors were present to make this "consent" invalid. As well as being temporarily incompetent, the consumer did not voluntarily consent to the procedure, although he voluntarily signed his name. It would seem that practitioners were less than frank in giving him information as to the nature of the procedure, and why they thought he should have it. The Court referred to the "ritual of the consent form", the relentless determination to have the document signed, regardless of how that is done. Courts and professional disciplinary bodies will discount consent forms where they are not convinced the consumer gave consent at least knowing the nature of the procedure, and freely consenting to it.

7.3 Intellectual disability

This term is used to describe the disability of a person who has a permanent or long-term intellectual impairment that renders her/him unable to lead an entirely normal life without some degree of assistance. Their impairment may be mild or severe but, although they may improve with care, it is not a disability that treatment will "cure". Unless otherwise assessed, a person with an intellectual disability is presumed to be competent to make an informed choice, give informed consent, and be capable of understanding the particular medical procedure proposed. They have the right under the Code of Health and Disability Services Consumers' Rights to decide whether to consent to treatment.[3] The law presumes competence, but greater care will be required when explanations are made to those with a

---

2   Cited in J O'Sullivan, *Law for Nurses and Allied Health Professionals in Australia*, Sydney, Law Book Co, 1983, 40-41.

disability. People with an intellectual disability also receive some protection under the Protection of Personal and Property Rights Act 1988. Under that Act, too, the law presumes that people are competent and can consent for themselves. That presumption is only displaced when they clearly cannot do so.[4]

The Protection of Personal and Property Rights Act 1988 is based on the idea that a person who is not fully competent should be encouraged to make their own decisions to the greatest possible extent. It recognises that those with an intellectual disability have the same fundamental rights as everyone else, including the right to self-determination (see chapter 5 for a discussion of these rights). People who are incapable of understanding the nature and implications of the treatment might not be competent to consent for themselves, but someone who is entitled to consent on their behalf may do so.[5] Someone simply exercising factual, but not legal, control over the person is not a person so entitled to consent. This is because:[6]

> "The law simply refuses to recognise that one adult may control the life of another, no matter how retarded, without express statutory or Court authority."

7.3.1 Welfare guardians and enduring powers of attorney

Where an adult is not considered capable of understanding what is involved, and is in a perilous condition, in an emergency the ordinary considerations regarding emergencies will apply (see chapter 6). If there is no emergency, someone else can apply to the Court asking to be appointed as a welfare guardian showing that for the purposes of medical care the person is unable to adequately make decisions regarding treatment.[7] This gives the guardian the right to permit treatment on behalf of the person. The power is given only after the Court has carefully considered the person's condition. A relative, social worker, doctor, hospital worker, or the person herself/himself can apply for the appointment of a welfare guardian. Any other person can apply with the leave of the Court. When necessary an appointment can be made very rapidly. The Court will endeavour to appoint the person best able to make decisions on behalf of someone who is considered incompetent.

The welfare guardian is given powers granted by the Court. In cases where a person is unable to manage their property, the Court may appoint a property manager. The same person can be appointed as both a welfare guardian and property manager. In some cases, the Court will appoint a different person or persons, or a trust company, as property manager.

---

3   The Code of Health and Disability Services Consumers' Rights (reproduced in Appendix 4) is in the Schedule to the Health and Disability Commissioner (Code of Health and Disability Services Consumers' Rights) Regulations 1996. At the time of writing (early 2009) the Health and Disability Commissioner Act 1994 and the Health and Disability Commissioner (Code of Health and Disability Services Consumers' Rights) Regulations 1996 are under review. These are currently reviewed every 5 years, though there is a recommendation that this be extended out to 10 years. Further information can be viewed on the Health and Disability Commissioner's website at www.hdc.org.nz/files/hdc/Report-on-the-Review-of-the-Act-and-Code-2009-Easy-Read.pdf.

4   Protection of Personal and Property Rights Act 1988, section 5. See also Right 7(2) of the Code of Health and Disability Services Consumers' Rights and chapter 5.

5   Right 7(1) of the Code of Health and Disability Services Consumers' Rights.

6   *Kirby v Leather* [1965] 2 All ER 441, discussed in S Hayes and R Hayes, *Mental Retardation: Law Policy and Administration*, Sydney, Law Book Co, 1982, 58.

7   Protection of Personal and Property Rights Act 1988, sections 7 and 12.

A Court will either make an order in general terms granting to the welfare guardian the exercise of general powers, or it will specify the particular aspects of a person's care and welfare on which the guardian may make decisions. Thus, decisions regarding consent to medical treatment can be made by the welfare guardian who has a general power with respect to matters of personal care and welfare.[8] It should be noted that such decisions will be subject to the limitations mentioned in paragraph 7.5.

The Act also provides for the granting of an enduring power of attorney by a person who is then competent to a person chosen to handle their affairs if they become incompetent. This is not a Court appointment. The power can only be created using a special form that is signed by the donor of the power and witnessed by a lawyer or legal executive independent of the person making the appointment, or by a trust company employee. In some cases, an enduring power of attorney will be made when a person realises that they may shortly become incapacitated. However, it may be made at any time. Nowadays, there is some encouragement to all people to grant an enduring power of attorney well before there is any sign of incapacity. The power does not take effect until the donor of the power becomes incompetent to make choices for herself/himself.[9] While an enduring power of attorney is granted by someone who is competent to make that appointment, an application for a welfare guardian is made to the Court on behalf of someone who has already become incapacitated.

Both welfare guardians and people who hold an enduring power of attorney as to personal care and welfare can consent to treatment on behalf of the person they represent, unless such power has been specifically excluded. They cannot refuse to grant consent to the administration of "standard medical treatment" intended to save a person's life, but there are some treatments where consent is prohibited.

Welfare guardians and persons holding an enduring power of attorney cannot consent on behalf of another person to electroconvulsive therapy ("ECT"), or to medical experimentation, or to any treatment that would destroy brain tissue.[10] ECT and brain surgery, carried out under the Mental Health (Compulsory Assessment and Treatment) Act 1992 ("Mental Health (CAT) Act"), is permitted only according to strict requirements (see paragraphs 7.4.8(4) and (5)).

If a person with an intellectual disability is incompetent to decide whether to receive treatment, health practitioners should always inquire whether a welfare guardian has been appointed. First though, the possibility of the consumer being capable of consent must be explored. It may in fact take longer, and involve much more careful counselling and explanation, but nevertheless is required by law. The same applies in relation to older persons who might, for example, have Alzheimer's disease, but who are still competent to give consent.

7.3.2 Parens patriae and the Court's guardianship jurisdiction

Where no welfare guardian has been appointed, no one has enduring power of attorney, and a consumer is unable to consent to treatment, treatment can be given without consent

---

8   Protection of Personal and Property Rights Act 1988, section 18(3).
9   Protection of Personal and Property Rights Act 1988, sections 93A and 94.
10   Protection of Personal and Property Rights Act 1988, section 18(1).

under Right 7(4) of the Code, or an application to the High Court or the Family Court can be made by any person who has a real interest in the client's welfare.[11] The High Court has inherent jurisdiction, called "parens patriae" (parent of the country), which gives it power to make orders in the interests of any of its citizens who cannot care for themselves. Also, the Family Court and in some cases the High Court, have jurisdiction to appoint guardians to a child under the age of 18 years.[12] The Mental Health (CAT) Act 1992 has provisions allowing a Court to make orders for the welfare of mentally disordered persons.

The High Court's parens patriae jurisdiction is very flexible. Orders made under it can override the wishes of family or guardians, as well as upholding them. Under the parens patriae jurisdiction, the Court can make orders for the care and maintenance of a person. The Family Court also has the power to override decisions made by welfare guardians and holders of an enduring power of attorney.

7.4 Mental illness

Just as there are many different types of physical illnesses, there are many different sorts of mental illnesses. At one end of the scale there are illnesses such as anxiety and depression, which are not necessarily as disabling as, for example schizophrenia or other severe psychoses. However, any mental illness in its acute stage can sometimes render a person unable to make an informed choice and be able to give informed consent.

Most people who have a mental illness are competent to make an informed choice and give informed consent to the provision of treatment for their illness and for the provision of other health and disability services. In an acute phase of an illness some people may become temporarily incompetent to consent to the provision of some or all services, and in some illnesses competency will fluctuate over time. A minority of people have such a severe degree of illness that it may come under the definition of mental disorder within the Mental Health (CAT) Act 1992. In that case it is likely that treatment can be given to them, even if they refuse to give consent. However, it is important to point out that even a person with a severe mental illness will not necessarily be mentally disordered.

7.4.1 Mental Health (Compulsory Assessment and Treatment) Act 1992

In New Zealand, the law relating to the compulsory assessment and treatment of people with a mental disorder underwent fundamental changes when the Mental Health (CAT) Act 1992 came into effect on 1 November 1992. Changes to the previous law, governed by the Mental Health Act 1969, had commenced in 1983 after the Oakley Committee of Inquiry report, and involved a lengthy succession of proposals, consultation, making of submissions and hearings. Among other changes, the Act:

- Provides a new definition of mental disorder;[13]
- Provides a definition of patient that applies only to persons who are required to be assessed, or who are subject to a compulsory treatment order, or who are special

---

11 This may be a nurse, doctor, social worker, or teacher.
12 Care of Children Act 2004, section 31 provides for the appointment of Court-appointed guardians for children. Section 8 defines children as those under 18 years.
13 Mental Health (Compulsory Assessment and Treatment) Act 1992, section 2.

patients — informal or "voluntary" patients who are mentally ill are therefore not patients under the Act. They are subject to the same laws as any other consumers;[14]

- Also applies to proposed patients for whom reasonable grounds have been found for believing they are mentally disordered;[15]
- Introduces a completely new procedure for compulsory assessment, designed to ensure that careful clinical decisions are made at critical times, that the patient is fully informed, and that their rights are protected;[16]
- Makes specific provisions concerning consent to treatment;
- Sets out the rights of patients;[17]
- Provides powers to nurses to detain a person who has been admitted as an informal/voluntary patient, that is someone who is not a patient under the Act, who they believed to be mentally disordered, for up to 6 hours to enable a medical practitioner to examine her/him;[18]
- Has a bias towards community compulsory treatment, rather than in-patient compulsory treatment.

7.4.2 Key personnel

Under the Mental Health (CAT) Act 1992, it is important to be aware of the functions of certain key personnel.

Director of Area Mental Health Services: A director, appointed under Ministry of Health guidelines, is appointed for each region. They are responsible for the administration of the Act in that region. Duties include the appointment of responsible clinicians and duly authorised officers.

Responsible clinician: A responsible clinician (a competent health professional, usually a psychiatrist) must be assigned to each compulsory patient. Although the responsible clinician will usually be one of a clinical team, they have the ultimate responsibility for making critical decisions concerning the care of a compulsory patient.

Duly authorised officer: Duly authorised officers are also appointed by the Director of Area Mental Health Services. They are health practitioners, usually nurses who have undergone appropriate training, who are available at all times to advise on and, where necessary, initiate the compulsory assessment and treatment procedure.

District inspectors: District inspectors are lawyers who are appointed to advise patients concerning their legal rights and status. They also make inquiries into complaints by patients that their rights have been breached, and inspect hospitals and other facilities where patients are treated.

Mental Health Review Tribunal: When a Mental Health Review Tribunal meets, there will be three members — a lawyer, a psychiatrist and one other person, each of whom have been selected from a panel of members. Its principal function is to provide a further review of

---

14   Mental Health (Compulsory Assessment and Treatment) Act 1992, section 2.
15   Mental Health (Compulsory Assessment and Treatment) Act 1992, section 2A as amended by Mental Health (Compulsory Assessment and Treatment) Amendment Act 1999, section 3.
16   Mental Health (Compulsory Assessment and Treatment) Act 1992, Part 1.
17   Mental Health (Compulsory Assessment and Treatment) Act 1992, Part 6.
18   Mental Health (Compulsory Assessment and Treatment) Act 1992, section 111.

a patient's compulsory status while a compulsory treatment order is in force, but the patient considers they should be discharged.

7.4.3 Definition of mental disorder

In a recent judgment, the Court of Appeal has held that the term "mental disorder", as defined in the 1992 Act, is wide enough to include conditions that not all psychiatrists regard as psychiatric illnesses. The reason for this is that the definition of "mental disorder" in the Act is somewhat wider than the definition of that term generally accepted by psychiatrists.

Case

Waitemata Health v A-G [2001] NZFLR 1112 (CA)

H had a long history of criminal offending involving serious assaults on women. He had spent much of his adult life in either hospital or prison. In 1998, he was made the subject of an Inpatient Compulsory Treatment Order, which became of indefinite duration after being in force for one year. When H applied to the Mental Health Review Tribunal during the following year, the Tribunal concluded that his severe personality disorder was insufficient to constitute "mental disorder" under the Act, and that H should therefore be discharged from compulsory status. In both the High Court and the Court of Appeal, it was held that the Tribunal's decision was incorrect. When considering the definition, the Court of Appeal said:

> "The Act avoids reference to mental or psychiatric illness. The words used in the definition of mental disorder are words in ordinary use, although their application is heavily dependent upon the assessment of clinicians".

There are two essential components to the definition of "mental disorder". The first is that there must be an abnormal state of mind, whether of a continuous or an intermittent nature, characterised by delusions or by disorders of mood, perception, volition, or cognition. The second part of the definition states a range of outcomes that the person's abnormal state of mind must produce, in terms of danger or diminished capacity for self-care. The outcome must be linked to the abnormal state of mind. It must be of such a degree that it poses one of the following four outcomes.

- *Serious danger to the health of others:* It may therefore be sufficient if a mentally disordered person induces serious emotional distress in others.
- *Serious danger to the safety of others:* Recent cases have made it clear that, while "mere nuisance type behaviour" is insufficient, it is not necessary to show that there is serious physical danger to others.

Case

Re I C [2001] NZFLR 895

I C had been diagnosed as having a schizophrenic illness, with associated erotomania. He had been harassing a particular woman, who had done her utmost to avoid his attentions, over a period of 16 years. Although I C had not been physically violent, his behaviour had at times been bizarre and sexually explicit. His conduct had frightened the elderly parents of the woman in question. The woman had taken out a restraining order under the Harassment Act 1997. On behalf of I C, it was argued that this should be sufficient for her protection. However, the Judge, William Young J was not satisfied that the restraining order on its own would deter I C from attempting to get in touch with the woman again. His Honour also held that "serious danger to the health of others," could include danger to the psychological health of the elderly parents of the woman in question.

- *Serious danger to the safety of that person:* Such dangers include suicide, attempted suicide, self-mutilation, and actions that place the person at grave physical risk, such as walking on busy highways or even refusing essential medical treatment.
- *Seriously diminished capacity for self-care:* In most cases this means a failure to secure the necessities of life, such as food, clothing, and shelter, or the failure to protect oneself from the risks of, say fire or poisoning. While mismanagement of money will not in itself lead to a finding of seriously diminished capacity for self-care, it may be a relevant factor.

7.4.4   The exclusionary rules

Section 4 of the Mental Health (CAT) Act 1992 provides that the procedures concerning compulsory assessment and treatment shall not be invoked in respect of any person *by reason only* of that person's:

- Political, religious, or cultural beliefs;
- Sexual preferences;
- Criminal or delinquent behaviour;
- Substance abuse;
- Intellectual disability.

However, this does not mean that the above matters are always ignored or discounted in determining whether a person suffers from mental disorder. If a person has psychiatric symptoms, criminal or delinquent behaviour may be relevant to the question of serious danger to the health or safety of others. In other cases, an intellectual disability coupled with a psychiatric disorder may be sufficient to meet the definition.

Case

In the matter of W [1994] NZFLR 237

W had an intellectual disability with a level of operation akin to a 5 or 6-year-old. He also had rapid mood swings, and received medication to keep these mood swings under control. Evidence was given to the Judge that, if W did not take the medication, he would be unable to care for himself. There was also a risk that he would make inappropriate sexual advances to others. Judge Boshier held that the definition was satisfied, as W did not only have an intellectual disability, but also a mood disorder that posed a serious danger to others.

7.4.5   Procedures for compulsory assessment and treatment

To enable compulsory assessment and treatment to be put in place,[19] there must be strict compliance with the procedures and time limits set out in the Mental Health (CAT) Act 1992. They are as follows:

---

19   Mental Health (CAT) Act 1992, Part 1.

(1) Application

The applicant for initiating committal proceedings must be aged 18 years or more, and have personally seen the proposed patient within the last 3 days.[20] In many cases, the applicant will be a relative or close acquaintance of the proposed patient, but a health practitioner or, say, a neighbour or a Police Officer is entitled to apply if no one else is available or willing. A duly authorised officer will normally be called to assist. The application must be accompanied by a medical certificate, which may be signed by any medical practitioner who has also seen the patient within the last 3 days.

(2) Assessment examination

When the application and medical certificate are received, a duly authorised officer will then arrange for an assessment examination to be conducted by a medical practitioner — usually a psychiatrist appointed by the director of area mental health services.[21] A notice providing details of the assessment examination must be handed to the proposed patient in the presence, if possible, of a family member or caregiver.[22] In most cases, the examination will be conducted at a hospital, but it may be conducted at the proposed patient's home, or at any other place specified, for example, a community mental health service base.

(3) Five days of further assessment

If the medical practitioner who has conducted the assessment examination reaches the view that there are reasonable grounds for believing the proposed patient is mentally disordered, and that it is desirable that the person be required to undergo further assessment and treatment, the patient will be given a notice requiring her/him to be assessed and treated at the place specified (either at their home or at hospital) for a period of 5 days from the date of the notice.[23] A responsible clinician must then be nominated for the patient, who is required to take such treatment as the responsible clinician directs. If, at any time before the 5 days has expired, the responsible clinician considers that the patient is fit to be discharged, this must occur immediately.[24] The patient must also be advised in writing of their legal rights, which include the right to apply to the District Court for a review under section 16 of the Act.

(4) Fourteen days of further assessment

Before the expiry of the 5-day period, the responsible clinician must complete a further formal examination to again determine whether the patient is mentally disordered, and the desirability of further assessment and treatment. This should be done in consultation with the patient's family or whanau, unless it is not in the patient's best interest or not reasonably practicable to do this. If the responsible clinician decides that further assessment or treatment is required, a further notice must be given to the patient. On this occasion the notice requires the patient to undergo a further 14 days' compulsory assessment and treatment.[25] Copies of the responsible clinician's certificate must be sent to a number of

---

20   Mental Health (CAT) Act 1992, sections 8-8B.
21   Mental Health (CAT) Act 1992, section 9.
22   Mental Health (CAT) Act 1992, section 9(2)(c).
23   Mental Health (CAT) Act 1992, section 11.
24   Mental Health (CAT) Act 1992, section 11(6).
25   Mental Health (CAT) Act 1992, section 13.

persons, including the patient's principal caregiver (who may be a family or whanau member or friend) and the district inspector. Again, the patient has the opportunity to apply for a review to a District Court Judge. The district inspector must talk to the patient during the 14-day period to ascertain the patient's wishes, and whether an application for review should be made. At any time during the 14-day period, the responsible clinician may discharge the patient if it is considered that they are fit to be released.

(5)   *Final assessment*

Before the end of the 14-day period, the responsible clinician must conduct a further formal examination.[26] If the patient is still unfit to be released from compulsory status, a certificate of final assessment is then issued. An application for a compulsory treatment order must then be lodged with the District Court. Again, copies of the certificate, along with a statement of its legal consequences and a statement of the right to appear before a Court, must be sent to a number of persons, including the patient's principal caregiver and a district inspector. The district inspector will again speak to the patient to ascertain the patient's wishes with respect to the making of a compulsory treatment order. The application for the compulsory treatment order must come before a Judge within 14 days from the expiry of the second (14-day) period of compulsory assessment and treatment. During this 14-day period the patient may continue to be assessed and treated on a compulsory basis.

Case

Re M [1993] DCR 658

In this case the second (14-day) period of further assessment commenced on 8 March 1993 and was therefore effective until 22 March 1993. On 18 March 1993, the responsible clinician issued a certificate of final assessment, but the application to the District Court for the making of a compulsory treatment order was not received by the Court until 30 March 1993. Judge Willy held that non-compliance with the time limits for the taking of the various steps leading to the making of a compulsory treatment order should be strictly observed, as these were matters that "critically affect the patient's freedom". Although the certificate of final assessment had been completed within the time permitted, it was also essential that the application for a compulsory treatment order be lodged with the Court within that time. The Court held that the application for a compulsory treatment order was a nullity. However, this did not prevent a further application for compulsory assessment and treatment being made immediately.

7.4.6   Compulsory treatment order

(1)   *Examination — consultation*

If practicable, the District Court Judge who presides at an application for a compulsory treatment order must be a Family Court Judge. The hearing will be informal, and will usually be conducted at a hospital or community mental health service base rather than at a Court. The Judge is required to examine the patient and explain directly to the patient the purpose of their visit, and to discuss with the patient the proposed course of treatment and find out the patient's views.[27] It is also a requirement that the Judge consults with the responsible

---

26   Mental Health (CAT) Act 1992, sections 14 and 14A.
27   Mental Health (CAT) Act 1992, section 18 (3).

clinician and at least one other health professional involved in the patient's care.[28] Although the Judge has had no medical training, some informal assessment of the patient's condition can be gained in this manner.

(2)   Hearing

The patient is entitled to be represented by a lawyer, and a district inspector may also be present at any hearing. Evidence that may be called on the patient's behalf will often be from the patient, but may include medical evidence or evidence from any other source, including relatives and friends. The Judge may call for a further report on the patient, or require any other person to be present as a witness. If, as is often the case, the patient indicates that they agree to the making of an order, there is no need for the Judge to proceed beyond the discussion with the patient and the consultation with the responsible clinician.

At the conclusion of the hearing the Judge may:

- Adjourn the hearing for up to one month from the date of the first hearing;
- Make a community compulsory treatment order or an inpatient compulsory treatment order, if it is considered that the patient is mentally disordered and it is necessary to make a compulsory treatment order;
- Discharge the patient, if it is considered the patient is not mentally disordered.

(3)   Community compulsory treatment order

The Act provides that a community compulsory treatment order is the first preference.[29] Such an order requires the patient to attend, at their own home or some other place in the community, for treatment. However, the Judge is directed not to make such an order unless satisfied that appropriate community care is available, and the social circumstances of the patient are adequate for care in the community.[30]

(4)   In-patient compulsory treatment order

Such an order directs the patient to be detained in the hospital specified in the treatment order.[31] At any time during the currency of the order, the responsible clinician may direct that the patient shall, from that time, be treated in the community rather than in hospital, thus changing an in-patient treatment order to a community treatment order.

(5)   Leave

At any time during the currency of any in-patient treatment order, the responsible clinician may grant leave for up to 3 months. Such leave may be extended for up to a total of 6 months.[32] In most cases leave will be granted subject to certain conditions, such as the

---

28   Mental Health (CAT) Act 1992, section 18(4). This is also the requirement under section 16 of the Mental Health (Compulsory Assessment and Treatment) Act 1992, when a judicial review is taking place. The Act does not stipulate that this second health professional needs to have any particular experience and concern has been expressed that some inpatient nurses are thrust into this role without any training or experience. See for example Fishwick et al "Unearthing the conflict between carer and custodian: Implications of participation in section 16 hearings under the Mental Health (Compulsory Assessment and Treatment) Act (1992)" (2001) 10(3) Australian and New Zealand Journal of Mental Health Nursing 187.

29   Mental Health (Compulsory Assessment and Treatment) Act 1992, section 28.

30   Mental Health (CAT) Act 1992, section 28(4).

31   Mental Health (CAT) Act 1992, section 30.

taking of regular treatment. Leave may also be cancelled at any time by the responsible clinician.

(6)   *Term of order*

Both the initial compulsory treatment order made for a patient and the first extension are for terms of 6 months.[33] However, if a compulsory treatment order is extended for the second time it will then be indefinite.[34] To become indefinite, the compulsory treatment order must therefore have already been in effect for one year.

(7)   *Extensions*

If it is desired that a compulsory treatment order be extended, an application for extension must be filed with the Court before the order has expired. The procedure then followed is the same as that followed for the initial making of the order.[35]

7.4.7   Reviews

A patient may apply to the Court under section 16 of the Act for a Judicial Review. Such an application is to be heard by a Judge as soon as practicable, usually within a few days. The patient will be released from compulsory status if considered fit for release by the Judge.

(1)   *Review by responsible clinician*

At any time when a patient is subject to compulsory status, whether during compulsory assessment and treatment or when subject to a compulsory treatment order, the responsible clinician may direct the patient's discharge if it is considered that the patient is fit to be released.

(2)   *Clinical review*

A formal clinical review must be undertaken by the responsible clinician within 3 months of the making of the compulsory treatment order, and if the order is indefinite, at 6-monthly intervals after the initial 3-month clinical review.[36]

(3)   *Mental Health Review Tribunal*

When a clinical review has been completed, copies of the certificate of clinical review are made available both to the patient and to others, including a district inspector who must then discuss the clinical review with the patient. The patient then has the right to apply to the Mental Health Review Tribunal for a review.[37] The Tribunal may, on its own motion, decide to review a patient at any other time. Hearings before the Tribunal are, in most respects, similar to judicial hearings. It is possible for the Tribunal to make only two decisions — either to discharge the patient if it is considered that the patient is fit to be discharged, or to direct that the patient not be discharged.[38] If dissatisfied with the Tribunal's decision, a patient may appeal to the District Court.

---

32   Mental Health (CAT) Act 1992, section 31.
33   Mental Health (CAT) Act 1992, sections 33 and 34(2).
34   Mental Health (CAT) Act 1992, section 34(4).
35   Mental Health (CAT) Act 1992, section 34(3).
36   Mental Health (CAT) Act 1992, section 76(1).
37   Mental Health (CAT) Act 1992, section 79(1).
38   Mental Health (CAT) Act 1992, section 79(7) and (8).

(4)   *High Court inquiries*

Judicial inquiries into the legality of a patient's detention, or any other matter, may be made by the High Court.[39] Such inquiries may be initiated either by a patient, or by any other person. In most cases, the High Court Judge will direct a district inspector to furnish a report before proceeding with the inquiry. The High Court may discharge the patient, and furnish a report to the Minister of Health.

7.4.8   Treatment

(1)   *Information*

Before the treatment is commenced, so far as possible, the patient must receive an explanation of the expected effects of any treatment offered, including the expected benefits and the likely side-effects.[40]

(2)   *Compulsory treatment — consent*

Even when a patient is subject to compulsory treatment, the responsible clinician is directed to seek, where practicable, the patient's consent to any treatment administered.[41] Throughout the period of compulsory assessment and treatment, and for the first month after the making of a compulsory treatment order, a patient is required to accept treatment for mental disorder as directed by the responsible clinician.[42]

(3)   *Compulsory treatment order — after one month*

After the first month of the order being in force, a patient is not required to accept any treatment unless, having had the treatment explained as set out above, the patient consents in writing.[43] However, the matter may then be referred to a psychiatrist (not the responsible clinician) nominated by the Review Tribunal. If the second psychiatrist agrees that the treatment is appropriate, the patient is then required to accept the treatment.[44]

(4)   *Electroconvulsive therapy*

There are similar provisions concerning electroconvulsive therapy, which may not be administered unless either the patient consents in writing after having the treatment explained, or a second psychiatrist appointed by the Mental Health Review Tribunal considers it to be in the patient's best interests.[45]

(5)   *Brain surgery*

It is worth noting that brain surgery intended to destroy any part of the brain or brain function is now rarely, if ever, undertaken. However, if it were contemplated, there are very strict requirements before it can be carried out.[46] Either the patient must consent and the Mental Health Review Tribunal must be satisfied the patient has given a free and informed

---

39   Mental Health (CAT) Act 1992, section 84.
40   Mental Health (CAT) Act 1992, section 67.
41   Mental Health (CAT) Act 1992, section 59(4).
42   Mental Health (CAT) Act 1992, sections 59(1), 58 and 15(1).
43   Mental Health (CAT) Act 1992, section 59(2).
44   Mental Health (CAT) Act 1992, section 59(3).
45   Mental Health (CAT) Act 1992, section 60.
46   Mental Health (CAT) Act 1992, section 61.

consent, or the surgery must be considered in the best interests of the patient by the responsible clinician, a further psychiatrist appointed by the Tribunal, at least one other medical practitioner, and one other health professional concerned with the patient's care.

(6) Urgent treatment

Consent is not required for any treatment that is immediately necessary to save the patient's life, to prevent serious damage to the patient's health, or to prevent the patient from causing serious injury to herself/himself or others.[47]

(7) Withdrawal of consent

In any case, where the Mental Health (CAT) Act 1992 does not authorise compulsory treatment and consent is required, a patient may withdraw that consent at any time.[48]

7.4.9 Patients' rights

(1) Information

In addition to receiving information concerning treatment,[49] every patient (and the term includes a proposed patient) is required to receive a written statement of their rights on becoming a patient. They must be kept informed concerning such matters as legal status, the right to seek the reviews set out previously, and the functions and duties of district inspectors.[50] A patient must be informed when it is intended to make any visual or audio recording, and they must consent to such recording.[51]

(2) Cultural identity and personal beliefs

Every patient is entitled to be dealt with in a manner that accords proper respect to that patient's cultural and ethnic identity, language, and religious or ethical beliefs, and with proper recognition of the importance and significance to the patient of the patient's ties with their family, whanau, hapu, iwi, and family group.[52]

(3) Treatment

Every patient is entitled to medical treatment and other health care appropriate to their condition.[53]

(4) Advice

Every patient is entitled to consult a psychiatrist of their own choice in order to get a second opinion,[54] and is entitled to access to legal advice.[55] It should be noted, however, that there is no provision for the payment of an independent psychiatrist's fee, unless approved on legal aid in relation to a hearing. Legal aid is generally available only for a hearing before a judge or the Mental Health Review Tribunal.

---

47   Mental Health (CAT) Act 1992, section 62.
48   Mental Health (CAT) Act 1992, section 63.
49   Mental Health (CAT) Act 1992, section 64.
50   Mental Health (CAT) Act 1992, Part 6.
51   Mental Health (CAT) Act 1992, section 68.
52   Mental Health (CAT) Act 1992, section 65.
53   Mental Health (CAT) Act 1992, section 66.
54   Mental Health (CAT) Act 1992, section 69.
55   Mental Health (CAT) Act 1992, section 70.

(5)   Company of others

Every patient is entitled to the company of others.[56] Seclusion must only be used, and only for so long as it is necessary, for the care or treatment of the patient or for the protection of other patients and with the responsible clinician's authority. Further requirements concerning seclusion are set out in Ministry of Health guidelines, which, in many cases, have been adapted to the requirements of the regional Mental Health Service. At the time of writing (mid-2009) the Ministry of Health guidelines for seclusion are under review.

(6)   Visitors and telephone calls

Every patient is entitled at reasonable times and at reasonable intervals to receive visitors and to make telephone calls, except in cases where the responsible clinician considers that it would be detrimental to the interests of the patient and to their treatment.[57]

(7)   Letters

Subject to a similar qualification as for telephone calls, every patient is entitled to receive and post unopened a letter or other postal article. However, letters to and from certain persons, including a Member of Parliament, a Lawyer and a District Inspector, may not in any circumstances be opened.[58]

(8)   Complaints

A complaint by, or on behalf of, a patient concerning any breach of rights conferred by the Act should be referred to a district inspector. The district inspector, after investigating the matter, is required to advise the complainant of their findings. They must also make a report to the Director of Area Mental Health Services.[59]

(9)   New Zealand Bill of Rights Act 1990

In cases where there is no specific provision in the Mental Health (CAT) Act 1992 (or any of its amendments), the provisions of the New Zealand Bill of Rights Act 1990 will apply.

Case
Re E (1994) 11 FRNZ 354; [1994] NZFLR 328

Judge Carruthers considered the case of a patient with a long history of paranoid schizophrenic illness. He had been admitted to Porirua Hospital in November 1993 following an incident in which he was charged with assault. There was also evidence of E having difficulties with his parents, assaulting his father, and becoming suicidal and desperate.

E stated that he was prepared to accept treatment in the community, and he was able to point to a history of community-based treatment, which had proved successful. However, his responsible clinician said that he was not prepared to treat E if placed under a community compulsory treatment order, principally because of the lack of resources in the community to cope. After deciding that the definition of mental disorder had been

---

56   Mental Health (CAT) Act 1992, section 71.
57   Mental Health (CAT) Act 1992, section 72.
58   Mental Health (CAT) Act 1992, sections 73, 123 and 124.
59   Mental Health (CAT) Act 1992, section 75.

satisfied and that it was necessary to make a compulsory treatment order, his Honour then considered whether the order should be a community treatment order or an in-patient treatment order. His Honour made it clear that he would prefer to make a community treatment order, as the thrust of the Act was in favour of treatment in the community, as was the New Zealand Bill of Rights Act 1990. However, there is a specific provision in the Mental Health (CAT) Act 1992 requiring that, before making a community treatment order, the Court must be satisfied that the care provided in the community is appropriate to the patient's needs and that the patient's social circumstances are adequate for the patient's care in the community. In this case, the Court could not be satisfied that adequate care and treatment could be provided on an outpatient basis. The Court was therefore obliged by the provisions of the Mental Health (CAT) Act to make an in-patient compulsory treatment order. The specific provision in the Mental Health (CAT) Act overruled the New Zealand Bill of Rights Act.

7.4.10   Consent issues

The basic principle is that a patient should not be treated without their consent (section 57). In every case, a patient is entitled to receive an explanation of the expected side effects of any treatment offered, including the expected benefits, before treatment is commenced (section 67). Even in cases where the Mental Health (CAT) Act 1992 authorises treatment without consent, an attempt should be made, wherever practicable, to obtain consent (section 59(4)).

As Judge Frater explained in *Coast Health Ltd v R* [1995] NZFLR 838 at page 844, "I do not see 'treatment' as a narrow concept. In the Mental Health context it must include all the remedies which mental health professionals — be they psychiatrists, psychologists, social workers, nurses or occupational therapists — have available to them to manage mental illness".

For patients under the Mental Health (CAT) Act 1992, written, informed consent to treatment is required, except at the following times:

- During the first 5 days of compulsory assessment and treatment under section 11.
- During the next 14 days of further compulsory assessment and treatment under section 13.
- During the period of no more than 14 days from the time an application for a compulsory treatment order has been made until the first appearance before the Judge (section 15).
- During the period of any adjournment of an application for a compulsory treatment order, provided compulsory treatment is authorised by the Judge (section 15).
- For one month after the making of a compulsory treatment order (section 59(1)).
- During the currency of a compulsory treatment order in cases where a second opinion obtained from a psychiatrist appointed by the Mental Health Review Tribunal (not the responsible clinician) considers the treatment to be in the patient's best interests.

The consent given must relate to the treatment to be administered. The Act gives no power to impose treatment for physical disorders that are unrelated to the patient's mental disorder. Although a person may be incapable of consenting to treatment for their mental disorder, they may still be competent to consent or refuse treatment for illnesses or injuries other than mental disorders.

Case

Re C (adult; refusal of medical treatment) [1994] 1 All ER 819; [1994] 1 WLR 290

C had a schizophrenic illness characterised by paranoia. He developed gangrene in his foot, which the surgeon considered would kill him if his foot were not amputated. C refused because he would prefer to die with two feet than live with one and so he sought an injunction restraining the hospital from amputating his leg without his written consent. The Court had to decide whether the patient's capacity was reduced by his mental illness so that he was unable to understand the nature, purpose, and effects of the amputation. Although the patient's capacity had been impaired by his schizophrenic illness, it was clear that he understood and had retained the information about the treatment, and had arrived at a decision regarding that treatment. Therefore, the Court held that his right to self-determination had not been displaced.

The common law right to administer treatment in an emergency, or under Right 7(4) of the Code of Health & Disability Services Consumers' Rights if the patient is not competent to consent and no one legally entitled to consent on their behalf is available, may apply in some circumstances. An example of this will be when a patient's mentally disordered thinking has resulted in their attempting to harm herself/himself and treatment is required for the resulting injury.

Section 66 of the Act contains a specific provision that the medical treatment and other health care administered to a patient under the Act must be appropriate to the condition of that patient. Section 9 of the New Zealand Bill of Rights Act 1990 contains a provision that no one must be subjected to "cruel, degrading, or disproportionately severe treatment". Whether the treatment is considered excessive will depend on the circumstances. It has been held in England in *B v Croydon Health Authority*[60] that the non-consensual force feeding of a woman, who refused to eat and who was seriously mentally disordered, was treatment authorised by the Mental Health Act 1993 (UK). In New Zealand, it has been accepted that, in serious cases of mental disorders such as anorexia nervosa, force-feeding by means of a nasal tube is treatment that the Mental Health (CAT) Act 1992 authorises in cases where the patient does not consent.

As discussed at 7.4.8(4) and 7.4.8(5), extra safeguards are considered necessary for the administration of electroconvulsive therapy ("ECT") and psychosurgery (see 7.3.1 and 7.4.8(5)). Under the Protection of Personal and Property Rights Act 1988, a welfare guardian may be appointed for a person who is not competent to make decisions concerning their personal care and welfare. Decisions made by a welfare guardian include decisions concerning medical treatment. A welfare guardian may not refuse consent to the administration of any standard medical treatment or procedure intended to save the subject person's life, or to prevent serious damage to that person's health. The legislation specifies

---

60   *B v Croydon Health Authority* [1995] 2 WLR 294; [1995] 1 All ER 683 (CA). B's appeal was dismissed and the CA stated that treatment included treatment to alleviate symptoms as well as to remedy the underlying cause.

some types of treatment to which a welfare guardian may not consent, including the administration of ECT and participation in any medical experiment.

The Mental Health (CAT) Act 1992 provides that consent to treatment, which is necessary after a compulsory treatment order has been in force for one month, may be withdrawn at any time. However, the treatment may be continued in cases where a second opinion is obtained from a psychiatrist appointed by the Mental Health Review Tribunal (other than the responsible clinician), who considers that the treatment is in the best interests of the patient.

7.5 Children and young persons

7.5.1 Consent by a child to medical procedures and other health and disability services

The law sees children as individuals and under the Code of Health and Disability Services Consumers' Rights there is no "age of consent". The word "consumer" applies to *all* consumers of health and disability services. There is no reference to age.

As seen in chapter 6, all consumers are presumed competent to make an informed choice and to give informed consent. This is extremely important in relation to all groups of people who could easily otherwise be discounted by health professionals when decisions are being made about their care and treatment. In the past, children have often been discounted.

The Code forces health practitioners to treat a child as an individual. The presumption of competence in Right 7(2), which forms the basis of the Code, means that a child is presumed competent until otherwise assessed. A competent child therefore has a right to make an informed choice, and give or refuse consent.

The Code operates on the basis that there is no age of consent, and it is the functional level of competency that determines whether a child is able to make an informed choice. However, the Code is subject to all other laws,[61] and in some cases treatment is authorised by another law and consent is not necessary. Also, in an emergency, treatment can be given without obtaining consent.[62] The Care of Children Act 2004 provides guidance around a child's consent.[63] Section 36 provides that a child who is of or over the age of 16 years or a younger child who is married, in a civil union or living with another person, such as a de facto partner, may provide a valid consent (or a refusal to consent) to any treatment and also to any blood donation. It is also provided, in section 38, that a female child of any age may consent (or refuse to consent) to an abortion. Section 37 also contains a special provision, which will be discussed later, relating to blood transfusions. The provisions mentioned above in the Care of the Children Act 2004 do not preclude a child under the age of 16 from giving a valid consent.

Case

Gillick v West Norfolk and Wisbech Area Health Authority [1985] 3 All ER 402 (HL)

---

61   Code of Health and Disability Services Consumers' Rights, right 7(1) and clause 5.
62   Code of Health and Disability Services Consumers' Rights, clause 3.
63   Repealed and replaced the Guardianship Act 1968.

A mother sought a Court ruling that parents and guardians have a right to make decisions on behalf of their children as to contraceptive advice or treatment. Her children, along with others, had been receiving information about contraception through the family planning clinic without the prior knowledge and consent of their parents. These children were under the age of 16.

The majority of the House of Lords held first, that minors may authorise medical treatment when they are old enough and mature enough to decide for themselves. It would be arbitrary and unreal, the Court held, to draw a line between childhood and maturity at a certain number of years, disregarding human development and social change:[64]

> "Provided the patient, whether a boy or a girl, is capable of understanding what is proposed, and of expressing his or her own wishes, I see no good reason for holding that he or she lacks the capacity to express them validly and effectively to make the examination and give the treatment that [the doctor] advises."

Secondly, the Court held that the rights of parents to control their child are for the child's benefit, and are recognised only so long as they are needed for the protection of the child. Absolute dominion over the child is now a thing of the past, and parental rights dwindle proportionately with the child's maturity. Accordingly, there may be occasions when the child's interest indicates that a parent's rights should be disregarded.

Lord Fraser made the useful suggestion that:[65]

> "[where a girl] refuses either to tell the parents herself or permit the doctor to do so ... the doctor will, in my opinion, be justified in proceeding without the parent's consent or even their knowledge provided he is satisfied on the following matters: (1) that the girl ... will understand his advice; (2) that he cannot persuade her [that her parents should be informed]; (3) that she is very likely to begin or to continue having sexual intercourse with or without contraceptive treatment; (4) that unless she receives contraceptive advice or treatment her physical or mental health or both are likely to suffer; (5) that her best interests require ... advice, treatment or both without the parental consent."

The House of Lord's judgment formed two tests in regard a child's competence to consent to medical treatment. The first is a general test provided by Lord Scarman, in which he states that:[66]

> "parental right to determine whether or not their minor child below the age of 16 will have medical treatment terminates if and when the child achieves a sufficient understanding and intelligence to enable him or her to understand fully what is proposed."

He then went on and set out a second test with a higher threshold in regard to contraception:[67]

---

64   *Gillick v West Norfolk and Wisbech Area Health Authority* [1985] 3 All ER 402, 409 per Lord Fraser.

65   *Gillick v West Norfolk and Wisbech Area Health Authority* [1985] 3 All ER 402, 413.

66   *Gillick v West Norfolk and Wisbech Area Health Authority* [1985] 3 All ER 402, 457.

67   *Gillick v West Norfolk and Wisbech Area Health Authority* [1985] 3 All ER 402.

"It is not enough that she should understand the nature of the advice which is being given: she must also have a sufficient maturity to understand what is involved. There are moral and family questions, especially her relationship with her parents; long-term problems associated with the emotional impact of pregnancy and its termination; and there are the risks to health of sexual intercourse at her age, risks which contraception may diminish but cannot eliminate."

The *Gillick* case and the Code appear to allow a child the right to consent to services being provided without their parent's consent. In New Zealand the Contraception, Sterilisation, and Abortion Act 1977 permits contraception to be given to children without their parents' consent. The Contraception, Sterilisation, and Abortion Amendment Act 1990 removed all restrictions on the advice and supply of contraceptives to those under 16 years of age. Young people of any age now have the right to access information about contraception and to be supplied with contraceptive products without parental consent.[68]

Thus, the first step in providing health and disability services to a child is to talk to the individual child where possible, and assess that child's competence. The key under the Code is to assess competency in relation to the *particular* service. The level of understanding required to be able to make an informed choice to have a broken bone set, may well differ from that required to understand the complexity and risks or serious consequences of making a choice about whether or not to undergo a regime of chemotherapy.

A number of factors must be taken into account, including how ill or frightened the child is. Age is only one of the factors that should be considered. Ultimately, assessment of a particular child's competency to make an informed choice about a particular procedure or treatment will depend on the understanding, maturity, and interest of the child, and the type and gravity of the proposed procedure or treatment.

7.5.2 How do you know whether a child is competent?

Sometimes it will be obvious that the child is incompetent, for example a baby or a very young child. As children get older though, they may well be competent to consent, even when quite young, especially if a procedure or treatment is a very simple one.

An English case set out a useful three-stage test for competency, which is the test the Courts now use.[69] A person is competent if they:

- Can comprehend and retain the necessary information about the procedure or treatment;
- Is able to believe it; and
- Is able to weigh the information, balancing risks and needs, and so arrive at a choice.

It is probably equally as important that the person is also able to communicate a decision.

---

68   By repealing Contraception, Sterilisation, and Abortion Act 1977, section 3. See also Barbara Collins, "Consistent or Conflicting? Sexual Health Legislation and Young People's Rights in New Zealand" (2000) 15 Social Policy Journal of New Zealand 1.

69   *Re C (adult; refusal of medical treatment)* [1994] 1 All ER 819; [1994] 1 WLR 290 (the Court starts with the presumption of self-determination).

While the views of the parent or carer as to the child's competence may be taken into account, it is the provider's responsibility to form an independent judgment about the child's competency.

Where a child is not competent to consent, then the provisions of section 36 of the Care of the Children Act 2004 apply and a guardian can do so. Where a guardian is not available, or if no guardian with reasonable diligence or capable of giving consent can be found in New Zealand, then consent can be given by anyone who has been acting in the place of a parent or guardian, for example a teacher or babysitter or even the partner of one parent.[70] If no one already mentioned who can legally consent on the child's behalf is available in New Zealand, then consent may be obtained from a District Court Judge or the Chief Executive of the Ministry of Social Development.

The Code appears to provide that a person entitled to make an informed choice on a child's behalf, for example their parent, can do so only if the child is not competent to do so herself/himself. This is not to say, however, that parents should not be involved. Parents can often assist health practitioners the most in deciding whether a child is competent to understand the information needed to make an informed choice.

In some cases, a child might to be too ill to be considered competent. Competency may fluctuate depending on how well the child is at a particular time, or a child might just not be interested, preferring to leave the decision-making to the parents. However, even where a child is not competent to make an informed choice, the Code provides that they retain the right to make an informed choice and give informed consent to the level of their competence. This means that a child might be able to consent to some procedures, although not all. Information therefore must always be provided to the level of the child's understanding and interest.

Therapeutic privilege should not be a ground for withholding information from a child about their illness. In some cases, however, it might be in a child's best interest to withhold information, for example in an emergency situation, but to ensure that this is discussed with the child afterwards where the child is competent to understand.

7.5.3   Can a child consent when there is a charge for the services?

A potentially difficult situation could arise when there is a charge for the service. Under contract law, a person under 20 years of age is a minor and is covered by the Minors' Contracts Act 1969. Under this Act, contracts with minors are not always enforceable (see chapter 12). Consequently, it would not always be wise for a health practitioner to enter into a contract for payment with a child or young person who does not have an income of their own. In these circumstances, there is no obligation on the health practitioner's part to provide the services, unless it is an emergency. Ethically, however, the health practitioner should assist the child to obtain alternative services at no cost if these are available.

Where a parent pays for a child who is competent to make an informed choice, that parent is not automatically entitled to health information about the child just because they are paying for the service. If the child consents to the parent receiving the information, the health professional can give it. However, if the parent is a primary caregiver a request for information could be treated by the health professional as a request made under

---

70   See also Code of Health and Disability Services Consumers' Rights, right 7(1).

section 22F of the Health Act 1956 and the information duly provided (see chapter 9). However, the information cannot be given if a competent child does not want it discussed.

It is suggested that at the outset this issue should be explained and fully discussed with both the child and the paying parent. A lot of parents would otherwise feel that they were entitled to the information about their child. In this way it may be possible to resolve some difficulties before the services are provided.

7.5.4   Can a child withhold consent or refuse treatment?

Under the Code, children have the right to make an informed choice, which means not only the right to consent, but also the right to refuse treatment. If a child does refuse treatment, what can a health professional do if a child has sufficient understanding to make an informed decision, but the health practitioner feels that the decision is not in the child's best interest?

The New Zealand Bill of Rights Act 1990 provides that everyone has the right to refuse medical treatment.[71] The Courts have upheld this right in a number of cases, but these involve adults.[72] Research has shown that very few children who are treated with respect, and who are appropriately informed and supported, will refuse consent to treatment necessary to save their life or their health from serious risk.[73]

On a strict interpretation of the Code, health professionals could give effect to the child's right to refuse, and certainly should not lightly override any person's choice, whether they are a child or not. However, Right 7(1) of the Code gives a consumer the right to make an informed choice and to give informed consent, "except where any enactment, or the common law, or any other provision of this Code provides otherwise". Thus, the Code is subject to the common law.

The Code has followed the common law in giving a child the right to consent to treatment. However, it appears that the test for competency to make an informed refusal at common law is much more rigorous than that for consenting. Where a refusal may result in death or severe disability, the common law cases show that a child's right to refuse medical treatment, even when the child is competent to make an informed decision, is not an absolute right. Also, rarely, where a child has refused to consent to lifesaving treatment, both here and overseas, the Courts have distinguished between the right of a child to consent to treatment and the right of a child to refuse it, and have allowed the treatment to be given. The Court

---

71   New Zealand Bill of Rights Act 1990, section 11.

72   See for example *Malette v Shulman* (1991) 2 Med LR 162; (1990) 67 DLR (4th) 321 (Ont CA) (see 6.5.3(1)) where the Court held that a blood transfusion should not have been administered to a card-carrying Jehovah's Witness even though there was a risk she would have died without it; *St George's Healthcare NHS Trust v S* [1998] 3 All ER 673 where it was held that detention in hospital and a caesarean section should not have been carried out even though both baby and mother were at risk of death; and *Re C (adult; refusal of medical treatment)* [1994] 1 All ER 819; [1994] 1 WLR 290, in which a man with a schizophrenic illness developed gangrene of leg — he refused amputation and the Court upheld his right to refuse treatment after finding he was competent to make a decision (see above 7.4.10).

73   P Alderson and J Montgomery, *Health Choices: Making Decisions with Children*, United Kingdom, Institute for Public Policy Research, 1996, pages 6-93, discussed in J Manning, "Parental refusal of life prolonging medical treatment for children: A report from New Zealand" (2001) 8(3) Journal of Law and Medicine 263.

either finds that the child is not competent after all (this is the most common reason given), or overrides the child's wishes on the basis that the treatment is in their best interests.

Case

Re W (a minor: medical treatment) [1992] 4 All ER 627 (CA)[74]

A teenager with a diagnosis of anorexia nervosa who understood her condition, but who wished to seek treatment in her own time, refused treatment for her condition. The local authority applied to the Court for an order for her treatment. The Judge held that although she had sufficient understanding to make an informed decision, he had inherent power under his parens patriae jurisdiction to order the treatment be given. W appealed.

By the time of the appeal, W was deteriorating, to the point where medical opinion estimated her reproductive capacity could be lost within a week, and her life a short time later. The Court of Appeal made an emergency order that W be removed to a specialist unit for treatment on the basis that her wishes were outweighed by the threat of irreparable damage to her health. The Court made it clear that it was not considering the importance of a young person's views generally, nor the weight it would have given her view earlier on when she was not so ill. However, it later said at a full hearing that its inherent jurisdiction over children meant that it could override the wishes of a person under 18 years. It also pointed out that although children can agree to treatment, they understand this does not mean an absolute right of *refusal* of treatment. It simply means that where parents have refused treatment and a child consents to it, the health practitioner is protected.

This does not mean that a child's wishes should not be taken into account. The Court in *Re W* made a strong statement to the effect that the refusal of treatment by a child, although not automatically legally actionable, is nevertheless of great importance for health carers in making clinical judgments and should reasonably be considered. Lord Balcombe said:[75]

> "In a sense [consideration of the child's wishes] is merely one aspect of the test that the welfare of the child is the paramount consideration. It will normally be in the best interests of a child of sufficient age and understanding to make an informed decision that the Court should respect [his or her] integrity as a human being and not lightly override [his or her] decisions on such a personal matter as medical treatment, all the more so if the treatment is invasive."

Case

Re M (medical treatment: consent) [1999] 2 FLR 1097

A 15-year-old girl needed an urgent heart transplant. She said that although she did not want to die, she did not want another person's heart in her body. A few weeks previously, she had been a healthy girl and was now close to death. Her mother was allowed to override her refusal and consent for her, even though the Judge found that the girl was intelligent. He said that she was "simply overwhelmed by the circumstances and the rapidity of events

---

74   The Court held that the teenager was competent yet overrode her refusal on the basis that consent from her parent was sufficient. The decision has been criticised: see Kennedy and Grubb, *Medical Law*, United Kingdom, Butterworths, 2000, 975-989.

75   *Re W (a minor: medical treatment)* [1992] 4 All ER 627, 643.

which had overtaken her so swiftly that she has not been able to come to terms with her situation".[76]

The Court therefore overrode her refusal in, what it said was her best interests.[77]

7.5.5 Where parents and child disagree

A competent child can consent to treatment without reference to an adult, but what should a health practitioner do where parents want the child to receive treatment, but the competent child objects and the treatment is not emergency treatment?

In this situation, health practitioners are not obliged to give any treatment that they consider unnecessary or unwise. To proceed with treatment could lead to complaints to the Health and Disability Commissioner for breach of the Code.

If the treatment is not urgent and alternatives are possible, these alternatives should be discussed with the child fully as part of making an informed choice anyway. Health practitioners need to be sure that the child fully understands the consequences of withholding consent, because making an informed choice that includes refusing treatment implies that any refusal be an *informed* refusal.

Health practitioners are in a difficult position because they need also to be aware that when the treatment is considered necessary to save the child's life, to fail to give it may leave the health practitioners exposed to criminal negligence if the child dies (see chapter 16). In such a situation the treatment can be given as emergency treatment, or the health practitioners could seek directions from a Court under the Care of the Children Act 2004. Where the child consents to treatment and is capable of doing so, but the parents (who are usually the legal guardians) do not want their child to receive the treatment, then it is clear that the treatment can still be given. If, however, the treatment is not urgent and alternatives are possible, the health practitioners should carefully consider these and discuss them with the child, especially where the treatment is complicated and really needs the ongoing input and involvement of the parents or guardian in ensuring the child's compliance.

7.5.6 Where parents refuse for a child who cannot choose

What can be done where a child is not competent to make an informed choice, the parents refuse to consent on their behalf, and a health practitioner believes the treatment is in the best interest of the child? Under the Code, the parent (who will usually be the legal guardian) is entitled to refuse treatment on behalf of the child where the child is not competent to make an informed choice, but the right is to make an *informed* refusal. In some situations the parents or guardian also might not be competent to make any informed choice.[78] If the parent is not competent, then services can be provided to the child under Right 7(4) of the Code.

If the parents or guardian are competent to make an informed choice and refuse the treatment for their child, and the practitioner believes that the treatment is in the child's best interests, all efforts should be made to communicate this to the parents or guardian

---

76   *Re M (medical treatment: consent)* [1999] 2 FLR 1097 (UK), 1100, per Johnson J.

77   The decision has been criticised, see Kennedy and Grubb, *Medical Law*, United Kingdom, Butterworths, 2000, 975-989.

78   They might be drunk for example.

and to keep the channels of communication open. A course of treatment over time might be needed, and the input and involvement of the parents or guardian in ensuring compliance with the treatment is often vital.

As a last resort, a provider can apply to Court for the child to have a Court-appointed guardian to consent to the treatment.[79] However, in this sort of situation there is always the risk that the family will disengage from the services. Where the treatment is not emergency treatment or treatment necessary to save the child's life, it is advised that this option should be exercised cautiously, and only after full consultation with other health practitioners and an ethics committee if there is time.

A Court can and has overridden parental consent or refusal when it considers it would not be in the child's best interests. This is within the Family Court and the High Court's guardianship jurisdiction. A child can be placed under the Court's guardianship, and the Court may appoint an agent to consent to the treatment.[80]

Case

Healthcare Otago Ltd v Williams-Holloway [1999] NZFLR 804[81]

Three-year-old Liam had a stage 4 neuroblastoma involving his jaw. He had already undergone two cycles of chemotherapy, and his parents had been distressed by his suffering. He was due for a third cycle of chemotherapy, but his parents refused this. The hospital applied to the Court and the treatment was ordered to be given. Liam's parents took him into hiding and tried alternative treatment with an electrical machine called a quantum booster. There was a large amount of media publicity, and a nationwide hunt for Liam followed. The Court then tried to promote a conciliatory approach with Liam's parents and suspended the treatment order. Later, the Court discharged the order altogether on the basis that as 4 months had passed, there was little likelihood that Liam would be able to benefit from the chemotherapy. His parents then brought him out of hiding, but took him to Mexico for natural therapy treatment. He died there in October 2000 aged 5½.

In other New Zealand cases the Court has authorised blood transfusions overriding parental refusal where there is a risk the child will otherwise die.[82] Also, there are cases where the Court has ordered surgical treatment overriding a parent's refusal.[83]

---

79   Care of Children Act 2004, section 27.

80   Care of Children Act 2004, sections 31-33.

81   For a full discussion of the legal position when parents refuse treatment for their children see J Manning, "Parental refusal of life-prolonging medical treatment for children: A report from New Zealand" (2001) 8 (3) Journal of Law and Medicine 263.

82   For example: *Re J (an infant)* [1996] 2 NZLR 134, a 3-year-old boy had a life-threatening nose bleed; *Re V* [1993] NZFLR 369, blood was needed during an operation to remove a kidney tumour; *Re CL* [1992] NZFLR 352, blood was needed during a congenital heart defect correction; *Re P* [1992] NZFLR 95, twins born at 26 weeks gestation needed blood transfusions.

83   For example: *THJL v SL &LL* 4/11/97, Salmon J, HC Auckland M708/97, a testicular biopsy ordered on a 2-year-old boy and an orchidectomy if it was malignant; *D-GSW v B* [1994] NZFLR 516, removal of cancerous tumour; *Auckland Healthcare Services v T* [1996] NZFLR 670, chemotherapy ordered for 12-year-old girl with malignant lymphoma; *Re Norma* [1994] NZFLR 516, chemotherapy ordered for 19-month-old Samoan girl with likely Ewing's sarcoma; *Auckland Healthcare Services v Lui* 11/7/96, HC Auckland M812/96, repair of partially detached retina ordered for 12-year-old boy.

This is similarly the case overseas.

Case

Re A (Children) (conjoined twins: surgical separation) [2000] 4 All ER 961 (CA)

Mary and Jodie were born conjoined at the pelvis. They were classified as ischiopagus tetrapus (four legs and joined at the pelvis). Their parents, who were strictly religious, had refused to consent to an operation to separate them because it would mean severing the common aorta through which one twin, Jodie, circulated oxygenated blood to both her own and to Mary's body. When the artery was severed it would kill Mary, whose heart and lungs could not sustain a circulation of her own. There was medical evidence that without separation, both twins would die within 3 to 6 months because Jodie's heart would fail.

The twins were placed under the Court's guardianship, which overrode the parents' refusal to separate them. Mary died when the common artery was severed.

The Court based its reasoning on the least detrimental choice and the doctrine of necessity. The decision is controversial and has been criticised.[84]

With the Court's permission therefore a hospital or health practitioner can apply either to the High Court for the child to be placed under the Court's guardianship or to the Family Court under the provisions of section 27(2) of the Care of Children Act 2004 for the appointment of a guardian for a specific purpose. The child's welfare is paramount and is the first consideration, which the Court must have regard to.[85] If it overrides parental refusal of treatment, the Court usually only places the child under the guardianship of the Court to allow the treatment to be given. For everything else, the parents remain the child's guardians.

7.5.7 Child under care of third party

A child may be in the care of someone other than a parent, for example a guardian, institution, teacher, babysitter, relatives, or neighbours. If a child requires emergency treatment while in such a person's care, there is no doubt that this can be given without consent (see chapter 6).

When a parent who is a guardian of a child is not available in New Zealand to provide a consent, the provisions of section 36 of the Care of Children Act 2004 apply to enable consent to be given either by someone who has been acting in the place of a parent or if no such person is available in New Zealand by a District Court Judge or the Chief Executive of the Ministry of Social Development. Decisions made are guided by the child's best interests and the paramountcy of his/her welfare.[86]

84　For example see G McGrath, "The killing of Mary: Have we crossed the Rubicon?" (2001) 8(3) Journal of Law and Medicine 322 and M Bagaric, "The Jodie and Mary (Siamese Twins) case: The problem with rights" (2001) 8(3) Journal of Law and Medicine 311.

85　Care of Children Act 2004, section 4: the welfare and the best interests of the child are paramount.

86　See n 83.

7.5.8   Research involving children

As stated above, if children are not competent to consent to treatment themselves, someone authorised to consent on their behalf may do so. However, this does not necessarily apply to research.

The New Zealand Bill of Rights Act 1990 has a provision in it that every person has the right not to be subjected to medical or scientific experimentation without that person's consent.[87] The words "*that* person's" might mean that only the particular person herself/himself can give a valid consent. If so, this would prevent parental consent and thus preclude children from being included in health research unless they are themselves competent to give informed consent.

This is a matter of legal uncertainty and requires further clarification by the Courts, or by Parliament. Ministry of Health guidelines advise practitioners and investigators undertaking research involving infants and children, to discuss relevant consent issues with an ethics committee.[88]

Ethics committees are allowing research to take place with parental consent, otherwise this could have considerable implications for therapeutic research and for safe non-therapeutic research that could be of benefit to a wide range of children. Interpretation of the word "experimentation" in section 10 New Zealand Bill of Rights Act 1990 is a crucial issue. Ethics committees interpret the word so that only non-safe, non-therapeutic research is prohibited by the section.[89]

Ethics committees are also trying to ensure that where research involves children and the child is competent to consent, the child makes the choice whether to participate. As compliance with a medication is often a crucial factor in child research, consent is asked for from both parent and child. Where one or other refuses, the child is not included in the research. Information sheets about the study and consent forms are directed to the children, as well as their parents. Ethics committees ensure that investigators take time to assess each child's understanding and competency, and involve an interested child as much as possible.

7.5.9   Children who are the subject of abuse

When it is suspected that a child is the subject of abuse, some jurisdictions require certain classes of people, such as doctors, nurses, teachers, and social workers, to report this to the authorities. In New Zealand, there are no mandatory reporting provisions. However, section 15 of the Children, Young Persons, and Their Families Act 1989 provides that abuse may be reported to a social worker or police officer. Section 16 provides protection from any civil, criminal, or disciplinary proceedings to any person reporting abuse, unless done in bad faith.

---

87   New Zealand Bill of Rights Act 1990, section 10.

88   Ministry of Health, *Consent in Child and Youth Health: Information for Practitioners*, Wellington, 1999.

89   Regional Ethics Committees accredited by the Health Research Council Ethics Committee under the Health Research Council Act 1990, review protocols involving proposed research on humans in their region. For further reading on the legal position of research involving children see N Peart and D Holdaway, "Legal and ethical issues of health research with children" (1992) 2(2) Childrenz Issues 42.

Under section 49 of the Children, Young Persons, and Their Families Act 1989, the Family Court may order a medical examination of a child or young person under the age of 17 years without the consent of either the child or young person or the child's guardian or parent. A social worker may take custody of the child and organise this examination.

7.5.10 Other situations in which services can be provided to a child without either child or parent consent

Services can be provided to the child in an emergency, as they can be to any person (see chapter 6).

Where a child is not competent to consent, and there is no one available who is entitled to consent on the child's behalf, then under Right 7(4) of the Code services can be provided to the child, just as they can be to any other person (see chapter 6).

Services can be provided to a child without consent under any other enactment, such as for example, the Mental Health (CAT) Act 1992 (see chapter 6).

Health practitioners who administer a blood transfusion without consent to a person under 20 are immune from any action against them for doing so, in certain circumstances.[90]

7.6 Special medical treatment — sterilisation of intellectually disabled clients

The first consideration must always be the person's own wishes, and the presumption of competence applies. Where this is rebutted then the Contraception, Sterilisation, and Abortion Act 1977 applies over and above the Code.

Parents do not have the power to consent to the sterilisation of their intellectually disabled children,[91] and welfare guardians would be wise to obtain a specific order from the Court before consenting to sterilisation of an adult for whom they act.

In *Re D (a minor) (wardship: sterilisation)*,[92] the Court refused to allow the sterilisation of a severely intellectually disabled girl, when the evidence was that the operation was medically unnecessary and that she might later be capable of making her own choice. By contrast, in *Re B (a minor) (wardship: sterilisation)*,[93] the Court allowed the sterilisation of an intellectually disabled woman when there was no possibility of her ever being capable of giving consent on her own behalf, and contraception would have proved impractical.

7.7 Further reading

D Bailey and C Coates, *A User's Guide to the Mental Health (Compulsory Assessment and Treatment) Act 1992*, Wellington, Department of Health, 1992.

S Bell and W J Brookbanks, *Mental Health Law in New Zealand*, Wellington, Brookers, 1998.

90　Care of Children Act 2004, section 37, where immunity will be provided to practitioners administering blood transfusions to children under 18 without consent in certain circumstances.

91　Contraception, Sterilisation, and Abortion Act 1977, section 7.

92　*Re D (a minor) (wardship: sterilisation)* [1976] 1 All ER 326.

93　*Re B (a minor) (wardship: sterilisation)* [1988] AC 199.

W J Brookbanks, "Electro-convulsive therapy and consent to treatment" [1993] New Zealand Law Journal 235.

W J Brookbanks, *Psychiatry and the Law*, Wellington, Brookers, 1996.

J Caldwell, "Parents, Courts and the sick child" [2000] Family Law Journal 129.

Dawson et al, *The Mental Health (Compulsory Assessment and Treatment) Act 1992*, Wellington, New Zealand Law Society, 1993.

M McDowell, "Medical treatment and children: Assessing the scope of a child's capacity to consent or refuse to consent in New Zealand" (1997) 5 Journal of Law and Medicine 81.

J Manning, "Parental refusal of life prolonging medical treatment for children: A report from New Zealand" (2001) 8(3) Journal of Law and Medicine 263.

Ministry of Health, *Consent in Child and Youth Health: Information for Practitioners*, Wellington, 1999.

J Morgan, Minors and Consent to Medical Treatment: "Reflecting on Gillick", Law Reform Commission of Victoria Symposium 1986, Melbourne, Globe Press, 1987.

N Peart and D Holdaway, "Legal and ethical issues of health research with children" (1998) 2(2) Childrenz Issues 42.

N Peart, "Health Research with Children: The New Zealand Experience", in M Freeman, and A Lewis (eds), *Law and Medicine: Current Legal Issues Vol 3*, Oxford, Oxford University Press, 2000.

C Rogers, "Proceedings under the Mental Health Act 1992: The legalisation of psychiatry" [1994] New Zealand Law Journal 404.

See also the further reading list for chapter 6.

Chapter 8

LIABILITY FOR PERSONAL INJURY

SUE JOHNSON AND ANNE O'BRIEN

Contents

8.1   Introduction

Although the "no fault" accident compensation scheme in New Zealand provides a large degree of protection from civil actions, health practitioners who fail to observe a reasonable standard of care, and as a result of that cause injury to a consumer, may still find themselves liable in the following ways:

- Where ACC determines that there is a risk of public harm following a finding of treatment injury under the ACC scheme, it will report to the appropriate authority (see chapter 4);
- A civil action (being sued) for compensatory damages for negligence where the aggrieved consumer is *not* covered by the ACC scheme (see 8.2);

- A civil action for exemplary damages (see 8.2 and 8.10.5);
- A civil action for mental trauma (nervous shock) on the part of someone who witnessed the death or injury of a loved one through negligent treatment by the health practitioner (see 8.4.5);
- A finding of breach of the Code of Health and Disability Services Consumers' Rights, especially Right 4, the right to services of an appropriate standard (see chapter 4);[1]
- Proceedings against the health practitioner in the Health Practitioners Disciplinary Tribunal (see chapter 15).

All these possible actions or findings can be brought or made because the health practitioner was not adhering to proper professional standards. In other words, the health practitioner was negligent. Negligence means the failure to observe a reasonable standard of care. It has been developed in law into a specific "cause of action". A person can sue another for damages in the tort of negligence. In New Zealand where a health or disability services consumer seeks financial redress for loss or injury caused by negligent treatment, their ability to sue a health practitioner for compensation is limited by the Accident Compensation Scheme.

8.2 The effect of the ACC scheme on personal liability

New Zealand is unique in providing a no fault accident insurance scheme for personal injury caused by accident since April 1974, with compensation being provided by a Crown-owned corporation, the Accident Compensation Corporation ("ACC"). The ACC is a statutory body funded through levies imposed on the employment sector, motor vehicle and driver registration, petrol, and various treatment providers, in particular, registered health professionals. Brought in initially as a cornerstone of a welfare State political philosophy, the accident compensation legislation has varied in accordance with the changing political climate in New Zealand. At the time of writing (December 2009) the current legislation is the Injury Prevention, Rehabilitation, and Compensation Act 2001, which came into force on 1 April 2002 ("the IPRCA").[2]

The IPRCA refers explicitly to the "social contract" represented by the ACC scheme whereby New Zealanders gave up the right to sue wrong doers for damages for personal injury in return for entitlements to compensation under the ACC scheme.[3] Although some of the earlier Acts included in their title the word "insurance", the current legislation specifically states that the business of ACC is not to provide insurance.[4] The focus of the IPRCA is on accident and injury prevention and the compensation aspects of earlier ACC legislation have been extended. The legislation focuses on prevention and rehabilitation

---

1   Code of Health and Disability Services Consumers' Rights (reproduced in Appendix 4) is in the Schedule to the Health and Disability Commissioner (Code of Health and Disability Services Consumers' Rights) Regulations 1996. The Code was reviewed in 2004 and Right 7(10) was amended. The Code can be viewed on the Health and Disability Commissioner's website at www.hdc.org.nz/theact/theact-thecodedetail. At the time of writing the Commissioner was undertaking a further review of the Code.

2   The recent change in Government is potentially going to change the scheme again and is currently being reviewed. An amendment bill by this Government has been introduced to parliament on 22 October 2009.

3   Injury Prevention, Rehabilitation and Compensation Act 2001, section 3.

4   Injury Prevention, Rehabilitation, and Compensation Act 2001, section 262(2).

and cover is provided for physical injuries and certain mental injuries suffered in most work and non-work situations. Under the ACC scheme:

- Generally, a person who suffers injury as a result of medical treatment is entitled to compensation;
- A person who is entitled to compensation under the Act may not sue for *compensatory* damages in respect of any personal injury that is covered by the scheme, although the right to sue for *exemplary* damages[5] still exists (see 8.10.5).
- If injury occurs because of negligence by a registered health professional, the registered health professional will not be liable to compensate the victim or the victim's estate if the claimant is eligible for ACC cover;
- ACC compensation will only be available if the claimant has cover under the IPRCA;
- If cover is accepted, compensation is paid without reference to whether any person has been negligent. Amounts paid in compensation are considerably less than the amounts that might otherwise have been sued for in a civil claim.

When consumers claim they have suffered personal injury caused by health treatment they may make a claim to ACC for cover and compensation. Cover is not automatic. If a registered health professional was involved in the provision or direction of the treatment then cover will only be available if the injury amounts to treatment injury.[6] Following a comprehensive review of the provisions of the IPRCA[7] the term "treatment injury" replaced the terms "medical misadventure", "medical error" and "medical mishap"[8] from 1 July 2005. The new criteria for treatment injury removes the requirement on ACC to find fault (medical error) with the actions of a registered health professional or organisation or to prove that a medical injury was rare or severe (medical mishap), before a patient is entitled to ACC cover. The focus now is on the outcome of the treatment rather than, as it was under medical error, on the fault of the person who carried it out. Registered health professionals are still expected to provide details of their involvement in a claimants care. Consistently with this focus reporting of findings of error on the part of a registered health professional occur only if ACC has identified a risk of harm to the public, although all claimants for treatment injury are given information about the Health and Disability Commissioner's services. The reasoning is that with the removal of the "fault" aspect and error reporting health practitioners involved in treatment injury claims are more likely to provide accurate and prompt information to ACC without fear of reprisal.

The IPRCA bars a claim for compensatory damages where cover is provided under the Act,[9] so a finding of treatment injury means that the claimant consumer will have ACC

5　　Are imposed to *punish* a defendant — the Privy Council in *A v Bottrill* [2003] 2 NZLR 721; [2003] 1 AC 449, para 43 — describe the ultimate touchstone for exemplary damages as "outrageous conduct by the defendant which calls for punishment".

6　　Injury Prevention, Rehabilitation, and Compensation Act 2001, sections 20 and 32. Section 34 deals with cover for personal injury by medical misadventure before 1 July 2005. For a detailed description of the provisions relating to medical misadventure see earlier editions of this book.

7　　A consultation document *Review of ACC Medical Misadventure* was published and 186 submissions were received. In addition a paper was commissioned by ACC from Wellington barrister, Bruce Corkhill, *Medical Misadventure, Development of the Statutory Concept and its place in the current medico-legal environment*.

8　　Medical misadventure was either medical error or medical mishap. Medical error meant the failure of a registered health professional to observe a reasonable standard of care in the circumstances and was thus a finding that the health practitioner was negligent. Medical mishap meant a rare and severe outcome of treatment that was properly given, and thus not negligence.

cover and be eligible for ACC compensation, but is barred from suing the negligent registered health professional for compensatory damages.[10]

The aim of this bar is to avoid compensation being recovered twice over.[11] The bar prohibits claims for compensatory damages (money), for negligent breach of duty of care causing the injury, and claims for assault and battery. In certain circumstances however, it does not prohibit claims for compensation for mental injury/nervous shock[12] caused by seeing the death or injury of another person, even if that other person has ACC cover (see 8.4.5). Nor does it prohibit claims for exemplary or punitive damages[13] (see 8.10.4).

The ACC legislation and the ACC regime thus provide what is termed a no-fault scheme for compensating people who are the victims of personal injury without having to sue for compensation. However, the principles of the tort of negligence and what amounts to negligent conduct guide the Health and Disability Commissioner when deciding if there is a breach of the right of consumers to be provided with services with reasonable care and skill and that meet professional, legal and ethical standards, ie Rights 4(1) and 4(2) of the Code of Health and Disability Services Consumers' Rights. As already stated, actions for exemplary damages for negligence are not barred by ACC and these involve proving negligence; claims for nervous shock also involve proving the defendant was negligent (see 8.4.5). Under the Health Practitioner's Competence Assurance Act 2003, the definition of professional misconduct (by a health practitioner) includes negligence.[14]

As the basis of most findings against health practitioners in nearly all the forums that can hold them accountable is negligence, and the principles underlying the law of negligence permeate every possible activity a practitioner may engage in, either on duty or off duty, it is important to discuss what is meant by negligence.

8.3 What is negligence?

Four elements constitute a "negligence action" in law. A person (A) in order to prove negligence on the part of another (B) must show that:

(1)   B owed a duty of care to A;

(2)   B has breached that duty of care, through some action or inaction by him or her;

(3)   A has suffered some physical or financial harm (often referred to as "loss");

(4)   B's breach of duty caused the harm.

---

9   Injury Prevention, Rehabilitation and Compensation Act 2001, section 317 bars compensation where there is cover under the Act.

10   ACC will, however, investigate claims to determine whether a sentinel event or serious event has occurred and there is a risk of public harm. In that case it will report the health provider to the appropriate authority. In those circumstances this may mean that the health professionals involved are investigated for breach of the Code of Health and Disability Services Consumers' Rights (see chapters 4 and 5) and/or a professional disciplinary charge could be laid against them (see chapter 15).

11   *Queenstown Lakes District Council v Palmer* [1999] 1 NZLR 549.

12   From 1 October 2008, Injury Prevention, Rehabilitation, and Compensation Act 2001, section 21B provides cover for work-related mental injury.

13   Injury Prevention, Rehabilitation, and Compensation Act 2001, section 319.

14   Health Practitioner's Competence Assurance Act 2003, section 100(1)(a).

All four elements must be proved on the balance of probabilities before negligence is proved, and it is up to the injured person (the plaintiff) to prove these elements, not the other party to disprove her/him. If the plaintiff fails to prove any one of these elements then the claim of negligence will fail. This means the plaintiff must do the work to prove that each of the elements of the defendant's negligence was more probable than not. The degree of probability needed will depend on the seriousness of the allegations and the consequences of proving them.[15]

8.4 Elements of negligence — duty of care

The "snail in a bottle case" clarifies the concept of "duty of care".

Case
Donoghue v Stevenson [1932] AC 562 (HL)
A woman's companion bought her a bottle of ginger beer and poured it out for her. The ginger beer contained the decomposing remains of a snail, which caused the woman both physical and mental harm, severe enough for her to sue the manufacturer of the drink.

This was a landmark case in establishing the modern definition of duty of care. The woman issued a writ, alleging negligence against the manufacturers, but they responded with a demurrer (a claim that the facts did not give rise to any action in law). This was because under law one could only have a duty of care in certain specific relationships, such as master and servant, parent and child, or carrier of goods or people. A manufacturer had no personal obligation to someone who bought their goods unless there was one of these special relationships, or a contract between the manufacturer and the purchaser. In this case, no such relationship or contract existed — any agreement had been between the retailer and the person who bought the drink. However, so many people had been harmed by faulty goods that they had purchased and not had redress at law that it was widely believed that it was time to change the law. The *Donoghue v Stevenson* case was in fact very important.

The trial Judge ruled that there was no case to answer, so the woman appealed to a higher Court. The case was taken, after further appeal, to the House of Lords, who in their ruling made a strong legal statement that changed the course of the law, and is influential even today. This ruling set out a new principle of negligence. The Law Lords established that the manufacturer of goods had a duty of care to all foreseeable users of his goods, whether they personally bought the goods from the manufacturer or not. The consequences of the case were more far-reaching than that. One of the Judges, Lord Atkin, in his judgment, stated what has become known as the "neighbour test":[16]

> "The rule that you are to love your neighbour becomes in law, you must not injure your neighbour; and the lawyer's question — 'Who is my neighbour?' — receives a restricted reply. You must take reasonable care to avoid acts or omissions which you can reasonably foresee would be likely to injure your neighbour. Who, then, in law is my neighbour? The answer seems to be — persons who are so closely and directly affected by my act that I ought reasonably to have them in contemplation as being

---

15   *Z v Dental Complaints Assessment Committee* [2009] 1 NZLR 1.
16   *Donoghue v Stevenson* [1932] AC 562, 580.

so affected when I am directing my mind to the acts or omissions which are called in question."

This test of "who is my neighbour?" was formally adopted in a later decision.

Case

Dorset Yacht Co v Home Office [1970] AC 1004 (HL)

Some young Borstal inmates, who escaped from a camp, damaged vessels from a nearby yacht club in their attempt to get away. The yacht club sued the Home Office, which was responsible for the Borstal.

The Home Office argued that, among other things, one cannot be held responsible for the acts of another who is of full age and capacity, and who is not one's servant or acting on one's behalf. The Court (again the House of Lords) rejected this. It held that it was not the action of the boys that was the negligence in question, but the failure of the officers to supervise them adequately. The issue was not the foreseeability of the harm resulting from a third person's acts, but the foreseeability of the consequences of one's own acts or omissions. The Home Office was found negligent. Lord Reid expressed the Court's view of the "neighbour test" thus:[17]

> "[Lately] … there has been a steady trend towards regarding the law of negligence as depending on principle so that, when a new point emerges, one should ask not whether it is covered by authority but whether recognised principles apply to it. *Donoghue v Stevenson* may be regarded as a milestone, and the well-known passage in Lord Atkin's speech should I think be regarded as a statement of principle. It is not to be treated as if it were a statutory definition. It will require qualification in new circumstances. But I think that the time has come when we can and should say that it ought to apply unless there is some justification or valid explanation for its exclusion."

The New Zealand Courts have endorsed this and the "neighbour" principal has become a cornerstone of the modern law of negligence.

The ramifications of both these cases are important for health practitioners. Health practitioners owe a "duty of care" to consumers because of the consumers' dependence on them for their physical and mental care and wellbeing. Thus, health practitioners must take reasonable care to avoid acts or omissions that would be likely to harm any consumer they ought reasonably to foresee as being so harmed by their conduct or omissions. If they fail to do this, they are negligent. If the health practitioner's act has been grossly negligent and as a result someone has died, a prosecution could be brought in the criminal Courts for manslaughter.[18]

Not only do practitioners have a duty of care to a consumer who is directly in their care leading to responsibility for their actions towards that person, but in some cases they may also have a duty of care to people of whose existence they may not even know, and so be responsible for the harm caused to third persons (see discussion on duty of care to third persons at 8.4.4 and nervous shock claims at 8.4.5).

---

17   *Dorset Yacht Co v Home Office* [1970] AC 1004, 1026-1027.
18   Criminal negligence is dealt with in chapter 16.

8.4.1 Proving duty of care

To limit those situations where a person may be found liable, within the bounds of justice and reason, the first requirement for establishing that liability exists for any action or omission under law is to prove that the defendant (for example, a health practitioner) owed a duty of care to the plaintiff (for example, a consumer). To do this, the plaintiff must prove that a reasonable person in the defendant's position would have foreseen the probable harm occurring to someone in the plaintiff's situation: that is, it would have been reasonable to foresee probable harm like this occurring to a person by carrying out the action in question, carelessly or at all.

It is also important to note that the harm foreseeable is to be probable, not possible. There is a recorded case of a person who regularly took a shortcut through a graveyard, being killed by an old tombstone that happened to fall on him just as he was passing beneath. While it was possible for the local council to reasonably foresee this might happen, it was not reasonably foreseeable that this would probably happen; we are expected by law to anticipate only the probable — something that has a significant probability factor.

As a generalisation the reasonable practitioner should use cautious common sense when considering whether a risk is worth avoiding in the particular circumstances that exist at the time. It must be remembered that health practitioners are recognised by law as being involved in busy schedules, emotionally and physically tiring work, and should, both because of that and despite it, act in the most effective, efficient, and harmless way that they reasonably can under the circumstances. With this in mind, and as far as they can reasonably foresee, health practitioners should guard against probable harm that could occur as a result of their actions. They do not have to take precautions against every remotely possible danger.

8.4.2 Duty of care is a question of law

Prima facie, protection from negligence seems to be limitless and undefined: no specific harm or interest need be involved. By allowing compensation for anyone who suffers harm from another's actions, we would certainly stifle initiative and suppress our avowed social policy of individualistic private enterprise. People would be either too frightened to do anything, or be required to pay compensation for any and every harm they caused. Therefore, the primary concern with negligence cases has been to limit claims by containing them within reasonable levels.

This gives the Judge, or whoever in a case decides whether an activity in question is within the bounds of the defendant's duty of care, the power to decide whether policy reasons should limit the duty of care being owed. Thus, even where the defendant's behaviour has been below a reasonable standard, and the activity has caused great harm to the plaintiff, there will be no negligence if it is found that a duty of care did not exist. Establishing whether a duty of care exists becomes all-important. If the test of foreseeability were simply applied, it would be no more than just having to determine whether a defendant breached her or his duty of care by acting unreasonably in the situation being considered. However, considerations of public policy have done much to limit the groups or classes of people to whom one owes a duty of care.

It would seem that although reasonable foresight of risk is a necessary condition for duty of care, it is not a sufficient one, nor does it automatically attract a duty of care. Anticipation of danger to others is a very useful test, but policy considerations involving many factors, such as history, morals, justice, convenience, and social practice have influenced judicial decisions with regard to the presence of duty of care.

There is no sure way to know exactly which activities give rise to a duty of care and which do not. All that can be done is to make educated guesses based on precedent (cases that have gone before) and reasoning from what the Judges have said. From this the practitioner must decide as best she or he can what is likely to apply to the situation at hand.

8.4.3 When a duty of care arises

It can be said that a duty of care will probably arise either when the reasonable person would become aware of potential harm to another from her or his activities, or when one accepts the care of another, whichever applies in the circumstances.

Case
Albrighton v Royal Prince Alfred Hospital [1980] 2 NSWLR 542 (NSW CA)

The consumer suffered from kypho-scoliosis and spina bifida from birth, and had a large hairy naevus on her lower back. She was admitted to hospital at age 15 for corrective surgery on her spine, and for possible halo-pelvic traction for straightening and lengthening it. Due to the hairy naevus, there was a recognised danger of "tethering" of the spinal cord (adherence to surrounding tissue) and consequent damage to the cord resulting in paraplegia from the traction. In fact, traction was applied and paraplegia resulted. She sued in negligence, but the question was, who was liable? A neurosurgeon was involved in the case, who had been asked to see the consumer to advise on traction, but who had not done so by the time the damage occurred.

There was not much evidence of what had happened to cause this unfortunate result. However, the medical records showed that the orthopaedic surgeon had written a consultation request to the neurosurgeon, who had received it and written in the consumer's medical notes: "As she has had (just) [sic] traction I will see her next week." (In fact, traction did not occur until 2 days later.) The Court held that although the neurosurgeon had not seen her, he both knew of the potential danger and had accepted the consumer into his care; therefore a duty of care existed.

8.4.4 Duty of care to third persons

A duty of care is owed not only to consumers and clients, but to any others whose personal wellbeing and property may be harmed by failure to take care.

Thus, care should be taken with a consumer who shows a tendency towards self-harm.

Case
Pallister v Waikato Hospital Board [1975] 2 NZLR 725 (CA)

A consumer being treated for suicidal tendencies was confined in a room. The door was left open for ventilation and in the hope the consumer would learn to cope with freedom of movement. He left the room and jumped from a window, killing himself. His widow sued the hospital in negligence.

The Court held that the hospital had breached its duty of care.[19]

A duty might be owed to people who would foreseeably be injured by potentially dangerous individuals. In such cases this duty would extend to ensuring they are properly supervised and cared for to prevent them from harming others and not carelessly allowed to leave an institution. In such cases, however, public policy considerations have limited the extent of the duty of care to those whom it is reasonably foreseeable would be harmed by the careless discharge of a potentially dangerous inpatient.

Case

Van der Wetering v Capital Coast Health 19/5/00, Master Thomson, HC Wellington CP368/98

A client of Capital Coast Health mental health services, who was a voluntary patient, was discharged on 26 February 1996. The patient carried out what has come to be known as the Raurimu massacre, killing his father and three others on 8 February 1997 and injuring others. The relatives of some of those killed and one of the wounded claimed that the defendant health services owed a duty of care to the public to take steps to protect them from the patient concerned.

The Court held that to impose a duty of care on the defendant in such circumstances would create "liability in an indeterminate amount for an indeterminate time to an indeterminate class" and also found that policy considerations applied, which meant that no legal duty of care should be imposed on the health service providers.

These same policy considerations were also found to apply in a subsequent case that initially came before the Master in the High Court.

Case

Maulolo & Ors v Hutt Valley Health Corp Ltd [2002] NZAR 375[20]

Leslie Parr was a client of Hutt Valley Health mental health services, and around 29 March 1996 he was discharged into the community. He met and became involved with a Fiona Maulolo. A little over a year after his discharge he killed her in horrific circumstances. He was charged with her murder, but found not guilty on the grounds of insanity. The deceased's children and brothers and a niece claimed that the defendant health services owed a duty of care to them, as they knew or ought to have known that Parr was a risk to them "being persons who would suffer distress and nervous shock if Parr were to murder Fiona and deal with her body in a bizarre manner".

---

19   The staff were on notice that special care was reasonable in these circumstances. Today, it is likely that the staff and the hospital would also be in breach of the consumer's rights under the Health and Disability Services Code of Consumers' Rights.

20   In the High Court, Masters, now known as Associate Judges, have jurisdiction to deal with preliminary matters in most civil proceedings. Their decisions can be reviewed by the High Court as happened in this case brought by the plaintiffs on appeal from Master Thomson's decision in *Re P [mental health]* (2001) 21 FRNZ 174.

The Court held that foreseeability of harm to the plaintiffs is not enough to found a duty of care to them. They must show "proximity" or a close relationship with the defendant in order to justify the imposition of a legal duty of care on them. There is no duty to prevent one person from causing deliberate harm to another unless there is a close and direct relationship and a right to control the actions of the person causing the harm. In this case, there was no evidence that the mental health services knew the plaintiffs or even the deceased. Also, there was no evidence that the mental health service knew Parr was a danger to any particular person as he had not expressed an intention to kill or injure the deceased. The same policy considerations considered in *Van der Wetering* and applied at the first instance hearing of the *Maulolo* case, reported as *Re P*,[21] were held to apply. These policy considerations are set out in the first instance judgment:

(a)   An intolerable burden would be placed on clinicians to divert attention away from focussing on the best interests of their patients, towards [cautious] self-protection, especially where patients can only be compelled to have treatment under the Act;

(b)   Clinicians would be overly cautious in issuing certificates for assessment and treatment under the Act;

(c)   Similar policy considerations were determinative in *Hill v Chief Constable of West Yorkshire* [1988] 2 All ER 238 (the *Yorkshire Ripper case*); *A-G v Prince and Gardner*;[22]

(d)   The far reaching scope and the inappropriateness of an unlimited duty; see Cooke P's comment in *South Pacific Manufacturing Co Ltd v NZ Security Consultants & Investigations Ltd* [1992] 2 NZLR 282 — "liability in an indeterminate amount for an indeterminate time to an indeterminate class".[23]

The matter may well be different if, for example the mental health services had been warned that a client was a potential risk to a particular person in his family and the deceased and her family were known to the mental health service. For example:

Inquiry

By the Health and Disability Commissioner into the Quality of Care provided to Mr Mark Burton

Southland District Health Board Mental Health Services February — March 2001, A Report by the Health and Disability Commissioner

Mark Burton was an inpatient of Southland District Health Board ("SDHB") mental health services and was being treated for relapse of a schizophrenic illness. Early on in his admission, his father wrote to the service expressing his concern that Mark had paranoid thoughts about his mother and his belief that "Mark is a real danger should he be discharged while still holding such views and that he could cause death or serious injury within the family home". He requested that particular note be taken of his concern as to Mark's mother's safety if Mark returned to the family home.

---

21   *Re P [mental health]* (2001) 21 FRNZ 174 appealed to the High Court on review where it is reported as *Maulolo & Ors v Hutt Valley Health Corp Ltd* [2002] NZAR 375.

22   *A-G v Prince* (1998) 1 NZLR 262.

23   Per Master Thomson in *Re P [mental health] (2001)* 21 FRNZ 174 applying the policy considerations he applied in *Van der Wetering*.

Mr Burton was discharged on a Friday morning to live in a flat in Invercargill, but that night he drove to his family home in Queenstown and killed his mother. He was charged with her murder and found not guilty on the grounds of insanity.

The Health and Disability Commissioner found SDHB and a number of the health practitioners had breached Mark Burton's rights under the Health and Disability Code.[24] However the Commissioner's role is limited to considering rights owed to consumers; he did not determine whether the DHB or the health practitioners owed a duty of care to Mr Burton's family. To date it appears no civil claim has been brought in the Courts.[25]

A recent decision of the Supreme Court has confirmed that the question of whether or not a duty of care exists in a particular situation will depend on all the circumstances of the case.

Case

Couch v Attorney-General [2008] NZSC 45

The plaintiff, Ms Couch, was seriously injured by William Bell when he robbed the Returned Services Association where she worked. Three other people, fellow employees of Ms Couch, were killed. Bell was convicted of their murders and the attempted murder of Ms Couch. At the time of the robbery, Bell was on parole after his release from prison having served two-thirds of a sentence of 5 years' imprisonment for the aggravated robbery of a petrol station. It was not suggested that the RSA knew that Bell was on parole when he was placed there for work experience. Ms Couch claimed exemplary damages against the Attorney-General for what, on her contention, amounted to grossly deficient supervision of Bell by the Probation Service of the Department of Corrections and the probation officer responsible for his supervision. Ms Couch said that her injuries would not have occurred if the Probation Service and the probation officer supervising Bell had acted with the standard of care reasonably to be expected of those with statutory obligations to supervise a known violent offender who had been assessed by the Probation Service psychologists as having a high risk of reoffending. The Attorney-General accepted that the Probation Services supervision of Bell was deficient but argued that her claim could not succeed because the Probation Service and its officer did not owe a duty of care to her. It asked the Court to strike Mrs Couch's claim out without having a full hearing.

The Supreme Court was not prepared to strike out Mrs Couch's claim. It held that whether the Probation Service may owe a duty of care to the victim of a criminal assault by a parolee under its supervision is not resolved by New Zealand authority. The majority of the Court (split 3/2) held that a duty of care would exist if, but only if, the plaintiff, either individually or as a member of "an identifiable and sufficiently delineated class" was known to the

---

24   Following findings by the Health and Disability Commissioner of breaches of Mark Burton's rights, the Director of Proceedings investigated the matter and commenced proceedings in the Human Rights Tribunal against SDHB for a breach of Mark Burton's rights. The Director of Proceedings also laid charges with the Medical Practitioners Disciplinary Tribunal against two medical practitioners. A Medical Officer of Special Scale who treated Mark Burton was charged with disgraceful conduct, but the Medical Practitioners Disciplinary Tribunal found him guilty of a lesser charge — that of professional misconduct. The other medical practitioner was found not guilty of professional misconduct. Disciplinary charges were also laid against a nurse, but were subsequently withdrawn by the Director of Proceedings.

25   In some cases in New Zealand and overseas such claims would not reach the Courts as they are the subject of out-of-court settlements, which are usually confidential.

defendar. · to be subject of "a distinct and special risk". At the time of writing (June 2009) the claim .vas still awaiting a full hearing.

8.4.5   Duty of care to the emotionally involved — nervous shock claims

In some cases where there is found to be a duty of care owed to a third person this gives rise to a claim for damages for nervous shock or mental trauma on the part of that third person. Such a claim is not barred by the ACC scheme except where cover is available because the mental injury is work-related.[26]

The Courts have found a duty of care exists in relation to two classes of victims — primary victims and secondary victims.

A primary victim is one who is psychologically injured by the negligent actions of the defendant, but who might also have been physically injured, for example a car crash victim.

A secondary victim is one who claims mental injury not from their being involved in the car crash but from observing its effect on someone else who was physically injured.

Case

Jaensch v Coffey (1984) 155 CLR 549 (HCA)

A police officer was seriously injured through the negligent driving of the appellant, Mr Jaensch. The police officer's wife was witness to the events at the hospital to which she was called. These involved several critical returns to theatre to repair internal injuries, and seeing her husband in considerable pain. She was told he was pretty bad and was urgently recalled later to intensive care as his condition had deteriorated. At this time she was told he had damaged kidneys and liver. She saw him with "all these tubes coming out of him". She feared her husband would die, and continued to do so for three to four weeks. As a result she suffered severe anxiety and depression, which led to gynaecological problems and a hysterectomy.

In the lower Court the Judge held that the defendant could foresee that his causing of harm to another could result in a wife having to go to the hospital, having to wait anxiously for her husband's recovery, and suffering mental harm as a result. The appeal by Mr Jaensch was disallowed in the Court of Appeal of South Australia, so he appealed to the High Court of Australia. There the original decision was again upheld. The implications of such a finding are clear — where a person can reasonably foresee harm to another, that person will be held by the Courts to also foresee psychological harm that close relatives may suffer as a result.

In order for a secondary victim who suffers nervous shock/mental trauma to succeed in a claim for damages they must also show that they:

•   Have suffered some kind of recognisable psychiatric illness;
•   Have some sort of connection to the person who was physically injured. Some "ties of love and affection"[27] must be proved;
•   Had some kind of connection to the accident or disaster either by being present at the time or seeing its aftermath.

---

26   Injury Prevention, Rehabilitation, and Compensation Act 2001, section 21B.
27   *Alcock v Chief Constable of South Yorkshire* [1992] 1 AC 310.

In England the House of Lords reviewed a series of cases arising out of the one disaster.

Case

Alcock v Chief Constable of South Yorkshire [1992] 1 AC 310 (HL)

Liverpool football fans travelled to Hillsborough Stadium in Sheffield, Yorkshire for an away match. The South Yorkshire police were responsible for policing the stadium, but allowed the fans to continue to enter it even when it became overcrowded. Ninety-five people, mostly Liverpool fans, were crushed to death and over 400 were injured. Relatives and friends of the victims claimed damages for nervous shock from seeing and hearing about the disaster.

The Court held that in order for a duty of care to be owed to the relatives and friends of the victims there had to be a close loving relationship, such as that between spouses or parents and children. No duty of care was found owing to brothers and brothers-in-law of the victims even though they were present at the stadium and saw what happened. The relatives who were found to have close ties of love and affection also needed to have been at the stadium or there in the "immediate aftermath" before it could be said that a duty was owed to them. Watching it on television was not sufficient and nor was seeing their deceased relation in the mortuary afterwards.

The same requirements are needed in New Zealand.

Case

Palmer v Queenstown Lakes District Council; Danes Shotover Rafts Ltd v Palmer [1999] NZLR 549

An American tourist saw his wife drown in a rafting accident in which he was also involved. His close proximity to the defendants, because he was also in the raft, and his ties of love and affection to his wife meant that he was able to make a claim for damages for mental trauma caused by seeing his wife drown.

Without a recognisable psychiatric injury a claim for nervous shock by a secondary victim will not be successful.

Case

Van Soest v Residual Health Management Unit [2000] 1 NZLR 179 (CA)

In 1992 surgeon Keith Ramstead performed operations at Christchurch Hospital on five patients. Four of them died and the fifth claimed she suffered unnecessary shock, distress and pain as a result of the surgeon's negligence. The relatives of the first four patients and the fifth patient herself brought claims against the surgeon and the Residual Health Unit (which accepted responsibility for staff employed by Christchurch Hospital before the major health reforms in 1993). The plaintiffs included allegations that they and their relatives had all suffered mental trauma as a result of the defendants negligence.

The Court held that the next of kin were sufficiently closely connected to the deceased (they were husband and sons), and also said that New Zealand Courts might not require that they must be present at the place of the injury or its aftermath. However, the claim could not succeed because none of the plaintiff's could show that the deaths of their loved ones had caused them to suffer a recognisable psychiatric illness.

8.4.6 Duty of care to the unborn

A duty of care is owed to a foetus, although it is not a legal person and cannot bring an action in law until it is born. Although the harm has been caused before the foetus is a person at law, the right to sue for harm caused before birth becomes exercisable once the foetus does become a person. When one cares for a pregnant woman, one owes a duty of care to her and to the foetus.

Case

Watt v Rama [1972] VR 353 (Vic SC)

A pregnant woman was involved in a car accident in which the other driver was at fault. The child, when born, had obviously suffered some physical harm from the accident. The child sued the driver in negligence.

The issue was whether the negligent driver owed a duty of care to the foetus. The Court held that as there are a significant number of pregnant women in the community and since pregnancy can be reasonably foreseen in others in the general community, not only do drivers have a duty of care to other drivers and passengers, but also to a potential child who may be harmed. This case was referred to in a later English case.

Case

B v Islington Health Authority [1991] 1 All ER 825

The plaintiff's mother had undergone a dilation and curettage. At the time, unknown to her, she was pregnant. She later gave birth to the plaintiff, a baby girl, who suffered numerous physical abnormalities, which impaired her future relationships with men and her earning capacity. She sued the health authority in negligence alleging that her injuries had been caused by the surgery on her mother, and that the staff should have ascertained whether her mother had been pregnant at the time of the operation. The hospital argued that they had no duty of care to the plaintiff, as, at the time the injuries were caused, she was an embryo which (under English law) lacked legal personality.

The issue was that at the time of the operation the plaintiff, by reason of being in utero, according to English law did not have an independent legal personality. Therefore no duty of care could be owed to her, nor could it be said that she suffered injuries. By some tortuous reasoning the Court held that the elements of negligence crystallise at the time of birth, and thus the requirements of negligence were fulfilled. This could be called a legal fiction, as the event causing the harm actually occurred before the duty of care would have arisen. The decision appears to be based on public policy, rather than established legal principle, for the purpose of providing a means by which a child can be compensated for harm before birth caused by another's fault.

In New Zealand, if a foetus is injured antenatal by or under the direction of a registered health professional, then, if the child is born alive but injured, they will have cover under the ACC scheme. Where the child is stillborn as a result of antenatal injury caused by a registered health professional, it might be assumed that the mother who suffers mental trauma, by way of a recognisable psychiatric injury, could sue the negligent health practitioner for damages for nervous shock. However, a Court of Appeal case makes this unlikely.

Case

Harrild v Director of Proceedings [2003] 3 NZLR 289

A mother claimed that the negligent treatment she received from her obstetrician caused the stillbirth of her child in 1997. Through the Director of Proceedings, a claim for compensatory damages was being brought by the mother against the obstetrician in the Human Rights Review Tribunal. Such claims cannot be brought if the claimant would be covered by the ACC scheme.[28] The issue was, therefore, whether an injury to the unborn child is a personal injury to the mother within the meaning of the ACC legislation.

The High Court held that an injury to the unborn child was not a personal injury to the mother. The High Court's view was that the child and the mother were separate people even though the child was inside and connected to its mother. The case was taken on appeal to the Court of Appeal. There a majority decision found that an injury to the child was a personal injury to the mother and that as the child is inside and connected to the mother, the mother and child are one person for the purposes of the ACC legislation. Injury to the child is therefore injury to the mother.

This decision means that a mother will not be able to bring a claim for nervous shock against a registered health professional, who negligently injures and causes the death of her unborn child even though she suffers a recognisable psychiatric injury as a result because she has cover for her personal injury under the ACC scheme. However the child's father could take an action for damages as he would not have cover under the ACC scheme.

A duty of care may even be owed to someone, even before they are conceived, where a health care worker would be reasonably able to foresee harm occurring to a foetus through negligent care of the potential parent. The most common situations that would come under this category of events are the negligent cross-matching of blood leading to disorders of a child later conceived; the negligent giving of x-rays; and negligent genetic counselling.

Case

Kosky v Trustees of the Sisters of Charity [1982] VR 961 (Vic SC)

The plaintiff, who was Rh-negative, had been negligently given Rh-positive blood by the defendant hospital after a car accident. There were no immediate effects, but 8 years later she gave birth to a child suffering from complications due to Rh iso-immunisation and the prematurely-induced birth that it required.[29]

The Court said there was a duty of care to the child, even though it was conceived many years after the initial, subsequently harmful, action.

8.4.7 Duty of care owed to rescuers

The Courts have held that where one negligently causes harm to a person and another is harmed in trying to rescue that person; one may be liable for the harm caused to the rescuer.

---

28   Health and Disability Commissioner Act 1994, section 52(2) prevents claims for compensation for personal injury being brought in the Human Rights Review Tribunal where the personal injury is covered by the ACC legislation.

29   *Kosky v Trustees of the Sisters of Charity* [1982] VR 961, 969, per Tadgell J.

> **Case**
>
> *Chapman v Hearse* (1961) 106 CLR 112 (HCA)
>
> Chapman, driving in bad weather conditions, negligently negotiated a right-hand turn at an intersection. This resulted in a pile-up of cars on the road, with Chapman being thrown onto the road, unconscious. A passerby, Dr Cherry, went to his aid, and was kneeling on the road administering assistance to Chapman. They were on the right side of the road. An oncoming car, also driven negligently, hit and killed Dr Cherry. His widow sued the driver of that car, a Mr Hearse, and Mr Hearse claimed contribution to the damages from Chapman, arguing that his negligence in the first place also contributed to Dr Cherry's death. Chapman argued that, negligent as he was, he did not have a duty of care to his rescuer, Dr Cherry, as he could not have foreseen that he would come to his aid.

The High Court of Australia disagreed with this argument. The Judges held that Chapman should have foreseen that if he drove negligently he might not only harm another, or himself, but also be the author of harm to a third person who came to his aid. The Court approved a US case, *Wagner v International Railway*, where Cardozo J said of this sort of situation:[30]

> "The risk of rescue, if only it be not wanton, is born of the occasion. The emergency begets the man. The wrongdoer may not have foreseen the coming of a deliverer. He is accountable as if he had."

8.4.8 Duty of care owed by rescuers

Health practitioners do not have a duty of care to go to the aid of those injured in an accident. However, if they do, then by their actions they establish a duty of care towards those they assist.[31] Overseas Courts have shown a tendency to be very understanding when dealing with rescuers, recognising that rescuers are to be encouraged. Thus, although the duty of care exists, every consideration is given to factors such as shock to all concerned at the accident, the speed with which decisions have to be made, and the difficult circumstances in which aid has to be rendered. In England, a distinction has been drawn between the duty of care owed by the ambulance service and other emergency services. Once a decision has been made to send an ambulance in response to an emergency call a duty of care is owed to those injured at the scene to ensure it arrives within a reasonable time.[32] In contrast, no duty of care is owed on the part of the fire service.[33]

8.5 Elements of negligence — breach of duty of care

8.5.1 Standard of care

Lord Atkins' "neighbour principle" in *Donoghue v Stevenson* also sets out the standard of care owed by a person who has a duty of care; that is, one of *reasonable* care.[34] A health practitioner does not have to be perfect, but has only to exercise the skill that a reasonable health practitioner in the circumstances would be expected to exercise. This is called the "objective" test — the Court does not look at, for example, the personality or actual

---

30   *Wagner v International Railway* 232 NY Rep 176 (1921), 180.

31   They are also expected to administer care to the standard of a health professional.

32   *Kent v Griffiths* [2000] 2 All ER 474.

33   *Capital & Counties plc v Hampshire CC* [1997] QB 1004.

34   *Donoghue v Stevenson* [1932] AC 562 (see 8.4).

intelligence of practitioner X on the particular day in question, but rather at a hypothetical "reasonable" practitioner in similar circumstances, and considers what they would do. To help it do this, other practitioners who are experienced in the field (called "expert witnesses") are called to give their opinion as to whether the actions in question were in fact reasonable under the circumstances. Standards of care such as protocols and policies and codes of practice will be of assistance in determining what amounts to a reasonable standard of care. However, ultimately, what is "reasonable care" is a decision for the Court.

It is impossible to set out a comprehensive explanation of what is a reasonable standard of care, which will cover every situation in one statement. No two situations are the same, and individual cases must be considered on their merits. The best way to understand is to consider past cases and examples, some of which are given in this chapter. The Health and Disability Commissioner's website contains reports of many of the Commissioner's opinions[35] and those that find a breach of Right 4(1) or (2) of the Code of Health and Disability Services Consumers' Rights are examples of cases where a practitioner has been found to be practising below a reasonable standard of care or has not complied with professional, ethical, and other relevant standards.[36] Likewise, the decisions of the Health Practitioners Disciplinary Tribunal published on its website[37] provide examples of practitioners who have been found guilty of failing to practice at a reasonable standard. However, as the duty to practise a reasonable standard of care covers provision of all health services, whether it is sponging consumers, giving medication, writing reports, or anything else, other chapters cover the standard of care for the particular health service dealt with there.

Case

Spivey v St Thomas' Hospital 31 Tenn App 12; 211 SW 2d 450 (1947)

Jesse Spivey was admitted to St Thomas' Hospital with pneumonia. He was febrile. His bed was on the first floor near a window. During the night, while he was delirious and unaware of his actions, he got out of the window, fell to the ground and, as a result of head injuries caused by the fall, died the next day. The Court was presented with the following facts:

6 pm: On admission, Spivey was delirious, and trying to get out of bed; the window was two or three feet from his bed, and there was conflicting evidence as to whether it was locked.

8.30-9.30 pm: Spivey's brother and friend had been sitting with him and they were told to leave several times between 8.30 and 9.30 pm, despite their request to stay and prevent him getting out of bed.

1 am: He was restless and tossing. Side-rails put on bed, sodium luminal IM was administered.

2.30 am: He was more restless, temp 105.8F, irrational, ankle and wrist restraints and canvas sheet to prevent his getting out of bed. This required two "strong" orderlies and took half an hour. Ten-minute visual checks through glass door panel.

---

35   Available at www.hdc.org.nz/complaints/complaints-intro.

36   Code of Health and Disability Services Consumers' Rights is set out in Appendix 4.

37   www.hpdt.org.nz. See also www.mpdt.org.nz for decisions of the Medical Practitioners Disciplinary Tribunal (one of the forerunners of the HPDT).

> 3.20 am: He was apparently sleeping.
> 3.45 am: He was out of bed, "sitting there looking out in the hall." Assistance called, but by the time it arrived he had fallen out of the window.

When his relatives sued the hospital for negligently causing his death, the Court looked at whether the staff had been unreasonable in not taking more precautions against harm that they could foresee (at least in general terms). It concluded that the failure to secure the window and to keep a closer watch on the consumer in view of his earlier violence was a breach of the nurses' duty of care to the consumer. Their care fell below the standard of care that a reasonable nurse would give.

What is reasonable will depend on the circumstances. It has been held that the use by staff of hot water bottles on a consumer who was anaesthetised, which resulted in burns, was not a dereliction of duty, because, under the circumstances (a very real danger of massive haemorrhage and no other means of heating available) the actions taken were reasonable.[38] Practitioners must weigh the harm that may result against the benefits one may confer, and the Court will look at both what harm could have been reasonably foreseeable by the reasonable health practitioner, and what safeguards a reasonable practitioner would take to prevent harm. Where it is considered that a risk should be taken and the benefits aimed at warrant the risk, the question becomes what measures ought to be taken to minimise any potential harm.

Although they consider evidence from experts as to what is considered reasonable care, Courts do not blindly follow the current practice. They reserve to themselves the right to rule that, although it may be current practice, the accepted procedure may be unreasonable.[39] However, where there is a difference of professional opinion:[40]

> "A judge's 'preference' for one body of distinguished professional opinion to another also professionally distinguished is not sufficient to establish negligence in a practitioner whose actions have received the seal of approval of those whose opinions, truthfully expressed, honestly held, were not preferred."

As long as a method of health service delivery is accepted as reasonable by health practitioners who are experienced and recognised as well qualified in the profession, although some (even a majority) might personally prefer another method, it could be acceptable at law. What is good health service provision is, of course, often open to debate. It would appear that in New Zealand if there is evidence of negligence, then even if the practice accords with a reasonable body of medical opinion it is open for a Court or tribunal to find negligence.[41]

---

38   *McDermott v St Mary's Hospital* 133 A 2d 608 (1957).
39   *Albrighton v Royal Prince Alfred Hospital* [1979] 2 NSWLR 165, where Lord Reynolds said it is incorrect to presume that actions cannot be considered negligence if they are according to the usual and customary practice but procedure is not correct: "it is plainly wrong, because it is not the law that, if all or most of the medical practitioners in Sydney habitually fail to take an available precaution ... then none can be found guilty of negligence."
40   *Maynard v West Midlands Regional Health Authority* [1984] 1 WLR 634. See *Bolam v Friern Hospital Management Committee* [1957] 1 WLR 582, 586 per McNair J: "there may be one or more perfectly proper standards of care and if a doctor conforms to one of those proper standards, then he is not negligent." This *Bolam* principle was rejected in Australia in *Rogers v Whitaker* (1992) 109 ALR 625, and it seems that in New Zealand Courts are of a similar view that if there is evidence of negligence, then even if the practice accords with a reasonable body of medical opinion it is open for a Court or tribunal to find negligence.

One of the reasons for delay in determining many cases is the scope for argument as to whether a particular activity is reasonable or not. When considering the reasonableness of an action, the following factors, among other things, will be taken into account.

8.5.2   Where the event occurred

Those attending an emergency that occurs in a rehabilitation centre, for example, where experience, equipment and preparation are not organised for this, would not be expected to react with the same efficiency as those in an accident and emergency department.

Care given to someone in an emergency is subject to the general principles of negligence law, in that those involved are expected to give reasonable care under the circumstances. Where staff are trained and prepared for emergencies, such as in emergency departments or intensive care, then a high standard of care is required. Where this is not the case, practitioners should at least be able to identify an emergency, and know how to get help. Occupational health practitioners, for example, should be prepared for reasonably foreseeable accidents, and have a plan of action prepared.

In some cases health practitioners may be justified in emergencies in carrying out procedures for which they are not trained or which are normally carried out only by doctors, but if they do, they must act reasonably under the circumstances.

Checklist

Preparation for emergencies

- Health practitioners should be able to identify emergencies and situations that are beyond their resources to handle.
- Health practitioners should be familiar with appropriate policies and procedures to be followed in reasonably foreseeable emergencies.
- A practitioner employed in, for example, occupational health, should obtain an agreement from the employer to prepare for and give emergency care. This ensures it is part of the conditions of employment.
- Health practitioners should ensure proper records of the treatment are kept.[42]

8.5.3   Statutory law

It goes without saying that a breach of statutory provisions is a prima facie (but not absolute) indication of unreasonable practice. The most obvious example here would be the statutory provisions for the administration of medicines (see chapter 10). These are intended, among other things, to protect consumers from harm (for example, provisions for the checking of, and signing for, those medicines that are given). In these provisions the legislation is setting out a general standard of reasonable practice. It is conceivable that breach of

---

41   See *R v Little* 12/6/01 Young J, HC Christchurch T17-01 Dr Little was found guilty of failing to provide the necessaries of life to a consumer who died during a face peel procedure using a product called Exoderm. He was found grossly negligent for not complying with the Australasian and New Zealand College of Anaesthetists guidelines for sedated patients, and for not having adequate resuscitation equipment on hand.

42   These may be rather unorthodox in extreme cases. Meg Wallace, one of the co-authors of the first edition of this book, remembers reading that during an earthquake in Newcastle, New South Wales the labour ward was transferred to the hospital lawn. Records of drug administration and observations were written in felt ink on the consumers' skin.

legislative provisions may not be negligent behaviour (for example, in an emergency or extraordinary situation) so other factors listed here may also be taken into account.

8.5.4 Official protocols and policies

Courts and tribunals and other investigative bodies will also consider procedure manuals, departmental directives, employer policies, and protocols, as evidence of recognised reasonable practice for those in the health care profession. Staff are expected to be aware of workplace policies and procedural checklists etc, and employers should make them available. In providing reasonable care, it is expected that staff would follow such advice, although there may be exceptional circumstances. The health practitioner would have the burden of proving that in those circumstances the actions taken were reasonable. For example, evidence that a practitioner acted contrary to a hospital policy in carrying out post-operative care would be prima facie evidence of negligence, and would place a heavy burden on her/him to convince anyone holding her/him accountable that the circumstances justified the deviation from established procedure.

8.5.5 General knowledge and practice of the profession

When an adverse event happens then a practitioner's practice is looked at through a "retrospectoscope" and it is easy to judge the conduct with the benefit of hindsight. However this is not acceptable in law. In the case below the Court found that no one in the doctor's position could have known of the possibility of seepage, although of course at the time of the trial it was well and truly known. The Court held that the state of knowledge of those involved at the time of the event, not hindsight, is what is considered by law. Therefore, the anaesthetist had not been negligent.

Case

Roe v Minister of Health [1954] 2 QB 66 (Eng CA)

An anaesthetist adopted a practice, developed in 1947, to prevent the danger of infection when administering spinal anaesthesia. This practice was to soak ampoules of the anaesthesia in phenol thereby rendering them sterile for use. On the day in question, he used two of these ampoules to provide two consumers with spinal anaesthesia for knee surgery. Both men subsequently became paraplegic as a result of corrosion of the spinal cord from minute amounts of the antiseptic leaking into the apparently intact ampoules and contaminating the drug.

In some cases, health practitioners may not be able to anticipate a consumer's actions.

Case

Wendover v State 313 NYS 2d 287 (1970)

An obese woman, who had a mental illness and epilepsy, was admitted for her second stay because of a suicide attempt. She was in a private room, but under close supervision. Despite this, and the fact that she was extremely restless, repeatedly letting down the side-rails, she managed to move the bed next to a radiator without staff's knowledge. As a result, she was badly burned when she had an epileptic seizure.

In this case the Court was satisfied that the nurses could not have foreseen the consumer moving her bed, and that there was no way the hospital could have prevented the accident.

169

The Court would have considered the consumer's past behaviour, her mental state, her medical condition, and the general nursing experience in this area to evaluate the reasonableness of the nurses not keeping an even closer watch on her. This case should be compared with that of *Spivey* (see 8.5.1). (Part of legal reasoning is to analyse two similar cases — as these are — and attempt to come to some principle that will reconcile the different outcomes.)

Where there are different accepted practices within the profession, it is recognised by law that a reasonable practitioner may follow any one of them without being held negligent. As long as there is a responsible body of practitioners subscribing to the method used by the defendant in a case and the method is applied according to that body of thought, then, despite the fact that some practitioners would not act in that way, it is open to the Court to find the defendant not liable.[43]

Departure from recognised practice may, as already stated, be indicative of negligence, although not necessarily so. In the case of *Hunter v Hanley* Lord Clyde stated that three things must be established to show negligence when the defendant has departed from recognised practice:[44]

- There is an established and usual practice;
- The defendant departed from that practice;
- No reasonable practitioner would have departed from the practice if they had been acting with ordinary care.

Case

Chasney v Anderson [1950] 4 DLR 223 (SCC)

A surgeon carrying out a tonsillectomy followed a common practice in that hospital of not using sponges with tapes attached to them, nor having nursing staff carry out a sponge count. Sponges with tapes attached were available; as were nursing staff to carry out the count had the surgeon requested this. The child suffocated to death because a sponge was left in situ. The issue was whether the hospital was negligent, and whether the doctor, by following a usual practice there, was also negligent.

In this Canadian case the Court held that the hospital was not negligent because it provided the means for reasonable precautions; the surgeon however was negligent (note that an employer will be liable for knowingly allowing employees to act dangerously — see vicarious liability at 8.7.6.). He had departed from a recognised and available practice for no good reason, despite expert evidence that the practice he adopted was a general one approved at the time. Where the defendant practitioner pleads common practice, the Court will take evidence of this into account as prima facie pointing to reasonable practice, but still could rule that such practice was, at least in the situation being considered, negligent.[45]

8.5.6 Other limiting factors

The condition of the consumer may cause one to act in ways that might otherwise be hazardous.

---

43   *Bolam v Friern Hospital Management Committee* [1957] 1 WLR 582.
44   *Hunter v Hanley* [1955] AC 200, 206.
45   See also *Sidaway v Bethlem Royal Hospital Governors* [1985] AC 871; [1985] 1 All ER 643 (see 6.5.1(7)).

Case

Mahon v Osborne [1939] 2 KB 14 (CA)

A surgeon operated on a young man with a burst Appendix under difficult circumstances: the consumer was having respiratory difficulty, it was 4 am, and there was not the usual number of staff available. After carrying out the surgery, it was revealed that respiratory difficulty was increasing, and the surgeon decided to "close up" as quickly as possible. Before doing so, however, he asked the theatre nurse whether the swab count was correct; she checked and told him it was. The consumer was returned to the ward in a satisfactory condition but some days later became very ill as the result of a pack that had been left inside him. After emergency surgery to remove it, he died. His family sued the surgeon and nurse in negligence (in those days a hospital was held not to be responsible for the actions of staff during surgery).

The plaintiffs argued that, among other things, the nurse was negligent in her counting of the packs and swabs, and the doctor was also negligent in this, as well as being the person responsible for the overall conduct of the surgery. At trial the jury found the doctor (but not the theatre nurse) negligent (there is no explanation as to why the nurse was not found negligent). He appealed, arguing, among other things, that the circumstances of the surgery as explained should have been taken into account in the trial, and that they had not. The Appeal Court agreed, stating that the difficult circumstances of the surgery may well have prevented the surgeon acting in what otherwise would have been a reasonable fashion, and remitted the case for retrial.

8.5.7   Probability of harm

The same statements apply here as were made regarding the foreseeability of the probability of harm. Here we are talking about harm that is foreseeable as likely to happen, but are now looking at the question of how likely it is to happen. A 70 percent chance of side-effects may warrant more drastic precautions than a 10 percent or 15 percent chance. This consideration is closely bound up with the following factors.

(1)   *Person suffering from specific disability*

A person will be held liable for harm that occurred because the victim had a specific disability, of which the person was, or ought to have been, aware. The standard of care will depend on the facts of the situation. The following two cases may assist in explaining this.

Case

Haley v London Electricity Board [1965] AC 778 (HL)

The plaintiff had been blind for many years. He conquered his disability to such an extent that the London County Council employed him. He routinely walked a short distance along the footpath, using a white stick to avoid obstacles, to a spot where he asked someone to assist him to cross the road to where he caught a bus to work. On the morning of the accident Electricity Board workers had dug a trench in the footpath. To prevent harm to pedestrians they placed a punner, which was a stick attached to a weight, across the footpath. The punner was attached to a railing on the inside of the footpath, so it sloped across the footpath from ground level to a height of about two feet. This was not the normal type of barricade used by the board. The plaintiff's stick did not detect the punner, and he tripped over it. As a result of his injuries he became deaf. He sued the Electricity Board in negligence.

The House of Lords held that the Electricity Board should have foreseen that some people using the footpath could be blind. The Board gave evidence that it did cater for blind people in the type of barricade normally used. The Court said it could accept that the Board would not have to take extra precautions if it could not foresee that blind people would be using the footpath at that time, or that the probability was so remote the board would be justified in not taking extra precautions. In this case these considerations did not exist, and the Board should have foreseen the possibility, and so were liable. Consideration of the inability or disability of those who are immature or feeble in mind or body is owed by those who know of, or ought to anticipate, the presence of such persons within the scope and hazard of their own operations.

Health practitioners, who deal with a section of the population that has a higher than average number of people with disabilities, need to be particularly conscious of anticipating their special needs. Where there is no clear indication of a person's disability however, one is not expected to foresee it.

Case

Bourhill v Young [1943] AC 92 (HL)

A woman who was 8-months pregnant heard the sound of a collision between a motorcycle and a car in which the motorcyclist was killed. She was about 45 to 50 feet from the accident and did not see it, but later saw blood on the road. She failed in an action against the motorcyclist's estate for the nervous shock she suffered as a result of the accident, on the grounds that she was not owed a duty of care by him.

The Judges considered whether a person had a duty of care to the public beyond ordinary health or susceptibility, and said that, unless there is knowledge of the disability, such a person cannot expect special treatment if they associate with the general population and suffers inordinately from what, to the general population, would not be a hazard:[46]

> "A blind or deaf man who crosses the traffic on a busy street cannot complain if he is run over by a careful driver who does not know of and could not be expected to observe and guard against the man's infirmity."

(2) *Magnitude of harm*

If a danger is remote but catastrophic if it occurs, more care should be taken than if it were just as remote but not so serious. An example given by the Courts is that of a car approaching a hill on a little used country road. If the car behind it overtakes while approaching the crest of the hill (the driver being unable to see any approaching car), there may be only a remote chance of it meeting another car, but if it does the results could be disastrous. The driver is unjustified in overtaking not so much because of the likelihood of meeting an oncoming car, but the magnitude of the harm if it did happen. This has been expressed in the maxim that the greater the magnitude of the foreseeable harm, the less the probability of its

---

46   *Bourhill v Young* [1943] AC 92, 109-110.

occurring is required before preventative measures are taken.[47] In health, this is an important consideration, which is not often articulated clearly.

(3) Necessity of the action

A dangerous action but one necessary to bring about more good than harm may be accepted as showing that the practitioner was not practising below a reasonable standard of care.

Case

Daborn v Bath Tramways Motor Co Ltd [1946] 2 All ER 333 (Eng CA)

During the Second World War, when London was being bombed, all ambulances that could be found were pressed into service as they were needed to attend to the injured.

Several old left-hand-drive vehicles without direction indicators were used, and because of difficulties in seeing the signalling driver, a bus collided with one of them, causing injury.

The Court held that the plaintiff, the ambulance driver, was not guilty of contributory negligence as the social need for ambulances outweighed the need to have only better equipped vehicles on the road.

8.5.8   Some special situations

(1)   Learners

Generally, the law will give no special consideration to beginners and learners.[48] For example, a student nurse is just as responsible for reasonable care as is the experienced nurse, provided, of course, that they only undertake to practise according to the level of experience to which they belong. Thus, a senior nurse should act as a reasonable senior nurse, a junior nurse as a reasonable junior nurse, and so on.

Case

Collins v Hertfordshire County Council [1947] KB 598 (HC)

A final year medical student was employed as a resident junior house surgeon, despite not being so qualified, because of the demands of wartime. She was asked by the surgeon in charge by telephone to obtain procaine one percent from the hospital pharmacy. She mistook the order to be for *cocaine* one percent and ordered cocaine orally from the pharmacy. It was given to the consumer, who died.

The Court said the junior practitioner had opportunities to consider and correct her mistake, and that she should be held to the standard of a junior house surgeon, as that was the position she held (even though she was not so qualified). This is in accord with the legal principle that if one holds oneself out to have a certain level of skill, or holds a particular position requiring it, one must operate as a reasonable person of the class of practitioners at that level. A junior house surgeon would have known (and in fact the student did know) what a lethal dose of cocaine was, and have followed more stringent measures in executing the surgeon's orders.

---

[47]   In *Welch v Dorrington* [1949] NZLR 871, at 872 Gresson J observed that "[o]ne is not called upon to take the same degree of care in pouring out a drink as in measuring a dose of medicine".

[48]   Principle set down in *Nettleship v Weston* [1971] 2 QB 691 CA, where a learner driver was expected to operate a motor vehicle with the same reasonable skill and care as an experienced driver.

It may be that a District Health Board or other employer will be found negligent for requiring or allowing a person to practise at a level at which they are manifestly not adequately trained or competent. For example, in the Health and Disability Commissioner's Report into Southland District Health Board ("SDHB") Mental Health Services and the care provided to consumer Mark Burton, SDHB was found to have breached Right 4(1) of the Code of Health and Disability Services Consumers' Rights by *failing in its organisational duty of care and skill.*[49] Proper supervision and allocation of responsibilities is a part of the function of an employer offering services to the public.[50]

Failure to provide proper and adequate information may be the basis of a complaint that a practitioner was negligent. This is dealt with in chapter 6 as part of the consideration of consent. What is said there also applies to advice in the form of treatment.

8.5.9 Obligation to question harmful orders

The duty of care owed to consumers by health practitioners includes the obligation to question those directions that they reasonably believe are likely to result in harm to consumers. An unusual medication order, for example, should be checked with the medical practitioner concerned (see chapter 10). This also applies to the failure of others to act where medical direction is believed to be necessary. Junior health practitioners should not adopt the attitude that they are only carrying out orders, and nurses should not blindly follow the directions of a doctor, but should use their knowledge and experience in rendering reasonable care to those who depend on them. This requires that they discuss any direction with which they are dissatisfied with the person concerned. If they are not comfortable with the result, the matter should be taken further.

Case

Darling v Charleston Community Memorial Hospital 211 NE 2d 253 (1965)

The plaintiff was a young man who broke his leg while playing football. He had a comminuted fracture of the right tibia and fibula. The attendant surgeon at the well-equipped and staffed hospital brought the bones into proper alignment and applied a plaster cast without underlying stockinette or padding. The consumer was admitted to a ward of the hospital, where, over a 2-week period, the leg deteriorated, until his family moved him to another hospital where the leg had to be amputated due to infection. The family sued the hospital and treating surgeon in negligence.

Nurses' notes contained repeated notations of increasingly oedematous, darkening, and insensitive toes, and of increasing pain and ineffectiveness of the analgesia that was ordered. The surgeon visited the consumer frequently at the request of the nurses, but did not call an orthopaedic specialist because, in his opinion, the situation was satisfactory. He cut back the plaster cast and removed a section of it to relieve pressure, but inadvertently cut the consumer's skin exacerbating the development of infection.

---

49   Health and Disability Commissioner, *Southland District Health Board Mental Health Services February-March 2001*, published by the Health and Disability Commissioner and available on the Commissioner's website at www.hdc.org.nz.

50   See also Opinion/05HDC11908, the Commissioner's report on the care provided to a consumer at Wellington Public Hospital.

The doctor admitted liability and settled out of Court, so the case proceeded against the hospital. The jury found the hospital liable because of the lack of action on the nurses' part. The hospital appealed, stating that it was not liable for the nurses' conduct because they were under the instructions of the doctor.

The Appeal Court dismissed the appeal. It held that the duty of care of nurses extends further than bringing to the attention of the responsible doctor the deteriorating condition of a consumer. The duty of care of nurses, the Court held, includes informing the hospital management of any departure from normal or proper care that puts a consumer's life or health in danger. The nurses could not say simply: "Well, we told the doctor and reported all unusual developments, we could not do any more." As well as some neglect in their observations and reporting, it said they were negligent in not taking the matter further by reporting it to the next appropriate person on the hospital staff who could take action and so on up the line of authority until they got satisfaction on behalf of the consumer. When the nurses were aware that there was a dangerous impairment to the circulation in the consumer's leg, which would become irreversible in a matter of hours:[51]

> "It became the nurses' duty to inform the attending physician, and if he failed to act, to advise the hospital authorities so that appropriate action might be taken."

Unfortunately, in the past nurses have often been considered the servants of the medical profession by the law, and where they have questioned orders they have been considered to have stepped outside of their role and even dismissed, or been subjected to harassment and even assault. Johnstone gives a detailed study of cases in which nurses have questioned the medical treatment of their consumers.[52]

Below is a checklist of the steps that should be taken for questioning orders according to legal and ethical principles. It is recognised that health practitioners may be unwilling to follow them because of the possibility of reprisals by those who could make their working life difficult (or non-existent).

Checklist

Questioning a superior's orders

- Discuss the matter with the person giving the order; explain your concerns and ask the person to clarify their reasons for the order.
- If the matter is not resolved, inform the person that you intend to discuss the matter with your supervisor or unit manager.
- Inform your supervisor or unit manager, in confidence, and in writing if time allows, of your disagreement with the order, and your reasons.
- If the supervisor or unit manager does not take action, and you still disagree with the order, tell your supervisor or unit manager that you disagree with the order and that you will take the matter yet further (for example, to the service manager or a person who is in an equivalent position). Obviously, the matter is a serious one to have got this far.

51   *Darling v Charleston Community Memorial Hospital* 211 NE 2d 253 (1965), 258. This account is taken from
      I A Murchisonn and T Nichols, *Legal Foundations of Nursing Practice*, London, Macmillan, 1970, 320.
52   M Johnstone, *Nursing and the Injustices of the Law*, Sydney, Saunders, 1994, chapter 6.

- Inform the service manager, again in confidence and in writing. If no satisfaction is gained you might at this stage consider a written application to the clinical director or appropriate body of management. Action at this level would have to be considered carefully, but persistence, courtesy, rationality, and most importantly confidentiality may convince others to listen to you.

8.5.10   The emergency department

Where a hospital operates an emergency department, it has a duty of care to all who pass through its doors, for, unless the contrary is made clear to the public, they are offered treatment there. Once a person's presence is made known to any of the medical staff they have a duty to provide diagnosis and first aid of a reasonable nature, and then to take reasonable care in referring the person for further care (for example to a ward or another doctor) or discharging the person with adequate information to protect him or her from danger.

There are no New Zealand cases directly on this point, but some cases from other jurisdictions can give some direction as to what our law would be. First, one could point to the case of *Barnett v Chelsea & Kensington Hospital Management Committee*,[53] where the Court upheld a doctor's expert opinion that "the duty of a casualty officer is in general to see and examine all patients who come to casualty". The doctor should not rely on the nurse's assessment although they may rely on the triage nurse as to the priority consumers should receive. Triage nurses should be well-trained for determining the severity of a client's condition (see 8.5.10(1)). This may be difficult if a consumer has been drinking, whether or not they appear intoxicated, but especially if a person has not been drinking but staff think they have.

Case

Methodist Hospital v Ball 362 SW 2d 475 (1961)

A 16-year-old boy was admitted to casualty, but was left unattended for 45 minutes. He was then sent, without examination, to another hospital. The doctor did not examine him because he accepted the opinion of several laymen that the boy was drunk. He later died of a ruptured liver, and expert evidence was heard by the Court to the effect that he would have lived if he had been diagnosed promptly.

Secondly, after diagnosis, Courts have held that the consumer should be offered reasonable first aid care.

Case

New Biloxi Hospital v Frazier 146 So 2d 882 (1962)

The consumer was admitted, bleeding heavily from gunshot wounds. Two nurses took his observations and called a doctor, but they did not attempt to stop the bleeding. The doctor attended the man; at that time there was a large pool of blood on the floor and his vital signs were poor. He was transferred to another hospital and died there soon after.

---

53   *Barnett v Chelsea & Kensington Hospital Management Committee* [1968] 1 All ER 1068, 1073 (see 8.7).

The Court found the hospital liable in negligence for the failure of its staff, including the nurses, to keep the consumer there and to offer the care necessary for his wellbeing.

Finally, once the consumer has been stabilised, staff must provide for proper reference to, or information about, after-care.

Case

Niles v City of San Rafael 42 Cal App (3d) 230; 116 Cal R 733 (1974)

A child who had suffered a blow to the head was examined, and after a time allowed to leave. The hospital failed to admit the child, or to give the father a card listing symptoms that would indicate that he should return. The child already had five of the seven symptoms listed on the card.

The hospital was found negligent. The staff had not properly considered the next step in the treatment programme.

The following checklist could really apply to all clients, but is particularly crucial for consumers who wish to leave the emergency department.

Checklist

Considerations when a consumer refuses further services

- Where is the consumer going?
- Does the consumer know how to care for herself/himself?
- Does the consumer know what symptoms indicate the need for further medical attention?
- Does the consumer know how to seek further attention?
- Does the consumer know what complications can occur?
- Does the consumer know how to deal with any complications that do occur?

(1) *Triage nurses*

Triage nurses are specialist nurses required to exercise special skills. If a complaint is made that a triage nurse is negligent, the level of training and expertise will be taken into consideration when deciding what the standard of care should have been. A triage nurse is expected to exercise care to the standard of a reasonable triage nurse of their training and experience. Triage nurses are generally expected to be able to assess a consumer in order to decide how soon that consumer needs to be seen by a doctor. This assessment is based on the taking of a good history, the appearance of the consumer, his or her vital signs, where indicated, and a sound clinical judgment. In some busy hospitals however, the policy is that a triage nurse's assessment is based on the presenting complaint only and any further assessment is carried out by another nurse after a triage category has been allocated. Most hospitals have various categories into which consumers are placed for priority of treatment. Each particular emergency department should have a clear set of categories and a process for training staff and assessing their competence. Hospitals in Australia and New Zealand adopt the Australasian Triage Scale (formerly the National Triage Scale) for categorising consumers by their symptoms as to how long they can wait to see a doctor.[54] This scale uses a number system.[55]

- *Triage category 1 (immediate need to be seen by a doctor):* For example, any immediate threat to life from a breathing airway or circulation problem.
- *Triage category 2 (can wait up to 10 minutes before being seen by a doctor — nursing treatment can be commenced within that 10 minutes):* A serious threat to life, limb, or bodily function for example; a pale, sweaty appearance with a subjectively very high pain rating or unconsciousness; a major chemical eye burn.
- *Triage category 3 (can wait up to 30 minutes before being seen by a doctor — again nursing treatment can be commenced within that time):* May be a potentially life-threatening problem, but one in which the differential diagnosis is unclear, for example subject has high pain rating with behaviour consistent with it to suggest, for example, severe headache, renal colic.
- *Triage category 4 (can wait up to 60 minutes before being seen by a doctor):* For example, a minor head injury with no loss of consciousness; minor limb trauma. Most consumers attending a hospital emergency department are self-referred and will fall into this category.
- *Triage category 5 (can wait up to 120 minutes before being seen by a doctor):* Will be seen by a doctor in the emergency department, but will have up to a 2-hour wait.

These times are recommended maximum waiting times and in some cases when an emergency department is extremely busy, consumers in categories 4 and 5 may find that they are having to wait longer than the recommended times.

(2) *Triage advice by telephone*

In some New Zealand emergency departments, including psychiatric emergency services, there is a practice of triage nurses giving telephone advice to consumers. It is important that any advice given is well documented. Distraught and ill consumers or their family will not necessarily remember instructions clearly and if there is any doubt that instructions might not be followed the consumer should be encouraged to go to the nearest doctor or emergency department. Advice should never be given without making a note of the name of the person requesting it, your name, the time of the call, and what advice was given. Carefully made notes may be important if the triage nurse is subsequently asked to state what advice was given and when.

Where consumers do not fit an established category, assistance should be sought in determining what care to give, and if a person is to be referred elsewhere, the consumer should be given a clear indication of where to go, and assured that they can and should do this. They should also be assured of what to do if their condition worsens. Often communication, particularly in the emergency department, can allay people's fear that they are being ignored and neglected. Assurances that staff are sympathetic, explanations as to why decisions are being made, and clear advice as to how appropriate treatment can be obtained can often mean the difference between whether consumers feel aggrieved or empowered to deal with the situation. For example, if callers are encouraged to delay

---

54   The Australasian College for Emergency Medicine Policy can be found at www.acem.org.au/media/policies_and_guidelines/P06_Aust_Triage_Scale_-_Nov_2000.pdf. Mental health consumers are also triaged using the Best Practice Evidence-Based Guideline issued by the Ministry of Health For The Assessment And Management Of People At Risk Of Suicide.

55   The Manchester Triage System developed in Manchester, England uses colour as an indicator of priority.

treatment until a visit to their GP can be arranged, they should also be reminded to request prompt attention from the receptionist when making that appointment.

(3) *Accidents and other incidents in the emergency department*

Consumers or visitors might suffer harm, faint, or collapse as a result of stress, or what they witness in casualty. Staff should be aware of this possibility and take as many precautions as they reasonably can. This might take the form of, for example, ensuring that if parents are with children receiving treatment such as stitches, they are seated, told they may leave for the duration, or encouraged to speak up if they feel faint. Where parents have been involved in the incident that injured their child but appear unharmed, they may nevertheless be ignoring their own injuries or weakness in their concern for their child. Although the possible situations are infinite, the point must be kept in mind that staff are only human, they cannot be expected to anticipate everything, and they need only act reasonably at the time. Further, the consumer is the person to whom care is to be given, and staff would thus be expected to be concentrating on him or her.

8.6 Elements of negligence — loss or harm

Where loss or harm has occurred and all the elements of a negligence claim are met (duty of care, breach, causation, and loss) monetary "damages" may be awarded. As stated at the beginning of this chapter, no claims can be brought in New Zealand for compensatory damages as a result of personal injury by accident if there is cover under the ACC legislation. If a negligence action is able to be brought against a health practitioner then loss or harm must be proved, no matter how careless the defendant's actions. One can give the wrong drug, fail to record crucial medical information about a consumer, or leave that person unattended when care is required, for example, causing her/him distress, worry, and discomfort. However, if no loss or harm in legal terms has been caused, they can do nothing to obtain compensation for this.[56] Similarly, of course, one cannot bring an action if one has suffered harm but cannot show that it was caused by another's negligence.

Loss or harm may vary from being very minimal to death. In the former case the law will not allow compensation where harm has been so slight or vague that it is considered a waste of the Court's time to pursue it. Previously, no damages were awarded for the death of a person either, as only the person harmed could bring suit (the action dies with the plaintiff). The obvious hardship to a bereaved dependent family was mitigated in the last century by legislation allowing particular close relatives to bring a claim where they can prove negligence, and that they have suffered pecuniary loss from the death of the victim.

8.6.1 Types of loss or harm

There are three types of loss or harm recognised at law.

---

56   Although a practitioner might still be found to have breached the consumer's rights under the Code of Health and Disability Services Consumers' Rights and/or be subject to disciplinary proceedings. In certain circumstances where a practitioner has been found to have breached the Code there is also the possibility of proceedings in the Human Rights Review Tribunal for damages for humiliation, loss of dignity, and injury to the feelings.

(1)   *Physical*

This is self-explanatory. It includes objective harm to the body that is measurable by a change in physical form or function or damage to mental faculties. Physical harm of the same magnitude may have more serious consequences for one person than for another. For example, minor damage to the nerves of the left hand may be of little importance to a right-handed academic, but may be a momentous handicap to a concert pianist or may be significant to a person who plays the piano for pleasure. These people could be harmed economically (the concert pianist) and/or emotionally (all three). It can be difficult to separate these categories.

(2)   *Economic/pecuniary*

The concert pianist could certainly suffer economic damage in the example discussed in 8.6.1(1). The Courts consider the loss of income, both past and future, as well as such things as expenses for medical treatment and replacement and acquisition of property that may be required due to the harm. Expenses such as those incurred in giving the plaintiff holidays from permanent hospitalisation to maintain their morale have been awarded by the Courts.[57]

(3)   *Psychological*

This is where damages may be awarded for nervous shock or mental trauma (see 8.4.5).

8.7   Elements of negligence — causation

There must be a causative link between a defendant's breach and the plaintiff's harm. This can best be illustrated by the following case.

Case
Barnett v Chelsea & Kensington Hospital Management Committee [1968] 1 All ER 1068 (HC)
Barnett and his fellow workers were nightwatchmen. One New Year's Eve they felt very ill after drinking their tea. They went to the local hospital, where the nurse thought they were drunk, but she was pressed to call the doctor. Unfortunately, he also felt sick and left instructions for them to contact their own doctor the next day. They left, but 5 hours later Barnett died. It seems arsenic had been put into the tea. Barnett's widow sued the hospital and the doctor, alleging that he had a duty of care to treat her husband and had failed to discharge this duty, causing his death.

It might seem just that the doctor pays for neglecting the man, but in fact he was not held liable. Let us consider why. First, a close and direct relationship was found between the hospital and the night watchmen, which imposed a duty of care onto the doctor, so he had an obligation to attend to Mr Barnett — the first requirement for proving negligence was fulfilled. A reasonable doctor would have foreseen that failure to see and treat the consumer could result in further harm. The doctor's failure to examine Mr Barnett breached his duty of care, the second requirement for proving negligence was met. However, he escaped liability because the doctor's failure to act was not the cause of Mr Barnett's death. His lawyer was able to convince the Court that, even if he had given Mr Barnett prompt

---

57   *Sharman v Evans* (1977) 138 CLR 563.

treatment it was unlikely that he would have found the cause of the poisoning and administer the antidote in time. Mr Barnett still would have died. All three elements of the negligence action must be proved for it to succeed, and Mrs Barnett had not been able to prove the third element, that of causation.

Another important fact to take from this case is that omissions, or failure to act, can be just as culpable in the eyes of the law as actions.

Case

Wilsher v Essex Area Health Authority [1988] 1 All ER 871 (HL)

A premature neonate suffered almost total blindness while in intensive care. During his time in intensive care a catheter was twice inserted into a vein rather than an artery, and in both cases he was given excess oxygen. The child (through its representatives) sued the hospital in negligence.

Both the trial Judge and the Court of Appeal ruled in favour of the plaintiff, and the defendant appealed to the House of Lords. That Court overturned the earlier decisions on the basis that causation had not been adequately proved. The child could have developed the blindness from several conditions he had suffered, such as patent ductus arteriosus, hypercapnia, intraventricular haemorrhage, and apnoea. Expert witnesses had differed on what had caused the blindness, and the Court was not satisfied that the plaintiff had proved, on the balance of probabilities, that the blindness had been caused by the excessive oxygen. The Court held that where there are a number of possible causes of harm, one of which is the defendant's breach of duty of care, the combination of the breach of duty and the harm is not enough to make them liable. It was not up to the defendant to prove they did *not* cause the harm: the plaintiff must prove that they did. On this basis the Court could not find the defendant negligent.

Case

Hotson v East Berkshire Area Health Authority [1987] 2 All ER 909 (HL)

The plaintiff injured his hip in a fall and was taken to the defendant hospital where they failed to correctly diagnose his injury and he was sent home. After 5 days he had severe pain and returned to the hospital where he was properly diagnosed and given treatment. Subsequently he developed avascular necrosis and sued the Area Health Authority in negligence. The plaintiff claimed that this was caused by the defendant not diagnosing his injury correctly at first instance.

The House of Lords heard expert evidence and decided that, even if the diagnosis had been made promptly, the plaintiff would still have developed the necrosis. The cause was not the failure to diagnose and treat the plaintiff's injury at first presentation to the hospital.

Another instructive case regarding negligence, which also gives good advice regarding coffee breaks and the standard of care to post-operative consumers, is *Laidlaw v Lion's Gate Hospital*.

Case

Laidlaw v Lion's Gate Hospital (1969) 70 WWR 727 (SC)

Cara Laidlaw was admitted to the post-operative room of the hospital after a routine cholecystectomy. There were eight stations in the room and two nurses on duty at the time. When Mrs Laidlaw arrived, Nurse M had left for coffee, and so Nurse S was alone with two consumers, a third arriving in Nurse M's absence before Mrs Laidlaw, and yet another consumer — R — arrived after her. This last consumer was accompanied by an anaesthetist and a nurse who then, it seems, left. Nurse S had interrupted her attentions to each consumer as the next arrived, not finishing their observations. By this time a consumer had left, so Nurse S was caring for four consumers. She left Mrs Laidlaw's observations to administer an injection to R, and after this answered the telephone before returning to Mrs Laidlaw who was in severe respiratory distress and required resuscitation. As a result, she sustained permanent, extensive brain damage.

This case is complex and only some of the nurses' actions are considered here. We will look at what the nurses later said about their behaviour to the Court. The nurses acknowledged that normally it was the practice of the hospital, and their practice, for two nurses to be on duty at all times when the room was in use. However, coffee breaks were taken when things were quiet and the remaining nurse could call on extra help if she needed it. The nurses said they did not expect the consumers to bunch up so rapidly. The Court responded that when five consumers were scheduled for surgery, nurses should be ready to receive them at any time, thus Nurse M should not have gone for coffee; or at least the nurses should have asked for someone to relieve her. Nurse S should have called for assistance, when things got busy. She could also have called on the staff entering the room with the new consumers. In giving their opinion with regard to the standard of care required, medical witnesses spoke in terms of constant and total care, with observation every minute or two, considering the particular vulnerability of post-operative consumers.[58]

These days a different situation may arise in post-operative care rooms. Modern technology provides machinery that automatically monitors vital signs such as blood pressure, pulse, and temperature, either constantly or at intervals, and sounds an alarm if these are abnormal. This means staff do not have to be physically at the bedside of consumers so frequently and can concentrate on other matters. The legal issues have changed as well. What is important from the legal point of view is the reliance one can place on the technology, which is translated into such questions as how reasonable it is to trust these machines, and under what conditions and for how long one can entrust a consumer to them.

8.7.1 When unable to give reasonable care

There may be occasions where a health practitioner feels that because, for example, of lack of staff in the ward, or lack of training or experience, they cannot offer a reasonable standard of care. It is suggested that the best course of action in these circumstances is to notify the directly responsible supervisor.[59] This shifts the legal responsibility of reasonable care to the employer (see chapter 13).

---

58 There is excellent commentary on this case in A Langslow, "The four elements" (1981) 10 (9) Australian Nurses Journal 20. (Langslow divides the causation element in two, listing the requirements for a negligence action as duty, breach of duty, harm, and direct cause, hence the title to her article).

59 Health and Disability Commissioner's Report into care provided to a patient at Wellington Hospital Opinion 05HDC11908, 22/3/07 where staff shortages were a significant factor.

This advice is based on the reasoning that when applying for a position as a health practitioner, applicants should have outlined their experience, preferably in writing, and include any particular lack of it, for example that they have no practical paediatric experience. They should quite clearly confirm the area or areas in which they might be required to work, and if they are likely to be asked to fulfil general duties, any areas where they lack practical experience.

Although an employer may require an applicant for a health practitioner position to carry out any duties as required from time to time, and the applicant may agree to do this, both the employer and the employee cannot relinquish their legal responsibilities to their clients or to each other (see chapter 13), including the:

- Employee's duty to the employer;
- Employer's duty to the consumer;
- Employee's duty to the consumer;
- Employer's duty to the employee.

8.7.2 Employee's duty to the employer

The employee has a duty to tell the employer of her or his experience and competencies, so that they can be appropriately placed for the employer to provide services to the consumer (see chapter 13 on the contract of employment).

8.7.3 Employer's duty to the consumer

The employer has a duty to provide reasonable services, including adequate and competent staff (see also chapter 13).[60]

8.7.4 Employee's duty to the consumer

The employee has a duty to provide reasonable care to the consumer, as outlined in this chapter.

8.7.5 Employer's duty to the employee

The employer has a duty to provide adequate facilities and training so that the employee can provide reasonable care to the client (see also chapter 13).

There is a duty of care on the part of the employer to provide adequate staff. Thus, they must ensure employees are competent but it is the employee's responsibility, as part of the employment contract, to let the employer know whether they have the necessary experience and competence.

When an employee informs the employer of their lack of competence, the employee is invoking the employer's, as well as their own, duty of care to the consumer, and placing on the employer the responsibility of finding, if they believe it is necessary and reasonable, someone else to provide the care for consumers. The employee has taken reasonable steps

---

60   *Wilsher v Essex Area Health Authority* [1988] 1 All ER 871 (HL) provides authority for this primary duty owed to the consumer by the hospital. That a hospital has a duty to provide doctors of sufficient skill and experience to give the treatment offered. This would be extrapolated out to all health practitioners within the hospital's employment.

to ensure proper care if the employer has been adequately and initially informed of their qualifications or lack of them: it is then up to the employer.

If the employer is told that an employee does not feel competent to work in a particular area and does not change the situation, the employer has taken the risk of lack of due care. The employee's responsibilities, in obeying the direction to work under these circumstances, are to give the best care possible in the circumstances, and to make sure that there is adequate evidence of advice to the employer. The employee should make a written report of the situation (an incident report is one effective way),[61] witnessed if possible.

An employee may feel so concerned at being required to work when not adequately experienced that they consider refusing to work under certain conditions. This is not recommended except in extreme cases — for example, where it is quite clear that the wellbeing of consumers is in real danger. In such an event the employer may theoretically resort to dismissal for breach of the contract of employment.[62] The matter could then be taken to the employee's union or professional organisation and an action for reinstatement by the employer instituted.

An alternative, and, it is suggested, a better approach would be to undertake the work as outlined above, and attempt to consult with management, or if that fails, an employee's association, union, or professional organisation, with the possibility of negotiations between that body and employer and improved conditions as a result. If an employee continues working under the unsatisfactory conditions, with documented evidence of having notified the employer, then in any negligence action that follows, provided his or her standard of work has been satisfactory under the circumstances, the employer may be made solely liable. There are some cases in the US and Canada where nurses have needed assistance and have not notified the employer, and they have been found at least partially liable (*Laidlaw*'s case (see 8.7) is an example of this).

Checklist

When you do not feel competent

- Always be courteous and calm and notify any person if you plan to take a matter to your superior.
- Tell your immediate superior of your concern.

If no response and the situation is urgent

- Put your concern in writing in an incident report (get a witness if possible).
- Tell colleagues on the ward, who may be able to advise and assist you.
- Carry out care as carefully as you can.
- Afterwards, write a letter stating that you were required to work when you believed you were not adequately experienced, give the details and send to the administration as soon as possible. Keep a copy.

---

61   Some institutions have highly structured and quite limited incident report forms. This should not deter practitioners from filling them in as best they can, attaching further pages if necessary. Most systems involve regular formal review of such forms by safety committees, quality assurance review committees, etc, so matters such as frequent allocation of insufficiently experienced staff or under-staffing must be addressed at a management level if they are reported as "incidents".

62   See chapter 13.

If no response and the situation is not urgent

- Attempt to take the matter to higher authority where relevant, in the least disruptive and offensive way.
- If no response, put your concerns in writing and send this to the administration.
- See if you can find others similarly concerned and enlist their support.
- Attempt to discuss the matter with senior staff members and administration.
- Record attempts and results in writing.
- If no response, consider taking the matter to your union representative, or employees' association, or professional organisation.

8.7.6 Vicarious liability

Negligence liability is personal — that is, it rests with the individual who caused the harm. There are, however, exceptions to this principle. Where a consumer suffers harm as the result of negligence on the part of an employee, that person may in fact sue the employer, not the individual health practitioner, as an employer is vicariously liable for the negligence of its employees. This also applies to someone who is acting as the agent of another (this is not to be confused with independent contracting, such as agency nursing).

Vicarious liability is based on the principle that you are responsible for the actions of those you engage to do your work for you. It stems from the earlier common law principle of responsibility of a master for his servant. This means that despite the utmost effort on the employer's part to ensure the best care is given to its consumers, and even a lack of knowledge on the employer's part of the negligent activity, so long as the employee is carrying out activities that are part of the employer's enterprise, the employer is responsible for the consumer's welfare.

Where a consumer suffers actionable harm caused by health care employees, that person can complain about both the health care facility (for example, a hospital) and any staff they believe responsible. The hospital is the first in the line of possible defendants for three reasons. First, the hospital or other provider has a duty of care to those who come under its care, and has undertaken to provide the necessary resources. Secondly, a contract may exist between the consumer and a hospital or other provider or health care facility that obliges it to give reasonable care. Finally, the facility is more likely to be able to pay damages to the consumer, because of its financial resources and insurance backing. There is no point suing someone who cannot pay. However, a consumer may choose to sue either, or both, the health practitioner and the hospital, in which case the Court may order respective damages payable by both parties.

The two questions involved in establishing the existence of vicarious liability are:

- Was the person involved an employee or agent at the time they caused the harm?
- Was the harm caused by actions carried out in the course of employment?

8.7.7 Who is an employee?

A person who works for another for pay may be either an employee or an independent contractor (see chapter 13).

Courts have distinguished between health practitioners who have been selected by clients to treat them in a hospital or other institution or clinic, and those selected by the treating body itself. The case of *Albrighton v Royal Prince Alfred Hospital*[63] addressed this issue. There it was held that where the consumer selects the treating health professional, the hospital is not responsible for the negligence of that professional; however, this principle must be qualified by the arrangements under which the professional works; if they are required to abide by hospital rules, standards, and procedures, for example, thereby submitting to some extent to the hospital's control, they may become part of the organisation and the hospital may well be found liable for their negligence. In *Albrighton* the Court considered that because the doctors accepted and complied with the hospital's forms and routines, and had abided by its bylaws, they were employees. A lot depends on the nature of the action that caused the harm: whether it was solely based on the visiting practitioner's professional judgment, over which the hospital may have had no control, or whether it was an action under hospital rules or standards by which the practitioner has agreed to be bound.[64]

8.8 Proof of the elements of a negligence action

When a person is the subject of a negligence action, the plaintiff must prove the four elements; duty of care, breach of that duty, loss, and causation on the balance of probabilities. The defendant may be able to bring evidence to rebut the allegations.

8.8.1 No duty of care

The defendant shows that the requirements for having a duty of care to the plaintiff did not exist. That is, it lacks proximity to the relationship[65] and a reasonable person would not have foreseen the likelihood of harm.

8.8.2 No breach of duty

The defendant admits there was a duty of care, but argues that there was no breach of that duty: all reasonable care was given under the circumstances.

Case

Whitehouse v Jordan [1980] 1 All ER 650 (Eng CA)

An obstetrician applied forceps during a difficult delivery and the child was born severely mentally handicapped. The plaintiff, the mother, claimed he had used undue force in delivering the child, and thus was negligent.

---

63   *Albrighton v Royal Prince Alfred Hospital* [1980] 2 NSWLR 542 (NSW CA) (see 8.4.3): when a duty of care arises.

64   Examples can be found on the Health and Disability Commissioner's website where a number of reports deal with the question of vicarious liability of employers, eg DHBs or rest-home owners for the actions of staff.

65   *Capital & Counties plc v Hampshire CC* [1997] QB 1004, 1035 — expressed in obiter that mere physical proximity between a doctor and a sick person, of itself, created no duty to treat. Another example: *Palmer v Tees HA* [1999] Lloyd's Rep Med 351; [2000] PIQRI; [2000] PNLR 87; [2000] 2LGLR 69 — the plaintiff was abducted and sexually assaulted by a patient being treated by the defendant hospital. It was found that there was not sufficient proximity between the plaintiff and the defendant to impose a duty on the HA.

The doctor was able to adduce evidence, through testimony of his colleagues, that he had not used unreasonable force. The Court accepted this, expressing the view that there is a difference between genuine mistakes and unreasonable behaviour. However, an error of judgement is only a defence if it is made while exercising reasonable care.[66]

Case

Hart v Herron (1984) Aust Torts Reports 80-201 (NSW SC)

The plaintiff sued a psychiatrist in negligence, assault, and battery. He had been given electroconvulsive therapy without his consent. He later became gravely ill with pneumonia. He alleged negligence for the following reasons: (1) he did not require psychiatric treatment at all; (2) proper care was not taken to obtain his informed and valid consent; (3) proper precautions for deep sleep therapy were not taken; and (4) timely diagnosis of pneumonia was not made and proper treatment for it not given. The defendant conceded negligence according to (3) and (4). The question of negligence in relation to (2) is mentioned earlier: see chapter 6 regarding informed consent.

The Court referred to *Whitehouse v Jordan* and applied it to this case. It was held that although the defendant differed in his opinion from another medical practitioner, this did not mean that he had been negligent.[67] However, it was held that so far as (3) was concerned, the fact that Hart was sedated so deeply that he could not be aroused for exercise or use of toilet facilities was backed by evidence that it was a departure from professional practice.

8.8.3 No causation

The defendant here argues that although there was a duty of care, and this was breached, the unreasonable behaviour did not cause the harm.

Case

X v Pal (1991) Aust Torts Reports 81-098 (NSW CA)

A woman who had untreated syphilis gave birth to a child with multiple abnormalities including intellectual disability, epilepsy, and dysmorphia. Two obstetricians and a paediatrician who were treating the mother at the time had failed to test her for syphilis, despite her symptoms. Expert medical evidence indicated that the abnormalities could not have been caused by congenital syphilis, for although it is possible for it to result in intellectual disability, this does not normally become evident until much later in the child's development. Other conditions, such as hepatosplenomegaly, skin rash, jaundice, or periostitis, which would have been pathognomonic[68] of syphilis, were not present, and the abnormalities the child did have were more likely to be the result of intra-uterine developmental abnormality.

---

66   J Manning in Skegg and Patterson et al, *Medical Law in New Zealand*, Wellington, Brookers, 2006, 98.

67   When considering the standard of care to be imposed, the Courts will usually start with the general principle "that the defendant must act in accordance with a practice accepted as proper by a reasonable body of medical men skilled in that particular art". Authority for this principle is found in *Bolam v Friern Hospital Management Committee* [1957] 1 WLR 582. Extended by *Bolitho v City and Hackney Health Authority* [1998] AC 232 (HL): the practice must also withstand logical analysis.

68   Pathognomonic means a sign or symptom that is so characteristic of a disease that it makes the diagnosis.

The Court held that although the child was born with congenital syphilis, many of the abnormalities were not caused by that condition but from another unspecified cause. Damages were limited to the fact that the child was, as a result of the defendants' negligence, born with the disease, and did not cover those abnormalities which the plaintiff could not show were caused by it. The sum awarded was $15,000.

8.8.4 No causation because of an intervening factor (novus actus interveniens)

Sometimes a defendant will concede that they acted negligently, and perhaps even caused some harm or damage, but nevertheless will bring evidence showing that following their negligent act, someone else did something that exacerbated the damage to such an extent that the defendant should not be considered liable. In such a case, the defendant is maintaining that the result of his or her action would have been different if the second person had not changed the course of events with a new intervening act (or novus actus interveniens as it is legally termed) that has broken the chain of causation between the breach of standard by the defendant and the harm or damage to the plaintiff. Negligent health provision can be a novus actus interveniens, but it is considered that where someone has negligently caused harm that necessitates medical treatment, that treatment would have to be *grossly* negligent before a Court would see it as breaking the chain of causation. A way of determining whether an action is a novus actus interveniens, which breaks the chain of causation, can be demonstrated by considering the following hypothetical situation.

> "Jack drives through a red light and injures Mary, who is driving carefully. Mary is taken to hospital and is now recovering. She is given prophylactic antibiotics, to which she develops a reaction, including severe diarrhoea that results in mild dehydration. To counteract this Mary is given parenteral fluids, but the nurse negligently administers the fluids too quickly. Mary develops emphysema and dies."

In this situation, as Mary was on the path to recovery, one could argue that Jack should not be liable for Mary's death — the original action was too remote from the resulting harm. Contrast this with another hypothetical situation.

After originally suffering an injury on a training exercise, a soldier is carried to the first aid centre, dropped several times (causing further injury), and finally given the wrong treatment, dying nevertheless as a result of the initial injury.

In this case the chain of causation has not been broken by the actions of those treating the soldier, as the original harm was still operative at the time of death. An intermediate situation can result where the Court considers that the subsequent acts did not break the chain of events but were contributing factors to the final harm. Liability is shared according to the estimated degree of causation of each act.

Case

Bugden v Harbour View Hospital [1947] 2 DLR 338 (SC)

The plaintiff was treated at the defendant hospital for an injury to his thumb. The doctor decided to set it and asked Nurse Bonnar, an experienced graduate nurse, for some novocaine. Nurse Bonnar asked Nurse Spriggs to get the novocaine. Nurse Spriggs handed Nurse Bonnar a labelled phial. Without looking at the label, Nurse Bonnar handed it to

> the doctor, who, also without checking the label, injected it into Bugden. The drug injected was in fact adrenaline, and Bugden died within an hour.

Each person involved argued that the other was in fact liable, as an intervening factor, but the Court held that the nurses should share the liability. Each nurse owed a duty of care to the consumer, and the subsequent breach of duty by another will not relieve one who has contributed to the harm. The more appropriate defence in this case would have been that of joint liability (see 8.9.4).

8.8.5 No loss

Where the plaintiff cannot prove harm or loss has been suffered a claim will be unsuccessful regardless.[69]

8.9 Other defences

8.9.1 Voluntary assumption of risk

The plaintiff may have knowingly undergone the risk of harm. That is, consent may have been given fully understanding the very risk that has materialised.

Consent may be expressed or implied from the plaintiff's actions and it must be quite clear that they have agreed to bear the risk of injury and so relieve the defendant from any liability for breach of duty of care. Examples would be where the plaintiff knowingly agrees to allow an inexperienced nurse to treat him or her, or participates in, or is a spectator at, a dangerous sport. The plaintiff expects the other person to act reasonably under the accepted circumstances, but cannot complain if those risky circumstances lead to disaster.

8.9.2 Expiration of limitation period

A person who wishes to claim under the ACC legislation must lodge a claim within 12 months of the date on which they incur the personal injury.[70] There is a standard limitation period of 2 years beyond which a civil claim generally cannot be brought for damages for personal injury.[71]

No matter how much harm is suffered, if the claim is not brought within the limitation period, it will not be heard. The limitation period runs not from when the accident happened, but from when the person is reasonably aware there is a problem. This may happen many years after the cause of the harm occurred — in the case of some cancers, for example, 20 to 30 years after the originating event.[72]

---

69   But the negligent practitioner may still be held accountable in different forums; eg Health and Disability Commissioner Investigation, or Health Practitioners Disciplinary Tribunal.

70   Injury Prevention, Rehabilitation, and Compensation Act 2001 section 53. However, ACC cannot decline a claim simply on the basis that it is late, unless the late lodging of the claim prejudices the Corporation's ability to make a decision on the claim.

71   Limitation Act 1950 section 4(7). However, the limitation period can be extended to 6 years with the consent of the defendant or with the leave of the Court.

72   See for example the case of *Pou v British American Tobacco (New Zealand) Ltd* 3/05/06, Lang J, HC Auckland CIV-2002-404-1729. Mrs Pou was diagnosed with lung cancer in 2001 after a lifetime of smoking and subsequently died. Her family sued the cigarette manufacturers alleging breach of a duty to cease manufacturing and selling cigarettes when they became aware of the dangers of smoking and to warn of the dangers of smoking. Although the claim failed on other grounds, the Court held the claim was not barred by the Limitation Act.

Where the plaintiff had no reasonable knowledge of the harm, for example, where the efficacy of treatment was misrepresented, symptoms of the harm were misdiagnosed, or facts were not available, the Courts are empowered to make exceptions to the limitation rules.[73]

The defences discussed above stop further action. There are other arguments that do not negate liability but which, if accepted, may reduce the amount of damages or costs awarded.

8.9.3   Contributory negligence

The defendant argues that the plaintiff, by her or his unreasonable behaviour, contributed to the harm.

Case
Brockman v Harpole 444 P 2d 25 (1968)
A registered nurse working in a doctor's surgery syringed a consumer's ears. His eardrums were punctured, but the nurse was able to show that she was badgered considerably by the consumer who did not want to wait.

The Court in this case held that the nurse did not have to pay full compensation, because the consumer had contributed substantially to his own harm.

8.9.4   Joint liability

The defendant is able to point to another person and show that, through their negligence, they are jointly liable, and should share the cost of compensation, as in *Bugden*'s case (see 8.8.4).

8.10   Damages

Where a claim in negligence has been successful and all the elements have been proved — duty of care, breach, loss, or harm, and causation — and no defences are available to the defendant then a Court will normally award a monetary payment termed damages. There are two recognised sorts of damages that may be sued for, compensatory damages and exemplary damages. Compensatory damages can only be sued for in New Zealand where such an action is not barred by the ACC legislation. Claims for exemplary damages are not ACC-barred.[74]

---

73   The case of *Kosky v Trustees of the Sisters of Charity* [1982] VR 961 involved a pregnant woman who had a routine blood test in 1975. This showed she had Rh iso-immunisation. Her son was born prematurely, and with brain damage. She happened to read a newspaper report some 8 years later about similar effects occurring after the administration of incompatible blood to another woman. She contacted the hospital where she had been treated after a car accident in 1967 to see if she had been given blood. That hospital reported that the wrong blood had been prepared for her, but had not been given. She persisted in her inquiries and found that this advice was a mistake. As she did not have all the information, and could not reasonably have had it within the limitation period, she and her son were allowed to bring the action for an event that occurred 13 years earlier, and 8 years before the son's conception: Dix et al, *Law for the Medical Profession*, Sydney, Butterworths, 1988, 234.

74   Injury Prevention, Rehabilitation and Compensation Act 2001, section 319.

8.10.1　Compensatory damages

Generally, compensatory damages are intended to compensate the victim, and the principle relating to how they are calculated is to place the victim in the same position as if the wrong had not happened to her/him. This, therefore, assumes an unharmed plaintiff so an injured plaintiff is entitled to compensation for all losses they have incurred that are consequent on the injury. Types of loss are pecuniary and non-pecuniary and special and general damages can be awarded.

8.10.2　Pecuniary and non-pecuniary loss

Pecuniary loss is financial loss arising directly from the defendant's action such as medical expenses or loss of earnings. Non-pecuniary loss are intangibles such as pain, distress, humiliation, injury to feelings, loss of expectation of life, loss of enjoyment of life, loss of a limb. Such loss is assessed in monetary terms.

8.10.3　Specific damages

Damages are usually claimed as either specific or general damages. Specific damages are those losses that can be calculated and added up, listed, item by item, with receipts for the amount paid. They include such things as medical expenses, cost of appliances or housing alterations, or specific loss of income through illness. They are generally expenses already incurred.

8.10.4　General damages

General damages are those that are not amenable to accurate assessment, loss or harm such as pain and suffering, anticipated loss of income, and medical expenses. They are necessarily estimates, based on such factors as:

- Actuarial calculations;
- Opinions as to future inflation rates;
- Likelihood of the lifespan of the plaintiff if they had not suffered the injury;
- The plaintiff's ability to earn in future years;
- The probable long-term progression of the plaintiff's condition.

The Court then, in assessing the amount of damages, will consider:

- Payment, past and predicted, for medical care and rehabilitation;
- Cost of amenities for both welfare and general living;
- Loss of earnings incurred up to the normally predicted retiring age;
- Any financial obligations such as family maintenance;
- Whether the claimant has undergone inordinate pain and suffering.

An example of an award of compensatory damages against a health practitioner in New Zealand is *L v Robinson*.

Case

L v Robinson [2000] NZLR 499

Dr Robinson was a psychiatrist who was treating a woman who had a number of psychological illnesses, including a major depressive illness and post traumatic stress

---

disorder. She had been sexually abused as a child and Dr Robinson was treating her with psychotherapy. She claimed both compensatory and exemplary damages against Dr Robinson alleging negligence, that sexual misconduct on his part that breached his duty of care towards her.

Dr Robinson was found to have caused prolonged and severe psychological damage to the plaintiff, which caused her to become suicidal. The Court found that Dr Robinson knew his client was extremely vulnerable to further psychological harm because of her psychiatric history. The Court awarded compensatory damages in the sum of $50,000.

L v Robinson was also the first time in New Zealand that an award of exemplary damages had been made against a health practitioner.

8.10.5 Exemplary damages

The ACC scheme specifically does not bar a claim for exemplary damages[75] and the reason for this is that exemplary damages are not regarded as compensation. Rather, the purpose of exemplary damages is to punish or deter and not to compensate the victim. In *McLaren Transport Ltd v Somerville*, Tipping J said:[76]

> "Despite the suggested inadequacies of the present scheme we have, for better or for worse, in New Zealand a no fault accident compensation scheme. Its purpose is to compensate. It is not, in my judgment, a proper function of the Courts to develop the law of exemplary damages so as to remedy any perceived shortcomings in the statutory scheme. If the scheme is regarded as being inadequate the proper remedy lies elsewhere and not by enlarging the scope of exemplary damages in what could only be an extremely imprecise way."

In *Ellison v L* it was held that while an oral surgeon was negligent in failing to remove packing from the site of a tooth he had extracted, it was not within the sphere of exemplary damages. In delivering the judgment of the Court, Blanchard J said:[77]

> "Exemplary damages are awarded to punish a defendant for high-handed disregard of the rights of a plaintiff or for acting in bad faith or for abusing a public position or behaving in some other outrageous manner which infringes the rights of the plaintiff. Negligence simpliciter will never suffice. We said in *Cable v Robinson* [10/5/96, CA125/95] at page 15:
>
> > 'New Zealand Courts are conservative in their approach to exemplary damages, reserving them for cases of truly outrageous conduct which cannot be adequately punished in any other way. They are awarded only in serious and exceptional cases.' "

In *L v Robinson* (see 8.10.4) exemplary damages were awarded to punish the psychiatrist's conduct in engaging in sexual misconduct with a vulnerable patient in circumstances that the Court described as completely outrageous. The sum of $10,000 was awarded.

The Privy Council has confirmed the availability of and the rationale behind an award of exemplary damages.

---

75   Section 319 of the Injury Prevention, Rehabilitation, and Compensation Act 2001.
76   *McLaren Transport Ltd v Somerville* [1996] 3 NZLR 424, 433.
77   *Ellison v L* [1998] 1 NZLR 416 (CA), 419.

Case

A v Bottrill [2003] 2 NZLR 721; [2003] 1 AC 449

Dr Bottrill was employed as a pathologist and was responsible for reading and reporting on cervical smear slides. Exemplary damages were claimed by Mrs A against him for his alleged misreading of her cervical smears. The High Court dismissed her claim, but a new trial was granted on the basis of new evidence. Dr Bottrill successfully appealed against the granting of a new trial in the Court of Appeal, which held that, as the new evidence did not address the defendant's knowledge, it could not have an important influence on the case. Mrs A appealed to the Privy Council, which in September 2002 overturned the Court of Appeal decision and ordered a retrial in the High Court.

The Court of Appeal had said that exemplary damages can only be awarded if the defendant is subjectively aware of the risk to which his conduct exposes the plaintiff and deliberately or recklessly takes that risk. The Privy Council held that this was incorrect. It went against the rationale behind an award of exemplary damages. It held that:

> "The ultimate touchstone … is that of outrageous conduct by the defendant which calls for punishment."

In some (rare) cases, there need be no subjective awareness on the defendant's part where the conduct of the defendant departs so far and flagrantly from the ordinary professional prudence that it satisfies the "outrageous" test.

Where exemplary damages are awarded, generally the amounts are low. In *Ellison v L*,[78] Blanchard J said:

> "As far as we are aware, Judges in this country have restricted such awards to a mere fraction of the sum claimed … Such awards are not intended as compensation."

In *McLaren Transport Ltd v Somerville*,[79] where apparently gross negligence in inflating a car tyre caused serious injury, $15,000 was awarded. In *L v Robinson* only $10,000 was awarded. The Courts continue to ensure that awards of exemplary damages are moderate.

Case

McDermott v Wallace [2005] 3 NZLR 661

Mr McDermott was badly injured in an air crash near Blenheim. He was a trainee in a light aircraft, undergoing instruction from Mr Wallace. Mr McDermott brought proceedings against Mr Wallace claiming exemplary damages of $75,000. The District Court awarded $50,000 in exemplary damages against Mr Wallace. Mr Wallace appealed to the High Court and the Court overturned the District Court decision. Mr McDermott appealed to the Court of Appeal.

The Court of Appeal restored the District Court decision but reduced the amount of exemplary damages to $20,000. The Court sets out in its judgment a schedule of past awards made in the New Zealand. It considered a "moderate but distinct" award of $20,000 marked out the outrageous behaviour of Mr Wallace.

---

78   *Ellison v L* [1998] 1 NZLR 416 (CA), 419.
79   *McLaren Transport Ltd v Somerville* [1996] 3 NZLR 424.

In determining whether to award exemplary damages and the amount of any such damages, the Court may have regard to whether a penalty has been imposed on the defendant for an offence involving the conduct concerned in the claim for exemplary damages and the nature of any such penalty.[80] In *McDermott* Mr Wallace had been fined $1,500 for breach of the relevant regulations and this was taken into account.

8.10.6   Damages under the Health and Disability Commissioner Act

Damages can be awarded by the Human Rights Review Tribunal where a breach of the Code of Health and Disability Services Consumers' Rights has been found. Claims can be brought through referral by the Health and Disability Commissioner to the Director of Proceedings, or if the Director declines to do so or Commissioner does not refer the matter to her, the aggrieved person can take proceedings herself/himself in the Human Rights Review Tribunal.

The "aggrieved person" is limited to the health consumer.

Case

Marks v Director of Proceedings [2009] 3 NZLR 108

SW died of injuries that he inflicted on himself in an attempt to commit suicide. Dr Marks, a consultant psychiatrist, had been treating him for 8 months previously. On behalf of SW's parents, the Director of Health and Disability Proceedings brought in the Human Rights Review Tribunal a claim under the Health and Disability Commissioner Act 1994 for compensatory damages. Dr Marks applied to the Tribunal to strike out the damages claim, contending that it had no jurisdiction to award damages payable to SW's parents, who were not consumers of his health services. The Tribunal refused to strike out the claim holding that the category of "aggrieved persons" extended beyond direct consumers. Dr Marks asked the High Court to review the decision. The High Court agreed with the Tribunal and held that the legislature plainly intended that rights in respect of breaches of Code should not be confined to health consumers but extended to persons who could show they were "injuriously affected" by the actions of the provider.[81] Dr Marks appealed to the Court of Appeal.

The Court of Appeal held that the meaning of the term "aggrieved person" under the Health and Disability Commissioner Act 1994 had to be ascertained from the Act. From that it followed that only consumers with rights under the Code could be "aggrieved persons". Once a breach of the Code was established, relevant humiliation, injury to feelings and loss of dignity could be inferred from circumstances of breach. The Court of Appeal referred the case back to the Human Rights Review Tribunal for determination in accordance with the judgment.

As long as a person does not have cover for personal injury under the IPRCA, the Human Rights Review Tribunal can award damages for pecuniary loss, loss of any benefit (whether monetary or otherwise), humiliation, loss of dignity and injury to feelings of the aggrieved person, and exemplary damages.

---

80   Injury Prevention, Rehabilitation, and Compensation Act 2001, section 319(3).
81   *Marks v Director of Proceedings* [2008] NZAR 168.

Section 57(1)(d) of the Health and Disability Commissioner Act 1994 provides that an award of exemplary damages can be made for *any action of the defendant that was in flagrant disregard of the rights of the aggrieved person*. This is a wider basis for allowing a claim of exemplary damages than under the current common law. However, in considering claims under this section the Tribunal has applied the principles set down by the Courts regarding exemplary damages. The High Court has agreed that this is the correct approach.[82]

It can be seen that even with the ACC scheme barring claims for compensatory damages in New Zealand Courts, health practitioners can still be held liable for personal injury. Where there is no ACC cover a claim for compensatory damages can be brought in the Court. Claims for exemplary damages can still be brought even if there is ACC cover.

Even where cover under the IPRCA bars a negligence claim for compensatory damages, the negligence may well be a breach of Right 4 of the Code of Health and Disability Services Consumers' Rights.[83] Failure to observe a reasonable standard of care in the circumstances causing injury to a consumer will be treatment injury under the ACC legislation. It will be reported to the appropriate authority (including the practitioner's professional body) for further investigation if ACC considers that there is a risk of public harm.

In conclusion, the following are examples of (generally) nurses' negligence, which may be of interest to illustrate some of the types of conduct that have been considered negligent:[84]

- Bath (ordered by the doctor) too hot: *Periowsky v Freeman* (strong prima facie case of negligence).[85]
- Consumer scalded: *Hillyer v St Bartholomew's Hospital*.[86]
- Hot water bottle allowed to come into contact with the consumer causing severe burns: *Hall v Lees*.[87]
- Tube left in the body: *Morris v Winsbury-White*.[88]
- Swab left in the body: *Fox v Glasgow South Western Hospitals*.[89] A lot of the older cases turned on swabs left in the body: *Dryden v Surrey County Council* (no negligence).[90]
- Swabs not checked: *Crotch v Miles*;[91] *Van Wyck v Lewis*;[92] *Urry v Bierer* (doctor and nurse to blame).[93]
- Failure to ensure instruments correct and sterilised: *Crotch v Miles*.[94]

---

82   *Director of Proceedings v O'Neil* (2000) 6 HRNZ 311; [2001] NZAR 59.
83   Code of Health and Disability Services Consumers' Rights (reproduced in Appendix 4) is in the Schedule to the Health and Disability Commissioner (Code of Health and Disability Services Consumers' Rights) Regulations 1996.
84   These examples have been taken directly from A Samuels, "The legal liability of the nurse: The lawyer's view" (1993) 33(4) *Medicine Science and the Law*, 305.
85   *Periowsky v Freeman* (1866) 4 F & F 977; 176 ER 873.
86   *Hillyer v St Bartholomew's Hospital* [1909] 2 KB 821.
87   *Hall v Lees* [1904] 2 KB 602.
88   *Morris v Winsbury-White* [1937] 4 All ER 494.
89   *Fox v Glasgow South Western Hospitals* [1955] SLT 337.
90   *Dryden v Surrey County Council* [1936] 2 All ER 535.
91   *Crotch v Miles* (1930) BMJ 620.
92   *Van Wyck v Lewis* 1924 ADSA 438 (South Africa).
93   *Urry v Bierer The Times*, 15 July 1955.
94   *Crotch v Miles* (1930) BMJ 620. See also "Doctors, surgeons, and consumers" (1936) 181 LT 247.

- Failure to notice defective equipment or drug or other substance: *Roe v Minister of Health* (though doctor defendant in that case, and no negligence established).[95]
- Excessive quantity of a drug (decicaine) given to a consumer lead to the consumer's death: *Fussell v Beddard* (misunderstanding can arise between doctor and nurse, but the primary responsibility must rest with the doctor).[96]
- Drug administered by a nurse with fatal consequences: *Strangways-Lesmere v Clayton* (nurse misread the written instructions (drachms not ounces), did not check the bed card, and administered a dose that she should have appreciated was excessive; negligence found).[97]
- Extra (34 instead of 30) unauthorised injections of streptomycin administered: *Smith v Brighton and Lewes Hospital Management Committee* (negligence found).[98]
- Rigid catheter was forced into the consumer and perforated an internal organ: *Powell v Streatham Manor Nursing Home* (negligence found).[99]
- Radiology treatment with insufficient protection causing injury to the consumer: *Gold v Essex County Council* (although defendant not a nurse).[100]
- Unskilful ultraviolet ray treatment: *Lavelle v Glasgow Infirmary*.[101]
- Failure to check the true nature of an infection, failure to protect incoming consumers, failure to inform the doctor of the situation: *Lindsey County Council v Marshall* (puerpera fever in maternity home).[102]
- Operating equipment became infected: *Voller v Portsmouth Corp* (breach of antiseptic technique, infected spinal injections, meningitis, and paralysis of both legs).[103]
- Failure to carry out proper monitoring during a Caesarean birth leading to oxygen starvation and cerebral palsy: *Martin v East Yorkshire Health Authority* (liability admitted).[104]
- Plaintiff rushed to hospital with severe chest pains. On the way to the hospital the ambulance was involved in an accident and the consumer was knocked unconscious. At the hospital he was put on a ventilator and a tracheotomy was carried out, inserting a tube directly into his windpipe to keep the air passage open. His heart stopped, depriving the brain of oxygen. The tube was found to be blocked with secretions. The brain was starved of oxygen for 20 minutes. The tube was replaced. However, he suffered another heart attack, and when left in intensive care suffered severe brain damage: *Blackburn-Newcastle Health Authority* (hospital liable).[105]
- Failure of nurse to turn to a senior colleague or a doctor in the event of difficulty: *Bull v Devon Area Health Authority* (negligence).[106] Contacting the doctor and acting on his or her instructions is likely to be sufficient to exonerate the nurse in the casualty

---

95   *Roe v Minister of Health* [1954] 2 QB 66 (Eng CA).

96   *Fussell v Beddard* (1942) 2 BMJ 411.

97   *Strangways-Lesmere v Clayton* [1936] 2 KB 11.

98   *Smith v Brighton and Lewes Hospital Management Committee*, *The Times*, 2 May 1958.

99   *Powell v Streatham Manor Nursing Home* [1935] AC 243.

100   *Gold v Essex County Council* [1942] 2 KB 293.

101   *Lavelle v Glasgow Infirmary* 1930 SC 123; 1931 SC (HL) 34; 1932 SC 247.

102   *Lindsey County Council v Marshall* [1937] AC 97.

103   *Voller v Portsmouth Corp* (1947) 203 LT 264. See also "Infected unsterilized GP equipment", *Sunday Telegraph*, 3 January 1993.

104   *Martin v East Yorkshire Health Authority*, *The Times*, 12 January 1993.

105   *Blackburn-Newcastle Health Authority*, *The Times*, 2 August 1988.

106   *Bull v Devon Area Health Authority* [1993] 4 Med LR 117.

or accident and emergency department, even though the nurse must exercise the care and skill to be expected in a difficult and demanding situation: *Barnett v Chelsea & Kensington Hospital Management Committee* (no negligence).[107]

- Consumer admitted to emergency department with non-specific abdominal pain was given parenteral tramadol but discharged before effect could be properly ascertained. Consumer readmitted within 48 hours suffering from sepsis and requiring ICU. Nurse and doctor liable for not assessing patient properly and a causative link found between this and the consumer's deteriorating condition. Also noted that the clinical notes both by the doctor and nurse were not adequate to show care and discharge information given to consumer: *Wright v WA Country Health Service.*[108]

- Consumer underwent colo-rectal surgery for a tumour and had only one functioning ureter. During the operation damage occurred to this ureter and the doctor was found to have breached the standard of care in not ensuring that he preserved the ureter: *Brown v Simpson.*[109]

- A mental health consumer (S) was raped by another mental health consumer. They were both patients in the same hospital. It was found that the DHB had breached its duty of care to S. A DHB owes a duty of care to each patient/consumer of their health services to prevent any act of violence from another consumer of their services: *S v Midcentral DHB (No 2).*[110]

- A woman was being monitored pre-labour but the baby was born without a heartbeat and eventually died 10 days later. The registrar was found to have breached his duty of care by failing to properly supervise the senior house officer and the midwife, as well as failing to communicate to the consultant the baby's increasing distress pre-birth: *McKenzie v Medical Practitioner's Disciplinary Tribunal.*[111]

- Death of consumer during a diagnostic hysteroscopy from an air embolism. A tube was incorrectly connected to the hysteroscope and nitrogen was pumped into the consumer's uterus causing the air embolism. The nurses assisting had no experience in the use of the hysteroscope — the nurses, doctor and hospital were found liable: *Chin v St Barnabas Medical Centre.*[112]

8.11 Further reading

Skegg and Patterson et al, *Medical Law in New Zealand*, Wellington, Brookers, 2006.

Todd et al, *The Law of Torts in New Zealand* (5th ed), Wellington, Brookers, 2009.

---

107   *Barnett v Chelsea & Kensington Hospital Management Committee* [1968] 1 All ER 1068.
108   *Wright v WA Country Health Service* [2009] WADC 46.
109   *Brown v Simpson* [2008] NSWDC 57.
110   *S v Midcentral DHB (No 2)* [2004] NZAR 342.
111   *McKenzie v Medical Practitioner's Disciplinary Tribunal* [2004] NZAR 47 (HC).
112   *Chin v St Barnabas Medical Center*, 312 NJ Super 81, 711 A 2d 352 (1998).

Chapter 9

HEALTH INFORMATION

KATHRYN DALZIEL AND SUE JOHNSON

Contents

9.1   Introduction

In the course of their work, health practitioners receive and hold large amounts of personal information about consumers and their families. It is important that health practitioners respect the sensitive and personal nature of such information, as the special relationship of confidence and trust between health practitioners and consumers is dependent on how health information is collected and used. Health practitioners need to consider how the information is:

- Collected;
- Disclosed or otherwise used;
- Accessed and corrected by the consumer;
- Stored; and
- For how long it is to be retained.

There are legal and ethical obligations required of health agencies and health practitioners that relate directly to health information. Starting with legal obligations, in New Zealand the Health Information Privacy Code 1994 ("HIPC") and the Health Act 1956 have immediate relevance in the way health information must be managed. Other legislation also has impact, for example the Children, Young Persons, and their Families Act 1989, Evidence Act 2006, Health (Retention of Health Information) Regulations 1996, Medicines Act 1981, Misuse of Drugs Act 1975, and the Official Information Act 1982. There are also Standards in the provision of hospital, residential disability, and rest home care which the Minister of Health has approved under the Health and Disability Services (Safety) Act 2001, including health and disability standards and mental health standards.[1] While these standards are designed to help health agencies in the implementation of the Code of Health and Disability Services Consumers' Rights, they also include protocols for the collection of health information (for example providing private areas), storage and security of health information, accuracy of health information, and disclosure of health information (for example coordinated care/discharge plans).

In terms of ethical responsibilities, the main ethical duty for health practitioners in respect of health information is the duty of confidentiality. As a starting point, health practitioners must protect and hold in strict confidence all information concerning the consumer. Confidential information may be disclosed in limited circumstances and health practitioners should refer to their professional code of ethics, relevant policies and procedures of their health agency, or seek peer review/support if they are not certain.

This chapter covers the collection, disclosure, use and retention of health information as well as the consumers' right to request access and correction of their health information. Under each heading is a discussion of the HIPC, any links to the Privacy Act 1993,[2] and reference to other legal and ethical considerations. This chapter cannot provide an answer to every situation, and it is important that health practitioners consult senior practitioners and/or their employer if they are faced with a health information dilemma.

9.2 Key definitions

The HIPC is a code of practice issued under the Privacy Act 1993. At its core are 12 Rules that apply to health information about identifiable individuals. In some part, these Rules codify what was already accepted as good and ethical practice, and they are useful for determining legal and ethical problems relating to health information. However, these Rules are not the only legislative guides in relation to health information, and health practitioners should be aware that the Rules are subservient to all parliamentary Acts and regulations. If another piece of legislation requires health information to be dealt with in a particular way, then this should be followed despite any apparent conflict with the HIPC.

The HIPC applies to *health agencies*,[3] which include:

- Health and disability service providers;
- A division within an agency which provides health or disability services;
- An approved counsellor or an accredited employer under the Injury Prevention, Rehabilitation, and Compensation Act 2001;
- An agency, including a professional body, for the training, registration, and discipline of health professionals;
- Health insurers;
- An agency providing health information services;
- District inspectors, or official visitors under either the Mental Health (Compulsory Assessment and Treatment) Act 1992; or Intellectual Disability (Compulsory Care and Rehabilitation) Act 2003;

---

1   See NZS 8143:2008 "Health and Disability Services (Core) Standards".

2   For example, the right to access health information is in the HIPC, but the grounds for refusing access to health information are in the Privacy Act 1993 (see also Appendix 3).

3   Note Privacy Act 1993, sections 3, 4 and 126. Health agencies are responsible for the actions of staff, agents, volunteers etc and so staff need to be aware and follow the agencies policies and procedures.

- An agency which manufactures, sells, or supplies medicines, medical devices, or related products;
- An agency which provides health and disability services consumer advocacy services;
- The Department for Courts in relation to documents for the Coroners' Court;
- Ministry of Health, Health Research Council, New Zealand Council on Healthcare Standards, Institute of Environmental Science and Research Limited, The Inter-church Council on Hospital Chaplaincy, Health Benefits Limited, The Mental Health Commission, Accident Compensation Corporation, The Regulator under the Accident Insurance Act 1998 and the Injury Prevention, Rehabilitation and Compensation Act 2001.

The HIPC applies to *health information* about an identifiable individual, including information about:

- A person's health or disabilities;
- A person's medical history;
- Any health or disability service provided to someone;
- A person that is collected while health and disability services are provided to that person;
- A person's participation in any body part or bodily substance donation, including anything derived from the testing or examination of a body part or bodily substance;
- An individual that is collected before or in the course of, and is incidental to the provision of any health or disability service to that individual.

In the provision of health services, it is recognised that consumers need support and both the HIPC and the Health Act 1956 refer to the role of the representative.[4] Under the HIPC the term "representative" is defined as:

- The person's personal representative where the person is dead;
- A parent or guardian where the person is under the age of 16;
- A person appearing to be lawfully acting on the individual's behalf or in their interests, when the person is not in the above categories and is unable to give consent or authority or exercise their rights.

A consumer can also appoint an agent, which should be in writing. This can include an Attorney under a power of attorney or a welfare guardian and/or property manager under the Protection of Personal and Property Rights Act 1988. The Court can also appoint an agent which will extend to lawyer for child under section 7 of the Care of Children Act 2004.

9.3 Collection

9.3.1 The Health Information Privacy Code

The HIPC sets out some of the legal obligations a health agency must consider when collecting health information. The following four Rules are about purpose, openness, and fairness. If a health agency is open about its information handling policies, and conveys these at the time of collection, consumers will know why information is being collected.

---

4   A representative is not automatically entitled to health information about the patient (see 9.4.3, 9.4.6(2), and 9.4.6(4)).

The agency should not have problems when the information is used or disclosed in accordance with those policies.

(1)   *Rule 1*

Health information must be collected only for the lawful and necessary purposes of the health agency.

(2)   *Rule 2*

Health information must be collected from the person concerned, unless the health agency believes on reasonable grounds:

- The individual authorises collection of information from someone else having been made aware of matters set out in Rule 3;
- The individual cannot give their authority and the health agency, having made the individual's representative aware of the matters set out in Rule 3, collects the information from the representative or the representative authorises collection from someone else;
- Compliance would prejudice the interests of the individual concerned, the purposes of collection, or the safety of any individual;
- Compliance is not reasonably practicable in the circumstances of a particular case;
- Collection is for the purpose of assembling family or genetic history of an individual, and information is collected directly from that individual;
- The information is publicly available;
- The information is used in a form in which the individual is not identified, is statistical information, or is research approved by an ethics committee (if necessary);
- Non-compliance is necessary to avoid prejudice to the maintenance of law;
- The Privacy Commissioner has authorised collection.

Emergencies are covered by the exceptions. For example, information may be collected from third parties if the consumer is unconscious, or is unable to give information. If admission information is needed, it may have to be collected from the representative, a family member, or a friend, but later it is wise to check its accuracy with the consumer.[5]

(3)   *Rule 3*

When health information is collected from an individual or from their representative, they must be made aware at the time or as soon as practicable after the collection of the following (unless an exception applies):

- That information is being collected;
- The purpose for which information is being collected;
- The intended recipients of the information;
- The name and address of the health agency collecting the information, and the agency that will hold the information;
- If collection of information is authorised by law, which law authorises it and if the supply of information by that individual is voluntary or mandatory;

---

[5]   See also 9.3.2(2) and 9.6.1(2).

- The consequences for that individual if all or any part of the requested information is not provided;
- The rights of access to and correction of health information provided in Rules 6 and 7.

The exceptions to Rule 3 are where the health agency believes on reasonable grounds:

- Compliance would prejudice the interests of the individual concerned or the purposes of collection;
- Compliance is not reasonably practicable in the circumstances of the particular case;
- Non-compliance is necessary to avoid prejudice to the maintenance of the law.

Rule 3 encourages openness at the point of collection of information. It encourages thinking ahead, so that there is no difficulty in sharing information with members of the clinical team or with family or caregivers. If the individual is informed at the outset about who may receive their information and if the individual consents or accepts that those people may receive information then, no further consent is required.

The Code does not necessarily require the consumer's consent to be obtained before the information can be used or disclosed for the necessary purposes of the agency. What the Code requires is for an agency to identify its "necessary purposes" (which may include disclosure to third parties like referred providers or the Ministry of Health) and to notify consumers about that necessary use of their health information. Further, Rule 3 has different requirements from the ethical and legal obligation to obtain informed consent.[6] Obtaining informed consent by explaining the consequences of a particular treatment may allow the procedure to happen, but may not necessarily fulfil the obligations under Rule 3 if, for example, the patient is not told where the information is going to be stored and who will have access to it.

Rule 3 requires a genuine attempt to inform, so health agencies need to think about appropriate language that reflects diversity of culture, age, physical or mental disabilities, and reading levels. There are many ways consumers can be informed about purposes, including direct explanations, letters, posters, notices, and pamphlets or brochures. It is not necessary to repeat a recent explanation every time information is collected for the same purpose (Rule 3(3)).

(4) *Rule 4*

Health information must be collected without intrusion to an unreasonable extent on the person's personal affairs, and must be collected lawfully and fairly. Examples of unreasonable, unlawful, or unfair collection may include digitally recording (audio or video) a consumer without consent, collecting information in an overbearing or threatening manner, or asking a consumer to provide personal details in a public area such as a front counter or a hospital bed in a ward. Health agencies need to consider how they ask consumers to provide their personal information, and to have protocols to ensure that consumers are comfortable with the situation.[7]

6　　See chapter 6.

9.3.2 Reports

The most obvious record of the collection of health information is the health report or health file. A health record, report or file contains information relating to assessment, investigations and results, diagnosis, plan of care, prevention, health promotion activities, treatments and medications, patient progress, other support services including referred services, evaluation and review (audit) and follow up.

There are two main purposes for collecting information from consumers and keeping a record of such information:

- A means by which the health team can provide good care for the patient. The records also become a historical account of the consumer's health care for future reference.
- A contemporaneous record of events that have taken place. They are therefore likely to be an accurate account of those events.

Both of these purposes have legal implications. As a means of consumer care, records can be used in legal proceedings to prove or refute a claim against a health practitioner. As a contemporaneous record of events, medical records can be used to enlighten the Court or Tribunal on what care was or was not given, and the condition of the consumer at any particular time. Practitioners should be aware of these uses by the law and should adapt their report writing to these needs.

The Health and Disability Commissioner Code of Health and Disability Services Consumers' Rights includes a right to services of an appropriate standard. The Standards (see 9.1) extend this to include an accurate and confidential record that promotes efficient and effective delivery of treatment and support is maintained for each person receiving the service:[8]

> "I have investigated several situations where such quality services have been jeopardised because standards were either not established or not adhered to. In one case a GP contacted after-hours made no notes about his conversation with a mental health consumer, explaining this was his 'usual practice'. In this case I recommended the GP amend his procedures and record all phone consultations, including information given by consumers."

Recognising the importance of record keeping, the Ministry of Health has prepared a Standard on Health Records (see NZS 8153: 2002 "Health Records"). Health practitioners should refer to this Standard in their record keeping although it is recognised that many health agencies have transferred their record keeping function to computerised electronic management systems (eg Medtech, Profile, MedCen and Housten), which should meet the requirements of the Health Records Standard.

---

7   Lawfully and fairly, will extend to the obligations under the Health and Disability Commissioner Code of Health and Disability Services Consumers' Rights and the Standards (see 9.1). Health practitioners should be familiar with a patient's right to support, the right to effective communication, and the right to be fully informed. The Standards also refer to obligations of physical privacy including separate rooms, adequate screening and private rooms for family meetings.

8   NZGP, November 1999, New Zealand Health and Disability Commissioner (Robyn Stent).

(1)   *Reports should be contemporaneous*

A report made soon after an event is more likely to be accurate, accepted as a true record of events, and admissible as evidence in Court. Also, prompt reporting shows efficiency and suggests honesty. The issue of the lack of contemporaneous notes comes up from time to time during investigations of the Health and Disability Commissioner.[9]

The following is an example of the acceptance of a contemporaneous report in preference to a witness's recollection of events.

Case
R v Adams, *The Times*, 5 November 1981[10]

Dr John Adams was tried for the murder of his patient, Mrs Morrell, who was being nursed at home. Mrs Morrell had been given barbiturates and other drugs, including morphia and heroin (legally permissible). The prosecution argued that combinations of morphia, sedomid, and heroin had been given over time in such quantities as to indicate that they had been given with the intent to kill the deceased, rather than the intent to relieve pain. One of the nurses gave evidence that Dr Adams would visit Mrs Morrell in the evenings about 11 o'clock. At these times Dr Adams would be alone with Mrs Morrell, she said, and would administer drugs in addition to those given and recorded by the nurses. The nurses were unaware of the nature of the drugs — the witness said she could recall giving no drug other than morphia at night. This evidence was damning to Dr Adams' case.

Dr Adams' counsel obtained a copy of the nurse's notes, and questioned her thoroughly on her memory of the events. She did not know at that stage that the notes were available. She swore to the events she had outlined, and no one doubted her honesty or integrity. What counsel was able to show, however, was that her ability to recall accurately was less than perfect. She could recall giving injections, but not the actual doses. The nurse's notes showed that:

* She had indeed given drugs other than morphia to the deceased;
* All injections administered to Mrs Morrell, on previous evenings, including those given by Dr Adams, were recorded;
* Dr Adams' visit on the night in question was recorded, as well as the drugs he had given;
* These were the same drugs and dosages as administered on at least one previous occasion;
* Mrs Morrell's condition had been recorded as "very low" a month before she died.

This evidence must have been crucial in the jury's decision to acquit Dr Adams, for as the doctor's counsel suggested "mistakes of memory can be made" and the nurse would not have recorded the administration of the drugs, or the doctor's visits, unless these events had happened.

---

9   See for example *Re Medical Office in General Practice, Dr B*, Case Note 07HDC01315, and *Re Midwife, Ms B* Case Note 07HDC03243. In both cases the lack of contemporaneous notes lead to the Health and Disability Commissioner casting doubt on the practitioners' recollection of events relating to the enquiry.

10   The discussion here is based on A Langslow, "High drama lay in nurses' notes" (1984) 13(7) Australian Nurses Journal 33.

For this important reason, witnesses may use medical reports to refresh their memories or, as in the case above, challenge the accuracy of others' testimonies. It is reasonable to assume that notes written at the time of the events would be more reliable than notes written later or recalled from memory months or years later at trial.[11]

(2) *Reports should be adequate and accurate*

While not including irrelevant material, reports should be carefully and fully made. As pointed out by one commentator: "Writing in a patient's chart should be taken as seriously as providing quality patient care."[12]

The ideas of accuracy and adequacy are recognised throughout the law on health records. In the Health Records Standard (NZS 8153:202) a key principle of health record documentation is that the health record is an accurate reflection of the interaction between the healthcare provider and the patient. Accordingly it is desirable to have the patent check the record as it is being made. Each entry in the individual clinical record is to be dated, signed (including designation), and to be legible. The obligation of accuracy is also a requirement of Rule 8 of the HIPC.[13]

Failure to report adequately may also constitute negligence, as it undermines the first purpose of record keeping as stated above — assisting good consumer care.[14] A point Greenlaw makes is that charting is a clinical, as well as a clerical, responsibility.[15] All health agencies must have a set of minimal requirements for reporting and means of ascertaining that these are maintained. Adequate time should be allowed on each shift for the making and receiving of reports, as they constitute one of the most important aspects of consumer care.

(3) *Reports should be objective*

Opinions are generally, not accepted in Courts, nor is hearsay. If a health practitioner did not see, hear, feel, smell, or taste something, but wishes to report its occurrence, they should state the source of information in the consumer's notes, for example, that "Mrs Jones claims she fell out of her bed"; or "Mr Api states he was attacked with a knife"; or "Ms Chan complaining of pain … says it has got worse". If the health practitioner thinks the consumer is suffering from shock, they should not say this, but should rather report signs and symptoms such as "Mr Smith is pale, sweating, has a feeble pulse with a blood pressure of 90/40", and add, if the health practitioner wishes, "Query shock" to alert other staff to its possibility. Obviously such reports as "usual day", "good night", "settled", etc are of little use to a Court, and may indicate carelessness on the part of other staff.

---

11   See also *Chan v Complaints Assessment Committee* [2001] DCR 1102 in which Judge Doogue held in the Auckland District Court that the medical practitioner's records were defective, and there was no room for arguing that the deficiencies they had could be remedied by the appellant supplementing them with his personal recollections.

12   J Greenlaw, "Documentation of patient care: An often underestimated responsibility" (1982) 10(3) Law, Medicine and Health Care 125.

13   See 9.6(2).

14   In *Whitree v State of New York* 290 NYS 2d 486 (1968) the defendant doctor did not make notes in the hospital record. The Court said: "It is this careless administrative medical procedure that, in our opinion, militates against adequate medical care."

15   J Greenlaw, "Documentation of patient care: An often underestimated responsibility" (1982) 10(3) Law, Medicine and Health Care 125, 126.

There may be times when opinion is needed. For example, a health practitioner may make a medical diagnosis but there may be other problems that should be addressed. These occasions will give rise to opinion, and it is valid to record this. However, the adequacy of the opinion is something that cannot be judged unless objective basis for the opinion are also expressed. Clinical data will therefore strengthen the statement of opinion. In these reports a health practitioner should be aware of the need to record objective data or clinical observations, as well as the opinions formed on the basis of this information. An indirect consequence of writing out the objective data first is that the opinion is more likely to be an accurate one, as the need to justify it will ensure that it is well considered.

(4)   *Reports should be legible and clear*

The need for clarity and legibility is obvious, and has been addressed to some extent by the development of computerised health information systems. Health practitioners still need to be careful with written records. Health practitioners also need to be careful in the use of abbreviations and popular terms. A health agency must be able to interpret acronyms and abbreviations for patient safety and for patients accessing their medical records.

(5)   *Errors should not be obliterated*

Where a mistake has been made, the mistake should be clearly identified and the correction clearly recorded with the erroneous words. The original record must still be legible and not be deleted. With modern computerised information systems, there is an ability to correct the mistake without deleting the original record. For written records, any correction should be signed or initialled and dated by the person making it, who should be the original report writer.

An additional sheet of paper may be required for the sole purpose of the correction if the record is in chronological order. This should, of course, be signed and dated. A marginal note should be made on the original that the addition has been made, the note also being initialled and dated. With digital records, the correction should be made, following the guides on the system.

A health practitioner should take these steps for the following reasons:

- It is a legal obligation and records must meet the stringent requirements of internal or external audit procedures;[16]
- Consumer safety and care must not be compromised by the alteration of a report;
- Records must meet the evidential requirements of any legal inquiry.[17] Obviously, alterations should not be made to falsify a report, but any detection of an alteration that is not clearly and openly made, no matter how innocent its intention, may lead to a suspicion that the writer intended to mislead. Clarity in establishing when and by whom the correction is made explains precisely what happened and provides evidence of the standard of care given by those concerned.

---

16   See Health Records Standard (8153:2002) which requires that information be recorded in such a way that text cannot be erased. See also Health Network Code of Practice (SNZ HB 8169: 2002) which recognises the principle of system integrity and that health systems/networks are required to ensure the record cannot be altered.

17   See 9.3.2(12).

(6)   Rewriting reports

Reports and charts should never be rewritten later. A similar approach applies to the rewriting of reports when they are untidy, hard to read, or where a health practitioner wishes to change them. Mistakes could be made.[18] Where a report has been rewritten, whether changed or not, the Courts could, where negligence has been alleged, consider the rewriting of a report as evidence of negligence:[19]

> "The value of a patient's medical record is that it is made contemporaneously with the events it documents; the existence of a 'rewrite' policy can call into question the accuracy of every patient record within the institution. If there is additional information which was forgotten at the time the entry was made, it should be included as an addendum …. A 'rewrite' policy reinforces the mistaken notion that charting is a clerical rather than a clinical responsibility."

(7)   Transcribing orders

Treatment orders should not be transcribed into a consumer's notes from the original order. They might be erroneously transcribed, and become the source of mistaken treatment. The consumer's notes should refer the reader to the medications chart, where a doctor has written the order, for example: "Seen by Doctor X: medication ordered as per chart". Staff should at all times refer to the original treatment order before carrying out the order, but transcribed orders may encourage failure to do this. Similarly, it is better not to rewrite a report from a note that has been scribbled on a piece of paper: it should be written straight into the consumer's notes (unless of course the health practitioner is so busy that to do so would endanger the consumer's welfare).

(8)   Integrity of reports

Reports should represent the knowledge of the person in whose name they are written or digitally recorded. The best way of ensuring this is never to write on behalf of another person or to enter data on behalf of another person. The person signing a report vouches for its truth and accuracy. Any evidence, that this was not the case, on even one occasion, will cast doubt on the whole report.

(9)   Hearsay

Under the Evidence Act 2006 a hearsay statement means a statement that was made by a person other than a witness; and is offered in evidence at a proceeding to prove the truth of its contents. Under section 17 of the Act, usually such statements cannot be admitted in Court. However, under section 18 of the Act, a hearsay statement can be admissible if the circumstances relating to the statement provide reasonable assurance that the statement is reliable; and the maker of the statement is unavailable as a witness; or the Judge considers that undue expense or delay would be caused if the maker of the statement were required to be a witness. This has significance in the use of clinical notes in evidence (see below).

---

18   J Greenlaw, "Documentation of patient care: An often underestimated responsibility" (1982) 10(3) Law, Medicine and Health Care 125, 126.

19   Ibid.

(10)   *Clinical reports/notes as evidence*

Generally, when asked to give evidence in Court or in an affidavit,[20] a person is required to give only an account of what was experienced by their senses. Reporting what one was told and asserting the truth of what was said is hearsay evidence and is not usually admissible. Practitioners should not use hearsay in their daily notes (this includes entries on charts and other reports) unless they identify it as such, because hearsay statements may be inaccurate.

Client's clinical notes and clinical records, as third-hand accounts are not first-hand evidence of what occurred at a particular time. Therefore, they would normally come under the hearsay rule in a Court of law. The Court would normally require the writer to swear to their accuracy in fact. However, the Evidence Act does allow the Court to admit business records as evidence.[21] Clinical reports and a client's clinical notes are regarded as business records and so this means that they are admissible in Court and can be sought by one of the parties to be produced as evidence, although issues of privilege and confidentiality may need to be addressed.[22] As they are written at the time of the care or treatment, they are taken to be the most accurate record of what happened at the time.[23] It is up to the Court to decide the usefulness of them.

Case

Albrighton v Royal Prince Alfred Hospital [1979] 2 NSWLR 165; on appeal: *Albrighton v Royal Prince Alfred Hospital* [1980] 2 NSWLR 542 (NSW CA)[24]

In the trial hearing the Judge prevented the plaintiff from tendering all the relevant records. It was argued that at least entries by junior medical staff and nursing staff should not be admitted as evidence. In addition, it was argued that entries that were illegible, unintelligible, heavily abbreviated, equivocal, or ambiguous should be excluded because their weight would be too slight to justify admission.

On appeal, it was held that all available records, no matter by whom they were made, are admissible unless the trial Judge should rule that they were not relevant to the issue, namely to liability or damages for pain and suffering. Hospital records are kept for the information of staff and treating doctors and are not therefore likely to be "repositories of the speculations of the inept." As to whether they were unintelligible etc, the Court held that they could still be admitted because defects could be overcome by oral evidence ("the unintelligible may be explained, the abbreviated may be expanded").[25] If, at the end of the day, some of the text is unintelligible to the jury, it is either harmless and can be disregarded,

---

20   An affidavit is a signed and sworn or affirmed statement made in writing, with the signature witnessed by a barrister and solicitor of the High Court of New Zealand. It must state that it is an affidavit. This means it has the same legal recognition as a statement made in Court under oath. A false statement in an affidavit and a false statement in Court both amount to perjury.

21   Evidence Act 2006, section 19.

22   See 9.4.

23   Reporting by quality assurance committees itself should follow specific guidelines. It should not contain names; attention should be given to the possibility of legal access to the report (although this should not undermine the purposes of quality assurance, such as the improvement of services); and the aim of the report, ie the change of procedures or policy, should be kept in mind.

24   The facts of this case are given at 8.4.3.

25   *Albrighton v Royal Prince Alfred Hospital* [1980] 2 NSWLR 542 (NSW CA), 568.

or if not, it can be corrected in the summing up or addresses of counsel. The jury (or Judge in the absence of a jury) is to determine what weight to place on them.

(11)   *Incident reports, accident and hazard registers*

The incident report is one of the tools used in risk management and quality assurance to ensure a coordinated and planned approach to the quality of consumer care. Serious incidents and accidents in the workplace must be reported in incident reports and in an accident register if it involves an injury. This is a requirement under the Health and Safety in Employment Act 1992. This register is required for compliance with reporting requirements in health and safety legislation, as well as good practice. The Health and Safety in Employment Act 1992 also requires the management of a hazard register to systemically identify and manage hazards in the workplace.[26]

Some incident reports will also be reported in the accident register or hazard register and others will not need to be. The former Health and Disability Commissioner Robyn Stent commented in her report on Canterbury Health "and I note that staff who fail to complete incident reporting forms act in an unprofessional and unethical way."[27]

Any accidents, other incidents, or hazards that are recorded and signed by practitioners are reviewed by the administration. From a legal point of view, where the reports indicate the need for it, the administration is subsequently obliged to take reasonable action, either to deal with any harm already caused, or to prevent future harm occurring. This becomes a matter of reasonable care in its administration of services to consumers as well as other people accessing the facility and provision of a safe and effective working environment for staff. All staff should be made aware of the existence and purpose of incident reports and the accident and hazard registers.

These reports have several uses and are potentially very important legal documents. They:

- Identify practices and work environments that give rise to an unacceptable level of risk of harm to consumers, other people accessing the worksite, and staff (for example, methods and equipment, or lack of it, for lifting consumers);
- Monitor the effectiveness of particular practices or equipment (for example, new staffing arrangements or procedures);
- Assist in satisfactorily dealing with an accident or hazard or unusual occurrence by the provision of information to those who need to know about it (for example, treatment of injuries, repair of equipment);
- Are a means of recording events and conditions (including the condition of an injured person), which can be used in the establishment of, or defence to, legal action (for example, identification of the cause of an accident, and standard of care given to the injured before and after it).

It can be seen that from an administration point of view the incident report is used at several levels to:

- Identify existing or potential problems;

---

26   Section 25(1).
27   Report on Canterbury Health Ltd available on www.hdc.org.nz/files/hdc/publications/other_canterburyreport.pdf, at page 36.

- Provide adequate remedies where these have occurred;
- Monitor the effect of remedies;
- Eliminate unsafe conditions or practices;
- Prevent accident compensation or other insurance claims;
- Prevent and/or protect in lawsuits.

Where an account of an incident or accident or hazard is documented, that document can be used, as can other medical records, to establish the facts for legal purposes. This means the report can provide protection for staff where it shows clearly that care was reasonable, and if the event was due to negligence, it can establish that reasonable steps were taken to remedy any harm caused, thus helping to lessen liability. Honesty and accuracy are advisable, as detection of anything that could indicate attempts to cover up the facts could exacerbate the liability of those concerned, and, if it is serious enough, lead to more serious action.

As these reports and the registers of reports are admissible in Court and accessible by Health and Safety Inspectors, the Health and Disability Commissioner, and Coroners etc, they should neither contain opinion, nor allocate fault. Opinions may indicate a less than reasonable approach on the part of health practitioners, especially if they are wrong, and the allocation of blame may be taken as a confession (even where the one confessing was not in fact negligent).

There is no limit to the content of these registers or reports, although a practitioner should try to record only the information that is relevant to the incident. Some forms may be drawn up in such a way that it appears only a limited amount of information is required. Where a form does not make allowances for a particular event, or give room for all the details to be included, practitioners should add a sheet of paper and include these.

Checklist

What to include in incident reports

Ensure the incident report is legible and includes where necessary:

- Name, designation, and experience of the writer;
- The name of the ward/service in which the incident occurred;
- Particulars of agency/employer;
- Location of place of work and place in it of accident/incident;
- Date and time of incident;
- Details of injured person (name, address, date of birth, gender, occupation or job title, relationship to worksite — consumer, employee, contractor, visitor etc);
- Period of employment of injured person if employee;
- Treatment of injury or any other action taken (for example doctor or relatives called or follow up to treatment required);
- Details of incident/accident (objective, full and accurate (no hearsay unless identified as such) including: what type of accident? how did it happen? what did it involve? was equipment involved (location, number, name of equipment)? which body part was affected? nature of injury? where did it happen?
- Condition of injured person before accident;
- Any investigation so far;
- Witnesses and their contact details;

- Was a significant hazard involved;
- Has any equipment involved been removed or made inoperable (ie hazard is eliminated, isolated, or minimised);
- Name and signature of writer.

(12) *Reporting a serious accident*

Where a serious incident or accident has occurred it is crucial that authorities are notified immediately, not only to provide care for anyone injured, but to comply with the Health and Safety in Employment Act 1992 (reporting of serious harm) and to enable the hospital insurer and solicitor to be contacted. This should be done within hours of the event — by phone at least. Staff involved should consider legal advice as soon as possible for the following reasons:

- There is a difference between the written documented incident report or accident register report and any statement made to a lawyer. The latter may be protected by legal privilege, which means that it would be inadmissible as evidence against the practitioner in any hearing. Thus, staff are advised to avail themselves of legal advice if they are asked to make a statement, or wish to do so, and are in any way concerned that they may be legally implicated by what they say. A free legal consultation may be available at a Citizens Advice Bureau, through a community law centre, or from a union or a professional organisation.
- If the practitioner is an insured independent contractor they can benefit by notifying the insurance company of the occurrence as soon as possible.

Health practitioners should resist attempts to get them to make statements that they do not believe are a true representation of the facts, or to alter their statements. This may be done to prevent unfavourable legal action being brought against the hospital staff.[28]

9.4 Disclosure

Health practitioners are frequently in a position where they hold information that should be kept confidential. There are ethical and legal obligations of confidentiality and it is important to remember that consumers trust health practitioners not to disclose all that they learn in the course of day-to-day care. Accordingly, consumers' health information should not be disclosed as a matter of course and if information is disclosed it should be only information relevant to the situation.

It has been suggested that the purpose of the right to confidentiality is not merely the protection of the special nature of the relationship between health practitioners and consumers, nor the peace of mind and reputation of the consumer, although these are certainly reasons for respecting consumers' privacy. The most important reason, it is argued, is the need to ensure a consumer can disclose facts that may be embarrassing, but are vital for their proper care and treatment.

The ethical obligation of confidentiality is recognised at common law and in equity. In other professions the giving of confidential information (such as the details of a customer's account by a bank) has been held to be a breach of confidence, for which the customer could sue. The Courts have held that in these circumstances confidentiality is required,

---

28   See 9.4.6(1) and n 43 in relation to disclosure to police.

either as an implied term of the contract entered into by the parties, or as the result of the relationship of trust, sometimes termed a "fiduciary relationship." There are similarities with the obligation in the HIPC and in other Acts of Parliament.[29]

9.4.1   What is confidential information?

Disclosures made to another person with the express condition that they be kept secret are, obviously, confidential. However, the practitioner gains a lot of information that is not specifically subject to this condition. Information, no matter how trivial, may be impliedly confidential by reason of the relationship between the practitioner and the consumer. Gossip during the tea break can be a breach of that confidentiality, and practitioners should be careful what they say on such occasions.

Many developments have created inroads into any absolute concept of confidentiality. Examples include the recognition of family and other health care providers in treatment and care, increased numbers of people working for health care providers, increased use of computers, more health insurance claims, and research. The result is that the provision of health care services includes the processing and filing of records by persons other than the doctor or nurse. It is important that health agencies and practitioners comply with Rule 3 of the HIPC and outline as far as possible the extent to which other people may see a consumer's record.[30] If a consumer has not been advised as to who may see the information and the agency is not required by law to release the information then, at first instance, it is better to regard that consumer's health information as confidential and protect it accordingly.

9.4.2   The extent of the duty

In *Seager v Copydex Ltd* it was established that:[31]

> "[A person who] has received information in confidence shall not take unfair advantage of it. He must not make use of it to the prejudice of him who gave it without obtaining his consent."

What this means in practical terms, however, is not clear. There are many debates in medical circles as to the extent of the duty of confidentiality. It is clear that in some cases disclosure is allowed, for example relevant discussions with colleagues directly involved in the consumer's case. However, the appropriate extent of disclosure to a consumer's relatives is not so clear. The law gives some guidance,[32] but a health agency should have a clear policy to deal with such matters. Practitioners should always consult the policy of their employer.

The duty of confidentiality applies to all personnel who come in contact with the information, including filing clerks and secretaries. The obligation does not cease when the professional relationship has ceased, nor with the death of the consumer. An unintended breach of confidence may still be the subject of a legal action by the consumer.

---

29   For example, the Health and Disability Services (Safety) Act 2001 (which gives legitimacy to the Standards described in 9.1). The Standards require consumer confidentiality to be maintained at all times.

30   See 9.3.1(3).

31   *Seager v Copydex Ltd* [1967] 1 WLR 923, 931 per Lord Denning, cited in Dix et al, *Law for the Medical Profession*, Sydney, Butterworths, 1988, 68.

32   See 9.4.6(4).

Health agencies should try and identify from the outset any possible disclosures. These can then be advised to the consumer in accordance with Rule 3 of the HIPC. Information can be disclosed if that is one of the purposes for obtaining it.[33] If the agency has not anticipated disclosure and advised the consumer about this pursuant to Rule 3 of the HIPC, then it should consider whether it:

- Must release the information by law; or
- May exercise a discretion to release the information.

9.4.3 Where an agency must release information

As stated in 9.1, the HIPC is subject to all other parliamentary Acts and regulations. If a law requires disclosure, the information must be made available. Words like "shall" or "must" indicate that disclosure is required.

Section 22F of the Health Act 1956 is an example of where a statutory provision requires disclosure, although it is not straightforward. It states that information must be disclosed on request to:

- The individual about whom the information is held;
- The individual's representative; or
- Any other person providing health or disability services to the individual. At first glance, family caregivers can use this section to obtain information, and health practitioners can use it to obtain relevant information from other health practitioners who are currently treating the consumer.

However, there are situations where a health agency does not have to release information to the above people:

- A request for information may be refused if there are reasonable grounds to believe that the consumer does not want the information to be disclosed to the representative or to the person providing health or disability services. In this situation the decision to release becomes discretionary and the health agency will want to consider its obligations of confidentiality and Rule 11 of the HIPC;[34]
- If the consumer makes the request, it must be treated as an access request under Rule 6 of the HIPC, which refers to the grounds on which an agency can refuse to disclose to the consumer;[35]
- If the consumer's representative makes the request, the agency may refuse the request if there would be grounds for refusing disclosure to the consumer. The agency may also refuse the request if:
  - Disclosure would be contrary to the consumer's interest; or
  - The agency has reasonable grounds for believing the consumer does not want the information disclosed.

In these latter two situations, the decision to release becomes discretionary and the health agency will want to consider its obligations of confidentiality and Rule 11 of the HIPC.

---

33   See 9.4.6(2).
34   Rule 11 is reproduced in Appendix 2.
35   See 9.5.6.

There are other Acts of Parliament requiring disclosure. For example, section 62 of the Health and Disability Commissioner Act 1994 can require health or disability service providers to make information available for an investigation conducted by the Health and Disability Commissioner. Also there are requirements for health agencies to report some infectious notifiable diseases (see chapter 17).

9.4.4 Impact of the Official Information Act 1982 on an information request

The Official Information Act 1982 must be considered by agencies subject to the Act, including public hospitals. If the agency receives a request from a third party for official information (which can include health information) held by the agency, then information should be provided. Again, there are withholding grounds,[36] including protection of:

- The privacy of natural persons (including deceased natural persons);
- Information subject to an obligation of confidentiality.

The Ombudsman (who reviews refusals of requests made under the Official Information Act 1982) has recognised that there are strong privacy interests attached to health information, and that the public interest in disclosure has to be particularly strong to outweigh the privacy interest.[37] However, if a public sector agency releases personal information in good faith in response to an Official Information Act request, no legal action (including an investigation by the Privacy Commissioner) can be taken against it.[38]

9.4.5 Court order to release information

There is no legally protected doctor-client relationship. Lord Denning in *A-G v Mulholland* stated:[39]

> "The only profession I know of which is given a privilege from disclosing information to a Court of law is the legal profession, and then it is the privilege not of the lawyer but of his client. Take the clergyman, the banker, or the medical man. None of these is entitled to refuse to answer when directed to by a Judge. The Judge will respect the confidence which each member of these honourable professions receives in the course of it, and will not direct him to answer unless not only it is relevant but also it is a proper, and indeed, necessary question in the course of justice to be put and answered. A Judge is the person … to weigh these conflicting interests … on the one hand the respect due to confidence in the profession and on the other hand the ultimate interest of the community in justice being done."

There are very limited instances where a registered medical practitioner or clinical psychologist must refuse to disclose information to a Court. Those instances are where a "privilege" applies, that is, a situation where information has been obtained in confidence and which cannot be disclosed to a Court unless the person for whom the benefit exists, waives that privilege.

---

36   Official Information Act 1982, sections 6 and 9.
37   Report of the Ombudsman for the year ended 30 June 1996, page 34.
38   Official Information Act 1982, section 48.
39   *A-G v Mulholland* [1963] 1 All ER 767, 771.

- Under section 59 of the Evidence Act 2006 there is a privilege which can be claimed in criminal proceedings for information obtained by medical practitioners and clinical psychologists. It only applies to a person who consults or is examined by a medical practitioner or a clinical psychologist to enable the medical practitioner or clinical psychologist to examine, treat, or care for the person for drug dependency or any other condition or behaviour that may manifest itself in criminal conduct. It does not apply in the case of a person who has been required by an order of a Judge to submit himself or herself to the medical practitioner or clinical psychologist for any examination, test, or for any other purpose.

- Disclosure may be made with the consent of the patient (the privilege belongs to the patient).[40]

In other cases, Courts do have a general discretion to excuse any witness from giving evidence if it would amount to a breach of confidence having regard to the relationship existing between the witness and the person from whom the information was obtained, the information to be protected or the necessity to protect the free flow of information in a particular activity.[41] The Court obtains the material in confidence and will consider a number of factors including whether or not the public interest in having the evidence disclosed to the Court is outweighed in the particular case by the public interest in the preservation of confidences between persons in the relative positions of the confidant(e) and the witness and the encouragement of free communication between such persons. It is important to note that nurses and counsellors, for example, are not automatically entitled to refuse to give evidence to a Court on the basis of confidentiality. In these cases the public interest in reaching the truth by the evidence being disclosed will normally outweigh the public interest in the preservation of confidences.

Case

M v L [1999] 1 NZLR 747

The plaintiffs issued proceedings in the High Court claiming exemplary damages for sexual abuse. The plaintiffs revealed there were "counselling notes," but claimed privilege from producing them on the basis that they were privileged and confidential. Privilege was also claimed for notes made by a medical practitioner and by a clinical psychologist. The defendants applied to the High Court for an order that the documents be revealed (discovery). The Court made the order with the restriction that inspection be limited to counsel for the defendants and any expert retained. The plaintiffs appealed.

The Court of Appeal held that there was no class privilege for counselling notes. The Court upheld New Zealand's case-by-case discretionary approach, whereby the competing interests are balanced. It was recognised however that to deprive the Court of relevant material was not a step to be taken lightly. The problem was that the High Court had not seen the counselling notes, so the Court of Appeal sent it back to the High Court to have it consider the notes. As for the doctor's notes and the notes of the clinical psychologist, it was held these notes should remain confidential.[42]

---

40   In relation to civil proceedings where disclosure is sought see Evidence Act 2006, section 63.
41   Evidence Act 2006, section 69.
42   Disclosure now covered by Evidence Act 2006, section 67.

9.4.6   Where an agency may exercise a discretion to release information

If a parliamentary Act or regulation uses the word "may" in relation to information, then it is over to the agency to decide if it will release the information. More often than not, the agency will refuse release because it will amount to a breach of its confidentiality obligations or agency policies. The agency should say this is the reason for refusing release, rather than relying on the Privacy Act 1993.

(1)   *Is the disclosure authorised by law?*

If information is released in accordance with a statute, the disclosure will not breach the HIPC. For example, section 22C of the Health Act 1956 states that agencies providing health or disability services are permitted to disclose health information to certain persons or official bodies to assist their functions (for example, the police, social workers, probation officers).[43] Civil, criminal, or disciplinary proceedings will not lie against a person who discloses information in good faith.

(2)   *Is disclosure allowed by Rule 11?*

If there is no law requiring or authorising disclosure of personal health information and an agency wishes to release information, it should consider Rule 11 of the HIPC,[44] which applies to living and deceased people although if the person has been deceased for over 20 years then a health agency is exempted from compliance.

Rule 11 says that health information must not be disclosed unless the health agency believes, on reasonable grounds:

- Disclosure is to the individual concerned, or to their representative where the individual is dead or cannot exercise their rights under the Rules; or
- Disclosure is authorised by the individual concerned, or their representative where the individual is dead or cannot exercise their rights under the Rules; or
- Disclosure is one of the purposes for which the information was obtained; or
- The information is sourced from a publicly available publication; or
- The information is in general terms concerning the presence, location, condition, and progress of a patient in a hospital on the day of disclosure, and the disclosure is not contrary to an express request from the individual or their representative; or
- The disclosure concerns death and is made by a registered health professional or a person authorised by a health agency, to a person nominated by the individual, or their representative, partner, spouse, principal caregiver, next of kin, whanau, close relative, or other person whom it is reasonable in the circumstances to inform; or
- The information is that the individual is to be, or has been released from compulsory status under the Mental Health (Compulsory Assessment and Treatment) Act 1992 and the disclosure is to the individual's principal caregiver.

---

43   If any of these officials request information ask the person to, specify the section of the Act or regulation or, alternatively, to show a Court order. There is no obligation to release information under the HIPC, but it may have to be released under other legislation.

44   Rule 11 is reproduced in Appendix 2.

Having an individual's authorisation to release information is not necessary where the health agency believes on reasonable grounds that it is not desirable or practicable to obtain authorisation from the individual concerned and:[45]

- Disclosure of the information is directly related to one of the purposes for which the information was collected;
- Information is disclosed by a health practitioner to a person nominated by the individual concerned, or to a principal caregiver, or a near relative of the individual concerned, in accordance with recognised professional practice, and the disclosure is not contrary to the express request of the individual or their representative;
- Information is required for statistical (no identification) or research purposes (with ethics committee consent if necessary);
- Non-compliance is necessary to prevent or lessen a serious and imminent threat to public or individual health and/or safety;
- The disclosure is necessary to facilitate the sale or disposition of a business as a going concern;
- Information to be disclosed briefly describes only the nature of injuries of an individual sustained in an accident, and the individual's identity, and the disclosure is by authorised hospital personnel to an authorised media representative for the purposes of publication or broadcast in connection with news activities, and is not contrary to an express request;
- Disclosure is required for the purposes of identifying whether an individual is suitable to be involved in health education, and so that individuals so identified may be contacted to seek their authority, and is by a person authorised by the health agency to a person authorised by a health training institution;
- Disclosure of the information is required for the purposes of a professionally recognised accreditation of a health or disability service, external quality assurance programme, or risk management assessment, and the disclosure is solely to a person engaged by the agency for the purpose of assessing the agency's risk and is published in non-identifiable form except where required by law;
- Non-compliance is necessary to avoid prejudice to the maintenance of law or for the conduct of any proceedings before a Court or Tribunal (commenced or in reasonable contemplation);
- The individual concerned is, or is likely to become, dependent on a controlled drug, prescription medicine, or restricted medicine, and the disclosure is by a registered health professional to a medical officer of health for the purposes of section 20 of the Misuse of Drugs Act 1975 or section 49A of the Medicines Act 1981;
- The Privacy Commissioner has authorised the use.

In these circumstances, disclosure is only permitted to the extent necessary for the particular purpose.

(3)   *Disclosure in the public interest*

The concept of disclosure in the public interest is not listed in Rule 11, but its meaning is covered. For example, it is in the public interest that a hospital is able to answer at reception

---

45   For example, the person is unconscious, is not competent, or has unreasonably refused to give an authorisation.

or over the phone a general inquiry as to the presence, location, condition, and progress of a consumer in a hospital on the day on which the information is disclosed. The consumer may veto this release of information.

Another example of disclosure in the public interest is where there is a serious and imminent threat to public or individual health and/or safety.

Case Note 2049[46]

1996

The Privacy Commissioner investigated a letter from a psychiatric nurse to an Opposition Member of Parliament in which health information of a patient was disclosed. The nurse had written to the Minister of Health expressing certain concerns about release of a particular and identified patient from the secure unit of a psychiatric hospital. This letter contained information about the patient, including allegations concerning earlier behaviour, some comments on the patient's psychiatric situation and state of mind, references to the patient's ability to cope with the outside world, and comments on the risk of release into the community. The nurse also sent a copy of this letter to the Minister of Police and the National Director of Mental Health. Some months later, the nurse sent to an Opposition Member of Parliament a copy of the letter to the Minister of Health.

The Privacy Commissioner said he found nothing in the evidence presented to him to indicate that the nurse considered whether the patient's authorisation should have been sought before disclosing the health information to the Member of Parliament. The Privacy Commissioner took the view that it was conceivable that with appropriate counselling and encouragement the patient would have been amenable to limited disclosures for limited purposes. The Privacy Commissioner thought an appropriate course of action may have been for the nurse to have discussed the issue with the community nurse looking after the patient, and to canvass the possibility of that nurse raising the issue with the patient to seek the patient's views.

The Privacy Commissioner accepted that disclosure to the Member of Parliament was for preventing or lessening a serious and imminent threat to public health or public safety. However, he took the view that a health agency can only rely on this purpose if it believes on reasonable grounds that the disclosure of the information is *necessary* to prevent or lessen the serious and imminent threat. It seemed to him, on the facts of the case that the Opposition Member of Parliament was unlikely to be in a position to assist. To address an imminent threat the recipient of a disclosure would need the power to act urgently to achieve a tangible result in a particular case. It should only involve the amount of information necessary for such a purpose to an appropriate or responsible authority.

Case

Duncan v Medical Practitioners' Disciplinary Committee [1986] 1 NZLR 513

---

46   This is an example of a case note that is issued by the Privacy Commissioner from time to time. Case notes are useful in illustrating the Commissioner's opinion as to how a rule of the HIP Code applies in an actual fact situation. The Commissioner can investigate a complaint and form an opinion about whether there has been an interference with an individual's privacy. The Commissioner does not give a decision and his opinion does not bind anyone. Only the Human Rights Review Tribunal can give a decision that could accurately be described as a ruling. See also 9.8-9.9.

Duncan was a registered medical practitioner in a small rural community. Henry, one of his patients, was a bus driver by occupation, and had operated a passenger service business for 30 years. In 1982 Henry suffered two heart attacks, and was attended by Duncan as his general practitioner. In December 1982, Henry underwent a triple coronary artery bypass operation. After the successful operation, Henry obtained a medical certificate from the surgeon, which enabled him to obtain a licence to drive passenger service vehicles. On 27 April 1983, Henry intended to take his bus to Auckland on a charter trip. On the day before the trip, Duncan spoke to a woman who was to be a passenger on the chartered bus, and told her that Henry was not fit to drive, and could have a heart attack at any time. Duncan also spoke to Henry, and on discovering that he had a licence to drive a passenger service vehicle, sought assistance from the local police constable to have Henry's licence revoked. Later Duncan asked a patient at his surgery to help him organise a petition to have Henry barred from driving passenger service vehicles; the patient refused. Henry complained to the Medical Practitioners' Disciplinary Committee that he was being unjustly victimised by Duncan, and that there had been a breach of patient confidentiality.

The Medical Practitioners' Disciplinary Committee found Duncan guilty of professional misconduct for breach of professional confidence and censured him. Duncan did not appeal against the decision, but made statements to the news media about Henry's heart condition and fitness to drive. As a result, Henry made a further complaint to the Medical Council, which Duncan unsuccessfully sought to have reviewed by the High Court, and later the Court of Appeal. Having considered the evidence, the Council adjudged Duncan to be guilty of professional misconduct by disclosing confidential information to the news media in breach of his professional responsibilities, and in respect of certain other charges, and ordered that his name be removed from the medical register.

The Medical Practitioners' Disciplinary Committee decision included the following reasons for censuring Duncan:[47]

> "The Committee accepts that Dr Duncan was motivated by concern for the welfare of his community, but considers that his actions and intervention were both unwise and unwarranted and amounted to professional misconduct ... he breached professional confidence in informing lay people of his patient's personal medical history. The Committee takes the view that professional confidence can only be breached in most exceptional circumstances and then only if the public interest is paramount. In such a case ... communication should be made only to the responsible authority[48] ... His breach of confidentiality on the 26th of April was serious; however, the Committee took a even more serious view of his breach of confidentiality one month after the first instance to an individual who, in no circumstances, could have been a responsible authority."

So, there may be occasions where a health practitioner receives information involving a consumer, which reveals that another's life is immediately endangered and urgent action is necessary. In those circumstances, there is no mandatory reporting of the situation (unless

---

47   *Duncan v Medical Practitioners' Disciplinary Committee* [1986] 1 NZLR 513, 518.

48   Under section 18 of the Land Transport Act 1998, medical practitioners and optometrists must notify the New Zealand Transport Agency if, in the interests of public safety, patients should not be permitted to drive, or should have limitations placed on their driving.

this is a policy or procedure of the agency for which the health practitioner works) but there is a choice. The health practitioner can choose to report the situation to someone who can do something about it (the responsible authority) even though this means a breach of confidentiality.[49]

(4)   Disclosure to relatives/whanau

Treating a consumer means that health practitioners come into contact with family/whanau. The Health and Disability Commissioner Code of Health and Disability Consumers' Rights promotes the right of a consumer to support, which includes family/whanau. The Standards (see 9.1) also promote family/whanau involvement and the sharing of information between people providing treatment and support to the consumer. Developing these relationships as part of a holistic approach to care does not change the confidentiality obligation. While it is important to involve family/whanau in the treatment and care of a consumer, any information released should be with the knowledge and/or consent of the consumer (see section 22F of the Health Act 1956[50] and Rule 11[51] for other circumstances in which information must or may be released).

The fact that the patient is a child makes little difference to this principle when considering what one can tell relatives. Although a parent or guardian of a child under the age of 16 is considered a representative under the HIPC, section 22F of the Health Act 1956 does not require disclosure to the representative if the patient does not want disclosure. There is still a choice although some of that choice will be directed by the professional obligation to obtain informed consent and a parent/guardian will need information to exercise informed consent on behalf of a child.

Rule 11 allows disclosure to the representative where the patient is unable to exercise their rights. Even in that situation there is still a choice. Because there is now greater recognition of family/whanau involvement in treatment and care, there will be few problems in involving parents, guardians, and caregivers in these processes. Health practitioners should be open and transparent about this. If there is a problem, health practitioners should refer to the policies and procedures of their agency for assistance and should seek peer support in the exercise of the choice.

(5)   The HIV-positive client

In New Zealand the need for strict confidentiality of HIV-related information has been recognised in the statutory form for notification of an AIDS diagnosis to the medical officer of health.[52] The patient is identified only by initials, sex, and date of birth.[53] However, there are arguably inadequate privacy safeguards for those who are HIV-positive or have AIDS, as Rule 11 permits disclosure of information held by a health agency, where that agency believes on reasonable grounds that the disclosure is necessary to prevent or lessen a serious and imminent threat to the life or health of another individual. This provision allows a doctor to warn a third party at risk of HIV infection from a patient. The New Zealand Medical Association has adopted the following protocol:

---

49   See 9.4.6(5) in relation to disclosure of HIV status to a sexual partner.
50   See 9.4.3.
51   See 9.4.6(2) and Appendix 2.
52   See chapter 18.
53   Health (Infectious and Notifiable Diseases) Regulations 1966, Amendment No 5, regulation 2.

- Take all reasonable steps to educate, counsel, and support the HIV-positive person to discuss their HIV status with sexual and intravenous drug sharing partner(s).
- If that person refuses to discuss their HIV status with their sexual partner(s) and there is a clear risk to the acknowledged sexual partner(s), the medical practitioner should discuss with a senior colleague, or the Central Ethical Committee if necessary, whether confidentiality should be maintained.
- The matter should be discussed with the practitioner's medical protection or defence adviser.
- Having reached a decision, the practitioner should consult with the HIV-positive person advising her/him of the practitioner's intention to disclose the information to the third person and to present her/him with written confirmation of this.
- A final opportunity should be given to the HIV-positive person to change their stance and inform the third party of their condition.
- If the person again refuses to respond, the practitioner should notify the third party of the risk. This would involve opportunity for a consultation, and to initiate steps to provide the third party with appropriate counselling and medical advice.

Only the information that needs to be released should be released.

Case Note 6998[54]

1997

The Privacy Commissioner investigated a case where two people had complained that the New Zealand Customs ("Customs") disclosed to Western Samoa Customs ("WS Customs") certain personal information about them. The events occurred after they left New Zealand for a holiday in Western Samoa. The complainants alleged that WS Customs was informed that one of them was a known drug user and HIV-positive, that the other was identified as travelling with the first complainant, and that their travel plans seemed suspicious. Customs disclosed information to the National Drug Intelligence Bureau ("NDIB"), requesting that WS Customs be contacted. The information was duly relayed to WS Customs. Following their arrival in Western Samoa, both complainants were detained and questioned by a number of authorities. The first complainant was subsequently requested to leave Western Samoa.

Customs argued that they disclosed information about one complainant's HIV status to prevent or minimise a serious and imminent threat to the life or health of another individual. They considered they had a reasonable belief that the first complainant could have been carrying used needles because of his history of IV drug use. In view of his HIV status, they considered the risk of infection from needle stick injury to a customs officer searching the baggage posed a serious and imminent threat to the life or health of that officer. Customs submitted that disclosure of this information was the only way to prevent or lessen the

---

54   This is an example of a case note that is issued by the Privacy Commissioner from time to time. Case notes are useful in illustrating the Commissioner's opinion as to how a rule of the HIP Code applies in an actual fact situation. The Commissioner can investigate a complaint and form an opinion about whether there has been an interference with an individual's privacy. The Commissioner does not give a decision and their opinion does not bind anyone. Only the Human Rights Review Tribunal can give a decision that could accurately be described as a ruling. See also 9.8-9.9.

threat to a WS Customs officer, as it would clearly indicate the nature of the risk and enable appropriate measures to be taken during any search.

The Privacy Commissioner took the view that a threat of needle stick injury would be serious and imminent only if there was a high degree of likelihood that the baggage contained used needles, and if a customs officer in Apia would search it. The information available to Customs suggested that the first complainant had never been found with needles or drugs in his possession. His past patterns of behaviour did not indicate that he would attempt to carry needles or drugs through Customs in his baggage. It was not clear that there was a serious and imminent threat in these circumstances.

The Privacy Commissioner took the view that the risk of injury from a needle stick is not limited to those with HIV. There are many blood-borne pathogens, such as hepatitis, which can be transmitted through used syringes. Furthermore, it should not be assumed that all people who are HIV-positive use intravenous drugs. Accordingly, he considered that the risk to WS Customs officials was more properly characterised by the use, or possible use, of intravenous drugs, rather than the presence of a particular pathogen. Information Privacy Principle 11(f) in section 6 of the Privacy Act 1993 requires that the disclosure be necessary to prevent or lessen the threat.[55] If an agency disclosed more than necessary, that disclosure would not be protected. In this case, Customs did not limit the disclosure to information about the first complainant's drug use or possible drug use. By disclosing his HIV status, Customs did not limit the disclosure to that information that was necessary to reduce the threat. For these reasons, the Commissioner formed the opinion that the disclosure of the first complainant's HIV status was not allowed by Information Privacy Principle 11(f) and that Customs had breached this principle.[56]

Checklist

Dealing with requests to disclose confidential information

Requests by:

a)   People for their own personal information (or requests by representatives) use:

  • Rule 6 of the Health Information Privacy Code 1994;
  • Section 22F of the Health Act 1956;
  • Health care providers (including GPs and family caregivers) and representatives: section 22F of the Health Act 1956.

b)   Other people:

  • Information must be disclosed if required by law (check for limits within the law);
  • If request is subject to the Official Information Act 1982 and no withholding grounds apply, the information must be disclosed;[57]
  • If disclosure is authorised by law then check for limits including ethical obligations;

---

55   Information Privacy Principle 11 also contains the exception to disclosure in relation to a serious and imminent threat to individual and public health and safety.

56   Customs and Excise Act 1996, sections 281 and 282 address most of, if not all, these issues should they arise in the future. That Act clarifies the information that can lawfully be disclosed to overseas customs agencies and the purposes for which it can be used.

- If disclosure is not authorised by law, then check Rule 11 and ethical obligations.

9.4.7 Consequences if health information is wrongfully disclosed

Equity, common law, and statute law provide relief for breach of confidence. The elements to be proved are: (i) there is a necessary quality of confidence about the information; (ii) the information was communicated in circumstances importing an obligation of confidence; (iii) there must have been unauthorised use of the information to the detriment of the person entitled to the benefit of the confidence(see *Hosking v Runting*).[58] Practitioners should be aware of the following actions at law: breach of confidence, breach of contract, negligence (see chapter 8), defamation, and interference with privacy (see 9.8). Practitioners should be mindful also of their ethical responsibilities as complaints can be made to the disciplinary committees of their professional bodies.

The obligation of confidentiality does not change even though the costs of providing medical support are being met by another person. If a practitioner is required to report to a third party such as a prospective employer or insurance company, the practitioner should make sure that the consumer is aware and consents to the information being released to these people. This will satisfy the health practitioner's professional obligations.

(1) *Equitable remedy — breach of confidence*

There is a remedy in equity for disclosure of confidential information that has been discovered through a relationship of trust, such as a marital relationship.

Case
Duchess of Argyll v Duke of Argyll [1967] 1 Ch 302 (Eng CA)
The Duke of Argyll sought to sell information about the private life of his estranged wife, the Duchess of Argyll, to the newspapers. This information involved secrets disclosed to him during their marriage. The Duchess applied to the Court for an injunction preventing him from doing so.

The Court held that within marriage, there is a duty for each spouse to maintain the confidence of the other. Note that this case was decided in equity, not common law, so there was no allowance for damages for harm or hurt reputation or feelings. If seeking an injunction, a claimant can also seek damages, or an account of profits (not both).[59]

There is a similar duty of confidence between a medical practitioner and a consumer.

Case
JD v Ross [1998] NZFLR 951

---

57 Note that with some of the withholding grounds under the Official Information Act, the existence of the withholding ground may not alter the fact that the information should be disclosed as the public interest outweighs the interest to be protected under the withholding grounds. See section 9 of the Official Information Act 1982.

58 *Hosking v Runting* [2005] 1 NZLR 1; for a discussion on this judgment see Katrine Evans, "Hosking v Runting Balancing Rights In a Privacy Tort" [2004] Privacy Law and Policy Reporter 28; also refer Todd et al, *The Law of Torts in New Zealand* (5th ed), Wellington, Brookers, 2009, 687-703.

59 See Todd et al, *The Law of Torts in New Zealand* (5th ed), Wellington, Brookers, 2009, 702.

Mr JD and his wife had a daughter who was exhibiting behavioural problems. They thought it best if she were removed from her current peer group and enrolled out of zone so they approached Mr Ross who was a registered psychologist employed in the Psychological Service of the Department of Education (as it was known then). Mr Ross agreed to write a letter supporting the out of zone enrolment. The daughter continued to have problems and ran away from home. The daughter then accused Mr JD of indecently assaulting her (the accusation was subsequently withdrawn) and the daughter was placed in the care of the Department of Social Welfare. During this time, Mr JD contacted Mr Ross to discuss the situation with his daughter and to discuss his own anxiety and distress. Mr Ross disclosed the details of that conversation to the Department of Social Welfare.

The Court held that Mr Ross owed a duty of confidence to Mr JD and did not have authorisation to discuss matters disclosed to him with the Department of Social Welfare. Mr Ross argued that it was in the public interest to disclose the information to the Department, however the Court held this was not necessary and the information was inconsequential in respect of the daughter's interests. The Court awarded damages in the sum of $7500 reflecting the fact that Mr JD had not suffered any economic loss however the breach needed to be recognised as a matter of policy.

(2) Common law remedy — breach of contract

The agreement between a medical practitioner and a consumer may specify that information received by the professional is confidential. If this is not present, the Courts will imply such a term in any agreement, particularly for medical care.

(3) Defences

If the elements of breach of confidence are able to be proved then there are 4 main defences to breach of confidence:

- The practitioner is required to disclose by law;
- The consumer has waived confidentiality;
- The information is in the public domain (although this defence will have limited application to practitioners who still may be required to keep information confidential, despite publicity surrounding the information); and
- There is a public interest in publication.[60]

(4) Defamation

Defamation is the publication of something that wrongfully tends to lower someone in the estimation of others. Communication may be either oral (slander), or in writing (libel). The law of defamation is found in legislation[61] as well as common law.[62] The sole interest allegedly harmed in a defamation action is the reputation of the person.

Defamation law is not concerned with invasion of privacy or hurt feelings; other actions mentioned above may be more appropriate if harm is sufficiently severe. The dead cannot legally be defamed, regardless of the extent of grief and distress caused to surviving relatives.

---

60   See Todd et al, *The Law of Torts in New Zealand* (5th), Wellington, Brookers, 2009, 695.
61   Defamation Act 1992.
62   For example, there is no statutory definition of defamation so the Courts turn to the common law for assistance.

What is to be considered is the reputation of the person involved. Examples of defamation may be an allegation that a colleague is incompetent,[63] or gossip about a patient having venereal disease, or of someone having committed a crime.[64] One must, however, consider the circumstances of the case. The fact that what is said may be true is not always an excuse for telling everybody.

(a) Subject of a defamatory statement

Any person or incorporated body may be the subject of a defamatory statement.[65] As well as an individual, a company or hospital[66] may bring an action as a single legal individual where the body as a whole has allegedly been defamed. Where more than one person alleges defamation, the statement would need to have been such that all those bringing the action could show that by imputation their reputation is besmirched, even though no specific assertion has been made against them individually. The statement may be contained in verbal comments or advice, nurses' notes, consumers' records or any other communication, whether as part of one's work or otherwise.

(b) Elements of a defamation action

The four elements of a defamation action are:

*   There must be a statement of fact or opinion or implied fact or opinion;
*   The statement of fact or opinion or implied fact or opinion must tend to harm a person's reputation;
*   The statement of fact or opinion or implied fact or opinion must have been published;
*   The statement of fact or opinion or implied fact or opinion must refer to the person alleging the defamation.

The statement: There is no established form prescribed for a matter to be considered defamatory. A potentially defamatory statement is a statement of fact or opinion (for example, a satirical cartoon, song, or play), made or implied, which expresses or suggests that the target is held in low esteem and invites the receiver to share that view. Circumstances surrounding the statement will be important: when, where, and how it is made determines its effect. Hurt pride is not enough. In the case of *Tolley v J S Fry & Sons Ltd* the English Court of Appeal held that:[67]

---

63   The Health Practitioners Competence Assurance Act 2003, which repeals the previous Acts that regulate and discipline health professionals has a provision (section 34) that allows practitioners to report any concerns of risk to public harm due to the incompetence of another practitioner to the practitioner's regulatory authority. Any report made in good faith will be protected against a claim of defamation.

64   In the case of *Kitson v Playfair*, 23-28 March 1896, *The Times*, an obstetrician informed the "head of his patient's household" that in his opinion she had had a recent miscarriage. The result of this was that she was cut off from family inheritance. She successfully sued the doctor in defamation.

65   However, unlike an individual, a company must show it suffered pecuniary loss or is likely to do so; otherwise its claim will not be successful: Defamation Act 1992, section 6.

66   It is not clear if a Government Department can bring an action in defamation. Despite section 6 of the Defamation Act, there is authority from England and Australia to suggest institutions of central and local government may be prohibited from this action. See Todd et al, *The Law of Torts in New Zealand* (5th ed), Wellington, Brookers, 2009, 756-757.

67   *Tolley v J S Fry & Sons Ltd* [1930] 1 KB 467, 479.

"To write or say of a man something that will disparage him in the eyes of a particular section of the community, but will not affect his reputation in the eyes of the right thinking man, is not actionable within the law of defamation."

Defamatory material: A defamatory statement must be shown to be one which the reasonable person would consider tends to bring the subject of it into contempt, ridicule, or diminished reputation. One can defame without intending to,[68] but in those circumstances an apology and retraction of the statement may satisfy the law. Health practitioners should not rely on this resolution. Implications made in general conversation that a patient has a socially unacceptable disease or lifestyle or that one's colleague or employer is incompetent or less than reasonable in their standard of care may amount to defamation.[69] The aggrieved party may seek more than just an apology.

Publication: A statement must be made, or in legal parlance, "published". It does not have to be public. Communication need only be between two people, for example in conversation, or handing over of a letter for typing. So long as one person (other than the person about whom the defamatory statement is made) has received the communication, there is potential defamation of the subject.

Reference to the subject: One does not have to refer directly to a person to defame her/him in a statement. It is only necessary that the reasonable person would be likely to associate the material with a particular subject.

Health practitioners need to be careful about disclosing confidential information as part of allegations against others, such as:

- The standards of treatment and care practised by their employer or other employees;[70]
- Reporting that the welfare of particular people or the public in general may be adversely influenced by the actions of someone else;
- Complaining about sexual harassment or other personal maltreatment by another.

In some circumstances it may be acceptable to make statements about others which could harm their reputations (such as incompetence), but this information should be restricted to those who have the authority to deal with the matter (such as management). There should be, if possible, details and documents to support the communication. Note that a person who successfully sues in defamation is entitled to compensation for damaged reputation.

---

68   For example, a newspaper article gave a fictional account of an English churchwarden's dallying with a "woman of bad character" in France. The warden bore the unusual name of Artemus Jones. A barrister from Wales, whose name also happened to be Artemus Jones, brought a defamation action: *Jones v E Hulton & Co* [1910] AC 20. A Victorian newspaper published details of allegations made against a certain police constable named Lee; the paper mistakenly named the police officer as Detective Lee. There were two detectives named Lee in the police force, and they both sued the newspaper successfully: *Lee v Wilson* (1934) 51 CL 276.

69   See n 65.

70   State sector health practitioners should also be aware of the Protected Disclosures Act 2000. Its purpose is to legitimise the disclosure of serious wrongdoing within/by an organisation. It protects employees who, in accordance with the terms of the Act, make such disclosures. Health practitioners should check that their organisation comes under the Act and check for the procedure to follow. If in doubt, contact the Office of the Ombudsman (www.ombudsmen.govt.nz).

(c)   Defences to an action in defamation

The exceptions in relation to defamation, however, have been expressed in the following terms.[71]

Truth: True disclosures are justified. Section 8 of the Defamation Act 1992 provides that an innocent belief in the truth of an actual untrue statement is not sufficient to amount to a defence. The statement itself has to be true, or the imputations contained in it must not materially differ from the truth. Thus, the truth of a nurse's revelation to a client that a doctor's negligent treatment was the cause of injury might be a defence to a defamation action by the doctor if in fact the nurse can show that what they said was true.

Absolute privilege: If this privilege is successfully claimed the person is protected from liability for making a defamatory statement. The law regards it as important that, on some occasions, disclosures can be made without fear of reprisal. Absolute privilege protects the defendant, even though the statements made were dishonest or knowingly false. The following communications and statements attract absolute privilege:[72]

- Statements made in the course of parliamentary proceedings, which include proceedings of parliamentary committees and statements given by witnesses appearing before these committees. It also includes statements made in petitions to Parliament.
- Statements made, including evidence given, in judicial proceedings, for example Court. This does not include Tribunals with non-judicial functions, for example polytechnic councils.[73] The Health Practitioners Disciplinary Tribunal accords witnesses and counsel the same privileges as a judicial proceeding.[74]
- Statements made by one officer of the State to another in the course of duty.

Qualified privilege: Section 16 of the Defamation Act 1992 confers a qualified privilege, which protects false assertions of fact.[75] Its basis is in the common law, where it applied to occasions when:[76]

> "The person who makes a communication has an interest or a duty, legal, social, or moral, to make it to the person to whom it is made, and the person to whom it is so made has a corresponding interest or duty to receive it. This reciprocity is essential."

The underlying justification for the existence of the defence is the "interests of the common welfare and convenience of society."

By virtue of section 19 of the Defamation Act the privilege is "qualified" in the sense that it may be lost if the plaintiff can show that the defendant was motivated by ill-will towards

---

71   The following list of defences is made with reference to "Defamation" (chapter 16) in Todd et al, *The Law of Torts in New Zealand* (5th ed), Wellington, Brookers, 2009, 733-844.

72   Defamation Act 1992, sections 13 and 14.

73   *Tertiary Institutions Allied Staff Association Inc v Tahana* [1998] 1 NZLR 41.

74   Being a tribunal or authority set up by another enactment: see Health Practitioners Competence Assurance Act 2003, sections 84-90.

75   This section creates qualified privilege for the publication of reports (eg fair and accurate reporting of Court proceedings) including matters in the Schedule 1 to the Act. Section 16(3) makes it clear that this does not rule out other law relating to qualified privilege.

76   *Adam v Ward* [1917] AC 309, 339 per Lord Atkinson.

the plaintiff or took improper advantage of the occasion of publication. Situations where qualified privilege applies may include:

- Answers to police questions;
- Communications between solicitor and client;
- Evaluations of work performance;
- References written for job applications;
- A report required as part of one's employment;
- Communication between employer and employee;
- Some newspaper reports, which are made in the public interest. The media can now rely on this defence in relation to published defamatory statements about actions and qualities of current or former elected members of Parliament, although some caution should be exercised. The circumstances and context will be significant in determining if the privilege applies and the range of situations that may apply has not been fully determined.[77]

Honest opinion: Beliefs should only be expressed for good and proper reason. Lord Atkinson elaborated on this point in the case of *Adam v Ward*:[78]

> "[The] authorities, in my view, clearly establish that a person making a communication on a privileged occasion is not restricted to the use of such language merely as is reasonably necessary to protect the interest or discharge the duty which is the foundation of his privilege; but that, on the contrary, he will be protected, even though his language should be violent or excessively strong, if, having regard to all the circumstances of the case, he might have honestly and on reasonable grounds believed that what he wrote or said was true and necessary for the purpose of his vindication, though in fact it was not so."

Defence of honest opinion, described and provided for in sections 9 and 10 of the Defamation Act 1992, is usually relied upon by journalists, and involves commentary on people and events in the public domain. At common law, it was called the defence of fair comment on a matter of public interest. The defence must show the statement is:[79]

- Based on true facts;
- Recognisable as opinion;
- Genuine; and
- On a matter of public interest (though there is academic debate about this).[80]

9.5 Client access to records

9.5.1 Rule 6

Where a health agency holds health information in such a way that it can be readily retrieved, the individual concerned shall be entitled (unless a ground for refusal applies) to:[81]

77   *Lange v Atkinson* [1998] 3 NZLR 424; also *Lange v Atkinson* [2000] 3 NZLR 385 (CA).
78   *Adam v Ward* [1917] AC 309, 318.
79   Todd et al, *The Law of Torts in New Zealand* (5th ed), Wellington, Brookers, 2009, 777, 16.8.
80   See *The Law of Torts in New Zealand* (5th ed), Wellington, Brookers, 2009, 788; cf *Laws of New Zealand: Defamation*, Wellington, Butterworths, para 133.
81   See 9.5.6.

- Obtain from the agency confirmation of whether the agency holds such health information; and
- Have access to that information and be advised of rights under Rule 7.

Consumers have a right to access their information, which can include medical records, letters of referral, test results, doctors' notes, nurses' notes, x-rays, and billing information. The right of access is not a right to possess original documents, although the concept of ownership of files seems irrelevant when consumers can access their health information.

9.5.2 Readily retrievable

In one case investigated by the Privacy Commissioner, a patient had requested his medical records. His GP had retired and a new doctor had taken over the practice. The old files were stored in the basement. The new doctor said the notes were not readily retrievable because the old files were not filed in any particular order. However, the retired doctor came in and found the notes without any difficulty. The Privacy Commissioner commented the term "readily retrievable" denoted information that can be located with reasonable ease. He considered that information about a person, which is collected in one file, should be readily retrievable even if several boxes have to be searched in order to find the files.

9.5.3 Health information

It is useful to remind health practitioners of the definition of health information (9.2). Consumers are entitled to access their health information, and it does not matter if information is spread over different files in different wards, or if the information is not written down. A person can request information stored in someone's memory, provided that information is readily retrievable (for example, a request for a written summary of what was discussed about a consumer during a ward meeting). A request for remembered information will have to be specific to help the agency respond.

9.5.4 Dealing with access requests

Part 5 of the Privacy Act 1993, sets out the procedural provisions relating to access.[82] From the outset it should be noted that the agency is to give reasonable assistance to the individual making the request.[83] Further, the agency can provide access to the individual by:[84]

- Allowing inspection of the documents;
- Providing a copy of the documents;
- Allowing access to hear or view audio or videotaped recordings;
- Supplying a written transcript of the document;
- Supplying a summary of the information;
- Supplying the information orally.

Access should be granted in the manner requested, unless it would:

- Impair efficient administration;
- Contravene a legal duty the agency has in respect of the document;
- Prejudice the interests protected by the withholding grounds set out in 9.5.6.

---

82   Privacy Act 1993, sections 33-45.
83   Privacy Act 1993, section 38.
84   Privacy Act 1993, section 38.

> ### Case Note 7602[85]
> ### 1997
>
> A client of the then Accident Rehabilitation and Compensation Insurance Corporation requested access to all the information it held about him. The information was contained in 20 Eastlight folders.

The Privacy Commissioner formed the opinion that, because the information consisted of 20 Eastlight folders, it was reasonable for the corporation to ask him to come in and read the information so he could select the specific documents he wanted to be copied.

The right of access is not a right of immediate access. The Privacy Act 1993 requires requests to be decided on as soon as practicable and within 20 working days.[86] If a consumer asks a nurse at 8 pm if they can read their medical notes, they do not have to be made available straightaway. The nurse can give the request to the privacy officer, or take responsibility for the request with the privacy officer's help. A consumer can request urgency, but must give reasons for this request.[87]

People can appoint agents to act on their behalf. An example of an appointment is the execution of an enduring power of attorney under the Protection of Personal and Property Rights Act 1988 although practitioners are reminded that these appointments do not come into effect until the consumer is deemed incompetent to exercise his or her rights. The attorney or agent may be a lawyer, friend, parent, guardian, or partner. The Privacy Act 1993 requires agencies to ensure that agents have written authorisation or are otherwise properly authorised to obtain the information.[88] This is important as an enduring power of attorney in relation to property may not be sufficient authorisation to release information in contrast with an enduring power of attorney in relation to welfare. Where a lawyer claims to act for a person, which should normally be sufficient for the Privacy Act 1993, because lawyers can be disciplined for claiming to act for someone when they are not.

9.5.5   Charging

Public sector agencies must not charge for providing information in response to a Rule 6 or Rule 7 request.[89] Private sector agencies are also prohibited from charging except in limited circumstances:[90]

- Provision of the same or substantially the same information as provided under an earlier request within a 12-month period;
- Providing a copy of an x-ray, video recording, or CAT scan photograph.

---

85   This is an example of a case note that is issued by the Privacy Commissioner from time to time. Case notes are useful in illustrating the Commissioner's opinion as to how a rule of the HIPC applies in an actual fact situation. The Commissioner can investigate a complaint and form an opinion about whether there has been an interference with an individual's privacy. The Commissioner does not give a decision and their opinion does not bind anyone. Only the Human Rights Review Tribunal can give a decision that could accurately be described as a ruling. See also 9.8-9.9.

86   Privacy Act 1993, section 40.

87   Privacy Act 1993, section 37.

88   Privacy Act 1993, section 45. This section also places an obligation to check the identity of any individual requesting access to information.

89   Privacy Act 1993, section 35(1) and Health Information Privacy Code 1994, clause 6.

90   Privacy Act 1993, section 35(2) and Health Information Privacy Code 1994, clause 6.

If there is to be a charge in these limited circumstances which will be more than $30, the agency has to provide the individual with an estimate before dealing with the request.

9.5.6   Reasons to withhold information

Where information is not held by the agency, but the agency believes it is held by another agency or may be closely connected to the functions of another agency then the request must be forwarded to that agency. The only reasons to refuse a request from the patient for access to health information about herself/himself are contained in sections 27 to 29 of the Privacy Act 1993:

- Release is likely to prejudice security, defence, and international relations of New Zealand;
- Maintenance and enforcement of law;[91]
- Disclosure would be likely to endanger the safety of any individual;
- The information is not readily retrievable, or it does not exist or cannot be found;
- Protection of trade secrets;
- Release will result in the unwarranted disclosure of another individual's affairs;[92]
- The disclosure is of evaluative material, thereby breaching an express or implied promise to keep it confidential;[93]
- Disclosure is likely to prejudice the mental health of the individual;[94]
- In relation to an individual under the age of 16, the disclosure is contrary to their interests;
- Disclosure would prejudice the safe custody or rehabilitation of a convict or detainee;
- Disclosure would breach legal professional privilege;
- Disclosure would identify a journalist's source;

---

91   This withholding ground can be used to protect the identity of an informant who has contacted a health agent. For instance, a patient is concerned that his neighbour abuses her children. He does not wish to go to the Department of Social Welfare, but thinks something should be done. He tells his doctor and asks her to look into the matter and contact the department if it seems appropriate. His identity could be withheld from the neighbour. Release will result in the unwarranted disclosure of the affairs of another individual is also applicable in this situation.

92   This is the most commonly used withholding ground in the health sector, and is often used in a psychiatric setting where the person making the request has participated in group therapy sessions. The hospital may consider that information relating to other consumers ought to be withheld. If the information about the other people can be separated, that can be withheld and the requested information supplied. If it cannot be separated, all of the information may need to be withheld, but consideration should be given to the factors that would make the disclosure unwarranted.

93   Evaluative material has a narrow definition under section 29(3). It means evaluative or opinion material compiled solely for the purpose of determining an individual's suitability, eligibility, or qualifications for employment; appointment to office; promotion in employment or office; continuance in employment or office; or removal from employment or office. It is also about material compiled to determine an individual's suitability etc for the awarding of contracts, awards, scholarships, honours, or other benefits; or for determining whether any contract, award, scholarship, honour, or benefit should be continued, modified, or cancelled. Finally, it includes material compiled to decide whether to insure any individual or property; or to continue or renew the insurance of any individual or property.

94   The agency must consult the requester's medical practitioner where practicable. The medical practitioner should be a person whose primary ethical obligation is to the requester. The agency is not obliged to adopt the views of the medical practitioner, but must consider them and weigh them with the other evidence.

- Disclosure would breach a condition by which information was given to a library or museum;
- Disclosure would amount to contempt of Court or Parliament;
- The request is frivolous or vexatious or the information is trivial.

9.5.7 Rule 7

A person may request correction (including deletion) of their health information or request a statement of correction be held with the information. Further:

- An agency must take steps on request or on its own initiative to correct information, as reasonable, to ensure information is accurate, up to date, complete and not misleading, having regard to the purposes for which the information may be lawfully used;
- If an agency is not prepared to correct the information upon request from the individual concerned, then the agency must take all reasonable steps to hold a statement of correction so that it will be read with the original information;
- If a correction is made an agency must take steps, if reasonably practicable, to inform agencies to whom the information has been disclosed of the correction.

Correction complaints normally arise where the consumer disagrees with a diagnosis. For instance, a consumer might not agree that they have a bipolar affective disorder. In such a case, it may be appropriate to offer to attach a statement of the correction sought. Agencies do not have to correct (alter or delete) information if they believe the information is correct. However, they must inform the individual why they will not correct the information, and must tell the individual that a statement of correction may be attached to the disputed information. The statement must be attached so that it will always be read with the disputed information.

Rule 7 links into the importance of accuracy of notes as discussed in 9.3.2(2) and 9.3.2(9). If a diagnosis in 1969 is found incorrect due to a test in 1975, it is important that the 1969 diagnosis is put into its historical context, but is not the basis for treatment after 1975.

9.6 Holding personal and health information

9.6.1 Rule 5

A health agency that holds health information must ensure:

- The information is protected by reasonable security safeguards against loss, access, use, modification, disclosure (except with the authority of the agency that holds the information), and other misuse;
- If it is necessary for the information to be given to a person in connection with the provision of a service to the health agency, everything reasonably within the power of the health agency is done to prevent unauthorised use or unauthorised disclosure of the information;
- Where a document containing health information is not to be kept, the document is disposed of in a manner that preserves the privacy of the individual.

Case Note 3984[95]

1995

On her son's behalf, the complainant requested a copy of a video recording of the boy taken while he was in hospital. The recording was made to assist diagnosis. The complainant required this information in order to obtain an independent medical assessment of her son's condition. The respondent hospital told her that it was not possible to give her a copy of the recording because of the difficulty involved in editing out other patients who appeared on the tapes. The complainant was not satisfied with this response, and made a complaint to the Privacy Commissioner. After he had commenced his investigation of this complaint, but before the completion of it, the hospital, having edited the 9-hour video recording to a 3-5 minute segment, erased the remainder of the tapes. The hospital told the Commissioner that it was "standard practice" to reuse tapes after editing the relevant information.

The Privacy Commissioner expressed serious concern about the destruction of information that was the subject of an access request under Rule 6 of the Health Information Privacy Code, which he was investigating. He referred the hospital to section 127 of the Privacy Act 1993, which makes it an offence to hinder the Privacy Commissioner in the exercise of their powers under the Act. He pointed out that Rule 5 of the Health Information Privacy Code 1994 appeared relevant to this complaint. Rule 5(1)(a)(i) of the HIPC requires a health agency to ensure that health information is protected by reasonable security safeguards against loss. Health information about the complainant's son had been lost. Health information is sensitive. Not all employees should be able to read entire patient files. Different information is needed for staff to carry out their functions, so appropriate levels of availability should be arranged. For instance:

- Administrators dealing with billing do not need to see clinical notes;
- Hospital chaplains and volunteer visitors do not need to see clinical notes or have details of treatment without patient authorisation;
- Clinical staff may not need to see the whole of the historical medical record;
- Medical records stored by an agency with a contractor, an agreement could be signed with the contractor that it will allow only duly authorised staff from the agency access to the records.

All staff should know storage and security policies.[96] They should be conscious of protecting the information as far as is reasonable. Some possibilities include:

- Keeping white boards that show patient details away from public areas;
- Physically securing the areas in which health information is stored;
- Locking filing cabinets and unattended rooms;

---

95   This is an example of a case note that is issued by the Privacy Commissioner from time to time. Case notes are useful in illustrating the Commissioner's opinion as to how a rule of the HIPC applies in an actual fact situation. The Commissioner can investigate a complaint and form an opinion about whether there has been an interference with an individual's privacy. The Commissioner does not give a decision and their opinion does not bind anyone. Only the Human Rights Review Tribunal can give a decision that could accurately be described as a ruling. See also 9.8-9.9.

96   The HIPC's commentary contains a recommendation from the Privacy Commissioner that medium to large health agencies develop suitable security plans which will have policies and procedures for staff to follow. Guidance can be found in the ISO Standards AS/NZS ISO/IEC 17799:2006 and AS/NZS ISO/IEC 27001: 2006 as well as the Health Records Standard (8153:2002) and Health Network Code of Practice (SNZ HB 8169: 2002).

- Restricting access to storage areas to authorised personnel;
- Implementing document tracking systems;
- Using screen savers and security screens so terminals cannot be seen by visitors;
- Encrypting sensitive files sent by email;
- Using passwords and restricting access to health information stored on computers;
- Implementing controls on the type of information which may be sent by fax;
- Pre-empting fax transmission with a telephone call;
- Programming fax machines with frequently called numbers to minimise the risk of incorrect dialling;
- Disposing of health information to ensure confidentiality.

9.6.2   Rule 9

Health information must not be kept longer than is required for the purposes for which it may lawfully be used. Documents may be kept if it is desirable for providing health or disability services to the individual concerned.

The Health (Retention of Health Information) Regulations 1996:

- Require health information to be retained for at least 10 years from the last date of treatment or care;
- Allow information to be transferred to another provider in this time. If a patient moves to another town, the records may be forwarded to a new agency;
- Do not prevent agencies from transferring information to the individual or (where the individual is deceased) to their personal representative.

If there is old information that should be retained, but it does not need to be accessed regularly by staff, health practitioners should put it in a separate file or in a sealed envelope. This could be done, for instance, where someone was admitted in 1969 for a psychiatric illness, but now only contacts the hospital for surgical matters.

9.6.3   Rule 8

Before using information, agencies must take reasonable steps to ensure information is accurate, up to date, complete, relevant, and not misleading. This can be particularly important where information has been obtained from a source other than the person concerned. Defining *reasonable* steps may depend on the proposed use for the information and its impact on the patient.

Case

P v J 27/10/98, HC Auckland HC117/98

This was an appeal from the Complaints Review Tribunal (now called the Human Rights Review Tribunal). The complainant was a university student who was concerned her mental health background would affect her ability to get a job. On advice from the University Careers Adviser, she decided to submit herself for a psychiatric examination to obtain a documented mental health clearance. The psychiatrist required a referral letter from a GP, and so the complainant saw an associate of her GP, as the GP was not available. The discussion at that consultation was the subject of conflicting evidence. The complainant thought she had made it clear that all she wanted was a referral for an

---

assessment, but the GP thought she wanted a referral for ongoing treatment. In the referral letter the GP included inaccurate history details. He said that he checked with the complainant before sending the letter, which she denied.

The High Court upheld the Complaints Review Tribunal's finding that there was no interference with the complainant's privacy. However, the case reflects the importance of exercising caution on referral notes and the danger of relying on inaccurate information.

9.6.4 Rule 10

Health information collected for one purpose should not be used for another purpose, unless the health agency believes on reasonable grounds:[97]

- Use of the information for that other purpose is authorised by the individual or their representative where the individual cannot give authorisation;
- The purpose for which the information was obtained is directly related to the proposed purpose for use;
- The information is publicly available information;
- Non-compliance is necessary to prevent or lessen a serious and imminent threat to public or individual health and/or safety;
- The purpose is for statistical purposes (no identification) or research purposes (approved by ethics committee if necessary);
- Non-compliance is necessary to avoid prejudice to the maintenance of the law (including the Inland Revenue Department and Income Support);
- The Privacy Commissioner has authorised the use.

9.6.5 Rule 12

Unique identifiers may be assigned only in situations where the assignment is necessary to enable the health agency to carry out its functions more efficiently.[98] Health agencies must take reasonable steps to ensure unique identifiers are assigned only to individuals whose identity is clearly established. Agencies must not require individuals to disclose unique identifiers assigned to them unless the disclosure is for a purpose about which the identifier was assigned, or is for a directly related purpose. Rule 12 also restricts agencies using the same unique identifier to identify an individual.

Rule 12 does not stop agencies from giving a number to a person, but individuals must remain a name, not a number. Unique identifiers may help to protect the privacy of each consumer's information, particularly when it is being transferred between providers, for example, from a hospital to a specialist, or from a laboratory to a health professional. However, overuse or improper use may work against individual privacy, particularly if agencies use the same number and information is improperly shared.

The National Health Index ("NHI") number is an example of a unique identifier. Traditionally, public hospitals made use of the NHI system, and they remain the main users of it. However, Rule 12 allows some health agencies to assign the NHI in their transactions

---

97   These exceptions are similar and on occasion mirror exceptions to other rules.

98   A unique identifier is an identifier that is assigned to an individual by an agency for the purposes of its operation that uniquely identifies the individual in relation to that agency. Examples are PINs (Personal Information Numbers) or serial numbers. An individual's name is not an unique identifier.

with agencies such as the Ministry of Health, District Health Board's hospitals, primary health organisations, health practitioners, NZ Blood Service, and Accident Compensation Corporation.[99] Rule 12 also allows the Director-General of Health to approve agencies and registered health professionals to assign the NHI. The Director-General must notify the Privacy Commissioner.

9.7   The role of privacy officers

Every agency must appoint a privacy officer to:

* Ensure that the agency complies with the Act;
* Deal with requests made to the agency about personal information;
* Work with the Privacy Commissioner when he investigates complaints.

9.8   An interference with privacy

An interference with the privacy of an individual occurs (other than in access and correction cases) if there has been a breach of a Rule in the HIPC and the Privacy Commissioner or the Human Rights Review Tribunal (formerly the Complaints Review Tribunal) considers the action has or may:

* Cause loss, detriment, damage, or injury to the individual concerned;
* Adversely affect the individual's rights, benefits, privileges, obligations, or interests; or Does not allow an individual access to their health information;
* Result in significant humiliation, significant loss of dignity, or significant injury to the individual's feelings.

In access and correction matters, all a complainant need establish is a breach of the relevant rule (either rule 6 or rule 7).

An interference with individual privacy may also occur if an agency acts as follows, and the Privacy Commissioner or the Human Rights Review Tribunal considers that there is no proper basis for the agency's decision:

* Does not allow an individual access to their health information;
* Does not allow correction of their health information;
* Does not make health information available within the statutory time periods;
* Does not make health information available in the way sought by the individual;
* Imposes an unreasonable charge;
* Imposes conditions on the use, communication, or publication of the information;
* Issues a "neither confirm nor deny" notice under section 32 of the Privacy Act 1993.

9.9   Privacy Commissioner's complaints procedure

When the Office of the Privacy Commissioner receives a letter of complaint, it may respond to the complaint in one of three ways:

* The complaint may raise an issue outside the Commissioner's jurisdiction. The Commissioner may then write to the complainant explaining why the matter cannot be investigated.

---

99   Further agencies are set out in the HIPC, Schedule 2.

- The complaint may raise issues already held not to breach the HIPC or the Privacy Act 1993 or it may be clear that the complainant has not suffered any adverse consequences. The Commissioner may write to the complainant explaining why the complainant may have difficulty establishing the substance of their complaint.
- The complaint may fall within the Commissioner's jurisdiction. The parties will be contacted by an investigating officer and brief details of the complaint will be provided to the respondent who is alleged to have breached the HIPC or the Privacy Act 1993. The parties will be invited to resolve the matter between them.

Once an investigation is completed, the Commissioner may form a provisional opinion as to whether an interference with privacy has occurred. The provisional opinion is sent to one of the parties or both (the complainant may not receive full details of a provisional opinion if it is about a request for access to information and the respondent wishes to continue to withhold information).

The Commissioner will invite comments from the parties who receive the provisional opinion, and will give them another opportunity to settle the complaint. In some cases, the parties' responses to the provisional opinion may highlight the need for some further investigation.

If a settlement is not achieved, the Commissioner forms the final opinion, including a conclusion about the substance of the complaint. The Commissioner's opinion is advisory only. It is not a ruling or a judgment. The Commissioner does not have the power to prosecute, award damages, or impose fines. In some cases, the Commissioner may discontinue the investigation, perhaps because the complainant does not want to pursue the matter, or because further investigation is not warranted in the circumstances.

With some very limited exceptions, allegations of breaches of the Rules cannot be heard in the ordinary Courts. They can be heard in the Human Rights Review Tribunal. A complaint can get to the Tribunal in two ways. If the Commissioner forms the opinion that a complaint has substance (this usually involves a breach of the Act and some adverse consequence), and it has not been settled, it may be referred to the Director of Human Rights Proceedings. The Director will normally try to settle the matter. If that is not possible he/she may issue proceedings before the Human Rights Review Tribunal. Alternatively, once the Privacy Commissioner has completed an investigation and closed the file, an aggrieved individual can bring proceedings before the Human Rights Review Tribunal.

The Tribunal has a hearing in which each side has the opportunity to present evidence and make submissions. Where the Tribunal is satisfied on the balance of probabilities that an interference with privacy has occurred, it has the power to award a number of remedies, including orders, declarations, injunctions, damages, and costs. In the few cases where damages have been awarded, the sums have been relatively low, notwithstanding the Tribunal's jurisdiction to award damages of up to $200,000.

9.10　Further reading

J Duffy, "Industrial focus: Reporting Incidents correctly" *Kai Tiaki: Nursing New Zealand*, July 1998.

E Longworth and T McBride, *The Privacy Act: A Guide*, Wellington, GP Publications, 1994.

Privacy Commissioner (Marie Shroff/B H Slane), *Health Information Privacy Code 1994*, Auckland, Office of the Privacy Commissioner, 2008.

Privacy Commissioner (B H Slane), *Mental Health Professionals and Patient Information*, Auckland, Office of the Privacy Commissioner, 1997.

Privacy Commissioner (B H Slane), *On the Record: A Practical Guide to Health Information Privacy*, Auckland, Office of the Privacy Commissioner, 1999.

R Stent, *Canterbury Health Ltd: A Report by the Health and Disability Commissioner*, Wellington, April 1998.

Skegg and Patersson, *Medical Law in New Zealand*, Wellington, Brookers, 2006.

For further information contact the Office of the Privacy Commissioner: 09-302 8680 (Auckland); 04-472 7590(Wellington); 0800 803 909 (other areas).

Chapter 10

PRESCRIBING AND ADMINISTRATION OF MEDICINES

SUE JOHNSON AND REBECCA KEENAN

Contents

10.1   Introduction

Health practitioners that can prescribe medicines are doctors, dentists, designated nurse prescribers, and registered midwives. They are referred to below as prescribers. Administration of medicines is carried out by a variety of health practitioners including nurses, midwives, physiotherapists, optometrists, and paramedics. This chapter will discuss the law relating mainly to the prescribing and administration of medicines. It should be noted, however, that there is also law relating to dispensing, and a regulatory regime for manufacturers, packers and wholesalers of medicines. From 18 September 2004 new regulations will govern the retail distribution of medicines, and establish a licensing regime for the ownership and operation of retail pharmacies.[1]

Medicines are drugs or other substances that are manufactured, imported, sold, or supplied for therapeutic purposes. The Medicines Act 1981 and its regulations and the Misuse of Drugs Act 1975 and its regulations govern legal and illegal use of all drugs, (including medicines), prescribing (such as who can prescribe and under what circumstances, as well as periods of supply), and labelling, dispensing, and administration of medicines.

The legislation that regulates all therapeutic products, including medicines, in New Zealand is administered by Medsafe, the New Zealand Medicines and Medical Devices Safety Authority (a business unit of the Ministry of Health). Medsafe has a useful website at www.medsafe.govt.nz, which is regularly updated.

There are also rules regarding pharmaceutical subsidies that prescribers need to be aware of. These are in the Pharmaceutical Schedule, which is produced by PHARMAC, the Pharmaceutical Management Agency that manages the health budget for subsidies. PHARMAC has an 0800 number (0800 66 00 50), which is answered during office hours for any questions related to subsidies for medicines. There is also an online facility at www.pharmac.govt.nz, with an interactive schedule that gives an approximate consumer cost of each medicine.

---

1   These regulations amended the principal Act (Medicines Regulations 1984) by inserting a new Part 7B — Supply of restricted medicine and pharmacy-only medicine.

10.2 Statutory law regarding medicines

10.2.1 Approved medicines

The Medicines Act 1981 and its regulations regulate the use of medicines. Before a drug is approved as a medicine, and is thus able to be marketed as such, its manufacturer must apply with supporting information to the Minister of Health for its registration in New Zealand. The minister's consent for approval is noted in *The Gazette*. When a medicine is approved, it is approved with a particular set of indications on a data sheet, as well as dosage instructions and routes of administration. Any proposed changes to the data sheet also have to be applied for.

Registered (ie approved) medicines are classified into four categories:

• Prescription medicines;
• Restricted medicines;
• Pharmacy only medicines; and
• Other medicines.

Section 3 of the Medicines Act 1981 defines the following:

• "Prescription medicine" is a medicine that can be sold only by retail under a prescription, or supplied in circumstances corresponding to retail sale under prescription or in accordance with a standing order.
• "Restricted medicine" is a medicine that can be sold or supplied only by a pharmacist in a pharmacy or a hospital. The pharmacist must record the sale and explain it to the patient.
• "Pharmacy-only medicine" is a medicine that can be sold or supplied in a pharmacy or hospital or in a shop with a licence to sell medicinal drugs.

Medicines must be registered in New Zealand to be sold and distributed in New Zealand, even if they are registered overseas. Letters of approval of registration to the pharmaceutical company state that the company must inform prescribers of the approval.

10.2.2 Unapproved medicines

As well as registered medicines, there are unregistered medicines whose distribution and use is unapproved, but that are nevertheless safe and effective and approved overseas. These medicines can still be prescribed, and exemptions under section 25 of the Medicines Act 1981 allow a prescriber to import an overseas medicine into New Zealand and prescribe it even though it has not been registered here.

Section 25 allows a prescriber to procure and supply an unapproved medicine to a particular "known and identifiable" patient in their care.

Section 29 of the Medicines Act 1981 permits an authorised supplier to sell or supply an unapproved medicine to a registered medical practitioner, but the practitioner must notify the Director-General of Health. The provisions are intended to allow treatment of a rare disease where an overseas medicine is available.

A prescriber who uses an unapproved medicine takes full responsibility for any adverse consequences of it. It is especially important to give effect to consumers' rights to make an informed choice and give informed consent to receiving the unapproved medicine. Advice and information should be provided about safety concerns, contraindications, side-effects, and precautions regarding the medicine's use. Information should also be provided about the degree and standard of support, if any, for the use of the medicine in New Zealand, and how much information the prescriber has or does not have about it.

Also, the Health Information Privacy Code requires that consumers are advised that their details will be sent to Medsafe and recorded on a database. This is a requirement of the Medicines Act 1981. Medsafe can then contact the prescriber if there are any future problems with the medicine that may require follow-up with the consumer.

In addition to a section 29 exemption, section 30 of the Medicines Act 1981 also provides for the Minister of Health to grant an exemption for the use and distribution of unapproved medicines in New Zealand in a clinical trial. The minister is advised by the Health Research Council's Standing Committee on Therapeutic Trials ("SCOTT"). Both SCOTT approval and an accredited ethics committee approval of the trial are required before the minister will grant the exemption. An application for a section 30 exemption must be made to Medsafe and to SCOTT. All drugs distributed under the section 30 exemption must be labelled "to be used by qualified investigators only" or words to that effect.

Section 30 exemptions must be applied for, if a prescriber intends to use herbal preparations to conduct any sort of trial as to a preparation's efficacy and:

- The herbal preparation is not approved as a registered medicine by the minister and its manufacturer claims it has a therapeutic effect; or
- Despite no therapeutic effect being claimed, toxic substances are contained in it, even if only in trace elements.

Ethics committee approval is also required for all research and studies carried out on humans.

10.3 Prescribing

Whether or not a medicine is approved, only a drug or substance classed as a medicine can be prescribed. This means it must be for a therapeutic purpose. Section 4 of the Medicines Act 1981 defines "therapeutic purpose" as:

(a) Treating or preventing disease; or

(b) Diagnosing disease or ascertaining the existence, degree, or extent of a physiological condition; or

(c) Effecting contraception; or

(d) Inducing anaesthesia; or

(e) Altering the shape, structure, size, or weight of the human body; or

(f) Otherwise preventing or interfering with the normal operation of a physiological function, whether permanently or temporarily, and whether by way of terminating or reducing or postponing, or increasing or accelerating, the operation of that function, or in any other way; or

(g) Cleaning, soaking, or lubricating contact lenses.

Not all drugs are medicines, or are regarded as being for a therapeutic purpose. The use of some drugs is strictly controlled.

10.3.1 Controlled drugs

The Misuse of Drugs Act 1975 categorises drugs according to their nature and effect into two classes: controlled drugs and non-controlled drugs.

Controlled drugs are those that are considered to require legal restrictions on their use. The Misuse of Drugs Act 1975 provides severe penalties for any unlawful prescribing of these drugs, and the supply or administration of these drugs is an offence.

All health practitioners dealing with controlled drugs should be aware of the different meanings of the following words, which are defined here very generally:

- "Illegal drugs" (generally a non-legal term) are drugs that are used for non-therapeutic reasons, and are not legally prescribed or are otherwise wrongfully obtained. Detailed provisions state which drugs are illegal, the best-known ones being cannabis in its different forms, cocaine, and heroin.
- "Possession" involves a substance in one's physical control, not necessarily on one's person. Certain drugs may only be in the possession of specified persons, such as emergency services personnel, appropriate staff in a health service institution, and community and industrial health practitioners under appropriate circumstances.
- "Supply" involves making a drug available to another person, and includes giving or selling. Legislation deems possession of more than a stipulated amount of illegal drugs to be possession for supply, no matter what the actual intention may be. Possession of a controlled drug for supply is a more serious offence than possession for personal use.

The Schedules to the Misuse of Drugs Act 1975 classify controlled drugs into three categories: Class A drugs, Class B drugs, and Class C drugs:

(1)   *Class A controlled drugs*

These are drugs that are considered to pose a very high risk of harm.[2] Most Class A drugs cannot be prescribed, and a prescription for those that can be prescribed, for example cocaine, must be on a form approved by the Director-General of Health. This class includes heroin, LSD, mescaline, and cocaine. It also includes drugs with known severe side-effects such as thalidomide.

(2)   *Class B controlled drugs*

These are drugs that pose a high risk of harm, but not a very high risk.[3] There are severe restrictions on the prescribing and dispensing of Class B drugs. They include drugs of dependence such as morphine, pethidine, amphetamine, and methadone. This class includes cannabis preparations. Prescriptions for these must also be written on a form provided by the Director-General of Health. (These forms are available from one of the regional Medsafe Control Offices — see 10.59.) Medsafe are considering adding benzodiazepines to this category of controlled drugs.[4]

---

2   Misuse of Drugs Act 1975, section 3A.
3   Misuse of Drugs Act 1975, section 3A.

(3)   Class C controlled drugs

These are drugs that are considered to pose a moderate risk of harm.[5] Class C drugs can be prescribed on the usual prescription form and include codeine, phenobarbitone, ipecacuanha, and codeine and opium powder mixture.

10.4   Form of prescription

The Medicines Regulations 1984 and the Misuse of Drugs Regulations 1977 state the form of prescriptions and who can prescribe medication. These set out the form of the prescription and require it to be legible, indelibly printed, signed, and dated with the prescriber's full address, rather than a Post Office Box number. Faxed prescriptions are commonly used, and a trial of electronic prescriptions is being undertaken. It is debatable whether these adequately meet the requirements of form.

The prescription must also contain the recipient's name, the medication dosage, the route, adequate instructions for use, and the number of times the medicine may be given or, for certain substances, the time between repeated administrations.

10.5   Who can prescribe?

This is provided for in the Medicines Regulations. Health practitioners currently authorised to prescribe for humans are medical practitioners, midwives, dentists, and independent nurse prescribers approved by the Nursing Council of New Zealand and prescribing according to the Medicines Amendment Act 1999 and the Medicines (Designated Prescriber: Nurse Practitioners) Regulations 2005.[6] These regulations no longer restrict nurse prescribers to two areas of nursing but open it up to all areas as long as the nurse fulfils the specified training. The Nursing Council has identified the training that must be undertaken and the competencies that need to be maintained for prescribing rights.[7] The regulations also determine the generic classes of medicines that nurses can prescribe. Nurse prescribing is regulated by the Nursing Council and from 18 December 2003 as the Nursing Authority established under the Health Practitioners Competence Assurance Act 2003. In September 2003 the Ministry of Health began consulting on a proposal to amend the current regulatory framework for designated prescribers. The proposal aims to streamline the current regulatory framework. It is proposed to amend the regulations to enable designated prescribers to have access to all medicines listed in the Schedules to the Medicines Regulations 1984, but require registration authorities to set limits on prescribing relevant medicines to defined designated scopes of practice. Regulation 39 of the Medicines Regulations 1984[8] does streamline conditions for authorised prescribers and does not limit access to the medicines within the Schedules. However different disciplines have had other regulations passed which relate specifically to their area of practice setting out what medicines are available to the designated prescriber. For example under the Medicines (Designated Prescriber: Nurse Practitioners) Regulations 2005, the substances that are able

---

4   At time of writing (early 2009) benzodiazepines are classified as a prescription drug only, unless specified in schedule 3 of the Misuse of Drugs Act 1975 — relates to ClassC drugs.

5   Section 3 of the Misuse of Drugs Act 1975.

6   This replaced the initial statutory regulations — Medicines (Designated Prescribers Nurses Practising in Aged Care and Child Family Health) Regulations 2001 — which restricted the areas of nurse prescribing.

7   See *New Zealand Gazette*, 10/11/2005, No 188, 4750.

8   Regulation 39 of the Medicine Regulations 1984.

to be prescribed by a designated nurse prescriber are listed in the Schedule to the Regulations.

The Nursing Council has developed a framework for nurse prescribing within the nurse practitioner framework. It includes a register for nurse prescribers, with specified requirements for application to enter the register and for ongoing competence. Nurse prescribers have to:[9]

- Be registered nurses under the Nurses Act 1977.
- Hold a current practising certificate.
- Have at least 4-5 years' experience in a particular field.
- Hold a Clinical Masters Degree, which includes required prescribing papers.
- Produce a portfolio that provides evidence that Nurse Practitioner and Nurse Prescriber[10] competencies have been met.
- Attend an interview with the Nursing Council Nurse Practitioner assessment panel.
- Possibly undertake a clinical site visit.
- Be approved by the Nursing Council as a nurse practitioner and a nurse prescriber within a specified scope of practice.

There are also strict requirements for the approval and monitoring of programmes for the development of specified competencies for advanced nursing practice and nurse prescribing.

10.5.1 What prescribers should know

(1) *Subsidies*

Some medicines in New Zealand are subsidised so that people can have access to medicines to meet reasonable health needs.

PHARMAC[11] manages the national Pharmaceutical Schedule that lists fully and partially subsidised medicines and related products, which together will be referred to below as pharmaceuticals. The Pharmaceutical Schedule is regularly updated, and the schedule and updates are available free of charge to prescribers.

The Pharmaceutical Schedule is published in April, August, and December and updates are published monthly. Each update contains a cumulative list of all changes to the Pharmaceutical Schedule over a 4-month period. These changes are then incorporated into the Pharmaceutical Schedule.

The update is sent to all prescribers on or about the 24th of each month. It is important for prescribers to read the update before the first of the next month, when the changes become effective, so they know of any changes that may affect their prescribing.

---

9   Information provided by Susanne Trim, Professional Nursing Adviser, New Zealand Nurses Organisation and the NZNO publication *Independent Nurse Prescribing*, February 2002, available on the NZNO website at www.nzno.org.nz.

10   For information on Nurse Practitioners see the Nursing Council of New Zealand website at www.nursingcouncil.org.nz and the NZNO website at www.nzno.org.nz.

11   www.pharmac.govt.nz.

A list of pharmaceuticals affected by changes for a current month is at the front of each update. Full details are listed in the body of the update, and months are cumulative. The news stories are also a good way to keep up to date with the month's changes.

On page 6 of the Pharmaceutical Schedule is a useful diagram that indicates what the different symbols etc mean in the Schedule.

All fully subsidised products are identified by a tick next to the brand name in the right-hand column. The product name is also in bold.

(2)   *Generic prescribing and substitution*

If prescribers prescribe generically, their patients are saved potential extra costs because the pharmacist should dispense the fully subsidised brand if one is available. Also, when a medicine is prescribed generically, pharmacists must dispense the preferred brand as designated by PHARMAC. This usually leads to additional savings at the national level. Generic prescribing also avoids prescribing brands that are only partly subsidised, or are not subsidised at all. Prescribers should inform their patients about the costs of the medicines and, where a subsidy is available, they should be told this as part of the information given to enable them to make an informed choice and give informed consent. If a brand that is not subsidised or not fully subsidised is prescribed, where there is a subsidised brand available and the patient has not been advised of this, the patient has a right to make a complaint to the Health and Disability Commissioner or the prescriber's disciplinary authority. It is best to be aware of this when responding to marketing and advertisements by pharmaceutical company representatives.

(3)   *Sole supply and preferred brand*

Where PHARMAC has entered into sole supply or preferred brand (preferred supplier) arrangements with pharmaceutical suppliers to keep the cost down, pharmacists can substitute the preferred brand over the brand prescribed. They can do this only if the prescriber authorised substitution[12] and the consumer has not chosen to pay for the non-sole supply brand or specifically requested the brand prescribed. This includes repeat dispensing where the brand prescribed is no longer subsidised or is partly subsidised. At the back of the Pharmaceutical Schedule are substitution forms that prescribers can fill out so that the pharmacist can substitute brands if necessary.

Preferred brand pharmaceuticals are highlighted in the Pharmaceutical Schedule by being blocked out. If a prescriber generically prescribes a preferred brand pharmaceutical, the pharmacist must dispense the preferred brand. The preferred brand will always be subsidised, but other brands of the same pharmaceutical may not be.

A sole supply product is the only brand of a pharmaceutical that is subsidised. To save consumers extra costs, prescribers should either have substitution forms in place if prescribing by brand name, or prescribe generically.

---

12   Pharmac Schedule September 2008 contains a change to the general rules that no other authorisation is necessary for the pharmacist to substitute to the subsidised medicine, as long as there is a generic authorisation which can be on the bottom of the prescription.

(4) Endorsements on prescriptions

Where a condition is specified for the pharmaceutical in section B of the Pharmaceutical Schedule, prescribers need to endorse the prescription to access the subsidy. It needs to be endorsed with the words "certified condition" or the condition of the patient unless the schedule states otherwise. There are some exceptions where specific words have to be used in the endorsement.

(5) Surcharges

Some medicines are not fully subsidised and have a manufacturer's surcharge. The consumer has to pay the difference between the manufacturer's price and the subsidy, plus a pharmacy mark-up. As a rough guide to the amount the consumer will pay, the following calculation can be used:

$$\text{Manufacturer's surcharge to patient} = (\text{price} - \text{subsidy}) \times 1.86$$

(6) Exceptional circumstances

In exceptional circumstances a particular consumer can have a medicine subsidised when it is not listed in the Pharmaceutical Schedule. The District Health Boards have criteria for when, and whether, this is appropriate. Applications and inquiries should be directed to the Regional Exceptional Circumstances Manager in the District Health Board office.

(7) Special authority

Some pharmaceuticals are subsidised only when a special authority application has been approved for a particular consumer. The criteria for approval of special authorities are below the pharmaceutical listing in the Pharmaceutical Schedule and are updated regularly. Applications must be sent to Health Benefits Centre, Private Bag 3015, Wanganui.[13]

The application must be in writing and include the:

• Patient's name and date of birth;
• Diagnosis and brief clinical details;
• Name of the medicine required and its *form and strength*;
• Duration of the course of treatment; and
• Alternative therapies that have been tried.

The application must:

• Be signed by the prescriber;
• Include the prescriber's printed name and full address;
• Show the prescriber's health practitioner registration number; and
• Provide evidence of the criteria as per special authority conditions for the medicine applied for.

(8) Restrictions

Some pharmaceuticals are restricted to being eligible for subsidy only if they are dispensed from retail pharmacies or from hospital pharmacies.

---

13   Inquiries by phone: 0800 243 666.

Note: if the prescription for the pharmaceutical is not dispensed by the specified pharmacies, it will not be eligible for subsidy. There are rules relating to retail pharmacy and hospital pharmacy restrictions: see the Pharmaceutical Schedule general rules.

(9)   *Practitioner supply order and wholesale supply order*

Prescribers can order supplies of some pharmaceuticals when these need to be administered personally to a consumer in an emergency, until a pharmacy can supply the consumer under a prescription. Generally, only the pharmaceuticals and quantities listed in section E, Part I of the Pharmaceutical Schedule will be eligible for subsidy. They must also be ordered on a form supplied by the District Health Boards or the ministry. It needs to be personally signed by the prescriber, setting out their address and the quantity of the pharmaceutical.

If a prescriber is working in a remote area, they can order supplies for administration to particular consumers in their care, not just in an emergency. These are listed in the Pharmaceutical Schedule.

(10)   *Quantities and prescriber endorsements (repeat prescriptions)*

Prescribers cannot prescribe more medicine than a patient reasonably requires for 3 months. Any more than that and any subsidy will not be available. For some Class B controlled drugs, only one month's supply will be subsidised. Where a 3-month supply is prescribed, pharmacies could until recently dispense all medicine only in monthly lots for it to be subsidised, unless the patient met the exemption criteria. Some medicines can now be dispensed in a 3 month supply.

Consumers who have difficulty getting to a pharmacy may receive an exemption from monthly dispensing, but the consumer must sign the back of the prescription certifying that they:

•   Have limited physical mobility; or
•   Live and work more than 30 minutes from the nearest pharmacy; or
•   Are relocating to another area; or
•   Are travelling extensively and will be out of town when the repeat prescriptions are due.

In other cases, a prescriber can endorse the prescription with the words "certified exemption" beside the prescribed item. In endorsing it, the prescriber is certifying that the consumer wishes to have more than a monthly lot of the medicine, that they have been stabilised on that medicine for a reasonable period of time, and that the prescriber believes the consumer is compliant and will continue on that medicine.

(11)   *Prescribing misconduct*

There are criminal sanctions in the legislation for the unauthorised possession, possession for supply, administration, and self-administration of controlled drugs, with some specifically named drugs of dependence having more severe penalties than others. There are also penalties for forging, fraudulently obtaining, or wrongfully giving prescriptions for controlled substances or drugs of dependence.

There is also prescribing conduct that, although not illegal, amounts to improper prescribing and could lead to disciplinary action. Examples include excessive prescribing, prescribing of inappropriate combinations of medicines, or reckless prescribing where potential harmful consequences are not even considered. Also, prescribing that does not take into account the particular consumer and their needs and condition could also be the subject of disciplinary action.

Case

Health Practitioners' Disciplinary Tribunal (HPDT)

Case Med06/44P

Dr C, a general practitioner, wrote an excessive amount of prescriptions for sudomyl — in excess of 46,000 tablets over a period of 2 years. Sudomyl is the generic name for pseudoephedrine which is the main precursor for making methamphetamine. To get the medication he used patient names and details of which they were unaware. He also had an agreement with a pharmacy for bulk supply. Regardless of the underlying illegal use for the drug the HPDT found him in breach of professional standards on the basis that his prescribing was in breach of regulations 39 and 40 of the Medicine Regulations 1984. He had used patient names and details for an improper purpose of which there was no clinical or medical use for them, and they did not receive any or only a minor number of the tablets prescribed. They rejected his explanation that it was for research reasons and cancelled his registration as well as imposing a $15,000 fine and order of costs of $25,000.

A Medical Officer of Health has the power to check up on any prescriber if improper prescribing is suspected. If asked, the prescriber must within 30 days provide the Medical Officer of Health information relating to the prescribing, administering, or supplying of any medicine prescribed by the prescriber including why it was prescribed and the age, diagnosis, and prognosis of the patient, details of any specialist referral, and any other treatments considered or tried. This checking on prescribers is in relation to all prescriptions,[14] not just for controlled drugs as it used to be.[15]

(12) *Drug seekers*

Prescribers must not treat drug addicts with addictive drugs. Many drug seekers will approach some prescribers often for narcotic analgesics, benzodiazepines, and codeine. There are Medsafe medical control officers who are available for advice. There is a head office and regional offices:[16]

Head Office, Medsafe	Northern Medicines Control Office
NZ Medicines and Medical	Private Bag 92 522
Devices Safety Authority	Wellesley Street
PO Box 5013	Auckland
Wellington	Tel (09) 580 9088
Tel (04) 819 6900	Fax (09) 580 9240

---

14   Regulation 44B of the Medicines Regulations 1984.

15   The Medical Officer of Health can look into prescribing of controlled drugs under section 19(2) of the Misuse of Drugs Act 1975.

16   Medicine control is no longer a part of Medsafe but now comes under Quality and Safety, Sector Funding and Accountability in the Ministry of Health.

Fax (04) 819 6806

Central Medicines Control Office	Southern Medicines Control Office
PO Box 5013	PO Box 5849
Wellington	Dunedin
Tel (04) 496 2437	Tel (03)4748592
Fax (04) 496 2229	Fax (03) 4748582

The medicine control offices can be contacted for advice about whether a patient is a restricted person under section 49 of the Medicines Act 1981, with regard to supplying a particular medicine, or whether the supply is restricted to one particular prescriber. Information can also be obtained about whether the person has been seeking drugs from other prescribers. General information is also available.

(13)   *Reporting of drug seekers*

Practitioners can also provide useful information to assist others about drug seekers they come into contact with. They will not infringe a patient's privacy rights by reporting drug seekers. Rule 11 of the Health Information Privacy Code provides an exemption to the rule against disclosure of information where it is not desirable or practical to obtain the individual's consent to disclose and they are, or are likely to become, dependent on a controlled drug, prescription medicine, or restricted medicine.

(a)   List of locally restricted people

Medsafe publishes a *Drug Abuse Newsletter* at least twice a year. It has a section on general information about drug seeking behaviour, as well as a local section. In the local section is a list of restricted people within the area and anyone else who has been notified to a medicine control office as an active drug seeker.

(14)   *Controlled drug prescription pads*

The medicine control offices also supply the controlled drug prescription pads.

10.6   Handling medicines

Health practitioners should be familiar with the legislation outlining the procedures required in handling medicines. Most hospitals and health service institutions have drawn up policies, to ensure that legal dictates are followed, but following them does not guarantee compliance with the law. Management should also be particularly aware of the law regarding the storing and handling of medicines.

Health practitioners have access to many drugs that need not be prescribed before being administered, such as paracetamol, kaomagma, laxatives, and many different creams and lotions, which they may administer and apply on their own initiative. It should be remembered that although the handling and administering of these medicines may not be the subject of legislation, practitioners should carefully follow any hospital policies, or they may be subject to disciplinary action and/or a complaint by a consumer.

There are criminal penalties in the legislation for the unauthorised possession, possession for supply, administration, and self-administration of controlled drugs, with some specifically named drugs of dependence having more severe penalties than others. There are also penalties for the forging or fraudulent obtaining of, or wrongful giving of, prescriptions for controlled substances or drugs of dependence.

Health practitioners have access to controlled and non-controlled drugs. They should be very careful that not only do they not misuse this privilege, but also that they are never tempted to cut corners and compromise the clear guidelines for handling drugs. Misuse of medicines by health practitioners is considered such a serious matter by the community that health practitioners should not give cause for doubt as to their integrity in handling them.

It is possible for a health practitioner to lose their registration if the privileged position of access to drugs is intentionally abused. Even where the law has technically not been broken, there may have been carelessness or negligence, which could lead to a breach of professional standards and disciplinary action.

Case

Health Practitioner's Disciplinary Tribunal (HPDT)

Case Nur07/69P / Misappropriation of drugs

Decision: 126/Nur07/69P

This case concerned an enrolled nurse who had been convicted of theft of morphine ampoules from her place of work. She subsequently appeared before the HPDT. The nurse had on two occasions completed the drug register and assigned drugs (morphine) to patients who had not been prescribed them and did not receive them. Instead she took the morphine for her own use. The case report of her conviction was clear that the evidence had been established and on this basis the HPDT found that her actions were not only illegal, but immoral and a breach of her professional conduct that adversely affected on her ability to practice. The nurse had her registration cancelled and had to pay 50 percent of the costs.

10.6.1 Medication order forms

A patient's medication order form is legally recognised as a prescription form for the purposes of medicine legislation, and it is suggested that health practitioners should not use this form for recording verbal orders given over the telephone, except where he/she has prescribed that medicine.[17] If other health practitioners wish to record a temporary oral order by a prescriber, they are advised to enter the administration of the medicine in the medication administration form. This indicates clearly that the medicine was given subject to a verbal order, and it prevents any mistake as to their record purporting to be a prescription as such, or the impression that the order was written by a prescriber, and no further action was required. It is also suggested that some clear and distinguishing marker,

---

17   Where hospital policy establishes the use of medication order forms for verbal orders, it is suggested staff should be very careful that a verbal order is clearly marked (preferably in a different colour pen). A suggested, perhaps more satisfactory, approach is that set out at 10.7.2.

such as a sticker, be applied to the consumer's notes with a clear notation on it that the order is to be written up, and the time by which this must be done.[18]

In an emergency, where there is not time to keep a proper record sheet of the medication given, a record should nevertheless be kept in whatever form is possible, for example writing the details in felt pen on the person's skin.[19]

10.6.2   Storage in a ward, clinic, etc

Storage of medicines and recording their use in a ward or unit is the responsibility of the charge nurse or team leader. They must maintain the prescribed security by ensuring that the medicine cupboard is locked when not in use. The key is always to be in the possession of the most senior nurse on the ward at the time, and must not be left where others have access to it.[20]

A register of all controlled medicines must be kept, with details of number and usage (including the consumer's name, date, and time of administration or destruction, prescriber, and signatures of the person giving the medicine and the witness) recorded. The nurse in charge of a ward is responsible for the maintenance of the register of such medicines kept in the ward.

Administration of controlled medicines must be witnessed by another person, for example the nurse preparing and administering the medicine, and at least one other witness (nurse or doctor) should sign the register. Any error must be corrected or witnessed, with the erroneous material carefully ruled through and not obliterated, and a marginal note with the correct details and the signatures of both parties legibly entered with the date (and preferably time) of the correction, and initialled by the witness. It is recommended that if it is possible to do so clearly and legibly, the names of the signatories should also be printed.

Where a controlled medicine is unusable it must be destroyed, and accounted for by at least two people, who record such destruction in the register. Loss must be recorded, and where a medicine is only partly used, the remainder of the medicine must be destroyed, again witnessed by two people and recorded in the register. Exact procedure differs, therefore practitioners should be aware of the precise requirements in their workplace.

The balance of controlled medicines should also be checked regularly by two people, and any unusable medicines destroyed as above. In emergencies, verbal orders for administration of a controlled medicine may be given by a prescriber, with the requirement that a prescriber must countersign it within an agreed time frame. Verbal orders should be accepted only in emergencies, or where the prescriber cannot reasonably attend to write

---

18   Administering a medicine under a verbal order is not specifically provided for in the legislation, but the Ministry of Health is of the view that if verbal approval from an authorised prescriber is given before charting and subsequently countersigned within an agreed period of time by an authorised prescriber, that is sufficient for legislative compliance. Verbal orders that are not retrospectively countersigned by a relevant doctor are open to challenge if there is some mishap. Therefore, anyone who carries out a verbal order exposes herself/himself to a legal risk.

19   This method of recording was used where obstetric patients were evacuated onto the hospital lawns during the earthquake in Newcastle, New South Wales in December 1989.

20   Today it is common practice for each nurse to have an electronic swipe card with their own identifying pass-code to access the secure drug cupboard. To be legally safe this should not be shared with others as the pass-code is the identifier informing who has been in the cupboard and can be counterchecked with the written records.

the prescription, ie verbal orders should not be based on convenience alone. In all cases the checklist on telephone orders (10.7.2) should be followed as closely as possible.

All those concerned with handling medicines should be familiar with the requirements at their workplace for storing them in their ward or unit or clinic, and the use and transport of them. They should also be aware of the possible offences that apply to the handling and possession of drugs outlined above. The charge nurse, team leader, or most senior nurse in smaller establishments, and industrial and community nurses have responsibility for overseeing the proper adherence to legislative and administrative requirements. They must also ensure that a regular and thorough inventory of the medicines in their possession is undertaken, immediately reporting any discrepancy in numbers to the appropriate authority. The only way to find out the detailed extent of these responsibilities is to have access to the legislation and workplace policies manual, both of which should be made available through an employer.

An important point to bear in mind is that medicines should never be put into a container different from that in which they were dispensed. The Medicines Regulations 1984 provide for the labelling of medicines by the dispensing pharmacist, giving their category and use, and this should not be altered. For some consumers monitored dosage systems are very useful with special containers, with compartments for different days such as blister packs, dosette boxes, or dispensing boxes. Preferably these should be filled and sealed by the dispensing pharmacist. Health practitioners such as community nurses, who will need to administer the medicines, should not take responsibility for filling their consumers' boxes from other pharmacy labelled containers. In cases where it is not possible for the boxes to be filled and sealed before supplying to the consumer, it is advisable that if necessary the nurse marks the containers with only the day and time the medicines are to be taken, rather than with the name of the medicines themselves. This means that they will not be undertaking that the medicines are specific ones, which technically could be dispensing[21] the medicines, but are rather providing for the medicine's administration. The consumer should be the only person to self-administer the medicine, and should be well instructed (preferably in writing in addition to verbal instructions) as to the name of the medicine, and given any information regarding the taking of it, side-effects, and contra-indications that are relevant. This provides necessary information for both the consumer and others who may need to deal with that person in an emergency. Nurses administering medicines from these types of containers that do not contain the pharmacy labelled names of the medicines run the risk of exposure to legal liability if something goes wrong, because the nurse will not be correctly administering the medicines. It is also not acceptable to tamper with a seal on a box between its closure by the pharmacist and time of administration.

10.7   Administration

Administration of medicines means the giving of the medicine, orally, by injection, per rectum, or by another route. Practitioners are permitted to administer medicines where they are required to do so as part of their duties.

---

21   *Dispensing:* This means making a medicine available from a central supply for individual use, a process usually carried out by a pharmacist. Those allowed to dispense medicines are specifically designated by the legislation and the process and recording of both storing and dispensing of medicines is set out in some detail.

The Medicines Act 1981 permits administration of prescription medicines only in accordance with the direction of the authorised prescriber who prescribed it, or according to a standing order.

Any health practitioner who administers a medicine should have an understanding of what its therapeutic purpose is, and should be able to justify its use. It is advisable to therefore:

- Insist on proper prescribing so to be able to read clearly the name of the medicine (not guess), the dosage, route, frequency, and any special instructions, as medicines must not be administered unless properly prescribed.
- Question the prescriber or pharmacist where necessary, for example regarding the dosage or route of administration if any of these are outside the set of indicators for the medicine's use.
- Refuse to prepare medicines for injection in advance of their immediate use.
- Refuse to administer a medicine that is not either in a pharmacy dispensed container, or placed in another container or drawn up by the administrator of it, or in their presence.
- Carefully follow established policy requirements.
- Not seek signatures of "witnesses" after the medicine has been given, to satisfy requirements.
- Make sure that any ampoules or tablets are really the medication prescribed, and not a substitute.
- Check the expiry date of the medicine.
- Ensure the consumer makes an informed choice about whether to receive the medicine.
- Consider whether the dosage and route and timing are still appropriate at the time of administration. (The medicine might have been prescribed at a much earlier time).
- Check there will be no interactions with other medicines the consumer is taking.
- Contact the prescriber if there are concerns about timing, contraindications, or interactions.
- Clearly record the date, time, dose, and route of the medicine's administration.
- Record in the consumer's notes, and let the prescriber know what the effect of the medicine was where appropriate, eg if an analgesic is administered, whether this has any effect on the type, intensity, and duration of the pain.[22]

Health practitioners administering medicines should be aware of their need to take reasonable care to prevent harm to patients from negligent handling and administration of medication. Medicine errors are common, and while the majority do not result in an adverse event, enough do to warrant scrupulous adherence to the standards of administration and checking with other staff where necessary. Practitioners should always:

- Check the order/prescription is clear before administering the medicine, especially if it is by way of an oral or telephone order;
- Check they administer the correct medicine;
- If rewriting, be very careful to write exactly what was prescribed in the clinical notes;

---

22   Most of the information in 10.7 has been taken with kind permission from the New Zealand Nurses Organisation from *Guidelines for Nurses on the Administration of Medicines* (2nd ed), New Zealand Nurses Organisation, PO Box 2128, Wellington, 2002 at pages 9 and 10.

- Check they give the right dose;
- Check they administer it to the right consumer;
- Check it is administered at the correct site, or by the correct route;
- Check for adverse effects.

The following examples of cases where there have been administration of medicine errors resulting in adverse results are nearly all from overseas. In New Zealand it is rare for a case to reach a Court, but medicine errors resulting in harm to consumers have to the writer's knowledge been the subject of findings of medical error by ACC, a breach of the Code of Health and Disability Services Consumers' Rights, and/or the subject of findings of professional misconduct.

10.7.1 Failure to check the order/prescription is clear before administering

---

Case

Norton v Argonaut Insurance Co 144 So 2d 249 (1962)

A 3-month-old baby was treated with lanoxin elixir, the original order being "2.5cc (0.125 mg) q6h × 3 then once daily". After the child was digitalised, the mother was instructed in administration and maintenance of the dose, and the child was treated at home. On second admission the admitting doctor noted that the mother was giving medication, but did not specify what it was. He increased the dose, telling the mother, and wrote "Give 3.0cc lanoxin today for 1 dose only", neglecting to specify the form of the medicine, the route, and the fact that the mother was giving the medication. Later that day the assistant director of nursing volunteered to assist in the ward due to its lack of staff, and began by checking the medications. On reading this order, and being unfamiliar with the fact that there was a paediatric suspension of lanoxin, she questioned other doctors and nurses about a written order for lanoxin that did not specify route, and appeared excessive. Due to their not fully understanding the nurse's lack of knowledge about the medicine, and the circumstances of its proposed administration (the mother had already given the day's dose), the nurse was advised by these people to give the medicine in the dosage written down. Wrongly believing that there is a presumption that unless specified, medicines are to be given intramuscularly, the nurse gave the child 3cc lanoxin intramuscularly. The child died.

The Court found the hospital, doctor, and nurse jointly liable for the child's death. Two specific and important points regarding the administration of medicines by nurses were made by the Court — where a medication order is not clear, nurses should make absolutely certain what the doctor intended; and this should be done by consulting the doctor who wrote the order, because, as this case shows, consulting others may lead to errors.

The further point could be made that the nurse in *Norton*'s case helped out in an area of specialty in which she was not competent. This shows that inexperienced practitioners should beware of undertaking specialist activities, even where attempting to help overworked colleagues.

10.7.2   Telephone orders

Most health service institutions have established protocols for the taking of telephone medication orders. The following is an advisable procedure to ensure that such orders are taken reasonably carefully.

Checklist

How to take a telephone medication order

- Write the order as it is being given.
- Read it back to the prescriber.
- Always get a colleague to hear the order from the prescriber and write it down, and repeat it to the prescriber.
- Resolve any discrepancy or difficulty in hearing the order before the telephone conversation is completed.
- The order should be written, preferably on the medication administration form (*not* on the medication order form), and clearly marked as an *administration of a medicine pursuant to telephone order* (preventing it being considered a written order by the prescriber, or the erroneous reading of the actual written order as a fresh order for repeat administration).
- Enter administration on the medication administration form as being given in the usual way, after checking and witnessing, as required.
- Record in that consumer's notes that special action is required, namely the writing up of the order by the prescriber.

The difficulties of identifying those situations where a telephone medication order may be misheard leads the writer to recommend that this form of ordering should only be used in emergencies, or where a written order would be extremely difficult to obtain. It should not be used as a tool of convenience.

10.7.3   Error in transcribing an order

It is not advisable to transcribe prescriptions and administration of medicines from the prescription chart or administration chart to other records. Where a prescriber, for example Dr Smith, has ordered a medicine, the other health practitioners writing in the consumer's notes are advised to write: "Seen by Dr Smith. Analgesia prescribed as per medication order form" — not, "Seen by Dr Smith. Pethidine 75 mgm imi hourly prn ordered." Mistakes can be made in the transcription. Someone may be tempted to rely on the secondary source rather than the original, and may end up giving the wrong medicine. Conversely, medicines must not be administered on the basis of any other written source than the original medication prescription on the prescription form or chart (such as the nurses' notes, doctor's consultation form, or a pharmacy dispensed label on a box).

Case
Pillai v Messiter (No 2) (1989) 16 NSWLR 197 (NSW CA)

A patient died from an overdose of phenytoin. The order for the medicine had been transcribed from an out-of-date prescription sheet onto a new one. The patient had been ordered phenytoin 230 mg daily, and tegretol 1,400 mg daily. In transcribing, the doctor wrote the new order as phenytoin 1,400 mg to be given three times daily. A number of other doctor and nurses had also not noticed the error in transcription. The transcribing doctor was struck off the register for misconduct in a professional respect, and appealed to the Supreme Court of Australia.

Although the Supreme Court held that the doctor's error was an "unfortunate mistake", it held that it was not enough to constitute misconduct to the extent of attracting the penalty of being struck off the register. Certainly such a mistake could lead to liability in negligence on the doctor's part, possibly also on the part of the other nurses and doctors who failed to detect the mistake.

10.7.4   Giving the wrong medicine

There could be several reasons for a consumer to receive the wrong medicine, for example:

*   The prescription is unclear (dealt with above);
*   A verbal order is misheard;
*   Failure to check the label on the medicine.

Case

Nurse: Report on Opinion — Case 97HDC9112

Health and Disability Commissioner's opinion, 31 August 1998

Reported on the website of the office of the Health and Disability Commissioner at www.hdc.org.nz

A nurse in a rest home was found to have breached a consumer's rights when she administered Batrafen solution into his eyes (which was for tinea between his toes), instead of his eye drops (Liquifilm). Both the Batrafen and the Liquifilm were solutions in drop form and were in labelled containers. The label on the Batrafen stated, "Not to be applied to or near the eyes". Both containers were kept in the same box as eye medications in drop form belonging to other residents. The nurse was found to be in breach of Right 4(2) and (4) of the Code of Health and Disability Services Consumers' Rights for failing to check the medicine was the correct one, and for failing to check the label.

10.7.5   Mistake in verbal orders

There is a responsibility on the part of health practitioners to carefully check a verbal order for treatment with which they are not familiar at the time of receiving it.

Case

Henson v Board of Management of Perth Hospital (1939) 41 WALR 15 (WA SC)

A resident doctor instructed a student nurse to administer glycerine and carbol eardrops to a patient. The nurse understood him to have ordered undiluted acid carbol, but when she went to question the doctor he was gone. She checked with a staff nurse, who was also unsure, but poured some carbolic acid into a bottle to give to the patient, instructing him to pour some of it into his ear. When he did so damage was caused to his eardrum and he sustained some permanent hearing loss.

The Court found both nurses and the doctor liable in negligence. It held that the student nurse, while not being expected to know as much as a staff nurse, should have exercised due care in ascertaining whether she had obtained the correct medication. The staff nurse, it seems, had even less chance of escaping liability, especially as it was shown that she burned her fingers when pouring out the carbolic acid. The doctor was also negligent, the Court said, because he failed to give adequate instructions when a student nurse was involved, and failed to record the order in writing.

10.7.6 Failure to check the medicine

This, of course, is a serious failure in the eyes of the law (see *Bugden v Harbour View Hospital*).[23]

In *Bugden*'s case Nurse S argued that Nurse B's failure to read the label was an intervening factor. Nurse B in turn pointed to the doctor's failure to read it as an intervening factor (see chapter 8). The Court did not accept either argument, holding that the foreseeability of harm to the patient was enough to require all involved to take care. It found the nurses liable, while exonerating the doctor.

This scenario is also highlighted by two New Zealand cases, both of which have been reported in the news media. In the first, a consumer was prescribed and administered augmentin, despite wearing a medic alert bracelet stating she was allergic to augmentin, and her medical records containing a reference to the allergy. The consumer had an anaphylactic reaction and died. The doctor who prescribed the augmentin was held accountable by the coroner. In the second case, the consumer wore a medic alert bracelet stating that she was allergic to stemetil. She was prescribed pethidine and maxolon for renal colic. However, stemetil was administered in error. Luckily, the error was detected straight away and a tragedy was averted. The registered nurse who checked the medicine and was supervising the enrolled nurse who administered the medicine was found to have breached the Code of Health and Disability Services Consumers' Rights.

10.7.7 Giving the wrong dose

There are cases where the wrong dose has been given for various reasons, such as not reading or not hearing the order correctly. This may be because of illegibility or carelessness on the prescriber's part, or carelessness on the part of those receiving the order.

This has been canvassed to some extent in this chapter. A case occurred in Victoria, Australia where a 19-month-old girl was given 500 mg of aminophylline for asthma, instead of 50 mg. The doctor ordering the medicine had been on duty for many hours, and had failed to write the order clearly. The two registered nurses on duty had failed to question the excessive dosage.[24] Health practitioners should check the label on the bottle or ampoule carefully, and the mode of administration — is the medicine to be given orally, intramuscularly, or per rectum? Of course, also they must always check when the last dose was given. In this type of case liability does not just fall on the doctor but also on the nurses administering the medication. Each of the health professionals involved have a duty to the client and will breach that duty if they fail to check a drug, its prescription, any allergies and administer it incorrectly.

---

23   *Bugden v Harbour View Hospital* [1947] 2 DLR 338 (see 8.8.4).

24   Described in J O'Sullivan, *Law for Nurses and Allied Health Professionals in Australia* (3rd ed), Sydney, Law Book Co, 1983, 192.

Case

Smith v Brighton, *The Times*, 2 May 1958

The patient was ordered to have 30 injections of streptomycin at 8-hourly intervals for a severe case of boils. She received 34 doses, and consequently suffered damage to the eighth cranial nerve, causing loss of balance. On investigation of the facts, it was found that there had not been an adequate record of the number of injections, and no cut-off date had been established. This was the ward sister's responsibility.

As a result the nurses who administered the extra injections were held not liable. An added feature of this case was that the ward sister, believing the nurses were the ones who would be held responsible, had attempted to shield the nurses by concealing from the doctor the fact that the extra doses had been given. This, the trial Judge held, was an "ugly and unfortunate feature" of the case, and may have prevented the woman from receiving the benefit of the doctor's knowledge of the circumstances. The hospital was found liable for significant compensation for damages based on the ward sister's negligence.

Case

R v Brown 6/5/94, Gallen J, HC Wellington, S-27/94

On 16 March 1994, a 73-year-old man underwent surgery at Wellington Hospital. The operation was successful and the patient was recovering. On 18 March, Nurse Brown was caring for the patient. He was receiving an antibiotic intravenously with saline via a Metriset at a rate of 100 ml an hour. He was also receiving an analgesic via an epidural through an Imed infusion pump at 5 ml an hour. At about 10.10 am, Nurse Brown administered the due dose of antibiotic into the Metriset running at the correct rate. She then altered the epidural pump setting from 5 ml to 100 ml an hour. The patient subsequently became unconscious and died on 24 March 1994.

Nurse Brown pleaded guilty. She was convicted of manslaughter and discharged by Gallen J in the Wellington High Court in May 1994. Nurse Brown was later called to appear before the Nursing Council. The Council took into account the presentence report, Nurse Brown's personal and family circumstances, and Gallen J's decision. They found that her care fell well short of the standard of care and skill expected of a reasonably prudent nurse in the same circumstances. She was ordered to practise subject to certain conditions for 3 years, and pay 50 percent of the council's costs. Details of the case were published in *The Gazette* and *Kai Tiaki: Nursing New Zealand*.[25]

10.7.8 Giving the medicine to the wrong patient

Even where it is thought that a consumer's name is known, their identity should be carefully checked. Some might always say, "Yes" when asked "Are you Mrs So-and-So?" just to be polite or helpful, when they did not hear the question correctly. Positive identification should be made by having the consumer state their name and date of birth. Special care should be taken where it is known or suspected that there are two clients with the same surname. This care should be taken even where the health practitioner feels familiar with the consumer's name, and embarrassed at going through the procedure. It is better to face

---

25   December 1994-January 1995.

some embarrassment over the apparent over-cautiousness of such a procedure (one may even make a joke of it), than to regret later that, for the sake of saving face, one has caused heartache and loss to others.

10.7.9   Giving the medicine in the wrong site

Special requirements for the administration of medicines must be known by, and/or communicated to, those administering medicines or consumers taking them. This is especially important for practice nurses giving vaccinations. It is a key requirement of any Vaccinators' Certificate.

Injections may cause harm if given subcutaneously, rather than intramuscularly.

Case

From *Medical Protection Society Report* 1974[26]

A general practice doctor prescribed kenalog (triamcinolene acetonide) for a patient. The nurse administering it was not aware of the manufacturer's warning that the medicine should be given by deep intramuscular injection to avoid subcutaneous fat atrophy. Due to the subcutaneous injection of the medicine and resulting fat atrophy, the woman sued the doctor. The Medical Protection Society settled on behalf of the doctor.

The nurse was not sued in this case, but it may well be that in New Zealand medical error[27] on the part of the nurse and the doctor would be found, as well as breach of the Code of Health and Disability Services Consumers Rights. Nurses, in particular, may also be interested in the following case.

Case

Cavan v Wilcox [1975] SCR 663 (SC)

A nurse administered an injection of bicillin into a patient's deltoid muscle. Despite the fact that she had pulled back the plunger to check that no blood vessel had been pierced, the substance entered the circumflex artery. Consequently, the patient developed gangrene of part of his hand.

The Court found the nurse not liable in negligence, as she had checked that she had not penetrated any blood vessel, which was satisfactory precaution under the circumstances. The Court also decided that knowledge of the proximity of the artery to the injection site was not part of nurse training and therefore not part of the body of knowledge that should be possessed by the reasonable nurse. Possibly today in New Zealand, ACC or the Health and Disability Commissioner would come to a different conclusion. Hitting of the sciatic nerve is, of course, a danger of which nurses should be aware. This was the conclusion of the following US case.

Case

Honeywell v Rogers 251 F Supp 841 (1966)

---

26   Described in A Langslow, "Drugs draw judicial fire" (1981) 10(10) Australian Nurses Journal 23.
27   See chapter 8 re the Injury Prevention, Rehabilitation, and Compensation Act 2001, medical error is no longer a requirement; instead it is treatment injury.

> A student nurse gave an injection of iron dextran to an 11-month-old child. The mother gave evidence that it was given towards the centre of the buttock, and not in the outer and upper quadrant.[28]

The Court took into account the training, supervision, and knowledge of student nurses in the giving of injections, and determined that the injection was negligently given by the student nurse in question.

10.7.10   Failure to check for adverse effects

It should be evident by what has been said that all health practitioners who administer any medicine should be aware of the likely adverse effects of it. This may be information:

*   Learned from lectures or textbooks;
*   Set out on the medicine label, or accompanying brochure;
*   Established by circular distributed by the employer;
*   Recorded in the consumer's notes by the prescriber.

Case

Chin Keow v Government of Malaysia [1967] 1 WLR 813 (PC)

A doctor ordered penicillin for a patient, whom he knew had been given penicillin previously. The doctor was aware of the possibility of an adverse reaction to penicillin. However, he had given many doses (as many as 100 per day) without any such reaction. In this case he went ahead and gave the injection. It was only after the death of the patient from an adverse reaction, that his outpatient card was consulted and found to be marked, "Allergic to Penicillin".[29]

The Court found the doctor liable. It said that it would take into account the probability of adverse reactions, and what the reasonable practitioner should know about them when considering what, if any, liability to impose. The doctor should have made further inquiries, and the fact that reactions are rare was not justification for his failure to do so. Medicines that require specific attention from health practitioners, such as digoxin and insulin, are the most obvious medicines about which they should take care, but as pointed out above, not the only ones.

10.7.11   Standing orders

Any prescription medicine or specified controlled drug[30] can be issued, supplied, and administered under a standing order that complies with the Medicines (Standing Order)

---

28   Note that even this "traditional" upper outer quadrant site risks the injection being placed too medially in the quadrant and the dorso-gluteal site is in fact the *upper outer aspect* of the upper outer quadrant. See articles by Ann Shaw, "Choosing the right injection site", *Kai Tiaki Nursing New Zealand*, December 2002/January 2003 and Wendy Scott and Mike Marfell-Jones, "Evidence alone is not enough to bring about practice change", *Kai Tiaki Nursing New Zealand*, February 2004.

29   Other cases involving the failure to take proper precautions to prevent adverse reactions include *Battersby v Tottman* (1985) 37 SASR 524, where the serious condition of the patient was held to warrant excessively large doses, despite the danger of adverse effects, and *Robinson v Post Office* [1974] 1 WLR 1176; 1974] 2 All ER 737, which established the accepted medical precaution of giving a test dose of anti-tetanus serum as a legal requirement. The likelihood of adverse effects of a medicine must be reasonably probable, and reasonably part of the knowledge of the profession for it to be necessary to be taken into account.

Regulations 2002. Standing orders allow for the supply and administration of specified medicines, by specified classes of health practitioners in specified situations such as emergencies, or as routine treatment for the patients of particular practitioners.

Section 2 of the Medicines Act 1981 (as amended in 2003 by Medicines Amendment Act (No 3) 2003 (2003 No 84) defines a "standing order" as:

> "(a)   A written instruction issued by a practitioner or registered midwife, in accordance with any applicable regulations, authorising any specified class of persons engaged in the delivery of health services to supply and administer any specified class or description of prescription medicines [[or controlled drugs]] to any specified class of persons, in circumstances specified in the instruction, without a prescription:"[31]

Even though the definition allows registered midwives to issue standing orders, this is only in accordance with regulations. The current regulations only permit practitioners to do so. A practitioner is defined as a medical practitioner, or a dentist. Registered midwives cannot currently issue standing orders. Nurse prescribers also cannot currently issue standing orders.

Standing orders should be developed in consultation between the medical practitioner or dentist issuing it, and the health practitioners who will supply and administer it, for example the pharmacist, registered midwife, registered nurse, physiotherapist, optometrist, or paramedic.

Standing orders must be *in writing*. They are a written instruction and *must*:[32]

- State the name of the doctor or dentist issuing it, and it must be signed and dated.
- Explain why the standing order is necessary.
- Identify the class of health practitioners (or other people) who can supply or administer a medicine under it, the level of competency and training required, and any additional competencies such as IV certification and whether a level of assessment and observational skills is required.
- List the medicines for which it applies (and use of the generic name will mean the orders will not need to be reissued where brand names change).
- Specify the indications for administration, recommended dose or dose range, contraindications, and validated reference charts for calculation of dose if required, route of administration, and the documentation required.
- Specify the time-frame for which the standing order applies, or a statement saying that it is to apply until it is replaced by a new one or cancelled in writing.
- Identify the groups of consumers to whom the standing order applies, and the treatments it applies to.
- Describe the circumstances in which it applies.

---

30   Medicine is defined in regulation 3 of the Medicines (Standing Order) Regulations 2002 to mean a prescription medicine or a specified controlled drug. Specified controlled drug means a controlled drug listed in Parts I and III of the Schedule 2 and Parts II to VII of the Schedule 3 to the Misuse of Drugs Act 1975.

31   Medicines Amendment Act (No 3) 2003, section 3(2).

32   Medicines (Standing Order) Regulations 2002, regulation 5.

- State the time period in which the charted treatment must be counter-signed by the medical practitioner or dentist.
- Describe the scope of the standing order, and define the terms used in it.
- Attach a copy of any existing policy relating to the standing order, which must have been signed by the issuer, everyone who will supply or administer under it, and an appropriate manager of the service.

Standing orders must be reviewed by the issuer of them at least 12-monthly. Health practitioners wanting to administer a medicine under a standing order can only do so if they have signed up on the standing order policy and have met the specified level of competencies.

In order to continue to administer under the standing order, the specified level of competency and any additional competencies must be reviewed by the issuer of it at least once a year from the date of issue.

The Ministry of Health has issued a document titled *Guidelines for the Development and Operation of Standing Orders*.[33] It contains a useful checklist,[34] and is available on the Ministry of Health's website at www.moh.govt.nz.

10.7.12   Outdated medicine orders

Medication charts should be periodically reviewed, and in any case anyone administering a medicine should check when it was charted. Sometimes a law or institutional practice may mean that an order is out of date. Other situations might arise where a certain number of administrations of a particular medicine are ordered and a proper check on those given is not kept (see the case of *Smith v Brighton* at 8.10.6).

10.8   Medicine and the internet

The internet is useful for obtaining and distributing medical information by health practitioners. Also, many consumers now access the internet to find out information and even advice about their illnesses and medicines. Medicines can be obtained through the internet.

There are issues arising from this including:

- Little or no protection available from poor quality or misleading information;
- Lack of protection from the sale of fraudulent or unsafe, or ineffective unapproved medicines;
- Consumers are able to obtain medicines without full consultation or a physical examination;
- The difficulties of contacting purchasers of medicines in the event of a recall;
- The lack of confidentiality of transmission of sensitive material.

---

33   *Guidelines for the Development and Operation of Standing Orders*, November 2002, Wellington, Ministry of Health. Revised and updated in 2006.

34   *Guidelines for the Development and Operation of Standing Orders*, November 2002, Wellington, Ministry of Health: available online at www.moh.govt.nz, page 8.

The Medical Council of New Zealand has put out guidelines setting out current minimum standards for New Zealand medical practitioners who want to advise and treat over the internet.[35] It will be updated as required. It includes the following advice:

- Prescriptions cannot be issued for anyone other than a patient under the medical practitioner's care. This means bulk prescriptions to individuals or groups overseas cannot be issued.
- Prescriptions by email alone do not comply with New Zealand prescribing laws.
- Prescribing requires a face-to-face consultation or verification by another medical practitioner of physical data and identity.
- The medical practitioner must be sure a physical examination is not going to be of use, and must be prepared to justify the reasons in the event of a complaint.
- Charges must be appropriate.
- The medical practitioner must not be the supplier of the medicine prescribed, nor have an arrangement with the supplier.

10.8.1   Sale or supply of medicines over the internet

There are approximately 30 internet pharmacies in New Zealand, with sales of over $50 m worth of products sold annually, mainly overseas. Before the law changed in November 2002, these pharmacies were able to take advantage of the loophole in section 33(b) of the Medicines Act 1981, which allowed any person to export prescription medicines for the purpose of sale without requiring a prescription. That loophole has now been closed.[36] Pharmacies, and anyone else, who want to supply or export medicines from New Zealand, can only do so under a valid prescription made by a person authorised to prescribe in New Zealand.

10.9   Further reading

Medical Council of New Zealand, *Medicine and the Internet*, June 2001 availble online at www.mcnz.org.nz.

Draft statement by the Medical Council of New Zealand on "Good prescribing practice" available online at www.mcnz.org.nz.

Ministry of Health, *Guidelines for the Development and Operation of Standing Orders* November 2002, Wellington, available online at www.moh.govt.nz.

New Zealand Nurses' Organisation, *Guidelines for Nurses on the Administration of Medicines*, Wellington, 2002.

---

35   *Medicine and the Internet*, June 2001, Medical Council of New Zealand. The document is available online on the Medical Council's website at www.mcnz.org.nz; also see medsafe: Prescribing and Buying Medicine on the Internet — A Risky Business, available online at www.medsafe.govt.nz.

36   Section 33 of the Medicines Act 1981 is now subject to regulation 44C of the Medicines Regulations 1984, as amended in November 2000. See also the case that prompted the need for new regulations, *Bell v Medsafe NZ Medicines and Medical Devices Safety Authority* [2000] DCR 60. Another case of interest in this area is *R v Standard 304 Ltd* [2008] NZCA 564. The Court in that case also makes an interesting comment (at para 44) in regard to regulation 44C, that the Executive through this regulation have considerably widened the scope of offending under ss 18 and 33 of the Medicines Act 1981 and also impose a penalty of imprisonment under delegated legislation, which goes against legislative guidelines.

New Zealand Nurses Organisation, *Standing Orders Regulations: Guidance and Information for Nurses* December 2002, Wellington.

M Wadsworth, "The pitfalls of verbal medication orders", *Kai Tiaki Nursing New Zealand*, September 1998, 24.

W Scott and M Marfell-Jones, "Evidence alone is not enough to bring about practice change", *Kai Tiaki Nursing New Zealand*, February 2004.

A Shaw, "Choosing the Right Injection Site", *Kai Tiaki Nursing New Zealand*, December 2002/January 2003.

Chapter 11

CONSUMERS' PROPERTY

Trevor Warr and Rebecca Keenan

Contents

11.1   Introduction

A person, hospital, or institution having custody of a consumer's property is legally bound to take reasonable care of it. Therefore, any employees will be required to deal carefully with it.

At law, the entrusting of one's property to another — for purposes such as dry-cleaning, repairs, safekeeping (including giving them to a hospital or another person when one is ill), or pawning or hiring one's goods — is called bailment. The person who gives the goods to another's care is called the bailor, while the person to whom the goods are given is called the bailee. From this it follows that the legal right to goods is composed of two elements — ownership and possession. Bailment involves the owner temporarily divesting possession of their goods, while retaining ownership of, ie title to them.

A health care facility may find itself caring for a person's property as the result of:

- Lodgment on admission (voluntary bailment, see 11.2 and 11.3);
- Admission of a person in an emergency (involuntary bailment, see 11.3.3 and 11.5.3);
- It being left by a person on discharge.

11.2 Bailment

The law of bailment is mainly covered by common law, which has generally been applied to cases involving commercial activities. Though it is somewhat complex, it contains important precepts for health practitioners. The act of bailment involves principles of contract. However, money is not always paid for bailment. The remedy of negligence is also available to the bailor. Thus, it is useful to consider bailment as a special area of law.

Before considering the rules relating to bailment, however, it may be useful to remember that as health practitioners come into contact with consumers' property, both when it is given to them for safekeeping and when they have to handle it on other occasions, there are two types of situations in which the law is interested:

- The wrongful interference with a person's goods; for example, the taking of a person's possessions or using them without permission of the owner;
- The careless or negligent treatment of a person's goods when they have been given for safekeeping.

11.2.1 Interference with goods

This generally involves the wrongful handling of another's goods, and is divided in law into three kinds of activity:

- The wrongful taking of goods out of the possession of another, for example, theft. In law, this is called *trespass to goods*.
- Dealing with goods in a manner inconsistent with the owner's rights, for example buying or selling another's goods; "borrowing" another's goods without their permission; or using goods in a way which is contrary to a person's wishes or instructions. In law, this is called *conversion*.
- Wrongfully refusing, after demand, to deliver goods to the person entitled to possession of them, whether that person is the owner or not. This would include a practitioner's refusal to return clothes or other possessions when the consumer has asked for them. In law, this is called *detinue*.

It can be seen that these categories might overlap in any given situation. The common element is that someone is wrongfully deprived of their lawful exercise of ownership or possession of their goods, without their consent.

Title to *ownership* of things is good against the whole world, that is no one else has a stronger legal claim to them. Title to *possession* of things is good against anyone, except a person who has a stronger claim to possession of them. That would be at least the owner, and one to whom the owner has given a stronger right to possess the goods.

11.2.2 The negligent handling of goods

Once possession of goods has been granted to a bailee, the goods must be kept secure and handled in a reasonable manner. Legal action can be brought against a bailee by someone where goods have been stolen, or are returned damaged or altered because of negligent handling.

Where it is proven that an employee has failed to take good care of the goods the employee's employer, for example a health care facility, will be vicariously liable for damages for any loss.[1]

The liability of an employer may include wrongful acts of an employee, such as theft.[2]

Liability will depend on there being a close association between the nature of employment and any particular wrongful act.[3]

11.3 Categories of bailment

For the purposes of duty of care, the law classifies bailments into three categories.

11.3.1 Bailment for reward

Here the bailee is paid for the bailment of the goods. Examples are the depositing of goods with someone for safekeeping in a bank, or in a railway station's "left luggage" department, or leaving clothes with a dry-cleaner, or a car with a car repairer. It is accepted that the bailment undertaken when a person hands over money or valuables to a health care facility is a bailment for reward, as even where they do not pay directly for their care, they are paying indirectly for treatment through taxes or levies to the government or other body.[4] There is a special duty of care in the case of bailment for reward: special care must be taken with the goods.[5]

On the death of a consumer, however, the health care facility becomes a gratuitous bailee.[6]

---

1   *Chesire v Bailey* [1905] 1 KB 237.
2   *Morris v C W Martin & Son Ltd* [1966] QB 716; [1965] All ER 726.
3   *Lister v Hesley Hall Ltd* [2002] 1 AC 215; [2001] 2 All ER 769.
4   In *Martin v London County Council* [1947] 1 All ER 783, a patient had handed over her jewellery on admission to hospital. The Court held that the hospital was liable as a bailee for reward because the patient paid indirectly through taxes. If this principle was to be applied to private health facilities in New Zealand, one could argue that health insurance contributors were similarly paying the facility indirectly for their care. It is directly analogous for a public health facility.
5   In the case of *Ultzen v Nichols* [1894] 1 QB 92 a waiter took a customer's coat and hung it on a nearby hanger. The coat was stolen while the customer was dining. The restaurant owner was found liable and required to replace the coat.
6   *Southland Hospital Board v Perkins Estate* (1986) 1 NZLR 373.

11.3.2 Gratuitous bailment

This occurs when the bailee offers to care for goods, but is not paid for this service. Loaning of one's possessions to another for their use is an example of this sort of bailment. The duty of care involved here is what is called the "ordinary" duty of care. It is based on the reasonable person, and requires one to take whatever steps are reasonable to secure and preserve the possessions. However, one is only liable for "gross" negligence or fraud.[7]

11.3.3 Involuntary bailment

This occurs when one finds oneself in possession of another's goods without prior notice or agreement.[8] An example is where a passer-by stops to assist someone involved in an accident, which results in the custody of the accident victim's possessions. In this case, the person is not under a duty of care to take special means to protect or preserve the goods. The only requirement at law is that no action is taken that will directly or indirectly harm the possessions.

11.4 Recommended procedure for health care facilities

11.4.1 The best rule — leave it at home

Obviously, consumers should be persuaded not to bring unnecessary property to a health service facility, or relations should be persuaded to take it away. However, this principle should be balanced with an appreciation of the emotional value possessions may have for consumers. Reasonable accommodation should be made for those possessions that are of importance to their comfort and wellbeing.

11.4.2 Careful recording of property received

As a health service facility is likely to be considered a bailee for reward, this means that property should be carefully recorded — both its nature and condition. This is a record for both the consumer and the hospital, and evidence of the transaction of handing over the property. Property should be stored in such a way that it is clearly identified as belonging to the consumer, and will not be in unreasonable danger of damage or theft.

11.4.3 Degree or standard of care

The health service facility must exercise reasonable care to prevent damage or loss of goods, but is not expected to take extraordinary security measures. Where there is any loss, the facility as bailee must prove that either it took good care of the goods, or that its failure did not contribute to the loss.[9]

---

7   *Moore v Morgue* (1776) 2 Cowp 479. The leading United Kingdom case on this type of bailment is *Gilchrist Watt and Sanderson Pty Ltd v York Products Pty Ltd* [1970] 1 WLR 1262. This was an Australian case that went to the Privy Council. The defendants were stevedores and lost two case loads of clocks. They were acting as sub-bailees between the owners and the shipping company. The defendants were found liable as expressed by Lord Pearson: "they took upon themselves an obligation to the plaintiffs to exercise due care for the safety of the goods, although there was no contractual relation or attornment between the defendants and the plaintiffs."

8   In *Property Life Insurance Ltd v Edgar* 15/3/80, Mahon J, HC Auckland A496/77 an involuntary bailee is described as a person who "has come into possession of goods without any volition on his part."

9   *Wilson & Horton v A-G* (1997) 2 NZLR 513; (1997) 6 NZBLC 102,245.

The degree or standard of care is the "care which a reasonable man would use in looking after his own chattels of the same kind in the same circumstances".[10]

The onus is on the facility to show that it had taken the necessary degree of care to keep the goods safe.[11]

11.4.4   Care of valuables

Special care should be taken with valuables, which should ideally not be kept in a ward, but in a central office in a safe. Less than this would not, in most cases, be considered by the Courts as reasonable care. Beware of being persuaded to take temporary custody of possessions, to move them from place to place, or to hand them over to anyone, without careful documentation and witnessing.

11.4.5   Witnessing by a third person

Personal possessions and a list of them should be checked by a third person, as well as the consumer, when the list is compiled. All three people should sign this list. If the consumer is unable to check the list, then a relation or friend should be asked to sign on the consumer's behalf. Those taking custody of items should describe them accurately. There have been two cases reported verbally to the author: one where a ring was described as gold, and one where a coat was described as fur — the clients refused to accept the platinum ring and fake fur coat respectively, which were returned to them, and threatened to sue the hospitals concerned for the real things. There was no evidence that the objects received by the hospital were anything other than as described.

11.4.6   Handing of property to relations

Health practitioners should be conscious of the fact that it is unlawful to deal with another person's property as if they were the owner of that property. That is, if a practitioner hands it over to any person (other than hospital personnel for safekeeping), without the owner's permission, this is considered in law to be exercising a right in that property to which the practitioner may not be entitled. It has not specifically been established at law, but it is a general policy of hospitals, that goods may be handed over to a person who is reasonably believed to be a relation or friend, or otherwise has entitlement to receive them. Where the goods are not valuable this would probably be legally acceptable, but careful recording of who receives them is advised and the person should sign for the goods. However, handing valuable property over to relations or friends (or police without a warrant) could be dealing unlawfully with the property. If in doubt, it should not be handed over to anyone other than the consumer. Management should deal with these matters and take steps to establish the validity of the claim.

11.5   Some special considerations

11.5.1   Valuable possessions

These should be transferred as soon as possible after recording to the hospital management, who should have proper means for safekeeping. If there is no such provision, or it is not

---

10   *Peterson v Papakura Motors Ltd* (1957) NZLR 495, 499.
11   *Conway v Cockram Motors (Chch) Ltd* (1986) 1 NZLR 381.

available after hours, then the valuables should be kept under lock and key until they can be transferred somewhere safer. Where, in spite of the advice given above, it is felt that valuables must be given to a relation or other representative of the consumer, record carefully and fully to whom they are being given, their particulars, and have this record signed and witnessed.

11.5.2 Money

Money may be deposited by the health care facility in a trust account, the amount deposited becoming a credit to the consumer, payable on demand. The money is not the subject of bailment in this case, as the exact notes given to the facility are not demanded in return. Rather, the consumer is a creditor, the facility a debtor, and the amount owing could be the subject of a suit for payment of a debt, or, where the money is deposited with the intention of benefit to a third person or body, the law of trust. The debt would apply absolutely, and the issue of negligence would be irrelevant in this case.

11.5.3 Emergency admissions

Where, due to lack of time or facilities, a consumer's possessions cannot be carefully checked and listed, it is suggested that they be quickly and carefully put in a bag or envelope, and sealed (for example, stapled) and put somewhere as safe as circumstances will allow. If possible have someone witness this, sign across the seal and date the signature, noting the time.

Subject to time permitting, where valuable property is contained in a wallet, purse, or other container and this is not opened by staff, a note should be made to that effect on the bag or envelope containing the goods. Where the container has been opened, staff may be liable for anything allegedly missing from it. If it was opened before coming into the possession of the staff, but there is a witnessed document stating that it was not opened by them, there is less likelihood that they will be held responsible. If it is opened — for example, a wallet is searched for identification — then the contents should be listed and witnessed again to establish what was there.

11.5.4 Possessions kept with consumer

These are kept at the consumer's bedside and at the consumer's risk. Thus, a watch or radio that disappears from the consumer's bedside is not the hospital staff's responsibility, unless the consumer is unable to care for such goods, in which case if they are to remain there, and ideally this should not occur, the staff must take reasonable measures to protect them. Otherwise they should be put in safekeeping. If, for example, X, who is perfectly competent, is to undergo surgery, then arrangements should be made for the care of valuables that have been kept at the bedside, for the duration of X's incompetency.

11.5.5 Transfer of consumer

Care should be taken to adequately check possessions when consumers are being transferred from one place to another. The list of possessions obtained on admission to the ward should again be checked against the possessions being transferred, and duly witnessed by the consumer or representative where possible, and hospital staff.

11.5.6   When a consumer becomes incompetent

Where a consumer becomes incompetent, the health care facility should not hand over valuable property to anyone other than the legal guardian of that person. If there is no such person, one should be appointed by the Family Court before their property can be dealt with. Staff should refer claimants of such a person's property to management. Where the consumer is a child, both parents are normally legal guardians, unless there is clear evidence to the contrary. They are entitled to deal with the property of the child. Where the parents were not married to each other and were not living together as husband and wife when the child was born, then the mother will be the sole guardian, unless a Family Court order has appointed someone else. A person's spouse is not the automatic owner of their property.

11.5.7   When a consumer dies

The law provides that when a person dies all that person's property becomes the possession of the estate's executor. The executor is nominated by the person in their will. Where there is no will, it is usually necessary for anyone interested in the estate, usually the next-of-kin, to apply to the High Court to approve an administrator. Relations may then have no right to possession of the deceased's belongings. If they are entitled under the will, that is for the executor to determine, and the executor must go through certain procedures before distribution of them. Of course a relation may be nominated the executor under the will, but health practitioners are not required to solve this legal question.[12] They should be wary of handing out the deceased's possessions to relations, and refer requests for property of any value to the hospital administration, whose duty it is to hand such property to the person demonstrating that they are the executor of the deceased's estate.

11.5.8   Exemption clauses

A health care facility may limit its liability for goods left with it by specifically providing that it will not be responsible for them. This would most likely be a clause in the contract of bailment (the form signed by the consumer) to the appropriate effect. It is important to note:

- Such a limitation must be specifically brought to the consumer's notice. Signs in a foyer are not enough,[13] and it must be reasonable notice under the circumstances, for example in a language that the consumer can understand. It must form part of the actual agreement made by the client. Unless all reasonable measures to bring the limitation of liability to the consumer's attention are taken, they will not be bound by it.[14]
- The clause must be clear and unambiguous. General phrases such as "all care and no responsibility" will have no effect.[15]
- The clause should be given its plain and natural, or ordinary meaning read in light of the contract as a whole. Any ambiguity should be construed against the interest of the party seeking to rely on the clause.[16]

---

12   Some health service institutions might provide for information regarding executorship of the client's will to be recorded on admission.

13   *Mendelssohn v Normand* [1970] 1 QB 177.

14   *Thornton v Shoe Lane Parking Ltd* [1971] 2 WLR 585; [1971] 1 All ER 686.

15   *Paterson v Miller* [1923] VLR 36.

Case

Sydney Corporation v West (1965) 114 CLR 481 (HCA)

West parked his car in a council car park. The ticket he received stated that the ticket must be presented for taking delivery of the car, and also that, "The Council does not accept any responsibility for the loss or damage to any vehicle or for loss of or damage to any article or thing in or upon any vehicle or for any injury to any person however such loss, damage or injury may arise or be caused." An unauthorised person claimed the car, stating he had lost the ticket, and the attendant allowed him to take delivery of the car. West sued for the replacement value of the car.

Despite the formidable exemption clause, the High Court held that although the council was relieved of liability for the consequences of negligence where it carried out acts that were authorised by the contract, the contract had specifically required that the ticket be produced for delivery of the car. In this case, the worker involved did not follow the authorised procedure. Thus, they concluded, the council was not covered by the exemption clause, and was liable.

Courts will accept exemption clauses so long as they have been brought to the awareness of the contracting party, or are reasonably available for that party to see. They will also construe them literally against the party seeking exemption, as they do not hold such clauses in favour. Therefore, the person or institution holding goods under bailment must show that they meticulously adhered to the terms of the bailment.

Case

Thomas National Transport (Melbourne) Pty Ltd v May & Baker (Australia) Pty Ltd (1966)
115 CLR 353 (HCA)

An interstate carrier regularly held May & Baker's goods in its warehouse overnight in Melbourne when storage was required, before sending them on to Sydney. They also used a subcontractor to transport the goods from May & Baker's premises to the warehouse. Some goods were destroyed while they were stored overnight, not while they were at the warehouse of Thomas National Transport (Melbourne) Pty Ltd ("TNT"), but at the subcontractor's premises. The contract had an exemption clause that said that TNT was not liable for harm occurring to goods while they were in transit or storage.

The Court said that TNT could rely on the exemption clause and so escape liability only if it was acting strictly according to the contract. It was found that the use of the subcontractor was not stipulated in the contract, and this was a deviation from the contract significant enough to prevent TNT from relying on its exemption clause. From this, one can extract the principle that a hospital will be liable for loss or damage to goods if staff do not take proper care of a consumer's belongings.

Exemption clauses protecting the facility when the consumer retains property may be ineffective on the death of the consumer. After death the consumer's control over property is terminated and the facility becomes a gratuitous bailee.[17]

---

16   *SGS (NZ) Ltd v Quirke Export Ltd* [1988] 1 NZLR 52.

17   *Southland Hospital Board v Perkins Estate* [1986] 1 NZLR 373 where the board was liable for the loss of a ring after a patient died despite by-laws limiting liability.

11.5.9   Unclaimed belongings

In New Zealand there is no specific Act of Parliament that deals with unclaimed money and personal effects left in hospitals.[18]

All unclaimed money and belongings found by nurses and other hospital employees should be handed into the hospital administration or the police with an explanation of the circumstances of the finding.[19]

Checklist

Dealing with consumer's property on admission or transfer

(Any reference to the consumer includes a reference to the consumer's representative where applicable.)

Have I:

- Informed the consumer about hospital policy?
- Listed each object by type and condition?
- Identified valuable property and separated it from other goods?
- Clearly identified the location of, or the person with, custody of all property?
- Secured the witness of at least one other staff member and the consumer, if possible?
- Given the consumer a copy of the list (receipt)?
- Made proper provision for the dispatch of property that is to go elsewhere in the hospital?
- Made proper provision for any goods that are to remain in the ward or under my supervision?
- Obtained a receipt on handing over goods to any person?

11.6   Further reading

Todd et al, *The Law of Torts in New Zealand* (5th ed), Wellington, Brookers, 2009.

---

18   The Unclaimed Money Act 1971 and section 59 of the Police Act 1958 are more general in their application and may be relevant depending on the circumstances.

19   See *Parker v British Airways Board* [1982] 2 WLR 503; [1982] 1 All ER 834 and *Southland Hospital Board v Perkins Estate* [1986] 1 NZLR 373.

Chapter 12

Contract

Sue Johnson

Contents

12.1 The provision of health services in New Zealand

The New Zealand Health Service today is governed by the New Zealand Public Health and Disability Act 2000, which saw a return to regional based purchasing of health and disability services. This had previously been the case up until 1993, when the system was restructured, and the Health and Disability Services Act 1993 split the purchasing aspect of health services from the provider aspect. A structure based on the market forces of competition was created and a national, central body, the Health Funding Authority ("HFA") purchased health services from providers who contracted with the HFA to provide those services. The result was that providers competed with one another for contracts with the HFA.[1] Now 21 District Health Boards ("DHBs") carry out the functions previously performed by the HFA. They receive funding from the Ministry of Health to purchase health services in their region. They are responsible for entering into contracts under which they purchase services from providers in their area. As well, the DHBs are responsible for running many of those services.[2]

Funding for the public health services comes mainly from taxation, and the funds are administered by government agencies. They provide funds to the DHBs based on population size, but also weighted according to local social needs. Age range in the region, ethnicity, and social wealth or deprivation is taken into account. DHBs are responsible for reporting to the Ministry of Health.

---

1   For example under section 51 of the Health and Disability Services Act 1993 (repealed) the old HFA gave public notice of all arrangements relating to payments for services it had purchased. Only accredited service providers could contract directly with the HFA. Until the section 51 (maternity) notice issued in 1998, registered midwives were not eligible to contract directly with the HFA. Midwives provided their services to obstetricians and/or gynaecologists and/or general practitioners, who were the only accredited service providers. Midwives were effectively subcontractors. The effect of the section 51 (maternity) notice was to put midwives on the same contractual footing with the obstetricians, GPs and gynaecologists, relative to the HFA. The result was fierce competition for maternity service provision. (The section 51 notice arrangement has continued under the superseding legislation. Such notices are now given under section 88 of the New Zealand Public Health and Disability Act 2000).

There are therefore contracts between DHBs and regional providers of health services. There are also contracts between consumers and providers. For example where a consumer enters a hospital, or makes an agreement for care from other health service facilities, or sees a private practitioner (for example, a specialist medical practitioner, a GP, an independent midwife, a dentist, a psychologist in private practice) then a contract has been entered into between the consumer and the practitioner. The consumer may undertake to pay a fee, and the facility or practitioner undertakes to provide reasonable care in the agreed treatment.

There are also contracts between DHBs and their employees. There are contracts between other providers and their employees. For example, a provider such as laboratory services contracts with the DHB to provide services, but also in order to carry out its part of the bargain with the DHB it enters into employment contracts with its staff.[3] These employees have a contract with the employer, but not with the consumer. Poor health service delivery, then, might not only be the basis of a potential Health and Disability Commissioner investigation, negligence action, or professional disciplinary action. It can also be a breach of that contract between the employee and the employer, and a breach of the employer's contract with the consumer, if the employer is at fault in not providing competent staff.

Where a consumer directly engages a practitioner, for example an independent midwife, GP or private specialist medical practitioner, dentist or psychologist, there is a direct contract between the health practitioner and the consumer. This chapter looks at the basic principles of contract law. The requirements for a valid contract are set out in the checklist at 12.2.

Health practitioners need to be aware of the distinction between liability in contract and liability for failing to observe a reasonable standard of care and skill under other laws. The duty to act reasonably in caring for consumers, that is, to observe a standard of care and skill reasonably to be expected in the circumstances and not to be negligent, always applies, whether or not a contract exists. Where there is a contract between a health practitioner and a consumer, the practitioner can be held accountable for breach of contract, as well as for liability under other laws, for example a medical error[4] finding by the ACC, a breach of the Health and Disability Services Code of Consumers' Rights, professional disciplinary action, and possibly a civil claim in tort law. Principles of contract law are different from those of say negligence, or failure to give effect to Right 2 of the Code of Consumers Rights — the right to appropriate services, or failure to observe a reasonable standard of care for ACC purposes. The basis of a contract is to carry out a bargain, rather than to apply a particular standard of care. One only has to give what one agreed to give — the standard

---

2   In January 2009 the Government set in place a Ministerial Review Group to assess the challenges that face the public health service. A result of the recommendations made is the establishment of a National Health Board to sit within the Ministry of Health. The main function of this new Board is to consolidate services in the DHBs by streamlining infrastructure, IT and administrative functions. It is proposed that this will result in the trimming of jobs in these areas and free up money to go into clinical areas. The National Health Board should be in place by December 2009 and it will be reviewed in 3 years. At this time there is no plan to merge any of the DHBs, though this may be revisited when the National Health Board is reviewed. For more information, see the Government's response to the Ministerial Review Group's Report 'Meeting the Challenge', available online at www.beehive.govt.nz/sites/all/files/MRG%20Decision%20Q&As%2021%2010%2009.pdf

3   See chapter 13.

4   Under the current ACC legislation — the Injury Prevention, Rehabilitation and Compensation Act 2001 — there is no requirement for a finding of medical error.

of service can be set by the parties involved. According to, say, the law of negligence on the other hand, the standard of care is set not by any agreement, but by an objective test — the "reasonable person" test.

12.2   What is a contract?

A contract is an agreement between two or more parties (individual persons or legal entities),[5] which, if it has certain features, will be legally binding. It need not be in writing. It can be oral, or even implied from a person's actions or overall conduct. When, for example, people ask the local car mechanic to fix their car, or the dentist to fix their teeth, they are entering into a contractual relationship. Unless it is otherwise agreed, there is an implied condition that, in exchange for payment of the prescribed fee, the mechanic or dentist will give appropriate professional services. The law of contract is covered by common law principles and by legislation.

Checklist

Requirements for a valid contract

- Intention by both parties to create a legal relationship.
- Identifiable offer and acceptance.
- Adequate identification of the parties.
- Consideration (something of value) exchanged between the parties, or an agreement recorded under seal.
- Genuine agreement on the part of each party.
- Legal capacity on the part of each party.
- Lawfulness of the activity involved.

If any of the above elements are missing, there is no legally binding contract and the agreement is defective. This means it will be void, voidable, or unenforceable.

Void agreements are those that have a serious defect, so that the law regards them as having no effect at all. Neither party can claim any rights under the agreement. All money and property must be returned, and no Court action is possible. Examples are illegal contracts (see 12.5.5), agreements where there was in fact no valid offer and acceptance, and agreements where there was no intention to create legal relations.

Voidable agreements are those that do not have such serious defects. One or both parties have a choice whether to carry out the contract, or end it. The contract is valid until it is cancelled. Examples are contracts where there has been misrepresentation, and cases of duress or undue influence.

Unenforceable contracts can be carried out by the parties, but cannot be enforced by a Court. Examples include contracts made by a minor (in some circumstances), or contracts that do not comply with the formal requirements of the Contracts Enforcement Act 1956.

---

5   A legal person can be an individual or a fictional person sometimes called an entity, such as a company. Legal entities have the same rights as an individual legal person, and can sue and be sued.

12.2.1 Intention to create a legal relationship

This means the parties are committed, that is, they intend to bind herself/himself to their obligations and benefits under the agreement or suffer legal sanctions. There used to be a presumption at law that several types of agreement are of themselves not legally binding. These included social arrangements, such as agreements between husband and wife, or parents and children (such as agreements to pay money, carry out chores, arrangements over childcare). The net effect of this was that their agreement was presumed not to be legally enforceable, because they did not intend it to be. However, this presumption could be readily rebutted if the evidence disclosed a contrary intention.

Case

Merritt v Merritt [1970] 1 WLR 1211; [1970] 2 All ER 760

Mr Merritt had left his wife. Mrs Merritt pressed him to finalise arrangements between them. They met, discussed matters, and Mr Merritt finally wrote, signed, and dated a note in the following terms:

> "In consideration of the fact that you will pay all charges in connection with the house … until such time as the mortgage repayment has been completed, when the mortgage has been completed I will agree to transfer the property in to your sole ownership."

In reliance on this undertaking, Mrs Merritt paid off the mortgage. Mr Merritt subsequently refused to transfer the house. Mrs Merritt sued.

The Court held that the parties had intended to affect their legal relations, and the agreement was contractually binding. Mrs Merritt was entitled to the transfer.

The parties' intention may be express or implied, but it must be mutual. It is determined by what a reasonable person apprised of the facts would deduce the parties' intentions to be from their actions, negotiations, and in some instances the background to the agreement (an "objective test"), rather than what one of the parties might have unilaterally wished or intended (a "subjective test").

The legal approach can be ascertained by comparing two cases, and the reasoning of the Courts in coming to different conclusions on somewhat similar facts.

Case

Balfour v Balfour [1919] 2 KB 571 (Eng CA)

A married couple had to part because of the wife's ill health. The wife remained in their homeland, England, and the husband returned to Ceylon to work. The husband agreed to pay £30 a month maintenance to the wife while she was in England. At some later stage, the wife decided she would not return to her husband, and when his payments stopped, she sued him for breach of contract.

Case

McGregor v McGregor (1888) 20 QB 529 (Eng CA)

A husband and wife, after making complaints against each other for assault, both agreed to drop the charges. They then separated, before the matter came to Court. This agreement

---

was made on condition that the husband would pay weekly maintenance, and the wife would support herself and the children. The husband later refused to continue the payments, and the wife sued him for breach of contract.

In *Balfour*, the wife did not succeed, but in *McGregor*, she did. The reasoning of the Courts is consistent. In the first case, the Court held that the couple did not wish to affect their legal relations. The agreement was part of their ongoing marriage, the better to manage it. In the second case, however, the Court held that the intention was to affect the couple's legal relations. They were no longer married and living together but separated; the money issue was to be addressed as part of the separation agreement. The Court considered not so much what the parties said, though that may come into consideration, but considered from an objective viewpoint what they intended to do in the circumstances.

Case

Jones v Padavatton [1967] 1 WLR 328; [1969] 2 All ER 616 (Eng CA)

The defendant was a divorced woman living in Washington in 1962. She gave up a good job on her mother's promise that if she went to London and studied for the Bar, her mother would pay her a regular allowance. After the defendant had been in London for 2 years, the mother bought a house there for her to live in. The house was big enough for tenants. The defendant rented the house, but did not send any rents to her mother, who was paying off a large mortgage. In 1965 the defendant remarried. In 1967 the mother claimed possession of the house, and the daughter counterclaimed for money she had spent on the house.

The Court held that the mother and the daughter had intended to create a legal relationship between them. The Court examined the circumstances of the negotiations and concluded that they both intended that the daughter should have a legal right to receive, and the mother a legal obligation to pay, the original allowance of $200 a month for a reasonable time for completion of the Bar exams. The new arrangement by which the mother bought the house for the daughter to live in was neither a variation of the original contract, nor, because of its vagueness, a new contract entitling the daughter to stay on in the house for an indefinite period of time. The mother could therefore have possession of the house. In setting out the reasoning to be followed in such cases, Salmon LJ stated:[6]

> "Did the parties intend the arrangement to be legally binding? This question has to be solved by applying what is sometimes … called an objective test. The Court has to consider what the parties said and wrote in the light of all the surrounding circumstances, and then decide whether the true inference is that the ordinary man and woman, speaking or writing thus in such circumstances, would have intended to create a legally binding agreement."

The English cases speak in terms of presumption. The range of circumstances in cases such as these is likely to be so varied that in any particular case a presumption, albeit of fact, is likely to be of limited assistance. Each case will turn on its own facts, and there is no substitute for a careful examination of those facts. The subject-matter and attendant

---

6   *Jones v Padavatton* [1969] 2 All ER 616, 621.

circumstances may well suggest that the parties had no intention of creating a legally enforceable obligation. The converse may equally be true.

In the leading New Zealand case *Fleming v Beevers*, the Court was reluctant to speak of presumptions, and preferred to examine each case on its facts.

Case

Fleming v Beevers [1994] 1 NZLR 385; [1994] NZFLR 108 (CA)

The appellant, Fleming, sought enforcement of an oral contract whereby her late de facto husband, Beevers, had agreed to leave her in his will, his half interest in a property at Queenstown that the parties had acquired as tenants in common in equal shares. Beevers died approximately 5 months later without having changed his will.

The Court held that there was a strong inference that each party intended a legally binding obligation. It held that the use of a presumption was not likely to assist, and each case must be carefully examined to determine whether the parties intended a legally binding obligation. The parties' intentions must be viewed objectively.

Most social agreements are just that, agreements that have little significance to the parties. They are unlikely to have any serious consequences. Breach of a social agreement is not usually a matter of gravity, and the Courts are therefore reluctant to find that such agreements were intended to be binding. However, they are not always without serious consequence and something that appears to be merely a friendly pact can go much deeper. Agreements to participate in competitions, lotteries, and the like are good examples.

Case

Simpkins v Pays [1955] 1 WLR 975

The defendant, her granddaughter, and the plaintiff regularly entered a fashion competition run by a Sunday newspaper. The entries were always made in the defendant's name and, although there was no fixed rule as to who would pay the postage and other expenses, they all contributed and there was an agreement that any prizes won would be shared. Eventually, one of the entries was successful, but when the prize was received, the defendant refused to share it. When the plaintiff sued her, she argued that there was no contract. The agreement between them was, she said, merely a friendly adventure and not something intended to create legal relations.

In the circumstances the agreement was enforceable. Its nature was such that the parties must have contemplated that it would be enforced in the event of any win. The plaintiff was, therefore, contractually entitled to her share of the prize.

Case

Welch v Jess [1976] NZ Recent Law 185

The parties went on a fishing holiday together and entered a contest. They agreed that if any prizes were won, they would be pooled and shared. The parties also agreed the expenses should be shared, and they all contributed to a "kitty". The defendant won $6,000 for the heaviest snapper, but refused to share the prize.

The Court held that there was a contract between the parties.

Where a person agrees to carry out the treatment of another, particularly a friend, or makes an informal arrangement, or where no payment is to be made at all, the parties should make it clear if the arrangement is to be legally binding, so that if breached by one party it can be enforced by the other. However, even if there is no legally binding contract for want of intent, the right to sue in negligence will remain.

The parties can specify that an agreement is not to be legally binding, or subject to legal enforcement. Many raffles, pools, and competitions have, as a condition of entry that they are not subject to legal enforcement.

Case

Appleson v H Littlewood Ltd [1939] 1 All ER 464 (Eng CA)

A alleged he won some money (£4,335) in a football pool. The defendants showed that the conditions of entry had stated that the competition was not subject to legal enforcement, and did not give rise to any legal relationship, rights, duties, or consequences. A was thus unable to claim the money. The Court held that the arrangement was one of honour only, and that the plaintiff had accepted it with his eyes open.

12.2.2   Offer and acceptance

Assuming legal relations were intended, where a contract is in dispute, the Court will consider whether one party made a clear offer of some benefit, and an acceptance of that particular offer was clearly and without qualification made by the other.

(1)   *Principles of offers*

(a)   Offers can be made orally, in writing, or by implication

An agreement does not have to be in writing, except where the law requires it, for example for contracts involving real property (land and buildings).

An example of an implied contract is where someone enters a hospital for emergency treatment. There is an implied offer by a hospital to give necessary life-saving treatment. The acceptance by the consumer of that offer, and of the conditions attached to it, are implied especially if a consumer is in need of emergency treatment and is unconscious. A consumer refusing treatment indicates withdrawal of the acceptance.

(b)   Offers may be withdrawn

Withdrawal of an offer must occur before it has been accepted, otherwise the withdrawal is ineffective. The person making the offer must ensure that the offeree knows or should in the circumstances know that the offer no longer stands. On this point, the Courts hold that the parties be *ad idem* (of the same mind). If they are aware that they are not of the same mind, then a contract cannot be entered into.

(c)   Offers must be communicated to the offeree

A person cannot accept an offer if they have no knowledge of it.

Case

R v Clarke (1927) 40 CLR 227 (HCA)

The Western Australian Government offered a reward for information leading to the arrest and conviction of the person(s) who murdered two policemen, and stated the Governor would pardon any accomplice, not guilty of the murders, who first gave such information. Clarke was arrested in connection with one of the murders. He gave police information, which indeed did lead to the conviction of two men for the murder of one of the police officers. Clarke gave evidence that although he was aware of the offer when giving the information, he had no intention of claiming the reward, and had not thought of it, but had instead given the information to prevent his own conviction. Nevertheless, he later claimed the reward. The Government argued it was not required to pay it.

The High Court of Australia reluctantly found in favour of the government on the basis that there could not be acceptance of an offer without knowledge of the offer, whether the ignorance stemmed from never having had knowledge of the offer, or of forgetting it. If Clarke had not so candidly acknowledged that he had forgotten it, he might have been successful.

This would suggest that a private health facility or practitioner cannot demand payment for services which have been carried out, but for which the consumer did not agree to pay in the first instance. An example would be where an Appendix is removed during a cholecystectomy, though the removal was not necessary. There was no offer to remove the Appendix that the consumer was aware of, so that there can be no acceptance, even implied.

(d)   Offers must be specific

An offer must be specific, that is, both parties must be quite clear on the benefits to be exchanged. For health practitioners, this means that treatment to be given must be clearly and fully explained to the consumer, and only the treatment agreed on must be given, except for any emergency treatment (see chapter 6).

(2)   *Conditions in offers*

Under some circumstances an offeree need not be aware of all the details of the offer to be said to have accepted it. The best example of this is where, after paying for goods or services, one is given a ticket or docket on which are written the conditions under which the goods or services are to be provided. So long as these conditions are reasonably available to be read before the contract is entered into, so that the company giving the ticket could reasonably assume that people would know it contained conditions of the contract on it, the purchaser is bound by those conditions, even if informed of them after paying. If it is in fact unreasonable in the circumstances to make that assumption, the company will need to notify each person receiving a ticket that the conditions are there, that is, the printing of such notice on the ticket will not be enough. Then, even if one is illiterate, one is taken to be aware of the conditions. One example of this type of contract in health service delivery is an agreement for diagnostic tests, where prerequisites such as fasting or taking certain medicines are required. Consumers have a right to be informed about these prerequisites so that they can decide whether to undergo the diagnostic test. However, the test is not offered without them, so once there is acceptance of the offer of the tests, the contract includes the consumer being bound by the prerequisites.

The legal test would be then, whether the offeror took reasonable steps to ensure that the reasonable person would be aware that conditions existed as to the offer. The Courts have held that there is no contract where an offeree reasonably believed that the piece of paper handed to her/him was merely a receipt, as it was given after they have committed to the contract. For instance, cases where a deck chair was hired[7] or where clothes were left at the dry-cleaners,[8] and the document containing the conditions was not handed in to the customer until after he had committed to the contract. The Court held that under those circumstances, it was not reasonable to expect someone to be bound by the conditions set out in that document. If a document is signed, however, then those signing it are held to have read and understood the contents of the document, whether they have or not, and whether the conditions in it are reasonable or not, and no matter how small the print is.

(3) Offers in bilateral contracts

A bilateral contract is a contract that creates obligations for both parties. It is the most common type of contract. An example is where a vendor, Anne Smith, offers to sell another person, Sue Jones, a boat for $2,000. Anne is the offeror and Sue is the offeree. The offer is clear: "Give me $2,000 and I will give you the boat." Sue may take up the offer, or turn it down. As soon as she says "yes", the two women have entered into a contract with obligations on both of them to perform: Sue must pay the money to obtain the boat, and Anne must give her the boat to obtain her money. Failure to honour the agreement by either of them may lead to an action in damages for breach of contract.

When displaying goods in a shop, or advertising, vendors are not in fact making an offer in the legal sense. Instead they are making "invitations to treat". It is the customer who makes an offer when asking for the goods. Technically, the vendor can then accept or refuse the customer's offer, although in the case of shopkeepers, there may be legislation that requires them to sell, and at the price advertised on the goods.

(4) Offers in unilateral contracts

Unilateral contracts are contracts where one party promises to do something on the other party performing a specific act. The offer is the promise, and the acceptance is the performance of the specific act. An example of a unilateral contract is where a person offers a reward for the return of lost property. The acceptance of the offer of a reward is the return of the property. The finder is under no contractual obligation to return the property, and the owner's obligation only comes into being when the property is returned.

(5) Gratuitous offers

Finally, one can make a gratuitous offer, for example, a promise to give one's health practitioner a gift of $1,000. Such a promise is only enforceable if it is made under seal, that is, made in writing and with the formalities creating a deed.[9]

---

7   *Chapelton v Barry Urban District Council* [1940] 1 KB 532.

8   *Causer v Browne* [1952] VLR 1.

9   It may well be unwise for the practitioner to accept such an offer, as accepting gifts from consumers may amount to professional misconduct: see chapter 15.

(6) *Principles on acceptance*

(a) Acceptance must be in full and unconditional

Nothing further must be left to be negotiated between the parties, and an acceptance of an offer will only be effective if the offeror agrees to the exact terms in the offer. If the offeree wants to include a new condition not part of the original offer, they make a counter-offer, and the roles are reversed.

This situation could arise in health where, for instance, a practitioner makes an offer to provide health services on the condition that the consumer provides certain facilities. The consumer accepts this offer and then says the facilities will not be available. Another could be where an offer is made to provide health services of a specific nature on the basis that the consumer undertakes certain preliminary tests, and the consumer accepts this offer, but then says they do not intend to have all the tests. In both of these cases the acceptances are not unconditional, but counter-offers. This means that the practitioner is not bound by the contract to continue attendance, although under statutes providing for consumers' rights or tort law or professional obligations, reasonable care may be required to prevent harm.

This principle also illustrates the need to fully inform consumers. If the treatment they received was either not what they agreed to, something additional to what they agreed to, or not given in the way agreed to, they may argue that there was no proper acceptance of an offer of health services, as the offer was not properly conveyed to them.

(b) Time limit for acceptance

Unless the time for acceptance is stipulated by the contract, it must occur within a reasonable time, otherwise the offer will lapse.

(c) Acceptance must be communicated

Acceptance is not operative until it is conveyed to the offeror. It can be communicated by words, or by conduct in the same way as offers.

(7) *Revocation of acceptance*

One can revoke an acceptance, but the revocation of the acceptance must reach the offeror before acceptance. Once acceptance has been received, the person accepting cannot change their mind without the consent of the offeror, because acceptance brings the contract into being.

(8) *Contracts by mail*

Health practitioners may at times enter into agreements by mail, or even by fax or email. There are certain rules for contracts by mail that may seem arbitrary, but have been adopted for convenience:

• An offer made by mail is not effective until it actually reaches the offeree — the person must know of it. The same applies to the revocation of an offer. It takes effect when the offeree receives it.

• An acceptance made by mail is effective when it is posted. The offeror need not know of its existence, to be bound by it. This is so even if the letter of acceptance is delayed, or never reaches the offeror.[10] The offeree should keep a record of having sent the letter, so that proof of this is available if required, otherwise the acceptance may not be provable. It is not clear whether one can effectively withdraw an acceptance one has sent in the mail by posting a letter of withdrawal.

These rules specifically apply to acceptances by mail[11] and by telegram. Attempts have been made to extend the operation of the rule to other means of communication, such as telex, but these have not been successful. The Courts have consistently held that the general rule of acceptance not being complete until it is received, applies to acceptances by telephone, telex, teleprinter, facsimile machine, and other forms of instantaneous or near instantaneous communication. Acceptance in those cases, therefore, occurs when and where the offeror receives the communication.[12]

In relation to contracts by email, the legal position is uncertain. Even though electronic mail can be virtually instantaneous, there can also be significant delays in transmitting messages. Most emails are sent by an individual through a service provider and then to the computer of the other person through their perhaps different service provider. Using two different service providers is therefore different to when a letter is posted through one medium — the post. The Electronic Transactions Act 2002 provides that where an information system has been designated for the purpose of receiving messages by the addressee, then the message is received when it enters that system. In all other cases, it is received when the message comes to the attention of the addressee — the email message is received.[13]

(9) Identification of parties

It must be possible to clearly identify the parties to a contract that is the offeror and the offeree. Where treatment is to be carried out by a hospital, the contract is made between the consumer and the hospital. Where the health practitioner involved is not employed by the hospital, there will be two contracts, one between the consumer and the practitioner for provision of requisite individual care, and another between the consumer and the hospital, for the care it provides. Where a health practitioner is in private practice, whether working in a hospital setting or not, the contract is between the individual private practitioner and the consumer.

12.2.3   Consideration

Unless the contract is under seal, it is called a simple contract, and must involve some form of consideration. This means that something of value (which can be qualified in monetary

---

10   *Household Fire Insurance Co v Grant* (1879) 4 Ex D 216.

11   The postal rules do not apply to international contracts for the sale of goods. The general rule applies, that the offer is complete upon acceptance.

12   *Entores Ltd v Miles Far East Corp* [1955] 2 QB 327. Entores Ltd was subsequently considered, approved, and applied by the House of Lords in *Brinkibon Ltd v Stahag Stahl und Stahlwarenhandelsgesellschaft mbH* [1983] 2 AC 34; [1982] 2 WLR 264; [1982] 1 All ER 293.

13   Professor Jeremy Finn in Burrows, Finn & Todd, *Law of Contract in New Zealand* (2nd ed), Wellington, LexisNexis, 2002, chapter 3, page 69, footnote 176, commented even before this Act came into force, the former part of the rule was problematic in that where the sender and addressee use the same information service provider the message will be deemed to have been received as soon as it is sent, yet where different information systems are used it will not be received as soon as it is sent, but only when it enters the addressee's information system. Professor Finn states that it could be unworkable and untenable. It is unclear as yet if this is the case.

terms) is to be conferred from one party on another, be it money, property, goods, services, information, etc. Most contracts involve a promise of a mutual exchange of benefit. For example, one party undertakes to work for, or to provide health services to, the other for a sum of money. Consideration is something capable of serving as the price of a promise, which another person is not otherwise bound to carry out. There must be specifically either a benefit to one party, or a detriment to the other. When considering whether a valid contract exists, the Court is not concerned with the adequacy of the consideration, so long as it is sufficient to indicate the parties were serious about the bargain.

Past consideration, that is, something done or paid for in the past, cannot hold someone to a promise to which the thing or money did not then relate. If a grateful consumer on leaving a practitioner's care promises a gift of $600, that is not an enforceable promise, as the care was given with no expectation of the money. It remains a gratuitous promise.

Only the person who has given consideration may enforce the contract. If, for example, a midwife is engaged to care for Mrs Jones, that does not create an obligation to attend to Mrs Jones's sister's care.

12.2.4 Deeds

Contracts under seal are called deeds. These are contracts made in writing that are signed, sealed, and delivered. In most cases, the parties' signatures need only be attested to by a witness, who is not a party to the deed, and the document is expressed to be a deed. Actual sealing with wax is rarely necessary. However, it may be used to sanctify mutual promises.

Deeds will be enforced in the absence of consideration. Promises of gifts embodied in deeds are enforceable. Deeds take effect at the moment of delivery. Physical delivery is not necessary, intention to deliver is enough — the promisor who puts a deed on a desk to be given to their lawyer, with a letter to be written to the promisee tomorrow, is bound by it. Neither knowledge on the part of the promisee who benefits from the promise, nor acceptance of the offer, as with simple contracts, is required.

One can sue for breach of contract based on a deed for up to 12 years after the deed has been made, whereas with a simple contract the limitation period is 6 years.[14]

(1)   *Contracts that must be in writing*

Generally, simple contracts need not be in writing. Legislation provides some exceptions to this principle. The following contracts need to be in writing to be enforceable:

* Bills of exchange, including cheques;
* Transfers of shares;
* Sale of land;
* Mortgages;
* Guarantees;
* Assignment of copyright;

---

14   This is currently regulated by the Limitation Act 1950. At present the Limitation Bill 2009 is before the select committee. The Bill aims to replace the present Act, to make the law clearer and more comprehensive, and to encourage claimants not to delay in bringing their suit. More information on the Bill is available online at www.parliament.nz/en-NZ/PB/Legislation/Bills/BillsDigests/8/5/0/49PLLawBD16951-Limitation-Bill-2009-Bills-Digest-1695.html

- Credit purchase agreements;
- Contracts for commission between a vendor of property and a real estate agent.

The requirement for these to be in writing is set out in the Contracts Enforcement Act 1956 and in other specific Acts, such as the Real Estate Agents Act 2008[15] and the Hire Purchase Act 1971.

Where terms of the contract are in writing, and there is no reason not to believe the parties meant the writing to constitute the whole of the agreement, the Courts will consider what is written down to be final and complete. The Courts will apply the plain meaning of the words contained in the contract, so that no party will be able to argue that they did not mean what the reasonable reader would take those words to mean. Only if there is some ambiguity or uncertainty as to the plain meaning of the words, will the Court consider other evidence, such as oral undertakings also made at the time, as to what the parties arranged.

12.3   Health service contracts

Most health service contracts between the DHBs and regional providers are in writing, but most contracts between consumers and providers are verbal or implied. Most health care consumers are unaware that they are entering a contract. The use of contract law as a means of compensation for unsatisfactory treatment is very rare. Where a practitioner falls below a reasonable standard of care and skill that results in injury, then there may well be cover under the Injury Prevention, Rehabilitation, and Compensation Act 2001.[16] However, not all failure to observe such a standard will provide cover. There are some instances where such cover will be declined. In these cases, actions against health practitioners tend to be brought in negligence, which is arguably easier to establish than a breach of the contract to provide treatment, and can result in compensation for such things as pain and suffering and loss of quality of life (chapter 8). Nevertheless, the law does recognise the consumer's right to receive what was implied or verbally agreed on in the way of treatment, and an implied term of that agreement is that the treatment will be of a reasonable standard. There is also the Consumer Guarantees Act 1993, which could be used to bring an action against a health practitioner where that person has not provided services with reasonable care and skill. The practitioner would probably have to be in private practice, as they have to be "in trade" providing professional services.

12.4   Capacity to contract — who can make a contract?

A person is obliged to fulfil a contract only if they have the legal capacity to agree to it. At law, this means the person must be 20 years of age, and competent to be able to agree. Thus minors, those under 20 years, and those who are not competent to agree, which may include those who are drunk, may be held not to have the capacity to enter into contracts. Unincorporated associations also do not have capacity to contract, while companies do. Contracts entered into by a party who does not have the required capacity are not void, but are voidable.

---

15   This Act came into force on the 16 November 2009 and the relevant section under this new Act is section 126.

16   See chapter 4.

12.4.1 Minors

Contracts entered into by minors are covered by the Minors' Contracts Act 1969. A minor is defined as a person who has not yet attained the age of 20.[17] The Act divides minors in to three categories — married minors; minors under 18 years of age; minors of and over 18 years of age. The time for classifying minors is when the contract is made.

The married minor is treated as an adult, and has full contractual capacity.[18]

Contracts entered into by minors less than 18 years of age are prima facie enforceable by the minor against the other party.[19] However, the contract cannot be enforced against the minor. The other party may apply to a Court for an order that the minor performs their part of the contract. The Court can make a variety of orders, although it cannot change the contract. The Court will take into consideration the circumstances in which the minor made the contract, for example, whether they had parental or other advice, the nature and value of the property, the age and means of the minor, and anything else of relevance. A Court may make an order requiring compensation be paid by either party, or for the transfer of property.

Minors of, and over, 18 have less legal protection. The contract is binding on the minor and is enforceable without any proof of fairness by the other party. If the minor considers that the contract is unfair, then they may apply to the Court to obtain an order in their favour. Such an order will only be granted if the minor can prove that the consideration given to her/him is so inadequate as to be unconscionable, or that a provision of the contract is harsh and oppressive.

If a minor is seeking treatment, does an agreement to give this treatment mean a contract exists? What is the consideration involved? If parents are paying, is the contract with the parents, or with the child? What if the parents agree to pay for what they believe is treatment for a sore throat, and the minor is in fact receiving contraception?

While these questions have not been specifically addressed by the Courts, it is arguable that a contract is entered into only if the minor promises to pay for treatment. If so, then the minor is bound by it. This is a different issue from consent to receive treatment — the issue here is the minor's obligation to pay. If the parents are the ones who will be paying, then there is an agreement by them, either specifically given or implied, that they will pay. The contract is then with the parents. Note that the law requires that parents provide adequate and reasonable maintenance of their children. In such instances, there would be a fiduciary relationship between the practitioner and the minor, but not a contractual one. Whether the parent will have access to their child's health information should be discussed beforehand where possible. Parents do not automatically have a right to their child's health information, and also the child might not want the parent to know. (See chapters 6 and 9.)

---

17   Age of Majority Act 1970, section 4.
18   Minors' Contracts Act 1969, section 4.
19   Minors' Contracts Act 1969, section 6.

12.4.2 Persons who are not competent

(1) *Who is legally not competent to agree?*

There are two categories of persons not competent to agree — those who have been recognised by the law as lacking capacity to enter into a contract, and those otherwise recognised as being incapacitated in particular circumstances.

Those who have been recognised by law as lacking capacity are, for example, people who are subject to property orders, or who have granted someone else an enduring power of attorney over their property. Contracts entered into by such persons are voidable, although the law protects the position of people who deal with them in good faith.[20]

People who might not be fully competent to, for example, give consent to receive treatment, are still presumed competent to enter into a contract, unless they can prove not only their incapacity in the particular instance, but also that the other party knew or should have known of the incapacity.[21] Unless these two elements are proved, they cannot escape liability. They must, for instance, pay for services provided to them.

(2) *Intoxication does not remove contractual obligations*

People who are drunk are also held to contracts, unless they can show that the other party to the contract knew, or should have been aware, that they were drunk at the time they entered into the contract.

(3) *Contracts for service for persons who are not fully competent*

In cases where there is no legal contractual incapacity, but a person is nevertheless not fully competent, for example drunk or temporarily incapacitated by a shock, they can be held to their agreement to receive services to the extent that they knew what they were doing. For example, such a person may be held to an agreement to pay for a taxi fare, as by getting into the taxi it can be inferred they understood they would have to pay for it.

12.4.3 Unincorporated bodies

Unincorporated bodies are groups of people, such as practitioners, acting together as one, but who are not a registered company. They include most common partnerships. The unincorporated body in itself is not a legal "person", and cannot be a party to a contract. Each individual member must be a party to the contract for it to be binding, either personally or through an agent. Partners are each other's agents, and so may bind each other. A group of practitioners may call themselves a "company" or have a registered business name without being incorporated under company law, and therefore the "company" or business is not a separate legal entity.

12.5 Unenforceable contract for misrepresentation

Those making an agreement must, at law, be ad idem, that is, regarding both the terms of the agreement and their consent to it, they must be of one mind and have freely consented to all the terms of the agreement. Consent to be bound by the contract must not, therefore, be affected by factors that, according to law, will make the agreement invalid such as:

---

20   Protection of Personal and Property Rights Act 1988, section 53; see also chapter 5.
21   *O'Connor v Hart* [1985] 1 NZLR 159 (PC).

- Misrepresentation of facts by another party;
- Mistake as to facts or terms by one or more parties;
- Duress suffered by a party;
- Undue influence on one or more parties.

12.5.1   Misrepresentation

A misrepresentation is a statement as to some existing fact that does not accord with the true situation, and/or can be said to be or likely to be misleading or deceptive in the circumstances.

The remedies for misrepresentation are found in the Contractual Remedies Act 1979 and the Fair Trading Act 1986. The remedies are available whether the misrepresentation was innocent or fraudulent. Fraudulent misrepresentation involves an element of dishonesty. Innocent misrepresentation involves the person honestly believing that what they said was true, but in fact for some reason is incorrect. The Contractual Remedies Act 1979 provides remedies by way of damages, that is, monetary compensation, or by way of right to cancel the contract. The Fair Trading Act 1986 also provides a wide range of remedies.

Some contracts, mainly insurance contracts, rely on the utmost good faith of the party applying for insurance to answer all questions which they are asked truthfully, and also to volunteer any other information that may be relevant to the risk being taken by the insurer. A failure to disclose material information will render the contract inoperative.

Fraudulent or negligent misrepresentation may lead to further action, either in criminal law or in tort (negligence).

12.5.2   Mistake

Mistake is another ground for holding a contract invalid. The relevant Act is the Contractual Mistakes Act 1977. One must distinguish a mistake at law from an error of judgment, or a mistake in personal assessment of facts. For example, the person who looks at a car for sale and decides it is worth $5,000 cannot have the contract of sale set aside if they later discover it is worth $500. The "caveat emptor" ("let the buyer beware") maxim applies.

The Contractual Mistakes Act 1977 applies to basic mistakes that occur in the process of making contracts at the offer and acceptance stage. Mistakes can be mistakes of fact or law:

- A mistake of fact is an error with regard to something in existence at the date of the contract, the subject-matter of the contract, or the identity of one of the parties.
- A mistake of law is an error about the legal aspects of the contract, or application of the law to the contract. Rights to relief might be limited if this kind of mistake is made.

There are three kinds of mistake of fact or law, one of which must have occurred before a Court will grant relief under the Contractual Mistakes Act 1977:

- *Common mistake:* Both parties make the *same* mistake about the *same* aspect of the contract.
- *Mutual mistake:* Both parties make a *different* mistake about the *same* aspect of the contract.

- *Unilateral mistake:* One party makes a mistake and the other party is aware of it, but does nothing to correct the impression.

(1) *Mistake as to the nature of the contract*

This is not to be confused with mistake as to the law regarding the contract, but rather, what sort of contract one is agreeing to. An example is the elderly gentleman who signed a bill of exchange thinking it was a guarantee.

(2) *Mistake as to the party one is contracting with*

Most cases involving mistake as to the identity of the other party are about rogues passing herself/himself off as someone else. If a person is mistaken as to whom they are dealing with, they may not be held bound to the agreement, as it will be void from the beginning. However, the Courts have held that unless the identity of the person in question is crucial to the carrying out of the contract, the contract remains enforceable.

An example in health services would include the engaging of Midwife Y to provide services to a consumer who believes Y is a registered midwife. If Y is in fact a registered midwife, but their name is Z, and if Z provides services as agreed, the contract would most likely be enforceable and the consumer would have to pay. If Y was the midwife's real name, but Y was not a registered midwife, that mistaken identity could be said to go to the heart of the contract. The consumer would have to show that they would not have agreed to be cared for by Y, if they had known the truth. Unless that is the case, Y can expect to be paid for services rendered.

Relief can be obtained under the Contractual Mistakes Act 1977 provided that the parties did not know of the mistake at the time they entered into the contract, and provided that the mistake was not just one of interpretation of the meaning of the contract.

12.5.3   Duress

Duress is a further ground for holding an agreement void. Traditionally, the Courts have restricted duress to acts or threats of violence to the person, of deprivation of liberty, and the unlawful detention of goods. Now duress has been extended to include economic duress, for example, the threat of having one's house burned down, or a valuable painting destroyed.

12.5.4   Undue influence and unconscionable bargains

If the situation falls short of the common law definition of duress, one may be able to invoke remedies available under the law of equity, which has developed remedies where one party holds an unfair advantage (moral or otherwise) over the other, through what is experienced as superior power or status.

(1) *Undue influence*

Where some special relationship of trust and confidence exists between the two parties at the time the contract is entered into, there is a presumption of undue influence by the stronger party on the weaker party. Examples of such relationships are those between solicitor and client, health practitioner and consumer, parent and child (in some instances), teacher and student, religious adviser and disciple (but not husband and wife, nor principal and agent). The stronger party can rebut the presumption if they prove there was no such influence, and that the consent was given freely. It will be a question of fact in each case. The Court will consider whether full disclosure of the facts was made by the stronger person, referred to as the fiduciary, whether independent advice was given, that is, advice by a third, impartial person with relevant knowledge, and the actual circumstances of the consent.

Where there is no special relationship, the person claiming undue influence will have the burden of proving that fact. The Courts will vary in their approach to the claim depending on circumstances. Where, for example, one of the parties suffers a personal or social disability, such as a physical or mental disability, or a language difficulty, the Court will take this into account.

It is not hard to imagine that undue influence may affect the relationship between health practitioners and consumers in many cases. Health practitioners and others must be careful not to dominate consumers to the point where their advice amounts to undue influence, but must allow the consumers to be free to decide, based on a fair and impartial disclosure of facts.

(2) Unconscionable contracts

Very similar to the doctrine of undue influence is that of unconscionable bargains, whereby the Courts will set aside contracts that impose harsh terms on one party due to inequality of bargaining power.

Case

Moffat v Moffat [1984] 1 NZLR 600; (1984) 1 FRNZ 211 (CA)

After 18 years of marriage, a husband and wife had instructed a solicitor to prepare a separation agreement. The wife, who was under stress and anxious to have the separation finalised, ceded in the agreement her entire interest in the matrimonial home, the furniture, and the fittings. Before signing, she acknowledged in writing that she had been advised by the solicitor to seek independent advice, but had chosen not to do so. She later sought to have the agreement set aside.

The Court considered this was a marginal case, but was satisfied that due to the strain on the wife, her ignorance of the value of the assets, and lack of independent advice created a serious disadvantage to her. Her husband knew of this situation, and took advantage of it. The agreement was set aside as being unfair and unconscionable.

This form of action has not been used widely in the health arena, but it may be only a matter of time before consumers bring action in the Courts complaining that they have been manipulated into agreeing to procedures, when they did not fully understand what was going on.

12.5.5 Illegal contracts

The Illegal Contracts Act 1970 deals with the kinds of contract that are illegal at law or in equity, such as contracts:

- To commit a fraud, crime, or tort;
- For sexually immoral purposes;
- Prejudicial to national security;
- Interfering with the administration of justice;

- Promoting corruption in public life;
- Depriving the government of tax.

There are also other statutes that make contracts illegal, for example the Commerce Act 1986 prohibits a variety of business practices that suppress competition.[22]

Some contracts that are illegal through performance are those in which the carrying out of the obligation under the contract breaches some other law, for example where a builder fails to observe a bylaw.

Some contracts are prohibited but not illegal, for example contracts made in restraint of trade where a person agrees to restrict their manner of carrying out their trade or profession. These are void, voidable, or unenforceable.

Section 7 of the Illegal Contracts Act 1970 provides for relief to those who have made illegal contracts. A Court is entitled to make an order, and will do so, after considering the parties' conduct and where the provisions of a statute are breached, the purpose of that Act, and the provision of penalties by it.

12.6   Discharge of contracts

A contract comes to the end of its life, that is, is discharged, on one of the following events:

- Performance of the obligations by both parties;
- Agreement to end the contract;
- Frustration by an outside event;
- Election to cancel the contract on breach;
- The occurrence of a specified event or condition provided in the contract.

12.6.1   Performance

Where parties have fully performed their promises in accordance with the terms of their agreement, the contract is discharged. Unless a specific time for the carrying out of one's obligations is stipulated, making time of the essence, these should be carried out within a reasonable time. Where activities are to be performed for a stated period of time, the contract is discharged at the end of that time. When a party has discharged their obligations under the contract, that party may demand discharge (often payment) by the other party.

12.6.2   Agreement

Where a contract has not been fully discharged, the parties may nevertheless agree to consider it discharged. This is a further contract and all elements, including consideration, must be present. Where no one has completed their part of the agreement, then the lack

---

22   The Commerce Act 1986 applies to all areas of the health sector, and to both public and private health and disability services provision. It prohibits collusive behaviour, price fixing, and market dominance. For further information see Commerce Commission, *The Commerce Act and the Health Sector: A General Guide*, January 1998. See also G Godlovitch, "Competition law in health care", in Alston et al, *Medical Practice Management*, Wellington, Brookers, 2002. Note also that the Commerce Commission has brought successful claims against the Ophthalmological Society and four other North Island eye surgeons. The Ophthalmological Society prevented competition in the cataract surgery market in Southland by preventing surgeons from outside New Zealand providing the service for a cheaper cost. The four North Island eye surgeons were found to have fixed the prices for surgery amongst themselves, preventing a competitive market for health consumers. For information see www.comcom.govt.nz.

of consideration is not an issue. Each party simply agrees to release their rights under the original contract, in consideration for a similar release by the other. Where one party has discharged some or all obligations required under the contract, but the other has not, then some further consideration is required for the agreement to be legally enforceable.

12.6.3 Frustration

Usually contracts are based on at least a presumption that those involved will carry out their promise as long as they remain able to do so, and that only ill health, unexpected events, accident, war, non-occurrence of a foreseen event, etc, which renders it impossible or unreasonably difficult for them to act, will excuse them from their obligation. In that case each party must fulfil those obligations that fell due before the frustrating event occurred. The contract is not void from the beginning. If the frustration is self-induced, the above does not apply. The Frustrated Contracts Act 1944 provides that when an external event not contemplated by the parties to the contract makes performance impossible, or difficult and different, there is a release of obligations. However, it does not apply to some types of contract, for example, most insurance contracts.

12.6.4 Election to cancel on breach

Where one party has breached a term of the contract, the other party may elect either to cancel the contract or to seek a remedy as outlined below, depending on the nature of the breach. The party may be able to claim for any damages suffered, but cannot thereafter seek specific performance of the contract.

12.6.5 Occurrence of a specified event or condition

This is self-explanatory. Where it is specified that if something happens or some stipulated condition occurs, the contract will be deemed discharged.

12.7 Remedies for breach of contract

There are three main remedies available for breach of contract.

12.7.1 Common law remedy — damages

The basic remedy for breach of contract is the award of an appropriate sum of money as compensation for loss of goods, business, or other value that has resulted from the breach. The Court considers the terms of the contract (written, oral, or implied), and the position the innocent party would have been in had there been no breach, that is, had the contract been performed.

Loss to a plaintiff who has been deprived of the benefit of a provision in the contract may be measured in different ways. It can be based on the difference in value between what was promised and what was supplied, or it can be based on the cost of curing the breach. The Courts take a pragmatic attitude and adopt whichever approach seems appropriate and reasonable.

(1) *Failure to provide services of a reasonable standard*

There is an implied condition in any contract for professional services, that not only will the services be those agreed on and consented to, but also that they will be of a standard reasonably to be expected of an ordinary person of similar experience and skill which the professional purports to have. If, for example, a health service is not provided by the health practitioner who contracted to provide it, whether there is any harm suffered or not, the consumer can sue for breach of contract. The consumer can claim for any financial or physical loss suffered as a result of the breach of contract, and can also claim that no fee is payable. The consumer can then be restored to the financial and physical position that existed before the contract was entered into, insofar as that is practicable. Under some circumstances, where the above remedies are inappropriate, the Court may make an order for specific performance. However, the Courts will not as a rule require any person to render personal service to another, as this smacks of slavery.

12.7.2   Equitable remedies

These are discretionary remedies granted by the Courts in accordance with the principles of the law of equity.

(1)   *Specific performance*

Specific performance is a Court order that a party performs their contractual obligations. The Court will only do this where the award of money would not be just under the circumstances, and the other party is still ready and willing to fulfil its part of the agreement. Specific performance is generally ordered where it would be impossible to get a similar good or service, and the unique nature of the particular good or service was relied on, such as a painting.

(2)   *Injunction*

This is an order by a Court forbidding, or ordering, a person to do something. It can be applied when there is a contract where someone has promised to refrain from some activity, and the other person is afraid the person will go ahead and do it, or it can be an interim measure where a further, more detailed Court hearing is to be held. Failure to pay damages ordered by the Court can lead to seizure of property, or garnishment of wages. Failure to comply with an order for specific performance, or an injunction, can lead to imprisonment for contempt of Court.

12.7.3   Statutory remedy

Relief can also be given under the Illegal Contracts Act 1970, Contractual Mistakes Act 1977, Frustrated Contracts Act 1944, Contractual Remedies Act 1979, and Fair Trading Act 1986. For example, the Court has a wide-ranging power to grant relief in the event of breach of contract by way of purported cancellation by one party.[23] Relief includes:

* Specific performance;
* Damages;
* Injunction;
* Prohibition.

12.8   Other relevant Acts

Two further Acts relating to contracts for the provision of services in the health sector are the:

---

23   Contractual Remedies Act 1979, section 9.

- Goods and Services Tax Act 1985; and
- Consumer Guarantees Act 1993.

These two Acts provide relief whereby the service specifically contracted for by the buyer (or consumer) is not provided as it was represented to that buyer. Breach carries severe penalties in the form of damages. These Acts require that health professionals provide the services they purport to provide.

12.9   Further reading

9 Halsbury's Laws of England, 1985.

Alston et al, *Medical Practice Management*, Wellington, Brookers, 2002.

Burrows et al, *Law of Contract in New Zealand* (3rd ed), Wellington, Lexis Nexis, 2007.

M Chetwin and S Graw, *An Introduction to the Law of Contract in New Zealand*, Wellington, Brookers, 2001.

Commerce Commission, *The Commerce Act and the Health Sector: A General Guide*, January 1998.

Chapter 13

THE CONTRACT OF EMPLOYMENT

ANNE O'BRIEN AND TREVOR WARR

Contents

13.1 Introduction

The basis of a health practitioner's relationship with an employer is the contract. Usually this is an employment agreement. Like any contract, an employment agreement consists of various terms agreed on between the parties to it. It must be certain in the sense that the parties have reached an accord on all the elements necessary to make the agreement work. The agreement creates obligations on each party to perform their part of the bargain.

Employment agreements are a special type of contract. The Employment Relations Act 2000 provides a specific set of rules to govern them. Other statutes also apply to such things as equal pay (Equal Pay Act 1972), mandatory holidays (Holidays Act 2003), parental leave (Parental Leave and Employment Protection Act 1987), minimum wages for employees (Minimum Wage Act 1983), savings schemes (KiwiSaver Act 2006), and how wages are to be paid (Wages Protection Act 1983).

The effect of these statutes, and the Employment Relations Act 2000 in particular, is to make the employment agreement unique among contracts. Before dealing with the nature of the employment agreement (referred to as a contract *of* service), it is important to distinguish it from another type of contract, which in a superficial sense it may resemble — the contract entered into by an independent contractor (a contract *for* services). Contracts for services are not subject to the rules set out in the Employment Relations Act 2000 or the other statutes mentioned above.

The most obvious examples of independent contracting are unlikely to be confused with employment agreements. A plumber who is engaged to fix a hot water cylinder is independent of the person who engages her/him. They are hired to perform a particular task, and neither party intends that the person engaging the plumber has any responsibility to him/her beyond the obligation to pay for the work done.

Other cases may be less obvious. A group of medical practitioners might wish to offer physiotherapy services at their medical centre. They could enter into an employment agreement with a physiotherapist, or for various reasons they might prefer to engage the physiotherapist as an independent contractor. They may rent a room to the physiotherapist at the medical centre, and have a referral service from the medical practitioners. In every sense the physiotherapist is in business on their own account, relieving the medical practitioners of the more onerous obligations that fall on an employer under an employment agreement. The outward appearance of the two relationships might be very similar, but at law they are very different.

The law does not provide a hard-and-fast rule to distinguish the two types of contract. However, the Employment Relations Act 2000 provides that, for the purpose of that Act, emphasis must be put on the real nature of the relationship between the person providing the work and the person to whom it is provided.[1] The question is sometimes put in these terms: is the person really in business on their own account? The Employment Relations Authority (the Authority) or the Employment Court (the Court) may determine whether a person is an employee.[2]

---

1   Employment Relations Act 2000, section 6(2).
2   See paragraph 13.8.1(2).

In practice, a contract may have a mixture of features from both categories. The mere fact that the contract contains a term saying that it is not an employment agreement will not determine the issue. Where there is a conflict over the nature of the parties' relationship, the Authority or the Court will take all the circumstances into account. It will weigh them up to decide into which category the contract falls, but it will have regard primarily to the reality of the relationship.

A "real" employment agreement or contract *of* service generally has the following features:

* The employer determines the work that is to be done, when it is to be done, and the employee makes herself/himself available by the hour.
* The employer also controls the premises and equipment, and how they are to be used.
* The employer has the power to hire and fire at their discretion.
* The employee is required to perform the work personally.
* The employee is paid regularly, and is entitled to recreation leave and other benefits.
* An employee, in most cases, serves only one employer.
* An employee is not required to register for GST for the services provided.
* An employee's employment contract cannot be terminated without justification.[3]

On the other hand, when an independent contractor is engaged:

* The contractor can be asked to carry out a specific task, the completion of which brings the contract to an end.
* The contractor generally owns the equipment, and maybe the premises, and determines how it is to be used.
* The contractor is usually free to employ others to perform the work under the contract.
* The contractor is free to provide services to more than one person.
* The contract can be terminated, without reason, if proper notice is given.
* The contractor has no claim for payment, unless special arrangements are made, until the work is completed.

13.2 When is a health practitioner an independent contractor?

It follows from the above discussion, that those who work in a health service establishment are generally employees, and those who work independently, for example, a dentist or an independent midwife, are independent contractors. If, for example, a rest home engages somebody as a temporary registered nurse through an agency to fill a staffing shortage, the nurse's status is not as clear. The employment agreement will be between the agency and the nurse, and there will be a separate contract between the agency and the rest home.

It is important to note that a health practitioner who supplies their services on a truly voluntary basis will not be an employee, and not entitled to the protection supplied by the Employment Relations Act 2000.[4]

---

3   See 13.8.2(5) on personal grievances.
4   *McCulloch v Director General of Social Welfare* [2000] 1 ERNZ 467.

A trainee health practitioner who is working in a hospital or other health care service purely as part of their training will not be an employee.[5] However, a person who is working part-time will be, regardless of whether they are also undertaking a course of study relevant to their employment. It is important to clarify the nature of the relationship before work commences.

13.3 Other relationships

There are other relationships in which one person may do work for another. Two relationships of particular interest to health practitioners are described below.

13.3.1 Principal and agent

An agent is one who is authorised to act for another, referred to in law as the principal, and who has power to create and effect legal relationships between their principal and third parties. An agent must act with the principal's approval, and, in so doing, may bind the principal by contract to the third party, for example real estate agents and commercial travellers. However, a specific contract of agency need not exist. Simply by placing another person in a position where, "according to ... law or ... the ordinary usages of mankind, [a person] is understood to represent and act for the person who has so placed him; but in every case it is only by the will of the employer that an agency can be created."[6] One difficulty in establishing agency as opposed to employment, is that many employees are, by the very nature of their work, agents of their employer. They may, in fact, be both.

The Court must examine the terms of employment, and consider the nature of the agreement. The difference, in effect, is that whereas a principal may direct an agent on what to do, an employer can also direct her/him on how, when, and where to do it. Health practitioners may be exercising the powers of agency when they commit their employer to some service for a client, for example community nurses signing up clients for treatment or rehabilitation services. Power of attorney is a form of agency, where a person authorises another to act on their behalf (see 6.5.1(3)).

13.3.2 Partnership

A partnership is where two or more people agree to combine for some object, such as providing a service. Health practitioners in private practice may decide to do this. A partnership is not a company, which is a legal "person" separate from the individuals who constitute it, but liability for debts and negligence may be shared jointly by the individuals involved. A partner is not an employee of the partnership, unless they specifically and separately enter into such a relationship by agreement. Partners are principals in their own right, and any work they do is not subject to employment law principles.

13.4 Terms of employment

Terms of employment may be expressly included in the employment agreement or they may be implied.[7] Terms may be implied by custom, by statute or by the courts into all contracts of a particular type. They exist just as if the parties specifically agreed on them.

---

5   *NZEI v Director General of Education* [1981] 1 NZLR 538.
6   *Pole v Leask* (1863) 33 LJ Ch 155, 161-162.
7   *Warwick Henderson Gallery Ltd v Weston (No 2)* [2005] 1 ERNZ 921; [2006] 2 NZLR 145 (CA).

This is because employment attracts common law and statutory duties and privileges for both the employer and employee. In some cases the courts may imply a term into a contract to remedy an omission in the contract.[8]

13.4.1 Terms required by the Employment Relations Act 2000

Fundamentally, the employer and employee may agree on anything but section 65(1) of the Employment Relations Act 2000 requires the agreement to be in writing[9] and to include:

- The names of the employee and employer;
- A description of the work to be performed;
- Where the employee is to perform the work;
- Hours of work;
- The wages or salary payable to the employee; and
- A plain language explanation of the services available to resolve employment relationship problems, and informing the employee of the 90-day limit for notifying a personal grievance.

An individual employment agreement must also contain clauses setting out:

- Payment on public holidays;[10] and
- An explanation of the process to be undertaken where all or part of an employer's business is transferred to a new employer, including the conditions on which an employee might transfer to the new employer.[11]

If the employment is for work in the cleaning services, food catering services, orderly services, or laundry services for the health sector or aged related residential care sector (among other specified industries), then the agreement should set out the additional rights of these "vulnerable" workers including the right to transfer to the new employer on existing terms and conditions of employment where all or part of an employer's business is transferred to a new employer.[12]

An individual agreement may not include any term that is unlawful or contrary to any of the provisions of the Employment Relations Act 2000.[13]

Section 4 of the Act implies into every employment contract a duty on the parties to deal with each other in good faith. Although "good faith" is not defined it is wider than the implied obligations of trust and confidence on the employer and employee and requires them to be active and constructive in creating and maintaining a positive working relationship. This term, which is an example of a term implied by statute, is fundamental to the employment relationship. It should be kept in mind in all dealings between the employer and the employee.[14]

---

8   See Burrows, Finn and Todd, *Law of Contract in New Zealand* (3rd ed), Wellington, LexisNexis, 2007 for a full discussion of implied terms.

9   Despite this, employment agreements that are not in writing are still enforceable to the extent that their terms can be proved: *Warwick Henderson Gallery Ltd v Weston (No 2)* [2005] 1 ERNZ 921; [2006] 2 NZLR 145 (CA).

10   Holidays Act 2003, sections 52 and 53.

11   Employment Relations Act 2000, section 69K.

12   Employment Relations Act 2000, Part 6A.

13   Employment Relations Act 2000, section 65(2)(b).

13.4.2   Terms implied by the common law

Some terms implied into all employment agreements that particularly affect health service employees include obligations to:

*   Carry out any lawful and reasonable order of the employer;
*   Carry out those orders with reasonable care;
*   Be faithful to the employer's interests;
*   Refrain from denigrating the service provided by the employer;
*   Refrain from misusing their employer's confidential information received by an employee in furthering the employer's interest; and
*   Account for the employer's property.

13.4.3   Carry out any lawful and reasonable order of the employer

An employee is obliged to carry out the lawful and reasonable instructions of the employer.

A health service employee should clarify with a prospective employer just what duties are to be involved in the position, and whether duties are limited to certain areas of care or are more general. If an employee is not prepared to carry out all instructions that the employer might give, for example they feel inexperienced or untrained in certain areas of care, this should be the subject of discussion when the employment is being negotiated. A health service provider has a responsibility to its clients to provide staff who are adequately trained and experienced.[15] However, this issue is not directly relevant to the employment agreement.

Employers must also consider the effect of the workload and type of work they are seeking from an employee in terms of workplace stress, which is now recognised as a hazard under the Health and Safety in Employment Act 1992.[16]

The requirement of obedience involves only lawful directions. Orders that endanger an employee's life or health, or which they reasonably believe would endanger their life or health, are not lawful orders. There is no obligation to obey them.[17] Presumably, this would apply to directions that it is believed would endanger the life and health of consumers or others. Likewise orders which conflict with a practitioner's professional or ethical obligations may not be lawful orders. These can place staff in an unenviable position, for example an enrolled nurse in an understaffed ward being instructed to carry out duties which are outside her/his scope of practice.

Refusal by staff to care for consumers with, for example, H1HI influenza, SARS or meningitis, where the employer has provided adequate protection and instruction, may be a breach of the employment contract. Whether it is reasonable to order staff to care for people with infectious diseases, even with the best of precautions, has never been tested. There have not been any significant epidemics since the introduction of modern employment law. In the event of such a situation, there is likely to be an obligation to work, provided all reasonable precautions have been taken.[18] There are obviously some jobs, such

---

14   Section 4 Employment Relations Act 2000 does not apply to dealings between an employer and an applicant for a position (other than a promotion): *Hayden v Wellington Free Ambulance Service* [2002] 1 ERNZ 399.

15   *Roylance v General Medical Council* [1999] 3 WLR 541 (PC).

16   See chapter 14.

17   *NZ Food Processing Union v Unilever NZ Ltd* (1990) ERNZ Sel Cas582; [1990] 1 NZILR 35.

as policing or bomb disposal, that carry an inherent risk that can only be minimised, rather than eliminated. In emergency situations, health service provision is one of them. It should also be remembered that discrimination against those with a physical or mental disability is prohibited in New Zealand (chapter 5).

13.4.4   Can health practitioners refuse to carry out work beyond their competence?

First, it is important to note that the employer is entitled to require an employee to carry out any lawful order, that is, any order reasonably related to the rendering of services contracted for. This is why it is important to inform an employer of anything one is unable or unwilling to do that could otherwise be expected of someone in the category under which one is employed. Unless otherwise stipulated, a health practitioner, for example a physiotherapist, is employed to carry out any of the duties it is reasonable to expect of someone with the training and experience they claim to have.

If the employee persistently refuses to carry out an instruction that is lawful and reasonable, the employer will in most cases have the right to dismiss the employee. Where the refusal occurs because the employee believes they cannot properly carry out a particular service or should not carry it out under the circumstances, insistence by the employer that the employee carry out the task (notwithstanding that belief) may be enough to make the instruction unreasonable. It is important for the employee to clearly state to the employer the reason for the refusal to carry out the instruction. In most cases, the problem can be resolved by discussion. If not, an attempt by the employer to dismiss an employee who genuinely believes that they cannot properly perform the task is unlikely to be justifiable. Any health practitioner who is contemplating refusing to follow any instruction should, if time permits, seek advice before doing so.

The case is not the same when one does not feel competent, a matter that was discussed in chapter 8. There the consideration was the practitioner's responsibility to the consumer which involves providing reasonable care. Here, the issue is the practitioner's responsibility to the employer, and the requirement that orders be obeyed. The two may not lead to the same answer. A practitioner may be lawfully obliged to care for someone in intensive care, according to the employment agreement, but feel that they cannot reasonably do so, lacking competence. There is a conflict of duties here, and no clear legal answer, because there is no priority of legal duties. Whatever choice is made, there is a potential legal sanction — the threat of an action in negligence, or the possibility of dismissal. The best solution under the circumstances is to consider the ethical ramifications of the issue, and decide for oneself the least culpable course.[19]

The responsibility does not rest solely with the employee. If the employer knows that particular practitioners may not be competent in certain areas of care, the employer has a

---

18   There is no general right of practitioners to refuse to provide health services. A refusal may breach the Human Rights Act 1993 and the Code of Health and Disability Services Code of Consumers' Rights. For information and advice on caring for consumers with pandemic infections, see the WHO website www.who.int for information on hospital infection control guidelines, the Ministry of Health Website www.moh.govt.nz and the New Zealand Nurses Organisation website www.nzno.org.nz for guidance on obligations in a pandemic or disaster.

19   See chapter 20 for two models to help with ethical decision making in clinical practice;

duty to consider employing alternative practitioners in order to fulfil its duty of reasonable care to the consumer. If it does not then vicarious liability becomes an issue.[20]

13.4.5 Carry out those orders with reasonable care

An employer can expect staff to carry out their duties with reasonable care. This is the same as, but separate from, the duty of reasonable care demanded by the law of torts and the Code of Health and Disability Services Consumers Rights. Here the duty is to the employer; in the law of torts and under the Code the duty is to the consumer. Even if there is no harm to a consumer action can be taken against an employee for not carrying out duties with reasonable care. The employer can discipline the employee for breach of a term of the employment agreement.

Where a consumer has been harmed by an employee's failure to carry out their duties with reasonable care the employer found vicariously liable may, in some circumstances, in turn seek indemnity from the negligent employee.[21] Generally, an employer is insured, and such insurance policies sometimes provide that action will not be taken against a negligent employee. Cases of such claims by employers against employees are extremely rare in New Zealand.

13.4.6 Be faithful to the employer's interests

The law has always recognised an obligation on the employee to act always in the interests of their employer. However, for many health practitioners they have other higher duties to consumers, or the ethics of their profession, that will always prevail in the event of a conflict.[22] It is difficult to comprehensively specify what being "faithful to the employer's interests" means, as situations vary. However, generally it would involve the duty of the employee to act in good faith towards the employer, and not do anything inconsistent with the agreement's terms, injurious to the employer, or inconsistent with the proper performance of the employee's duties under the agreement. Obvious examples of conduct that fall into this category are dishonesty and insubordination. It could also arise in the following circumstances.

(1) *Denigrating the standard of health services provided by the employer*

This could be done by actions or words that undermine consumers' or prospective consumers' confidence in the standard of health services offered by the employer. This may be regarded as a type of insubordination. It may involve only one consumer, or be a public communication or action, or participation in debate. This duty, like the duty to carry out lawful orders, is not based on one's personal views as to the harm that may be involved in carrying it out.

The position of the health practitioner, who is genuinely concerned about seriously inadequate standards of health service delivery, has been strengthened by the Protected

---

20 See, for example, *Opinion 05HDC11908* (Health and Disability Commissioner, 22/3/07) district health board criticised for failure to address shortages of medical and nursing staff. Junior medical staff were asked to make decisions beyond their level of competence and an enrolled nurse was inadequately supervised and required to care for a consumer with complex needs that were outside the scope of her practice.

21 *Lister v Romford Ice & Cold Storage Co Ltd* [1957] AC 555.

22 *Birthcare Auckland Ltd v McFarland* [2000] 1 ERNZ 674.

Disclosures Act 2000.[23] The Act applies to allegations of serious wrongdoing by an organisation, and that term is defined so as to include within it wrongdoing that constitutes a serious risk to public health and safety.[24] An employee is expected to take their concern through any established internal procedures.[25] However, in some circumstances, they may take their concerns directly to the head of the organisation. If the use of established channels does not or cannot satisfactorily resolve the employee's concerns, there is provision for access to outside entities, including a Cabinet Minister or Ombudsman. There is no protection for an employee who makes disclosure to the media. False allegations or disclosures (even if true) made in "bad faith," for example out of personal animosity, are not protected by the Act.[26]

The Act makes it unlawful for the employer to carry out any retaliatory action against an employee who makes a protected disclosure. It also provides for immunity from prosecution, civil liability, or professional disciplinary action.[27] However the Act will not protect an employee who does not comply with its provisions.

Plainly, recourse to the Act is reserved for very serious circumstances, and the employee must be very careful to ensure that they are protected before embarking on disclosure. Guidance for any person considering disclosure under the Act can be obtained from the office of the Ombudsman. That would be an advisable first step in every case.

Although public criticism of the employer will not amount to insubordination in every case[28] any such action should be considered very carefully, especially when there is a direct instruction from the employer that no public comment is to be made. It is important to remember that the Protected Disclosures Act 2000 offers no protection for disclosures to media organisations.

(2)   *Misuse of any information received by a health practitioner while furthering the employer's interest*

There are two sorts of knowledge one acquires in a job — general knowledge, necessarily acquired while carrying out one's duties, and knowledge gained through special access to documents, plans, procedures, and scientific information that is specific to the employer. It can be hard to distinguish between the two. Generally, the first is knowledge one can take and use elsewhere, while the second is specific, confidential information and trade secrets that would not normally be lawfully usable elsewhere. The law protects the latter because it recognises that it is valuable property belonging to the person who created it. It

---

23   This legislation followed publicity surrounding the case of Neil Pugmire, a nurse employed by Good Health Wanganui. Mr Pugmire wrote to the Minister of Health allegedly documenting his concerns about the Mental Health (Compulsory Assessment and Treatment) Act 1992. Before sending his letter he showed it to other hospital staff including his unit manager. There was publicity about the conviction for a serious offence of a former patient of Lake Alice Hospital following that patient's release into the community. When the opposition spokesperson for Justice called for a public inquiry into these events Mr Pugmire sent him a copy of his letter. The letter was released to the news media. As a result Good Health Wanganui commenced disciplinary action against Mr Pugmire.

24   Protected Disclosures Act 2000, section 2.

25   Public Sector organisations are required by section 11 of the Protected Disclosures Act 2000 to establish internal procedures for this purpose (see section 11).

26   Protected Disclosures Act 2000, section 20.

27   Protected Disclosures Act 2000, sections 17-18.

28   *Hobbs v North Shore CC* [1992] 1 ERNZ 32; *Beesley v NZ Clerical Workers Union* [1991] 2 ERNZ 616.

is often referred to as intellectual property. Contractual terms may specify information that is not to be used or disclosed.

Lawful disclosure may also be made where an employee is in charge of their employer's documents or files, and is subpoenaed to produce them in Court.

13.4.7 Account for the employer's property

This includes the duty to reasonably protect an employer's property from harm; to account for all money and goods received in the course of employment; and to indemnify the employer for any financial loss caused. An employee cannot use an employer's equipment or stock of goods for personal gain outside working hours, or for purposes that are not related to employment, such as an employee helping herself/himself to equipment or drugs for the purpose of treating their own or their family's minor injuries and illnesses. As well as being forms of theft, such actions are breaches of an employee's employment agreement.[29] Inventions made in the course of employment belong to the employer, unless otherwise stated in the employment agreement.

13.4.8 Disclosure of information to the employer

There is an obligation at common law to inform the employer of anything essential for the employer's business. Thus, incompetence or wrongdoing on the part of other staff should be disclosed, according to law, if it is in the employer's interest to know of this.[30] Also included in this principle, is the requirement to answer questions, except where to do this would incriminate oneself unless such protection has been removed by statute. Where it has, an employee might be expected to answer questions, even where these may render her/him liable for criminal prosecution. However, such a situation is rare. Where a health practitioner is asked to disclose information, and is unsure of their obligation to do so, the practitioner should seek independent legal advice.

13.4.9 Implied undertakings of employer

A number of the terms implied into employment agreements place obligations on employers. These may arise from statute or common law and include obligations relating to:

- Payment of wages;
- Provision of work;
- Provision of a safe system of work;
- Fair and reasonable treatment.

---

29   In addition, such actions may also have professional disciplinary consequences. See, for example *PCC v Wallace* (HPDT, 221/NUR08/110P, 13/10/08). Mr Wallace, a nurse, was summarily dismissed from his employment and also found guilty of professional misconduct for taking a number of grocery items for his employer.

30   Section 34 of the Health Practitioners Competence Assurance Act 2003 imposes obligations on practitioners to report incompetence in certain circumstances.

13.4.10   Payment of wages

This is straightforward. The employer's obligation to pay wages is controlled by a number of statutory provisions.[31] An employer may not make deductions from an employee's wages expect with the employee's explicit agreement.

13.4.11   Provision of work

In New Zealand, it has been recognised that an employee has a right to more than wages. They have a contractual right to work, and, until the contract is terminated or validly suspended, the employer is bound to provide it.[32]

13.4.12   Provision of a safe system of work

While there is a common law duty on the employer to provide a safe system and place of work, this obligation is substantially affected by legislation, in the form of the Health and Safety in Employment Act 1992. A breach of that legislation by the employer will also amount to a breach of the employment agreement. It may give rise to a personal grievance,[33] and it gives rise to a right to strike in certain circumstances.[34] The Employment Court has recognised that failure to provide an ergonomically safe environment to an employee, who developed occupational overuse syndrome, was a breach of the employment agreement. The Court awarded punitive damages against the employer for persistently failing to act on the employee's concerns about her workstation.[35]

The likelihood of punitive damages, which are awarded solely to punish the wrongdoer, being awarded for a breach of an employment agreement is much reduced since the Privy Council decision in *A v Bottrill*[36] because of the high degree of negligence before such awards will be appropriate. Remedial orders will still be available under the Employment Relations Act 2000, where the employer's failure has caused the loss of a position or thwarted a career.[37]

Many health practitioners, particularly those involved in the provision of accident and emergency services, are required to witness the aftermath of serious injury and death. Employers may not assume that they will take it in their stride. Assistance should be readily available, and for their part employees should seek it when it is required. When an employee notifies their employer that they are suffering from work-related stress the employer has an obligation to take all practical steps to alleviate the stress. From 1 October 2008, compensation for work-related mental injury is available under the Injury Prevention, Rehabilitation, and Compensation Act 2001 in certain circumstances.[38]

The primary means of addressing a failure to keep employees safe is through the provisions of the Health and Safety in Employment Act 1992.[39] Increasingly, the Department of

---

31   As well as the Employment Relations Act 2000, there is the Minimum Wage Act 1983 (13.9.1), the Equal Pay Act 1972 and the Wages Protection Act 1983 (13.9.2).

32   *Hill v NZ Rail Ltd* [1994] 1 ERNZ 113.

33   See 13.8.2(5).

34   See 13.7.1.

35   *Morritt v Jespersen* [1998] 3 ERNZ 1.

36   *A v Bottrill* [2003] 2 NZLR 721; [2003] 1 AC 449.

37   *A-G v Gilbert* [2002] 2 NZLR 342; [2002] 1 ERNZ 31.

38   Section 21B of the Injury Prevention, Rehabilitation, and Compensation Act 2001.

Labour is initiating prosecutions against employers who fail to comply with its provisions and the Courts are imposing significant fines on convicted employers.[40]

13.4.13 Fair and reasonable treatment

Employers and employees both have obligations to treat each other fairly and reasonably, but the employer's obligation is the most often tested. The common law duty of fair and reasonable treatment has become subsumed within the more general statutory obligation for the parties to act in good faith towards each other. It recognises that the employment relationship is one involving a special relationship of trust and confidence, and just as the employee must refrain from acts that destroy that trust and confidence, for example by engaging in dishonesty, the employer must also not act in a manner that is likely to destroy it.[41] It most commonly arises in the obligation of employers to treat employees fairly when engaging in a disciplinary process but extends to an obligation to communicate with employees about all matters likely to affect them in their employment, including restructuring and redundancy.

13.5 The Employment Relations Act 2000

There are two types of employment agreement recognised in New Zealand. The Employment Relations Act 2000 controls both. An *individual employment agreement* is one entered into between one employer and one employee. A *collective employment agreement* is entered into between one or more employers and two or more employees. Under the Employment Relations Act 2000, collective agreements can be negotiated only through a registered trade union.

One of the objects of the Employment Relations Act 2000 is the promotion of collective employment agreements, but while it encourages this form of agreement, it does not compel it.

Before offering employment to the chosen applicant, the employer must consider whether there is already a collective agreement in place that covers the kind of work the applicant is to do. If there is such a collective employment agreement, the employer must give the prospective employee notice of that document and the details of how to contact the union that is party to it, unless the prospective employee is already a member of a trade union.

For the first 30 days of employment, the terms of that employee's employment agreement will incorporate the terms of the existing collective document, and they will override any inconsistent terms agreed on individually by the employer and employee. No other term agreed to by the employer and employee will be of any effect if it is inconsistent with the terms taken from the collective agreement. Even if the employee decides not to join the collective agreement, the terms borrowed from the collective document will remain until the employer and employee mutually agree to change them.

If there is no collective agreement, the employer can offer an individual employment agreement. A copy of that document must be given to the prospective employee, and they

---

39   See chapter 14.

40   See for example *Dept of Labour v Nalder and Biddle (Nelson) Ltd* 13/4/05, Judge McKegg, DC Nelson CRN04042500; *Talleys Frozen Foods Ltd v Department of Labour* (2008) 6 NZELR 267.

41   *Auckland Shop Employees Union v Woolworths (NZ) Ltd* [1985] 2 NZLR 372; (1985) ERNZ Sel Cas 136 (CA).

must be advised that they are entitled to seek independent advice and be given a reasonable time to do so.

13.5.1 Individual employment agreements

The employer and employee may deal directly for the purpose of entering an individual employment agreement, just as they could under the previous legislation. However, the Employment Relations Act 2000 provides special protection for certain persons who are at a disadvantage in that process.

If the employer was aware of the employee's disadvantage, the agreement may be challenged as the product of an unfair bargaining process. That will also apply if the employee is not given the required information about their right to seek advice.[42]

Employment agreements are normally for an indefinite period. The employee may terminate them by resignation. The employer may terminate them by dismissal, but only if the employer can prove that the dismissal is justified.

Probationary periods have always been popular with employers, and they are permitted under the Employment Relations Act 2000 provided that the provisions of section 67 of the Act are followed. The probationary period must be specified in writing in the agreement. The employer is under no less an obligation to treat the employee fairly when contemplating ending employment during or after the probationary period, than when contemplating a dismissal. That will include giving reasonable warning that the probationary period is not going well enough, and a fair opportunity for the employee to do something about it.

However for employers who employ fewer than 20 people this provision has been substantially modified from 1 March 2009 by an amendment to the Act.[43] This allows the employer to enter into an agreement with a new employee which contains provision for a trial of up to 90 days from the date of employment. During the trial the employer may dismiss the employee and the employee cannot bring a personal grievance based on the dismissal. In all other respects however the employee and the employer must deal with each other as if there was no provision for a trial.

An employer may ask a potential employee to perform a small amount of work without payment solely for the purpose of determining whether they will be suitable, but this should be only for a brief period. For example, if there is likely to be heavy lifting involved, the employer may want to see if the employee has sufficient strength. The prospective employee will not become an employee if the services they provide are solely for this purpose, but the Employment Relations Authority will be astute to prevent unscrupulous employers using this as an opportunity to obtain free services. The employer must make it clear to the employee at the outset that it is a pre-employment assessment and that they will not be paid.

13.5.2 Collective employment agreements

Collective employment agreements are the creation of the Employment Relations Act 2000. Were it not for the Act, the law would not recognise them. They cannot come into

---

42 Employment Relations Act 2000, sections 68 and 69.
43 Employment Relations Act 2000, , sections 67A and 67B.

existence other than by the process of collective bargaining that is set out in the Act. They can be entered into only between one or more employers and one or more registered unions.

What they are is less complicated than how they come about. A collective employment agreement is in many respects similar to an individual agreement, but it binds at least one employer, one union and at least two employees to the same terms and conditions. In the interests of avoiding complication, this chapter will not consider separately the collective agreements that involve more than one employer or more than one union, which may be referred to as multiple agreements or multiple employer collective agreements (MECA's). There are some points of difference that will be identified, but not explained in detail.

Like an individual agreement, a collective agreement must be in writing. It must also be signed by each employer and each union that is party to it. The agreement can contain anything that the parties can agree on, provided it is not unlawful or contrary to any provisions of the Employment Relations Act 2000. Some features that must be present are:

- A coverage clause — a clause setting out what work the agreement covers either by reference to the work, type of work or employees or types of employees;
- A plain language explanation of the services available to resolve employment relationship problems, and informing the employee of the 90-day limit for notifying a personal grievance;
- A clause stating how the agreement may be varied; and
- The expiry date of the agreement.

The latter point is one of the most important features of the collective agreement. Unlike an individual employment agreement it cannot run on indefinitely. It can last for up to 3 years, with a possible extension of 12 months if, before the expiry date, the union party has given notice to bargain for another collective agreement in its place.

Since registered unions alone can bargain for and enter into collective agreements, it follows that employees must be members of a union to be bound by them. The union signs the agreement on behalf of its members, but it must have a process by which entry into the agreement is ratified by the employees to be bound by it. Unions are obliged to follow a democratic process. If an employee resigns from the union, which they have the right to do, they remain bound by identical terms.

13.5.3   Registered unions

Unions have been a constant feature of industrial relations in New Zealand for well over 100 years. Under the previous legislation, their role was diminished because of the emphasis on direct bargaining between employers and employees. They are back in the ascendancy under the Employment Relations Act 2000, with an integral and exclusive role in the bargaining process.

Unions are incorporated societies, which mean that they must have at least 15 members. To participate in collective bargaining, they must be registered with the Registrar of Unions. Among other things, in order to register, a union must satisfy the registrar that the union has a set of rules that are reasonable, democratic, and not unfairly discriminatory or prejudicial; that its object is the advancement of its members' collective employment interests; and that it is at arm's length from any employer.[44] This last requirement is to prevent the development of "tame" unions set up by, or for the benefit of an employer. The union must be in a real sense independent of the employer.[45]

Once a union has a certificate of registration under the Act, it is entitled to recognition as the representative of its members in all matters concerning their collective employment interests. It does not have to provide any further proof of its authority.

In addition to the ability to initiate and pursue bargaining for its members, unions have significant ancillary rights.

(1) *Access to the workplace*

A union representative may gain access to a workplace for many purposes, including meeting with members, monitoring compliance with a collective agreement, recruiting new members, and distributing information about the union. A union representative can gain access only if the union either has members on site, or reasonably believes that there are employees who might come within its membership rules. Access must be undertaken at a reasonable time and in a reasonable way. An employer may set reasonable conditions for entry if they are necessary for the purpose of ensuring health and safety, or security of the premises.

Many health sector workplaces will need to have such conditions. Health and safety is not a reason to deny access, but the employer is entitled to require the union representative to follow the guidelines that apply for employees and other persons in the workplace.

There will be occasions where access would be considered inappropriate at any time. Any parts of a hospital where a sterile environment is being maintained, where contagious diseases are being treated, or where the safety and proper treatment of consumers requires that there be no disturbance (such as an intensive care unit) ought to justify exclusion. The employer will nonetheless be expected to make appropriate alternative arrangements so that meaningful access can occur between the union and its members.

Union representatives exercising the right of access must identify herself/himself and the purpose of their visit to the employer. If they cannot find a representative of the employer, they must post a notice to that effect. A workplace discussion between employees and a union representative is not a "union meeting" and an employee engaged in such a workplace discussion must be paid for that time, provided the time taken is reasonable.[46]

The Employment Court has held that unreasonably delaying the right of access will be a breach of the good faith requirement.[47]

(2) *Organising union meetings*

In addition to workplace visits, the union has the right to organise two paid meetings per year for its members in any given workplace. There is no limit on the time a meeting may take, but the employer has to pay only for the first 2 hours. Payment is at the employee's ordinary rate of pay. The union must come to an arrangement with the employee to ensure

---

44   Section 14 of the Employment Relations Act 2000.

45   *Meat & Related Trades Workers Union of Aotearoa Inc v Te Kuiti Beef Workers Union Inc* (2002) 6 NZELC 96,473.

46   *Terry Young Ltd v NZAEPMU Inc* [2007] 1 ERNZ 533.

47   *National Distribution Union Inc v Carter Holt Harvey Ltd* [2001] ERNZ 822.

that sufficient employees remain at work to enable the employer's business to continue, including making its own members available for that purpose.

(3)   *Union education leave*

The Employment Relations Act 2000 reintroduced the concept of leave allocated to employees for union-related education. This had disappeared under the Employment Contracts Act 1991. Under Part 7 of the Act a union is entitled to allocate education leave to employees who are members of the union. The Act provides a table for calculating the total number of education leave days that the union will be entitled to allocate depending on the number of union members employed in a workplace. The union is obliged to calculate the number of days and notify the employer of the number of days allocated. Once an employee is selected for this leave by the union and, on proper notice being given, they are entitled to be paid for the leave. The maximum amount of education leave allocated to an individual employee each year cannot exceed 5 days, and unused leave cannot be carried forward without the employer's permission. An employer may decline a request for education leave if it is satisfied on reasonable grounds that it would unreasonably disrupt the employer's business for leave to be taken on the dates applied for.

13.5.4   Union membership

When the Employment Contracts Act came into force in 1991, for the first time in many years, membership of a union became a matter of choice. Before that, an employment agreement could contain a clause that gave a preference to members of a particular union, and unions usually insisted on its inclusion. If a job was within a union's coverage clause, a person could not do it unless they belonged to the union, and they were required to join the union, unless they objected on valid grounds of conscience.

Under the Employment Relations Act 2000, although one of the objects of the Act is to promote collective bargaining, union membership remains voluntary and preference clauses are illegal. Membership of a union is essential in order to participate in a collective agreement, and the Act ensures that employees are made aware of their right to join one, but there is no compulsion or coercion. Most unions will require their members to make a weekly or fortnightly payment of their union subscription, and to authorise the employer to deduct that amount from their wages and pay it to the union. An employer must respect that arrangement.

13.5.5   Initiating collective bargaining

Bargaining for a collective agreement may be initiated either where no collective agreement has previously existed, or where an existing collective agreement is due to expire. Only a union can initiate bargaining where no collective agreement exists. Either an employer or a union may initiate bargaining for a replacement collective agreement.[48] If no collective agreement exists, the union can begin bargaining at any time. If there is an existing collective agreement, the union cannot initiate bargaining more than 60 days before the agreement expires. An employer who initiates bargaining cannot do so until 40 days before the existing agreement expires. There are different time periods for multiple employment agreements.[49]

---

48   Employment Relations Act 2000, section 40.

THE CONTRACT OF EMPLOYMENT

The union or employer commences the process by delivering a notice to the other party, specifying the parties with which it wishes to enter into a collective agreement, and the work that it wants to cover. The notice does not have to contain any other information. If an employer gets such notice, it has 10 days in which to bring the notice to the attention of all employees, whether union members or not, who perform work that would be covered. Bargaining is deemed to have started on the day the notice is sent.[50] This is important, because strikes and lockouts are prohibited for 40 days after bargaining begins.

13.5.6 Bargaining in good faith

The Act does not tell unions or employers how to bargain but requires them to do so in good faith. Obviously, they must include in the process discussion of the required elements of a collective agreement, but beyond that they may seek to determine any terms and conditions that they wish for the employees covered. Pay and hours of work are likely to be frequent topics. However, the Act contains some specific direction about what good faith means in this context. Section 32 of the Act is not a code, but it provides the framework:

"**32 Good faith in bargaining for collective agreement**

"(1) The duty of good faith in section 4 requires a union and an employer bargaining for a collective agreement to do, at least, the following things:

"(a) the union and the employer must use their best endeavours to enter into an arrangement, as soon as possible after the initiation of bargaining, that sets out a process for conducting the bargaining in an effective and efficient manner; and

"(b) the union and the employer must meet each other, from time to time, for the purposes of the bargaining; and

"(c) the union and employer must consider and respond to proposals made by each other; and

"(ca) even though the union and the employer have come to a standstill or reached a deadlock about a matter, they must continue to bargain (including doing the things specified in paragraphs (b) and (c)) about any other matters on which they have not reached agreement; and

"(d) the union and the employer—

"(i) must recognise the role and authority of any person chosen by each to be its representative or advocate; and

"(ii) must not (whether directly or indirectly) bargain about matters relating to terms and conditions of

---

49   Employment Relations Act 2000, section 41.

50   Employment Relations Act 2000, section 44. Note that the later of the dates of notice apply if more than one notice is required under section 42 of the Act.

> employment with persons whom the representative or advocate are acting for, unless the union and employer agree otherwise; and
>
> "(iii) must not undermine or do anything that is likely to undermine the bargaining or the authority of the other in the bargaining; and
>
> "(e) the union and employer must provide to each other, on request and in accordance with section 34, information that is reasonably necessary to support or substantiate claims or responses to claims made for the purposes of the bargaining …"

The term "best endeavours" means more than to do everything that one can reasonably do to achieve the outcome and sets a high standard for entering into a bargaining process arrangement.[51] The Act makes it clear that an obligation to bargain in good faith does not create an obligation to agree, nor does it mean that parties must meet indefinitely until they have agreed; however if parties are deadlocked on one matter they must still continue to bargain on those matters over which they are not deadlocked. Parties are required to conclude a collective agreement unless there is a genuine reason based on reasonable grounds not to do so.

13.6 Codes of good faith

The Employment Relations Act 2000 allows for the approval by the Minister of codes of good faith. Once approved, a code provides guidance as to the performance of the good faith obligations set out in section 4 of the Act. The situations in which these obligations arise include, but are not limited to, collective bargaining. The Code of Good Faith for Bargaining for Collective Agreement[52] was developed by agreement between the Employers Association, the Council of Trade Unions, the State Services Commission, and the Government. It provides guidance for employers and unions on the concept of "good faith" in bargaining for a collective agreement or variation to a collective agreement. The code largely follows, but expands on the principles set out in section 32 of the Act. A separate Code of Good Faith (covering collective bargaining and other issues) has also been developed for the public health sector, and is set out in Schedule 1B of the Employment Relations Act 2000.[53] The Authority or the Court may have regard to the relevant Code when determining whether parties have dealt with each other in good faith during collective bargaining.

In *Christchurch City Council v Southern Local Government Officers Union Inc*[54] the Court of Appeal discussed the requirements of section 32, and its relationship with the more general good faith provisions in section 4 in the context of recognition of bargaining agents and undermining the bargaining process.

---

51   *Assn of University Staff Inc v Vice-Chancellor of the University of Auckland* [2005] 1 ERNZ 224 (EC).
52   The *Code of Good Faith in Collective Bargaining* current at the time of writing was approved by the Minister of Labour on 9 August 2005. It can be accessed at www.ers.dol.govt.nz/goodfaith/code.html.
53   Section 100D Employment Relations Act 2000.
54   *Christchurch City Council v Southern Local Government Officers Union Inc* [2007] 1 ERNZ 37; [2007] 2 NZLR 614 (CA).

Although the concept of good faith bargaining is relatively new in New Zealand it has been a feature of industrial relations in other jurisdictions, notably the US and Canada. The overseas jurisdictions show, for example, that a "take it or leave it" stance will not be in good faith. There is a distinction recognised between that approach (which indicates a closed mind) and mere hard or even ruthless bargaining, where the party concerned is still listening to the other point of view, but does not yield to it.

More difficult to detect, but nonetheless indicative of bad faith, is pretence of willingness to negotiate, when there is in fact no intention to listen. Persistently being late for meetings, cancelling meetings at the last minute without explanation, sending bargaining personnel without the necessary authority to bargain, and imposing unreasonable preconditions to meeting are all likely to be seen as indications of bad faith.

One of the most important influences on the process is the requirement for parties to share information relevant to the negotiations, particularly about wage increases. Employers cannot retreat behind the balance sheet saying "we can't afford it," without being required to disclose information by which that statement might be tested.

If a union or employer requests information, the party to whom the request is made may require it to be referred to an independent reviewer, who must be agreed on by both parties. The reviewer can determine whether a claim to confidentiality is warranted. If it is, the reviewer can also decide how the information that the other party is entitled to see can be made available without unduly compromising the confidentiality.[55] The Code of Good Faith recommends agreeing on the process for appointing a reviewer when the bargaining protocols are being settled at the start of the process.

13.7   Strikes and lockouts

Despite the emphasis on negotiation, the Employment Relations Act 2000 preserves the two most potent tools for coercion between employer and employee.

13.7.1   Strikes

A strike is a concerted action by more than one employee to temporarily withdraw from the proper performance of their obligations under their employment agreement. It may involve refusing to carry out any duties, but it need not do. Employees may simply refuse to do some of their normal work or "work to rule" (a partial strike). A strike in New Zealand is lawful only if it complies with the conditions set out in the Employment Relations Act 2000.[56]

To be lawful, a strike must not be "unlawful" under section 86 of the Act and must relate to the bargaining of a collective employment agreement, or be reasonably grounded on a belief that it is justified in the interests of health or safety. Additional requirements apply to strikes in "essential services."[57]

With the availability of the Occupational Safety and Health Service ("OSH") and the broad powers it has to address health and safety issues, strikes on this ground have become

---

55   Section 34 of the Employment Relations Act 2000; as an example see *NZ Resident Doctors Assn v Auckland etc DHBs* 30/6/08, R Arthur (member), AA225/08.

56   Section 83 and 84 of the Employment Relations Act 2000.

57   See para 13.7.3.

infrequent. Those cases which have reached the courts have generally failed to establish the high level of justification required.[58]

Strikes during the bargaining process are the most common. The right to strike cannot lawfully be exercised until 40 days after bargaining has been initiated. There is nothing in the legislation to prevent a strike or lockout taking place while the parties are in mediation, as long as the required 40 days have elapsed.[59] The only employees who can lawfully strike are those who will be bound by the collective agreement being bargained for.

It is unlawful to take strike action over any matter that is the subject of a personal grievance, or a dispute between the parties.[60]

During a strike, the employer may suspend any worker who is a party to the strike, which means the employer is not required to pay the employee's wages during the strike. The suspension continues until the strike ends. The employer also has the right to suspend non-striking employees if, by reason of the strike, the employer cannot offer them work. In either case, the employer must treat the employment as continuous for the purpose of calculating holiday pay and other benefits. There is a specific requirement for the employer to tell an employee suspended because of a strike under which section of the Act the suspension is made. Non-striking employees have a right to challenge the suspension and seek a compliance order and other remedies, including arrears of wages, in the Authority. Employees who are not suspended during a strike are entitled to continue to be paid. It is unlawful to dismiss an employee for participating in a lawful strike.

While the employer may suspend employees, it may not replace them with temporary staff. Existing staff who do not wish to participate in the strike may be asked to perform the services of the strikers but cannot be compelled to do so.

An employer may not employ new staff to do the work of striking employees except in the case of work that must be done for health and safety reasons. This is a distinct possibility in the case of a strike involving health practitioners, where consumer safety is a concern. The notion of necessity suggests that other avenues must also be considered. For example, a hospital will be expected to use other means of addressing the risk, such as cancelling or postponing non-urgent treatment. The additional staff hired may perform only those tasks that are necessary to abate the risk to health and safety.

If a strike is unlawful then none of these restrictions apply.

13.7.2 Lockouts

A lockout is the act of an employer closing its place of business; discontinuing the employment of some or all of the employees; breaching some or all of the employment agreements the employer is party to; or failing or refusing to engage employees for work for which the employer normally employs employees. Unlike a strike, a lockout may affect a single employee. The lockout must be for the purpose of compelling employees to accept terms of employment, or comply with the employer's demands. As with strikes, lockouts are lawful only if they are not unlawful under the Act and they relate to negotiating a collective agreement or the employer believes on reasonable grounds that the lockout is

---

58   See for example *Tranz Rail Ltd v Rosson* 30/9/03, Shaw J, WC30/03.
59   *Ports of Auckland Ltd v NZ Waterfront Workers Union* [2001] 1 ERNZ 564.
60   Section 86 of the Employment Relations Act 2000.

justified for reasons of health or safety. A lockout is subject to similar conditions as to timing and notice. As with strikes, employers may request other employees to perform the work of locked out employees but cannot compel them to perform that work.

13.7.3   Essential services

Of particular note for those working in health services is the requirement for a strike or a lockout to be preceded by formal notice where it involves an "essential service." The essential services, which are listed in the First Schedule to the Employment Relations Act 2000, include ambulance services, hospitals, the manufacture or supply of surgical and dialysis solutions, the manufacture or supply of prescription medicines, welfare institutions, and prisons.

In the essential services which affect health practitioners, at least 14 and no more than 28 days' notice of an intention to strike or lockout must be given in writing to the employer or employees affected if the proposed action will affect the public interest. The notice must specify where and when the proposed strike or lockout will occur. It must also specify the kind of action that will be taken, including whether it will be continuous.

Not every strike or lockout in essential services will require notice but since a strike or lockout involving essential health services will usually affect the public interest, notice is best regarded as a necessary prerequisite.

It is important that the notices comply with the Act, as a defective notice can lead to the notice, and therefore the lockout or strike, being declared invalid.

Notice of an intended strike or lockout in an essential service must also be given to the Chief Executive of the Department of Labour, who is then obliged to make mediation services available to the parties for the purpose of assisting them to avoid the intended strike or lockout.

13.7.4   Effect of lawful strikes and lockouts

If a strike is lawful, an employer cannot take civil action against the employees participating in it for breach of contract, or to recover damages for harm caused to the business. Similarly, employees cannot bring proceedings against an employer for breach of contract, or to recover arrears of wages if they have been lawfully locked out.

Strike action is often accompanied by picketing, which itself can amount to strike action because it involves inducing other employees to breach their employment agreements. Pickets can be restrained by injunctions, but before doing so, the Court will take into account the rights of peaceful assembly set out in the New Zealand Bill of Rights Act 1990.

The Employment Court alone may hear and determine proceedings seeking injunctions to prevent a strike or lockout that is occurring or is threatened. However, if the Court finds the strike or lockout is lawful it must dismiss the proceedings, and the proceedings cannot then be pursued in the District Courts or High Court.

There is no protection from prosecution for those who engage in unlawful activities on a picket line.

13.8   Problems in the employment relationship

The Employment Relations Act 2000 provides a comprehensive regime for resolving disputes and grievances that arise in the course of an employment relationship. The Act sets up specialist institutions—the Mediation Service, the Employment Relations Authority, and the Employment Court which have exclusive jurisdiction to deal with issues arising from employment relationships.[61]

13.8.1   Institutions

(1)   *Mediation Service*

Under the Employment Contracts Act 1991, nominated Employment Tribunal members provided mediation services. Although they were considerably less formal than adjudication hearings, these mediations followed a very structured format.

Under the Employment Relations Act 2000 mediation services are now provided separately from the adjudication function under the Act, which is carried out by the Employment Relations Authority. Mediation services are provided by the Department of Labour through Workplace Services. Mediators are appointed by the Chief Executive of the Department and are specifically trained and highly skilled in resolving workplace disputes. They must abide by the Code of Ethics for Mediators Employed by the Department of Labour.[62]

Access to mediation services is informal. No form of documents is required, and it is not necessary to have started a proceeding in the Employment Relations Authority in order to use mediation. Every employment agreement must contain a plain English explanation of the procedure for resolving employment problems. This includes advice on how to access mediation if a problem can't be resolved by discussion between the employer and the employee. The Act also allows the Department of Labour to provide dispute resolution services, including mediation, to parties who are in a work-related relationship that is not an employment relationship.[63] Mediation is voluntary and a party cannot be forced to attend.

The object of mediation is to enable the parties to an employment relationship problem, with assistance of an independent mediator,[64] to isolate disputed issues in order to develop options, consider alternatives and reach agreements that will accommodate their needs and allow them to move on. This process may occur by telephone, by email, in the workplace, or in a mediation room.[65]

One of the key benefits of mediation is that the dispute is explored in private. Unless the parties consent to disclosure, information provided to a mediator for the purpose of mediation is strictly confidential. It cannot be used in any subsequent proceedings before the Employment Relations Authority or the Employment Court.[66] There is an exception where the mediation is convened for the purpose of assisting the parties in a bargaining

---

61   Subject to limited rights of appeal from the Employment Court to the Court of Appeal and Supreme Court.

62   Copies of the Code are available from the Department and can be accessed at www.ers.dol.govt.nz/problem/code-of-ethics.html;

63   Employment Relations Act 2000, section 144A. For example, a contractor and principal or between partners in a partnership.

64   Employment Relations Act 2000, section 153.

65   Employment Relations Act 2000, section 145.

process. However, the mere fact that information is used in the mediation, does not make it inadmissible if it was otherwise available to the parties outside the mediation process.

Usually the parties will agree their own terms of settlement (or not) but if all parties agree in writing the mediator will make a binding decision on the outcome. Settlements agreed in mediation cannot be appealed.

(2)   Employment Relations Authority

Where the parties are unable to resolve an employment relationship problem, either directly or through mediation, they may file proceedings in the Employment Relations Authority.

The Authority has a wide jurisdiction, including the most common types of employment relationship problems — personal grievances, disputes, and claims for arrears of wages and, where the parties are having serious difficulties, facilitating collective bargaining. It can also investigate allegations of unfair bargaining and can set the redundancy payments to be made to vulnerable workers under section 69O of the Act.

The Authority's powers of investigation are wide ranging. It may require persons to give evidence before it, obtain relevant documents, and adopt such procedure as it thinks best suited to resolving the problem. It must have regard to the law, but it can make decisions consistent with equity and good conscience. It can accept any evidence or information, whether or not that information would be admissible in a court of law. However, it is obliged to observe the principles of natural justice, and act in a manner that is reasonable having regard to its investigative role.

The Authority is not a Court and does not operate after the fashion of a Court. Its processes are inquisitorial, rather than adversarial. That means that the Authority takes the responsibility not only for deciding on the outcome of the case, but investigating it as well, rather than dealing with the problem simply on the basis of the evidence the parties choose to put before it. The Authority has its own set of rules and regulations.[67] A party (the applicant) makes an application to the Authority to determine a relationship problem by filing and serving a "Statement of Problem" in the form prescribed by the regulations and paying a fee.[68] The other party (the respondent) has 14 days from the date the Statement of Problem is served on them to file a statement of reply.

The Act sets out the Authority's powers to deal with the applications made to it. If they have not already done so, the Authority will direct that the parties attempt mediation, unless it is satisfied that no useful purpose would be served by mediation or urgency requires that mediation be dispensed with.

In order to give effect to its decision, the Authority can make a wide range of orders, including reinstatement of a dismissed employee, the payment of compensation, compliance, and penalties. The Authority also has power to award costs.

---

66   Employment Relations Act 2000, section 148; and see *Just Hotel Ltd v Jesudhass* [2007] NZCA 582; [2007] ERNZ 817; [2008] 2 NZLR 210 (CA) and *Te Ao v Chief Executive of the Dept of Labour* [2008] ERNZ 311.

67   Schedule 2 to the Employment Relations Act 2000 and the Employment Relations Authority Regulations 2000.

68   At the time of writing the fee for filing a statement of problem was $70. No fee is payable by the respondent.

A party who is dissatisfied with the Authority's determination may challenge all or part of the determination by asking the Employment Court to rehear the original application.

(3) *Employment Court*

The Employment Court operates in a similar way to the ordinary Courts, but it has a special jurisdiction to deal with certain problems that arise in employment relationships. Any dispute that arises out of a strike or lockout must be resolved in the Employment Court. It also has jurisdiction to determine whether a person is an employee for the purposes of a number of statutes where that issue can arise. It can make any orders that other Courts can make, and can also order compliance and impose penalties in respect of those parts of the Act over which the Court has direct jurisdiction. Its procedures are formal and the Court is governed by its own set of rules and regulations.[69]

A significant part of the Employment Court's work arises from cases that begin in the Employment Relations Authority. The Authority can refer issues of law to the Court for determination and parties have a right to challenge determinations of the Authority and have the original problem reheard by the Court.

(4) *Other Courts*

On issues of law only, there is a right of appeal from the Employment Court to the Court of Appeal provided the Court of Appeal grants leave for an appeal. It will do so only where the intending appellant can establish that the appeal will give rise to a matter of general or public importance.[70] There is a further right of appeal from decisions of the Court of Appeal to the Supreme Court, again with leave. For leave to appeal to the Supreme Court to be granted, the intending appellant must establish that the appeal will give rise to a matter of general or public importance or a matter of general commercial significance.[71] In exceptional circumstances parties can appeal directly to the Supreme Court if the Supreme Court grants leave to do so.[72]

13.8.2 Mechanisms for resolving problems

(1) *Compliance orders*

The parties can be kept to their duties and obligations under the employment agreement and the Act by means of a compliance order from the Employment Relations Authority or the Employment Court that they comply.

The Employment Court's jurisdiction is confined to enforcing compliance with its own orders and with Part 8 of the Employment Relations Act, which deals with strikes and lockouts. The Authority deals with almost everything else.[73]

---

69   Schedule 3 to the Employment Relations Act 2000 and Employment Court Regulations 2000.

70   Employment Relations Act 2000, section 214.

71   Section 13 of the Supreme Court Act 2003 and see *Buchanan v Chief Executive of the Dept of Inland Revenue* [2006] NZSC 37; [2006] ERNZ 512; (2006) 18 PRNZ 79 (SC).

72   Employment Relations Act 2000, section 214A. The right is subject to section 14 of the Supreme Court Act 2003.

73   The District Court has jurisdiction to deal with offences under the Health and Safety in Employment Act 1992 and enforcement of compliance orders.

Any party affected by the alleged non-compliance, including unions and employer organisations, may apply for a compliance order. The order is only available if it is established that non-compliance has occurred.

Once a compliance order is made, it must be followed. A persistent failure to do so can result in fines and even imprisonment.[74]

(2)   Disputes

In some cases, there may be confusion about what the obligations under the agreement are, or how they should be applied. Such a dispute is classified as an employment relationship problem.

If the parties cannot resolve the dispute themselves, it can be referred to the Mediation Service or the Employment Relations Authority for resolution. Unless the parties have already engaged in mediation or a compelling reason exists to dispense with it the Authority is likely to refer any dispute to mediation initially.

The disputes procedure enables a doubtful provision in an agreement to be tested without risking the consequences of breaching it.

A health practitioner, who was concerned about the lawfulness of an instruction, could invoke the disputes procedure as a way of resolving the problem without having to face the risk of disobeying the instruction and disciplinary action.

(3)   Arrears of wages

A special procedure is available for employees to recover money due under the agreement, but which has not been paid. A claim for arrears of wages or other money due under an employment agreement may be referred to a labour inspector, or brought directly in the Employment Relations Authority. Again, the parties are encouraged, and may be directed by the Authority, to use mediation first.

The employer has an obligation under the Act to keep records of time and wages, and the employer must produce these for inspection within 14 days of a request being made to see them. Claims for arrears of wages must be brought within 6 years of the money becoming payable.

(4)   Penalties

As an additional incentive for parties to an employment agreement to comply with their agreements, the Authority or Court can fine a party who breaches the agreement or specified sections of the Act. That fine can be up to $5,000 for a natural person and up to $10,000 for a body corporate such as a company or incorporated society. An order can be made that, some or all, of the penalty is to be paid to any person.

An action for a penalty must be started within 12 months of the breach occurring.

(5)   Personal grievances

The Employment Relations Act 2000 provides for a unique procedure available only to employees, a personal grievance, where the employee has been unjustifiably dismissed or

---

74   Employment Relations Act 2000, section 140(6).

disadvantaged in their employment. A personal grievance is the only way for an employee to challenge a dismissal but a personal grievance may arise in several ways including sexual harassment, discrimination, and more general forms of unfair treatment.[75]

A personal grievance must be submitted to the employer within 90 days of the grievance arising or coming to the employee's notice. If the grievance is to be taken to the Employment Relations Authority, an application must be filed with the Authority within 3 years of it being raised with the employer.

Parties to the employment relationship are encouraged to resolve the personal grievance either between themselves or with the assistance of a mediator.

If the grievance cannot be resolved and the employee wishes to pursue it, it must be determined by the Employment Relations Authority.

The Act provides for a range of remedies for personal grievance, including orders for the employer to pay compensation for distress and anxiety caused, reimbursement of wages lost as a result of the grievance, and the loss of any benefit which would not have occurred but for the personal grievance. Where the grievance arises from unjustified dismissal, the employer can be ordered to reinstate the employee to their job.[76] Reinstatement is described as the primary remedy, so it must be considered first and allowed, unless there is good reason not to. The Authority also has the power to order interim reinstatement pending the outcome of the Authority's investigation.

Where conduct by the employee has contributed to the grievance arising, the Authority may reduce the remedies to take account of that contribution.[77]

(6) Sexual or racial harassment

The Employment Relations Act 2000 provisions relating to sexual or racial harassment are additional to the rights recognised in the Human Rights Act 1993. They apply specifically to employment relationships. The kind of conduct that can give rise to a personal grievance includes all the forms that are recognised in the Human Rights Act 1993, but a personal grievance arises where the conduct is connected with a promise of favourable treatment in the victim's employment or a threat of unfavourable treatment in the case of sexual harassment by the employer or representative, or is hurtful and detrimental to the employee's employment, job satisfaction or performance. If an employee complains to the employer about racial or sexual harassment in the workplace by someone other than the employer then a personal grievance will arise if the employer does not take all practicable steps to prevent a repeat of the behaviour. An employee who suffers racial or sexual harassment at work may choose to complain to the Human Rights Commissioner and bring proceedings in the Human Rights Review Tribunal rather than raising a personal grievance but cannot do both.[78]

---

75   Employment Relations Act 2000, section 103 sets out a comprehensive definition of "personal grievance".

76   Employment Relations Act 2000, section 123.

77   Employment Relations Act 2000, section 124.

78   Human Rights Act 1993, sections 79A and 92B.

(7)   Discrimination

The provisions relating to discrimination are additional to those set out in the Human Rights Act 1993. Discrimination against an employee in their employment occurs if there is discrimination as to the terms and conditions of employment, or the circumstances of his or her dismissal, on a ground prohibited under the Act such as the employee's membership, or non-membership, of a trade union, their race or sex. As with harassment the employee may choose to raise a personal grievance or complain to the Human Rights Commissioner.

(8)   Unjustified dismissal

An employer may dismiss an employee only where there are good grounds for doing so. When contemplating a dismissal, the employer must adopt a procedure that is fair to the employee. This is the case notwithstanding anything in the contract to the contrary. If the employer does not satisfy both requirements, the employee will have been unjustifiably dismissed, and they may bring a personal grievance. The Employment Relations Act 2000 sets out the test for justification:

> "**103A   Test of justification**
>
> > "…the question of whether a dismissal or an action was justifiable must be determined, on an objective basis, by considering whether the employer's actions, and how the employer acted, were what a fair and reasonable employer would have done in all the circumstances at the time the dismissal or action occurred."

Case
Air NZ Ltd v V 3/6/09, Colgan CJ, Travis, Shaw, & Couch JJ, AC15/09

V had failed a random drug test and was summarily dismissed for serious misconduct. V bought a personal grievance against his employer, on the grounds that his dismissal was unjustifiable. The Employment Relations Authority found that his conduct was serious misconduct but the employer's refusal to provide a rehabilitation programme rendered the dismissal unjustifiable. Consistent with previous decisions the Authority had applied section 103 to all aspects of the dismissal. This was the primary ground of challenge, that once serious misconduct is found section 103 should not be applied to the consequential actions of the employer.

The full Employment Court (unusually with a full panel of four Judges) reviewed and restated the application and interpretation of this test. The NZCTU and Business New Zealand were given leave to appear. The Court upheld the approach taken in previous decisions and held that section 103A imposes an obligation on the Authority or Court to judge the decision of the employer to dismiss against the objective standard of a fair and reasonable employer.[79]

It should be noted that section 103A applies not only to dismissals but also to actions of an employer giving rise to a disadvantage in the employee's employment.

---

79   See as examples *Air NZ Ltd v Hudson* [2006] 1 ERNZ 415; *Fuiava v Air NZ Ltd* [2006] 1 ERNZ 806; *X v Auckland DHB* [2007] 1 ERNZ 66; and *Housham v Juken NZ Ltd* [2007] 1 ERNZ 183.

(9)   *Grounds for dismissal*

Grounds for a summary dismissal, that is, dismissal without notice, will exist where the employee has been guilty of serious misconduct. Actions that constitute serious misconduct must be such that they irreparably damage the trust and confidence that is essential to the employment relationship. Examples of this conduct include assaulting a workmate, being intoxicated at work, gross insubordination, a persistent refusal to carry out lawful instructions, gross negligence, and dishonesty (including falsifying time sheets or patient records). What will amount to serious misconduct may be set out in an employment agreement and will always be affected by the type of work being performed.

For health practitioners, misconduct that endangers consumers' health may amount to serious misconduct. However, an employer needs to be wary of putting too much emphasis on the potential or actual consequences. The degree of negligence or carelessness will also be relevant, as will the employee's working conditions if they have contributed to the error.

An employee may also be dismissed for less serious misconduct, but they will be entitled to be given notice of the dismissal and will be liable to dismissal only if the misconduct persists after the employee has been given a warning.

Inadequate work performance is often put forward as a ground for dismissal. An employer is not required to put up with poor performance, but must ensure that the standard set is reasonable; that the employee is properly aware of what is required and is given a fair opportunity to perform at that level including being given training if required.

If a health practitioner is dismissed for reasons relating to competence then their employer must give the notice of the dismissal and the reasons for it to the registrar of the authority responsible for the practitioner's registration.[80]

(10)   *Redundancy*

Redundancy is unique among the grounds for terminating an employment relationship, in that it does not involve any fault on the employee's part. It is often incorrectly said that employees become redundant. In law, it is the job that becomes redundant, and the employee who performed it has their employment terminated as a result of the redundancy. For that reason, it is not permissible to terminate, on the grounds of redundancy, the employment of any person other than the one who was performing the job that has disappeared. When some health service providers have undergone internal restructuring, some personnel have been required to apply for the position they already occupy, along with others who may wish to apply. This practice, while often a result of a genuine attempt to be fair, is unlawful. If the position has not become redundant, the incumbent is entitled to retain it.

Where a number of similar positions become redundant, and it is necessary to choose who remains and who does not, unless there is some provision for that in the employment agreement, that decision is a matter for the manager of the organisation. In a hospital, for example, there would be no obligation to select first those employees who had been recruited overseas to fill staffing shortages, unless their contracts specified that they were

---

80   Health Practitioners Competence Assurance Act 2003, section 34.

temporary replacements. The employer must, however, follow a fair process in deciding who will remain in employment.

The parties to an employment agreement can agree on a formula for payment of compensation in the event of redundancy, but unless there is such a formula, there is no obligation to make a payment. A collective employment agreement must contain provisions setting out what will happen in the event of the sale or transfer of the employer's business, which is one of the reasons that a redundancy (a "technical redundancy") may arise, but that does not have to include a compensation payment for those employees.[81]

A redundancy dismissal will be unjustified if it is not genuine. An employer may not use redundancy as a pretext to dismiss an employee. It must be the result of a position becoming surplus to requirements. The Authority or Court may not go any further than examining the genuineness of the decision. It may not listen to arguments that the redundancy might have been avoided by other measures. If the basis for redundancies is financial, it is not enough for the employer to point to a commercial need to reduce costs. The employer must establish that there were genuine commercial reasons to do this, by the laying off of staff.[82]

Redundancies generally arise for economic reasons, or because of advances in technology. If the employer's business can be carried out more efficiently without a particular job, the employer may treat it as redundant. Provided the decision to make a position redundant is genuine, it is not open to the Employment Relations Authority or Employment Court to look behind that decision and question the reasons for it.[83] The Authority or Court is however entitled to look at the process followed by the employer in deciding which employee's employment should be terminated.

If a redundancy dismissal is made for a genuine reason, but is implemented in a manner that the Authority or Court finds to be unfair, perhaps through lack of consultation or inadequate notice, remedies may be given to the employee. However, this can not include any component for the loss of the job itself. The inclusion of good faith obligations under the Employment Relations Act 2000 has not brought any significant change in the law in that respect. It has, however, meant that in almost all cases, consultation in some form will be required.[84]

13.8.3   Procedural fairness and good faith

It has long been recognised in New Zealand that to be justified, a dismissal must not only be founded on just grounds, but it must also be carried out in a manner that is procedurally fair to the employee.

The requirements of procedural fairness will be assessed against the circumstances of each case. Inevitably, they will include the obligation to give the employee a fair hearing, and a

---

81   But see the requirements set out in section 69A to 69O of the Employment Relations Act 2000 for employees who are defined as "vulnerable workers" under those provisions.

82   *NZ Nurses Union v Air NZ Ltd* [1992] 3 ERNZ 548.

83   See *Simpsons Farms Ltd v Aberhart* [2006] 1 ERNZ 825, para 67 where the Chief Judge of the Employment Court held: "So long as an employer acts genuinely and not out of ulterior motives, a business decision to make positions or employees redundant is for the employer to make and not for the Authority or the Court, even under section 103A."

84   *Coutts Cars Ltd v Baguley* [2002] 2 NZLR 533; [2001] ERNZ 660 (CA).

genuine opportunity to influence the employer's decision. The most common way for this to be compromised is for the employer to arrive at a decision before hearing from the employee. Where some default on the employee's part is alleged, the employee is entitled to fair advance notice of what is alleged so that they can answer the allegation. The employer should inform the employee that they may have someone else present in support at the interview. If there is a collective agreement, the obligation of good faith or a specific term of the agreement may require that the union be informed before any decision is made. It is a good practice to inform the union in any event. Dismissals for poor performance will almost always be found to be unjustified if the employee has not received a warning. Even where warnings have been given failure to do what a fair and reasonable employer would have done in the circumstances will make the dismissal unjustified.[85]

13.9 Other statutes affecting the employment relationship

13.9.1 Minimum Wage Act 1983

This Act gives the Government the power to set a minimum wage. That rate is adjusted from time to time, and is expressed as an hourly, daily, and weekly rate. The rates are reviewed annually. An employee who is not paid the minimum wage is entitled to bring an action to recover arrears of wages.[86]

13.9.2 Wages Protection Act 1983

Employees are entitled to receive their wages or salary in cash. This Act prevents employers from requiring employees to take their remuneration in any other form,[87] and prevents unauthorised deductions being made from wages.[88] For security reasons, most employers request employees to accept their wages by way of direct lodgement into a bank account. Deductions may be agreed on, for example, to repay a loan to the employer, or to pay for board and lodgings, but these must be authorised in writing. The authority can be withdrawn by the employee at any time by notice in writing to the employer.[89] This does not affect deductions that are specifically authorised by statute, such as the Income Tax Act 1994 or the Child Support Act 1991.

Some employers attempt to deduct sums owed by the employee from the final pay of an employee who is leaving. This is unlawful without written authority. The employer is obliged to pay wages and holiday pay in full, and must recover the money owed by the employee by some other means. If they do not, then they may be liable for a penalty under the Employment Relations Act 2000.[90]

13.9.3 Holidays Act 2003[91]

The Holidays Act 2003 provides minimum holiday and leave entitlements for all employees, except those in the armed forces. The key minimum entitlements under the Act are:

---

85   *Air NZ Ltd v Hudson* [2006] 1 ERNZ 415.
86   Section 11 of the Minimum Wage Act 1983.
87   Wages Protection Act 1983, section 7.
88   Wages Protection Act 1983, section 4.
89   Wages Protection Act 1983, section 5.
90   Wages Protection Act 1983, section 13.
91   On 3 June 2009 the Minister of Labour appointed a working group to review the Holidays Act 2003. The group is due to report to the Minister in December 2009.

- 4 weeks paid annual holidays per year;
- 11 public holidays per year;
- 5 days sick leave per year; and
- bereavement leave.

An employer and employee may agree to entitlements more beneficial than those set out in the Act but cannot agree to anything less. An employer is required to maintain accurate leave records that include the entitlements, leave, and holidays taken by an employee. Employees can request access to, or a copy of, any record relating to them.[92]

(1)   *Annual holidays*

After 12 months of continuous employment, an employee becomes entitled to a minimum of 4 weeks paid annual holiday leave. The 12-month qualifying period may include any periods of annual holidays, parental leave, weekly compensation from ACC, bereavement leave, sick leave and any other unpaid leave which lasted no more than one week.[93] An employee's entitlement to annual holidays remains in force until the employee has taken all of the entitlement.[94] An employee has the right to take holidays within 12 months after the date of entitlement, and if the employee wishes to do so, the employer must allow the employee to take at least 2 weeks of the entitlement in one continuous period.[95]

The employer and employee should agree between themselves when the employee's leave is to be taken. Employers are not allowed to unreasonably withhold consent to an employee's request to take leave.[96] Employers may also allow an employee to take an agreed portion of the leave entitlement in advance.[97]

Where the employer and employee cannot agree when the leave should be taken, the employer can require that the employee take it at a certain time, but must give the employee at least 14 days' notice.[98] The employer can also require that the leave be taken during a closedown period, which is a period when the employer customarily closes down business.[99]

(2)   *Public Holidays*

The purpose of public holidays is to allow employees time off work to observe significant dates in the calendar. The 11 public holidays listed in the Act are Christmas Day, Boxing Day, New Year Day, the second day in January, Good Friday, Easter Monday, Anzac Day, Queen's Birthday, Labour Day, Waitangi Day and the appropriate provincial day.[100]

Entitlement to take the day off on a public holiday only arises if the public holiday occurs on a day that would otherwise be a working day for the employee. In the past, particularly with rostered employees, there were often disputes over whether the day of the public

---

92   Holidays Act 2003, section 82.
93   Holidays Act 2003, section 16.
94   Holidays Act 2003, section 16(4).
95   Holidays Act 2003, section 18.
96   Holidays Act 2003, section 18(4).
97   Holidays Act 2003, section 20.
98   Holidays Act 2003, section 19.
99   Holidays Act 2003, sections 29 and 32.
100   Holidays Act 2003, section 44.

holiday was a day that would otherwise have been a working day. The Act now sets out factors to take into account where there may be doubt, including the employee's roster and work pattern.[101] An employee who does not normally work on a Monday would therefore not be entitled to a holiday in respect of a public holiday that fell on a Monday.

An employer can only compel an employee to work on a public holiday if the day would otherwise be a working day for the employee *and* the employment agreement requires the employee to work on public holidays.[102] Employees who take the public holiday off as leave are to be paid for that day at no less than their "relevant daily pay."[103] What is meant by "relevant daily pay" is set out in the Act and is the amount the employee would have received had the employee worked the day concerned. An employment agreement may specify a special rate of relevant daily pay.[104]

Employees who work on a public holiday must be paid the greater of one and a half times their relevant daily rate of pay for the time actually worked or the portion of the relevant daily rate that relates to the time actually worked.[105] All employment agreements must contain this provision. In addition, employees who work on a public holiday, that would otherwise be a working day, are to be provided another day's "alternative holiday."[106] Any employee who is employed solely to work on public holidays is not entitled to this alternative holiday.

An alternative holiday is to be taken on a day agreed between the employer and employee, and it must be a day the employee would normally work and be a whole day off regardless of time worked on the public holiday.[107] If the employee and employer cannot agree on when to take the holiday, the choice can be made by the employee. If 12 months has passed since the entitlement to the alternative day arises and there is no agreement then the employer can require the employee to take the alternative holiday on a particular day, provided 14 days' notice is given to the employee.[108]

Alternative holidays are to be paid at no less than the employee's "relevant daily pay."[109] Payment for public holidays must be made in the pay that relates to the period when the holiday occurs.[110]

Many health service employees are required by their employer to be on call. Employees on call who are called back to work on a public holiday are entitled to an alternative holiday. Employees on call and who are not called back to work might still be entitled to an alternative holiday if their freedom to otherwise do things on that public holiday has been so restricted by the on-call arrangements, because for all practical purposes they have not had a whole holiday.[111] Pay for an alternative holiday is to be no less than the employee's "relevant daily pay." If the alternative holiday has not been taken within 12 months of

---

101   Holidays Act 2003, section 12.
102   Holidays Act 2003, section 47.
103   Holidays Act 2003, section 49.
104   Holidays Act 2003, section 9.
105   Holidays Act 2003, section 50 and see *NZALPA Inc v Air NZ Ltd* [2008] 1 ERNZ 62.
106   Holidays Act 2003, section 56.
107   Holidays Act 2003, section 57.
108   Holidays Act 2003, section 58.
109   Holidays Act 2003, section 60.
110   Holidays Act 2003, section 55.
111   Holidays Act 2003, section 59.

accruing it, the employee can request the employer to exchange the holiday for a payment.[112]

An employee who agrees to work on a public holiday but does not do so because of sickness, injury or bereavement must have the day treated as a public holiday on which they did not work rather than as sick leave or bereavement leave.[113]

(3)   *Sick leave and bereavement leave*

Entitlements to sick leave and bereavement leave are separate under the Act. Employees who have worked for a continuous period of 6 months are entitled to a minimum of 5 days sick leave. In the case of employees with an intermittent work pattern, such as casual employees, they are entitled to the leave if over a 6 month period they worked for the employer for an average of 10 hours per week or no less than one hour in every week, or no less than 40 hours in every month during that period.[114] This provision extends sick and bereavement leave to casual staff that, under previous legislation, were not entitled to paid leave.

Sick leave can be taken for periods of sickness or injury of an employee, spouse or dependant.[115] Sick leave which has not been taken can be carried over into subsequent years to provide a maximum of 20 days in any year.[116] Employers can request proof of illness or injury for any period of 3 days or more whether or not the days are working days. Therefore, an employee sick on the day prior to days off and sick on the next day of work can be requested to provide proof of sickness. Employees do not have an entitlement to be paid for sick leave which has not been taken.

Employees are entitled to three days bereavement leave on the death of an employee's child, parent, sibling, spouse, spouse's parent, grandparent, or grandchild, and one day for the death of any other person, if the employer accepts that the employee has suffered bereavement because of the death.[117] An employee need not take all 3 days at once and may, for example, take 2 days at the time of the death then a further day to attend an unveiling 12 months later.

Factors the employer should take into account when deciding if the employee has suffered bereavement are cultural responsibility, closeness of association, and the employee's responsibilities for ceremonies related to the death.[118] This provision, though not confined to Maori, will enable an employee to attend a funeral or tangi for people outside of the immediate family.

An employer and employee can agree for an employee to take sick leave or bereavement leave in advance of entitlement. Where sick leave is taken in advance it is deducted from the employee's entitlement.[119]

---

112   Holidays Act 2003, section 61.
113   Holidays Act 2003, section 61A.
114   Holidays Act 2003, section 63.
115   Holidays Act 2003, section 65.
116   Holidays Act 2003, section 66.
117   Holidays Act 2003, section 69 and 70.
118   Holidays Act 2003, section 69(3).
119   Holidays Act 2003, section 63.

Payment for sick and bereavement leave is the amount equivalent to the employee's "relevant daily pay" for each day of sick or bereavement leave.[120]

(4) Calculation of annual holiday pay

The amount of pay that an employee receives for annual holiday leave must be the greater of the employee's "ordinary weekly pay" as at the start of the holiday, or the employee's "average weekly earnings" for the 12 months prior to the annual holiday.[121] Ordinary weekly pay is what the employee is normally paid and includes allowances and normal overtime. The Act sets out how to work out the ordinary weekly pay in cases where it is unclear.[122] Average weekly earnings are calculated by dividing the gross earnings over the previous 12 months by 52.

The Act sets out how holidays are to be paid when holidays are taken in advance and where employment ends before holidays are taken.[123] Unless an employee agrees otherwise, the employee is to be paid for holidays before the holiday is taken.[124]

Prior to the enactment of the Holidays Act 2003, the Court of Appeal confirmed that an employer and employee could agree to incorporate holiday pay into the hourly or weekly pay.[125] This "pay as you go" practice is still permissible under the Holidays Act 2003, but only in the following limited circumstances:

- Where an employee is employed on a fixed-term agreement for less than 12 months; or
- Where the employment is so intermittent as to make it impractical for the employer to provide 4 weeks holiday leave.

In these circumstances the employment agreement may allow for holiday pay to be paid with the employee's pay, provided the holiday pay is an identifiable component of the pay and is not less than eight percent of gross earnings.[126]

(5) Interface between annual holidays and other entitlements

The Act clarifies entitlements when sickness or bereavement arises before or during annual holidays. Holiday leave is designed to allow employees rest and recreation. With the employer's agreement, if an employee is sick or injured during annual holidays the days when the employee is sick may be taken as sick leave if the employer agrees. Where the employee is bereaved during annual holidays then the employer must allow the employee to take the time as bereavement leave. Similarly, where sickness or injury of the employee, spouse or dependant arises *before* the annual holiday, the employer must allow the employee to take that time as sick or bereavement leave.[127]

An employee who has exhausted their entitlement to paid sick leave may ask to take those days as part of their holiday leave entitlement.

---

120   Holidays Act 2003, section 71.
121   Holidays Act 2003, section 22.
122   Holidays Act 2003, section 22(3).
123   Holidays Act 2003, sections 22-24.
124   Holidays Act 2003, section 28.
125   *Drake Personnel (NZ) Ltd v Taylor* [1996] 2 NZLR 644; [1996] 1 ERNZ 324.
126   Section 28(1) of the Holidays Act 2003.
127   Holidays Act 2003, sections 36-38.

13.9.4   Parental Leave and Employment Protection Act 1987

This Act provides for both paid and unpaid parental leave.

(1)   *Unpaid parental leave*

There are four types of unpaid parental leave. These include:

*   Maternity leave for up to 14 weeks continuously for the mother;
*   Paternity (or partner's) leave of up to 2 weeks for the mother's spouse/partner;
*   Extended leave of up to 52 weeks; and
*   Special leave of up to 10 days for a pregnant mother before maternity leave begins.

This means that both parents can take leave at the time of the birth or adoption and then a second period of leave to care for the child. In total, they are entitled to up to 52 weeks' leave between them. Partner means a person in a married, civil union or de facto relationship (including same-sex partners) with the mother or the primary carer who assumes the care of the child they intend to jointly adopt with their spouse/partner. They do not need to be the natural parent of the child.

To qualify for leave under this Act an employee must have been employed by a single employer continuously for at least an average of 10 hours per week and at least 1 hour each week or 40 hours each month for a period of either 6 or 12 months prior to the expected date of delivery or care of the child to be adopted; entitlements to leave differ depending on whether the 6 or 12 month criteria is met. Junior doctors who are required to rotate between different DHBs as part of their compulsory training are entitled to treat the DHBs as a single employer.[128]

Maternity leave commences either on the date of confinement, or some earlier date determined either by the employee, the employer, or in some cases a medical practitioner. It is also available to an employee adopting a child under the age of 6 years.[129] In addition to maternity leave, a pregnant employee may take up to 10 days' special leave for reasons connected with her pregnancy.[130]

Partner/paternal leave is available to an employee who is to assume the care of their child from birth or adoption. The period of leave normally commences at the time of the partner's confinement, although the employee can have the period of leave commence up to 21 days before the expected date of delivery or adoption.[131]

Extended leave is available to both parents, provided they each take their leave in one continuous period, and the total between them does not exceed 52 weeks. Maternity leave taken by the mother will be included in the calculation of this time, but paternity leave will not.[132]

Where an employee intends to take parental leave the employee is obliged to notify the employer of their intention in writing including the period of leave proposed, a certificate from a medical practitioner or midwife confirming that the employee (or spouse) is pregnant

---

128   Parental Leave and Employment Protection Act 1987, section 2AB.
129   Sections 7-14 of the Parental Leave and Employment Protection Act 1987.
130   Parental Leave and Employment Protection Act 1987, section 15.
131   Parental Leave and Employment Protection Act 1987, sections 17-22.
132   Parental Leave and Employment Protection Act 1987, sections 23-30.

and the expected date of delivery, and in the case of her partner, a written assurance from the pregnant woman that she or he is her spouse and intends to assume the care of the child.[133] Three months notice of intention to take parental leave is generally required but the notice requirements for adoptive parents depend on the type of evidence of adoption provided.[134] The employer must respond in writing confirming the leave or sets out reasons why it is not allowed.[135] Once leave has commenced, the employer must notify the employee in writing of the date when it commenced and the date it is due to expire.[136] No later than 21 days before it is due to expire, the employee must notify the employer whether they intend to return to the job at the end of the leave period.[137]

The Act places an obligation on the employer to hold the employee's position open for her/him during the period of leave, unless the employer is unable to do so for reasons specified in the Act. It treats the employment as continuous, notwithstanding the taking of that leave.[138]

It is presumed the employer can keep the job open for the employee for the first 4 weeks of parental leave, unless there is a redundancy affecting the position.[139] For any subsequent leave, there is a presumption the job can be kept open except in the case of redundancy, or if the employer can show that it was not reasonably practicable to hire a temporary replacement, due to the job being a key position in the organisation.[140]

It is permissible to hire an employee as a temporary replacement for an employee on parental leave, but that temporary employee must be informed in writing of the nature of the employment and the fact that the permanent employee may return at any time.[141]

Other than the circumstances allowed for, that is, redundancy, or the need to find a permanent replacement to a key position, it is unlawful to dismiss an employee solely on the grounds of pregnancy, or taking parental leave. Such action would give rise to a personal grievance.[142]

(2) Paid parental leave

For parents who meet the criteria for maternity or partner/paternity leave this Act also provides for State-funded paid parental leave[143] of up to 14 weeks in total for:

- Female employees who give birth to a child; or
- Either parent where a couple has assumed the care of a child under six they intend to jointly adopt.

---

133 Parental Leave and Employment Protection Act 1987, section 31. The Parental Leave and Employment Protection Regulations 2002 sets out the manner and form in which various applications and notifications are to be made.
134 Parental Leave and Employment Protection Act 1987, section 33.
135 Parental Leave and Employment Protection Act 1987, section 36.
136 Parental Leave and Employment Protection Act 1987, section 38.
137 Parental Leave and Employment Protection Act 1987, sections 31 and 39.
138 Parental Leave and Employment Protection Act 1987, section 43.
139 Parental Leave and Employment Protection Act 1987, section 40.
140 Parental Leave and Employment Protection Act 1987, section 41.
141 Parental Leave and Employment Protection Act 1987, section 48.
142 Parental Leave and Employment Protection Act 1987, section 49.
143 Parental Leave and Employment Protection Act 1987, Part 7A.

Only one person is entitled to receive the payment but an employee may transfer all or part of their paid parental leave to their spouse/partner as long as they also meet the eligibility criteria.[144] The rules governing entitlement to payment, the rate of payment, and the manner in which it is to be paid are set out in the Act and in Regulations made under the Act.[145] Payments are made directly to the employee from Inland Revenue and are treated as income in the hands of the employee.

13.9.5 Employment Relations (Flexible Working Arrangements) Amendment Act 2007

This amendment to the Employment Relations Act 2000 inserted a new Part 6AA which came into force on 1 July 2008.

Part 6AA provides a right for employees who have the care of any person to request a variation in their working arrangements (including their time and place of work). An employer is obliged to deal with such a request as soon as possible and in any case within 3 months. The grounds on which an employer may refuse such a request are set out and the Act provides a process for dealing with an alleged failure of an employer to deal with such a request according to this Part.[146]

Employees may only make a request for flexible arrangements after they have been employed by the employer for 6 months and may not make more than one request in any 12-month period.[147]

The Act is due for review after the middle of 2010.[148]

13.9.6 Employment Relations (Breaks, Infant Feeding, and Other Matters) Amendment Act 2008

From 1 April 2009, all employees are entitled to paid rest breaks and unpaid meal breaks for a minimum period of time in each shift or "work period" of 2 hours or longer.[149] Timing of meal breaks can be agreed between the employer and employee but if they cannot agree then breaks must be spread across the work period as far as is reasonable and practical.[150]

The Employment Relations Authority can order compliance with these provisions of the Act and impose a penalty on any employer who fails to provide the required minimum breaks.[151]

The same amendment to the Employment Relations Act 2000 also provides for unpaid breaks to enable employees to breastfeed their babies.[152] Employers are required, as far as reasonable and practical, to provide facilities to enable them to do so. These minimum entitlements are in addition to the rest and meal breaks provided under the Act.[153]

---

144   Parental Leave and Employment Protection Act 1987, section 71E.
145   The Department of Labour website provides comprehensive information about both paid and unpaid parental leave entitlements including a parental leave calculator at www.ers.dol.govt.nz/parentalleave.
146   Section 69AAA of the Employment Relations Act 2000.
147   Employment Relations Act 2000, sections 69AAB and 69AAD.
148   Employment Relations Act 2000, section 69AAL.
149   Employment Relations Act 2000, section 69ZD.
150   Employment Relations Act 2000, section 69ZE.
151   Employment Relations Act 2000, section 69ZF.
152   Employment Relations Act 2000, section 69Y.

13.9.7 KiwiSaver Act 2006

"The purpose of this Act is to encourage a long-term savings habit and asset accumulation by individuals who are not in a position to enjoy standards of living in retirement similar to those in pre-retirement. The Act aims to increase individuals' well-being and financial independence, particularly in retirement, and to provide retirement benefits."[154]

The Act provides for the establishment of privately managed KiwiSaver schemes and is a voluntary regime aimed at establishing a simple long term savings habit for employees. It is not guaranteed by the Government and employees assume the risk of their investment in a scheme. Incentives for joining or remaining in a KiwiSaver scheme include a government payment of $1000 to "kick-start" an employee's account, regular contributions from employers and annual tax credits.

Savings are generally locked in until retirement but in certain circumstances early withdrawals may be made.[155]

The Act is administered by the Inland Revenue Department and the Ministry of Economic Development.

13.10   Further reading

Brookers Employment Law, Wellington, Thomson Reuters.

Brookers Employment Law Handbook 2009, Wellington, Thomson Reuters, 2009.

J Brown and G Davenport, *Good Faith in Collective Bargaining*, Wellington, LexisNexis NZ Ltd, 2002.

Burrows, Finn and Todd, *Law of Contract in New Zealand* (3rd ed), Wellington, LexisNexis NZ Ltd, 2007.

Employment Law Guide (7th ed), Wellington, LexisNexis NZ Ltd, 2005.

Department of Labour website, www.ers.dol.govt.nz.

---

153   Employment Relations Act 2000, section 69Z.
154   Section 3 of the KiwiSaver Act 2006.
155   KiwiSaver Act 2006, Schedule 1.

Chapter 14

ACCIDENTS AT WORK AND OCCUPIERS' LIABILITY

LOUISA CLERY AND AUSTIN POWELL

Contents

14.1 Accidents to consumers

Accidents to consumers may be the result of negligence by the management of a health service facility or its staff or, in other situations, by a health practitioner (chapter 8). Where there is an accident to a consumer, this should be reported as soon as possible, no matter what the cause. "Accident" here includes receiving the wrong treatment. From a legal point of view, apart from the need to avoid allegations of negligence, there is an issue of veracity in prompt reporting. Also, as most health care institutions are also workplaces, there are reporting requirements for any accidents that cause injury under the Health and Safety in Employment Act 1992.

In any event, delay, or lack of full and frank disclosure of events, can give rise to the suspicion that facts have been hidden. The sooner after the event the report is given, the more likely it is to be an accurate account of what happened in the eyes of the Court or the disciplinary body, as memories are not served well by time. Some details may not be so important for the consumer's immediate health but may be vital to establish, perhaps years later, what happened.

Under the Health and Safety in Employment Act 1992,[1] employers must record accidents that harmed any person who was in a place of work controlled by that employer. Such accidents must be recorded in the accident register kept by the employer (see *Recording and reporting accidents* below).

In addition to the details required to be recorded in the accident register, the names of witnesses to the accident, or the whereabouts of the nearest person or people should be recorded. If there is any possibility that the event may give rise to legal action, a written account, apart from any official incident report, can be made and kept for future use. If there is likely to be a contradiction between your written account and that of any other person, if you are absolutely certain of the facts, consider making a sworn statement (an affidavit), as soon as practicable after the event. (See the footnote 18 on affidavits at 9.3.2(9)).

14.2 Accidents to staff

The right to a safe working environment is given statutory force by the Health and Safety in Employment Act 1992.[2] This Act places a primary responsibility on employers to provide a safe working environment. Compensation for work-related injuries, and illnesses caused by gradual processes is provided for under the Injury Prevention, Rehabilitation, and Compensation Act 2001. These issues are considered below.

14.3 Occupational safety and health

The object of the Health and Safety in Employment Act 1992 (the Act) is set out in the Act itself.[3]

---

1   Section 25(1)(a)(ii).

2   See section 6 — Employers to ensure safety of employees.

3   See also *Central Cranes Ltd v Department of Labour* [1997] 3 NZLR 694; [1997] ERNZ 520; this case reinforces that the object of the Act is to promote safety in the workplace and that this duty falls on employers and others associated with the workplace.

"5   Object of Act

"The object of this Act is to promote the prevention of harm to all persons at work and other persons in, or in the vicinity of, a place of work by—

"(a)   promoting excellence in health and safety management, in particular through promoting the systematic management of health and safety; and

"(b)   defining hazards and harm in a comprehensive way so that all hazards and harm are covered, including harm caused by work-related stress and hazardous behaviour caused by certain temporary conditions; and

"(c)   imposing various duties on persons who are responsible for work and those who do the work; and

"(d)   setting requirements that—

"(i)   relate to taking all practicable steps to ensure health and safety; and

"(ii)   are flexible to cover different circumstances; and

"(e)   recognising that volunteers doing work activities for other persons should have their health and safety protected because their well-being and work are as important as the well-being and work of employees; and

"(f)   recognising that successful management of health and safety issues is best achieved through good faith co-operation in the place of work and, in particular, through the input of the persons doing the work; and

"(g)   providing a range of enforcement methods, including various notices and prosecution, so as to enable an appropriate response to a failure to comply with the Act depending on its nature and gravity; and

"(h)   prohibiting persons from being indemnified or from indemnifying others against the cost of fines and infringement fees for failing to comply with the Act."

The Act includes most places of employment and it binds the Crown. Under the Crown Organisations (Criminal Liability) Act 2002, certain Crown organisations, but not the Crown itself, may be prosecuted under the Act.[4]

Under the Act, responsibility for controlling hazards and responding appropriately to accidents can fall on more than one person. For example, hospitals often contract out some ancillary services, such as catering or cleaning, to independent operators. Those independent operators will in turn employ staff to carry out the duties. If an accident occurs through an employee's actions, responsibility under the Act may fall on the employee, the contractor, and the hospital (as principal to the contract).[5]

---

4   Health and Safety in Employment Act 1992, section 3.
5   Health and Safety in Employment Act 1992, section 2(2); *Central Cranes Ltd v Department of Labour* [1997] 3 NZLR 694; [1997] ERNZ 520.

14.3.1   Employer obligations

Under the Act an employer must take all practicable steps to:[6]

- Provide and maintain a safe working environment;
- Provide and maintain facilities for the health and safety of employees at work;
- Ensure machinery and equipment in the workplace is designed, made, set up, and maintained to be safe for employees;
- Ensure employees are not exposed to hazards in the course of their work;
- Develop procedures for dealing with emergencies that arise while employees are at work; and
- Provide adequate safety training facilities for employees.[7]

These obligations are expressed in general terms and have been described as "uncompromising and onerous".[8]

The Act sets out specific duties on employers in relation to hazards in the workplace. They must identify them;[9] take all practicable steps to eliminate them;[10] and if they cannot practicably be eliminated, isolate them.[11] If they cannot be isolated, the risk they pose must be minimised and any employees exposed to them must be monitored.[12] Monitoring information must be given to the employee.

One of the express obligations in minimising hazards is to provide appropriate protective clothing and equipment and ensure that it is used. It is no longer acceptable for employers to provide an allowance for protective equipment with the employee's wages. An employee who genuinely wants to provide their own clothing (but not equipment) is still allowed to do so.

The obligation to deal with hazards will arise regularly in health sector environments. For instance, medical radiation technologists and radiologists working with x-rays and in nuclear medicine should be monitored for signs of adverse effects, as well as being provided with specific training and clothing. Health workers who have to handle radium or other radioactive substances that are used in the treatment of some cancers also need careful monitoring.

The general language of the Act requires a broad approach by employers to potential hazards. For example, a health practitioner employed in a penal institution may be required to deal directly with some inmates who have an established propensity for violence. In the language of health and safety, their presence in the workplace could constitute a hazard.

---

6   The term "all practicable steps" is important and is repeated throughout the Act. It is the measure taken to decide if the duty under the Act has been breached. Lord Reid in the House of Lords (*Marshall v Gotham Co Ltd* [1954] AC 360; [1954] 2 WLR 812; [1954] 1 All ER 937, para 35) defined it in the following way: "... as essentially one of objective fact, viewing the matter at a stage shortly before the injury through the eye of an employer conducting the respondent's operation and with the knowledge that such employer could reasonably have been expected to possess as to the nature of prospective harm from the machine."

7   Section 6 of the Health and Safety in Employment Act 1992.

8   *Tranz Rail Ltd v Department of Labour* [1997] ERNZ 316.

9   Health and Safety in Employment Act 1992, section 7.

10   Health and Safety in Employment Act 1992, section 8.

11   Health and Safety in Employment Act 1992, section 9.

12   Health and Safety in Employment Act 1992, section 10.

Likewise, the staff at an Accident and Emergency Clinic may be regularly exposed to intoxicated persons. Even before the definition of hazard was widened in 2003 to include "a situation where a person's behaviour may be an actual or potential cause or source of harm", the Employment Court held that in some circumstances psychiatric clients could be a significant part of the hazard in an institution that cares for them.[13] Violence has become such a recognised hazard within the healthcare industry that the Department of Labour has published guidelines — *Managing the Risk of Workplace Violence to Healthcare and Community Service Providers*.[14] The Department of Labour recommends that healthcare staff should be given training in the management of workplace violence before exposure to potential hazards, followed by refresher training within the first year.[15]

The Act provides that employers must inform, train and supervise employees to ensure their safety. This includes providing relevant information about emergency procedures, hazards and available safety equipment[16] and providing training in the safe use of plant objects and substances in the workplace and supervision from a person who is knowledgeable and experienced in safe procedures.[17]

In health care facilities employers should train employees to handle needles and blood so as to minimise any risks associated with the contraction of viral Hepatitis B and HIV. Handling of other infectious material must be analysed, and guidelines and training provided to employees. The use of theatre equipment and methods of lifting consumers that might cause injury to health practitioners, must be assessed to prevent all recognised potential risks. The duty to supervise and train employees implies safety mechanisms are put in place by the employer, which must be monitored on an ongoing basis to ensure compliance.[18]

The Act also imposes a wide duty on employers to ensure that non-employees in the workplace are not harmed by the actions or inactions of employees.[19] This creates an obligation to ensure the safety of consumers, visitors, and other people who might reasonably be in the workplace.

14.3.2   Duties of employees

Employees are also required to take all practicable steps to ensure their own safety in the workplace, including a specific obligation to use safety equipment provided by the employer, and to ensure that their actions do not harm anyone else.[20] However, the fact that an employee fails to do this does not affect the employer's responsibility for the accident, unless the employee was solely to blame for the accident. There are many instances where both the employer and the employee responsible were successfully prosecuted for the same incident.[21]

---

13   *Healthlink South Ltd v Flanagan* [2000] 1 ERNZ 63.
14   *Managing the Risk of Workplace Violence to Healthcare and Community Service Providers*, Department of Labour, 2009, www.osh.dol.govt.nz/order/catalogue/preventing-violence.html.
15   *Managing the Risk of Workplace Violence to Healthcare and Community Service Providers*, Department of Labour, 2009, www.osh.dol.govt.nz/order/catalogue/preventing-violence.html.
16   Section 12 of the Health and Safety in Employment Act 1992.
17   Health and Safety in Employment Act 1992, section 13.
18   *Department of Labour v Alexandra Holdings* [1994] 1 CR 50.
19   Section 15 of the Health and Safety in Employment Act; *Punts Painting & Waterblasting Ltd v Burt* 21/12/95, Greig J, HC Nelson M32/95.
20   Section 19 Health and Safety in Employment Act 1992.

14.3.3 Duties of other persons

A person who controls a workplace has duties to protect the people there, and people in the vicinity from hazards arising in or emanating from the workplace.[22] Self-employed persons and principals all have obligations to ensure that their actions do not harm other people in the workplace.[23] Persons, who supply plant, by sale or hire, must take reasonable steps to ascertain whether the plant is to be used in a workplace, and if so, to take all practicable steps to ensure that it is safe.[24]

The Act contemplates that the duties may overlap so more than one person may be liable where harm is caused. The primary responsibility is on the employer,[25] but that does not diminish the responsibility of other persons who have a concurrent duty not to harm others in the workplace.[26]

14.3.4 Employer/employee cooperation

The Act requires employers to provide their employees with reasonable opportunities to participate in the ongoing management of health and safety in the workplace.[27]

Specifically, employers are required to develop an employee participation system if they employ 30 or more employees. When the employer employs less than 30 employees, they must develop an employee participation system if any employee or union representative asks them to.[28] If that is not done, there is a default scheme that will apply. This will incorporate provisions for the selection and training of health and safety representatives drawn from the employees, who qualify for special leave to attend health and safety training.[29]

Areas for participation include the development of health and safety systems, ongoing hazard identification and hazard management, and emergency procedures.

14.3.5 Recording and reporting accidents

(1) *Accident register*

The Act requires employers, principals, and self-employed people to keep an accident register.[30] The particulars that must be recorded are set out in regulations.[31]

---

21   For example: *Bellett (H&S Inspector, Department of Labour) v Haddow & Annor* 30/11/07, Judge Weir, Greymouth DC CRI-2006-018-689. In this case the employee of a mine died from an inrush of water while digging access tunnels. Not only was the company charged and fined but also the mine manager who was injured in the same incident. A third employee who had provided consultant advice on where to dig was also charged and fined.

22   Health and Safety in Employment Act 1992, section 16.

23   Health and Safety in Employment Act 1992, sections 17 and 18.

24   Health and Safety in Employment Act 1992, section 18A.

25   *Department of Labour v De Spa & Co Ltd & Ors* [1994] 1 ERNZ 339.

26   *Central Cranes Ltd v Department of Labour* [1997] 3 NZLR 694; [1997] ERNZ 520.

27   Section 19B of the Health and Safety in Employment Act 1992.

28   Health and Safety in Employment Act 1992, section 19C.

29   Health and Safety in Employment Act 1992, section 19E.

30   Health and Safety in Employment Act 1992, section 25.

31   Health and Safety in Employment (Prescribed Matters) Regulations 2003.

The register must record every accident that harmed or might have harmed an employee or any person in a workplace controlled by the employer. The information that must be entered in the register is as follows:

- The place of work, giving specific details such as the relevant shop, shed, floor, building, street number, street, locality, suburb, and postal address, or, where applicable, a reference to the identification of a vehicle, ship, or aircraft;
- The time and day of the incident (and the shift, if the incident was during a shift);
- A description of the nature of the incident;
- The cause of the incident;
- Details of any investigation that was carried out;
- Any significant hazard involved;
- If anyone has been injured, the following details;
  - The person's name, residential address, date of birth, and sex;
  - Whether the person was an employee, self-employed person, or someone else;
  - If the person was an employee, the person's occupation or job title, and length of employment by the employer, and the time between the person's arrival at work and the occurrence of the harm;
- If the person was a self-employed person, the person's occupation or job title, and the time between the person's arrival at the place of work concerned and the occurrence of the harm;
- The treatment the person was given (whether at the place of work or elsewhere);
- The part or parts of the person's body harmed;
- The nature of the harm; and
- The name and position of the person recording the details.

The form that is used for notifying the Department of Labour of serious harm incidents can also be used for the accident register.[32]

The definition of "accident" in the Act includes an event that, "in different circumstances, might have caused any person to be harmed",[33] so "near misses" must be recorded.

"Harm" includes illness,[34] so the accident register must record work-related illnesses.

(2)   *Accident reporting*

The Department of Labour must be notified by employers if an accident in their place of work results in serious harm.[35] Notice must be given as soon as possible after the occurrence of an accident/illness (eg by telephone or fax) and in writing within 7 days of the occurrence. It must be given in the form prescribed by regulations.[36]

The nearest Department of Labour health and safety office can be notified of serious harm incidents by calling 0800 20 90 20.

"Serious harm" means a death or a harm that result in either:

---

32   This form can be downloaded from www.osh.govt.nz.
33   Health and Safety in Employment Act 1992, section 2.
34   Health and Safety in Employment Act 1992, section 2, as well as injury.
35   Health and Safety in Employment Act 1992, section 25.
36   Health and Safety in Employment (Prescribed Matters) Regulations 2003.

- Permanent loss of bodily function or severe temporary loss of bodily function that has been caused by:
    - Respiratory disease;
    - Noise-induced hearing loss;
    - Neurological disease;
    - Cancer;
    - Dermatological disease;
    - Communicable disease;
    - Musculoskeletal disease;
    - Illness caused by exposure to infected material;
    - Decompression sickness;
    - Poisoning;
    - Vision impairment;
    - Chemical or hot-metal burns to the eye;
    - Penetrating wounds to the eye;
    - Bone fracture;
    - Laceration or crushing; or
- Amputation of a body part; or
- Burns requiring referral to a specialist registered medical practitioner or specialist outpatient clinic; or
- Loss of consciousness from lack of oxygen; or
- Loss of consciousness or acute illness requiring treatment by a registered medical practitioner, from absorption, inhalation, or ingestion of any substance; or
- A person being hospitalised for a period of 48 hours or more, starting within 7 days of the harm occurring.

(3)   *Accident scene*

Where a person is seriously harmed at work, the Act[37] provides that nobody may, without a Department of Labour inspector's approval, remove or in any way interfere with or disturb any wreckage, article, or thing related to the incident. Except for limited reasons, such as saving someone's life, preventing harm to a person or damage to property, or relieving someone's suffering.

14.3.6   Institutions

The Department of Labour administers the Act. Its role includes coordinating the development of codes of practice, enforcing compliance with the Act and regulations made under it, through inspectors employed by it, and it acts as the principal prosecuting authority for offences under the Act.

14.3.7   Codes of Practice and other standards

Provisions exist under the Act for the Minister of Labour to approve statements of preferred practices and arrangements in relation to work methods, plant design, and safety equipment. It may also develop "approved codes of practice".[38] These codes are the result of

---

37   Health and Safety in Employment Act 1992, section 26.
38   Health and Safety in Employment Act 1992, section 20.

consultation between the Department of Labour and affected industry members, including employers and employee organisations. Compliance with the codes may be evidence of good practice should an employer be prosecuted. Some of the codes published to date are relevant to hospital activities. There are codes of practice for noise in the workplace, handling of hazardous substances, pressure equipment, and use of visual display units.

The codes are not the only evidence of appropriate standards. For example, there are industry protocols for handling chemotherapy drugs. These protocols will not be as decisive as a code but an employer who allowed them to be ignored would be taking a substantial risk.

14.3.8   Inspectors

Inspectors are employees of the Department of Labour who are specially trained and certified in workplace safety. Under the Act, inspectors may enter workplaces to carry out examinations and tests and require employers to provide statements about the conditions, materials, or equipment affecting employees in the workplace.[39]

When enforcing the Act, inspectors can:[40]

- Issue an *improvement notice*, which requires the employer to comply with the Act by a given date;
- Issue a *prohibition notice*, which requires the employer to stop operations until the Act has been complied with;
- Issue an *infringement notice*, which fines the employer up to $4,000 for breaching the Act;
- Bring a prosecution against the employer at the District Court, which usually results in a fine and an order of reparation (paid by the offender) to the victim.

14.3.9   Departmental medical practitioners

Departmental medical practitioners are registered medical practitioners who have been certified by the Chief Executive of the Department of Labour. They have the same powers as inspectors, and may issue supervision notices to employees whose health has been detrimentally affected by hazardous work processes. If satisfied that an employee has been exposed to or harmed by a significant hazard, a departmental medical practitioner may require the employee to submit to medical examination and provide samples for testing.[41] In some circumstances they may direct that the employee be suspended.[42]

14.3.10   Health and safety representatives

The trained employee representatives have a specific power under the Act to issue their employer with a hazard notice if they have drawn the hazard to the employer's attention.[43] They may also advise an employee that the work they are doing is likely to cause serious harm, which will enable the employee to refuse to perform the work.[44] The employee

---

39   Health and Safety in Employment Act 1992, sections 29-31.
40   Health and Safety in Employment Act 1992, section 41.
41   Health and Safety in Employment Act 1992, section 36.
42   Health and Safety in Employment Act 1992, section 37.
43   Health and Safety in Employment Act 1992, section 46A.
44   Health and Safety in Employment Act 1992, section 28A.

does not require that advice in order to exercise their right to refuse to perform work. It is likely that most employees will resort to it, because of the protection it offers for their decision to refuse.

14.3.11　Offences and penalties

Under section 49 of the Act fines of up to $500,000 and 2 years imprisonment may be imposed for non-compliance with the Act where the prosecution can prove that the defendant knew that their failure was likely to cause serious harm. Otherwise, under section 50, the maximum penalty for a breach of the Act is a fine of up to $250,000.

For offences under section 50, the prosecution does not have to prove that the defendant was negligent, or that they knew that harm was likely to be caused. Although the offences are classed as "strict liability" offences, many of the Act's provisions that an employer might be charged with breaching refer to a failure to take all practicable steps. The prosecution will fail unless the prosecutor can prove that there were practicable steps that could have been taken, but were not.

The Act provides a definition of practicable steps that requires the Court to have regard to — among other things — the nature and severity of the harm that might result from a failure to take steps, the current state of knowledge about harm of that type, and the availability and cost of any preventative steps.[45]

In most health service workplaces, there will be a considerable body of knowledge and expertise among those who control the workplace and the work that is carried out about the types of hazards that may be present. Restrictions on funding will inevitably impact on health and safety measures, as they do on other aspects of management but a pure cost-benefit analysis is inconsistent with the purpose behind the Act. Once potential harm is identified, unless the type of harm is minor, the risk of it occurring is slight, and the cost of preventing it disproportionately large, it is unlikely to be regarded as impracticable.

Inspectors have the power to issue infringement notices in respect of offences under section 50(1) of the Act.[46] This is a summary process similar to the issue of a traffic infringement notice. This covers most of the obligations under the Act. It can only be issued if the person has received a prior warning, and the inspector has 14 days to issue the notice after becoming aware of the infringement. The scale of infringement fees ranges from $100 to $4,000. It is unlawful for any contract of insurance to indemnify any person against the cost of meeting fines or infringement fees imposed under the Act.[47]

14.4　Accident compensation

New Zealand has a no-fault accident and illness compensation scheme that was introduced in 1974. It has gradually been revised and extended to provide continuous cover for all people in New Zealand for personal injury by accident and occupational illness. The latest version of the scheme is set out in the Injury Prevention, Rehabilitation, and Compensation Act 2001, most of which came into force on 1 April 2002. It reinforces what is now routinely referred to as the social contract that arose from the first scheme in 1974. The people of

---

45　Health and Safety in Employment Act 1992, section 2A.
46　Health and Safety in Employment Act 1992, sections 56A-56H.
47　Health and Safety in Employment Act 1992, section 56I.

New Zealand surrendered the right to sue for personal injury, in exchange for a statutory right to compensation that would be funded from a levy on employers. It replaces the Accident Insurance Act 1998, which had allowed private insurance providers to compete with the Accident Compensation Corporation ("ACC").

14.4.1　Injury Prevention, Rehabilitation, and Compensation Act 2001

The ACC is funded principally by levies charged to employers, earners, and self-employed persons. There is a system for determining the amount of levy that employers and self-employed persons pay, which is based on the accident record of the industry they operate in and adjusted to reflect their particular accident history.

The ACC's role is not to act purely as an insurer. Its main aim is the prevention of accidents, and it assumes a significant educational role in order to pursue that aim.

For the purpose of this chapter, the emphasis is on the compensation for accidents. Part 2 of the Act deals with two important issues under this heading — the definition of what constitutes a personal injury for the purpose of the Act, and in what circumstances a person suffering that personal injury is entitled to cover under the Act.

14.4.2　What is a personal injury?

A personal injury is defined in section 26 as any of the following five events: death; physical injuries; mental injuries arising because of physical injuries, a single traumatic event that is directly experienced by the person during the course of their employment, or because of certain criminal offences committed against that person; or damage to any dentures or prostheses that replace a part of the human body other than wear and tear.

14.4.3　When does a person have cover under the Act?

If a person has suffered a personal injury under the definition in section 26, then they will have cover if that injury was caused by any of the events set out in section 20 of the Act. The most common events that are likely to apply in a health service environment are accidents, medical misadventure, gradual process, disease, or infection that is either work-related, a consequence of medical misadventure, or a consequence of treatment for a personal injury, or cardio-vascular or cerebro-vascular episodes that result from medical misadventure.

14.4.4　Accidents

Accidents for the purpose of the Act are defined by section 25 to include the following:

> "(a)　a specific event or a series of events, other than a gradual process, that—
>
> > "(i)　involves the application of a force (including gravity), or resistance, external to the human body; or
> >
> > "(ii)　involves the sudden movement of the body to avoid a force (including gravity), or resistance, external to the body; or
> >
> > "(iii)　involves a twisting movement of the body:
>
> "(b)　the inhalation of any solid, liquid, gas, or foreign object on a specific occasion, which kind of occurrence does not include the inhalation of a virus,

353

bacterium, protozoan, or fungus, unless that inhalation is the result of the criminal act of a person other than the injured person:

"(c)   the oral ingestion of any solid, liquid, gas, fungus, or foreign object on a specific occasion, which kind of occurrence does not include the ingestion of a virus, bacterium, or protozoan, unless that ingestion is the result of the criminal act of a person other than the injured person:

"(d)   a burn, or exposure to radiation or rays of any kind, on a specific occasion, which kind of occurrence does not include a burn or exposure caused by exposure to the elements:

"(e)   the absorption of any chemical through the skin within a defined period of time not exceeding 1 month:

"(f)   any exposure to the elements, or to extremes of temperature or environment, within a defined period of time not exceeding 1 month, that,—

"(i)   for a continuous period exceeding 1 month, results in any restriction or lack of ability that prevents the person from performing an activity in the manner or within the range considered normal for the person; or

"(ii)   causes death."

14.4.5   Work-related gradual process, disease, or infection

Diseases, infections, and gradual processes will be covered under the Act if they are work-related.

To be work-related, the employment task being performed by the employee or the environment in which they were working, must have had a particular property or characteristic that caused or contributed to the personal injury. From 1 October 2008, the Act was amended to provide that if a person had both work and non-work exposure, they will be covered if the work exposure was the more likely cause. ACC is responsible for proving that the work task or work environment placed the claimant at no significantly greater risk of developing the condition than a person who does not work in that environment or undertakes that employment task.[48]

Personal injuries caused by air conditioning systems, passive smoking, and non-physical stress were specifically excluded under the previous legislation but are not excluded under the Injury Prevention, Rehabilitation, and Compensation Act 2001.

Gradual process injury and an increased risk of communicable disease is of particular concern to health workers based in hospitals. If a person has been diagnosed as suffering from a gradual process disease, or infection, the causation must be established using the following criteria:

•   The person performs an employment task or works in an environment that had a particular property or characteristic; and

---

48   See section 10 of the Injury, Prevention, Compensation and Rehabilitation Amendment Act 2008 which amends section 30 of the principal Act.

- The particular property or characteristic causes or contributes to the person's injury; and
- If the person has both work and non-work exposure to the particular property or characteristic, the work exposure is more likely to have caused the personal injury.

However, certain occupational diseases do not require the causation criteria to be met.[49] Examples of those that relate to the healthcare industry include:

- Exposure to mercury (eg dental workers), which may cause mental illness or kidney damage;
- Exposure to ionising radiation (eg radiologists), which may cause leukaemia and non-Hodgkin's lymphoma;
- Exposure to ethylene oxide (eg hospital and healthcare workers), which may cause leukaemia; and
- Exposure to sensitising agents (eg doctors, nurses, dentists), which may cause occupational dermatitis.

14.4.6 Claims process for work-related personal injury

A work-related personal injury includes an injury suffered while an employee is at any place of work for the purpose of their employment. It also includes injuries suffered when travelling to work in transport provided by the employer, injuries while on rest or meal breaks and travelling, or between the place of work and a place for getting treatment for a work-related personal injury.

Like all persons claiming any benefits under the legislation, employees who suffer work-related personal injuries must complete the prescribed forms indicating that they are seeking cover under the Act. Some employers may be accredited by ACC to handle claims directly, if they meet the criteria in the Act. This will only occur if there is an accreditation agreement. That agreement may involve the employer exchanging a greater responsibility for payment of claims, in exchange for a reduced levy.

The claim for cover must be lodged with the Corporation or accredited employer if there is one, in the manner required by the Corporation. It must specify a method that is reasonable for the claimant to comply with. A treatment provider may lodge a claim on behalf of a claimant. If they do so, they must act promptly.

A claim for cover must be lodged within 12 months of the injury, but the Corporation may not decline a claim by reason of lateness unless it has prejudiced the Corporations ability to make decisions.[50] The circumstances that might amount to such a prejudice are not specified. The most likely circumstances are those that prevent the insurer from gathering evidence to evaluate the claim. This might occur where a witness has died, or where evidence of the accident has since been destroyed. Logically, any such events would need to have occurred after the end of the 12-month period to cause any prejudice for the purpose of that section of the Act.

---

49   Injury Prevention, Rehabilitation, and Compensation Act 2001, Schedule 2.
50   Injury Prevention, Rehabilitation, and Compensation Act 2001, section 53.

The claimant is required to assist the Corporation in processing the claim. This includes the provision of a certificate from any registered health professional who has dealt with her/him, and to undergo further medical examination at the Corporation's expense.

Under the Act the Corporation was required to draft, after proper consultation, a Code of Claimants' Rights to govern its relationship with claimants under the Act. It was also required to ensure the delivery of service that is consistent with the aims of the Act. The Code of Claimants' Rights came into force on 1 February 2003.[51]

There are rights to review and appeal the Corporation's decisions. The Corporation has exercised its right under the Act to form a subsidiary company, Dispute Resolution Services Ltd, to carry out the review functions under the Act. Both the Corporation and the claimant have a right of appeal and those appeals are heard in the District Court.

The compensation available to persons who have cover includes:

(a) Rehabilitation, which comprises treatment, social rehabilitation, and vocational rehabilitation;

(b) First week compensation;

(c) Weekly compensation;

(d) Lump sum compensation for permanent impairment;

(e) Funeral grants, survivors' grants, weekly compensation for the spouse, children and other dependants of a deceased claimant, and child care payments.

First week compensation arising from work-related injuries is payable by the employer. The Corporation pays other entitlements. The reintroduction of lump sum compensation applies only for claims arising after 1 April 2002.

14.5 Occupiers' liability for accidents on their property

An occupier of premises has a duty of care to those who come onto those premises. In New Zealand, the Injury Prevention, Rehabilitation, and Compensation Act 2001 diminishes the importance of this duty by placing a bar on the ability to sue for compensation for personal injuries. Occupiers remain liable for property damage.

14.5.1 Who is an occupier?

Occupiers are those who have control of the premises, and they may or may not be the owner:[52]

"Wherever a person has a sufficient degree of control over premises that he ought to realise that any failure on his part to use care may result in injury to a person coming lawfully there, then he is an 'occupier' and the person coming lawfully there is his 'visitor' and the 'occupier' is under a duty to his 'visitor' to use reasonable care ... [an occupier need not] have entire control over the premises. He need not have exclusive occupation. Suffice it that he has some degree of control."

---

51 The following link provides access to the Code and is provided in several languages: www.acc.co.nz/ publications/index.htm?ssBrowseSubCategory=Code%20of%20claimants%20rights.

52 *Wheat v E Lacon & Co Ltd* [1966] AC 552, 578, per Lord Denning.

Management of health service facilities would normally be the occupiers of the premises. However, this quote could lead to the argument, for example, that a nurse or pathologist is in control of premises in which they work to the extent that they have knowledge of, and can affect the safety of, those premises. The duty of care normally owed to one's "neighbour" (see 8.4) would apply as well. These two duties merge into the test of foreseeability of harm.

14.5.2   Standard of care of an occupier

Until 1962 the standard of care an occupier owed to those entering premises depended on the category of the entrant. An entrant may be:

- *An invitee* or person with whom the occupier has a special relationship based on pecuniary, material or business interests. It would include consumers, their visitors (although there is some difference of opinion about this),[53] messengers, florists, chaplains, or those delivering goods. It would exclude those entering purely for social reasons, or reasons unrelated to the occupier's enterprise;

- *A licensee* or person who enters with the occupier's permission, express or implied,[54] and who does so for reasons other than those mentioned above. This would include those entering to use amenities, as a short cut in their journey, or travelling salespeople seeking to become invitees by creating a business relationship;

- *An entrant as of right* or person who enters under some statutory power, not requiring the occupier's permission to do so. Such people are inspectors, meter readers, police under warrant or other powers of entry, and the general public where the premises (or part of them) are open to the public. Only designated areas of a public hospital are available to all-comers;

- *A trespasser* or person who enters premises without the occupier's express or implied consent. Where there is no forewarning that a person is forbidden entry, and there is access to the premises, for example a gate or path, a person may enter. They are a licensee that is, has implied permission until told clearly they are not welcome. They then immediately become a trespasser and should exit with reasonable speed. If not, the occupier can use reasonable force to eject her/him. There is an implied consent for members of the public to enter business premises such as hospitals, nursing homes, and clinics, and be in areas clearly designated for public access.

An occupier does not have to make premises totally safe but they must prevent harm to those entering, or warn of dangers that a person entering would not be expected to know about. These categories originally carried different duties of care. However, it can be seen that this leads to difficulty and even absurdity in the attempt to determine the status of an entrant. As suggested above, an entrant may change categories at any moment, for example when told that they are welcome or unwelcome, or when friendly discussions become more seriously businesslike. Divisions between the categories are also hard to draw, for example does a dinner party for a friend who happens to be a more senior colleague, which may lead to favourable references or promotion, make her/him an invitee or a licensee?

---

53   *Western Suburbs Hospital v Currie* (1987) 9 NSWLR 511.
54   Where occupiers know (or ought to know) of someone's use of their premises and do nothing about it, the person becomes a licensee. In one case the continual crossing of an owner's paddock as a short cut by people, which the owner tolerated, resulted in their becoming licensees and the subjects of a duty of care by him.

The Occupiers' Liability Act 1962 abolished distinctions between categories of lawful visitors, and it extended a common duty of care to all entrants on to land. However, trespassers are outside the scope of the Act. The duty imposed by the Act is to take "such care as in all the circumstances of the case is reasonable to see that the visitor will be reasonably safe in using the premises for the purpose for which he or she is invited or permitted to be there".[55]

The categories described above are no longer relevant to the fact that a duty of care may exist to the entrant upon the premises but they will remain important in determining the foreseeability of harm and the reasonable chance of prevention from harm.

14.5.3 Position of trespassers

If an occupier is aware of the likelihood of trespassers, for example children who play in hospital grounds, the occupier is held to foresee that they may be harmed by dangerous structures or other hidden dangers.[56] The occupier is also obliged to make sure the trespassers know of the danger; that is, tell them or make the premises inaccessible.

An occupier has a duty to warn visitors of any hidden danger in the property, for example faulty steps that they know about, and which is likely to cause harm if no warning is given. Thus, slippery floors in a home or a hospital can result in liability to a consumer, visitor, or community nurse (all invitees). Of course a community nurse who is aware that a client being visited is not well enough to keep the premises in good order would be foolish to trust in this legal principle and not keep a reasonable lookout for danger. They could be considered contributorily negligent, and partially responsible for any harm suffered. As all premises are different, people enter them, to some extent, at their own risk.

14.5.4 Community workers and occupiers' rights

The legal principles involved here affect everyone, but are most relevant to health practitioners who are community workers, such as district nurses or mental health key workers or visiting GPs. The owner or anyone in legal occupation of premises, for example a tenant or a friend using someone's home, has the right to control who is allowed on those premises. This means that anyone may be excluded from premises for any reason, unless they have a statutory right to enter, such as a police officer with a warrant.

The owner or occupier of property is entitled to enjoyment of that property to the exclusion of all others, unless permission is granted to others to enjoy its use as well.

Where premises have an unlocked gate or door or an unobstructed path and there is no sign to indicate that a person is not welcome, a health practitioner may enter the premises and take reasonable steps to determine whether they are welcome. They may remain until permission to stay is revoked. Where there is no indication on whether the health practitioner is welcome, they are there on sufferance as a licensee. If welcomed, the practitioner remains a licensee unless it is established that there is a benefit to be gained by the occupier. The practitioner then becomes an invitee. If unwelcome, the practitioner becomes a trespasser, and the occupier has the right to either remove her/him with

---

55   Occupiers' Liability Act 1962, section 4(2).

56   *Southern Portland Cement v Cooper* [1974] AC 623.

reasonable force, or sue. Health practitioners may be confronted by refusal of entry by an occupier where someone on the premises, for example a sick or abused child, needs care.

If the occupier asks the practitioner to leave the premises, even though someone (the occupier or any other person) needs care, the practitioner should consider leaving. Where there is concern that people might suffer as a result, however, the practitioner may remain or consider notifying relevant authorities, or take some other form of useful action. In either case, care should be taken for the safety of all concerned.

14.6 Further reading

A Scott-Howman and C Walls, *Workplace Stress in New Zealand*, Wellington, Brookers, 2003.

Todd et al, *The Law of Torts in New Zealand* (5th ed), Wellington, Brookers, 2009.

Department of Labour publications:

- Best Practice Guidelines for Occupational Safety and Health in Dental Therapy;
- Practice Guidelines for the Provision of Facilities and General Safety in the Healthcare Industry;
- Health and Safety Guidelines for Home-Based Health Care Services;
- Managing the Risk of Workplace Violence to Healthcare and Community Service Providers.

Chapter 15

REGISTRATION, NOTIFICATIONS OF COMPETENCE, HEALTH AND DISCIPLINE

CLARE PRENDERGAST AND SUE JOHNSON

Contents

15.1   Introduction

As a New Zealand citizen the health practitioner is subject to the laws of the land. However, the special occupation of a health practitioner gives rise to legal considerations peculiar to that occupation. As with most other professions, for example law and accountancy, each health profession is self-regulated. Professions set their own standards, and put in place mechanisms to ensure that health practitioners are competent and fit to practise those professions.[1] Many health professions are subject to the Health Practitioners Competence Assurance Act 2003 (HPCA Act).

---

1   Health Practitioners Competence Assurance Act 2003, section 3.

The HPCA Act repealed the 11 existing regulatory statutes dealing with health professionals. The HPCA Act covers health professionals, who are termed health practitioners and who are registered with an authority.

Regulatory authorities were continued in existence for some existing regulated professions and new authorities were appointed for dentistry, midwifery, osteopathy, and pharmacy.[2]

The HPCA Act also provides for the inclusion of other health professions where the provision of health services by that profession poses a risk of harm to the public or where it is otherwise in the public interest that the profession is regulated.[3] In October 2007 the Psychotherapists Board was established to regulate psychotherapists. A number of other health professions have applied to the Ministry of Health for regulation including, amongst others, anaesthetic technicians and medical herbalists.

Health practitioners may be accountable for their professional conduct outside of professional disciplinary proceedings. This has been discussed in chapter 4.

15.2   Professional accountability

For the purpose of outlining legislation and practice in relation to the process of professional accountability, the nursing profession is chosen as a model. Other health professions, for example medicine, dentistry, physiotherapy, etc, are similar in most respects.

15.2.1   Functions of the Authorities

The functions of the Authorities appointed in respect of each health profession are to:

- Prescribe the qualifications required for scopes of practice within the profession;
- Accredit and monitor educational institutions and degrees, courses of study or programmes;
- Authorise the registration of health practitioners and maintain registers;
- Consider applications for annual practising certificates;
- Review and promote the competence of health practitioners;
- Recognise, accredit and set programmes to ensure the ongoing competence of health practitioners;
- Receive and act on information from health practitioners, employers and the Health and Disability Commissioner ("the Commissioner") about the competence of health practitioners;
- Notify employers, ACC, the Director-General of health, and the Commissioner that the practice of a health practitioner may pose a risk of harm to the public;
- Consider cases of health practitioners who may be unable to perform the functions required for the practice of the profession;
- Liaise with other authorities about matters of common interest;
- Promote education and training in the profession;
- Promote public awareness of the responsibilities of the authority;
- Exercise or perform any other functions powers and duties imposed by this Act or any other enactment.[4]

---

2   Health Practitioners Competence Assurance Act 2003, section 114.
3   Health Practitioners Competence Assurance Act 2003, sections 115 and 116.
4   Health Practitioners Competence Assurance Act 2003, section 118.

15.2.2 Composition

Under the HPCA Act the Minister must appoint between five and 14 members for each of the authorities. The membership of an authority must include two laypersons if the authority has eight or fewer members and three laypersons if there are nine or more members. The authority must have a majority of members who are health practitioners. Organisations and individuals are invited to nominate appointees. The Minster of Health appoints each member by notice published in the New Zealand Gazette (the Gazette). The aim is to achieve an experienced and balanced body that can adequately deal with the many functions of the authority to protect public safety.[5]

The Minister may also regulate to provide for the election by the profession of one or more practitioners to an authority. In 2009 the Minister decided that two members of the Nursing Council would be elected by the profession and that, by the end of 2010, three of the six professionals would be elected and three would be lay appointments. To be eligible for election or to vote, nurses must hold a current practising certificate at the time of the election and have a New Zealand address. Regulations for medical practitioners were made under the HPCA Act in 2009 for the provision of elected members in an election conducted by the authority.[6]

15.2.3 Education

Under the HPCA Act, Authorities are required to describe the contents of a profession in terms of one or more scopes of practice, and to prescribe the qualifications for each scope of practice.[7]

The qualifications may include:

- A degree or diploma from an accredited educational institution;
- Completion of a degree, course of studies, or programme accredited by the authority;
- A pass in an examination or assessment set by the authority or an approved organisation;
- Registration with an overseas organisation equivalent to the authority.

The authority is required to monitor every accredited New Zealand educational institution, and it may accredit and monitor overseas institutions.

15.2.4 Registration

The Authorities register practitioners under a scope of practice. Each authority must, by notice in *The Gazette*, describe the contents of a profession in terms of one or more scopes of practice. A scope of practice may be described in any way the authority thinks fit, including reference to a name or words, an area of science or learning, tasks commonly performed or illnesses or conditions to be diagnosed, treated, or managed.[8] The authority also has to prescribe the qualification or qualifications for every scope of practice by notice in *The Gazette*.[9] The authority is required to take into account protection of the public, and

---

5   Health Practitioners Competence Assurance Act 2003, section 120.
6   Health Practitioners Competence Assurance (Election of Members of Medical Council of New Zealand) Regulations 2009.
7   Health Practitioners Competence Assurance Act 2003, sections 11 and 12.
8   Health Practitioners Competence Assurance Act 2003, section 11.

to ensure that the qualifications do not unnecessarily restrict registration, or impose undue costs on the practitioner or public. Before the authority publishes a *Gazette* notice, it must consult with those it considers represent the view of health practitioners, and organisations affected by the proposal or whose members will be affected by the proposal.[10]

After consultation with the sector and the profession the Nursing Council prescribed four scopes of practice:

- Registered nurse;
- Enrolled nurse;
- Nurse assistant;
- Nurse practitioner.

Authorities are expected to consult and review these scopes of practice to ensure that they continue to meet the health needs of the New Zealand public. The original scopes of practice and prescribed qualifications for the eleven authorities established or continued by the HPCA Act were published in 2004.[11]

15.2.5 Requirements for registration

The authority must be satisfied that an applicant is:

- Fit for registration; and
- Has the prescribed qualifications; and
- Competent to practise.

(1) *Fitness for registration*[12]

The Authority must not register an applicant if he or she:

- Does not satisfy the authority that the applicant is able to communicate effectively for the purposes of practising;
- Does not satisfy the authority that the applicant's ability to communicate in and comprehend English is sufficient to protect the health and safety of the public;
- Has been convicted (in New Zealand or elsewhere) of any offence where the penalty is 3 months imprisonment or more, taking into account all the circumstances of the offence, including when the offence took place and whether it reflects adversely on the applicant's fitness to practise;
- Is unable to perform the functions required to practise because of a mental or physical condition (including a condition or impairment caused by alcohol or drug abuse);
- Is under investigation or the subject of professional disciplinary proceedings (in New Zealand or elsewhere) and the authority believes that the investigation or those proceedings reflect adversely on his or her fitness to practise;
- Is the subject of a disciplinary order of a professional disciplinary tribunal (in New Zealand or elsewhere) or an order of an accredited educational institution or an order

9   Health Practitioners Competence Assurance Act 2003, section 12
10   Health Practitioners Competence Assurance Act 2003, section 14.
11   *New Zealand Gazette*, 2004, Issue No 120, Notice of Prescribed Scopes of Practice and Related Qualifications for Health Practitioners, 2893.
12   Health Practitioners Competence Assurance Act 2003, section 16.

of a authority in another country and does not satisfy the authority that the order does not reflect adversely on fitness to practise; or

- The authority believes that the applicant may endanger the health and safety of members of the public.

An authority may include conditions in a practitioner's scope of practice to ensure the competent practice of that applicant. The HPCA Act does not provide for provisional or temporary registration, but enables an authority to register a practitioner with conditions included in his or her scope of practice.[13]

In order to satisfy itself that the applicant is fit for registration the Nursing Council may require a certificate of good standing (or similar) from a nominated institute or body in New Zealand or overseas. An authority may also require the applicant to pass an approved examination or assessment to ensure that the applicant is competent to practise in New Zealand and his or her ability to communicate in and comprehend English is sufficient to protect the health and safety of the public.

New Zealand applicants for registration as a nurse obtain a certificate from the head of the nursing school that they are in good standing with the school. Overseas applicants are generally required to provide a certificate of good standing from their regulatory authority.

(2) Declining registration

Once an application in the correct form that contains the information required by the Authority has been received, the Authority may register the applicant or decline registration on the grounds specified in the HPCA Act.[14]

The Nursing Council has delegated the decision to decline registration to a Committee of Council (the Registration Committee).[15] Before making a decision to decline registration the Registration Committee must provide the applicant with an opportunity to provide written and/or oral submissions in support of his or her application. An applicant who has been declined registration may apply for a review of that decision by the full Nursing Council.[16] A review looks at the information provided with the application and any written submission the applicant wishes to make. Alternatively, the applicant may appeal this decision to the District Court.[17] This right of appeal to the District Court includes decisions where the authority has declined registration, declined to issue a practising certificate, suspended registration, cancelled registration, or included or varied conditions in the person's scope of practice.[18] The appeal is by way of rehearing, and the Court may confirm, reverse or modify the decision.[19]

Case

Williams v Auckland Hospital Board, 6 March 1981 (HC)

---

13   Health Practitioners Competence Assurance Act 2003, section 22.
14   Health Practitioners Competence Assurance Act 2003, section 16.
15   Health Practitioners Competence Assurance Act 2003, Schedule 3, clause 15.
16   Health Practitioners Competence Assurance Act 2003, Schedule 3, clause 18.
17   Health Practitioners Competence Assurance Act 2003, section 106(1)(a).
18   Health Practitioners Competence Assurance Act 2003, section106.
19   Health Practitioners Competence Assurance Act 2003, section 109.

Williams was a nursing student who became involved in drug misuse. Twice he deceived his fellow nurses and used a hospital medication order form to obtain medicines for his own use.

The head of his school of nursing declined to recommend him as being of good character, and a fit and proper person to sit the State final examination. The Nursing Council would not let Williams sit State finals because of the absence of that recommendation. Williams appealed to the High Court.

This was an appeal under the previous legislation, the Nurses Act 1977. As the appeal could not be heard until after the date for the State finals, Williams was allowed to sit the examination. His papers were kept sealed until the appeal was heard. When the appeal was heard, the Judge upheld the Council's decision and the examination papers were destroyed. The Court found that although Williams was well-motivated towards a nursing career, he was not a fit and proper person to sit the State examination or, if successful, to be registered as a nurse. This was not just because of obtaining medicines for his own use, more particularly it was because of his deceiving his fellow nurses and the subsequent denials he made about what he had done.

(3) Cancellation of registration

Under the HPCA Act, an authority has the power to cancel registration if the practitioner:

- Obtained registration by a false or misleading representation, or was not entitled to be registered;[20]
- Asks for their registration to be cancelled, unless there are criminal or disciplinary actions pending against that practitioner;[21]
- Has been found guilty of one of the grounds of discipline listed and where the Health Practitioners Disciplinary Tribunal has made a disciplinary order to that effect;[22]
- Was originally registered overseas but the educational establishment granting the qualification or the overseas authority has cancelled or suspended that registration.[23]

15.2.6 Annual practising certificates

Practitioners must renew their practising certificates annually if they wish to continue practising. If they are not working, they may stay on the register but cannot practise. A Registrar on behalf of the Authority may decline to issue an annual practising certificate where there are reasonable grounds to believe that the applicant:

- Has not maintained a required standard of competence;
- Has failed to comply with a condition on their scope of practice;
- Has not completed a competence programme;
- Is unable to practise because of a mental or physical condition;
- Has not held an annual practising certificate, or lawfully practised within the 3 years preceding the application date;

---

20   Health Practitioners Competence Assurance Act 2003, section 146.
21   Health Practitioners Competence Assurance Act 2003, section 142.
22   Health Practitioners Competence Assurance Act 2003, sections 100 and 101.
23   Health Practitioners Competence Assurance Act 2003, section 147.

- Has provided information that is false or misleading.[24]

The Registrar is also able to decline to issue a certificate where there are fines or costs outstanding, following a disciplinary order.[25] The Nursing Council relies on a declaration made by the nurse on his or her application for a practising certificate that he or she has maintained the required standard of competence, and completed the required number of professional development hours and practice hours within the previous three years.

To assess the competence of registered health practitioners a random audit is completed by the regulating Authority each year. For example, the Nursing Council randomly audits 5 percent of practising nurses to assess their competence. Under section 41 of the HPCA Act recertification programmes are put in place to assist in the audit, enabling each Authority to create assessments to test the health practitioner's competence.

15.2.7 Restricted activities and unqualified providers

The HPCA Act prohibits an unqualified person from using words implying that they are a health practitioner, unless registered. It also prohibits anyone from doing anything calculated to suggest that they practise as a practitioner unless registered and hold a current practising certificate. The penalty for doing so, on summary conviction, is a fine not exceeding $10,000.[26] Prosecutions under this section are carried out by the Ministry of Health.

The HPCA Act allows the Minister of Health to declare an activity that forms part of a health service, a restricted activity, where he or she is satisfied that members of the public risk serious or permanent harm if unqualified persons perform the activity.

The list of restricted activities put in place from 1 August 2005 is as follows:[27]

- Surgical or operative procedures below the gingival margin or the surface of the skin, mucous membranes or teeth;
- Clinical procedures involved in the insertion and maintenance of fixed and removable orthodontic or oral and maxillofacial prosthetic appliances;
- Prescribing of enteral or parenteral nutrition where the feed is administered through a tube into the gut or central venous catheter;
- Prescribing of an ophthalmic appliance, optical appliance or ophthalmic medical device intended for remedial or cosmetic purposes or for the correction of a defect of sight;
- Performing a psychosocial intervention with an expectation of treating a serious mental illness without the approval of a registered health practitioner (under review);
- Applying high velocity, low amplitude manipulative techniques to cervical spinal joints.

Authorities may include an activity in a practitioner's scope of practice if that practitioner is qualified and competent to perform it. However, it is not necessary for a scope of practice to specifically refer to a restricted activity; only that the scope covers or clearly includes that activity. The penalty for an unqualified person performing such an activity is a fine not

---

24   Health Practitioners Competence Assurance Act 2003, section 27.
25   Health Practitioners Competence Assurance Act 2003, section 26.
26   Health Practitioners Competence Assurance Act 2003, section 7.
27   Health Practitioners Competence Assurance (Restricted Activities) Order 2005.

exceeding $30,000 on summary conviction.[28] A health practitioner who acts outside his or her scope of practice may be subject to proceedings initiated by his or her registration Authority.[29]

15.2.8   Fitness to practise

(1)   *Health*

The HPCA Act places a mandatory duty on the following classes of people; the person in charge of an organisation providing health services; any health practitioner; an employer of health practitioners; or a medical officer of health to notify the relevant authority if they have reason to believe that a practitioner is unable to practise because of a mental or physical condition.[30] There is also provision for any person to inform the relevant Registrar, in writing, but this is only a voluntary duty.[31] An impairment that may cause the health practitioner to be unable to perform his/her functions would include any impairment caused by drug or alcohol abuse. The HPCA Act also requires the person in charge of an educational programme to notify the relevant authority when they have reason to believe that a student would be unable to practise because of a mental or physical condition.[32]

The different Authorities have an ability to delegate these inquiries to a committee.[33] An example of this is the Nursing Council, which has delegated the function of considering nurses with a health condition to a Health Committee. This Committee does not have a disciplinary function. Its role is to protect the public by ensuring that nurses are fit to practise, recognising that these nurses are unwell and may require supervision and counselling to be able to return to safe practice. Through its Health Committee, the Nursing Council may require a medical examination of a nurse's mental or physical fitness to practise. This examination and report is paid for by the Council. The relevant Authority must endeavour to consult with the practitioner about the medical practitioner who is to conduct the examination.

Many nurses referred to the Health Committee have a mental health or alcohol or drug abuse problem. Physical reasons that may mean a health practitioner is not fit to practise might include contracting an infectious disease that would endanger the health of consumers or a serious head injury that impacts on his or her fitness to practise. The Authority must provide the practitioner with a reasonable opportunity to make written and/ or oral submissions on the notification and the medical report obtained. The Authority may suspend the practitioner's registration, or order that conditions be included in the scope of practice where it is satisfied that the health practitioner is unable to perform the functions required for the profession because of a mental or physical condition.[34]

The HPCA Act also allows an Authority to suspend, or place conditions on a practitioner's practice *before* receiving the medical report or receiving submissions from the practitioner for 20 working days and then a further 20 days, if required for the completion of a medical

---

28   Health Practitioners Competence Assurance Act 2003, section 9.
29   Health Practitioners Competence Assurance Act 2003, section 100.
30   Health Practitioners Competence Assurance Act 2003, section 45.
31   Health Practitioners Competence Assurance Act 2003, section 45(3).
32   Health Practitioners Competence Assurance Act 2003, section 45(4) and (5).
33   Health Practitioners Competence Assurance Act 2003, Schedule 3.
34   Health Practitioners Competence Assurance Act 2003, section 50.

examination.[35] This interim suspension can be imposed without notice on the health practitioner, but must be in writing, contain the reasons it is based upon and be signed by the Registrar.

(2) Competence

The HPCA Act also allows an Authority to review the competence of a practitioner where it has received notification that a practitioner may pose a risk to the public by practising below the required standard of competence.[36] There is a voluntary obligation on health practitioners to notify the Authority of any competence issue regarding another health practitioner if they think that particular person poses a risk of harm to the public.[37] A mandatory obligation exists for the Health and Disability Commissioner and Director of Proceedings to notify the Authority where they have reason to believe that a practitioner may pose a risk of harm to the public; and on an employer where an employee has been dismissed or resigned for reasons relating to competence.[38] Competence reviews can only be carried out if the practitioner holds a current practising certificate.

These reviews can be delegated and an example of how this may be done is shown by the Nursing Council. It has formed competence review panels made up of two nurses and a layperson. The Nursing Council requires one of the nurses to be practising in the same general area of practice as the nurse being reviewed. The competence process is not a disciplinary process and is intended to protect the public by determining whether a practitioner requires further education or supervision to practise safely. If after carrying out a review, the authority believes that the practitioner fails to meet the required standard of competence, it must make orders that the practitioner undertakes a competence programme, include conditions in the practitioner's scope of practice, order that the practitioner sits an examination or assessment and/or order that the practitioner is counselled or assisted in practice.[39]

If there are reasonable grounds for believing that the practitioner poses a risk of serious harm to the public the relevant authority may suspend the practitioner or change the health services a practitioner is permitted to perform or include a condition in the practitioner's scope of practice, pending a review.[40] This may only occur after providing the practitioner with a reasonable opportunity to make written or oral submissions on the proposed suspension.[41] Any such suspension may continue until the review has been completed or the practitioner has passed any examination or assessment ordered by the authority.

15.2.9 Discipline — complaints

Whenever an authority receives a complaint alleging that the practice or conduct of a practitioner has affected a health consumer, that authority must refer the complaint to the

---

35   Health Practitioners Competence Assurance Act 2003, section 48.
36   Health Practitioners Competence Assurance Act 2003, section 34.
37   Health Practitioners Competence Assurance Act 2003, section 34(1); this voluntary notification is contrasted with the mandatory notification required under section 48 where a health practitioner reasonably believes another health practitioner is unfit to practise because of a physical or mental condition.
38   Health Practitioners Competence Assurance Act 2003, section 34(2) and (3).
39   Health Practitioners Competence Assurance Act 2003, section 38.
40   Health Practitioners Competence Assurance Act 2003, section 39(2).
41   Health Practitioners Competence Assurance Act 2003, section 39(3).

Health and Disability Commissioner.[42] The Commissioner may either investigate the complaint or may refer it to the relevant authority when it appears that the complaint relates to competence or fitness to practise, or where the appropriateness of the practitioner's conduct may be in doubt.[43]

The Health and Disability Commissioner may deal with complaints occurring before 1 July 1996 (when the Code of Health and Disability Services Consumers' Rights came into force), where the action would have been a ground for bringing disciplinary proceedings against the practitioner at the time of the conduct.[44]

An Authority is not able to take any disciplinary action against a practitioner (except interim suspension or a restriction on practice pending investigation or prosecution) until the Commissioner notifies the authority that:

- He or she is not investigating the matter;
- The complaint or matter has been resolved;
- The matter is not to be referred to the Director of Proceedings; or
- The Director of Proceedings informs the authority that he or she has decided not to lay charges.[45]

Where the Commissioner investigates and believes that there has been a serious breach of the Code of Health and Disability Services Consumers' Rights,[46] the Commissioner may refer the matter to the Director of Proceedings (DoP).[47] The DoP will decide whether to institute proceedings, either under the HPCA Act and/or before the Human Rights Review Tribunal.[48]

An aggrieved person may also bring proceedings before the Human Rights Review Tribunal, where the Commissioner has found a breach of the Code of Health and Disability Services Consumers' Rights, but has not referred the matter to the Director of Proceedings, or the Director of Proceedings declines or fails to take proceedings before the Human Rights Review Tribunal.[49]

15.2.10   Professional conduct committees

The Professional Conduct Committee's (PCC's) role is to investigate complaints, convictions, or information they have received that raises questions about a practitioner's conduct or safety to practise.[50] An authority may also appoint a PCC to consider cases of a particular class.[51] For instance the Nursing Council has appointed a PCC to consider convictions; nurses practising without practising certificates; and nurses alleged to be

---

42   Health Practitioners Competence Assurance Act 2003, section 64.

43   Health and Disability Commissioner Act 1994, section 34(1)(a).

44   Health and Disability Commissioner Act 1994, section 40.

45   Health and Disability Commissioner Act 1994, section 42.

46   The Code of Health and Disability Services Consumers' Rights (reproduced in Appendix 4) is in the Schedule to the Health and Disability Commissioner (Code of Health and Disability Services Consumers' Rights) Regulations 1996.

47   Health and Disability Commissioner Act 1994, section 45(2)(f).

48   Health and Disability Commissioner Act 1994, section 49.

49   Health and Disability Commissioner Act 1994, section 51.

50   Health Practitioners Competence Assurance Act 2003, power of appointment is through schedule 3, clause 16 and 17; and at section 68 is the power for the Authority to refer to the PCC.

51   Health Practitioners Competence Assurance Act 2003, section 71(1).

practising outside their scope of practice. A PCC must consist of two health practitioners and one layperson, and they may include an authority member.[52] A PCC may appoint an investigator to investigate complaints and collect information required by the PCC. It may also appoint a legal adviser to advise it on matters of law, procedure and evidence.[53]

The PCC must provide the practitioner and the complainant with a reasonable opportunity to make written or oral submissions on the complaint and the information gathered during its investigation before making any decision on the complaint.

Within 14 days of completing an investigation, a PCC must make recommendations or determinations.[54] It may recommend that the authority:

- Review the practitioner's competence;
- Review the practitioner's fitness to practise;
- Review the practitioner's scope of practice;
- Refer the matter to the police;
- Counsel the practitioner.

A PCC may also determine that:

- No further action will be taken on the matter;
- A charge is to be brought against the practitioner before the Health Practitioners Disciplinary Tribunal (HPDT);[55]
- The complaint is submitted to conciliation.

15.2.11   Suspension of practice — discipline

If, during an investigation into a nurse's conduct or a conviction, a PCC has reason to believe that a nurse's practice poses a risk of serious harm to the public, it must inform the Council of that belief and the reasons for it. It may either recommend that the Authority suspend a practitioner's practising certificate or the inclusion of one or more conditions in the practitioner's scope of practice.[56] The Health and Disability Commissioner or Director of Proceedings may also recommend interim suspension or a restriction on practice on the same grounds.[57] The Council must offer the nurse a reasonable opportunity to provide written and oral submissions before any orders are made.[58]

15.2.12   Health Practitioners Disciplinary Tribunal

Under the HPCA Act a disciplinary hearing is conducted before the Health Practitioners Disciplinary Tribunal. The charge against the practitioner will be laid by the Director of Proceedings or a PCC. The HPDT is made up of a Chairperson or deputy chairperson; who must be a barrister or solicitor of the High Court who has practised for no less than

---

52   Health Practitioners Competence Assurance Act 2003, section 71(1) and (2).
53   Health Practitioners Competence Assurance Act 2003, section 73.
54   Health Practitioners Competence Assurance Act 2003, section 80.
55   Health Practitioners Competence Assurance Act 2003, section 84; discussed at 15.2.12.
56   Health Practitioners Competence Assurance Act 2003, section 79.
57   This was inserted through an amendment Act in 2003 to the Health and Disability Commissioner Act 1994; see sections 39 and 45.
58   Health Practitioners Competence Assurance Act 2003, section 69(3)(b).

7 years; three professional peers of the practitioner whose conduct is under consideration; and a layperson.[59]

It is important to note that the primary intention of disciplinary procedures carried out under registration legislation is neither to punish those involved (the function of criminal law), nor to compensate those harmed (the function of civil law). The primary intention of disciplinary procedures is the protection of the public, and the setting and maintenance of standards within the profession. Any practitioner who is being dealt with under disciplinary provisions, or who is the subject of a competency review or a review of fitness to practise, is advised to seek legal or professional advice.

(1)   Disciplinary action

The grounds[60] for professional misconduct which result in disciplinary action are because of an act or omission that:

- Amounts to malpractice or negligence in relation to the practitioner's scope of practice at the time of the conduct; or
- Has brought or is likely to bring discredit to the profession practised at the time of the conduct.

Additional to these grounds are the following:

- A court conviction (in New Zealand or elsewhere) that reflects adversely on a practitioner's fitness to practise;
  - Must be in relation to an Act listed;[61] or
  - For an offence punishable by a term of imprisonment of 3 months or longer;
- Practising without holding a current practising certificate;
- Practising outside a practitioner's scope of practice;
- Failing to comply with conditions included in his or her scope of practice; or
- Breach of an order of the HPDT.

The first step the HPDT takes is to consider whether the acts or omissions of the practitioner constitute malpractice or negligence. There is no guidance in the Act to these terms, so the HPDT must look to the common law.[62] For some clarity of these concepts Gendall J discussed them in *Collie v Nursing Council of New Zealand*,[63] where his Honour said:[64]

> "Negligence or malpractice may or may not be sufficient to constitute professional misconduct and the guide must be standards applicable by competent, ethical and responsible practitioners and there must be behaviour which falls seriously short of that which is to be considered acceptable and not mere inadvertent error, or oversight or for that matter carelessness."

---

59   Health Practitioners Competence Assurance Act 2003, section 86.
60   Are set out in full at section 100 of the Health Practitioners Competence Assurance Act 2003.
61   Health Practitioners Competence Assurance Act 2003, section 100(2)(a).
62   For a discussion on negligence and the common law, see chapter 8.
63   *Collie v Nursing Council of New Zealand* [2001] NZAR 74.
64   *Collie v Nursing Council of New Zealand* [2001] NZAR 74, para 21.

So the test as to what constitutes negligence requires a determination of whether or not the practitioner's conduct fell below the standard of care, which would reasonably be expected of a practitioner in the circumstances of the person appearing before the HPDT. Whether or not there has been a breach is judged by the standards of the practitioner's colleagues, of what is thought to be reasonably competent care in the circumstances. Malpractice is usually considered to be immoral, illegal or unethical conduct or neglect of professional duty.

The second step of the process requires the HPDT to be satisfied that the practitioner's acts or omissions require a disciplinary sanction. The Nursing Council has listed examples of conduct that might attract a disciplinary sanction in its Code of Conduct. This list includes accepting gifts from patients, misappropriating money or entering into a sexual or inappropriate relationship with a patient or ex-patient. For further examples the HPDT publishes its decisions on its website.[65] The following cases can be used to illustrate conduct that was found to amount to professional misconduct and court convictions that reflect adversely on fitness to practise.

Case

Ongley v Medical Council of New Zealand [1984] 4 NZAR 369

A doctor wrongly issued medical certificates that were relied on by the Accident Compensation Corporation ("ACC") to pay earnings-related benefits to a patient of the doctor. At the time that at least two of the certificates were issued, the doctor knew the patient was in hospital suffering from terminal cancer. When asked for an explanation by ACC, the doctor failed to respond. He was found guilty of professional misconduct and referred to the Court.

Jeffries J said when speaking of professional misconduct:[66]

> "The test the Court suggests ... could be formulated as a question. Has the practitioner so behaved in a professional capacity that the established acts under scrutiny would be reasonably regarded by his colleagues as constituting professional misconduct? ... The test is objective and seeks to gauge the given conduct by measurement against the judgment of the professional brethren of acknowledged good repute and competency."

Case — negligence

Henry 22/Nur05/07D

Decision dated 14 December 2005

Mr Henry was a registered nurse who was the director and manager of a nursing and homecare agency. An elderly patient was discharged from hospital into his care on 14 August 2000. The patient died on 19 November 2001 from complications arising from septic pressure sores and anaemia. Mr Henry was charged with and pleaded guilty to failing to ensure that an adequate nursing care plan was undertaken, documented or reviewed, failing to ensure that adequate measures were taken to prevent pressure areas, or to treat

---

65   www.hpdt.org.nz.
66   *Ongley v Medical Council of New Zealand* [1984] 4 NZAR 369, 374-375, per Jeffries J.

the patient's pressure sores or ischaemic ulcer, and failing to ensure appropriate staffing levels to ensure adequate nursing care.

The HPDT found that Mr Henry had failed to ensure that caregivers received the appropriate training in dementia and challenging behaviour or adequate training in the prevention of pressure sores. The HPDT held that, viewed cumulatively, Mr Henry's actions and omissions justified a finding of professional misconduct on the grounds of negligence and was severely below the standards expected of a nurse in his circumstances. The HPDT ordered that Mr Henry should not practise as a sole practitioner in the aged care sector and he should undergo a competence assessment and satisfy the Nursing Council that he was safe and competent to practise in any area and that these conditions would be in force for 3 years from the date he returned to practice. Mr Henry was not ordered to pay a fine or costs because of his financial circumstances. Publication was ordered on the HPDT website and in *Kai Tiaki: Nursing New Zealand*.

Case — malpractice

Taylor v Nursing Council of New Zealand

Noted *Kai Tiaki: Nursing New Zealand*, September 1997

Mr Taylor dragged a consumer into a room yelling, "Stop your f***ing noise." He also dragged another consumer with his fist against their ear, administered medication to a consumer in an unreasonable way and pushed another one in such a manner that the consumer lost his footing and his toenail was ripped off. He threatened a consumer with a pocketknife, but believed he did this in a joking manner. He verbally abused other staff while in a primary nursing role.

The Nursing Council held that dragging, pushing, and abusing of consumers was improper treatment amounting to malpractice, and that the threatening with a pocketknife amounted to professional misconduct, notwithstanding that Mr Taylor believed he was joking. His attitude towards the staff fell below the standard of conduct reasonably expected of a psychiatric nurse.

The Nursing Council said Mr Taylor had a responsibility to provide a safe environment for staff and vulnerable consumers in a challenging practice area. It found him guilty of three charges of professional misconduct. The Nursing Council removed Mr Taylor's name from the register of psychiatric nurses, and ordered him to pay $17,500 in costs. He was ordered to return to the Council Registrar every certificate and badge issued to him under the Nurses Act 1977.

Case — negligence and malpractice

Check v Nursing Council of New Zealand

20 January 1999, noted *Kai Tiaki: Nursing New Zealand*, September 1999

Mr Check, an enrolled nurse, took observations of a consumer admitted with pneumonia. He noticed a slightly raised temperature, increased pulse, and an oxygen saturation of 75 percent. He did not record the oxygen saturation. Two hours later he found the consumer collapsed, with no radial pulse. He did not commence resuscitation or initiate emergency protocols. The consumer was later declared dead.

The Council found that Mr Check had been negligent in not appreciating the significance of the two previous recordings, and in not seeking advice on the apparent inconsistency with his assessment that the consumer was not compromised by the oxygen saturation recording. The Council also found him guilty of malpractice, in that his actions were unethical and likely to bring discredit on the profession because he did not follow standard procedures on discovering a collapsed consumer. He also did not make adequate assessment of the consumer's condition, and he unilaterally made the decision not to initiate resuscitation procedures. His name was removed from the roll, and he was ordered to pay 40 percent of the total costs of $26,662.24.

Case — discredit to the profession

Collie v Nursing Council of New Zealand [2001] NZAR 74

In September 1999, the Nursing Council found Ms Collie guilty of professional misconduct for accepting gifts totalling $25,000 from an elderly couple. The couple had met the nurse in her capacity as a practice nurse. The Council considered that she had breached the principle that consumers should have trust and confidence in the nursing profession. As a result, the nurse's actions had discredited the nursing profession, and her name was removed from the register. Ms Collie appealed to the High Court.

The High Court dismissed her appeal, and held that conduct that brought discredit on the nursing profession did not have to be conduct during the actual practice of the profession. The conduct had to bear a direct relationship to the nurse's professional behaviour or standing, or have some connection with her professional position. Justice Gendall also held that a nurse was in a fiduciary relationship with a patient, and the essence of such a relationship was the vulnerability of the patient to whom the nurse owed special duties.

Another nurse employed in the same practice, Raelene Moore, accepted gifts of money from the same couple amounting to $20,000. She was found guilty of professional misconduct and her name was removed from the register. Her appeal to the High Court was also dismissed. Gendall J held that the duty to the patient arose "out of the professional responsibility to advance the patient's interests and not to harm them."[67]

Case — court conviction

Martin 45/Nur05/19P

Decision dated 16 June 2006

Ms Martin was convicted in the High Court on 26 August 2003 of one charge of attempted murder laid pursuant to section 173 of the Crimes Act 1961 after deliberately administering an overdose of Morphine to her terminally ill mother. She had been sentenced to 15 months imprisonment. She was charged by a PCC with having a conviction that reflected adversely on her fitness to practise.

The HPDT found that her conviction did reflect adversely on her fitness to practise and that her actions in attempting to end the life of her mother were not compatible with the fundamental obligations of all health practitioners to respect the sanctity of life. The HPDT noted that Ms Martin's actions were premeditated and clearly designed to cause her mother's

---

67   *Moore v Nursing Council of NZ* 18/12/00, Gendall J, HC Wellington AP100/00, 13.

premature death. Ms Martin was trusted to administer appropriate levels of morphine to achieve pain relief and to carry out the responsibility of being her mother's primary caregiver because of her nursing experience. The HPDT noted that Ms Martin had shown no remorse, steadfastly believed she had done the right thing and asserted she would offend in the same way if placed in the same circumstances. After taking into account mitigating circumstances the HPDT decided not to cancel her registration but to include conditions in her scope of practice. One of those mitigating circumstances was the HPDT's view that Ms Martin had already been appropriately punished by society and saw no reason to impose a penalty designed to punish.

The PCC appealed the penalty to the High Court. The High Court determined that although cancellation or suspension of registration may punish a practitioner it is ordered for the primary purpose of protecting the public and community by upholding professional standards, deterring other practitioners and ensuring that only those who are fit to practise are entitled to do so. The High Court ordered that Ms Martin's registration be cancelled.[68]

The case of *Duncan v Medical Practitioners' Disciplinary Committee* (see 9.4.6) illustrates that a practitioner can be guilty of professional misconduct even if they have good intentions, and what amounts to professional misconduct is behaviour that is not approved of by other practitioners.

The case of *Oborn v Nursing Council of NZ* shows conduct that was not regarded as professional misconduct.

Case

Oborn v Nursing Council of New Zealand 1/7/93, Greig J, HC Wellington AP174/191

Oborn was charged with leaving her post for 15 minutes without ensuring another nurse would cover for her. She also failed to record a post-operative consumer's temperature and pulse readings. No harm came to any consumers. Oborn was found guilty by the Nursing Council of professional misconduct by malpractice. She was censured and ordered to pay costs. She appealed against the Council's findings.

Her appeal was successful. Greig J in the High Court held that the incidents that gave rise to the charge of professional misconduct were both isolated, with no continuing conduct. His Honour stated that while they amounted to improper practice, they did not amount to professional misconduct.

Under the HPCA Act these charges would probably be considered under the competency section and her practice would have been reviewed by a competency panel — this was not available under the Nurses Act 1977.

(2) Penalties

Each case is decided on its own facts and circumstances. It does not always follow that the more serious the consequences of the action for the patient, the more serious the outcome will be for the practitioner. The actions taken by the practitioner after the initial incident is also relevant to the penalty, for example if the practitioner does not tell the truth or deliberately conceals the truth or falsifies the truth, the penalty is more likely to be severe.

---

68   *PCC v Martin* 27/2/07, Gendall J, HC Wellington CIV-2006-485-1461.

The penalties that may be ordered where the HPDT has found the conduct proven and that the conduct amounts to professional misconduct (or one of the other grounds set out in the Act) are as follows:

- The registration of the practitioner is cancelled;
- The registration of the practitioner is suspended for a period not exceeding 3 years;
- The practitioner may only practise with conditions as to employment, supervision or other conditions specified for a period not exceeding 3 years;
- Censure;
- Payment of a fine not exceeding $30,000 (fines cannot be imposed for court convictions);
- Payment of part or all of the costs of the Commissioner or PCC's investigation, prosecution and the HPDT hearing.[69]

Where the practitioner's registration is suspended he or she is permitted to practise again once the period of suspension has elapsed. Where the HPDT has made an order cancelling the registration of a practitioner it may impose one or more conditions the practitioner must satisfy before applying for reinstatement to the register. Those conditions may require the person to complete a course of education, or undergo medical examination or treatment or a psychological or psychiatric examination, counselling or therapy, attend a course of treatment for alcohol or drug abuse or any other condition designed to address the issue that gave rise to the cancellation. The conditions regarding medical or psychiatric examination or treatment/therapy cannot be imposed unless the person consents to those conditions.[70] It is worth reiterating that the object of removing a practitioner's name from the register is not to punish the practitioner, but to protect the public, which promotes the primary purpose of the legislation. Where the Human Rights Review Tribunal has heard the matter, and is satisfied on the balance of probabilities that there is a breach of the Code of Health and Disability Services Consumers' Rights, it may:[71]

- Declare that there has been a breach of the Code;
- Order the practitioner to restrain from continuing or repeating the breach;
- Order the practitioner to redress the loss or damage suffered by the complainant;
- Order payment of compensation (damages) to the complainant;[72]
- Order any other relief as it thinks fit.

(3) *Appeal from HPDT decisions*

Any order made by the HPDT may be appealed to the High Court by the practitioner, or by the Director of Proceedings, or the PCC, whichever laid the charge.[73] The appeal is by way of rehearing — a reconsideration of the facts.[74] The Court may confirm, reverse, modify, or substitute the decision with any order that the body appealed against could have made.[75] Though there is provision for an appeal the courts are reluctant to change decisions

---

69   Health Practitioners Competence Assurance Act 2003, section 101.
70   Health Practitioners Competence Assurance Act 2003, section 102.
71   Health and Disability Commissioner Act 1994, section 54.
72   Health and Disability Commissioner Act 1994, section 57.
73   Health Practitioners Competence Assurance Act 2003, section 106(2).
74   Health Practitioners Competence Assurance Act 2003, section 109(2).
75   Health Practitioners Competence Assurance Act 2003, section 109 (3).

made by a specialist tribunal. It is arguable that the likelihood of the court changing a decision or order in favour of the appellant is minimal.

Checklist

Typical steps of disciplinary procedures for practitioners

- The complaint or information is brought to the Authority's notice, and referred to the Health and Disability Commissioner.
- The Commissioner investigates the matter, or refers that matter to the Authority for investigation.
- If the Commissioner reaches an opinion that there is a serious breach of the Code of Health and Disability Services Consumers' Rights, the matter is referred to the Director of Proceedings.
- The Director of Proceedings reviews the evidence, calls witnesses, considers the practitioner's defence, and may bring a prosecution before the HPDT and/or the Human Rights Review Tribunal. If a PCC appointed by the Authority has conducted the investigation, that PCC lays the charge before the HPDT.
- If the practitioner is found guilty by the HPDT, it takes disciplinary action, either by:
    - Censuring the practitioner or;
    - Placing the practitioner on conditional practice, for example supervision or;
    - Cancelling or suspending the practitioner's registration or;
    - Fining the practitioner or;
    - Ordering that the practitioner pay all or a proportion of the costs of the investigation, prosecution and hearing.
- The practitioner, Director of Proceedings or PCC may appeal the HPDT decision to the High Court.
- An appeal will result in the Council's decision either being:
    - Upheld;
    - Reversed;
    - Substituted with another decision.
- The practitioner, Director of Proceedings or PCC may appeal this decision on a question of law to the Court of Appeal.

15.3   Further reading

M E Burgess, *A Guide to the Law for Nurses and Midwives*, Auckland, Pearson Education New Zealand Limited, 2002.

Kai Tiaki: Nursing New Zealand, the official journal of the New Zealand Nurses' Organisation.

P D G Skegg, R Paterson, *Medical Law in New Zealand*, Wellington, Thomson Brookers, 2006.

See also www.hpdt.org.nz for HPDT decisions and the websites of the regulatory authorities.

Chapter 16

CRIMINAL ACCOUNTABILITY

SUE JOHNSON AND REBECCA KEENAN

Contents

16.1   Introduction

Health practitioners may be accountable for their professional conduct through prosecution for breach of the criminal law. Criminal law deals with wrongs committed against the community as a whole, rather than against individuals. This is reflected in the fact government officers, such as the police, Inland Revenue Department, or Crown Prosecutor prosecute offenders. The interest of criminal law is in the punishment of the perpetrator, not in the fate of the victim, who must pursue remedies in civil actions. This lack of interest has been mitigated somewhat by the development of accident compensation legislation and the Victims' Rights Act 2002 (see 3.2.1).

The basic outline of a criminal action and the proof required for a conviction is dealt with at 3.2.6. It is important to have this in mind when considering more specific actions under criminal law.

It should be noted that in criminal law, assault and battery are generally grouped together, both in statute and in case law, and called "assault". To avoid confusion in this chapter the term "assault" includes the concepts of both assault and battery.

Apart from its general application to all people with its prohibition of interference with another person's physical integrity (for example, homicide and assault), or property (for example, forms of theft and fraud), criminal law involves some offences that are of particular interest to health practitioners. These are:

- Murder (see 16.4.2);
- Manslaughter (see 16.4.3);
- Intentionally accelerating a consumer's death (see 16.5.4);
- Negligently accelerating a consumer's death (see 16.5.4(4));
- Failing to provide the necessaries of life (see 16.5);
- Aiding and abetting suicide (see 16.5.4(7));
- Procuring an abortion (see 16.5.6);
- Female genital mutilation (see 16.6);
- Offences related to infectious diseases (see 16.10.3);
- Medicines offences (see 16.10.5);
- Assaulting a consumer (see 16.8);
- Acting improperly in respect of human remains (see 16.9).

There are also some legal duties affecting health practitioners, including the duty:

- To provide the necessaries of life(16.5);
- Of persons in charge of dangerous things (16.5);
- To avoid omissions dangerous to life (16.5).

Before these are dealt with, however, some important principles of criminal law will be considered.

16.2   Principles of criminal law

16.2.1   Criminal offences must be established by law

New Zealand has a number of Acts that establish criminal offences and penalties for them.[1] As New Zealand inherited the common law from England, we also inherited our initial set of criminal offences and defences. Now all offences and some defences are statute-based, but the common law continues to be a source of other defences.[2]

There is nothing inherent in an act that makes it criminal. Crimes are defined as such by law and established by statute, as it is considered important that where one may be deprived of liberty and property and subject to a criminal record, offences must be clearly established and available for all to identify.

Criminal law comes from the establishment of two kinds of offences. First, there are the general catalogues of criminal offences, for example in the Crimes Act 1961 and Misuse of Drugs Act 1975. Those in the Crimes Act are dealt with in this chapter. For offences against the Misuse of Drugs Act, see chapter 10. Secondly, there is a body of offences created in the multitude of Acts, regulations, and bylaws, which are not part of the criminal law as such, but do attract penalties. These offences are an adjunct to the main thrust of the legislation in which they appear, and generally are not considered bad enough to classify the offender as "criminal", even though the penalties might be quite severe. They may cover anything from using a hose at prohibited times to polluting water, or from misusing computer information to parking in the wrong place.

16.2.2   Elements of an offence

It should be borne in mind that in most cases the prosecution (for example, Crown, police etc) must prove all the elements of the offence beyond reasonable doubt (see 16.2.6). There are a number of elements common to most offences:

*   The actus reus — the physical act, such as killing, taking property, driving too fast. This also includes the identification of the accused as the offender.
*   The mens rea — the mental component, for example *intending* to kill or *wilfully* taking property or *recklessly* driving too fast.

16.2.3   Actus reus

This is the element in the offence that requires the prosecution to prove the alleged offender has performed some conduct, or been in a certain situation. With some offences, a result must also be proved, for example that a death has occurred. When both conduct and a result are required to be proved, the prosecution must also prove the conduct caused the result, for example that shooting the victim (conduct) caused his death (result).

(1)   *The act must be voluntary*

One cannot be found guilty of an act over which one does not have physical control. In these cases, there is no actus reus because the person did not "do" the act — it just

---

1   The main ones are the Crimes Act 1961, Misuse of Drugs Act 1975, Summary Offences Act 1981, and Land Transport Act 1998.
2   Crimes Act 1961, section 20.

happened. However, where an accidental action cannot be isolated from other voluntary actions, one cannot plead involuntariness.

Case

Ryan v The Queen (1967) 121 CLR 205; [1967] ALR 577 (HCA)

Ryan took a loaded and cocked rifle into a service station, pointed it at an employee, Taylor, and demanded money, which he was given. About to tie Taylor up, Ryan was startled by Taylor's sudden movement. Ryan's finger involuntarily squeezed the trigger and Taylor was killed. Ryan argued that he should not be found guilty of murder because the squeezing of the trigger was involuntary. He was found guilty by the Supreme Court of New South Wales, appealed unsuccessfully to the Court of Appeal, and applied for leave to appeal to the High Court.

The Australian High Court said the death was caused by a combination of events that was carried out with the intention to rob. All actions, including the loading and cocking of the gun, were as much a part of causing death as was the actual pulling of the trigger. This final act could not be isolated from the earlier ones, and so it could not be held to have been purely accidental and unforeseen.

(2) Omission

Generally, it has been held that a crime cannot be committed by omission, that is, by a person's failure to act. This is not always the case, however, for failure to act may make a person open to conviction for aiding and abetting, thus as a party to the offence.[3]

Case

R v Coney (1882) 8 QB 534

Coney was in a crowd, watching an illegal prize-fight. He took no part in it, nor in the management or encouragement of it. He said and did nothing. He was convicted of assault as a party, although the jury found that he did not aid or abet the fight.

Hawkins J stated:[4]

> "It is no criminal offence to stand by, a mere passive spectator of a crime, even of a murder. Non-interference to prevent a crime is not itself a crime. But the fact that a person was voluntarily and purposefully present witnessing the commission of a crime, and offered no opposition to it, though he might reasonably be expected to prevent and had the power so to do, or at least to express his dissent, might [provide prima facie evidence] … that he wilfully encouraged and so aided and abetted."

In some cases an omission can satisfy the actus reus element and give rise to criminal liability where a person has failed to fulfil a duty of care. There is a legal duty of care in section 155[5] of the Crimes Act 1961, which declares that those who undertake to administer surgical or medical treatment are under a duty to have and use "reasonable" knowledge, skill, and care. The standard of care is that of a reasonable health professional in those

---

3   Crimes Act 1961, section 66(1). For a person to be guilty of aiding and abetting there must be an offence committed by the principal offender: *R v Bowern* (1915) 34 NZLR 696.
4   *R v Coney* (1882) 8 QB 534, 557-558.
5   Duty of persons doing dangerous acts.

circumstances. If there is a major departure from that standard, the person is criminally responsible for the consequences of omitting, without lawful excuse, to discharge that duty.

16.2.4   Mens rea

This is the mental element in the offence requiring the prosecution to prove that the accused carried out the actus reus with a particular state of mind, for example intending to do it, being reckless about it, or being wilful, knowing, or negligent. Each offence describes, either expressly or impliedly, the state of mind that the prosecution must prove was present. For example, for a charge of murder, the prosecution must prove the accused *intended* to kill, or was *reckless* as to whether death ensued.

In the case of a breach of the legal duties of care imposed by the Crimes Act 1961,[6] the prosecution must prove gross negligence, that is, that there was a major departure from the standard of care expected of a reasonable person to whom that legal duty applies in those circumstances (16.5.4(4)).[7]

While a major departure from the standard of care is regarded as gross negligence, for criminal liability there must also have been an untoward consequence of the major departure. If death ensues, a person may be charged with manslaughter. This is often termed "medical" manslaughter. In rare cases if more than gross negligence can be proved, for example if intention or recklessness can be proved, there may be liability for murder.

16.2.5   Concurrence of actus reus and mens rea

Generally, an accused will not be liable for an offence, unless the required mens rea was present at the same time as the actus reus. Exceptions to this general rule are continuing offences, the one transaction approach, and the causation approach.

(1)   *Continuing offences*

Continuance of an accidental act becomes a criminal act if the prosecution can prove the accused had the requisite mens rea at any time during the continuance of the act.

Case
Fagan v Commissioner of Metropolitan Police [1969] 1 QB 439; [1968] 3 WLR 1120; [1968] 3 All ER 442
Fagan accidentally drove his car onto the foot of a police officer who was directing him how to park it. The police officer said several times "Get off, you are on my foot". Fagan indicated that he could wait, and after the police officer repeated his order several times, slowly turned on the ignition and moved the car. The Court was undecided as to whether the initial driving onto the officer's foot was a deliberate act, but the accused argued that he had not intended any assault when he actually drove onto the officer's foot. Therefore, he argued, the required mens rea (intention) was absent at this time. Later, when he had that required mens rea he did not carry out any act, and thus he could not be convicted of assault. He was convicted and appealed.

---

6   Section 156 of the Crimes Act 1961 imposes a duty to take reasonable precautions and care on persons responsible for dangerous things. Section 157 imposes a duty on persons who undertake to do an act to carry it out if not doing so will endanger life.

7   Crimes Act 1961, section 150A.

The Court decided that where an act was a continuing one, there did not need to be mens rea at the inception of that act, so long as at some stage while it was ongoing, the accused formed the mens rea. He was convicted.

(2) One transaction approach

In some cases, if the prosecution can prove that a series of acts by the accused can be regarded as one act (that is, "one transaction") and there was the required mens rea present during any one of those acts, the accused will be held to have had the requisite mens rea for the whole transaction.

Case

Thabo Meli v R [1954] 1 WLR 228; [1954] 1 All ER 373 (PC)

Four people formed a plan to kill the victim, then fake an accident. One of them struck the victim with intention to kill, and then all of them, believing the victim was dead, pushed him over a cliff. The victim was still alive, and eventually died of exposure at the foot of the cliff. It was argued that there was no mens rea for murder at the time of pushing the victim over the cliff.

The Privy Council held that it was "impossible to divide up what was one transaction in this way". The requisite mens rea had been present during the transaction, and that was sufficient for the four people to be convicted of murder.

(3) Causation approach

In some cases, a series of acts cannot be regarded as one transaction. However, if the required mens rea for one act was present and that act is an operating and substantial cause of the result, then there was the requisite mens rea for the result.

Case

R v McKinnon [1980] 2 NZLR 31 (CA)

The accused delivered a blow to the victim's head, rendering the victim unconscious. The accused did not intend to kill, but to rob. The victim died, and the immediate cause of death was due to inhalation of blood from an injury to the nose.

The Court held that where there is more than one injury to the victim, death can be said to be from the original injury if that injury is still an operating and substantial cause of the victim's death, and the immediate cause was not so overwhelming as to make the original injury merely part of the history.

16.2.6 Presumed mens rea

The definition of some offences is silent as to a mens rea element. In these cases a Court will categorise the offence. There are three categories: presumed mens rea offences, absolute liability offences, and strict liability offences. The first is *presumed* or, as it is sometimes termed, *implied* mens rea. Into this category go the offences that the Court declares must contain a mens rea element, based on the presumption that Parliament would have intended such an element to be proved before convicting a person, because of the nature of the offence and the severity of the penalty. If a person is charged with an offence that is fitted into this category by the Court, the accused must raise some evidence that they did not have a guilty mind at the time of the actus reus. The Court will then "read in" or imply into the offence a mens rea element (usually recklessness). This element must be proved by the prosecution, beyond reasonable doubt, before the accused person can be convicted.

16.2.7   Absolute liability

In other cases where the statute is silent, a Court might not presume mens rea. Instead, the Court will categorise the offence as being one of strict or absolute liability. In an absolute liability offence, a person may be found guilty even where that person did not have a guilty mind at all. Such offences require only that the person has committed the prohibited act. Their state of mind is irrelevant. The Court will decide if the offence is to be placed in the absolute liability category by looking at the wording of the offence, the penalty (which is unlikely to be one of a term of imprisonment), and the type of offence. Absolute liability usually applies to traffic offences (for example, parking or activity on licensed premises). The person charged need not even be aware that the offence has occurred.

16.2.8   Strict liability

The other possible category of silent offences is called "strict liability" offences. These are usually offences of a public welfare regulatory type, not as serious as the presumed mens rea type of offence and yet carrying a more severe penalty than the absolute liability offences. The Courts therefore consider that Parliament would not have intended a person to be able to be convicted on mere proof of the actus reus alone, and so this category is a "half-way house" between the other two categories. The prosecution has to prove the actus reus, and then the accused will escape liability only if they can prove, on the balance of probabilities, that they were not at fault. Although this has been criticised as a rejection of the fundamental principal (that it is for the prosecution to prove guilt not for the accused to prove innocence), the Courts have held that in these types of offence it is the accused who knows their own business best and is in the best position to prove there was lack of fault. Lack of fault includes acting with all due diligence. Offences such as polluting waterways or health and safety offences often fall into this category.

16.2.9   One cannot normally be vicariously guilty in criminal law

The general principle is that a person can only be found guilty of an offence they personally committed, as mens rea is normally required.

Case

R v Huggins (1730) 2 Ld Ryam 1574; 92 ER 518

In 1730 a prison superintendent, Huggins, was convicted of murder. His underling, Barnes, had placed a prisoner in a cell in conditions that eventually caused his death. Huggins was not fully aware of the conditions of the deceased's incarceration.

On appeal, the Court held that Huggins could not be found guilty because only the one who immediately does the act is guilty. If it is the act of an employee, unless it is done by the command or direction of the employer or superior, or they are an accomplice to the crime (16.2.9(3)) the latter is not guilty.

Exceptions to the general principle where an accused may be found guilty, even though they did not personally carry out the offence, are where a Court finds they are liable through:

- Others;
- Incitement, aiding, or abetting;
- Delegation.

(1) Liability through others

A person may carry out a crime through another person who does not have the appropriate mens rea. For example, a woman who wishes, with her lover, to kill her husband might deceive her children into putting poison into his drink. The woman and her lover might be found guilty of murder but the children, who unknowingly carried out the act, would not be guilty.[8]

(2) Liability through incitement, aiding, abetting — accomplices

When a person incites another to commit a crime, that person will, in most circumstances, be guilty of the completed crime as an accomplice. An accomplice to a crime assists in the event, and may be either a party who is present during the act, or an accessory that is not present during the act, but has been of assistance before or after the act. The distinction is of little comfort to the accomplice, however, because parties whether present during the act or accomplices before the act are liable to the same punishment as a principal offender.[9] The means for inciting this are not important; rather the Court is interested in determining whether the accused sought to reach and influence the mind of the other person towards commission of a crime. It is not essential that the person who incites the other is successful in so doing: where the inciter does not reach the mind of the prospective incitee (for example, a letter goes astray), the offence will be one of attempted incitement. Where the incitee's mind is reached, but not influenced enough to commit the offence, the incitement has still occurred. The intentions and actions of the person inciting are vital to the proof of the offence, regardless of any action or otherwise of the prospective perpetrator.

(3) Delegation

The case of R v Huggins[10] (see 16.2.9) dealt with this situation, but there the Court held that delegation did not exist. However, where one delegates responsibilities to an employee that involve certain statutory offences, such as the serving of liquor to underage drinkers, one remains accountable for the breach of responsibility by that employee. It is suggested that where a person delegates a function, and that function is bound by a licence, the person cannot complain that they were unaware of the delegate's knowingly carrying on the enterprise in contravention of the licence (it has yet to be considered by the Courts whether this would apply to a health facility, especially with the handling of drugs).

---

8   *Female Poisoner's Case* (1634) Kelyng 53; 84 ER 1079. This ancient principle has been adapted into legislation regarding, for example, murder.

9   Sections 66 and 71 of the Crimes Act 1961 (respectively party liability and accessory after the fact).

10   *R v Huggins* (1730) 2 Ld Ryam 1574; 92 ER 518.

16.2.10   The precise act for which one is charged must have been committed

A person cannot be found guilty of an offence, unless the act specified in the charge against her/him has been committed. Even where one believes one is committing a crime, and intends to do so, if the act has not been established by law to be criminal, there is no crime.

Case

Haughton v Smith [1975] AC 476; [1973] 3 All ER 1109 (HL)

Smith was convicted of attempting to handle stolen goods. In fact, the goods had been seized by the police and were in their custody in a van. Smith, ignorant of the police involvement, met the van and arranged for disposal of the goods. The Crown conceded that the goods were, while in the custody of police, no longer "stolen goods" in the strict sense of that term, when the alleged offence was committed. Smith appealed on the ground that as the goods were no longer stolen, he could not be convicted of attempting to handle stolen goods.

The House of Lords agreed. Lord Morris said: "the presence of a guilty mind does not transform what a man actually does into something that he has not done."[11]

Viscount Dilhorne added:[12]

> "A man cannot attempt to handle goods which are not stolen. A man taking his own umbrella from a club thinking it the property of someone else does not steal. His belief does not convert his conduct into an offence if his conduct cannot constitute a crime."

Criminal law cannot be retrospective, that is, any offence for which a person is charged must have been established as such before the commission of the act.

16.2.11   Ignorance of the law is no excuse

Conversely, it must be noted, where a person carries out a criminal act but does not know that it is prohibited, they may nevertheless be found guilty, for intention goes to the action not the guilt. Ignorance of the law is no defence.

16.2.12   Presumption of innocence

(1)   *"Innocent until proven guilty"*

All readers are probably familiar with the aphorism that one is "innocent until proven guilty". This is one of the fundamental principles of criminal law, and leads to the rule that the prosecution must prove the guilt of the accused — the accused does not have to prove anything.

In the courtroom the accused attempts to throw doubt on the prosecution's case, in adducing evidence, but at no stage, with the exceptions below (16.2.12(2)) does the accused have to present proof of not having committed the offence. Thus, if Nurse Jane Doe is accused of murder, it is not her lawyer's task to prove she did not commit the offence; it

---

11   *Haughton v Smith* [1975] AC 476; [1973] 3 All ER 1109 (HL), 501;1122.
12   *Haughton v Smith* [1975] AC 476; [1973] 3 All ER 1109 (HL), 506;1126.

is the prosecution's task to prove she did. The proof must be strong enough to convince a jury *beyond a reasonable doubt* that Doe was the person who caused the death and that she had intended to do so. Her lawyer's task is to produce evidence that will cause the jury to have *reasonable doubt* as to her guilt. Even if the members of the jury believe on the balance of probabilities that Doe committed the murder, unless they are convinced of her guilt beyond a reasonable doubt they must enter a "not guilty" verdict.

Case

Woolmington v Director of Public Prosecutions [1935] AC 462; [1935] 3 All ER Rep 1 (HL)

Woolmington had an argument with his wife. He told the Court that he threatened to kill himself, and produced a loaded gun. Somehow, in the ensuing activity, it went off, killing her. The jury convicted him of murder, the Judge having told them that if they were satisfied that he killed his wife, the killing was to be considered murder unless the defendant convinced them that it was something less, for example manslaughter or excusable homicide. Woolmington appealed, basing his argument on error in the Judge's instructions. The Appeal Court upheld the conviction, but the case went to the House of Lords, where the conviction was quashed.

The House of Lords, in one of the most quoted statements of criminal law, stated that:[13]

> "Throughout the web of English Criminal law one golden thread is always to be seen, that it is the duty of the prosecution to prove the prisoner's guilt subject to … the defence of insanity and subject also to any statutory exception. If, at the end of and on the whole of the case, there is a reasonable doubt … whether the prisoner killed the deceased with a malicious intention, the prosecution has not made out the case and the prisoner is entitled to an acquittal."

(2)   *Exceptions*

Exceptions to this principle, that is, situations where the accused has the onus of proof, include:

- Strict liability offences (see 16.2.8), where the accused must prove on the balance of probabilities that they lacked fault;
- Where an accused offers the defence of insanity (16.3.1);
- Where a statute expressly provides for this.

16.3   Defences to a criminal charge

A successful defence either justifies the wrongful act or excuses the actor (the accused). For example, an insanity defence will excuse the accused, whereas the defence of acting in self-defence justifies what the accused did.

A defence to a criminal charge may, if successful, lead to a finding of "not guilty" (for example, where a jury finds a person insane at the time of an alleged offence, they are to find the person "not guilty on the grounds of insanity"). These defences are absolute defences compared with a defence that provides partial relief only in that it does not acquit.

---

13   *Woolmington v Director of Public Prosecutions* [1935] AC 462; [1935] 3 All ER Rep 1 (HL); 481-482, 8, per Viscount Stanley LC.

For example, a successful defence of provocation does not acquit a person of a murder charge but reduces it to one of manslaughter.

16.3.1 Insanity

Section 23(1) of the Crimes Act 1961 provides a presumption of sanity that must be rebutted by the accused for a defence of insanity to succeed. The defence, as stated, is always an absolute defence, in that a person who successfully pleads insanity is not guilty of the offence on that ground. This does not mean that person is allowed to go free, but instead of being convicted and punished for a crime, they will be dealt with according to their illness. The defence has the onus of proving insanity on the balance of probabilities. In practice, insanity is mainly used as a defence to a charge of homicide, and the general result is that the accused will be kept in a psychiatric hospital, as a special patient.

(1) *M'Naghten rules*

The rules relating to establishment of insanity were formulated in 1843 by the House of Lords, who had to decide how to establish whether one Daniel M'Naghten, charged with murder, was insane according to law. He had attempted to shoot the Prime Minister, Sir John Peel, but mistakenly shot his secretary. M'Naghten was allegedly suffering delusions of persecution. The Lords decided that jurors should be instructed that every person is to be presumed sane, and to possess normal responsibility for their crimes, unless the contrary is proved to the jury's satisfaction.

To establish insanity, the accused must prove on the balance of probabilities that at the time of committing the act they had a disease of the mind. They also have to prove that the disease of the mind caused her/him to have such a defect of reason that they either did not know the nature and quality of the act (that is, they did not know what they were doing) or, if they did know, that they did not know that what they were doing was wrong (for example, knowing that they were killing someone but wrongly believing it was in self-defence or that the person was a wartime enemy).

The wording of the rules, including the requirement that the person be suffering from a "disease of the mind", has caused much confusion and legal argument, and also liberal and loose application of the rules.[14] Lawyers argue that they are an incomplete formulation, and do not take account of the diversity of situations that may arise, and psychiatrists argue that they are based on faulty principles of psychology, omitting important conditions from which one might suffer.[15]

---

14   R Roulston, *Introduction to Criminal Law in New South Wales* (2nd ed), Sydney, Butterworths, 1980.

15   C R Williams, *Brett and Waller's Criminal Law*, Australia, Butterworths, 1983, page 683; P Gillies, *Criminal Law* (3rd ed), Sydney, Law Book Co, 1993, page 257. Gillies states (at page 248): "The insanity defence has in a number of jurisdictions been supplemented in more recent times by the statutory defence of diminished responsibility. This defence may only be pleaded in relation to a charge of murder. In not being [as is the defence of insanity] confined to disruption of the cognitive process resulting from disease of the mind (it is formulated in terms of a mental impairment of D's mental responsibility for D's conduct, resulting from abnormality of mind), [diminished responsibility] does, however, help to suggest the terms in which a more broadly based statutory defence of mental illness might be cast."

16.3.2 Diminished responsibility

This defence is not available in New Zealand,[16] although it is in England and some Australian States, where it is a defence to a charge of murder. Diminished responsibility generally requires proof by the accused of an abnormality of the mind that had substantially impaired the accused's mental responsibility at the time of the offence. If this defence was available in New Zealand it could well go some way towards resolving some of the problems posed by the M'Naghten rules.

Insanity is an exception to the rule that the accused does not have to prove innocence. Other defences, which are raised to discredit the prosecution arguments, follow.

16.3.3 Automatism

This defence is used where a person acts through their body, but without its control by their mind. It gives to someone who is relying on the fact that at the time they were incapable of knowing the nature of the act, but who does not fit the criteria of insanity, the chance of a "not guilty" verdict.

Automatism is a temporary condition of mind, that may have one of many causes (which must be external rather than internal), and results in a person carrying out acts of which they are totally unconscious.

It may be drug-induced, for example a hypoglycaemic episode caused by too much insulin or the result of injury (for example, concussion):[17]

> "The jury might not accept the evidence of a defect of reason from a disease of the mind, but at the same time accept the evidence that the prisoner did not know what he was doing. If the jury should take that view of the facts they should find him not guilty."

It has been held that a self-induced incapacity will not excuse a person, nor will one which could have been reasonably foreseen as the result of an action or omission.

Case

R v Quick [1973] 3 All ER 347 (Eng CA)

Quick was a nurse who suffered from diabetes, requiring regular doses of insulin. On the morning in question he turned up to work having taken the prescribed insulin, but no food and some alcohol, something he knew was dangerous. He later assaulted a patient and, on trial for assault, adduced evidence that at the time he was suffering from hypoglycaemia, causing him to be unconscious of his acts. He was convicted and appealed to the above Court.

---

16   There is academic comment that judicial interpretation is allowing an emergence of this defence but within of the defence of provocation. See *Principles of Criminal Law* (2nd ed), Wellington, Brookers, 2002, 334.

17   *Bratty v A-G (Northern Ireland)* [1963] AC 386, 403, per Lord Lilmuir. For a good introductory discussion of automatism, see R Roulston, *Introduction to Criminal Law in New South Wales* (2nd ed), Sydney, Butterworths, 1980, page 99; and G Bennett and B Hogan, "Criminal law, criminal procedure and sentencing" [1989] All ER Annual Review 94.

The Court of Appeal held that whatever the malfunctioning of his mind, it was caused by an external factor, not a disease of the mind, so the jury should consider automatism, not insanity. However, the Judges also said that events that could be foreseen by the accused as arising from his act or omission, such as hypoglycaemia from failing to have regular meals while taking insulin, may not excuse him: the jury would have to consider how much he could have foreseen and decide his responsibility. This defence of automatism failed and his appeal was dismissed.

(1)   Intoxication and automatism

The response in New Zealand to the question of responsibility for crimes committed while under the self-induced influence of alcohol relates to the defence of automatism, but intoxication has never been held to be a defence in itself.

Case

R v Kamipeli [1975] 2 NZLR 610 (CA)

Kamipeli was charged with murder. He had been drinking large amounts of beer and had hit and kicked the victim, who later died in hospital. Kamipeli was convicted, but appealed on the ground that the jury had been misdirected by the Judge regarding the accused's defence of intoxication. The Judge had misdirected the jury that Kamipeli was drunk, and that the onus was on the prosecution to prove that he was capable of forming the intent to murder.

The Court of Appeal held that intoxication was not a defence in itself. It could only be so if it amounted to insanity or automatism. The Court held that the onus is on the prosecution to prove that the accused intended to kill, even though he was drunk. A new trial was ordered, at which Kamipeli was found guilty. Therefore, the question for the Court is not, was the accused *capable* of forming the required intent, but *did* the accused form the required intent?

Case

Burnskey v Police (1992) 8 CRNZ 582

Burnskey had been drinking since 9.20 am on the day in which he indecently assaulted a 13-year-old girl at Trentham Railway Station on a train.

It was accepted by the Court that for the last 14 years, alcohol had played a large part in Burnskey's life and had affected him adversely. He became "very, very intoxicated" when drinking, and his unacceptable behaviour in Hutt Valley hotels had led him to acquire the nickname of "Nuisance".

The medical evidence for the accused was given by Dr Marks who testified that it was possible that Burnskey was in a state "of what we would medically call automatism" at the time of the acts complained of. However, the Court found Burnskey guilty and he was convicted. Burnskey's appeal was allowed as it was held by the Court of Appeal that the prosecution had not proved that he acted with full knowledge and intent.

However, in that case, self-induced intoxication was held to amount to a defence of automatism, as the Court found that Burnskey also had a brain injury from birth, which, combined with the alcohol, caused a disassociated state. Elizabeth MacDonald has questioned this decision.[18]

16.3.4　Compulsion

Compulsion, or duress as it was called at common law, is a defence to a criminal charge and is provided for in section 24 of the Crimes Act 1961. However, that section also provides a list of offences to which the defence is not applicable:

- Treason;
- Communicating secrets;
- Sabotage;
- Piracy and piratical acts;
- Murder and attempt to murder;
- Wounding with intent;
- Injuring with intent to cause grievous bodily harm;
- Abduction;
- Kidnapping;
- Robbery;
- Aggravated robbery;
- Arson.

To all other offences the defence is available, and will be successful if it is shown that the accused, at the time of the offence, believed a threat by another that death or grievous bodily harm would be unlawfully inflicted on someone, usually herself/himself. The defence is not available to any party to an offence who knowingly exposed herself/himself to a risk of being threatened. In addition, the threat has to be operational at the time of the offence. There is no requirement that the prosecution proves that the accused should have tried to escape or have taken the first opportunity to seek help from the threatened danger. However, this consideration may be relevant to whether the threat was operational at the time of the offence.

16.3.5　Self-defence

Self-defence may be offered as a defence to a criminal charge in some circumstances.[19] It is the commission of an offence undertaken to preserve one from threatened harm by another.

Self-defence may be so well balanced that the action taken precisely prevents the harm (called here "reasonable self-defence") or it may be excessive. What is necessary for the defence to succeed is that the accused only used such force as was reasonable in the circumstances. However, although the proportion of force used should be weighed against the force threatened, it is recognised that the force used may be more than appears reasonable in the courtroom so allowance must be made for the heat of the circumstances.

Case

R v Kerr [1976] 1 NZLR 335 (CA)

18　"Acquittal for the intoxicated automaton? Case notes on Burnskey v Police" [1993] NZLJ 44.
19　Section 48 of the Crimes Act 1961.

Kerr approached four men, including one he knew was a member of a rival gang. He was carrying a knife, which he said was for his protection. Three of the four men ran off, but the fourth aimed a blow at Kerr with his fist. Kerr hit back with the hand with the knife in it, and the fourth man died. Kerr argued that he was acting in self-defence.

Richmond J reminded the Court that if a person in a moment of unexpected anguish had only done what he honestly and instinctively thought was necessary, that would be potent evidence that only reasonable defensive action had been taken.

The Court held that a defence would fail only if the prosecution proves beyond reasonable doubt that the accused did not act in self-defence. The case was retried, as the defence of self-defence had not been presented to the jury.

16.3.6   Provocation[20]

Provocation was not a defence to any offence other than murder, and could only reduce the charge to one of manslaughter if it was successfully pleaded. It did not acquit.

Provocation was defined by Devlin J in 1949:[21]

"[It] is some act, or series of acts, done by the dead man to the accused, which would cause in any reasonable person, and actually causes in the accused, a sudden and temporary loss of self-control, rendering the accused so subject to passion as to make him or her for the moment not master of his [sic] mind."

The defence was provided for in section 169 of the Crimes Act 1961 and required that a person loses self-control and that the provocation must come from or be attributable to the accused's victim. The test for a jury is whether the accused herself/himself lost control and whether a reasonable person would have lost control when so provoked. When deciding this, a jury must take into account any peculiarities or characteristics of the accused that would have made the provocation be felt more keenly. A successful plea of provocation will reduce a murder charge to one of manslaughter.

The rationale behind this defence was to allow for mitigating circumstances surrounding the offence of murder. Historically murder had a mandatory punishment, which was initially death and on repeal of this, life imprisonment. As it was mandatory there was no room for discretion at the time of sentencing and so the defence was available to be raised at the time of trial.

In 2002 there was a change to the Sentencing Act,[22] which allows the judge to use his/her discretion if a sentence of life imprisonment would be *manifestly unjust*, in the circumstances of the case. This change coupled with two recent cases[23] in New Zealand that have received adverse publicity in the use of the defence of provocation, were behind the current government's push to amend the Crimes Act 1961 and repeal the defence of provocation.

---

20   This statutory defence was successfully repealed in December 2009 and it also abolished any residual common law defence available; Crimes (Provocation Repeal) Amendment Act 2009.

21   R v Duffy [1949] 1 All ER 932.

22   See section 102.

23   R v Weatherston (see sentencing decision: R v Weatherston 15/9/09, Potter J, HC Christchurch CRI-2008-012-137) and R v Ambach 10/7/09, Winkelman J, HC Auckland CRI-2007-004-027374.

For offences other than murder, provocation cannot be raised as a defence, but can be a mitigating factor at sentencing. A plea of mitigation is made after conviction, and is an argument for lenient treatment by the Judge in sentencing. Matters that do not excuse the defendant or justify their act, but have worked unfairly to her or his disadvantage, either in regard to the actual offence or the personality of the accused, and which therefore in the name of justice should be taken into account, are raised at this point. They may include such matters as emotional or economic hardship, abuse as a child, etc.

16.4 Substantive offences

16.4.1 Culpable homicide

Homicide is the killing of one human being by another. It may be legally justified, for example:

- War;
- Execution as the result of a conviction where this is prescribed;
- Self-defence.

Where a killing is not legally justified it is termed culpable homicide.

Culpable homicide is the unlawful killing of another person. It may be murder or manslaughter. It is provided for in Part 8 of the Crimes Act 1961. Culpable homicide may be murder or manslaughter.

Homicide is culpable:[24]

> "When it consists in the killing of any person—
> "(a)   By an unlawful act; or
> "(b)   By an omission *without lawful excuse* to perform or observe any *illegal duty*; or
> "(c)   By both combined … ." (Emphasis added.)

16.4.2 Murder

Culpable homicide is murder[25] where the offender means to cause the death of the person, or where the offender means to injure the person, knowing that death is likely and is reckless whether death ensues or not.

The common law has a rule that where death occurs after one year and a day of the injury, a charge of murder cannot be laid. This is because of difficulty in proving cause. This rather arbitrary rule has been adopted in New Zealand. However, with the development of better means for identifying the causes of death, and the recognition that actions may cause death more than a year later (an example is deliberately exposing a person to a lethal disease with a long incubation period), some overseas jurisdictions have abolished the "year and a day" rule.

The penalty for murder is life imprisonment. Except in the case of infanticide, culpable homicide not amounting to murder is manslaughter.[26]

---

24   Crimes Act 1961, section 160.
25   Crimes Act 1961, sections 167 and 168.
26   Crimes Act 1961, section 171.

16.4.3　Manslaughter

Manslaughter[27] is also an unlawful causing of the death of another. If a person unlawfully causes someone's death with no intention to kill or no recklessness as to whether death will ensue where the injury they cause her/him is likely to result in death, then they will not have murdered because the requisite mens rea will not have been present at the time of the killing. Such an unlawful killing will be manslaughter. It is technically called "involuntary manslaughter" as opposed to "voluntary manslaughter", which is committed by a person who had the requisite mens rea for murder but has a successful defence of provocation so that the charge has been reduced from murder to manslaughter (see 16.3.6).

The penalty for manslaughter is anything up to life imprisonment. Life imprisonment is the maximum penalty, but a good plea in mitigation may result in the imposition of a significantly reduced penalty. In some cases persons found guilty of manslaughter have been discharged without conviction.

The victim of homicide must be a human being, generally defined at common law as any being having been born by being completely extruded from the body of its mother and having an independent existence in the sense that it does not derive its power of living from its mother. Statutory law, however, does not require independent existence or severing of the umbilical cord.[28]

This means that the killing of a foetus (abortion) or unborn child (16.5.6) or a child in the process of being born may be subject to different considerations.

16.4.4　Infanticide

Infanticide is the killing of a child by its mother who is suffering from the consequences of its birth or lactation subsequent on it.[29]

16.5　Legal duties

Section 160 of the Crimes Act 1961 refers to "legal duties". Anyone who, without legal excuse, omits to perform a specified legal duty may be liable to a charge of culpable homicide. The Act sets out a number of legal duties, of which the following may apply to individual health service practitioners:

- A person in charge of another person who cannot provide himself or herself with the necessaries of life has a duty to provide that person with the necessaries of life.[30]

Case
R v LauFau [2001] NZLJ 82
This case concerned a child who had a cancerous tumour on his leg. His parents had a legal duty to provide him with the necessaries of life. They were informed

---

27　Crimes Act 1961, section 171.
28　Crimes Act 1961, section 159.
29　Crimes Act 1961, section 178.
30　Crimes Act 1961, section 151.

> that if they did not seek medical treatment for it he would die. Instead the parents used prayer and the child died six months later.

The parents were found guilty of neglecting their child and failing in their legal duty to provide the necessaries of life. A sentence of imprisonment was handed down but because of the circumstances of the case Potter J suspended the sentence as there was little chance of reoffending.

- There is a duty (except in case of necessity) to have and to use reasonable knowledge, skill, and care in administering surgical or medical treatment.[31]
- Persons in charge of or who have under their control dangerous things have a duty to take reasonable precautions against, and to use reasonable care to avoid, such danger.[32]
- If a person undertakes to do any act and omitting to do that act is or may be dangerous to life, they have a duty to avoid such omissions.

Until recently, the standard of care required for persons performing specified legal duties was not high. In a number of cases, the Courts held that doctors whose mere negligence had resulted in patients' deaths had omitted to perform or observe legal duties and were guilty of manslaughter.

Case

R v Yogasakaran [1990] 1 NZLR 399

Yogasakaran was an anaesthetist who was attending a patient who had undergone surgery but had developed complications. Yogasakaran went to administer dopram — he withdrew a drug from a draw and administered it. Instead of administering dopram he gave dopamine, which proved fatal in the circumstances. He was convicted of manslaughter and appealed this decision.

The Court of Appeal held that there was no special protection for doctors — ordinary negligence needed to be proved beyond reasonable doubt. A person who is in charge of a thing that may endanger life if care is not taken owes a duty to exercise reasonable skill and care. They found that a reasonable doctor in these circumstances would check the label before administering the drug — appeal dismissed.

Now, in respect of the specified duties, the omission or neglect must be "a major departure from the standard of care expected of a reasonable person to whom that legal duty applies in those circumstances."[33] The Court of Appeal in *Yogasakaran* required ordinary negligence to be proved but the requirement of a major departure imposed by s150A points towards gross negligence, a higher standard. It is arguable then, that if applied to the circumstances of Yogasakaran's the departure would not be a *major* departure and his conviction would have been quashed.

16.5.1 Act or omission is cause of death

It is not an excuse to say that the consumer was dying of something else and the practitioner's act or omission was not the cause of death. Section 164 provides:

---

31 Crimes Act 1961, section 155.
32 Crimes Act 1961, section 156.
33 Crimes Act 1961, section 150A.

"Everyone who by any act or omission causes the death of another person kills that person, although the effect of the bodily injury caused to that person was merely to hasten his death while labouring under some disorder or disease arising from some other cause."

This section applies in cases where a consumer is dying and their life is abruptly ended by administering a drug, withholding medication, or switching off a life support system.

16.5.2   Consumer cannot consent to homicide

Nor is it an excuse if the consumer requested or consented to an act done with the intention of ending the consumer's life.[34]

16.5.3   Where treatment causes death

If a person causes dangerous bodily injury to another and the injured person receives medical treatment applied in good faith and then dies as a result of the treatment, the law presumes that the cause of death was the initial injury.[35] The person who caused the initial injury will be regarded as having killed the person.

16.5.4   Fact situations

There are a number of situations where a practitioner may risk being charged with murder or manslaughter. Usually, they are variations of those examples set out below.

(1)   *Pain relief*

"Consumer is dying and in extreme pain. The practitioner administers a drug to relieve the pain, knowing that it may also hasten the consumer's death."

Generally, in this situation, there should be no criminal law consequences. In *R v Adams (Bodkin)* Devlin J instructed the jury as follows:[36]

"If the first purpose of medicine, the restoration of health, can no longer be achieved, there is still much for a doctor to do, and he is *entitled to do all that is proper and necessary to relieve pain and suffering, even if the measures he takes may incidentally shorten life.*" (Emphasis added.)

This principle is known as the doctrine of double effect. It safeguards a practitioner who, in accordance with what is accepted good medical practice, administers drugs to relieve pain and suffering. "Good medical practice" is discussed at 16.5.4(8) in the context of taking consumers off life support systems. One of the key aspects is adhering to "the prevailing medical standards, practices, procedures and traditions which command general approval within the medical profession."[37] In the present situation, it may, for example, be good medical practice to administer a drug that is recognised for its pain relieving qualities. It would not be good medical practice to administer a drug that relieves pain only by killing the consumer.

---

34   Crimes Act 1961, section 63.

35   Crimes Act 1961, section 166.

36   *R v Adams (Bodkin)* [1957] Crim Law Rev 365 (CCC).

37   *Auckland AHB v A-G* [1993] 1 NZLR 235, 251, per Thomas J.

(2) Hastening death

The consumer is in extreme pain and pleads with the practitioner to administer a drug to "put an end to it all".

If the practitioner administers a drug or does some other positive act with the purpose of ending the consumer's life, they may be liable to a murder charge. It is no defence that the act was done with the consumer's consent.[38]

In *R v Cox*,[39] an elderly woman who was terminally ill and in extreme pain asked Dr Cox to end her suffering by killing her. Dr Cox administered a lethal dose of potassium chloride, which has no curative properties. The woman died almost immediately. Dr Cox was charged with attempted murder and convicted. In summing up to the jury, Ognall J said that it is never lawful to use drugs with the primary purpose of hastening the moment of death. The House of Lords endorsed his Honour's comments in *Airedale NHS Trust v Bland*,[40] although their Lordships were troubled by the illogicality of distinguishing in law between a positive act of killing (administering a drug) and a passive act (withdrawal of life-sustaining treatment).

Dr Cox was charged only with attempted murder. The prosecution generously took the view that the cause of death may have been the illness from which she was suffering. As a result, the Judge had a wide discretion in imposing penalty and was able to take into account mitigating factors. Dr Cox did not go to prison and was able to resume his medical practice. It would be unwise for any practitioner to assume that in New Zealand in a similar situation the outcome would be the same. In all circumstances, a practitioner should follow the dictates of good medical practice.[41]

(3) Consumer refuses treatment

The consumer refuses to undergo medical treatment. The practitioner complies and, as a result, the consumer dies.

Every competent adult has the right to refuse treatment, and is endorsed by section 11 of the New Zealand Bill of Rights Act 1990, which provides that: "Everyone has the right to refuse to undergo any medical treatment." A practitioner who complies with a competent consumer's refusal to undergo medical treatment should not be liable to criminal consequences.

The situation may be different if the consumer is a child, generally this right is not extended to children and their choice to refuse treatment will be overridden either by their parent or the court as legal guardian. Or if the consumer is not competent to make such a decision, or, if they are competent, makes the decision without having been fully informed as to the consequences. The doctor may be in breach of the duty under section 151 of the Crimes Act 1961 to provide the necessities of life (paragraph 16.5) if he complies with the refusal to accept treatment. The practitioner may also be in breach of their duties under the Health Practitioners Competence Assurance Act 2003. Also there might be a breach of the Health

---

38   Section 63 of the Crimes Act 1961.
39   *R v Cox* (1992) 12 BMLR 38 (Winchester CC).
40   *Airedale NHS Trust v Bland* [1993] AC 789; [1993] 1 All ER 821; [1993] 2 WLR 316 (HL).
41   This concept is discussed in 16.5.4(8) in respect of taking a patient off a life support system.

and Disability Commissioner (Code of Health and Disability Services Consumers' Rights) Regulations 1996.[42]

(4)   *Practitioner's negligence when providing treatment*

"In the course of providing medical treatment, the practitioner's negligence results in the death of the consumer."

If the practitioner's conduct amounts to gross negligence, they may be said to have omitted without lawful excuse to have performed their legal duty under section 155 of the Crimes Act 1961 and to have thereby committed manslaughter.

Section 155 provides:

"Everyone who undertakes (except in case of necessity) to administer surgical or medical treatment, or to do any other lawful act the doing of which is or may be dangerous to life, is under a legal duty to have and to use reasonable knowledge, skills, and care in doing any such act, and is criminally responsible for the consequences of omitting without lawful excuse to discharge that duty."

If a practitioner's breach of this duty results in a consumer's death, the practitioner may be charged with manslaughter. However, a recent amendment to the Act (section 150A) provides that section 155 and other sections specifying legal duties apply only where:

"The omission or neglect is a *major* departure from the standard of care expected of a reasonable person to whom that legal duty applies in those circumstances." (Emphasis added.)

In any Court case in which a practitioner is alleged to have failed in their duty under section 155, much will depend on the evidence of that practitioner and of their peers as "expert witnesses" as to:

- The standard of care to be expected of "a reasonable person to whom that legal duty applies in those circumstances"; and
- Whether the practitioner's conduct was a "major departure" from the standard.

The words "except in the case of necessity" in section 155 are intended to cover the case of persons unqualified or insufficiently qualified, who in emergencies undertake medical or surgical treatment or the like. They are not intended to emancipate a professional medical practitioner from the exercise of reasonable professional care and skill in an emergency.[43]

(5)   *"Sanctity of life" principle*

The sanctity of life is a principle established by law.[44] It states that life has an absolute value, and one cannot dispense with a life even when it is considered an inferior one. However, there is also a right to be free from unwanted or harmful actions.[45] Active killing is forbidden, but so are omissions that adversely affect someone whose welfare is one's responsibility.[46] However, the Courts have stated that the sanctity of life principle is not

---

42   See chapter 6 (Consent).
43   *R v Yogasakaran* [1990] 1 NZLR 399, 405.
44   The prohibition of murder applies for all human beings: Z Lipman, "The criminal liability of medical practitioners for withholding treatment from severely defective newborn infants" (1986) 60 Australian Law Journal 286.

absolute and have recognised that sometimes a life may be so awful that one may be justified, at least morally, in not extending by extraordinary means what amounts to a painful and unbearable existence.[47] In *Airedale NHS Trust v Bland*[48] (16.5.4(8)). Lord Keith of Kinkel spoke for the majority when he stated the well-established legal principle:

> "The principle [of the sanctity of life] is not an absolute one. It does not compel a medical practitioner on pain of criminal sanctions to treat a patient, who will die if he does not, contrary to the express wishes of the patient. It does not compel the temporary keeping alive of patients who are terminally ill where to do so would merely prolong their suffering."

Lord Keith recognised two categories of persons where the sanctity of life principle may not apply absolutely:

- Those who do not wish to live;
- Those who are terminally ill and suffering by being kept alive.

(6)   *Consumers who do not wish to live — the right to refuse services*

A competent person has the right to refuse medical treatment and all services. This right is enshrined in the New Zealand Bill of Rights Act 1990 and Code of Health and Disability Services Consumers' Rights.[49]

The right to refuse treatment comes within the definition of choice in the Code of Health and Disability Services Consumers' Rights and all choices should be informed choices. The clinical team should provide full information about the consequences of the choice before the choice is made. Other options should also be discussed and every effort made to ensure an *informed* refusal is given.

(7)   *Assisting those who do not wish to live*

As has been stated above, a person who understands the implications of such a decision can refuse treatment necessary for the continuation of life. A person may be able to refuse treatment, but at law consent to being killed does not necessarily exonerate the perpetrator. It is an offence to aid and abet suicide.[50]

---

45   This right is protected by criminal sanctions against assault and battery (P Skegg, *Law, Ethics and Medicine: Studies in Medical Law*, Oxford, Clarendon Press, 1984, page 32ff; and C R Williams, *Brett and Waller's Criminal Law*, Australia, Butterworths, 1983, chapter 4) and civil actions available for assault and battery (J Fleming, *Law of Torts* (8th ed), Sydney, Law Book Co, 1992, chapter 2) as well as statutory provisions aimed at stopping child abuse.

46   Z Lipman, "The criminal liability of medical practitioners for withholding treatment from severely defective newborn infants" (1986) 60 Australian Law Journal 286; P Skegg, *Law, Ethics and Medicine: Studies in Medical Law*, Oxford, Clarendon Press, 1984, chapter 7.

47   That this could be acceptable at law was suggested by Templeman J of the English Court of Appeal in *Re B (a minor) (wardship: medical treatment)* [1981] 1 WLR 1421 (see 16.5.4(9)).

48   *Airedale NHS Trust v Bland* [1993] AC 789; [1993] 1 All ER 821; [1993] 2 WLR 316 (HL).

49   Section 11 of the New Zealand Bill of Rights Act 1990; Right 7(7) of the Code of Health and Disability Services Consumers' Rights. The Code of Health and Disability Services Consumers' Rights (reproduced in Appendix 4) is in the Schedule to the Health and Disability Commissioner (Code of Health and Disability Services Consumers' Rights) Regulations 1996.

50   Section 179 of the Crimes Act 1961.

Case

R v Ruscoe (1992) 8 CRNZ 68 (CA)

Ruscoe pleaded guilty in the High Court to a charge of aiding and abetting his friend, Nesbitt, to commit suicide. Nesbitt had been left with tetraplegia as a result of a work accident and wished to die. Ruscoe assisted him by feeding him sleeping and pain-killing tablets that had been prescribed for Nesbitt. He also ensured that death had taken place by placing a pillow over Nesbitt's face.

Both the Judge in the High Court and the Judges in the Court of Appeal who reduced Ruscoe's sentence from one of 9 months' imprisonment to one year's probation made passing reference to mercy killing, as though it was a separate offence. The Court of Appeal said there are very exceptional cases where a non-custodial sentence is appropriate.

The active causing of death, such as the giving of lethal treatment, could, of course, be murder.

Case

R v Stead (1991) 7 CRNZ 291 (CA)

Stead was charged with murder after stabbing his mother to death. She had told him on numerous occasions that she wanted to commit suicide, and had made previous attempts to do so. To assist her, he put her in the front seat of a car, closed the garage doors, and turned on the car's engine. When he returned to her, she was still alive. Together, both Stead and his mother tried other ways to kill her. Eventually, in desperation he stabbed her. Her consent to the killing did not exonerate Stead. He was convicted and sentenced to 3½ years' imprisonment for manslaughter. Nevertheless, the Court of Appeal made reference to mercy killing as though Stead's manslaughter of his mother was somehow a different type of offence.

Although the Court of Appeal in both these cases recognised that the defendants were motivated by compassion and that the deceased had consented, the defendants were still charged with the killings. The difference between the cases was that Ruscoe was charged and convicted of aiding and abetting suicide whereas Stead was charged with murder, although the jury returned a lesser verdict of manslaughter. Why were the charges different in the two cases? The Court of Appeal in *Stead* said:[51]

> "The case is very significantly more than an aiding of suicide: it is more akin to a mercy killing with the unusual feature of persistence in the attempts."

A recent case was that of Lesley Martin[52] who attempted to end the life of her mother and was found guilty of attempted murder. She was a registered nurse caring for her mother who had bowel cancer. She was entrusted with 100mg of morphine by her mother's GP to administer for pain relief. Instead she acted on a promise made to her mother to end her life and intentionally administered 60mg of morphine. Wild J followed the reasoning on the above two cases and said that Ms Martin fell firmly within the area of mercy killing along the lines of *Stead*. Ms Martin's intention was to kill her mother; her failing to do so

---

51   *R v Stead* (1991) 7 CRNZ 291, 295.
52   *R v Martin* [2004] 3 NZLR 69.

was not a result of a lack of determination. At no time did she show any remorse for her actions and her book only underlined this intention.[53]

Where a person ends their life, medical personnel are not implicated unless they assist the person to do so. Leaving the means to suicide, such as drugs or instruments, with the intention of assisting the suicide may be an offence. Without that clear intention proved, negligence or carelessness might be alternative findings by a Court.

(8) Life support

The consumer is on a life support system. The consumer is taken off the life support system and, as a result, dies.

The consumer may be in a persistent vegetative state or almost completely non-sentient, but with virtually no prospect of meaningful improvement. In these situations the Courts generally recognise that, in accordance with good medical practice, the life support system may be withdrawn and the practitioner responsible for this action will not be liable to criminal prosecution.

The leading UK authority discussing this principle was a case involving a survivor of the 1989 Hillsborough Football Stadium disaster in England.

Case

Airedale NHS Trust v Bland [1993] AC 789; [1993] 1 All ER 821; [1993] 2 WLR 316 (HL)

Bland, a 21-year-old patient in the care of the applicant health authority, had been in a persistent vegetative state for 3½ years after suffering a severe crushed chest injury that caused catastrophic and irreversible damage to the higher functions of his brain. He was being fed artificially and mechanically via a nasogastric tube. The unanimous opinion of all doctors was that there was no hope whatsoever of recovery or improvement of any kind, or expectation that Bland would ever recover from his persistent vegetative state.

The consultant specialist reached the conclusion that it would be appropriate to cease treatment, including the withdrawal of the nasogastric tube and thus nutrition, as well as such treatment as antibiotic therapy. Others supported this view, and the health authority applied to the Court for declarations that it and the responsible physicians could lawfully discontinue all life-sustaining treatment and support measures designed to keep Bland alive, including ventilation, nutrition, and other medical treatment. This was to be for the sole purpose of enabling him to end his life and die peacefully with the greatest dignity and the least pain. Bland's parents and family supported the plaintiff's action.

The Official Solicitor appealed to the Court of Appeal, which affirmed the Judge's decision. The Official Solicitor then appealed to the House of Lords. The argument was that the withdrawal of life support was a breach of the doctor's duty to care for Bland, indefinitely if need be, and a criminal act.

The House of Lords held that where a patient is incapable of deciding whether to consent to treatment, health practitioners are under no absolute obligation to prolong the patient's life regardless of the circumstances. Medical treatment, including artificial feeding and the administration of antibiotic drugs, could lawfully be withheld from an insensate patient who

---

53   L Martin, *To Die Like a Dog: The Personal Face of the Euthanasia Debate*, M Press, Wanganui, 2002.

had no hope of recovery when it was known that the patient would shortly thereafter die, provided reasonable and competent medical opinion was of the view that it would be in the patient's best interests not to prolong their life by continuing that form of treatment and that such treatment was futile and would not confer any benefit on the patient.

This is a landmark case in that it established that a person can have life-preserving measures removed with the sole intent that they should die. It also broke with common law precedents by rejecting the formerly accepted notion that only extraordinary measures can be withdrawn from a person by allowing the discontinuance of life support by removal of hydration and nutrition. In doing this, the Court accepted the argument of expert witnesses that nutrition and hydration were treatment just like any other, as it substitutes a function that has naturally failed. The removal of the feeding tube, they said, did not amount to a criminal act because if the continuance of an intrusive life support system was not in the patient's interests, the doctor was no longer under a duty to maintain the patient's life but was simply allowing the patient to die of the pre-existing condition and the death would be regarded in law as exclusively caused by the injury or disease to which the condition was attributable. Throughout the extensive consideration of the law, the Law Lords also expressed their dissatisfaction with the common law as it stands. They recognised its inappropriateness in many cases, and its inability to cope with modern medical knowledge and technology, as well as changing social attitudes.

As a result some of the Judges made the following points:

- Active steps to end a patient's life are unlawful.
- Doctors should from time to time seek the Court's guidance in all cases before withholding life-prolonging treatment from a patient in a persistent vegetative state. This should be by way of declaratory relief. In time, a body of expertise would develop, and only exceptional cases would need to be brought to Court.
- Lords Browne-Wilkinson and Mustill declared that it is imperative that the moral, social, and legal issues raised by the withholding of treatment from an insensate patient with no hope of recovery should be considered by Parliament (that is, that legislation clarifying the law be passed).

In New Zealand the principle of prolonging life by extraordinary means was discussed by the Court in a case where, unlike *Bland*, the consumer was not in a persistent vegetative state, that is, insensate, but rather had what has come to be known as "locked in" syndrome.

Case

Auckland AHB v A-G [1993] 1 NZLR 235

"L" was suffering from Guillain-Barré syndrome. He was unable to communicate or respond in any way to his environment. He was not brain-dead, but the extent of denervation meant that his brain was not connected with any part of his body, except perhaps with the visual pathways. He required ventilatory support in order to exist. The Board and L's doctor sought a declaration from the New Zealand High Court that disconnecting the ventilator would not be a criminal act.

This case, as in *Airedale NHS Trust v Bland*,[54] caused the Judges some concern that the legal principles that have been developed are not suitable to modern medical technology and knowledge. Strict adherence to the principle that removal of so-called "life-preservation" is a crime poses problems. Thomas J expressed his concern by stating that the issues before the Court could not be resolved by legal logic, but required rather the application of the common principles of humanity. The Court stated that while it could make a declaration to this effect, it would have to do so very carefully. It said that the question to answer was whether the doctor had a legal duty to continue life support, or whether there was justification in removing it. Justification in ceasing treatment is its futility. The Court declared that a doctor who removes life support from a patient who is effectively lifeless should not be held responsible for the person's death. In this case, the ventilation was deferring death rather than preserving life. The Court held that removing it would not be a criminal offence, provided the discontinuance was in accordance with good medical practice. Of the phrase "good medical practice", Thomas J said that its perceived content, not its meaning, was what was important, and before good medical practice could be held to have been demonstrated for the purpose of the case before him, various things had to be established:

- A decision was made in good faith that the withdrawal of the life support system was in the patient's best interest;
- There was conformity with prevailing medical standards and with practices, procedures, and traditions commanding general approval within the medical profession;
- There was consultation with appropriate medical specialists and the medical profession's recognised ethical body;
- The fully informed consent of the patient's family was gained.

His Honour Thomas J's comments on the terms "lawful excuse" and "good medical practice" are worth noting.

"Lawful excuse" has no defined meaning. However, "doctors have a lawful excuse to discontinue ventilation when there is no medical justification for continuing that form of medical assistance."[55] It is not unlawful to discontinue if this accords with good medical practice.

As to "good medical practice", Thomas J commented:[56]

"A phrase such as 'good medical practice' may not have the precision of meaning that the medical profession or the public would desire. But that imprecision is inherent in the problem itself. There can be no single or fixed rule as to exactly when a doctor may withhold a life support system which would cover the infinite variety of factual situations arising in practice. Consequently, the criterion can only be a general phrase such as 'good medical practice'."

Nor is it imperative that the phrase "good medical practice" be accepted in any exclusive or dogmatic sense. It has been selected because it already enjoys some currency. But any description such as "sound medical practice" or "proper medical standards and procedures"

---

54   *Airedale NHS Trust v Bland* [1993] AC 789; [1993] 1 All ER 821; [1993] 2 WLR 316 (HL).
55   *Auckland AHB v A-G* [1993] 1 NZLR 235, 250.
56   *Auckland AHB v A-G* [1993] 1 NZLR 235, 250-251.

would serve equally well. What is important is its perceived content. Clearly, it must begin with a bona fide decision on the part of the attending doctors as to what, in their judgment, is in the patient's best interests. Equally, it must encompass the prevailing medical standards, practices, procedures, and traditions that command general approval within the medical profession. All relevant tests would need to be carried out.

In making vital decisions of the present kind, specialist opinions and agreement will no doubt be required and extended consultation with other consultants is likely to be appropriate. Consultation with the medical profession's recognised ethical body is also critical. It must approve the doctors' decision. Finally, the patient's family or guardian must be fully informed and freely concur in what is proposed. It is knowledge of this practice, and the assurance that the procedures are conscientiously followed, which will provide the public with the confidence to accept the decisions that are then made.

Withholding treatment is not the same as not providing treatment in the first place, and in some cases a failure to provide treatment is not a breach of section 151 (duty to provide necessaries of life).

Case

Shortland v Northland Health Ltd [1998] 1 NZLR 433; (1997) 4 HRNZ 121 (CA)

Rau Williams was a 63-year-old man with end stage renal failure and brain damage due to hyperglycaemia. Both of these conditions were complications of Type II diabetes, which Mr Williams had had for many years. Between November 1996 and June 1997, Mr Williams' condition had deteriorated such that on 20 June 1997 he had an irreversible non-functioning kidney. Over an extended period between June and September 1997, Mr Williams' suitability for acceptance onto a dialysis programme was assessed; that assessment included interim dialysis. On 3 September 1997 Northland Health confirmed to Shortland, the family spokesperson, that Mr Williams had not been accepted onto the programme and that interim dialysis treatment would be discontinued on 17 September 1997.

Shortland went to Court claiming that not providing dialysis treatment was a breach of legal duties owed by Northland Health to Mr Williams. He also claimed that there was a breach of section 8 of the New Zealand Bill of Rights Act 1990 ("no one shall be deprived of life except on such grounds as are established by law and are consistent with the principles of fundamental justice"), and a breach of the requirements of good medical practice laid down by Thomas J in *Auckland AHB v A-G*).

The Court of Appeal rejected Shortland's claims. It held that the decision not to accept Williams onto the dialysis programme was a clinical one and was made on the basis of good medical practice. As far as Thomas J's criteria for good medical practice were concerned, these are not necessarily applicable in their entirety to a different situation and the fact that the fully informed consent of the patient's family was not obtained in this case was clinically appropriate:[57]

> "To require the consent of the patient's family to the cessation of a particular form of treatment, or to a decision not to give the patient a particular form of treatment,

---

[57] *Shortland v Northland Health Ltd* [1998] 1 NZLR 433; (1997) 4 HRNZ 121 (CA).

gives the family the power to require the treatment to be given or continued irrespective of the clinical judgment of the doctors involved. The law cannot countenance such a general proposition. While the criterion may have been appropriate in the content of the proposed removal of a life support system, as in the *Auckland* case, it cannot apply to a decision not to put the patient on a long term dialysis, following a period of assessment, which demonstrated that long term dialysis was clinically inappropriate."

The Court of Appeal also held that there were difficulties with the criterion of obtaining family consent in deciding who should be included as members of the patient's family, and that in a case such as this, that criterion should not be to require consent from the patient's family but to expect, where circumstances permit, that there will be a reasonable consultation with the patient and such members of the family as are available, and when a patient wishes them to be involved.

The Court decided that there was no evidence that Northland Health, or any of its doctors, failed in their responsibilities either legally or from the point of view of good medical practice. Also, because of the careful assessment process adopted by Northland Health and the clinical judgment to which that led, there was no breach of the duty in section 151 of the Crimes Act 1961 to provide the necessaries of life. The Court also held that refusing to provide dialysis did not deprive Williams of life in terms of section 8 of the New Zealand Bill of Rights Act.

In each of the above cases, the consumer dies as the result of an intentional act by practitioners. Without the Courts' sanction, practitioners run the risk of breaching their legal duty under section 151 to "provide the necessaries of life". If they have no "lawful excuse", they may be guilty of murder or manslaughter.

Clearly, there are no absolute standards of good medical practice. However, in the above two recent New Zealand cases where the Courts have discussed good medical practice at length, the Courts have indicated the standards that apply in the types of situations they were reviewing. In other situations, where proposed action by health service practitioners is likely to result in a consumer's death, application to the High Court for a declaratory judgment or the exercise of its parens patriae jurisdiction is recommended.

(9) *Withdrawing treatment from newborn infants*

When a baby is born with serious disabilities or of very low birth weight, the prognosis and expected quality of life (in any meaning of the term) of the child may be a more critical issue in determining whether to institute treatment. As it is not always possible to make a rapid assessment of the baby's condition and the extent of their disabilities, health carers must sometimes make quick decisions relating to resuscitation and commencing or continuing treatment based on incomplete information. Different policies have been adopted to deal with this problem — some facilities insist on full care for all babies over, say, 23 weeks gestation; others withhold treatment from all babies under a nominated weight or with specified ailments; yet others adopt a case-by-case decision-making approach, in consultation with parents. The English Court of Appeal clarified the term "quality of life" where severely disabled neonates are concerned.

Case

Re B (a minor) (wardship: medical treatment) [1981] 1 WLR 1421 (Eng CA)

An infant was born with Down's syndrome, intestinal blockage and certainly with severe mental and physical handicaps, though it was probable she would have some sapient functions.[58] The parents had refused consent to the operation to clear the intestinal blockage — without this B would die. The local health authority had B made a ward of the Court and sought consent through the Court. The Court saw the question as being whether it was in the *best interests* of the child to be allowed to die within the next week, or to have the operation required to correct the bowel problem. If she did have the operation it was not certain whether she would suffer any handicap or whether she would have any quality of life.

The Court ruled:[59]

> "At the end of the day it devolves on this Court to decide whether the life of the child is demonstrably going to be so awful that in effect the child must be condemned to die, or whether the life of this child is still so imponderable that it would be wrong for her to be condemned to die."

Lord Templeman went on to say that there might be other instances where damage is so certain and the child's life bound to be so full of pain and suffering, that the Court might be moved to rule that treatment be withdrawn. However, he found too little certainty of such a future for the child under consideration. The Court ordered that the required treatment be given. The novel point here, for English law, is the possibility that the certainty of a very poor quality of life may be accepted by the English Courts.

In New Zealand the very poor quality of a baby's life was accepted as a reason for withdrawing life support. However, in this case the Court was of the opinion that a ventilator was not prolonging life, but prolonging the baby's death.

Case

Auckland Healthcare Services Ltd v L & L (1998) 17 FRNZ 376; [1998] NZFLR 998

Baby L was born with Nobius Syndrome, a very severe abnormality of the brainstem. She had an extreme example of this to the extent that her brain was atrophied and there was extensive calcification of it. This abnormality meant that she was unable to control the muscles of her face, which were paralysed. In addition, she was deaf, could not breathe properly on her own, could not swallow or clear secretions from her mouth, and was developing signs of cerebral palsy.

She had been on a ventilator for 8 weeks and her condition was deteriorating. Her clinicians and others from whom medical opinion was sought were of the opinion that despite any treatment they might offer she would die sooner or later and before her first birthday,

---

58 The term "sapient" is given the meaning established in *Re Quinlan* 348 A 2d 801 (1975); 365 A 2d 647 (1976): a "permanent vegetative state".

59 *Re B (a minor) (wardship: medical treatment)* [1981] 1 WLR 1421, 1424. Since then the English Courts have recognised the lawfulness of managing some neonates "towards their deaths", giving them treatment to make them comfortable rather than to extend their lives: *Re C (a minor) (wardship: medical treatment)* [1989] 2 All ER 782; *In re J (a minor) (wardship: medical treatment)* [1990] 2 All ER 930; *In re J (a minor) (wardship: medical treatment)* [1992] 4 All ER 614.

even on the ventilator. None of her problems could be reversed, and it was felt that she was dying in a most unpleasant and painful manner and that the ventilator was not prolonging her life but prolonging the process of dying.

Baby L's parents, while accepting the medical evidence that Baby L was dying, believed it was still appropriate to give her a chance of some family life. Neither parent would give their consent to turn off the ventilator. Auckland Area Health Care Services applied to the Family Court for it to be appointed as Baby L's guardian in place of the parents, with the paediatricians to be appointed agents of the Court for the purposes of managing Baby L, including making the decision to switch off the ventilator.

The Court granted the application and Baby L was made a ward of the Court and the doctor the Court's agent. The ventilator was switched off and Baby L's parents took her home where she died.

The paramount consideration for the Court was the welfare of the child.[60] After considering cases including *Re B* and the *Auckland AHB* and *Shortland* cases, the Court concluded that there was authority both in New Zealand and overseas which shows that in extreme circumstances the welfare of the child requires the discontinuance of life support. It countenanced the view that to prolong life is not the sole objective of the Court, and to require it at the expense of other considerations may not be in a person's best interest.

When deciding what was in Baby L's best interest, the Court looked at Thomas J's criteria for best medical practice in the *Auckland AHB* case and held that all the criteria apart from the parents' consent favoured the making of the order sought. The Court took notice of the *Shortland* decision, and a practice note from England, and commented that the parents' wishes, while of the greatest significance, cannot always be a determining factor.[61]

(10) *"Do not resuscitate" orders*

Since the development of cardio-pulmonary resuscitation for consumers with particular heart conditions, this procedure has been adopted in most situations of sudden cardiac failure in hospitals and elsewhere. The result has been the prolongation of life, which in many cases is of a quality so poor that the resuscitation is recognised as not being in the consumer's best interest.

The legal issues for practitioners involve those discussed throughout this chapter. Is the failure to resuscitate a criminal act? Are there some circumstances that make it a criminal act? As can be seen, the answers are not certain. Practitioners should take into account the consumer's wishes, their prognosis, and what they can reasonably expect the outcome of cardio-pulmonary resuscitation to be on this particular person in the circumstances.

Given the fact that at the time of cardiac arrest the consumer's condition is terminal and resuscitation could be considered as extraordinary treatment, the culpability or otherwise of practitioners in not carrying out the resuscitation is difficult to assess. A central consideration is that there are times when treatment becomes futile,[62] and people should

---

60   This is a statutory requirement in relation to all applications made under section 23(1) of the Guardianship Act 1968.

61   It was also held by the Court that there was no breach of section 8 of the New Zealand Bill of Rights Act 1990 (the right to life), because switching off the ventilator would not "deprive" Baby L of her life as she was dying even on the ventilator.

be allowed to die despite the fact that resuscitation would revive them, either for a short period or with a severely diminished quality of life.

There should not be a policy of disguising "Do not resuscitate" orders, for example by using codes or stickers. This creates distrust, not only on the part of the consumer, but also on the part of those who must consider the legal implications of such an instruction. Where a code or unspoken instruction has been issued, it may be open to a Court to find that the reasons for the order may not have been properly considered, or could be malicious or reckless, whereas the full recording of reasons, with the result of consultation with the consumer and/or family if this has occurred,[63] indicates an intention to abide by ethical and legal principles.

16.5.5   Euthanasia

Euthanasia ("good death") is the deliberate bringing about of the death of a person to end what is considered an intolerable existence. Euthanasia is defined here as either an active measure to cause death ("active euthanasia") or the withholding of treatment, which results in death ("passive euthanasia"). The former may be the criminal offence of homicide; the latter is more problematic. Some commentators say it cannot be homicide as there is no act to cause the harm, but it has been quite clearly established that an omission can amount to criminal negligence at least. It could also, of course, constitute civil negligence.

Technically, whether active or passive, euthanasia can amount to the crime of culpable homicide. With passive euthanasia as shown above, the Courts have granted relief from the harshness of such provisions by developing principles that nevertheless are vague and unable to deal satisfactorily with the advances of modern technology. This has resulted in intense legal debate and calls by law reform bodies for change. If practitioners are concerned that their action in withholding treatment or removing life-saving machinery could be regarded as a crime they should seek legal advice. It is possible to seek a declaration from a Court that the passive euthanasia would not be a crime as in *Bland* and *Auckland AHB v A-G*.

Currently in New Zealand, even though it is the subject of active lobbying by some citizens and MPs, active euthanasia is still prohibited and may amount to culpable homicide.

16.5.6   Abortion

(1)   *Procuring abortion, killing an unborn child*

The law regarding abortion is contained in the Crimes Act 1961,[64] as well as some case law. An abortion is the untimely expulsion of the foetus from the womb, either spontaneously by natural means, or by external influences (induced abortion). There are six main elements to the law:

---

62   Treatment is considered normatively futile if and only if it fails to produce any benefit or fails to promote any reasonable purpose of treatment;

63   This is an important part of the process of making an informed refusal by a person who is considered in danger of cardiac arrest. Hospitals must develop policies that include involvement of patient and family in "Do not resuscitate" decisions to comply with the Code of Health and Disability Services Consumers' Rights.

64   Section 182 of the Crimes Act 1961.

- The woman need not actually be pregnant (the intention to abort is the crucial factor);
- The prohibition is against the unlawful procuring of miscarriage;
- A woman must not unlawfully bring about her own miscarriage;
- A person must not aid another in unlawfully procuring a miscarriage;
- An attempt by any person to procure an unlawful miscarriage is just as serious an offence as if it were successful;
- A person must not supply the means for procuring an unlawful miscarriage; the means may be "any drug or noxious thing, or any instrument or thing whatsoever".

"Unlawfully" is defined in section 187A of the Crimes Act 1961. Any act in which a person intends to procure abortion is done unlawfully unless:

- In the case of a pregnancy of not more than 20 weeks gestation where the person doing the act believes continuation of the pregnancy would result in serious damage to the woman's life or physical or mental health, or there is a substantial risk of the child being born seriously handicapped, or the pregnancy was the result of sexual intercourse between a parent and a child, a brother and a sister, or a grandparent and a grandchild, or the woman is severely subnormal, or is under 20 and has been sexually violated;
- In the case of a pregnancy of more than 20 weeks, the person doing the act believes the miscarriage is necessary to save the woman's life or to prevent serious permanent mental or physical injury.

(2)   *Who may carry out an abortion?*

Any person may offer the defence that they carried out a procedure in an emergency, and it was intended to prevent a real and imminent danger of death or serious harm, so long as it is done in a responsible way and there is no better medical help available.[65] The person must weigh the dangers and not aggravate the existing condition. Where there is no emergency, it is advised that a nurse should not carry out an abortion unless supervised by a doctor, as it is considered a medical procedure, although there may be no criminal sanction against this.

Hospitals and clinics themselves may have guidelines and rules determining procedures for carrying out the termination of pregnancy.[66] Practitioners involved in assisting with terminations should be aware of these.

(3)   *Does the foetus have any rights?*

The short answer to this question would appear to be "no". The foetus is not a person until it has lived independently outside the mother's body (see chapter 7). Until then, it is regarded as an unborn child. The Courts have considered the question of whether the unborn child has a right to live in several cases.

Case
F v F (1989) FLC 92-031 (FCA)

---

65   At common law this constitutes the defence of necessity.

66   For example, a hospital may require certain procedures, such as certification of the need for the termination by two doctors, procedure for legal abortion is governed by the Contraception, Sterilisation, and Abortion Act 1977.

> A husband applied to the Family Court for an injunction to prevent his estranged and pregnant wife from terminating the pregnancy of their prospective child. He argued, among other things, that the foetus had a right to protection against abortion, and that he could enforce that right on its behalf.

The Court considered precedent, and made the following important points:

- A Court does not make ethical judgments — it is concerned with legal rights. Its task is to interpret and apply the law, not particular moral or ethical precepts;[67]
- "The foetus has no right of its own until it is born and has a separate existence from its mother." This was held by the English case of *Paton v British Pregnancy Advisory Service*,[68] and the Australian High Court case of *A-G (Qld) (Ex rel Kerr) v T*.[69] Both those cases involved the father of a foetus attempting to prevent the mother from having an abortion.
- It was also considered by the European Court of Human Rights in *Vo v France*[70] whether Article 2 — the right to life — protected the unborn child. There was no consensus on the moral status of the foetus, but it was common ground that it was a member of the human race. However the capacity to become a person did not make it a person with a right to life protected by Article 2.

(4) *Do others have any rights?*

In the case of *F v F*, the Court also addressed the right of third parties to determine whether a termination will be undertaken. The Court followed those cases mentioned in determining that a father has no right to stop the mother having a legal abortion:[71]

> "To grant the injunction would be to compel the wife to do something in relation to her own body which she does not wish to do. That would be an interference with her freedom to decide her own destiny."

16.6 Female genital mutilation

Female genital mutilation is prohibited, and so is sending a child out of New Zealand to be operated on in a manner prohibited under New Zealand law.[72] Health professionals will come across women, usually from African countries such as Somalia, who have been circumcised. For many years this practice has been culturally acceptable in those countries, and it is only recently that the practice is actively being outlawed on a worldwide scale.

Despite the fact that the practice is prohibited, some members of some cultures will continue the practice and millions of young girls are circumcised in parts of Africa each

---

67   Readers may compare this approach with the use by many Courts of public policy (see 3.4.4(3)). See also S Watson, "Rashomon of science: The legal position of the foetus in New Zealand" [1994] NZLJ 338.

68   *Paton v British Pregnancy Advisory Service Trustees* [1979] QB 276, [1978] 3 WLR 687, [1978] 2 All ER 987. Note also the case of *K v Minister for Youth & Community Services* [1982] 1 NSWLR 311, where an application was sought to be brought in the name of a foetus to prevent an abortion, Street CJ (with whom the other Judges agreed) said: "I am not, as at present advised, satisfied that the unborn child or foetus has the requisite status to participate as a party in proceedings of a character of those before the equity division or in those such as are sought to be brought before this Court."

69   *A-G (Qld) (Ex rel Kerr) v T* (1983) 57 ALJR 285; (1983) 46 ALR 275.

70   *Vo v France* (53924/00) [2004] 2 FCR 577, (2005) 40 EHRR 12, (2004) 17 BHRC 1.

71   *F v F* (1989) FLC 92-031, 77-438.

72   Sections 204A and 204B of the Crimes Act 1961.

year. It is not uncommon for the practice to continue in refugee populations in other countries, and while there have been no prosecutions to date under the Crimes Act 1961, it is believed that some young girls are sent out of New Zealand to be circumcised.

Practitioners should be aware of this, and that Somali refugees and other women patients living in New Zealand may have been circumcised. Many of these women are sensitive about their circumcisions, and are not sure how much knowledge their health professionals have. Recent research suggests a growing awareness on the part of many health practitioners, but more education of the health professionals generally is still needed.

16.7 Causing or producing in another person any disease or sickness

Section 201 of the Crimes Act 1961 provides that:[73]

> "Everyone is liable to imprisonment for a term not exceeding 14 years who, wilfully and without lawful justification or excuse, causes or produces in any other person any disease or sickness."

This section is directed more at people who are infected with a disease and wilfully pass the infection on to others. It may also apply to health practitioners conducting private medical research that is not authorised by an ethics committee.

16.8 Assaulting another person

A person convicted of assault under section 196 of the Crimes Act 1961 is liable to up to one year of imprisonment. If the charge is assault with intent to injure under section 193, the maximum penalty is 3 years' imprisonment. A person may also be charged with common assault under section 196 of the Crimes Act, the maximum penalty being one year imprisonment. Alternatively the Summary Offences Act 1981 also has a charge of common assault under section 9, in which case the maximum penalty is 6 months' imprisonment or a fine of $4,000.

Assault is defined in section 2 of both Acts as:

> "the act of intentionally applying or attempting to apply force to the person of another, directly or indirectly, or threatening by any act or gesture to apply such force to the person of another, if the person making the threat has, or causes the other person to believe on reasonable grounds that he has, present ability to effect his purpose ..."

In the case of a surgical operation, a medical practitioner is protected from charges of assault if the operation is performed with the patient's consent and reasonable care and skill:

* For the patient's benefit and the performance of the operation was reasonable, having regard to the patient's state at the time and to all the circumstances of the case;[74] and
* With the consent of the patient or a person lawfully entitled to consent on the patient's behalf.[75]

---

73 See *R v Mwai* [1995] 3 NZLR 149; (1995) 13 CRNZ 273 (CA), discussed in chapter 18 under Acquired Immunodeficiency Syndrome.

74 Crimes Act 1961, section 61; Summary Proceedings Act 1957, section 3(1)(d).

75 Section 61A of the Crimes Act 1961; section 3(1)(d) of the Summary Proceedings Act 1957.

Generally, in respect of any proper clinical procedures, a health practitioner should not be liable to a charge of assault if they are conducted with the valid consent of the consumer or of the person entitled to consent on their behalf. Informed consent is discussed in detail in chapters 6 and 7. Nor should a practitioner be liable to a charge of assault in circumstances where consent cannot be obtained, and the practitioner is doing what they consider necessary and the procedures would be accepted by an appropriate body of medical opinion.[76]

16.9   Misconduct in respect of human remains

Section 150 of the Crimes Act 1961 provides:

> "**150   Misconduct in respect of human remains**
>
> "Everyone is liable to imprisonment for a term not exceeding 2 years who—
>
> "(a)   Neglects to perform any duty imposed on him by law or undertaken by him with reference to the burial or cremation of any dead human body or human remains; or
>
> "(b)   Improperly or indecently interferes with or offers any indignity to any dead human body or human remains, whether buried or not."

Failure to perform duties in respect of human bodies or human remains under the Burial and Cremation Act 1964, Coroners Act 2006 and Human Tissue Act 2008 (see chapters 17 and 19) may amount to misconduct in respect of human remains under section 150.

Mere possession of human remains where they were not mutilated has been held to be insufficient to constitute the crime of interference with human remains.[77]

16.10   Offences under Acts other than Crimes Act 1961

Apart from the Crimes Act 1961, a number of other Acts contain provisions that are of particular significance to health practitioners. These include the:

- Births, Deaths, and Marriages Registration Act 1995;[78]
- Coroners Act 2006;[79]
- Health Act 1956;[80]
- Human Tissue Act 2008;[81]
- Medicines Act 1981;[82] and
- Mental Health (Compulsory Assessment and Treatment) Act 1992.[83]

There are also offence provisions in the Health Practitioners Competence Assurance Act 2003 (HPCAA), which regulates and disciplines health practitioners. This Act replaced

---

76   *F v West Berkshire Health Authority* [1989] 2 All ER 545 (HL).
77   *Police v Entwhistle* [1972] 13 MDC 277.
78   See chapter 17.
79   *Police v Entwhistle* [1972] 13 MDC 277.
80   See chapter 18.
81   See chapter 19.
82   See chapter 10.
83   See chapter 7.

the Nurses Act 1977, the Medical Practitioners Act 1995 along with other Acts that regulated other health practitioners, and it came into force in September 2004.[84]

16.10.1 Offences under Births, Deaths, and Marriages Registration Act 1995

Various offences and penalties are set out at section 89 of the Births, Deaths, and Marriages Registration Act 1995. Of particular significance to health practitioners are those that relate to making false statements when providing information required under the Act, tampering with or misusing information stored for the purposes of the Act, and failing to provide information required under the Act.

Section 89(3)(a) refers to section 42, which sets out a duty to notify the Registrar when a body is disposed of or removed for disposal outside New Zealand or removed for anatomical examination under the Human Tissue Act 2008.

Section 89(3)(b) refers to section 41 and provides that no person shall dispose of a body or cause or permit a body to be disposed of unless the person in charge of the disposal has obtained a doctor's or coroner's order.

16.10.2 Offences under Coroners Act 2006

Offences and penalties prescribed by this Act are set out in sections 134-139.

(1)   *Failing or refusing to give to a coroner a report required under the Act — reporting of deaths*

A medical practitioner, who fails or refuses to give a Coroner a report required under the Act, is liable on summary conviction to a fine not exceeding $1,000.[85] This offence does not apply to any health practitioner other than a doctor or pathologist.

(2)   *Failing to comply with directions relating to removal or disposal of a body*

Section 20 of the Coroners Act 2006 authorises the coroner to give directions relating to the removal or disposal of a body. Section 136 provides that a person who fails or refuses to comply with a direction under section 20 or who hinders or prevents any person from complying with such a direction commits an offence and is liable on summary conviction to a fine not exceeding $2,000.

A person who fails to comply with directions relating to the removal or disposal of a body may also be liable under section 150 of the Crimes Act 1961, misconduct in respect of human remains[86]

(3)   *Publishing details of self-inflicted deaths or of evidence given at an inquest in respect of which a coroner has prohibited publication*

Under section 71(1) of the Coroners Act 2006, where a death may have been self-inflicted, no person may make public details relating to the death before the completion of the inquest. Where the coroner has completed the inquest and found the death to be self-

---

84   See chapters 4 and 15.
85   Coroners Act 2006, section 137.
86   See 16.9.

inflicted, no person may make public any particulars of the death other than the name, address, and occupation of the person concerned and the fact that the coroner has found the death to be self-inflicted.[87] Section 71(3) allows an exception to be made if the coroner believes it is unlikely to be detrimental to public safety. He or she must have regard to the characteristics of the person who has died, any practice notes issued by the Chief Coroner and any other matters the coroner considers relevant.[88]

Under section 74, a coroner may prohibit the publication of any evidence given at an inquest or any other part of the inquest proceedings if satisfied that it is in the interests of justice, decency, or public order to do so.

Under section 139, it is an offence to publish or permit to be published information in contravention of section 71 or information that has been prohibited under section 74. The penalty on summary conviction is a fine not exceeding $5,000 in the case of a body corporate, or $1,000 in the case of an individual.

(4)   *Falsely identifying a person in respect of whom the coroner decides not to hold an inquest*[89]

A person who commits this offence is liable under section 138 to a maximum of 7 years imprisonment. For the offence to be committed, the statement must have been in writing and it must have been made knowing it to be false and with the intention of misleading persons who might rely on it.

16.10.3   Offences under the Health Act 1956

The Health Act 1956 prescribes offences in respect of conduct relating to public health. Of particular significance to health practitioners is section 80(1)(b). This provides that every person commits an offence who:

> "[w]hile in charge of any person suffering [from an infectious or communicable disease], takes him into or allows him to be in any public place without having taken proper precautions against the spread of infection."

The penalty is a fine not exceeding $500 and, if the offence is a continuing one, a further fine not exceeding $50 per day may be imposed: section 136.

16.10.4   Offences under Human Tissue Act 2008

Any person who intentionally or knowingly does an act that contravenes one of the following is liable on summary conviction to a fine not exceeding $20,000 or to imprisonment for a term not exceeding 3 months:

- Performs a post mortem that is not by or in accordance with the instructions of a medical practitioner;[90]
- Performs an anatomical examination of a body at a place where or at a time when that examination is prohibited by this Act;[91]

---

87   Coroners Act 2006, section 71(2).
88   Coroners Act 2006, section 71(4).
89   Relates to section 64; duties of coroner who decides not to hold an inquest.
90   Section 49 of the Human Tissue Act 2008.

- Not being authorised under this Act to practise anatomy, practises anatomy or, otherwise than on behalf of a person so authorised, receives or has in his possession anybody for the purpose of anatomical examination.[92]

The provisions of the Human Tissue Act 2008 are subject to section 150 of the Crimes Act 1961, under which it is an offence to neglect to perform any duty with reference to the burial or cremation of any dead human body or human remains, or to improperly or indecently interfere with or offer any indignity to any dead human body or human remains, whether buried or not.[93]

(1)   *Trading in human blood and controlled substances*[94]

Trading in human blood and controlled substances is covered by Part 2 of the Human Tissue Act 2008,[95] which includes provisions that prohibit a person from:

- Trading in his or her own blood or any controlled human substance: section 56. The penalty is a term of imprisonment not exceeding 1 year or a fine not exceeding $50,000.
- Providing money or other consideration for the taking of blood or any controlled human substance from the body of a person for administration to another person: section 57(1). The penalty is a term of imprisonment not exceeding 6 months or a fine not exceeding $20,000: section 57(2). Collecting blood or any controlled human substance unless that person is an authorised "appointed entity" or employee or agent of an appointed entity: section 57(3). The penalty is a term of imprisonment not exceeding 6 months or a fine not exceeding $20,000: section 57(2).
- Charging for administered blood or any controlled human substance: section 59(1). The penalty is imprisonment for a term not exceeding 1 year or a fine not exceeding $50,000: section 59(2).
- Distributing an advertisement relating to the purchase or sale in New Zealand of blood or a controlled human substance: section 61(1). The penalty is imprisonment for a term not exceeding 3 months or a fine not exceeding $20,000: section 61(2).

The terms "blood" and "controlled human substance" are defined in section 55.

16.10.5   Offences under Medicines Act 1981

The Medicines Act 1981 is concerned with the law relating to the manufacture, sale, and supply of medicines, medical devices, and related products. A number of provisions set out offences in respect of these activities. However, under section 25, practitioners are exempt from many of these provisions where they are dealing with medicines for particular patients.

There are no exemptions in the case of offences relating to the adulteration of medicines (section 39) and failure to comply with standards that are prescribed in respect of a medicine (section 40).

---

91   Human Tissue Act 2008, section 52: examination must be performed at a school of anatomy; however section 53 provides for an exception if authorised.
92   Human Tissue Act 2008, section 53.
93   See 16.9.
94   This was formerly under the Health Act 1956 but was repealed and incorporated into the Human Tissue Act 2008.
95   Human Tissue Act 2008, sections 55-65.

Other offences that may relate to medical practitioners are:

- Section 46 — a person in charge or in possession of a medicine must, other than removing it for effective and lawful use, keep it in a container conforming to relevant requirements or in the labelled container in which it was acquired;
- Section 47 — a person in possession or in charge of a prescription medicine or restricted medicine must not store it in a place where food or drink is stored or kept for ready use, or in a place to which young children or unauthorised persons have ready access, or in an unattended building or vehicle unless they have taken reasonable steps to secure the building or vehicle;
- Sections 56 to 62 — restrictions on medical advertisements in respect of medicines, medical devices, and the use of any method of treatment;
- Sections 66 and 67 — a person required to do so by the Director-General of Health or Medical Officer of Health must supply the name or address of any person from whom they obtained a medicine or medical device that is subject to investigation.

The general maximum penalty for these offences is 3 months imprisonment or a $500 fine and, if the offence is a continuing one, a further fine of $50 per day.[96]

16.10.6 Offences under Mental Health (Compulsory Assessment and Treatment) Act 1992

The Mental Health (Compulsory Assessment and Treatment) Act 1992 provides for the following offences:

- Intentional neglect or ill-treatment of a mentally disordered person — on indictment a penalty of imprisonment not exceeding 2 years: section 114;
- Intentionally assist a patient to be absent without leave — liable to a term of imprisonment not exceeding 3 months or a fine not exceeding $1,000: section 115 and section 115A;
- Unlawful publication of reports of proceedings before the Review tribunal — liable to a fine not exceeding $10,000: section 116;
- Obstruction of an inspection by a district inspector or an official visitor — liable to a fine not exceeding $2,000: section 117;
- Supplying false or misleading particulars in any certificate under the Act — liable to a fine not exceeding $5,000: section 118;
- Otherwise supplying false or misleading documents under the Act — liable to a fine not exceeding $2,000 fine: section 119.

16.10.7 Victims of crime

Where the consumer is apparently a victim of a criminal offence (for example, assault or rape), the attending practitioners should be aware that evidence of the offence might be required (for example, vaginal smears, samples of clothing, and photographs and descriptions of wounds). Police, or other investigators appointed by them, will want to collect such evidence, so it is important that the patient be undisturbed as much as possible after any urgent treatment has been given. To best preserve evidence, a victim of sexual assault should not bathe or shower, no matter how desirable this may be from a personal

---

96   Section 78 of the Medicines Act 1981.

point of view. It should be borne in mind, however, that the person must not be forced against their will in this matter, but should be reminded that prosecution by the police will be very difficult without this evidence. Reassurance and comfort will therefore be an essential part of the practitioner's caring for victims of violence, who are likely to be distressed and uncomfortable.

Those working in emergency and other receiving wards should be familiar with the hospital's procedures for dealing with such consumers, and should be aware of any special personnel for handling the collection of evidence or liaison with police.

Where there are no specially trained personnel for gathering forensic evidence, it may help the client if health carers consider how they might retain useful evidence (for example, descriptions of injuries and events, samples of blood, tissue, hair, and clothing). However, caution is advised: they should not adopt the role of detective.

Due to their close relationship with the victims of crime, practitioners may find that they possess information and witness events and facts that may make them useful witnesses in later Court cases. They may have received a dying statement that can later be admitted in evidence. It is suggested that while they should not shirk their civic duty to assist in the process of justice, they should not actively involve themselves in potential criminal cases by undertaking activities for the patient that are not part of their normal caring duties to the patient (such as getting or giving information, contacting people, discussing the case with others, or intervening in private disputes).

It is equally important for practitioners to remember the requirements of confidentiality, no matter how much one might be tempted to discuss exciting details of criminal events with others. Potential witnesses in a case are warned by lawyers involved in the case against discussing certain matters with other witnesses or the press. Spreading allegations about the guilt of specific or identifiable persons may amount to defamation.

16.11   Consumers allegedly the perpetrators of crime

Similar advice applies to those caring for people who are charged with, or accused of crime, with several further important points.

A person is not guilty at law until they have been convicted by a Court. It is for a Court to determine guilt, not health care staff. Even where the consumer has been convicted of a crime, it is not for practitioners to determine and carry out their punishment. That is the task of law enforcement agencies. Practitioners should give the same standard of treatment to every person they care for. Failure to give this standard may result in a complaint to the Human Rights Commission or to the Health and Disability Commissioner.

16.12   Further reading

A Alston, "Legal aspects of gender reassignment" (1998) 5 JLM 279.

A Alston, "Transgender rights as legal rights" (1999) 7 Canterbury Law Review 329.

M Bagaric, "Active and passive euthanasia: Is there a moral distinction and should there be a legal difference" (1997) 5 JLM 143.

I Bassett, "Liability of health professionals for a breach of the abortion law of New Zealand" (2001) 9 JLM 115.

F Bates, "Males, mutilation and the law: Some recent developments" (2001) 9 JLM 68.

Boyle et al, "Circumcision of healthy boys: A criminal assault?" (1999-2000) 7 JLM 301.

D Collins, "Prescribing limits to life-prolonging treatment" [1994] New Zealand Law Journal 246.

I Freckelton, "Withdrawal of life support: The 'Persistent Vegetative State' conundrum" (1993-1994) 1 JLM 35.

G Gillett, L Goddard QC, and M Webb, "The case of Mr L: Legal and ethical response to the Court-sanctioned withdrawal of life-support" (1995) 3 JLM 49.

A Hooper and I McColl, "Mercy killing in the new millennium" (2000) 40(3) Medicine Science and the Law 189.

J Keown, "Restoring moral and intellectual shape to the law after Bland" (1997) 113 LQR 481.

Lord Carlisle of Berview QC, "The ethics of euthanasia: Devil without a cause" (2000) 40(3) Medicine, Science and the Law 185.

C Mason, "Exorcising excision: Medico-legal issues arising from male and female genital surgery in Australia" (2000) 9 JLM 58.

N Peart and G Gillett, "Re G: A life worth living?"(1998) 5 JLM 239.

J B Robertson (ed), Orchard, Finn, Mahoney, *Adams on Criminal Law* (3rd ed), Wellington, Brookers, 1992.

P D G Skegg, "Omissions to provide life-prolonging treatment" (1994) 8 Otago Law Review 205 (discussion of *Auckland AHA v A-G*).

G Williams, "The principle of double effect and terminal sedation" (2001) 9 (1) Medical Law Review 41.

Chapter 17

BIRTHS, DEATHS AND CORONERS' INQUIRIES

SUE JOHNSON

Contents

17.1   Introduction

There are times when matters concerning individuals must be reported to the State. These include births, deaths, child abuse and neglect, and the knowledge that someone has an infectious or sexually transmitted disease. There are also deaths that, because of their unusual or unexplained nature or other circumstances defined by statute, should come to the Coroner's notice, usually via the police. Child abuse and domestic violence, in particular, are matters of public concern. Also, those practising in rural areas, or taking part in home births or other aspects of health service delivery which have become increasingly concerned with matters of life and death, will be involved in reporting to the authorities concerned. The notification of births and deaths, as well as Coroners' inquests, will be dealt with in this chapter. The reporting of infectious diseases and child abuse is dealt with in chapter 18.

17.2 Notification of births

The Births, Deaths, Marriages, and Relationships Registration Act 1995 and its amendments establish a register of births, deaths, and marriages, which is maintained by the Registrar of Births, Deaths, and Marriages. All births must be recorded in the register, along with the parentage of the child (parentage of artificially conceived children is determined by statute — see 19.6.4). There is a requirement that a preliminary notice of a birth, including a still-birth (see 17.2.2) is given within 5 working days to the Registrar by the doctor or midwife who attended the birth, or by the occupier of the premises where the birth took place.[1]

- Both parents of a child born in New Zealand are required to register the birth.[2] If they have failed to do so, or are unable to do so, the child's guardian can register it.[3] The time limit is "as soon as is reasonably practicable after the birth".
- There is a penalty for failure to report a birth to the Registrar, but there is also the defence that the person reasonably believed the birth had already been reported by some other person.
- The sex of a person is notified on the birth certificate.

17.2.1 Sexual/gender reassignment

The Births, Deaths, Marriages, and Relationships Registration Act 1995 provides for the Family Court to make declarations relating to:

- Persons of 18 years or older who have a gender identity contrary to the information relating to the sex that appears on the person's birth certificate;[4]
- Children of ambiguous or complicated genital conformation declaring that it is in the child's best interests to be brought up as a person of the sex specified in the application (based on medical evidence).[5]

In both cases the Family Court may declare that a birth certificate issued for the applicant shows the information relating to the new gender, which replaces previous information in that person's birth entry. Health practitioners may be asked to give evidence of medical procedures that the applicant has undergone or, in the case of children, are likely to be in the child's best interests.[6]

---

1   Births, Deaths, Marriages, and Relationships Registration Act 1995, section 5A.
2   Births, Deaths, Marriages, and Relationships Registration Act 1995, section 9.
3   Births, Deaths, Marriages, and Relationships Registration Act 1995, section 10.
4   Births, Deaths, Marriages, and Relationships Registration Act 1995, section 28.
5   Births, Deaths, Marriages, and Relationships Registration Act 1995, section 29.
6   For a discussion of the law affecting adults who undergo gender reassignment see A Alston, "Legal aspects of gender reassignment" (1998) 5 Journal of Law and Medicine 279.

17.2.2 Still-births (children not born alive)

"Still-born child" is defined in the Births, Deaths, Marriages, and Relationships Registration Act 1995 as meaning a dead foetus that weighed 400 g or more when it issued from its mother, or that issued from its mother after the 20th week of pregnancy. The Act specifically does not include miscarriage. "Dead foetus" means a foetus that, whether or not the umbilical cord had been severed or the placenta had detached, at no time after issuing completely from its mother breathed or showed any other sign of life, such as beating of the heart, pulsation of the umbilical cord, or definite movement of the voluntary muscles.[7]

Still-births must be notified to the Registrar in the same way as births, with the same people being responsible. It is not necessary to register the death of the child.

In every case of still-birth and foetal death after the 20th week of pregnancy, the medical practitioner or midwife in attendance has to provide to the Registrar a certificate stating their belief as to the cause of death.

It is an offence to fail to give notice of a birth or still-birth, or to give false information.

Checklist

When practitioners have a responsibility to notify the Registrar of the birth of a child

To determine a birth for the purposes of registration:

*   Is the foetus of at least 20 weeks' gestation?
*   Was the child alive at the time of delivery?
*   If "yes" to both, then it is a "child" for the purposes of notification, and it is a live birth;
*   If "yes" only to the first question, the delivery is a still-birth for the purposes of notification.

Rarely, a health practitioner might be unsure whether the birth was a still-birth or a live birth, as it may be unclear whether the child was alive at the time of delivery or died shortly afterwards. This is not merely an academic point, as a Coroner has no jurisdiction to hold an inquiry into a stillbirth, but only for a child who died after birth.[8] However, where there is doubt a Coroner can direct that a post mortem be performed to find out whether a child was still-born or born alive. Health practitioners, who are uncertain whether or not the birth was a live or a still-birth, should contact the Coroner.

Live birth is not defined in the Act, but the definition used by the World Health Organisation (WHO) is used in regular Ministry of Health Reports on Maternity:[9,10]

> "Live birth is the complete expulsion or extraction from its mother of a product of conception, irrespective of the duration of pregnancy, which, after such separation, breathes or shows any other evidence of life, such as beating of the heart, pulsation

---

7   Births, Deaths, Marriages, and Relationships Registration Act 1995, section 2.

8   Coroners Act 2006, section 9 (definition of "body").

9   For example: Ministry of Health Report on Maternity 2004 New Zealand Health Information Service Ministry of Health. Available on the Ministry of Health's website at www.nzhis.govt.nz/moh.nsf/ pagesns/73?Open.

10   WHO website at www.who.int/whosis/indicators/compendium/2008/3mr5/en.

of the umbilical cord, or definite movement of voluntary muscles, whether or not the umbilical cord has been cut or the placenta is attached. Each product of such a birth is considered live born."

17.3 Notification of death

The Births, Deaths, Marriages, and Relationships Registration Act 1995 provides that all deaths in New Zealand must be notified on the register of deaths. This includes perinatal deaths, where a child dies within 28 days of birth. Notification is normally done by the funeral director or someone from the immediate family or whanau attending a registry office, and taking along a death certificate signed by a medical practitioner. The death is then noted in the register of deaths. The cause of death is noted and this is based on the certificate as to cause of death issued by a medical practitioner or by a certificate from the Coroner once he or she has established the cause of death. The Registrar supplies cause of death information to the New Zealand Health Information Service (NZHIS) of the Ministry of Health. The NZHIS assigns an underlying cause of death in accordance with World Health Organisation classification and produces cause of death statistics. These statistics are used to monitor causes of death, for research and policy development.

Only about twenty percent of deaths in New Zealand must be reported to the Coroner. The other eighty percent are the sorts of deaths we all hope for our loved ones and ourselves: where our doctor knows what the cause of death is and is able to issue a certificate.

The cause of death certificate is a legal document and it is important that doctors have full information before they complete it. They need to be satisfied as to the likely cause of death. Also unlike some jurisdictions there is no requirement that the deceased had to have been seen by the doctor within a certain time frame before death. There are resources to assist doctors including the Ministry of Health publication, *A Guide to Certifying Causes of Death*.[11] Where a doctor is in doubt as to whether the death is one that needs to be reported to the Coroner he or she should seek advice from senior colleagues or telephone the Coroner to discuss. Coroners' office numbers are in the local White pages of the telephone directory under Coronial Services Unit. In case of emergency and where a death needs to be reported to a Coroner at night, weekend or a public holiday there is a 24 hour Coroner service — telephone 04 910 4482.

17.4 Coroners

Coroners have a long history dating back to the 12th century, the first undoubted reference to "Coroners" appearing in the *Articles of Eyre* in 1194. The office was established as a means of safeguarding the important revenue generated by the execution of justice. The Coroner's primary interest then, as now, was the investigation of violent or sudden deaths.

The Coroners Act 2006 is the principal legislation in New Zealand governing the work of Coroners. It replaced and reformed the Coroners Act 1988.

---

11   *A Guide to Certifying Causes of Death*, New Zealand Health Information Service 2001 Ministry of Health, Wellington. For updated information see www.nzhis.govt.nz/ moh.nsf/pagesns/216.

17.4.1 Coroners Act 2006[12]

The Coroners Act 2006 was prompted by a Law Commission Report produced in 2000, which identified a number of issues with the Coroners Act 1988. The Ministry of Justice undertook a series of reforms relating to the Coroners Act 1988. The Bill, to replace the 1988 Act, was introduced into Parliament in 2004 and was passed into law in August 2006. It came into force on 1 July 2007. The Act was designed to enhance public confidence in the integrity and independence of the coronial system.

(1)   *Key features of the Act*

- Appointment of the Chief Coroner;
- Provision for up to 20 legally qualified full-time Coroners rather than 55 mostly part-time Coroners;
- Establishment of the Coronial Services Unit (CSU);
- Clarification of the role of Coroners and other agencies involved in investigating deaths;
- Structured and standardised training for coronial staff nation-wide to provide greater consistency of practice across the country;
- Addressing problems of timeliness, lack of collegiality, and lack of standardised processes;
- Clarity of deaths that must be reported to the Coroner;
- Better recognition of the different cultural and spiritual needs of families and those with a close relationship to the deceased; and
- Enhancing the inquiry and inquest processes and allowing greater public access to information

There is a Chief Coroner and currently 14 full-time Coroners covering nine regions. The Chief Coroner's main function is to help ensure the integrity and effectiveness of the coronial system[13] by training Coroners, designation of Coroners, approving pathologists to carry out Coroner's post mortems, achieving consistency by issuing practice notes, maintaining a register of Coroner recommendations and by education and liaison with the public.

Coroners in New Zealand are legally qualified sworn judicial officers appointed by the Governor General on advice from the Attorney General.

(2)   *Coronial Services Unit*

The Coronial Services Unit was established under the Coroners Act 2006 for the delivery of support to the Chief Coroner and the Coroners. It provides case management, inquest hearing management, administrative, secretarial, research and judicial support as well as Registry support services for the Coroners. For more information go to www.justice.govt.nz/coroners.

---

12   Paragraph 17.4.1 is reprinted from the website of Coronial Services of New Zealand www.justice.govt.nz/courts/coroners-court/coronial-services-of-new-zealand/background-of-coronial-services with kind permission of the Ministry of Justice.

13   Coroners Act 2006, section 7.

17.4.2 The Role of the Coroner

Anyone in New Zealand who finds a body must notify the Police. The Police must report some deaths to the Coroner. Where a death occurs in hospital and a health practitioner attends, then it must be reported to the Police or the Coroner if it is one that is reportable. Reportable deaths are those:

- That appear to have been without known cause, are unnatural, violent or suicides; or
- Where no doctor has given a cause of death certificate; or
- That occur during a medical, surgical or dental procedure or similar operation or procedure; or
- That appear to be the result of a medical, surgical, dental or similar procedure; or
- That occurr while the person was affected by an anaesthetic or that appear to have been the result of the administration of an anaesthetic or medicine;
- That occurr while a woman was giving birth or that appear to have been a result of a woman being pregnant or giving birth; or
- Where the person had been in custody or care. This means:
  - A person detained under section 9 of the Alcoholism and Drug Addiction Act 1966;
  - A child or young person placed in a residence under section 365 of the Children, Young Persons, and Their Families Act 1989;
  - A child or young person in the custody or care of an Iwi Social Service or Cultural Social Service;[14]
  - A mental health patient (special or committed);[15]
  - A care recipient or proposed care recipient[16] (with an intellectual disability);
  - A prisoner[17] either in
    - (a)   Police custody; or
    - (b)   Under the control of an officer[18]—

whether or not the death has occurred in that place of custody or care; for example, if a prisoner dies of natural causes in a public hospital the death must be notified to the Coroner.

(1)   *The Coroner's role involves*

- Taking notification of deaths from Police and doctors;
- Directing Post Mortem examinations;

---

14   Pursuant to sections 43, 78, 110, 139, 140, 141, 234, 238 or 345 of the Children, Young Persons, and Their Families Act 1989.

15   "Patient" is defined in section 2 of the Mental Health (Compulsory Assessment and Treatment) Act 1992 (Mental Health (CAT) Act) to mean only persons who are required to be assessed or who are subject to a compulsory treatment order or who are special patients. Informal or "voluntary" patients who are mentally ill are therefore not patients and their deaths are not required to be reported to the Coroner.

16   As defined in section 6(1) and 6(4) of the Intellectual Disability (Compulsory Care and Rehabilitation) Act 2003.

17   As defined in section 3(1) of the Corrections Act 2004.

18   Corrections Act 2004, section 3(1).

- Talking to immediate families[19] of the deceased person about all significant matters, including post mortems and whether or not they have a right to object;[20]
- Authorising who can view, touch and remain with the body prior to post mortem examination;[21]
- Authorising who may attend the post mortem;[22]
- Releasing a body once it is no longer necessary to examine it;
- Conducting an inquiry which may including holding an inquest in some cases;
- Making written Findings.

17.4.3   Coroner's inquiry

There are three purposes for conducting inquiries. The first[23] is to establish so far as possible:

- That a person has died; and
- The person's identity; and
- When and where the person died; and
- The causes of the death; and
- The circumstances of the death; and

The second purpose is to make specified recommendations or comments that, in the opinion of the Coroner, may if drawn to public attention, reduce the chances of the occurrence of other deaths in such circumstances.[24]

The third purpose is to determine whether the public interest would be served by the death also being investigated by other investigating authorities. Such authorities include the Health and Disability Commissioner and any of the authorities established under the Health Practitioner's Competence Assurance Act 2003.

In inquiries involving health practitioners, often the principal focus will be the causes of the death and/or the circumstances of the death and the making of recommendations or comments to reduce the occurrence of similar deaths.

A Coroner has jurisdiction to open an inquiry in respect of any body that is in New Zealand or, where the body has not been found, where the Coroner is satisfied that it is likely that the person concerned is dead and the person's body is destroyed, irrecoverable, or lost (for example down a crevasse) and the person was alive in New Zealand immediately before it was unable to be found. Also a Coroner has jurisdiction to hold an inquiry in New Zealand where, although the body is not in the country, death occurred on or from an aircraft or ship and the Solicitor General has authorised the inquiry.

A Coroner need not always open an inquiry but *must* do so if the death appears to have been self inflicted or is one where the person who died had been in custody or care.[25]

---

19   Section 9 of the Coroners Act 2006 provides for a very wide definition of immediate family.
20   There is a right to object in some cases, see section 33(2) of the Coroners Act 2006 and paragraph 17.4.5 below.
21   Coroners Act 2006, section 25.
22   Coroners Act 2006, section 38.
23   Coroners Act 2006, section 57(2).
24   Coroners Act 2006, section 57(3).
25   Coroners Act 2006, section 60(1).

With other deaths a coroner has a discretion whether to open an inquiry and will consider the following criteria when deciding whether to open an inquiry:[26]

- Whether or not the causes of the death appear to have been natural;
- Where unnatural or violent, whether or not it appears to have been due to the actions or inaction of any other person;
- The existence and extent of any allegations, rumours, suspicions, or public concern about the death;
- The extent to which the drawing of attention to the circumstances of the death may be likely to reduce the chances of the occurrence of other deaths in similar circumstances;
- The desire of any members of the immediate family of the person concerned that an inquiry should be conducted;
- Any other matters the Coroner thinks fit.

An inquiry is not the same as an inquest. The inquiry begins from the moment the Coroner decides to open one and finishes when the coroner makes her or his Findings. Nowadays most inquiries are completed without holding an inquest (the public hearing). The only time a Coroner *must* hold an inquest is when the death is one where the person who died had been in custody or care. This is because there is a public interest in knowing what happens to people whose liberty is curtailed by the State and there has to be transparency about what goes on in our institutions.

However, where there are issues that need to be canvassed, or where someone wishes to give evidence in person, then an inquest will be held.

Where a person is charged with an offence, or some other investigation is to be held, the provisions of section 68 and 69 of the Coroners Act 2006 apply. A Coroner may postpone opening an inquiry or open it and then adjourn it until criminal proceedings or the other investigation (for example, conducted by the Department of Labour or the Health and Disability Commissioner or the Maritime Safety Authority) have been finally concluded. However, the Coroner may proceed if satisfied that the person is no longer to be charged/investigated or that the inquiry would not prejudice the person.

If the other investigation clearly establishes everything the Coroner has to establish under section 57 (the purpose of inquiries section) then the Coroner may decide not to open or resume an inquiry. This now avoids duplication of some investigations.

17.4.4   Medical and other reports to the Coroner

Coroners have wide powers and may require people to provide information or documents or other things.[27] So statements can be asked for from people involved in the care of the person who has died. Also telephone records can be accessed as well as text messages and information held on computer. The provisions of the Privacy Act 1993 and the Health Information Privacy Code 1994 allow for such disclosure because the Coroners Act 2006 overrides them and because there is specific provision in them for disclosure where there is a lawful purpose and it is necessary for that purpose.[28] Unless there are reasonable grounds

---

26   Coroners Act 2006, section 63.
27   Coroners Act 2006, sections 40 and 120.
28   See privacy Principle 1 and Rule 11: www.privacy.org.nz/privacy-principle-one/.

for refusing to supply the information (and these are set out in the Act)[29] then it is an offence not to comply with a notice to supply the information.[30]

17.4.5   Post mortems

Under section 31 of the Coroners Act 1988, a Coroner may direct a Pathologist to carry out a post mortem examination of the body. This can be directed either if the Coroner has decided to open an inquiry, or so that the Coroner can decide whether or not to open an inquiry. If a body is to undergo a post mortem or the person's death is the subject of an inquiry then, even if the deceased requested that their body parts or other tissue be donated for research or transplantation, these cannot be removed without the Coroner's consent.[31] However, even where a post mortem is possible the Coroner may, if satisfied it will not prejudice the inquiry, permit removal of the body parts for such purposes.

Body parts or body samples cannot be removed during the post mortem unless the Pathologist reasonably believes it is necessary and then they must be put back unless the Coroner has authorised otherwise and the Coroner must also explain this to family members.[32]

The Coroners Act 2006 signalled a major trend away from post mortem examinations, and section 32 provides criteria for deciding whether a Coroner should authorise one. It includes reference to minimising distress to those, who by reason of their ethnic origins, social attitudes or customs, or spiritual beliefs, customarily require bodies to be available to family members as soon as possible after death; or who find post mortem examinations offensive. The weight to be attached to the various criteria is a matter for a Coroner to determine in the particular circumstances of each case.

Section 33 of the Coroners Act 2006 provides for the right in some cases for family to object to post mortem unless the death is likely to have been the result of a criminal offence or where other laws require a post mortem to be performed.

The Coroner must therefore let the family know that she or he wishes to direct a post mortem and whether they have a right to object. This will often mean the Coroner will talk to the family about what a post mortem involves. Families have twenty-four hours to decide if they do object and the reasons for that. If they do, there is a process set out in section 34 of the Coroners Act 2006. Under it, the Coroner then has a further twenty-four hours to decide whether or not to uphold the family's objection or still direct the post mortem. The Coroner must let the family know the decision and then if it is that the post mortem should still be directed, the family has a further forty eight hours to appeal this decision to the High Court.

During this time the body will normally have to stay in the mortuary. Post mortem examinations are normally conducted during "office hours". So a death on a Friday would likely mean the post mortem would be carried out on the following Monday morning or even Tuesday or Wednesday if there are public holidays. This means the body could remain in the mortuary for a number of days. However, the Coroner can authorise that family/

---

29   Coroners Act 2006, section 121.
30   Coroners Act 2006, section 134.
31   Human Tissue Act 1964, section 3(5) or Human Tissue Act 2008, section 48(2).
32   Coroners Act 2006, section 48.

whanau remain with, view, and even touch the deceased,[33] as such delay can cause enormous distress. Section 37 of the Coroners Act 2006 allows a Coroner to direct the post mortem examination to be performed "immediately." This can be done where the person concerned is an infant, or where delay would limit the pathologist determining the cause of death, or where family /whanau have the ethnic origins, social attitudes or customs, or spiritual beliefs, which customarily require the body to be available to family members as soon as is possible after death.

17.4.6   Statements

Many inquiries into deaths are made by the police on behalf of the Coroner. The police need to gather information and interview those concerned. In carrying out this role, the police are acting as the Coroner's agents. The Coroner frequently makes direct inquiries, and asks for reports.

As soon as health practitioners are aware that an inquest may be held, or earlier if the circumstances of a particular death may be subject to inquiry, it is in their interest to write personal statements as to what happened, date them, and keep them. This may be used to aid their memories when they give evidence later, sometimes much later.

Health practitioners and other staff involved in a deceased's care may be asked by the Coroner or police to make a statement. They must provide it but they may seek legal advice if they are concerned about what to say, and provide a written statement rather than be interviewed by the police. They may decide to consult a lawyer if they are in any way concerned that they may be implicated in the death of the person. In this case, they should consider legal advice before making any statement. If they feel there is likely to be a contradiction between their statement and that of any other person, and they are absolutely certain of their facts, they should consider making a sworn statement as soon as practicable after the event.

17.4.7   Inquests

Inquests are public hearings and are not always held nowadays during a coroner's inquiry. Where they are, Coroners have wide powers to direct evidence to be placed before them. This includes the testimony of witnesses, records, and exhibits.

The Coroner may call for independent expert opinion evidence and this is provided in accordance with the High Court Rules for expert witnesses. The expert witness may be subject to cross-examination.

On the recommendation of a Coroner, the Chief Coroner may appoint a specialist adviser to sit with and help the Coroner at an inquest by giving advice.[34] The specialist adviser's appointment continues until the Coroner's findings are given.[35] The specialist adviser is not subject to cross-examination.

---

33   Coroners Act 2006, section 25. The Coroner will normally authorise such viewing or remaining with or near the body but must take certain matters into account first. These are set out in section 26 of the Coroners Act 2006 and include whether there is a risk of contamination of evidence or a risk to the security of the body or insufficient facilities or suitable staff available to supervise visitors.

34   Coroners Act 2006. section 83(1).

35   Coroners Act 2006, section 83(4).

Health practitioners may be required to give evidence at an inquest, in which case they answer questions under oath if so required. It should be remembered that the inquest process is inquisitorial rather than adversarial and is not a trial. The purposes of any Coroners inquiry do not include determining civil, criminal or disciplinary liability.[36]

All witnesses, except in the case sometimes of expert witnesses, will receive a summons to appear as a witness. Failure to turn up, or refusal to give evidence when required to, is an offence, with a penalty.

(1)   *Legal representation*

Any person or organisation with a sufficient interest, or whom the Coroner has directed be notified, has the right to appear or be represented by legal counsel at an inquest. A Coroner will notify any person or organisation, such as a District Health Board, or Resthome whose actions are likely to be called into question. Those with a "sufficient interest" include the deceased's immediate family and any medical practitioner who attended the person before the death, or during an illness that preceded death.

The Coroner may require clinical records, or any other documents. Health practitioners may be called as witnesses, and be required to testify to their having written the documents and to explain them. Well-written and legible medical notes are often crucial to a proper investigation of the circumstances of a death (see 9.3.2).

(2)   *Procedure*

The Coroner is required to examine witnesses on oath or affirmation. This means that any false testimony is perjury, and is subject to punitive action. Evidence of a witness is often given in written form by way of a statement (or brief of evidence), that the person is asked to read out in Court. The witness has the opportunity to add to (verbally), or to amend the evidence. Witnesses may be excluded from the Court until they have given their evidence.

Coroners' inquests are usually open to the public.[37] A Coroner may exclude any person from the entire inquest, or from any part of an inquest if satisfied that it is in the interests of justice, decency, or public order to do so.[38]

The media can attend Coroners' inquests, but where the finding is one of suicide, publication is prohibited without the Coroner's authority.[39] The Coroner has the power to prohibit publication of any evidence given at an inquest, or any other part of the proceedings of an inquiry, if satisfied that it is in the interests of justice, decency, public order, or personal privacy to do so.[40]

(3)   *Answering questions*

When giving evidence in any hearing, witnesses should keep in mind that questioning is often designed to test the accuracy and truth of their answers. Some general rules to follow are:

---

36   Coroners Act 2006, section 57(1).
37   Coroners Act 2006, section 85.
38   Coroners Act 2006, section 86.
39   Coroners Act 2006, section 71.
40   Coroners Act 2006, section 74.

- Speak slowly and clearly.
- Consider answers carefully. It is better to pause and collect one's thoughts, than to rush into answers. Backtracking, correcting oneself or being corrected by others, and stumbling through the answer give a bad impression. However, don't pause for too long — you may appear to be concocting an answer. If it is difficult to remember precisely how something happened, or to express things clearly, say so.
- It is no disgrace to forget. The best approach is to be honest and say that one cannot remember something, or cannot recall precisely how it happened, than to answer untruthfully or to fabricate an answer. One is not in the witness box to please the person asking the questions, nor to appear efficient and helpful, but to answer questions to the best of one's ability.
- Remain calm, despite attempts to test one's self-control.

Witnesses are required to answer all questions, except those where the answer might incriminate them (see 17.4.8). It is an offence to refuse to answer other questions, even on the ground of breach of confidence. It is also an offence to refuse to take the oath or affirmation, to refuse to produce documents, or to impede or disrupt the proceedings. Such actions may be contempt of Court, attracting fines or even imprisonment. It is also an offence to disrupt proceedings, or to misbehave during them.

17.4.8 Incriminating evidence

An important rule that is maintained is the rule against self-incrimination. A witness, who thinks that to answer a question would incriminate them, or implicate them in some criminal offence, may refuse to answer on that ground.

This may occur in two ways:

- A person may be asked a question, such as: "Did you remove the oxygen mask?", the answer to which may directly indicate that they committed a crime;
- A question may be asked that the witness perceives is part of a pattern of questioning, which, if continued, might lead to the inference that they committed a crime. This perceived trend may only be a suspicion, but the witness may, nevertheless, claim the privilege. It may be that the Coroner requires an investigation into why the question is not being answered. A reasonable apprehension of the danger of incrimination is grounds for not answering.

17.4.9 Findings of a Coroner

Frequently in inquests that examine medical or mental health issues, the complexity of the evidence and the issues require the inquest to be adjourned, in order that the Coroner can give a written finding.

A Coroner may not comment adversely on any living person without taking all reasonable steps to notify the person of the proposed comment, and giving that person a reasonable opportunity to be heard in relation to the proposed comment.[41]

Inquiries, whether or not they include holding inquests, are concluded by the Coroner making Findings, which are delivered either orally or made in writing. Where oral Findings

---

41   Coroners Act 2006, section 58(3).

are made a written transcript of these will be made available to the family and all those other interested persons.

After the Findings are made the inquiry is concluded and the Coroner then becomes "functus officio", which means that he or she is no longer acting on the matter and this also means they cannot respond to any comments or questions about their Findings or recommendations.

17.4.10   Release of bodies for burial or cremation

For a body to be released by the Coroner, a funeral director must have either a certificate as to cause of death under section 25 of the Births, Deaths, Marriages, and Relationships Registration Act 1995, or an order for release of the body from the Coroner.

There may be circumstances where a medical practitioner will issue a certificate as to cause of death, but nevertheless an inquiry is opened and the Coroner may require a post mortem. In these circumstances, the inquiry takes priority and the certificate as to cause of death should not be registered.

Sometimes there is a delay in a Coroner issuing an order for release of the body, for example in homicide cases. If a person has been charged with an offence, or is about to be charged, then generally the Coroner will ensure that no further access to the body is required for forensic purposes before giving the order for release of the body. In this situation, it is a matter of balancing the wishes of the family for release of the body, against the rights of any person charged or about to be charged with an offence. The Coroner keeps in close contact with the Forensic Pathologist and the police in these circumstances.

17.5   Guidance for health practitioners in relation to sudden deaths and Coroners' inquests

Sometimes when an unexpected, suspicious or sudden death occurs the police will be notified by an attending doctor, in some cases by telephone from the hospital ward or unit where the death occurred. In some of these cases, the police attend straightaway and may take photographs. They may also seize clinical notes, TPR and blood pressure charts, and fluid balance charts. They might also seize equipment such as ampoules and syringes.

The police at this stage are acting as agents of the Coroner, but might also be investigating to determine if a crime has been committed. It is therefore important to remember that once the clinical notes and other documents have been returned to the hospital, that the police will have photocopied them. Entries written subsequently should never be written as though they were written at an earlier date, but it is especially important to remember in this situation. If this is even done inadvertently, and then later is discovered by the police or Coroner (as it inevitably will be, because the police and Coroner will have a copy of the original notes) then suspicion of covering up could be directed at the writer of the notes.

In cases where the police do not attend a death immediately, the clinical notes could be sealed straight after the death to prevent backdated notes being inadvertently written. If it is necessary to write a later note, it is best to put "written in retrospect" at the top of it and clearly write the date and time of writing it.

The police may want to interview the health practitioners who were caring for the deceased immediately prior to his or her death. This is often a traumatic time for these health practitioners, who might have developed a therapeutic relationship with the deceased and may be distressed. No one has to talk to the police straightaway, even if the police want them to do so. It is perfectly permissible to tell the police that you are happy to assist them but you cannot do so right away. It is also permissible not to have to stay behind on a shift to give a statement. It can be done the next day, or even given in writing. Some health practitioners might want to wait until they have sought legal advice and readers are advised to do this if they have any concerns about what the giving of a statement could mean in terms of their own care of the deceased.

The police will give all the statements to the Coroner, who will then decide if he or she needs more information and also whether to hold an inquest as part of his or her inquiry and if so, whether to call the makers of the statements to give evidence as witnesses. Many health practitioners who are requested to make statements by the police are not called to give evidence at an inquest. Often, the Coroner will have sufficient information from a statement and will not need to ask further questions of the person who made the statement. In other cases however, the maker of a statement will be called to give evidence. This may be because the Coroner needs clarification of some points, or the deceased's family wish to ask questions, or the inquest is into a death where the cause or circumstances of it are in the public interest.

As discussed in chapter 4, in these latter inquests the media may be present in the courtroom during the giving of evidence, and a Coroner may allow witnesses to be filmed giving their evidence.

Inquires begin the moment the Coroner opens one and conclude with the Coroner's Findings, but inquests are only *part* of this process and are nowadays often not held. Many inquiries are finalised without holding an inquest by what are called Chambers Findings,[42] which are not made in public and usually means the Coroner makes a written Finding based "on the papers" (all the evidence she or he has received in writing). If an inquest is held it is usually open to the public and is often, but not always, held in a courtroom. Health practitioners might be understandably anxious if they are not used to giving evidence.

It is suggested that they talk with someone else who has done so or with a lawyer from their professional organisation, who can advise them on the process. If the lawyer thinks it necessary, he or she will attend the inquest with them and represent them as legal counsel. Legal advice and representation is expensive, but it is normally covered by the health practitioner's professional indemnity insurance. Professional indemnity insurance is sometimes provided as one of the benefits of membership of a professional organisation, for example the New Zealand Nurses Organisation and the New Zealand College of Midwives have insurance policies that provide their members with professional indemnity insurance.

If a reader is ever required to make a statement or give evidence at an inquest, it is sensible to act cautiously. The Coroners' Court is fact-finding and is not an adversarial process, and a Coroner's role is not to blame individuals. Some families however, use a Coroner's inquest to "test a case". Coroners have the power to make adverse comments on the conduct of

---

42   See Coroners Act 2006, section 77.

any person, when establishing the circumstances of death. Thus, blame can be implied. This could mean that a Coroner's inquest would not be the end of the matter for the health practitioner.

Evidence gathered by a Coroner can be used by, for example, the Health and Disability Commissioner. Occasionally at inquests that have a strong public interest element, investigators from the Health and Disability Commissioner's office might be present at the inquest hearing and take notes. An adverse comment about a health practitioner in the Coroner's Findings might also lead to a civil claim against the health practitioner in some rare cases (see chapter 8).

Generally, it can be stated that if an adverse comment is made about a health practitioner at an inquest, the health practitioner should be prepared for the matter to go further in another forum (see chapter 4). The family of the deceased may make a complaint to the Health and Disability Commissioner, if they have not already done so before the inquest. Any finding by the Commissioner of a serious breach of the Code of Health and Disability Services Consumers Rights can be referred to the Director of Proceedings, who has the power to bring a professional disciplinary charge against the practitioner. Health practitioners, who are at all concerned about their care of the deceased, are advised to seek legal advice before talking to the police or making any statement.

17.6   Burial and cremation

The law regarding burial and cremation is to be found in the Burial and Cremation Act 1964 and its subordinate regulations.[43] The Act does not apply to Maori burial grounds.[44] Under the provisions of the Act, local authorities may make by-laws for any cemetery under their control, regulating and restricting the position of graves, prohibiting the burial of more than one body in any grave, and prescribing conditions under which more than one body may be buried in any grave. The by-laws may also regulate the burial in the cemetery of the ashes of the dead and control or restrict the times when burials may be carried out.[45]

The local authority is responsible for public health and for preventing the escape of any noxious exhalation in the cemetery. Therefore, it has power to make by-laws directing the depths of graves and the construction of coffins.

A local authority may also erect a crematorium, either within or outside a cemetery's boundaries. The manner in which cremations are to be carried out is provided for in the Cremation Regulations 1973.

Part 8 of the Burial and Cremation Act 1964 provides for offences. Section 54 makes it an offence on penalty of $400 to bury a body in any land that is not a cemetery or private denominational burial ground, or a Maori burial ground if there is any such burial ground within 32 km of the place where the death has occurred, or the body has been taken for lying in state. If there is no burial ground within 32 km, the body may be buried in other

---

43   Burial and Cremation (Removal of Monuments and Tablets) Regulations 1967; Cremation Regulations 1973; Exhumation Licence Fee Order 1991; Waipori Cemetery Order 1977.

44   Burial and Cremation Act 1964, section 3.

45   A stillborn child cannot be buried unless a certificate that the child was born dead has been provided to the person burying it.

land, but a District Court Judge must be notified within 3 days after the burial of the buried person's name if known, the supposed cause of death, and the place of burial.

Exceptionally, with a District Court Judge's permission or with the permission of a mayor or two councillors, any body may be buried in any private burial place used for burials before the Burial and Cremation Act 1964 came into force. It will only be when such a burial would be prejudicial to public health or decency that permission could be refused.

All burials and cremations must be registered in a register provided and kept by the local authority. The registers are to be kept open for public inspection, upon payment of a small fee.

No body or body remains may be removed from its burial place without authority from the Minister of Health. Any person removing a body or its remains commits an offence, and is liable for a penalty of up to $400 or imprisonment for 3 months.[46] There are fines of up to $1,000 and 12 months' imprisonment for breaching the cremation regulations by burning or taking part in the burying of a body, except in accordance with the regulations.[47] Also, any person who wilfully makes a false statement or certificate with a view to procuring the cremation of a body is liable to a term of up to 2 years' imprisonment.[48] There is also a fine of up to $40 for allowing an animal to enter any cemetery or burial ground of any sort, and a further fine of $10 in respect of every animal entering.[49]

17.7   Further reading

C Dorries, *Coroners' Courts: A Guide to Law and Practice*, London, Blackstone Press, 2004.

I Freckleton, *Regulating Health Practitioners*, Sydney, Federation Press, 2006.

I Freckleton and D Ransom, *Death Investigation and the Coroner's Inquest*, Melbourne, Oxford University Press, 2006.

Matthews and Foreman J (eds), *Jervis on the Office and Duties of Coroners* (12th ed), London, Sweet & Maxwell, 2002.

T P Smith and Rudolf Ludwig Karl Virchow, *Post Mortem Examinations: With Especial Reference to Medico-Legal Practice (1896)*, Montana, Kessinger Publishing, 2008.

Stefan Timmermans, *Post Mortem: How Medical Examiners Explain Suspicious Deaths*, Chicago, University of Chicago Press, 2007.

---

46   Burial and Cremation Act 1964, section 55.
47   Burial and Cremation Act 1964, section 56(1).
48   Burial and Cremation Act 1964, section 56(2).
49   Burial and Cremation Act 1964, section 57(1).

Chapter 18

PUBLIC HEALTH AND CARE AND PROTECTION

DAVID KERSLAKE, REBECCA KEENAN AND SUE JOHNSON

Contents

18.1   Regulating public health

There have in the past been questions raised as to the manner in which Parliament regulates public health, and under what circumstances, if at all, a person should be detained and treated against their will on the basis of a doctor's diagnosis.

New Zealand has legislation dealing with diseases subject to government intervention: the Health Act 1956 and Regulations made under the Act. This legislation is, in a number of respects, considered to be dated, and has for some time now been undergoing a review. It is anticipated that the legislation will eventually be superseded by a new Act: the Public Health Act.[1] Progress on advancing with this legislation is continuing. The intention of the Public Health Bill, as introduced by the former Labour-led government, is to update existing public health legislation — in order to "improve, promote, and protect, public health, and to help attain optimal and equitable health outcomes for all population groups across New Zealand".

In December 2007, the Bill, introduced into Parliament the previous month, was referred to the Health Select Committee. The Committee proceeded to hear submissions during March and April 2008, and in June of that year the Bill was "reported back to Parliament" by the Committee. In mid-2008, the then Minister of Health suggested that the Bill would "future-proof" public health for generations to come. The Minister noted that the Public Health Association and The Office of the Children's Commissioner were amongst those supporting the Bill. At the time of writing this text, the Bill is still awaiting its second reading. Parliament's last sitting day for 2008, under the Labour-led government, was Friday, 26 September. The Bill was one of those "carried over" into the newly-elected National-led government.

---

1   A draft version of this can viewed at www.legislation.govt.nz/bill/government/2007/0177/latest/ DLM1049327.html.

18.1.1 Category of diseases

Certain categories of disease must be reported to a Medical Officer of Health, and, in some cases, to the local authority. They have powers to ensure the containment of any threat to public health.

New Zealand law currently classifies diseases in different ways. Obligations and powers apply according to how a disease is classified. Five categories are used:

- Notifiable diseases;
- Infectious diseases;
- Communicable diseases;
- Venereal diseases; and
- Quarantinable diseases.

Notifiable diseases may be reported to the Medical Officer of Health for many reasons, including infectiousness, while infectious diseases may or may not be notifiable. Venereal diseases come under powers more specifically related to the nature of such a disease. Communicable diseases are any infectious disease, for example tuberculosis, or venereal disease, and have specific but minor provisions in relation to them.[2] Quarantinable diseases also have specific provisions.[3]

18.2 Notifiable diseases[4]

The government has an interest in people's affairs when their illnesses or activities pose a threat to the health of others. A person may have a contagious disease that requires isolation and special treatment, or may be engaged in activity potentially or actually dangerous to the health of others. The government's role, therefore, involves prevention, as well as cure.

There are many ways in which the government acts to maintain public health, which include the following:

- Regulating standards in places such as camping grounds;[5]
- Licensing the preparation and serving of food;
- Developing community public education and awareness programmes;
- Maintaining an awareness of international health issues that may impact on the health of New Zealanders;
- Encouraging regular health checkups and providing specialised clinics and information centres; and
- Providing immunisation programmes.

The government goes further, however, when dealing with infectious, communicable, and quarantinable diseases. It reserves the right to intervene in people's private lives, and where necessary, to isolate or quarantine them and subject them to compulsory treatment.[6]

---

2   Health (Infectious and Notifiable Diseases) Regulations 1966 and Infectious and Notifiable Diseases Order 1966.
3   Health (Quarantine) Regulations 1983 and Health (Quarantine Inspection Places) Notice 2005.
4   Primarily governed by the Health Act 1956.
5   Health Act 1956, section 120B and Camping-Grounds Regulations 1985.
6   As shown by the recent (2009) swine flu pandemic that saw people quarantined in their homes.

This raises the issue of the relative weight to be given to the freedom of the individual. As with mental health, there may be conflict between the "medical" model and the "rights" model. However, there is much less conflict regarding the nature, cause, and treatment of diseases in the public health arena. The acquired immunodeficiency syndrome ("AIDS") and the increasing numbers of people infected with the human immunodeficiency virus ("HIV"), and Severe Acute Respiratory Syndrome ("SARS"), and most recently (at the time of writing, September 2009), the global Influenza A H1N1 "swine flu" pandemic, have each raised a lot of questions — for the government, healthcare providers, and communities across New Zealand — bringing into the public arena many issues that had hitherto been given little attention. Both swine flu and SARS have emphasised the increased vulnerability of all people to communicable diseases that can be spread rapidly due to the ease of international travel.

18.2.1 Pandemics

At the time of writing,[7] many countries — including, to a lesser extent, New Zealand — are still within the grasp of a "pandemic". At the centre of this health crisis, unprecedented in modern times, is the Influenza A H1N1 virus, or — as it has come to be known colloquially — swine flu. In the early months of 2009, Mexican public health authorities reported increased levels of respiratory disease, including reports of severe pneumonia cases and deaths. Subsequent testing of specimens revealed the Influenza A (H1N1) strain.

H1N1, a newly-identified strain of the influenza A virus, can cause, and has caused, both illness and death. Early laboratory testing reportedly showed that many of the genes in the virus were similar to the strain of H1N1 influenza virus that normally occurs in pigs in North America — hence it swiftly became referred to globally as "swine flu". Further tests revealed that, as well as avian and human influenza virus genes, H1N1 has two genes from flu viruses that normally circulate in pigs in Europe and Asia.

In June 2009, The World Health Organization (WHO) declared a global pandemic, and put the world on the highest of pandemic alerts: Phase Six. At that point, it had been established that the virus had spread globally through human-to-human transmission. While the greater proportion of cases was reported to be mild, severe illness and death were confirmed amongst victims of swine flu. As at mid-June 2009, countries reporting cases of Influenza A (H1N1) infection numbered in the seventies, with almost 36,000 cases of infection having been reported, and 163 resulting deaths.

(1)   *Community transmission*

Once community transmission of the virus had been confirmed in New Zealand, containment measures at international borders were implemented. Those suspected of having Influenza A (H1N1) were requested to stay in isolation, and to take anti-viral medication.

The numbers of confirmed cases continued to increase, with the first community transmission reportedly recorded in the country's capital, Wellington, on 14 June. In response, the Ministry of Health increased the pandemic alert status to Phase 6: Scenario 6.2 (Code Yellow/Red). Within days, after further cases of community transmission had

---

7   June-September 2009.

been confirmed, the Ministry revised its pandemic status to one of *managing* (rather than containing) the virus and its spread. District Health Boards (DHB's) are the lead agencies, on a local and regional basis, for planning and responding to a pandemic. They follow major incident and emergency plans, and regional incident co-ordination plans specifically focused on the outbreaks of pandemics.

Activities at the country's borders continued, but quarantining, the dispensing of anti-viral drugs, and individual (H1N1) testing, were reduced. Given, however, that the southern hemisphere was at the time about to encounter its typical arrival of seasonal influenza — with the potential to further exacerbate pressure on the health system, as well as disruption to everyday business and community activities — containment of the virus was integral to avoiding simultaneous impact of the *two* influenza viruses.

The Ministry of Health advised households to stock up on essential goods and fever-reducing medicines, and businesses were advised to encourage their staff to be prudent — particularly those who may have travelled off-shore in recent times. It was progressively anticipated that the majority of Influenza A (H1N1) cases would recover at home, without the need for medical intervention.

As at September 2009, the number of deaths from swine flu in New Zealand reportedly stood at 17, with more than 3100 cases of the virus having been confirmed.[8] WHO, in the same month, acknowledged that transmission of the virus was in decline globally.

(2)   *Planning for pandemics*

In November 2006, the Ministry of Health produced the New Zealand Pandemic Action Plan.[9] The Plan outlines national scenarios based on the WHO suggestions for various phases of alerts, and gives corresponding alert codes and strategies.

A (New Zealand) parliamentary support research paper explains that pandemics are characterised by the global spread of a novel type of virus. Three conditions, the paper notes, must be present for a disease to cause a pandemic: a new virus subtype emerges to which the population has little or no immunity; the new virus can cause serious illness in humans; and it spreads efficiently between humans.[10]

The Ministry of Health, which takes the lead role in planning for a health-related emergency, has established an internal Pandemic Emergency Group. Reporting to the National Health Emergency Plan (NHEP) steering group, the Group oversees and co-ordinates pandemic planning for the health sector. The Pandemic Emergency Group and the NHEP steering group report to the Ministry of Health Executive Team and the Minister of Health.

(3)   *Relevant legislation*

As explained in the parliamentary support research paper, it is the Epidemic Preparedness Act 2006 that allows the Prime Minister, with the agreement of the Minister of Health, "to enable special powers". These become operative once the Prime Minister issues an "Epidemic Notice" in the Gazette. Before doing so, the Prime Minister must be satisfied

---

8   As at January 2010, NZ swine flu statistics stood at 3175 confirmed cases and 20 associated deaths.

9   www.moh.govt.nz/moh.nsf/indexmh/nz-influenza-pandemic-action-plan-2006.

10   For more information go to this government link: www.parliament.nz/en-NZ/ParlSupport/ ResearchPapers/c/1/8/00PLSoc09041-Human-Influenza-A-H1N1-Swine-Flu.htm.

that the effects of an outbreak of a stated infectious disease are, "likely to disrupt or continue to disrupt essential governmental and business activity in New Zealand (or stated parts of New Zealand) significantly."[11]

The Epidemic Notice, explains the parliamentary support research paper, activates the special powers of the Medical Officers of Health, as covered under sections 70 and 71 of the Health Act 1956. The paper also explains that, acting under section 71A of this Act, the Police have special powers to do anything reasonably necessary (including the use of force) to assist Medical Officers of Health.

18.3 Reporting

All notifiable diseases should be reported. At this time (2009), it is pertinent to note that medical laboratories may be required to give notice of cases of disease during an epidemic.[12] The Schedules to the Health Act 1956 list the diseases that are infectious and notifiable, and those that are not infectious, but are notifiable. Some examples of notifiable diseases are:

- Acute gastroenteritis;
- AIDS;
- Campylobacteriosis;
- Creutzfeldt Jacob Disease and other spongiform encephalitis;
- Decompression sickness;
- Hepatitis A;
- Hepatitis B;
- Hepatitis C;
- Highly Pathogenic Avian Influenza (including HPAI subtype H5N1)
- Measles;
- Meningitis (Neisseria meningitis invasive disease);
- Mumps;
- Pertussis;
- Poisoning arising from chemical contamination of the environment;
- Rheumatic fever;
- Rubella; and
- SARS.

Generally, only notifiable diseases have to be reported to the Medical Officer of Health for the area, and, in some cases, also to the local authority of the district. Most infectious diseases are also notifiable, but there are some, for example (seasonal) influenza, that are not notifiable, and so need not be reported.

18.3.1 Who must notify?

The Health Act 1956 requires notification of certain diseases to a prescribed authority. Any medical practitioner who has attended a person, and has reason to believe that person has a disease or symptoms that create a reasonable suspicion that it is a notifiable disease, or

---

11   Epidemic Preparedness Act, section 5(1).
12   Health Act 1956, section 74AA.

who attends a deceased person, that is, at a post-mortem, who had the disease, must notify the District Medical Officer of Health. In some cases, a pathologist, who certifies that a person had the disease, must notify the Medical Officer of Health and the local authority if required. In limited circumstances, infectious and communicable diseases that are not listed as notifiable should also be reported:

1.   Where it is suspected a person who is living in premises and is suffering from a notifiable infectious disease, it is the *occupier's* duty,[13] or whoever may be in charge of the premises, to consult a medical practitioner, or to notify the local authority.

2.   The *master of a vessel*[14] carrying any person who is suffering from a sickness, that is reasonably suspected to be a notifiable infectious disease, has a duty to notify the Medical Officer of Health of the existence of the disease.

3.   A *funeral director* or other person having charge of a funeral, where the deceased died of an infectious disease, must notify the Medical Officer of Health.

4.   Every *vet*[15] who has reason to believe that any animal professionally attended to by them is suffering from a communicable disease must also give notice to the Medical Officer of Health.

18.3.2   What information must be given?

The infectious nature of the disease, and the precautions that must be taken, should be explained to the client. Personal information must be obtained from the client, including, in some cases, the details of any contacts. In the case of a child with a very infectious disease, this might include facts such as the school attended by the child, and details of the child's contacts there.

18.3.3   What can authorities do?

There are powers in the Health Act 1956 allowing the Medical Officer of Health to pursue several courses of action.[16] They may cause the inspection of premises where the person is residing, or elsewhere.

In some cases, property may be seized and/or dealt with (for example, disposed of or fumigated), and the person and any other person may be required to undergo tests, and/ or be removed, by force if necessary, to a specified place, to undergo specified treatment or be effectively isolated.

18.4   Venereal diseases

Venereal disease includes gonorrhoea, gonorrhoeal ophthalmia, syphilis, soft chancre, venereal warts, or venereal granuloma.

---

13   Health Act 1956, section 75.
14   Health Act 1956, section 76.
15   Health Act 1956, section 87A(2).
16   Health Act 1956, section 71.

18.4.1 Reporting

The aforementioned provisions in regard to notifiable diseases, as well as powers to examine and detain people (18.3.3) apply generally to venereal diseases, but there are some specific requirements that apply to this type of disease.[17]

The diseases defined as venereal diseases are all categorised in the Health Act 1956 as infectious diseases. They are not defined as notifiable, but as "Other infectious diseases".[18] Consequently, they need only be reported as outlined in 18.3. However, if a medical practitioner has reason to believe a consumer they have been treating for a venereal disease has had intimate sexual contact with another person, and the medical practitioner becomes aware of the other person's name and address, they may communicate these facts to the Medical Officer of Health.[19]

18.4.2 Compulsory examination and treatment

The legislation provides powers allowing the compulsory examination and treatment of people suffering from venereal diseases when they do not willingly undertake treatment of their own volition. Prescribed treatment must be followed until a person is certified as being free of the disease, and notification must be given of change of address or medical practitioner.

The Health Act 1956 makes it an offence to knowingly infect any other person with a venereal disease.[20]

Every medical practitioner who attends any consumer with any venereal disease must, in written form:[21]

- Direct the consumer's attention to the infectious character of the disease, and to the penalties prescribed by the legislation for infecting any other person;
- Warn the consumer against having sexual intercourse until they are cured of that disease in a communicable form; and
- Give the consumer printed information relating to the disease and to their legal obligations as a person with that disease.

18.4.3 Confidentiality must be maintained

The legislation requires all letters are sent through the post, if relating to any person suffering from a venereal disease, to be conspicuously marked with the word "confidential".[22]

A medical practitioner, who attends a child (a person under the age of 16) who is suffering from a venereal disease, must notify the child's parents or guardian, unless the practitioner decides it would be undesirable to do so in the interests of the child's health, or in the wider interests of public health.[23]

---

17   Health Act 1956, sections 88-92 and the Venereal Diseases Regulations 1982.
18   Health Act 1956, Schedule 1, Part 2.
19   Venereal Diseases Regulations 1982, regulation 7(2).
20   Health Act 1956, section 92, and a penalty on summary conviction of a fine not exceeding $1000 or a term of imprisonment not exceeding 1 year, or both.
21   Health Act 1956, section 89.
22   Venereal Diseases Regulations 1982, regulation 14.
23   Venereal Diseases Regulations 1982, regulation 7(5).

18.5 Acquired immunodeficiency syndrome

Acquired immunodeficiency syndrome ("AIDS") is one of the most serious infectious diseases. It is also of concern because of its social and psychological ramifications, and the stigma attached to it.[24]

18.5.1 Legal requirements

The Health Act 1956 categorises AIDS as an infectious disease notifiable to the Medical Officer of Health. The requirements for the reporting of AIDS are the same as for other notifiable infectious diseases (see 18.3). The inclusion of AIDS as a notifiable infectious disease begs the question of what stage the disease must be at to become notifiable. There are several systems of categorisation by which stages of the illness have been divided by the medical profession. The presence of HIV-positive serum tests is not notifiable; therefore a person with HIV-positive serum tests is not classed as having an infectious disease within the meaning of the Health Act 1956.

Case
R v Mwai [1995] 3 NZLR 149; (1995) 13 CRNZ 273 (CA)
Mwai had sexual intercourse with several women when he knew he was HIV-positive. Two of the women became infected, allegedly from him. He was charged under the Crimes Act 1961 with causing grievous bodily harm, with reckless disregard for the safety of others and with criminal nuisance.

Mwai was convicted on both charges. On appeal, these convictions were upheld, as was the sentence of 7 years' imprisonment. Mwai was deported back to Africa before his prison term had been fully served, and he died there.

The "year and a day" rule[25] will act to limit potential liability for the death of someone who has been maliciously infected with AIDS. The victim must die within a year and a day of the malicious act before the offence could possibly amount to murder. This would also apply to the malicious, actual, or threatened injection of a person with HIV-positive blood, or other attempts to infect a person.

There has been recent heightened awareness in the national newspapers of men being alleged to have unprotected sex without disclosing their HIV status. They had not been diagnosed with AIDS, but their HIV status was known to health authorities. In May 2009, it was reported that the government may consider changing the law after a man believed to be infecting others with HIV was not reported to police because of patient confidentiality. Health authorities were told the HIV-positive man was allegedly infecting people in Auckland and Wellington with the virus months previously but were not obliged to tell police, a newspaper reported. The Public Health Bill makes HIV a notifiable disease and would to an extent close this loophole, names and details of the person infected do not need to be notified but it does provide an exception to this. However the Public Health

---

24   Health (Infectious and Notifiable Diseases) Regulations 1966, Amendment No 5, Form 1 in Schedule 1 requires that the person is identified only by initials, sex and date of birth (as under Health Act 1956, section 74).

25   Crimes Act 1961, section 162; and chapter 16 (16.4.2).

Bill is not progressing at this time (September 2009) though it has completed its Select Committee process.

18.5.2 Discrimination against people with AIDS

It is a breach of consumer confidentiality to disclose the identity of a person with any form of disease, subject of course to notification requirements. This also applies to people with AIDS.[26] Discrimination against people with AIDS takes many forms, from refusal to treat them, special categorisation of consumers, unwarranted isolation, and special methods of handling food and equipment. It also extends to many day-to-day matters that are incidental to the lifestyles of those concerned.

The Human Rights Act 1993 prohibits discrimination on the basis of the "presence in the body of organisms capable of causing disease".[27] It is also in breach of the Act to discriminate on the basis of a person's sexual orientation.[28] Although it is unlawful to discriminate on the basis of someone having in their body organisms capable of causing illness (which includes AIDS), in some circumstances discrimination against people with AIDS, may be allowed. An example may be where the presence of the organism would endanger another — for instance, if the person was applying for a job handling blood. However, it is only in limited circumstances that such discrimination may be acceptable (see chapter 5).

Anti-discrimination legislation would therefore appear to establish that health practitioners cannot refuse a client treatment, nor give inferior treatment, simply because a person is HIV-positive or has AIDS, and that a consumer can attempt to obtain redress for discrimination on the grounds of their sexual orientation. This poses a challenge for those who have objections to caring for these clients. Also involved in the issue is the rule that an employee should obey the employer's reasonable and lawful directions (see chapter 13). A health practitioner contemplating refusing to treat a consumer who has an infectious or notifiable disease could be in breach of anti-discrimination legislation, and should seek medical and legal advice. Questions that should be addressed relate to the consequences of treatment or non-treatment:

- The chances of the health practitioner contracting the virus;
- Whether the risk of infection can be reasonably reduced if care is given;
- The consequences of non-treatment for the consumer (and others, if relevant);
- The balance between harm to the health practitioner by *giving* care, and to the consumer by *not giving* it;
- Any less drastic solution to the problem than not giving care; and
- The course of action indicated by authorities on the issue.

Discrimination can best be dealt with by educating health professionals and their clients, and by carefully considered programmes where special treatment is required for the safety, comfort, convenience, and wellbeing of those concerned. Where health professionals genuinely fear for their safety, or they believe conditions are not such that proper care can be given, they should discuss the matter with their supervisor, and/or management.

---

26   See 9.4.6(5) with regard to disclosure to sexual partners.
27   Human Rights Act 1993, section 21(1)(h)(vii).
28   Human Rights Act 1993, section 21(1)(m).

18.5.3   Compulsory isolation to prevent the spread of AIDS

As is the case with all those who have a notifiable disease, a person with AIDS must undergo medical examination if required by the Medical Officer of Health. A person may be removed to a hospital or other suitable place, and isolated, if the Medical Officer of Health believes they are likely to cause the spread of an infectious disease.[29] HIV sero-positivity is not an infectious disease within the meaning of the Health Act 1956.[30] However, engaging in unprotected sexual intercourse while HIV-positive, can cause the spread of AIDS. In May 1999, the Medical Officer of Health for the Canterbury District isolated two men he believed were likely to cause the spread of AIDS, and who were HIV-positive, but who did not themselves have AIDS. The two men were engaging in unprotected sexual intercourse with a number of people who did not know the men were HIV-positive. The men were also charged with criminal nuisance, convicted, given a suspended sentence, and placed in the care of the Medical Officer of Health. This enforced isolation will continue until such time as the Medical Officer of Health is satisfied they are no longer likely to cause the spread of AIDS.[31]

18.5.4   Compulsory blood testing for AIDS on admission to facilities

There is no legislation providing for the compulsory blood testing of consumers on admission to hospital or other health facilities, although there have been calls to pass such legislation. There are many arguments for and against such measures — some of the major considerations being the cost, doubtful value, and emotional disadvantages on the one hand, and protection of staff and other consumers on the other. Health care providers should carefully consider the legal implications of whatever policy they adopt:

- What is reasonable care for all consumers should be established;
- Compulsory testing should not make consumers careless where tests are negative (considering that sero-conversion can take up to 3 months);
- Treating every consumer as potentially positive could be cumbersome, expensive, and unduly distressing to the consumer, but could be the only reasonable way of preventing the spread of the disease;
- Consent to the taking of blood is not automatically consent for the specific tests that may be made on it; and
- Special provision for proper counselling is essential, as not only would those who are HIV-positive be confronted with an unexpected disaster to cope with in addition to the illness they have been admitted for, but also the very fact of their being tested could cause undue anxiety and distress to consumers in general.

---

29   Health Act 1956, section 79.
30   Health Act 1956, Schedule 1.
31   The complexity here is that one of the men involved was mentally handicapped and apparently unaware of the consequences of his actions — he was still in isolation in 2003.

18.6   Diseases in general

18.6.1   Cervical cancer

In the wake of the Cartwright report on cervical cancer,[32] the Health Act 1956 was amended to create a national cervical screening register.[33] In March 2005 the relevant section of the legislation was repealed by Health (National Cervical Screening Programme) Amendment Act 2004, section 3.

The principal Act was amended by inserting, after Part 4, Part 4 A: National Cervical Screening Programme.[34] The purpose[35] of this Part is to "reduce the incidence and mortality rate of cervical cancer by providing for the continuation of the NCSP" and to "facilitate the operation and evaluation of that national cervical screening programme by enabling access to information and specimens by the persons operating the programme" and "enabling access to information and specimens by screening programme evaluators appointed to evaluate that programme". Sections 6 and 7 of the Amendment Act provide transitional provisions relating to the National Cervical Screening Programme.

18.6.2   Compulsory treatment and isolation

The Health Act 1956 provides health authorities with wide powers, including the power to require those with a prescribed disease to undergo compulsory medical tests and treatment, and, if necessary, to be removed to a hospital or other suitable place, and be isolated there until they are no longer likely to cause the spread of the infectious disease.[36] The Health Act 1956 also provides that in no case of exercising this power shall the Medical Officer of Health or any person assisting the Medical Officer of Health incur personal liability by reason of anything lawfully done by her/him under the powers of the Act.[37] The powers are very wide, and will allow many things to be done lawfully which otherwise would not be lawful.

There is concern that these provisions allow for detention of people without proper legal process. There are no specific provisions for time limits on isolation, or appeal to the Courts. There are no provisions for rights while in isolation.[38] One would have to rely on the New Zealand Bill of Rights Act 1990, common law, and/or administrative law rights to appeal a decision to detain.

The Health Act 1956 allows the Minister of Health to specify areas of quarantine, prevent entering or leaving these areas by any person, cause the arrest without warrant and detention of persons within the area, and the seizing, disinfecting, or destroying of property.[39] Section 95 of the Health Act 1956 allows the Minister of Health to declare any place in

---

32   *The Report of the Committee of Inquiry into Allegations Concerning the Treatment of Cervical Cancer at National Women's Hospital and other Related Matters*, 1988.

33   Health Act 1956, section 74A.

34   Health (National Cervical Screening Programme) Amendment Act 2004, section 4.

35   Health Act 1956, section 112A.

36   Health Act 1956, sections 70 and 79.

37   Health Act 1956, section 70(3).

38   The Public Health Bill allows for appeal against orders made and includes the principle of least restrictive measure; clause 267 of the Bill allows for safeguards for those people quarantined or isolated and provides a right of review.

39   Health Act 1956, Part 4.

New Zealand to be an infected place on the grounds that the place is infected with a quarantinable disease. Quarantinable diseases are defined as avian influenza (capable of being transmitted between human beings), plague, cholera, yellow fever, and non-seasonal influenza (capable of being transmitted between human beings). Once a place is declared infected, the authorities have powers to isolate the place, and to do whatever is necessary to contain the spread of the disease.

18.6.3 Prescribed diseases — offences

As well as the offence described at 18.4.2 and those of not complying with the specific legislation on notification and treatment of prescribed diseases generally, it is an offence to obstruct the Medical Officer of Health in the carrying out of their functions and powers under the Act.[40] The Medical Officer of Health also has powers in the event of an outbreak of any infectious disease while an epidemic notice is in force.[41]

Health practitioners should all be generally aware of the legal requirements regarding prescribed diseases. If the disease is notifiable, notification by medical practitioners is required, and in some cases by the health facility involved, but employees should make sure that suspected disease is brought to the notice of management. They may also explain the requirements of the law and its purpose to a consumer; it is important to acknowledge that the consumer may well already be distressed, confused, and feeling isolated.

18.6.4 Disclosure by health practitioners with a disease

There is much controversy around whether employers or clients should be informed when a health care worker is HIV-positive, has AIDS, or has any other disease. There has been no definitive legal pronouncement on this point, but the general thrust of the Privacy Act 1993 and government policy is that confidentiality should be given priority, and that disclosure of the fact should not be mandatory. As long as health professionals ensure they are not posing an unreasonable risk to consumers, there is no legal requirement to tell them or the employer.[42] Any lesions would have to be properly sealed and other precautions taken to prevent infection.

(1) *Infection control*

There are many publications providing guidance on how to prevent and reduce the spread of infection. In hospitals and other health and disability care facilities, it is most important that precautions are taken to plan, introduce, and implement an infection control strategy. In 2000, Standards New Zealand published a standard for infection control,[43] which was available from the Ministry of Health. All organisations providing health and disability services needed to be familiar with the standard, and ensure their policies around infection control were consistent with it.

The Standard has been superseded, as of June 2009, by NZS 8134.3:2008 — Health and Disability services (infection prevention and control) Standards. These standards, are to be

---

40   Health Act 1956, sections 71 and 79(6).
41   Health Act 1956, section 70.
42   Though there has been no legal pronouncement in relation to health workers a general principle from the sex cases can be that if reasonable precautions are taken to prevent risk of transmission then disclosure is not required. See *Police v Dalley* (2005) 22 CRNZ 495; [2005] NZAR 682.
43   New Zealand Standard Infection Control NZS8142:2000, Ministry of Health.

read in conjunction with NZS 8134.0:2008 Health and Disability services (general) Standard, which "contains the definitions and audit framework information applicable across the health and disability suite".[44] NZS 8134.3, notes the Ministry's website, is the result of the first revision of NZS 8142:2001 Infection control. "The main intent of Part 3 is to facilitate consistently safe and quality health and disability services, by identifying principles designed to reduce the rate of infections in the health and disability sector." The standard provides the following: "guidance on infection control management, implementing the infection control programme, policies and procedures, education, surveillance, and antimicrobial usage".[45]

18.7 Domestic violence

The many manifestations of domestic violence are being reported more frequently than in the past. Although they are not required to report domestic violence, health practitioners are often the first to learn of it, and can assist the victims in preventing it from happening again.

18.7.1 Child abuse

Section 14 of the Children, Young Persons, and Their Families Act 1989 provides the definition of a child or young person in need of care or protection. The section identifies various situations in which the child or young person can be said to be in need of care or protection. The section is wide-ranging, and includes:

- Harm to the child or young person, either physically, emotionally, or sexually;
- Neglect of the child's physical or mental wellbeing;
- Where the child and caregiver have serious relationship difficulties;
- Where the child has committed an offence giving cause for concern as to the wellbeing of the child;
- Where the caregivers have abandoned the child or are unable to take care of the child; and
- Where the child is being moved around and cannot bond with any one person, impairing the child's development.

18.7.2 Notification

The Children, Young Persons, and Their Families Act 1989 provides that any person who believes that any child has been or is likely to be harmed, ill-treated, abused, neglected, or deprived, may report the matter to a social worker or a constable.[46] There is no mandatory requirement to do this. Any person who makes such a disclosure concerning a child is immune from prosecution, unless the information was disclosed in bad faith.[47]

(1) *Accompanying evidence of abuse*

Those reporting should be objective in the reasons for their conclusion that a child has been abused. One of the difficulties with reporting child abuse is that the response by the

---

44   Can be accessed through www.moh.govt.nz/moh.nsf/indexmh/certification-standards.
45   NZS 8134 Parts 0 to 3 are sold as a loose-leaf set, for use in a binder.
46   Children, Young Persons, and Their Families Act 1989, section 15.
47   Children, Young Persons, and Their Families Act 1989, section 16.

authorities may result in the child being in a worse situation than if the matter were not reported. This should not lead to tolerance of child abuse, but to attempts to deal more appropriately with it.

18.7.3   Care of an abused child

Either welfare officers or a medical officer may if necessary direct that a child be detained in a hospital for examination and immediate treatment. This may be done by a medical practitioner against the parents' will. Depending on the situation, the child may be made a ward of the Court, or alternative action may be taken to ensure the child's welfare. The Family Court has jurisdiction to make decisions generally for the child's welfare at the instigation of welfare officers.[48]

(1)   *Care of Children Act 2004*

The purpose of the Care of Children Act 2004 is to promote children's welfare and best interests, and to facilitate their development, by helping to ensure that appropriate arrangements are in place for their guardianship and care. Its purpose is also to recognise certain rights of children. The Act defines and regulates the following: parents' duties, powers, rights, and responsibilities, as guardians of their children; parents' powers to appoint guardians; and Courts' powers in relation to the guardianship and care of children. Also, amongst other things, the Act acknowledges the role that other family members may have in the care of children; respects children's views, and, in certain cases, recognises their consents (or refusals to consent) to medical procedures; and encourages arrangements for, and provides for the resolution of disputes about, the care of children.[49] The intention of the Care of Children Amendment Act 2008, which amends the principal Act, is that Family Court proceedings will become more open, and that there will be enhanced efficiency and effectiveness within the Family Courts.

At the time of writing this text, another Bill has recently been introduced to Parliament: The Child and Family Protection Bill.[50] It amends three principal Acts: the Domestic Violence Act 1995, the Care of Children Act 2004, and Adoption Act 1955. The explanatory note to the Bill outlines that it is to enhance the protection of children from physical and psychological abuse, adapt the law to cope with the ease of movement of children to or from the country and to ensure the Court processes are effective and clear, and to reduce administrative barriers. The Bill also contains the last legislative amendment required for New Zealand to ratify the Optional Protocol to the United Nations Convention on the Rights of the Child on the sale of children, child prostitution and child pornography.[51]

The Justice Minister, on introducing the Bill, noted that it supports the Domestic Violence (Enhancing Safety) Bill, which is also, at the time of writing this text, before Parliament.

---

48   Children, Young Persons, and Their Families Act 1989, sections 49-58.
49   It also incorporates into New Zealand law Hague Convention on the Civil Aspects of International Child Abduction and reforms and replaces the Guardianship Act 1968 and its amendments.
50   See www.legislation.govt.nz/bill/government/2009/0072/4.0/DLM2295903.html.
51   New Adoption Act 1955, section 27C.

18.7.4 Crimes (Reasonable Parental Control and Correction) Amendment Bill

In August 2009, the Crimes (Reasonable Parental Control and Correction) Amendment Bill was proposed to the House. The purpose of this Member's Bill is to repeal and replace section 59 of the Crimes Act 1961.[52] At the time of writing this text, there is considerable and ongoing parliamentary, community-based, and media attention being given to this section of the Act — specifically as to whether it should be amended to provide clarity on the law's present intent. Parents, says the Explanatory Note of the Bill, have obligations to their children, including an obligation to teach them, and to provide guidance. Sometimes, the Note continues, this requires parents to correct their children's behaviour for the children's own benefit, to help them grow into maturity. In many cases, it says, parental guidance and correction will be non-physical. However, in some cases, the Note continues, "a parent may reasonably decide that correcting their children's behaviour requires some degree of physical action".

In such cases, "section 59 of the Crimes Act 1961 states that parents are committing the crime of assault". Section 59(2), says the Note, states that "Nothing ... justifies the use of force for the purpose of correction." This applies to any physical contact by a parent where the intention is to correct their child's behaviour. "It includes, for example, lifting up an unwilling child to put them into their room for 'time out' as well as giving a light 'smack'."

As explained in the Explanatory Note to the Bill, Section 59 of the Act "is intended to provide children with greater protection against violence and abuse." However, acknowledges the Note, "reasonable physical correction is not violent or abusive". It continues: "Allowing parents to use reasonable physical correction, with clear limits on what is reasonable written into the law, will protect children from harm, while offering parents appropriate legal protection."

This Bill, it says, "will allow parents, and those in the place of parents, to use reasonable force to correct their children's behaviour, while providing clear limits on what is

---

52   Section 59 of the Crimes Act 1961 (as amended in 2007):

"59   Parental control

"(1)   Every parent of a child and every person in the place of a parent of the child is justified in using force if the force used is reasonable in the circumstances and is for the purpose of—

    "(a)   preventing or minimising harm to the child or another person; or

    "(b)   preventing the child from engaging or continuing to engage in conduct that amounts to a criminal offence; or

    "(c)   preventing the child from engaging or continuing to engage in offensive or disruptive behaviour; or

    "(d)   performing the normal daily tasks that are incidental to good care and parenting;

"(2)   Nothing in subsection (1) or in any rule of common law justifies the use of force for the purpose of correction;

"(3)   Subsection (2) prevails over subsection (1);

"(4)   To avoid doubt, it is affirmed that the Police have the discretion not to prosecute complaints against a parent of a child or person in the place of a parent of a child in relation to an offence involving the use of force against a child, where the offence is considered to be so inconsequential that there is no public interest in proceeding with a prosecution."

reasonable." Although section 59 "bans physical correction," continues the Note, "it is often unclear to parents whether using reasonable force is permitted or whether it breaks the law. Its intention is to remove that confusion by adding *correction* to the list of permitted purposes." It is also the intention of the Bill to remove the reliance on Police discretion, in relation to the deciding of instances in which parents, and those in the place of parents, may be in breach of Section 59.

In September 2009, Prime Minister John Key released Terms of Reference for a review of policies and procedures used by the New Zealand Police and Child, Youth and Family, in relation to the issues surrounding smacking. "This review", reported a media release at the time, "will look at the policies and procedures of the Police and CYF, including the referral process between the two agencies, to identify any changes needed to ensure good parents are treated as Parliament intended." The review, is to be conducted by the Chief Executive of the Ministry of Social Development, the Commissioner of Police, and a well-known clinical psychologist, was, at the time of writing this text, scheduled to report to the Prime Minister, Minister of Police, and Minister of Social Development, by 1 December 2009.

18.7.5   Families Commission

Established in 2004, the Families Commission is an autonomous Crown agency governed by a board of commissioners. The Commission has specific functions under the Families Commission Act 2003, and aims to promote a better understanding of family issues and needs among government agencies and the wider community.

The Commission's specific functions under the Act include: encouraging informed debate about families; increasing public awareness and promoting better understanding of matters relating to the interests of families; playing a part in shaping government policies that promote or serve the interests of families; and consulting with, or referring matters to, other official bodies or statutory agencies. Under the Act, the Commission is mandated to focus on families generally, and cannot advocate on behalf of individual families or cases.

18.7.6   Partner or spousal abuse

Health practitioners may be confronted by cases of partner or spousal abuse. Domestic violence may involve child abuse, but covers wider occurrences of violence other than child abuse. It includes partner abuse (including spouses, de facto partners, and same-sex partners), and increasing recognition of violence by any person against another in their domestic environment (for example, relatives who assault and abuse, and parental abuse). Despite common misconceptions, partner and child abuse occur across the social spectrum.[53] As the problem has been increasingly recognised, governments have attempted to give the victims of domestic violence more appropriate protection through the law. Many victims of abuse feel humiliated and ashamed, and fear the consequences of disclosure. Health practitioners who come across such situations can help by being aware of the possibility for victims to seek legal assistance, and, by pointing this out, helping them to take control of the situation.

---

53   J Scutt, *Even in the Best of Homes: Violence in the Family*, Ringwood, Penguin, 1985.

18.7.7 Domestic violence as criminal activity

Partner abuse, as is the case with child abuse, is a crime. There is no excuse for violence against another except self-defence, even though one may feel some sympathy for a person's condition. Provocation will not exonerate a person from being answerable to the law for their actions (see 16.3.6).

18.7.8 Punishment after the event

(1) *Prosecution*

Assault is a crime invoking the possibility of prosecution. The victim of spousal or partner abuse has the right to pursue criminal action, but may fear that this will make matters worse.

If police believe, and have evidence to show, that there has been domestic violence, they can arrest a person and take her/him to the police station to be charged. The police and/or a Court can release such a person on bail. Strict conditions can be imposed to minimise the chance of violence occurring, for example: non-contact terms. If the bail conditions are breached, the person can be arrested and detained.

Police acknowledge they cannot prosecute unless they have proof of the event. It is often one person's word against another's. Even where the victim is obviously wounded, this evidence is often considered insufficient. Police argue that:

- There is difficulty in obtaining proof;
- The victim often drops the claim, and often will not give evidence or testify against the accused;
- Prosecution does not solve the underlying issues; and
- There may have been provocation (this approach can lead to stereotyping of the nature of domestic violence, and raises a false defence for it).

The police have enhanced powers of arrest and entry into homes where they believe domestic violence has taken place or is threatened.[54] There are also units of specially-trained police officers to deal with domestic violence and child abuse.

Once a protection order exists, it is easier for the Police to arrest a person who creates a potential threat. However, police can generally only arrest in response to offences already committed, or to an order issued by a Court.

18.7.9 Protection from future domestic violence

(1) *Orders*

Where a person fears violence from someone they are in a domestic relationship with, that person can apply to the Family Court for an order to restrain that person. This pertains to whether the fear is for their own safety or the safety of a child of the family. The person can apply for a protection, occupation, tenancy or furniture order, or a combination of these orders. This approach to the problem is different to that of criminal law, because:

---

54   When an order under the Domestic Violence Act 1995 is in force.

- The burden of proof for establishing abuse or potential abuse is the balance of probabilities. This standard is more easily met than the standard required for proof of a criminal offence — proof beyond reasonable doubt;
- Action can be taken before an offence is committed;
- The offence is wider than criminal law offences of assault and battery; and
- The effect may be more restrictive than that offered by criminal law.

There have been efforts made to streamline the issuing of injunctions where violence is either experienced or anticipated. The law makes several avenues available.

The Domestic Violence Act 1995 was enacted to provide greater protection from domestic violence, and to reduce and prevent violence in domestic relationships. The Act enables people in a wide range of domestic relationships — including marriage, heterosexual, and same-sex relationships, close friends, and family relationships — to apply for a protection order.

The definition of domestic violence under the Act includes physical abuse, sexual abuse, and psychological abuse, including (but not limited to) intimidation, harassment, damage to property, and threats of physical, sexual, or psychological abuse. Under the Act, a person is deemed to have psychologically abused a child if that person causes or allows the child to see or hear the physical, sexual, or psychological abuse of a person with whom the child has a domestic relationship, or if that person puts the child at risk of seeing or hearing that abuse.[55]

(2)   Protection orders

The purpose of a protection order is to prevent violence or bodily harm being caused or threatened against the applicant or "child of the applicant's family".[56]

Before a Court can grant a protection order, two criteria must be fulfilled:

- The respondent must be using or have used domestic violence against the applicant and/or a child of the applicant's family; and
- The making of an order must be necessary for the protection of the applicant and/ or a child of the applicant's family.[57]

(3)   Standard conditions of a protection order

A protection order is made with a number of standard conditions. When a protection order is made, the respondent must comply with a number of standard conditions. The respondent must not:

- Physically or sexually abuse the protected person, or threaten to do so;
- Damage, or threaten to damage property of the protected person;
- Engage, or threaten to engage, in other behaviour, including intimidation or harassment, which amounts to psychological abuse of the protected person; or

---

55   Domestic Violence Act 1995, section 53(3).
56   The phrase "child of the applicant's family" is defined in Domestic Violence Act 1995, section 2 as "a child who ordinarily or periodically resides with the applicant (whether or not the child is a child of the applicant and the respondent or of either of them)".
57   Domestic Violence Act 1995, section 14.

encourage any person to engage in behaviour against a protected person, where the behaviour, if engaged in by the respondent, would be prohibited by the order.[58]

The Act does allow the respondent and the protected person to continue their relationship, and even live in the same house with the express consent of the protected person. Consent can be withdrawn at any time.

Unless the protected person's consent is given, the respondent must not:[59]

- Watch, loiter near, or prevent or hinder access to or from the protected person's place of residence, business, employment, educational institution, or any other place that the protected person visits often;
- Follow the protected person about or stop or accost the protected person in any place;
- Enter or remain on any land or building occupied by the protected person;
- Where the protected person is present on any land or building, enter or remain on that land or building in circumstances that constitute a trespass;
- Make any other contact with the protected person, including contact by telephone or correspondence, except that which is reasonably necessary in an emergency, or authorised by an order or written agreement relating to custody or access to a minor.

Where the Court makes a protection order, it may impose special conditions that it considers are reasonably necessary to shielding a protected person from further domestic violence by the respondent, by an associated respondent, or by both. A condition may relate to arrangements for contact with a child, or to how a respondent, or an associated respondent, may make contact with the protected person.[60]

The Court may specify the period during which the special condition is to have effect. In the absence of such a direction, the special condition has effect for the duration of the protection order, unless it is varied or discharged, or unless it is suspended for any period during which the protected person and the respondent — with the express consent of the protected person — live in the same dwelling.[61]

(4)   Occupation orders/tenancy orders

The purpose of a tenancy or occupation order is to give the applicant the right to live in the domestic household to the exclusion of the other person to whom the order relates.[62]

The Courts will grant an occupation order if:[63]

- They think it is necessary for the protection of the applicant; or
- It is in the best interests of a child of the applicant's family.

---

58   Domestic Violence Act 1995, section 19(1).
59   Domestic Violence Act 1995, section 19(2).
60   Domestic Violence Act 1995, section 27.
61   See Brookers Online, *New Zealand Law Partner*, synopsis of section 27 of the Domestic Violence Act 1995.
62   Domestic Violence Act 1995, sections 52-61.
63   Domestic Violence Act 1995, section 53(2).

(5)   *Ancillary furniture orders*

An application for an ancillary furniture order can be made at the same time as an occupation or tenancy order is made.[64] The Court has to be satisfied before making an ancillary furniture order that the applicant and the respondent have lived together in the same house specified in the order, and that a child of the applicant's family is or will be living in that house.[65]

(6)   *Without notice applications*

All the above orders can be applied for without the party to whom the order relates being told such an order is being sought, that is, on a without notice basis. The particular circumstances of domestic violence and often the urgency involved mean this is important for the applicant's protection. Any protection order made without notice will be a temporary order.[66] A temporary order will become final 3 months after the date on which it is made, unless the respondent takes steps to defend the application. Before granting a temporary order, the Court must be satisfied that the delay in proceeding by giving the respondent notice would or might entail a risk of harm or undue hardship to the applicant or a child of the applicant's family.

(7)   *Programmes*

When a protection order is made, the applicant can request that a programme or counselling be provided to her/him. This service can be utilised by any children of the applicant's family, and is optional. The Court must, however, direct the respondent to a specified programme unless there is good reason for not making that direction. Usually the specified programme for the respondent is one to stop violence. If direction to attend a programme is made by the Court, non-attendance at that programme amounts to a breach of the protection order.[67]

(8)   *Penalties for breach of a protection order*

Notice of any protection order must be given to the Police. Details of the place and time when the order is served on the respondent must also be given to the Police if a standard condition relating to weapons is included in the order.

When a protection order is in force, any member of the Police may arrest, without warrant, any person suspected of breaching the order.[68] Where a person is arrested and charged with breaching a protection order, the police are not able to release that person on bail during the 24 hours immediately following the arrest. Application for bail may be made during that period, but must be made to a Judge.

It is an offence to contravene a protection order or any condition thereof, and is punishable by up to 6 months' imprisonment or a fine not exceeding $5,000 on first occurrence. For a third or subsequent offence occurring within 3 years of the first, the penalty is increased on conviction to imprisonment of up to 2 years.[69]

---

64   Domestic Violence Act 1995, section 62.
65   Domestic Violence Act 1995, section 63(2).
66   Domestic Violence Act 1995, section 13(3).
67   Domestic Violence Act 1995, sections 29-44.
68   Domestic Violence Act 1995, section 50.
69   Domestic Violence Act 1995, section 49.

The Domestic Violence Act 1995 makes provision for the enforcement overseas of protection orders made in New Zealand. It also provides for the enforcement in this country of orders made overseas conferring protection similar to the protection order.[70]

(9)   *Caring for those with domestic protection orders*

If a client has a protection order restricting access to her/him by another person, those attending the client may lawfully refuse to assist that person in access. Hospital authorities may deny such a person entry on to premises, on the ground that they have a duty of care to the client involved, which involves protecting the client from those who may cause her/him harm. However, health practitioners are advised that the law is not theirs to administer, and, if the person insists on access, they should contact the police (through administrative channels where appropriate) on the client's behalf. While not getting directly involved in others' domestic concerns, health practitioners should assist in the lawful protection of their clients.

18.8   Further reading

Janet Y Lin MD, MPH, Dr Lisa Anderson-Shaw PH,MA,MSN, *Rationing of Resources: Ethical Issues in Disasters and Epidemic Situations*, available on the Ministry of Health website.

M Henaghan et al, *Family Law in New Zealand*, (13th ed, academic & practitioners), Wellington, Lexis Nexis, 2007.

Families Commission website: www.familiescommission.govt.nz.

M Henaghan, *Care of Children*, Wellington, Lexis Nexis, 2005.

M Henaghan and B Atkin, *Family Law Policy in New Zealand* (3rd ed), Wellington, Lexis Nexis, 2007.

B D Inglis, *New Zealand Family Law in the 21st Century*, Wellington, Brookers, 2007.

Ministry of Health, *SARS (Severe Acute Respiratory Syndrome): Advice for Health Professionals*, www.moh.govt.nz.

Ministry of Health: *Health Act Review and Proposed Public Health Bill*, www.moh.govt.nz.

Ministry of Health: *Pandemic Influenza*, www.moh.govt.nz.

The National Division of Infection Control Nurses (a specialist Section of the New Zealand Nurses Organisation) website: www.infectioncontrol.co.nz.

Parliamentary Support Research Papers: Human Influenza A (H1N1) (Swine Flu), Parliamentary Library, 19 June 2009, www.parliament.nz.

G P Sampson (ed), *Role of the World Trade Organisation in Global Governance*, Tokyo, United Nations University Press, 2001.

Trapski's Family Law, Vol VI, Matrimonial and De Facto Property, Marriage, Domestic Protection, Wellington, Brookers, chapter 7.

P Davos and T Ashton (eds), *Health and Public Policy in NZ*, Auckland, Oxford University Press, 2001.

---

70   Domestic Violence Act 1995, section 96.

An Integrated Approach to Infectious Disease: Priorities for Action 2001-2006, Wellington, Ministry of Health, 2001.

D Patten, *HIV/Aids and Prisons: A Study of Knowledge, Attitudes and Risk Behaviours*, Wellington, Department of Health Research Service, 1991.

Chapter 19

HUMAN BODY PART REMOVAL AND TRANSPLANTS AND REPRODUCTIVE TECHNOLOGY

REBECCA KEENAN AND SUE JOHNSON

Contents

19.1 Legislative background and cultural practices

Laws and guidelines exist in New Zealand regarding the removal, use, and transplantation of body parts from both live and dead donors. The law relating to this has recently undergone extensive consultation and revision. The underlying ethical tensions when considering reform in this area are; respect for the individual and autonomy and the need to assist others with providing an environment that promotes the donation of organs. This is usually supported through a utilitarian[1] concept — the greater number of people helped outweighs the rights of the individual.

The discussion on the reform focussed on informed consent, which has been borne out in the new legislative regime. It does provide exceptions for use of organs or bodily tissue when informed consent has not been obtained. The reform process outlined the current concerns as the law being outdated and did not provide enough guidance in relation to informed consent, and it lacked an effective definition of human tissue and a framework around the therapeutic and non-therapeutic use of human tissue.[2]

The current legislation falls under the Human Tissue Act 2008,[3] the Code of Health and Disability Services Consumers' Rights,[4] and under common law.[5] Prior to the new legislation the Ministry of Health approved guidelines for all health service providers that were developed by Te Puni Kokiri, the Ministry of Maori Development ("TPK") in 1999.

During the consultative process of forming the Human Tissue Act 2008, input was obtained from Maori and Pacific Island groups. This was important as informed consent is formed from the principle of autonomy, which is usually used to promote the rights of the individual. However for both Maori and Pacific Islanders this concept does not fit easily with their cultural practices in decision making.

For Maori the use of body parts has significance to their whakapapa as the body is seen as symbolic of atua and tipuna and cannot be spiritually separated.[6] This for Maori, then means that informed consent cannot occur without input from the extended family and how it may affect the whanau/hapu/iwi. The extended family also has a major role in the cultural practices of Pacific Island people. Not in the same way as Maori but in the belief that the family will know what is right, for the family member after death.[7]

---

1   See chapter 20.

2   See *Regulatory Impact Statement: Human Tissue Review*, accessible at www.moh.govt.nz/moh.nsf/ 238fd5fb4fd051844c256669006aed57/eee1fef1668f0a80cc2571230076e47a?OpenDocument.

3   Section 93 of this Act repealed the Human Tissue Act 1964 and Part 3A of the Health Act 1956.

4   The Code of Health and Disability Services Consumers' Rights (reproduced in Appendix 4) is found in the Schedule to the Health and Disability Commissioner (Code of Health and Disability Services Consumers' Rights) Regulations 1996. Note that the Code is subject to the common law.

5   Code of Health and Disability Services Consumers' Rights, Right 7 (1), provides the right to make an informed choice and give informed consent *except where any enactment, or the common law, or any provision of this Code provides otherwise* (emphasis added).

6   *Review of the Regulation of Human Tissue and Tissue – based therapies: Submissions summary* (August 2004), page 15.

7   Ibid, page 17.

The Act requires that, in the informed consent process, cultural practices are taken into account.[8] Taking account of the cultural, spiritual needs and beliefs of the immediate family also form part of the overall purpose of the Act.[9]

19.2   Human body part removal and transplants

Part of the "mischief" the Human Tissue Act 2008 remedies is the lack of guidance around defining body parts or tissue. Under the Act there is now a specific definition for human tissue in section 7.

> "7   **Human tissue defined and illustrated**
>
> "(1)   Human tissue or tissue means material that—
>
> "(a)   Is, or is derived from, a body, or material collected from a living individual or from a body; and
>
> "(b)   Is or includes human cells; and
>
> "(c)   Is not excluded, for the purposes of some or all of the provisions of this Act, by subsection (2) or (3).
>
> "(2)   A human embryo or human gamete is not human tissue for the purposes of any provision of this Act.
>
> "(3)   Cell lines derived from human cells are human tissue for the purposes of the following sections, but not for the purposes of any other provisions of this Act:
>
> "(a)   Sections 47 and 74 (which relate to standards for collection or use of human tissue for non-therapeutic purposes);
>
> "(b)   Sections 66 and 75 (which relate to standards, etc, for export and import of human tissue).
>
> "(4)   Examples of human tissue therefore include the following:
>
> "(a)   All or any part of a body;
>
> "(b)   Whole human organs (for example, hearts, kidneys, livers, and lungs) or parts of them (for example, heart valves);
>
> "(c)   Human stem cells or other human cells (for example, stem cells obtained from human embryos);
>
> "(d)   Human blood;
>
> "(e)   Human bone marrow;
>
> "(f)   Human eyes;
>
> "(g)   Human hair, nails, and skin;
>
> "(h)   Human lung washouts;
>
> "(i)   Human mucus, sputum, or urine."

8   Human Tissue Act 2008, section 42.
9   Human Tissue Act 2008, section 3(a).

This definition thus provides clarity over what is and what is not included and it does include blood and blood products. It does not include human embryos, gametes,[10] or cell lines. These have been incorporated into the Human Assisted Reproductive Technology Act 2004 and will be discussed separately at 19.6.3. In concert with the new Act the term *human tissue* will be used to include all body parts and tissue. Human tissue may be regenerative, for example blood or bone marrow, which is naturally replaced in the body after it has been removed, or they may be non-regenerative such as a kidney, liver, heart, or cornea.

Human tissue is usually removed for the following reasons:

- Donation (live donor or brain dead donor);
- Medical reasons (amputation to prevent the spread of infection — hip replacement);
- Forensic purposes (requested by police /coroner as part of a trial);
- Testing or research purposes;
- Educational purposes (schools of anatomy);
- Cosmetic purposes (liposuction);
- By a natural process (delivery of placenta during childbirth).

19.3 Removal of regenerative human tissue

Regenerative human tissue such as blood and bone marrow can be donated.

The law concerning blood donation and transfusion is covered by the general sections related to informed consent for the taking and use of human tissue. Part 2, subpart 6 (Trading in blood, controlled human substances, or other human tissue) of the Human Tissue Act 2008, covers how and by whom blood can be taken and used — there is no consideration to be given for any collection of blood, and trading in human tissue is generally prohibited.

19.3.1 Blood donation

Any competent adult[11] may donate blood for therapeutic medical or scientific purposes. Consent should be obtained in accordance with the Code of Health and Disability Services Consumers' Rights.

Special requirements to protect the public require that donors sign a declaration regarding sexual practices and intravenous drug use.[12] Also people who travelled to or lived in the UK between 1 January 1980 and 31 December 1996 for 6 months or longer can no longer donate blood. This latter requirement is to try to minimise the risk of transmission of variant Creutzfeld-Jacob disease ("VCJD") into the blood supply. VCJD is believed to be the human form of bovine spongiform encephalopathy ("BSE"), a disease affecting cattle, which was first reported in the UK in 1996. Although the disease is very rare, it has a long incubation period, possibly 40 years. It is not possible currently to estimate the number of people who might be affected by it.[13]

---

10   The definition of gametes in Human Assisted Reproductive Technology Act 2004, section 5 includes an egg or sperm.

11   The age of consent in the Human Tissue Act 2008 is 16; see section 26 — a person of 16 years or older is assumed to be capable.

12   For a list of common reasons for a person's blood not being acceptable see www.nzblood.co.nz/?t=49.

13   For further information on VCJD see the Ministry of Health's website www.moh.govt.nz or www.cjdfoundation.org.

19.3.2 Blood removal for testing

Statutory provisions permit the taking of blood for testing in certain circumstances without consent, for example:

1. Where a person has been involved in a motor accident and is in hospital, an ambulance, or a doctor's surgery, blood can be taken for alcohol testing;[14]

2. Where a preliminary breath test at the roadside is positive, a blood test may be requested in certain circumstances;[15]

3. When ordered by the Court for determination of paternity or for any other reason, such as suspicion of a crime;[16]

4. When ordered by a medical officer of health in the prevention of an outbreak or spread of any infectious disease.[17]

For example, a person unconscious in hospital does not have to consent to a blood sample being taken for blood alcohol testing, nor is consent required from the person's relatives. Medical practitioners are immune from legal action where blood samples are taken for testing if they have reason to believe a police officer has directed the samples be obtained. They are not compelled to take the blood samples.

Under previous legislation Registered nurses and medical practitioner's were persons authorised to take blood samples with the person's consent if the sample was taken under the provisions of the Criminal Investigations (Blood Samples) Act 1995.[18] However, this was amended in 2004 so that it is a "suitably qualified person"[19] who is authorised to take the bodily sample, which may be blood.[20] Once again, this suitably qualified person is not compelled to take the sample.[21] Blood samples compulsorily taken cannot be used for any other purpose than that for which they were taken, either by consent or by statutory exception. For example, a blood sample taken for the purpose of alcohol testing cannot be tested or DNA analysed in the investigation of a crime without express consent for the DNA testing.[22]

19.3.3 Transfusions

Anyone may agree to the administration of a blood transfusion to herself/himself. The law in this respect is the same as that applying to all provision of health services to adults (see chapter 6).

---

14   Land Transport Act 1998, section 72.
15   Land Transport Act 1998, section 72.
16   Family Proceedings Act 1980, sections 54-55; Status of Children Act 1969, sections 7-10; Criminal Investigations (Bodily Samples) Act 1995, section 5.
17   Health Act 1956, section 70.
18   Amendment in 2004 changed the title to the Criminal Investigations (Bodily Samples) Act 1995.
19   Defined in the Interpretation section of Criminal Investigations (Bodily Samples) Act 1995 as: (i) a medical practitioner; or (ii) a nurse; or (iii) a medical technologist with a degree in medical laboratory science; or (iv) a person trained in phlebotomy in accordance with the national standard for training phlebotomists adopted by the Association of Community Laboratories Incorporated.
20   Amended in 2004 and now Criminal Investigations (Bodily Samples) Act 1995, section 49.
21   Criminal Investigations (Bodily Samples) Act 1995, section 51.
22   Criminal Investigations (Bodily Samples) Act 1995, Part 3, relates to taking a bodily sample for DNA.

Anyone may refuse a blood transfusion, even if that refusal puts their life in jeopardy. However, the person or relatives might take action against health practitioners for not treating someone when they needed the treatment, arguing that refusal was either not voluntary or not properly informed. When a health practitioner is considering a refusal of treatment they ought to consider the elements of a valid and binding refusal,[23] which are:

1. The consumer must be an adult;

2. They must have capacity;

3. It must be their own independent decision (voluntary); and

4. If in the form of an advanced directive, it must be intended to cover the situation concerned.

The ethical, and possibly legal, duty to treat someone should also be considered. Emergency or necessity could be used as a defence by health practitioners. Such an approach, it is suggested, should not be used paternalistically. The issue is whether one respects individual autonomy, or is prepared to substitute paternalism.

The question is not a legal one. The legal issues are clear — health practitioners who have to decide whether to give treatment against the consumer's will, choose between the possibilities of being in breach of the Code of Health and Disability Services Consumers' Rights[24] and/or sued in tort if they act or not. The decision is fraught with ethical dilemmas, and is not an easy problem to solve. Community discussion, as well as discussion among health practitioners, is essential for establishing an accepted approach to deciding one's values. Giving a transfusion to an adult of "sound mind" against that person's will is a breach of their legal right to refuse it. Therefore, it should be carefully considered (see *Shulman*'s case at 6.5.3(1)).

19.3.4 Children

Normally parents, as guardians, can give or refuse consent for medical treatment of their children where the child is not competent to do so. However, where parents refuse to allow emergency or lifesaving treatment, medical staff can act against their wishes (see chapter 7). Specific legislation provides for the giving of a blood transfusion to a person under 18 years where their life is in danger, and parents cannot be reasonably contacted.[25] Where the parents of a child refuse consent, a blood transfusion can still be given if it is considered medically necessary to save the child's life.[26]

---

23 A UK case that offers judicial guidance on this is *Airedale NHS Trust v Bland* [1993] AC 789; [1993] 1 All ER 821; [1993] 2 WLR 316 (HL): "it is established that the principle of self-determination requires that respect must be given to the wishes of the patient, so that if an adult patient of sound mind refuses, however unreasonably, to consent to treatment or care by which his life would or might be prolonged, the doctors responsible for his care must give effect to his wishes, even though they do not consider it to be in his best interests to do so" (per Lord Goff).

24 Code of Health and Disability Services Consumers' Rights, Right 7(7).

25 Care of Children Act 2004, section 37 exempts health practitioners' from liability if administering a blood transfusion without consent, except by leave of a High Court Judge. If leave is granted then the reasonableness of the health practitioner's actions will be taken into account in the circumstances of the case and whether the child's life was at risk. However, when making the decision a health practitioner should be aware that section 36 enables a child of 16 years to either refuse or consent to a blood transfusion or medical treatment.

Case

Director- General of Social Welfare v B [1995] 3 NZLR 73; (1995) 13 FRNZ 441

The child, J, had been admitted to hospital with a nose bleed and his condition was worsening. The parents were refusing to consent to a blood transfusion. Initially application had been made to the District Court under the Children , Young Persons, and Their Families Act 1989; however this case confirmed that jurisdiction was under the High Court pursuant to the Guardianship Act 1968 (which is replaced by the Care of Children Act 2004). The Judge confirmed that the court will always intervene to overrule a parent's refusal either with its statutory jurisdiction or inherent jurisdiction of parens patriae to give consent where a child's life was seriously threatened. This intervention is also reinforced by the child's right to life under s8 of the New Zealand Bill of Rights Act 1990 which overrides the parents' right to religious freedom.[27]

Though it was under the previous legislation (Guardianship Act 1968), it is still relevant today. A child's right to life and medical treatment, where their life is threatened without it, will always be paramount. Blood transfusions given under these circumstances will generally be sanctioned by the Court, but it is preferable the application is made before the treatment is given. Having a court order before giving treatment not consented to will protect the health practitioner from liability.

19.3.5 Blood transfusions and HIV

Due to the danger of transmitting HIV and other blood-borne diseases through blood donations, blood donors are requested to sign declarations stating they have not been involved in activities placing them at risk of being infected, not to their knowledge been infected with the virus.

All blood donated is tested for HIV antibodies. If the result is positive the donor is informed. Care should be taken when informing the donor as negligent communication to a person resulting in mental trauma or other harm could lead to legal action. Staff in blood donation centres should be aware of this issue when informing those whose declaration as to donor suitability indicates the possibility they could have been infected with the virus. They will be advised to have a blood test for HIV antibodies.

Where it is likely that the results may be positive, those who are giving the blood should be counselled as to this possibility. Of course those donating blood who have testified to being suitable donors are indicating they are extremely unlikely to be HIV positive, and one would expect that these considerations would not have as much priority as, for example, in an AIDS clinic. Staff in the New Zealand Blood Service donation units should still be aware of this issue.

---

26   Care of Children Act 2004, section 16, identifies a non-exhaustive list of powers, duties and responsibilities that parents/guardians have for the children in their care. Section 16(2)(c) identifies that one of these responsibilities includes medical treatment. If there is dispute over decisions of medical treatment then an application can be made to the High Court under section 44(2) for an order to be made in terms of that medical treatment.

27   New Zealand Bill of Rights Act 1990, section 13.

19.4 Non-regenerative human tissue

19.4.1 Removal from live consumers

The law relating to consent for the removal, storage, and utilisation of non-regenerative human tissue from a live consumer is covered by the Code of Health and Disability Services Code of Consumers' Rights.[28] The Code requires that:

1. Consumers have the right to make a decision about the return or disposal of any human tissue removed or obtained in the course of a health care procedure;[29] and

2. Any human tissue removed or obtained in the course of a health care procedure may be stored, preserved, or utilised only with the informed consent of the consumer, or for the purposes of research that has obtained ethics committee approval, or an activity that is undertaken to assure or improve quality of services — such as an audit.[30]

When human tissue is to be removed from live consumers, it is important that *all* the provisions of the Code of Health and Disability Services Consumers' Rights are complied with. This means the right to respect, taking into account cultural needs and beliefs,[31] and the right to be provided with full information[32] in a manner and environment that enables the consumer to understand it, ask questions, and communicate concerns.[33] The consumer should be informed why the body part is being removed, how it will be done, what it will be used for, and the options the consumer has in relation to its disposal or return. If tests are to be performed on it, then the consumer has a right to know what they will be, and why they are to be carried out. If the removed human tissue is to be used for research or teaching, then consent must be in writing[34] (and see 19.3.3).

19.4.2 Return of removed human tissue

Consumers have the right to decide whether they want their human tissue returned to them, or disposed of.[35] This is a right to choose. It should be given effect to as a right to *choose*, and not an automatic assumption that human tissue *must* be returned. Not all consumers will wish to have the human tissue returned.

Though Maori have a different perspective on removed human tissue and how they relate to their whakapapa it should not be automatically assumed that all Maori wish human tissue to be returned. The previous guidelines provided by the Ministry of Maori Development cite as an example the return of a foetus to a young Maori mother. She did not want to have it returned, and was very distressed at the "brusque manner" in which it was returned.

---

28 The Code of Health and Disability Services Consumers' Rights (reproduced in Appendix 4) is in the Schedule to the Health and Disability Commissioner (Code of Health and Disability Services Consumers' Rights) Regulations 1996. At the time of writing (mid-2009) the Health and Disability Commissioner Act 1994 and the Health and Disability Commissioner (Code of Health and Disability Services Consumers' Rights) Regulations are under review.

29 The Code of Health and Disability Services Consumers' Rights, Right 7(9).

30 The Code of Health and Disability Services Consumers' Rights, Right 7(10).

31 The Code of Health and Disability Services Consumers' Rights, Right 1.

32 The Code of Health and Disability Services Consumers' Rights, Right 6.

33 The Code of Health and Disability Services Consumers' Rights, Right 5.

34 The Code of Health and Disability Services Consumers' Rights, Right 7(6).

35 The Code of Health and Disability Services Consumers' Rights, Right 7(9).

Sensitive and culturally appropriate communication of information about the options is vital. The way in which requested human tissue is returned is also important — when returned it should be returned in an appropriate container.

19.4.3 Donation of human tissue for research purposes

Competent consumers can donate their human tissue for research purposes with their informed consent. It has to be in writing,[36] and the research must be approved by an ethics committee.[37]

There are now tissue banks that store donated tissue and organs from both live and dead donors. For example, the Christchurch Tissue Bank was established in 1997 at Christchurch Public Hospital. It has a curator and it is controlled and regulated by a local Tissue Bank Board, set up specifically for that purpose. All tissue donors give their consent for storage, and for the sort of research that can be carried out on the tissue. There is a special consent form and information sheet developed by the Tissue Bank Board and the Canterbury Ethics Committee. Research can then be carried out on the stored tissue, without having to go back each time to the donor for further consent. However, it must first be approved by both the Tissue Bank Board and the Canterbury Ethics Committee. They monitor and regulate the type and amount of research conducted on the material.

In Auckland there is a brain bank — The New Zealand Neurological Foundation Brain Bank, at the University of Auckland Department of Anatomy and Radiology. People can donate their brain when they die. Research is regulated in the same way as it is in Christchurch, by a Brain Bank Board and the Auckland Ethics Committees.

19.4.4 Donation of human tissue for transplant

Currently, there is no legislation specific to the donation of non-regenerative tissue for transplantation by live donors.[38] It is neither specifically allowed by legislation, nor specifically prohibited, however an amendment to the Health and Disability Commissioner Act 1994 amended the definition of a "health treatment," and it was changed to read:[39]

> "To avoid doubt, includes treatment of a person (A) that is, or is related to, the taking of human tissue from A for all or any of the following purposes:
>
> "(a)   transplantation, or another therapeutic purpose, for the benefit of 1 or more persons other than A; or
>
> "(b)   educational purposes or research purposes."

At present, only the following non-regenerative human tissue can be removed for transplantation:

1.   Kidney — one kidney can be donated to a family member or friend;

2.   Liver — a segment of a liver can be donated to a family member.

---

36   The Code of Health and Disability Services Consumers' Rights, Right 7(6).

37   The Code of Health and Disability Services Consumers' Rights, Right 7 (10).

38   During consultation for the Human Tissue Act 2008, it considered that the Code of Health and Disability Services Consumers' Rights provided enough safeguards for live donation, especially with the change to Right 7(10) in 2004, so the new legislation focused primarily on dead donors.

39   Human Tissue Act 2008, section 90.

In Australia, most states allow transplantation of non-regenerative tissue from competent adults. There are additional safeguards such as requiring a medical practitioner other than the surgeon who is to carry out the transplant, stating the terms of the consent, that it was freely given, the person was of sound mind, and proper information was given. Another legal safeguard is that there must be a cooling-off period, and therefore removal cannot occur less than 24 hours after consent is given.[40] Children are banned from donating non-regenerative tissue in three Australian states,[41] while in others it is prohibited by implication. In the Australian Capital Territory it is permitted, but with strict safeguards including referral to a Ministerial Committee for a decision.

There are no such legislative safeguards in New Zealand. It is important health practitioners remember that removal of human tissue for transplantation is non-therapeutic for the live donor. This means that it is vital to ensure that detailed information is provided to the prospective donor. This includes all information about the surgery, and the possible social and psychological impact of it. Practitioners should be careful to ensure there is a freely given consent, with no undue pressure, or coercion where a family member would otherwise die without the transplant. Recipients should be offered the opportunity for discussion in accordance with Right 6.

They need to be fully informed about all the potential consequences of being a recipient, including emotional changes. Sometimes there may be a need for some procedure so the recipient can appropriately feel the body part is "acceptable" to her/him in a cultural sense. The previous guidelines provided by the Ministry of Maori Development gave the following comment by a recipient as an example:

> "We do need to think about whakapono and taha wairua especially at a crucial stage. After I had my transplant I wished I had someone there to have blessed it before the specialist had put it in. Had I known, I could've easily blessed it myself. I don't know what taputapu it might have, or what the donor's whakapapa is."

19.5   Human tissue from the dead

The issues, both legal and ethical in this area mainly concern:

1.   Who can give consent for removal of human tissue?

2.   How valid is the deceased's request to be a donor?

3.   What conditions apply to the removal of human tissue?

4.   Removal of human tissue during post-mortems, should they be returned?

5.   Financial consideration for human tissue?

---

40   On 2 October 2002, the Attorney-General the Hon Margaret Wilson announced that the Ministry of Health will undertake consultation and review the legislation governing both therapeutic and non-therapeutic uses of human tissue, including the Human Tissue Act 1964; This resulted in the Human Tissue Act 2008.

41   South Australia, Victoria, and Western Australia; for discussion see also "Ethical issues in donation of organs or tissues by living donors: Ethical issues in organ donation, Discussion paper No. 2", access at www.nhmrc.gov.au/_files_nhmrc/file/publications/synopses/e30.pdf.

19.5.1   Who can consent to removal?

The Human Tissue Act 2008 governs how and when tissue and other human tissue can be removed from the dead for transplant purposes, and for research and teaching. This new Act has informed consent as its primary principle; it clearly defines informed consent along with informed objection and over-riding objection.[42] Though the Act provides for a definition it does not provide guidance on what information or the depth of information needed that would meet — "in the light of all information that a reasonable person, in that person's circumstances, needed in order to raise an informed consent."[43] This is the difficulty that health practitioners in this field will face when they are seeking an informed consent for the use of human tissue.

No one owns a body.[44] There is no legal right of ownership in a body. The highest right is a possessory one. The Human Tissue Act 1964 had a section where it described a person who is "lawfully in possession of a body" and that person could then approve activities governed under the Act.

This term came under consultation in the review and the Human Tissue Act 2008 now describes this person as the *Responsible Person* (as defined in section 12). This is a person lawfully in possession of the body, but does not include a person entrusted with the body only for its burial, cremation, or lawful disposal.[45] A *Responsible Person* may be contacted when a person dies by the person responsible for removal of tissue to ascertain if there is consent or if that consent had subsequently been withdrawn.[46] The *Responsible Person* has a mandatory obligation to assist if consulted under section 14(2) and to take all steps reasonably practicable.[47]

Under the Human Tissue Act 2008, informed consent for the removal of human tissue is split into two categories, the first for general purposes[48] and the second for use for anatomical examination or public display.[49] Both sections allow for several people to give consent and they are listed in decreasing order of importance. Of primary importance is the person from whose body the tissue is being removed, if that person has either not given consent or not raised an objection to the use of his/her tissue, it then falls to either of the following class of person:

1.   That person's nominee;[50] or

2.   An immediate family member; [51] or

---

42   Human Tissue Act 2008, section 9.
43   Human Tissue Act 2008, section 9.
44   This is well established law, see the Australian case of *Doodeward v Spence* [1908] 15 ALR 105; 6 CLR 406; 9 SR (NSW) 107 (HC), where Pring J states: "There can be no property in a human body, dead or alive. I go further and say that if a limb or any portion of a body is removed that no person has a right of property in that portion of the body so removed."
45   Subsection (2) describes the different people who would fill that role depending on if the body was lying in either a hospital, was a patient as defined under the Mental Health (CAT) Act 1992 and in a hospital, in a secure facility, in a prison, or in a school of anatomy.
46   Human Tissue Act 2008, section 14(2).
47   Human Tissue Act 2008, section 15.
48   Human Tissue Act 2008, section 31.
49   Human Tissue Act 2008, section 32.
50   Regulated by Human Tissue Act 2008, sections 38 and 39 , the nominee must give their consent in writing to act as a nominee.

3.   A close available relative.[52]

Any informed consent, informed objection or overriding objection or nomination given for the purposes of this Act may be made orally in the presence of two witnesses present at the same time, or in writing, with or without witnesses,[53] and finally an informed consent, informed objection or overriding objection or nomination may be contained in a person's Will if it relates to tissue from that person's body.[54]

Any person giving either informed consent, informed objection or an overriding objection has a duty to take into account the immediate family's cultural and spiritual needs, values, and beliefs.[55] The person responsible for taking or using the tissue is entitled to assume that this duty has been fulfilled unless there is evidence to the contrary.[56] However, the person who takes or uses the human tissue must also take into account the immediate family's cultural and spiritual needs, values, and beliefs.[57]

19.5.2   How valid is the deceased's request to be a donor?

Now, statutory requirements for either informed consent, informed objection or overriding objection take into account cultural and spiritual beliefs of the immediate family. If the deceased's wishes have been gained prior to their death and it should be noted so that it shows these aspects of consent were considered at the time. Then these wishes will have a stronger legal basis and will not be as easily overturned by a family's objection after death has occurred.

The Act also provides for an affirmative defence for health practitioners who take or use human tissue from a dead body because they believed on the balance of probabilities that informed consent was either given (with no overriding objection) or not required under the Act.[58]

In regard to research, informed consent is required under general purposes and nothing will be used without this informed consent. However, section 20 provides exemptions for informed consent and one of those is use for a secondary purpose — including research that has been approved by an ethics committee.[59]

Prior to these rigorous requirements, in practice, next of kin were asked for their agreement before human tissue was taken, and only human tissue the next of kin had consented to be taken was removed, irrespective of the wishes expressed by the deceased.

Informed consent is the primary principle and includes considering one's immediate family's cultural and spiritual beliefs. Thus, a computer record of a person's consent to

---

51   Human Tissue Act 2008, defined in section 6, has a wide interpretation to include different cultural beliefs and practices.

52   Human Tissue Act 2008, defined in section 10 and provides for two meanings depending on whether the deceased person is over 16 years (subsection(1)) or under 16 years (subsection (2)).

53   Human Tissue Act 2008, section 43(1).

54   Human Tissue Act 2008, section 43(2).

55   Human Tissue Act 2008, section 42.

56   Human Tissue Act 2008, section 28.

57   Human Tissue Act 2008, section 18.

58   Human Tissue Act 2008, section 25.

59   Human Tissue Act 2008, section 20(e).

organ donation will not be sufficient as it was under s 3 (1A) of the Human Tissue Act 1964 to show consent to donation.[60]

The 2008 Act also repealed sections of the Land Transport Act 1998[61] that enabled a person's request to be recorded at the time of renewing their driver's license as this would not have met the now rigorous requirement contained in the Act for informed consent/objection. The Act does allow for the establishment of a register that would show either a person's informed consent or objection.[62] However, this has not been acted upon by the Government and there is no Bill in process, at this time.[63] There is a lack of consensus as to the effectiveness of a register in increasing the number of organs for donation and the primary drawback of such a system is the cost of establishing and maintaining it.

As stated above at 19.5.1, there is no ownership of a body. The highest right to a body is a possessory one, and not a proprietary one. In New Zealand there is no legislative definition of the person lawfully in possession of the body (PLIP), except in respect of the body of a patient lying in a hospital or prison (as discussed as 19.5.1). In all other situations, the common law position applies:[64]

> "The person who has actual physical custody of the body has lawful possession (and the duty of disposal) of it until someone with a higher right (eg an executor or parent) claims the body … In the absence of executors there is a common law duty to see that the body is buried and the person lawfully in possession is normally the occupier of the premises where the body lies or the person who has the body."

Therefore, a family who are in possession of the body that has been removed from a hospital or prison can decide for themselves whether human tissue can be removed, and the wishes of the deceased are irrelevant legally.

All those who request to donate body parts, either in writing or orally, may revoke their consent at any time. Authorisation of the removal of body parts from a deceased person, by the PLIP, may also be revoked. This revocation of consent may take place at any time, and is absolute. It would seem a legally sound argument that a health practitioner who is aware of a consumer revoking consent or a relative revoking consent, should promptly inform those who propose to carry out the removal of human tissue.

Perhaps one of the most challenging situations for health practitioners is dealing with the family of those who have died suddenly and violently and who are brain dead, but on a ventilator. To their family, these people may seem to be alive, and the work of the ventilator keeps up this appearance. The important thing for all to remember is that a person must be *legally dead* before human tissue can be removed. The Human Tissue Act 2008, only states that a person collecting tissue should take into account the cultural and spiritual needs of the immediate family[65] but does not provide guidance on what these may be. The guidelines previously provided by Te Puni Kokiri stated that:[66]

---

60   See the previous edition of *Health Care and the Law.*
61   Human Tissue Act 2008, sections 87-89.
62   Human Tissue Act 2008, section 78.
63   The Organ Donor Registry Bill was scrapped in 2007.
64   J Kennedy and A Grubb, *Medical Law* (3rd ed), London, Butterworths, 2000.
65   Human Tissue Act 2008, section 18.
66   Te Puni Kokiri, *Hauora o te tinana me ona tikanga : a guide for the removal, retention, return and disposal of Maori body parts and organ donation*, Wellington, Te Puni Kokiri, 1999, page 18.

"It is considered inappropriate for medical staff to discuss body part donation with the patient's whanau before the patient has been certified as being brain dead."

The guidelines stated that whanau/family may be consulted and their consent gained, but this should not be until after at least the first set of tests for brain death has been carried out. Health practitioners should discuss with them the concept of brain death, as well as the tests. Human tissue donation should be sensitively explored. The whanau or next of kin should be reassured that no consent will be sought until after the final tests to confirm brain death have been completed, and the patient has been declared brain dead.[67] Human tissue may be removed only by a "qualified person," defined as:[68]

"(a)   A person who is, or is acting under the supervision of, a medical practitioner collecting the tissue for the purposes of the practice of his or her profession;

"(b)   A person authorised in writing by or on behalf of the New Zealand Blood Service, the New Zealand National Eye Bank, or a body that is a successor to that Service or Bank, as suitably qualified to collect tissue of that kind for the purposes of that Service, Bank, or successor body;

"(c)   A person who the Director-General has, by notice in the *Gazette*, authorised as suitably qualified to collect tissue of that kind for 1 or more specified purposes."

There is no legal definition of death for the purposes of organ donation. Before a qualified person can remove any part of the body, they must personally examine the body and be satisfied that life is extinct.[69] The decision as to whether a person is dead will be a medical one, based on either the irreversible cessation of brain function, or irreversible cessation of blood circulation.

All health service institutions should have policies requiring that where a prospective donor is on life support, there are certain requirements regarding the number and seniority of medical personnel who may declare the person dead, and specific clinical tests must be completed, as well as the certification required of them as to the cessation of blood circulation or brain function.

19.5.3   What sort of non-regenerative human tissue can be transplanted?

In New Zealand the following human tissue can be transplanted from brain-dead donors. Potentially, anyone up to the age of 80 years can be a donor and in the case of a donation of a cornea, up to the age of 85 years.

1.   Kidney — up to 80 years old.

2.   Liver — up to 80 years old.

3.   Heart — up to 60 years old.

4.   Lungs — up to 60 years old.

---

67   Ibid.
68   Human Tissue Act 2008, section 50(3).
69   Human Tissue Act 2008, section 50(2).

5. Pancreas — up to 40 years old.

6. Cornea— up to 85 years old.

7. Skin — up to 80 years old.

8. Bone — male up to 65 years old, female up to 50 years old.

9. Heart valves — up to 60 years old.[70]

19.5.4 Post-mortems, inquests, and anatomical examinations

Before removal of any tissue from a corpse, a medical practitioner must first rule out any situation where the coroner will have jurisdiction over the body. If there is a possibility that an inquest may be required, or a post-mortem examination of the body might be requested or ordered by the coroner, then no tissue can be removed without the coroner's consent.[71] Even where a post-mortem is possible, the coroner may, if satisfied it will not prejudice the coronial inquiry, permit removal of tissue from the body.

Use of a body for scientific, anatomical teaching, or other medical or research purposes is subject to similar requirements to those outlined above for the donation of tissue after death.[72]

Recently, there have been a number of discoveries of what has been revealed as a long-standing and widespread practice of removing and retaining human organs without consent following post mortem examinations. The report of the inquiry into children's heart surgery at the Bristol Royal Infirmary, in England,[73] led to a number other discoveries and inquiries, most notably the inquiry into the largest collection of children's hearts, which were kept at the Royal Liverpool Children's NHS Trust (Alder Hey Hospital in Liverpool, England).[74]

The inquiry discovered there had been systematic full-scale removal of hearts, especially in the period from 1988 to 1995.[75] These removals had taken place without consent from parents. The majority of the retained organs were preserved and stored, but not used in research. They were largely ignored.

In February 2002, it was revealed that Green Lane Hospital in Auckland had been retaining children's hearts following post-mortem examinations up to as recently as 1996. Also, at the Institute of Forensic Medicine in New South Wales, long bones and joints were removed from adult cadavers.[76] The medical profession had justified retention of body parts for the

---

70   Information obtained from the donor website at www.donor.co.nz.

71   Human Tissue Act 2008, section 48(2).

72   Collection of tissue for this purpose is regulated by Human Tissue Act 2008, Part 2, subpart 6 and therefore covered by the usual consent process.

73   Bristol Royal Infirmary Inquiry, *Learning from Bristol: the Report of the Public Inquiry into Children's Heart Surgery at the Bristol Royal Infirmary 1984-1995*, Bristol, Crown Copyright, 2001.

74   *Report of the Royal Liverpool Children's Inquiry*, 10/1/01, Her Majesty's Stationary Office, London, England, available at www.rlcinquiry.org.nz.

75   The author (Sue Johnson) recalls seeing many preserved hearts in the period 1977 to 1980 in the mortuary in Myrtle Street Hospital (the Royal Liverpool Children's Hospital (RLCH) in Mulberry Street, Liverpool), which was closed some years later when services were all transferred to the Alder Hey site. The RLCH was at the time a regional centre for the treatment of congenital heart defects. The hearts were on shelves in jars of preserving fluid and were occasionally used for teaching purposes.

76   B Walker, *Inquiry into the matters arising from the post mortem and anatomical examination practices of the Institute of Forensic Medicine*, Sydney, The Government of the State of New South Wales, August 2001.

purposes of research. Their reasoning for not obtaining consent from relatives was that grieving parents and families would not wish to know about retention of organs and the uses of these. All the inquiry reports that have followed discovery of the body parts recognised this paternalistic approach is not appropriate, and openness and frankness be required and must prevail.

19.5.5 Conclusion

It may well be that in the future organs for transplant are derived from stem cells,[77] or manufactured artificially. Until then, health practitioners should become familiar with all the legal rights of both donors and recipients, and the procedures in their workplaces that deal with human tissue.

A knowledge of cultural practices, beliefs, and attitudes of both donor (or donor's whanau or next of kin) and recipient (and their whanau) is essential, so that the process of donation and acceptance of transplanted human tissue promotes the recipient's health and respects the grieving practices of the donor's family. Sensitive communication with cultural awareness on the part of health practitioners working in this area is vital.

19.6   Assisted conception and reproductive technology

The term "assisted conception" is used to include all the various means of transplanting material from one person to another for the purposes of bearing a child. It is included in this chapter because it is a form of human tissue transplantation.

Around 600 babies, out of the approximately 63,000 born each year in New Zealand, are conceived using some form of artificial conception. It is likely this figure is higher, as it is unknown how many babies are conceived at home with donated sperm using objects such as pastry brushes and turkey basters to implant the sperm into the vagina. Artificial insemination, or implantation of seminal fluid into the vagina or uterus through means other than natural physical copulation, has been used for many years as a means of promoting conception where sexual intercourse is not desired. It has become an accepted way of dealing with conception.

The known assisted conceptions usually take place within fertility clinics, and are possible because of modern reproductive technology. The clinics are carefully controlled, overseen, and monitored by a number of bodies, including the Advisory Committee on Assisted Reproductive Technology (ACART) and Ethics Committee on Assisted Reproductive

---

77   Stem cells are those that have the ability to continuously divide and develop into a variety of different kinds of tissue. Sources of stem cells are early embryos, spare embryos, cloned embryos, cord, blood, and adult tissue as well as foetuses from pregnancy terminations. Stem cell research has been taking place since the 1998 published account by James Thomson of the development of plurpotent embryonic stem cells from human blastocysts. Discussion of the legal and ethical issues arising from it is outside the scope of this chapter but interested readers are referred to the Royal Society of New Zealand web page that discusses stem cells and human cloning at www.rsnz.org/news/stem.

Technology (ECART)[78], the Reproductive Technologies Accreditation Committee[79], and the local regional Ethics Committee.

Assisted conception and reproductive technology raises difficult social and legal questions that touch the nature of parenthood, and less fundamental questions of succession and inheritance. The law in New Zealand has undergone recent development and is regulated by the Human Assisted Reproductive Technology Act 2004 (HART Act) .

The general purposes of this Act was to provide a robust framework to regulate assisted reproductive procedures and research in this area, prohibit certain procedures and research, and to establish an information-keeping regime for those children conceived using assisted reproductive technology, providing them with an ability to find out about their genetic origins.[80]

To regulate the status of children born as a result of assisted reproduction is the Status of Children Amendment Act 2004. As well as determining the status of the child it also determines who the parent is depending on what type of donor material or procedure has been used.

The issues in relation to reproductive technology and assisted conception include:

1. Who are the child's parents;

2. Surrogacy agreements;

3. Storage and use of gametes, zygotes and embryos, including use of frozen embryos and sperm after death or divorce;

4. The rights of children to know their biological parents;

5. The psychological need for such information, as well as the need for proper medical histories where these may have significant effects on children;

6. Cloning;

7. Genetic screening of embryos and genetic modification of embryos.

19.6.1 Who are the child's parents

The Status of Children Amendment Act 2004 determines the status of children born from various forms of artificial conception. These are:[81]

1. Artificial insemination by a donor;

2. Use of donor semen in an implementation procedure;

3. Use of a donor ovum;

---

78   These two committees replaced the National Ethics Committee on Assisted Human Reproduction ("NECAHR").

79   Fertility clinics prior to this Act coming into force were accredited through this committee but they are now regulated under the Health and Disability Services (Safety) Act 2001, by being incorporated into the definition of "specified health or disability services" (section 80(1) of the Human Assisted Reproductive Technology Act 2004).

80   Human Assisted Reproductive Technology Act 2004, section 3; also, section 48 requires the provider of the fertility service, after a live birth, to provide the Registrar-General with all information of the donor of the donated cell or donated embryo and the Registrar-General must keep this information indefinitely.

81   Defined in Status of Children Amendment Act 1969, section 15.

4.   Use of a donor embryo;

5.   Use of donor semen in an intra-fallopian transfer procedure;

6.   Use of donor ovum in an intra-fallopian transfer procedure;

7.   Use of embryos in an intra-fallopian transfer procedure.

These procedures cover forms of in vitro fertilisation such as ZIFT (zygote intra-fallopian transfer), PROST (pro-nuclear stape ovum transfer), TEST (fallopian embryo transfer), and GIFT (gamete-intra-fallopian transplant). No provision is made for hyper-ovulation treatments or research on adults, gametes, and embryos.[82]

The Act quite clearly establishes that where a woman gives birth to a child as the result of any of the procedures outlined above, the child is the child of that woman[83] and her spouse (including a de facto husband, or a same-sex partner), if the spouse has given his/her consent to the procedure.[84] Conversely, the law states that a person donating ova or sperm has no legal connection whatsoever with any resulting child.[85] This means that where the spouse does not consent to the procedure or there is no spouse, the genetic father does not then become the legal father of the child. It seems there is a gap created in the child's parental relationships.

The result of the legislation is that a donor of gametes has no legal claim whatsoever on a child born as the result of an artificial conception procedure, and the child also has no legal right to the parentage of that person. This applies even where donors are known.

Case

P v K [2003] 2 NZLR 787; (2002) 22 FRNZ 677; [2003] NZFLR 489 (FC) (HC)

The sperm donor agreed with the mother of a child that following the child's birth he would have access to the child. Both the man and the woman were in same-sex relationships. The woman had become pregnant after forty-eight attempts using the man's sperm, which the woman inserted into herself after the man put it in a glass and passed it to her in the next room. Once the child was born he had access to his child for a while, then this ceased. He applied to the Court for access and to be a guardian. The case eventually went to the High Court to decide if the man had any parental rights to make such applications. The High Court decided that the Status of Children Amendment Act 1987[86] removed the man's rights, even though he was the donor father. The Court said that had the child's conception resulted from a single act of sexual intercourse, the father would have parental rights and that the Act produced an unfair result for the father.[87] The Court, however, went on to find that the agreement between the man and the mother was

---

82   Guidance on research is now covered by the Human Assisted Reproductive Technology Act 2004 and the Advisory Committee and Ethics Committee that is formed through this legislation.

83   Status of Children Act 1969, section 17.

84   Status of Children Act 1969, section 18, also the Act talks about a "partnered" woman and this could mean either, married, or living with a defacto partner or another woman (section 14).

85   Status of Children Act 1969, sections 17, 19, 21, 22. The father only has a legal connection if, after the conception, he becomes the woman's partner; any liability does not incur until this time, unless there is prior agreement (see sections 19, 20, 22).

86   The 2004 Amendment also does this, see above.

87   P v K [2003] 2 NZLR 787; (2002) 22 FRNZ 677; [2003] NZFLR 489, para 94.

relevant, and was a starting point in deciding what was best for the child. The Court referred to the United Nations Convention on the Rights of the Child and said:

> The father in this case is undoubtedly the child's biological father and has been recognised as such in the parties' agreements. The child has an international law right, which New Zealand's domestic law must enhance, to know and be cared for by his parents (Article 7(1) and to maintain personal relations and direct contact with his parents on a regular basis (Article 9(3)).[88]

The Court found that there was no reason that a Family Court cannot "structure appropriate orders designed to promote a child's welfare through parental sharing".[89] This case was the first test case on the rights of a sperm donor in New Zealand to have recognised parental ongoing contact with his child.

The Care of Children Act 2004 appears to set this result in statutory form. Section 41 of the Act provides for agreements between parents and donors about the donor's contact with the child, or their role in bringing up a child conceived by an assisted human reproductive procedure. Such agreements will not be enforced under the Act, but if all parties consent, an order that embodies some or all of the agreement can be made and that order can be enforced.[90] Thus, if there is a dispute between parties as to the role of the donor in the upbringing of the child, either of them can apply to the Court for directions and the Court may "make any order it thinks proper."[91]

19.6.2   Surrogacy agreements

Surrogacy agreements are agreements whereby a woman agrees to bear a child that will be given to another person or couple at birth, to be taken as their child. A surrogacy arrangement now has a legal definition provided by the HART Act as:[92]

> "an arrangement under which a woman agrees to become pregnant or to seek to become pregnant; for the purpose of surrendering custody of a child born as a result of the pregnancy."

This topic is dealt with as if such agreements are a part of reproductive technology, but in fact, from the point of view of the law, the main interest is in the substitution of parentage that is involved. The woman giving birth is legally, as well as gestationally, the child's mother.[93] Surrogacy agreements involve an agreement to substitute one set of parents with another, thus bringing into focus the issues of the legal parenthood of the child, the welfare of that child, and the use made of the physical and emotional relationship that a woman has with the child to whom she gives birth.

There is no legal or ethical restraint on natural intercourse surrogacy arrangements. Such arrangements have been entered into for centuries. In vitro intercourse surrogacy is not regulated by any law either[94], however HART does prohibit commercial surrogacy while

---

88   *P v K* [2003] 2 NZLR 787; (2002) 22 FRNZ 677; [2003] NZFLR 489, para 137.
89   *P v K* [2003] 2 NZLR 787; (2002) 22 FRNZ 677; [2003] NZFLR 489, para 135.
90   Care of Children Act 2004, section 41(3); or, if the parties' cannot agree, one party to the agreement can apply to the court for direction (section 41(1)(b)).
91   Care of Children Act 2004, section 41(6).
92   Human Assisted Reproductive Technology Act 2004, section 5.
93   See discussion in 19.6.1.

allowing for fertility service providers to be paid for expenses incurred for the following purposes:

1. Collecting, storing, transporting, or using a human embryo or human gamete:

2. Counselling one or more parties in relation to the surrogacy agreement:

3. Insemination or in vitro fertilisation:

4. Ovulation or pregnancy tests.

It also allows for legal expenses to be paid for the woman who might become pregnant under the agreement to enable her to get independent advice.[95] ACART has developed guidelines for fertility clinics that provide this service.[96] These guidelines include:

1. Being guided by the principles set out in section 4 of HART —

   (a) Health and wellbeing of a child born using an assisted reproductive technique must be an important consideration in all decisions;

   (b) Human health, safety and dignity of future generations should be preserved;

   (c) Women are more directly and significantly affected by these procedures and their health must be protected;

   (d) An informed choice must be made and informed consent be given before any procedure or research is undertaken;

   (e) Donor offspring should be made aware of their genetic origins and be able to access information on these origins;

   (f) Needs, beliefs and values of Maori should be considered and treated with respect;

   (g) The different ethical, cultural and spiritual perspectives of society should be considered and treated with respect.

2. That ECART in its determination of a surrogacy arrangement by a fertility services provider should consider:

   (a) A preference that one or both of the intending parents be genetic parents;

   (b) That the intending mother —

      (i) has a medical condition preventing or precluding conception, or which meant if she got pregnant it would damage the child;

      (ii) A medical diagnosis of unexplained infertility that has not responded to other treatments;

   (c) Discussion and declared intentions on the day-to-day care, guardianship and adoption of the resulting child and any ongoing contact;

---

94   Section 14(1) of the Human Assisted Reproductive Technology Act 2004, states that these arrangements are not illegal but they are not enforceable.

95   Human Assisted Reproductive Technology Act 2004, section 14(4)(b).

96   Guidelines on Surrogacy Arrangements involving Providers of Fertility Services (Nov 2007). Prior to these were guidelines developed by NECAHR in 1997 when it approved non-commercial surrogacy using IVF.

(d)   Each party has received independent medical and independent legal advice;

(e)   Each party has received counselling in accordance with the Code of Practice for Assisted Reproductive Technology Units or the Fertility Services Standard.

It also sets out relevant factors that ECART should take into account; such as — whether the intending surrogate has completed her family and whether all parties clearly understand the legal issues surrounding surrogacy. An aspect of this is that the surrogacy arrangement will not be completed until the intending / commissioning parents have either adopted the child or sought a parenting / guardianship order under the Care of Children Act 2004.

If a dispute occurs between the commissioning parents and the biological mother, the relevant law relating to such agreements is at present governed by the laws relating to parentage, adoption, and child welfare.[97] The famous *Baby M* case illustrates this.

Case

In the Matter of Baby M 525 A 2d 1128 (1987); A 2d 1227 NJ (1988)

A middle class couple, the Sterns, commissioned Mary Beth Whitehead to carry their child, which was conceived using Mr Stern's sperm. The agreement between them was that Mrs Whitehead would give up the baby to Mr Stern and his wife at birth, and she would be paid $10,000 for a live birth and less if the child was stillborn. Mrs Whitehead refused to give up the child. Mr and Mrs Stern took the matter to Court to enforce the agreement.

The agreement was found to be for the sale of the child, and this was not sanctioned by law. Therefore, it was null and void. The decision as to who should have the child was made on the basis of the child's best interests. The Court eventually gave custody to the Sterns. It appears this middle class couple, with their emphasis on education, were seen as preferable to the Whiteheads, who were economically poorer and had three other children.

The prohibition on commercial surrogacy is reinforced by the enactment of the HART Act as discussed above.

19.6.3   Storage and use of gametes, zygotes, and embryos, including use of frozen embryos and sperm after death or divorce

Law applying to the use, storage, and disposal of embryos, is covered jointly by the HART Act, the Human Assisted Reproductive Technology Order 2005 (HARTO),[98] and guidelines produced by ACART.[99] The HART Act requires that any embryo may not be stored for

---

97   Care of Children Act 2004; Status of Children Act 1969; Adoption Act 1955 and Births, Deaths, Marriages, and Relationships Registration Act 1995. For discussion on surrogacy and the law surrounding this see *Report on the Regulatory Framework Governing Assisted Reproductive Technologies in New Zealand* 2006, available at www.acart.health.govt.nz/moh.nsf/indexcm/acart-resources-publications-regulatoryframeworkreportaug06. The Law Commission has also put out a paper entitled *New Issues in Legal Parenthood*, NZLC R88, Wellington, New Zealand Law Commission, 2005.

98   HART Act, section 6 states that certain medical procedures/treatments may be declared as established procedures — these do not require ethics committee approval. This Order was made to declare what those established procedures are and was updated in July 2009.

99   Guidelines on Embryo Donation for Reproductive Purposes (Nov 2008) and Guidelines on Donation of Eggs or Sperm by certain Family Members (Nov 2007).

more than 10 years unless there has been an ethics committee approval sought before this deadline.[100]

The HARTO, in schedule one, outlines uses through the established procedures and these procedures also include the disposal/discarding of eggs, sperm and embryos. Part two of the schedule states that if a donor has died, the stored sperm cannot be used unless specific consent has been obtained.

In relation to eggs, these cannot be used if collected from a dead person or if that person dies prior to collection. It is silent on the use of stored embryos where the donor may have died. ACART guidelines do not add to this other than to note that the parties to embryo donation must agree to the use, storage and disposal of unused donor embryos. This agreement would to some extent bypass the difficulties outlined in the case below, unless one of the parties sought to vary their original consent.

A dispute between the gamete owners over the future of an embryo is a difficult issue. It has been addressed in England, where the Human Fertilisation and Embryology Act 1990 states that unless both parties consent to storage and use, the embryos must be destroyed. On 1 October 2003, a High Court in England ruled that two women who had tried to challenge this law were unsuccessful. The ruling was felt to be landmark, as it prevents one of the parents of the embryo from using it to have children without their former partner's consent.

Natalie Evans and Lorraine Hadley both underwent IVF treatment with their respective partners, and had a number of embryos in storage. The couples separated, and the partners withdrew consent for the use of the embryos. The women went to Court to stop the embryos being destroyed.

The women said it should be up to them to decide whether to carry the child to term, just as it would be if the embryo had been created naturally. Evidence was given that it was Natalie Evans' last chance to have children because her ovaries had been removed after they were found to contain pre-cancerous cells. Though the High Court refused the two women leave to appeal, they can apply directly to the Court of Appeal to request it to grant them leave to appeal.

Prior to the HARTO, there were no guidelines where a woman wished to use her dead husband's sperm to have a child. This Order now states that unless there is specific consent for its use after death it cannot be used.[101] In England, the Human Fertilisation and Embryology Act 1990 also requires consent before sperm can be used after death.

Case

R v Human Fertilisation and Embryology Authority, ex p Blood [1997] 2 All ER 687

Mrs Blood wanted to collect sperm from her dead husband to have a baby. He had died before there was any chance for him to consent. Mrs Blood was successful only insofar as she could go to another country to do it. This was on the grounds that she should be able to seek "medical treatment" in Belgium, where its laws did not require her husband's consent.

---

100   Human Assisted Reproductive Technology Act 2004, section 10.
101   Human Assisted Reproductive Technology Order 2005, at Part 2, clause 5.

19.6.4   The rights of children to know their biological parents

Until 1984 all sperm donors in New Zealand were anonymous. This has led to some children feeling they were conceived to heal the pain of their parents' inability to conceive naturally, and that little or no thought was given to the pain they feel at not knowing who half their ancestry is and what half their medical history is.[102]

As discussed above (at 19.6), the HART Act brought changes to this aspect of the law. Where a child is born using an assisted reproductive technique, the provider of fertility services must retain all information concerning the donor[103] and must also give this to the Registrar — General (Births, Deaths, Marriages and Relationships) on the earlier of the following events: either 50 years have passed since the live birth or the provider is no longer a provider and has no successor; then the Registrar must retain this information indefinitely.[104] If the child wishes to access this information he/she may do so on their own account once they have reached the age of 18 years. If under 18, then their guardian can request the information on their behalf.[105]

If aged between 16 and 18 the child may apply to the Family Court for an order for the child to be treated as if they are 18 years.[106] However, the entity holding the information does have a right of refusal if they think on reasonable grounds that disclosure may endanger any person.[107]

19.6.5   Cloning

The HART Act defines a cloned embryo as: "a human embryo that is a genetic copy (whether identical or not) of a living or dead human being, a still-born child, a human embryo, or a human foetus."[108] The HART Act only prohibits cloning for reproductive purposes,[109] so it appears to leave open the possibility of research using cloned embryos (therapeutic cloning).[110]

Cloning of human embryos is possible by using developed embryonic stem cells with the capacity for differentiation. Stem cells and cell lines (in limited circumstances) now come within the definition of human tissue by the Human Tissue Act 2004[111] and therefore must be collected in accordance with the consent procedures of this Act. It also provides for collection for non-therapeutic use such as research. If this is to occur it must have ethical approval and meet the ethical requirements of the Human Assisted Reproductive Technology Act 2004.[112]

---

102   See the poignant statement from a child born as a result of anonymous sperm donation in Professor Mark Heneghan's article titled "When biotechnology and law collide: assisted human reproduction and family law (Part II — the legal perspective)" [2003] 4 *Butterworths Family Law Journal*, 143.

103   Human Assisted Reproductive Technology Act 2004, section 3 and Part 3, sections 47-66.

104   Human Assisted Reproductive Technology Act 2004, sections 48, 52 and 55.

105   Human Assisted Reproductive Technology Act 2004, section 50 and 57; section 58 relates to a donor offspring accessing any information about siblings.

106   Human Assisted Reproductive Technology Act 2004, section 65; this decision will be based on the best interests of the child.

107   Human Assisted Reproductive Technology Act 2004, section 50(4).

108   Human Assisted Reproductive Technology Act 2004, section 5.

109   Human Assisted Reproductive Technology Act 2004, Schedule 1.

110   Cloning to produce stem cells.

111   Human Tissue Act 2004, section 7.

112   Human Tissue Act 2004, section 74.

A number of ethical issues are being debated around the world, such as whether it is ethical to prohibit the artificial production of cloned embryos for research that could lead to health improvements in future generations. At present some embryos that would otherwise be discarded are being used for other types of research.

In the United Kingdom when the case of Quintavalle[113] was ruled on at first instance it seemed to indicate a gap in UK legislation that did not allow for embryo cloning or their use. This was because the definition of an embryo under the current legislation was, "a live human embryo where fertilisation is complete." [114] A cloned embryo is not fertilised it is created by cell nuclear replacement and because of this a license could not be authorised for their use.[115]

This led to the Human Reproductive Cloning Act 2001 (UK), which broadened the definition of embryo so it covered all areas of embryo creation not done by fertilisation. It made permissible reproductive cloning for therapeutic research only, however, when the case made it to the House of Lords[116] their decision made the legislation unnecessary as they decided on a purposive interpretation of "embryo" that brought cloned embryos within the statutory framework.

19.6.6   Genetic screening of embryos and genetic modification of embryos

Designer babies, in terms of eye colour, hair colour, sex, perhaps even personality and temperament, may well appear to be the stuff of science fiction, but clearly technology will make this possible in the future:[117]

> "This is the beginning of the end of sex as the way we reproduce. We will still have sex for pleasure but we will view our children as too important to leave to a random meeting of eggs and sperm."

Whether this is acceptable, both legally and ethically, is the subject of debate. The law in New Zealand now regulates pre-implantation genetic diagnosis, or prenatal genetic diagnosis through the HART Act and the Human Assisted Reproductive Technology Order 2005, which has this listed as an established procedure. Pre-implantation genetic diagnosis (PGD) is useful, for example when couples who know they carry genes for inherited diseases are deciding which embryos to implant. Reproductive technologies such as IVF and artificial insemination are the only means to enable the use of pre-implantation gene diagnosis. The HART Act prohibits fertility clinics from offering sex selection to their IVF consumers, and it is punishable by either a term of imprisonment not exceeding 1 year or a fine not exceeding $10,000 or both.[118]

---

113   R *(on the application of Quintavalle) v Secretary of State for Health* [2002] EWCA Civ 29; [2002] QB 628; [2002] 2 WLR 550; [2002] 2 All ER 625.

114   Human Fertilisation and Embryology Act 1990 (UK), section 1.

115   Human Fertilisation and Embryology Act 1990 (UK), section 3(3)(d).

116   R *(on the application of Quintavalle) v Secretary of State for Health* [2002] EWCA Civ 29; [2002] QB 628; [2002] 2 WLR 550; [2002] 2 All ER 625.

117   Professor G Stock, as quoted in P Dixon, "IVF Latest News — Truth About IVF: Summary of IVF San Diego conference" *Daily Express*, 27 October 2000, www.globalchange.com/ivfnews.htm.

118   Human Assisted Reproductive Technology Act 2004, section 11.

Other ethical issues the law will need to grapple with are whether pre-implantation genetic diagnosis should be used to produce a child who can act as a human tissue donor for a sibling. In 2001 in the UK, consent was given by the Human Fertilisation and Embryology Authority (HFEA) to do just that.

A boy with thalassaemia required a blood transfusion or bone marrow transplant from a closely genetically matched donor. None of his siblings were a match and the mother had conceived two children trying to get a match — one had thalassaemia and she elected an abortion, the second was a healthy child free of the disease but not a match. This prompted her to approach the HFEA for a license to have her embryo tested not only for thalassaemia but also to be tissue typed so the resulting child was a match to her son. This was an extension for the HFEA as the licence was not just for PGD but also for HLA (tissue typing), before the mother could go ahead a pro-life group lodged a challenge stating that the HFEA did not have the authority to give a license for tissue typing. This went all the way to the House of Lords, who dismissed the pro-life group's challenge and allowed the HFEA decision to stand.[119]

In New Zealand under the HART Act as tissue typing is not an established procedure the fertility service provider would have to seek ethic committee approval, the guidelines provided by ACART[120] states that the provider must seek approval by ECART and it is decided on a case by case basis.

19.6.7 Conclusion

It is important to point out that some proceedings involved in the field of assisted reproductive technology are experimental in the sense that they may have a less than 20 percent chance of resulting in a viable pregnancy. For this reason, health practitioners should take particular care to ensure clients are adequately informed of the nature, risks, and success rate of the technology. Counselling is advisable and is recommended by the guidelines produced by ACART.

The right to reproduce is a fundamental right and there are issues as to how far it extends, and whether and to what extent the law should limit it. These issues are important and will continue to be debated as more technologies are developed.

19.7 Further reading

S Coney and A Else (eds), *Protecting our future: The case for greater regulation of Assisted Reproductive Technology*, Auckland, Women's Health Action Trust, 1999.

K Daniels, "Assisted human reproduction in New Zealand: The contribution of ethics" (1998) 8 Eubios Journal of Asian and International Bioethics 79.

G McGee, *The Perfect Baby: Parenthood in the New World of Cloning and Genetics* (2nd ed), Maryland, Roman and Littlefield Publishers, 2000.

---

119   R *(on the application of Quintavalle) v Human Fertilisation and Embryology Authority* [2003] EWCA Civ 667; [2004] QB 168; [2003] 3 WLR 878; [2003] 3 All ER 257. Also for interest there is a fictional book called "My Sister's Keeper" by Jodi Picoult that traverses the ethical dilemmas once a child who has been born specifically typed to match a sibling with a genetic disorder is born, and raises questions about when that child stops being a donor and the different rights involved.

120   www.acart.health.govt.nz/moh.nsf/indexcm/acart-resources-guidelines-preimplantation.

N A Olbourne, "Ethical considerations underpinning the donation of alive, non-regenerative organs" (2001) 9 Journal of Law and Medicine 76.

F M Sim, "Retrieving semen from a dead patient" (1998) BMJ 317.

Te Puni Kokiri Ministry of Maori Development, *Haurora o te Tinana me ona Tikanga: A Guide for the removal, retention, return and disposal of Maori body parts and organ donation*, Wellington, 1999.

S Watson, "Gifts to strangers: Organ donation in New Zealand" [2002] New Zealand Law Journal 291.

R Fisher, "When biotechnology and law collide: Assisted human reproduction and family law (Part I — the medical perspective)" [2003] Butterworths Family Law Journal 139.

M Henaghan, "When biotechnology and law collide: Assisted human reproduction and family law (Part II — the legal perspective)" [2003] Butterworths Family Law Journal 143.

Chapter 20

Ethics

Glenys Godlovitch

Contents

20.1   Background, facts, and values

From a very early age most of us are taught and encouraged to distinguish between what is right and what is wrong. We learn through stories and lived experiences how to make moral judgments and how to incorporate moral thinking into our action plans. We learn by example and lesson. We come to share, to respect others and so on in much the same way as we learn to talk. It is part of being socially acculturated and situated. Moral thinking is often encapsulated in aphorism, such as "do whatever will maximize good outcomes" or "act for the right reasons" or "behave as a good person would". These ideas are all well and good but they need content if they are to guide us. We recognize while there is a generic sense of ethical thinking common in all our ordinary daily lives, some people's lives take on special moral significance because of the role they occupy in society.

Health professions carry social responsibilities that import special content for moral considerations. Edmund Pellegrino, a noted bioethicist and medical doctor, has said that skill, self-effacement and fidelity to trust are required to be an ethical health professional, given the vulnerability and dependence of those who seek or need the specialised help and the powerful position of health professionals to affect lives and wellbeing. So much hangs on a health practitioner being not just a good person, but a good health care provider.[1] It is therefore essential that practitioners learn not just the specialised knowledge of their chosen calling but also learn to identify, think about, and act on ethical considerations. But this is not simply a matter of doing an electronic literature search or picking up a few books at the library.

As health practitioners, readers will readily identify examples where something occurred that they thought was wrong, or are not sure what the right course of action was. Examples include:

- The difficult, obstructive or aggressive patient who is left waiting longer to be helped back from the toilet to the hospital bed or is given faster attention than another patient just to prevent an outburst;
- Parents who want to discontinue interventions for their newborn with neurological deficiencies following birth trauma;
- The use of an anaesthetised person, or the body of a recently deceased person for surgical or procedural practice, or for exhibition;
- The use of a patient's health information and images without their consent.

Other examples include activities that have typically occurred over extended periods, such as:

- The management practice of staff rostering that rotates nurses through a series of different wards with no home ward assignment;
- The double booking or rescheduling of appointments as a common way of managing case load;

---

1   Edmund D Pellegrino, (1) "Character, Virtue and Self Interest in the Ethics of the Professions" (1989) 5 *The Journal of Contemporary Health Law and Policy* 53; (2) "Towards a Virtue-Based Normative Ethics for the Health Professions" (1995) 5 *Kennedy Institute of Ethics Journal* 253.

- The systemic lack of support and oversight for those working in isolation or rural communities;
- The institution of a policy banning smoking that precludes dying patients from that small pleasure or from meeting a craving;
- Drug or alcohol problems in colleagues;
- Institutional policy that instructs employees not to admit errors.

Readers probably know from experience in the health care setting that both the resolution and the process used to reach a resolution are very important to the integrity of the health care. This makes it crucial that practitioners have a stronger grasp on the theoretical nature and application of ethics as a cornerstone to good clinical practice.

This chapter will introduce some concepts that may not be familiar to readers but which – without their knowing it — they may be using when faced with issues about what to do in any given setting. The chapter addresses ethical principles, and their place in the decision-making process. It outlines various approaches to moral thinking. It does not give a final answer as to how a person should act in any given situation. A model for clarifying values is offered, with suggestions for reasoning so that one may reach an acceptable decision on how to proceed. As this is a book about law, it is not intended that this analysis be other than an outline of some of the main ethical issues, an indication of their relationship to the law, and a brief guide to ethical decision-making.

20.1.1 Moral values and prescriptions

Although we often hear people and their actions described as ethical or unethical, few of us have a clear idea about what ethics is. Few doubt, however, that in making moral statements we are doing more than simply describing objective physical characteristics; rather we are making value judgements, and usually recommending (prescribing) or condemning (proscribing) certain actions or character traits. Something would be extremely odd about a person who said "X is unethical and I recommend you do X." These twin aspects, value and prescription, are thought to be hallmarks of moral statements.

Moral judgements are not straightforward. The facts they involve are not like physical facts about objects, such as size, shape, or colour. Consider the example where a class is just coming out of an exam and two students are talking about a third student whom they saw cheating in the "closed book" exam.

A: Did you see that?

B: Yes.

A: What a dreadful thing to do, cheating like that!

B: I agree.

A: I've never seen anything so wrong before!

B: I didn't see anything wrong.

A: How can you say that?

B: Well, let's go over it. I saw C sneeze, reach into his pocket, pull out a handkerchief with a sheet of paper folded up inside it, open the paper, read the piece of paper, and copy from it into his exam book. I didn't see anything wrong.

Seeing the wrongness of C's actions is not simply *seeing* X, where X is an obvious objective feature. It is unlike seeing the size or colour of the handkerchief, or the number of folds in the cheat's crib sheet. The kind of *seeing* in what A and B saw C do was a *seeing that* C did something wrong. It is a judgment that depends on the interpretation of the facts relative to values.

20.1.2   Moral statements

There is no simple way of identifying a statement as a moral statement. Certain grammatical and semantic characteristics should be looked on as symptomatic of moral statements, but the presence or absence of those characteristics is not definitive. Moral statements are typically context dependent too. The entire setting needs to be considered along with the particular sentential form. Many moral statements do in fact take the form: "In situation X, person P ought to do Y." Moral statements may also take the form of instructions, but this form too will also occur as the instructions for any practical skill, such as a recipe for cooking ("If the batter is too runny, add more flour"). The statements have this in common — they are all hypothetical generalisations, ("If X, then Y"). To understand them and address the issue involves determining:

- The conditions under which the statement is applicable;
- What is to be done;
- Who is to do it?

(1)   *Expressive statements*

Often people believe they are making a moral statement, when in fact they are not. What they are doing is just expressing an emotive personal reaction to a particular situation. That is, they are making an *emotive or expressive statement* (or "gut reaction"), for example:

> "I don't want to tell patients they are dying."

We can find if there is more to this statement than personal feeling fairly quickly by asking "Why is that?" Opinions and feelings, though strongly sensed, may not have the rational underpinning that we expect of moral judgments. So we can say that there is something extra at work when we make *value or moral statements*. The person may even begin to develop a moral framework and rationale for their expressive statement just by being asked the question "why?" So we can next distinguish moral statements as a class of value statements.

(2)   *Value statements*

To have validity as a moral statement, one should be able to establish the reason(s) for it. This becomes a *value statement*:

> "People should not be told they are dying (because …)."

A value statement appeals to reasons that set out what is "good" or "bad", "right" or "wrong". So in our example, the reasons might be "because it will make them die sad, despairing and depressed and it would be better to die not feeling that way." But compare that reason with "because it makes me uncomfortable". The latter sounds very like "I just don't like how it feels when I tell people they are dying." So a good test of what reasons are moral reasons as distinct from other explanation is to see whether it involves an essential reference to the speaker. If it does, then it is merely a personal expression (but that needs supportive empathy nonetheless). If it does not, and applies to people in general, then it is a much stronger candidate for being a moral value statement.

(3)   Prescriptive statements

Value statements that pass the sniff test as moral value statements embody moral principles. But notoriously different moral principles can cohabit within a single situation, yet only one decision can be made and acted on. In determining whether there is more to the value statement, it may become apparent that there should be some qualifications to it. Often the qualifications are in the form "[Value statement] unless …" One can then turn the value statement into a *prescriptive statement* — one that qualifies the value statement. There are arguably few, possibly no, value statements than can be applied absolutely without qualifications. Moral dilemmas often arise precisely because various people take incompatible positions about what qualifications are appropriate and about how they rank them when there are two different value statements at work in the same set of circumstances. For example:

> "Truth telling is fundamental to building and maintaining a good relationship."

and

> "It is wrong to hurt people's emotional wellbeing when they are ill and vulnerable."

These two statements support incompatible prescription statements as conclusions — one where the patient should be told, the other where the patient should not be told that they are dying.

> "In situation X (or every situation) person P (or every person) ought not to tell someone if they are dying."

A prescriptive statement turns the principle into an "ought" statement that sets out an apparent obligation or duty. It also stipulates situations and conditions under which the action ought to be carried out.

(4)   Duty statements

The *duty statement* would be:

> "One — (You) must not tell a person if they are dying."

The reader will have recognised that there is a close association here with the tenet of truth telling. Although we have framed our statements as negatives ("do not tell …") there is a professional pull to challenge the validity of the statements precisely because of the emphasis we place on truth telling. We value truth telling both as a fundamental principle of social life (required, in fact, to make language learning and linguistic communication possible) and as an instance of respect for the integrity of the vulnerable patient.

A good tip for working through the rationale underpinning what might be just emotive expressions or grounded prescriptions is to see whether one can find a counter-example, something that flies in the face of the general prescription. One might ask oneself whether a situation could arise where a health practitioner may have a duty to tell someone if they are dying. Some have argued that there are different cultural approaches to telling a person they are going to die, which would place exceptions on health practitioners directly giving this news to her/him. Should we be influenced by the belief that such information would

491

make a person depressed? Is it more important to tell them anyway, so that they can prepare themselves and their affairs, and not find out in a way that makes them feel the truth was wrongly withheld from them? (It may be instructive to consider other general statements such as "I feel health practitioners should never disclose to a third person that another person is HIV positive".) In considering exceptions to the original statement, one can identify duties arising from prescriptive statements, and rank them in order of importance.

Another way of determining whether one can advance from an expressive statement to a prescriptive statement is by asking the question: What would happen if the proposed prescriptive statement were to be applied? Would all the consequences be acceptable, given *other* moral values that one holds, and also form the basis of prescriptive statements, such as "You should never harm another by your actions" or "You should treat all people equally"? One might modify the statement about telling a person they have cancer to reflect the different situations. The modification will be a refinement so it is compatible with other statements. Alternatively, one might change the other statements, if the duty to tell the person they have cancer is considered to apply at all times in all situations.

20.1.3   Moral claims, truth, and reality

One common tendency is to think that ethics is relative or subjective — relative to one's upbringing, or subjective as a matter of personal opinion. People speak of moral views as personal opinions or cultural outlooks. This position is called *relativism*, and two versions of it are *ethical relativism* and *subjectivism*.

Relativism is attractive at first look, but it does not stand up to close scrutiny. As an attempt at a moral theory, it is naive. It appears at first to reflect the variations in beliefs and practices across times and cultures. It seems to foster acceptance and tolerance of differences. To do the former, namely identify differences, involves nothing more than objective data collection. To do the latter, namely endorse social and cultural tolerance, involves more. It involves making a judgement about different social practices. It goes beyond the claim, "This is how they do it there," to say, "They are right to do what they do. It is right for them." So, for example, if one group or society practises aggressive, expansionist supremacist oppression of others, the moral relativist would logically be committed to the conclusion that aggressive, expansionist oppression is right for that group. That is scarcely what we usually have in mind when we promote tolerance. Needless to say, such an implication is not what naive relativists have in mind either when claiming that relativism fosters tolerance.

Relativism cannot be correct as a moral theory, even if it is correct as comparative cultural anthropology. There is a logical gap between reporting that, as a matter of fact, people do things differently and making a value judgement about the different practices. It is one thing to state that group A does X and group B does Y, and another thing to say that group A ought to do X and group B ought to do Y. Or, put another way, the rightness or wrongness of any particular course of action cannot be established simply by the practice. That would mean that no group was ever morally wrong, no group could ever improve, no member in a group could ever rationally dissent on moral grounds. If cultural and social factors do correctly influence moral judgements, they do so not by endorsing moral relativism. The role cultural and social beliefs and practices play is that of being relevant factors among others in moral reasoning.

If relativism were morally correct, there could be no such thing as a moral dilemma, or a moral disagreement in any interesting or useful way. It could never be wrong for a slave owner to beat a slave, or even to own a slave in a slave-owning society. Yet it is precisely the practice that has been challenged. The belief that slavery is right, and the practice of owning slaves, no more makes it right to own slaves than does the belief that the practice of eating stinging nettles cures cancer. Believing something does not make it true. Practising something does not make it right. Relativism flies in the face of seeing a dilemma. Dilemmas and disagreements presuppose that at least one position is wrong. The very existence of moral dilemmas and moral disagreements is sufficient to establish that morals are not just something personal, or something particular to one group of people.

Philosophers argue whether moral claims are objectively true. Those who are persuaded that matters of value are objective are called *realists*. Those who hold that matters of value are social constructs and conventions are called *anti-realists* or *conventionalists*. Anti-realists do not hold that there is no truth about morals; rather they hold that morals are conventions in much the same way that money is a convention, or the organisation of the letters on a keyboard, or the notes on a piano go higher from left to right.

20.1.4 Moral philosophy, semantics, and ethicists

There are at least three levels of moral discourse. The highest level, most removed from practice, is called meta-ethics. It deals with the question "What is Ethics"? The middle level is called normative ethics or moral philosophy. Moral philosophers ask the question "What makes actions right/wrong"? They try to develop moral theories. We will look at some of these theories below at 20.2. Then at the practice level there is applied ethics which addresses the practical question "What should be/ought to be done herein this situation?"

We can sketch the relationships like this:

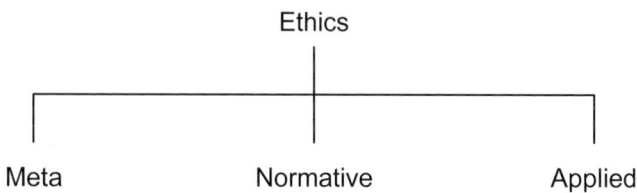

Ethics

Meta   Normative   Applied

(1)   *Meta-ethics*

Over the centuries, some philosophers have tried to analyse conceptually our moral pronouncements into coherent, unified theories about our language of morals. Philosophers in this group concentrate on semantic questions about the vocabulary we use in moral discourse and comparing those uses with uses in other contexts, for example "what does 'good' mean in expressions like 'good action', 'good idea', 'good person', 'good friend', 'good food', 'good dog', 'good weather'?". They are said to be engaging in meta-ethics, which is theorising about moral vocabulary and moral concepts. They also consider examples involving modal verbs especially "ought" and "should." The range of examples is extensive, from "I ought to cross the road at the pedestrian crossing," "she ought to apply iodine to those cuts", "they ought to help the victims of the earthquake," to "he ought to write more neatly," and "no-one ought to put up with that!" They look for common core meanings to the use of "ought" in these sentences. However, they are not advocating some specific moral stand or perspective.

(2)   *Normative*

By contrast, other philosophers have proposed and analysed particular ethical theories, trying to identify the strengths and weaknesses within each theory. These philosophers are called ethicists or moral philosophers. So, whereas meta-ethicists focus on the meaning of words and the underlying concepts, moral philosophers concentrate, for example on what kind of person one has to be to be a good person, or what makes actions right or wrong.

We will focus on the three main approaches to thinking about ethical issues, what their strengths and weaknesses are, and how they relate to the health service.

(3)   *Applied*

This is the deliberative application of ethics to actual practical situations. Health professionals are probably aware of the roles played in their own institutions by bioethicists, sometimes called clinical ethicists. Clinical ethicists or bioethicists are practitioners whose field of expertise is health care ethics. These professional ethicists bring together their knowledge of normative ethics and the health care setting and help resolve issues or at least help clarify what the issues are and how they can be approached ethically. Some bioethicists specifically give advice about what would be the appropriate course(s) of intervention; others stop short of giving advice beyond identifying and exploring a range of possibilities.

20.2   Normative ethics: moral rules, principles, and theories

Many people associate facts and values by applying a rule. A classic example of a set of rules is the biblical Ten Commandments, believed by some to be God's law and requiring unwavering compliance. Rules demand and command certain conduct. However, some argue that adherence to rules is misplaced or even impossible. Those who think it is a mistake to follow rules say that the rule adherents are too blinkered. Such thinkers hold that in order for a command to be compelling, it must be grounded in a principle, and hence the value of each of the Ten Commandments depends on whether it exemplifies a sound principle.

Principles are generalisations of a special kind. They are not just statistical reports. They prescribe conduct. Appeal to principles is integral to most approaches to ethics. A single, unified set of principles constitutes a moral theory. In the cheating example given above, one theory might be: fairness and respect for others are fundamental values, which are to be promoted. Deliberate misrepresentation in the form of cheating is neither fair nor respectful. Cheating is inconsistent with the promotion of those values. Therefore, cheating is wrong.

20.2.1   Three traditional types of moral theory

There are three main types of moral theory:

- *Consequentialism*, associated with utilitarians[2] and cost-benefit analysis. This kind of approach is causal in nature and focuses on outcomes of actions;
- *Deontological ethics*, a "rational moral duties" view associated with Kant[3] and others. This approach is rational in nature and focuses on moral obligations or moral rights;
- *Virtue theories*, or "moral character" theories, associated with Aristotle and others, this approach has been revived in the last forty years. It focuses on the character of the person as moral agent.

All three approaches assert that there are objective moral truths.

20.2.2 Consequentialism

Consequentialist moral theories hold that the moral worth of an action is gauged in terms of the consequences. So consequentialist theories are causal theories. Broadly speaking, they hold that an action is morally right if its good consequences outweigh its bad consequences relative to some value. As Bentham, one of the founders of utilitarianism, asserted, "Nature has placed mankind under the governance of two sovereign masters, *pain* and *pleasure*." This sounds like an innocent claim and something with which one can concur. People try to avoid pain and pursue pleasure. He continues, "It is for them alone [ie pain and pleasure] to point out what we ought to do, as well as to determine what we shall do."[4]

On its face, it seems to say that what a person should do is make the world a better place for everyone. As a moral theory, utilitarianism is frequently characterised by the term, *the greatest happiness principle*, advocating the greatest happiness of the greatest number of people possible. Happiness is thus the value to pursue, and pain the contrary value to avoid. Some other utilitarians, Mill among them, argue that Bentham was too narrow in identifying a single value, happiness, as the ultimate measure of the goodness of an action. Mill,[5] and utilitarians like him, subscribe to the view that there is more than just one single intrinsic value. For that reason, they are said to be pluralist utilitarians.

Values are said to be either intrinsic (needing no further justification) or instrumental (justified in terms of an intrinsic value). The moral value of specific action is construed in terms of the part it plays towards promoting some ultimate, intrinsic value. Values are classified as instrumental values (for example, being inoculated) and as intrinsic values (for example, being healthy). Consequentialist theories are what we appeal to when we ask: "Does the expected overall good outweigh the expected overall harm?" This way of thinking is obviously very common in the health service setting. We need only consider the venerable Hippocratic Oath to see how well entrenched is the principle of preventing harm and promoting wellbeing.

---

2   Key figures in the development of utilitarianism are Jeremy Bentham (1748-1832) and John Stuart Mill (1806-73).

3   Immanuel Kant (1724-1804). Theories based on Kant's approach are called "Kantian". Among those who owe Kant an intellectual debt of gratitude are the present day "rights" theorists. Kant's own model was grounded on the notion of moral duties, but many later thinkers have reinterpreted duties in terms of rights, where one person has a right, another person has a duty.

4   J Bentham, *An Introduction to the Principles of Morals and Legislation*, 1789, public domain.

5   J S Mill, *Utilitarianism*, 1863, public domain.

There are some significant shortcomings to a utilitarian approach. For example, imagine a derelict with no relatives — no one who cares about him. He could disappear and nobody would miss him. Assume he is utterly dejected and does not care whether he lives or dies. There he is, a potential organ donor, a walking research subject. Others would benefit enormously from his participation in their health service, even his involuntary participation, even from his death.[6] On the simplest version of utilitarianism, the greater good of the greater number justifies it. No doubt, more good would result if he were used instrumentally in these ways — including maybe good to other derelicts who would then get a larger meal at the soup kitchen — than if he were left in his current situation. The good of the many would definitely outweigh the harm to the one. Indeed his despair and dejection will be cut short by an early end. But many people find it thoroughly objectionable to think that people should be treated simply as nothing more than a means to an end, as causal cogs in causal machines to be used by others for their own ends.[7]

Other problems with consequentialist theories arise in connection with the following:

- *The assignment of comparative value and issues of commensurability:* Who is to say that their ranking scores 3, 73 or 200000000014? How are numbers attached? Who is to say that the value one person attaches to eating strawberries is commensurable with a 16-year-old girl's at solving a differential equation, or with Sir Edmund Hillary's thrill at being first to climb Mt Everest? In the health service context, this problem relates directly to surgery waiting lists and prioritisation within them.
- *Whose interests are to be considered?* Do we need to consider future (possible) generations, only existing people, or all sentient creatures?
- *There is a logical flaw:* Maximizing for two disparate factors (greatest number/greatest happiness) is logically flawed where the factors are not inherently coextensive.
- *The free-rider problem:* Provided the overall gain is maximized, it should not matter that some individuals are taking advantage of others. For example, as long as enough people do not pick the flowers, it is right to pick the flowers when to do so would increase that person's happiness. Similarly, as long as everybody else pays the correct bus fare, it is right for one person not to pay, especially if they otherwise would not be able to travel.

However, even given counter-examples and problems like these, we still want to make moral space for the ideas of preventing harm and increasing wellbeing. That notion still has a strong influence as a moral factor.

20.2.3 Deontological ethics

The deontological approach ignores the consequences and the outcomes. It focuses instead on the reasoning process of moral agents, and looks at people's intentions coupled with making one's best effort to carry them out. In its most famous version, it says that *one must act only in accordance with reasons which are capable of being completely universal, tantamount to utterly*

---

6   Hollywood recently used this long-standing example in the movie *Extreme Measures*.
7   The classic examples are of the experiments done on concentration camp inmates by German clinicians during the Nazi period. Finding out how long a person could survive if thrown into ice-cold water was extremely relevant to downed German air force personnel. Maybe on a purely numerical basis, the good of the aircrews would and did outweigh the harm done to the victims. However, many argue that that does not justify the practice and is counted by some as a refutation of simplistic consequentialist theories.

rational law.[8] As the reasoning is thought to have the character of universal moral law, the deontological theories are often framed in terms of moral duties and rights. The universalisability[9] requirement removes from the consideration all personal preferences, inclinations, personal favourites, and even consideration of whether one's actions result in an increase in wellbeing over harm.

In outlining his theory, Kant tells us always to act so as to treat others as *ends in themselves* and never as a means to some other end — to recognise the *autonomy* of all rational beings. He says we are to think of ourselves as if we were creating rational moral law, but in the roles both of legislator and of subject simultaneously. His is a scheme where all people are self-determining and rational. The choices they make would all be the same no matter who actually makes the decision. He insists this is the only logical way to determine what is right. In health care, this theory is recognised as autonomy and respect for all involved.

There are some major conceptual problems with Kant's approach, especially the universalisability requirement and his notion of rationality. However, to examine these would take us outside the scope of this chapter.

The major drawbacks that critics raise include the following:

- *Kant's system is utterly impracticable:* We cannot and maybe even should not discount all the local preferences and inclinations involved — it might be better to look after the sick neighbour, than to say that you have an equal obligation to look after the sick unknown resident of a far-off country.
- *Lack of conflict resolution potential:* Kant's theory provides no guidance when we discover conflicting moral obligations. He appears to believe that if we reason properly, conflicting duties could not arise.

And, most importantly:

- *Disregard of all consequences:* Kant's moral outlook pays no attention whatsoever to the results of one's actions: Actual outcomes are to be disregarded as irrelevant — if harm results, that is regrettable, but not a matter to be factored into one's preliminary decision-making. From a medical perspective, it allows for incompetence, so long as the practitioners try their best and act on the best principles.

The positive aspect of deontological theories is the demand for recognition of autonomy and the respect for the rights of others.

20.2.4   Virtue theories

In response to the longstanding difficulties and dissatisfaction with consequentialist and deontological approaches, there has been a rebirth in recent decades of the virtue ethics approach where the aim is to foster the development of virtuous people. It is safe to think of this as *the good social role model* approach, where a person is encouraged to analyse and emulate the behaviour of a good person.

---

8   I Kant, *Groundwork of the Metaphysics of Ethics*, 1785, public domain.
9   The reader's attention is drawn to the term, universalisability, as distinct from the term, universality, in connection with a person's reason for acting. By the former, universalisability, Kant means to provide a logical test for distinguishing moral precepts. It is not whether one does universalise one's reason, but whether one's reason is capable of being universalised to all rational creatures, at all times.

Over 2,000 years ago the great philosopher Aristotle was one of the first writers on virtue theory.[10] He said, "It is a difficult business to be good." Aristotle saw ethics as inextricably connected and interdependent with one's place in society, the overall wellbeing of the society and of its individual members. He saw moral conduct as a skill a person could learn by practice, by following others who are more skilful and by hard thinking, where one's job was to hone one's virtues in practice.

Virtue theory for Aristotle then is a functional theory: it couples skill and prudential reasoning within the biologically and socially determined parameters of aiming for a common goal, namely wellbeing. For Aristotle, an individual's wellbeing and societal wellbeing are inseparable. Aristotle does not tell his readers exactly what they must do nor what skills they must acquire. He emphasises the need for continual self-monitoring, close factual investigation of the circumstances, analysis of the character and conduct of a good person, and the avoidance of extremes.

In later years Christianity adopted Aristotle's perspective and Christianised it as The Golden Mean. However, it is a mistake to identify the two too closely. Aristotle did not advocate a "meek and mild" or "submissive" approach. In fact, he urges that it is sometimes right to be angry or demanding. The trick for Aristotle is in knowing when and to what degree these are appropriate. For Aristotle the worst general characteristic is the failure to guard against one's own ignorance, and acting in ignorance without even willingness and an enthusiasm to learn.

The difficulties with virtue theory approaches include the following:

- There are no inclusion and exclusion criteria for identifying virtues;
- There is no method for determining excess or shortage;
- There is no prescribed method for acquiring the virtues;
- It is also open to charges of medical paternalism;
- It fails to address misplaced esteem, the fallen hero syndrome where someone who was admired lets one down — the loss of confidence could be calamitous;
- When confronted with a situation, for which one has no suitable role model, one is left adrift.

However, on the positive side, virtue theory as it has emerged in the modern writings of people like Pellegrino does encourage the emulation of good conduct.[11] It doesadvocate learning from an acknowledged master and it does give us reason to try to think better, be better, and do better in our social conduct. We see these components in the health care practitioner who has the practical and practitioner competence coupled with the trust and respect of patients, participants, staff, and fellow practitioners. In the medical context, it is more difficult to say what might count as being a virtuous patient. From one perspective, some might suggest it is the person who adheres to the prescribed regime and makes no unreasonable demands of the health practitioners, but that smacks of medical paternalism — of "doctor knows best". A better candidate is actually mentioned in the

---

10   For readers wanting to go into more depth, the key work on virtue theory by Aristotle is found in his *Nicomachean Ethics*. This is a tough read — though at a superficial level it might seem straightforward — and is best approached and understood through taking a theory course on Moral Philosophy.

11   See for example: Edmund D Pellegrino and David C Thomasma, *The Virtues in Medical Practice*, New York, Oxford University Press, 1993.

Hippocratic writings, namely the person who strives to get better by neither surrendering to, nor ignoring the health problem.

20.2.5   Pluralism approaches

Over the last three decades new approaches have emerged in response to the perceived deficiencies of the classical approaches to ethics. We will not be able to consider them all and indeed they are too recent to have stood the test of time but readers should be aware of the changing landscape.

20.2.6   The Belmont Principles

The Belmont Report of the late 1970s was the official response in the United States to some egregious research.[12] One example is called the Tuskegee Study that went on for decades in Florida. Although it started in the pre-penicillin days the observational longitudinal study continued for about 20 years after penicillin became standard first line treatment for syphilis. Penicillin was withheld from men in the study. But to make matters worse, they were led to believe they were being treated. One should pause for a moment and reflect on the effect this might have for sexual partners as well as the men themselves! The situation was further compounded by the overall demographic profile of the participant population drawn as it was from traditionally deprived and disempowered African-Americans and Hispanics some of whom were prisoners and the offering of incentives (such as free burial) to enhance recruitment.

When the Tuskegee experiment finally became public knowledge a committee was mandated to identify the ethical underpinnings of health research in the US. The committee members identified core values. The Belmont Principles, as they came to be called, are:

* Autonomy;
* Beneficence/non-malfeasance; and
* Justice.

These principles are well discussed by the authors who influenced the Belmont Report, authors such as Beauchamp, Childress and Veatch.[13] These four values reflect the ancient Hippocratic tenets (the "do good/do no harm" dyad) and the modern recognition of the role of self-determination but sets them within a just society that makes special place for addressing social inequities. Yet, as we shall see the principles can and do conflict in application.

(1)   *Autonomy*

Autonomy — deciding for oneself what treatments one will or will not refuse or accept — occupies the primary position in the Belmont model. Autonomy is closely allied with rights theories and deontological approaches to ethics. It is based on the recognition of the inherent worth of others as self-managing, self-interested actors with goals and life plans.

---

12   The National Commission for the Protection of Human Subjects of Biomedical and Behavioral Research, *The Belmont Report*, Washington, DC: DHEW Publication OS 78-0012, 1978.

13   See for example: Tom L Beauchamp and James F Childress, *Principles of Biomedical Ethics*, (5th ed), New York, Oxford University Press, 2001; James F Childress, *Practical Reasoning in Bioethics*, Bloomington, Indiana, Indiana University Press, 1997, especially chapters 4-7; Robert M Veatch, "Resolving Conflicts Among Principles: Ranking, Balancing and Specifying" (1995) 5 *Kennedy Institute of Ethics Journal* 199.

With few exceptions autonomy has been thought to trump other values even if it results in less than a best outcome. Consent as a central component in the relationship between practitioner, patient and proposed intervention is grounded on two features: one in ethics and one in law. The ethical importance of autonomy arises from respect for the independence of individuals. The legal importance is as a defence: having consent or the sincere reasonable belief that one has consent from a patient turns what would otherwise be criminal battery into a non-criminal action. Great emphasis is therefore placed on seeking and obtaining informed consent from patients before undertaking a procedure or implementing a care plan both for ethical and legal reasons.

Consent to be meaningful requires information, understanding and freedom to choose or refuse. Insufficient information, lack of understanding or coercion strips away the veneer of consent.

But autonomy and securing consent are problematic. Mental health, for example is rife with cases of superimposing the decision of others over a patient's sustained informed refusal to accept treatment. It is argued that although the refusal sounds like an exercise in autonomy it is flawed, coming from a person who because of his or her mental condition is not capable to decide on the matter. Here beneficence overrides apparent self-determination. After all, from an abstract perspective, doing good is what the healing arts are about.

Another problem with autonomy — even when restated by authors such as Childress as "respect for the principle of autonomy" — is that it is in sharp contrast with the ways in which people decide in fact much of the time. The "macho" individual model is at patent odds with reality, where decisions are often made as collective decisions or for reasons other than self-interest. These points are well discussed in feminist bioethics and the ethics of care where compassion and solidarity, ignored completely in Belmont models, play central parts.

(2)   *Beneficence and non-malfeasance*

These are two values that derive from Consequentialist approaches, focussing as they do on promoting good consequences and eliminating or limiting bad consequences. The earliest known professional health care oath, the Hippocratic Oath still recited today, opens with the declaration "First, do no harm." The Oath continues by declaring that "I will use my skills for the good of my patient." But while these are good precepts to adopt they can quickly lead to medical paternalism, trumping other values. Allowing paternalism to trump other factors compounds the vulnerability of the patient who is already in questionable health and not with equal knowledge. Medical paternalism disenfranchises the patient as a person and converts him or her to "a case" presenting certain conditions.

(3)   *Justice*

Issues of justice arise in health care. Access to resources and resource rationing are an example. Many readers will be able to identify circumstances where for instance there are fewer rooms available in facilities than patients who need them or where there are more people wanting an organ transplant than there are donated organs.

In health care, justice is about determining the most just distribution. Aristotle called this "distributive justice" and contrasted it with "corrective justice", which is akin to correcting a wrong. Aristotle's starting place for distributive justice is that like cases should be treated alike and different cases differently. Therefore, on a distributive justice account, two patients with the same condition at the same stage should be offered the same care and treated in the same way. Although this is helpful it is not definitive or exhaustive let alone easy to apply. Sometimes it is downright impossible, for example when there is only one organ available for transplant and two equally eligible potential recipients.

Even deciding which respects to consider as the relevant ones for decision-making precludes other respects. In most cases the least contentious respects surely are the clinical factors, assuming we can say what is and what is not, a clinical factor. Once clinical respects have been considered there remain all sorts of other factors that could be countenanced in reaching a decision on fair distribution.

In the early days of the use of "the iron lung" for kidney failure treatment, far more patients had chronic kidney disease than could be accommodated on iron lungs. Again in the US a committee was struck to determine priority eligibility. After some time it was noted that although unintended and subconscious in the decision making, the profile of those patients who got access to iron lungs was remarkably like that of the membership of the priority committee, namely white, male, young-to-middle-aged, educated, employed head of households. So we must recognise that there may be unintended predispositions or unrecognised assumptions working to bias the distribution patterns and the decision on what to take into consideration is contentious and policy laden.

Fair, equitable distribution does not tell us how far afield we should set the boundaries; should patients outside the immediate health authority be treated just like their counterparts within the catchment area? Problems abound, for example about whether living at a distance from a cancer centre should be addressed not by having patients travel but by creating lots more local centres. Nor does the bald statement of treating likes alike distinguish between different types of care. Should more health care resources — including money — be devoted to providing relief for life-style induced common problems like type 2 diabetes and obesity or should those resources go to treating inherited disorders like Duchennes? Should funding be directed towards neo-natal or end-of-life care?

With respect to cases that happen at the individual level (who gets the transplant organ, for example) similar policies are required. There are many different theories of distributive justice, including the following identified by Beauchamp and Childress:[14]

1. To each person an equal share.

2. To each person according to need.

3. To each person according to effort.

4. To each person according to contribution.

5. To each person according to merit.

6. To each person according to free-market exchange.

---

14   Tom L Beauchamp and James F Childress, *Principles of Biomedical Ethics*, (5th ed), New York, Oxford University Press, 2001, chapter 6, 228.

In response to challenges about how to make a distribution of limited health care services both reasonable and just, Norm Daniels et al have proposed a 4-point evaluative method. It is often referred to as "A4R", "Accounting for Reasonableness".[15] The goal is to ensure that everyone has "fair equal opportunity" (Daniels' expression) at benefiting from social resources to attain "ordinary species functioning". A reasonable and fair system of distribution requires

1.   Decisions made for relevant reasons (Relevance).

2.   An open, systematic decision process (Publicity).

3.   Decisions are reviewable (Revision).

4.   The system is enforceable either as a voluntary scheme or as a regulatory scheme (Enforcement).

Readers might want to think about how Daniels' A4R fits with each of the 6 versions of distributive justice outlined above.

20.2.7   The Ethics of Care

The focus on the Belmont Principles and on autonomy in particular has been significantly undermined more recently by arguments from feminist writers such as Sherwin,[16] and Gilligan[17] and by global collectivist writers such as Dwyer,[18] Chadwick, ten Have and others.[19] The feminist approaches are many and varied. One common theme is the rejection of models of society as just an aggregate of individuals; as self-standing, self-determining silos. People do not come in isolation from one another; they are situated in groups where concern for the wellbeing and welfare of others in the group and for the group as a whole is a non-deniable empirical, biological feature. The upshot is a restructured approach to the analysis and role of autonomy in decision-making in health care.

Sherwin, for example, sees the nexus of interrelated people as fundamental in producing a relativised concept of autonomy. In her view, autonomy is not one person's rational decision, but is a group decision reflecting the group's values and core concepts that make that group the group it is. She terms this "relational autonomy". Here we can clearly see how the "ethics of care" plays a key role. There is a strong ethnographic and cultural component that from a New Zealand perspective resonates well, for example with traditional Maori emphasis on the whanau and the iwi. One can even say that western thinking is beginning to catch on to an idea that has informed Maori identity and practice from time immemorial, although in fairness we should note that the same approaches in western thinking can be found in the eighteenth century writings of Hume.[20] The shift of

---

15   Norm Daniels and James Sabin, *Setting Limits Fairly*, New York, Oxford University Press, 2002, 45.

16   Susan Sherwin, "A Relational Approach to Autonomy in Health Care" in S Sherwin, F Baylis et al (eds), *The Politics of Women's Health: Exploring Agency and Autonomy*, Philadelphia, Temple University Press, 1998; S Sherwin, *No Longer Patient: Feminist Ethics and Health Care*, Philadelphia, Temple University Press, 1992.

17   Carol Gilligan, *In a Different Voice*, Cambridge, Massachusetts, Harvard University, 1982.

18   James Dwyer, "Global Health and Justice" (2005) 83 Bioethics 875

19   Ruth Chadwick, Henk ten Have and E Meslin (eds), *Health Care Ethics in an Era of Globalisation*, London, Sage Press, 2009.

20   David Hume, *Enquiry Concerning the Principles of Morals*, 1751.

focus from self to others has meant that formerly marginalised groups find advocates in many feminist positions.

20.2.8   Global Ethics

Without necessarily adopting a feminist perspective, writers such as Dwyer[21] have moved our thinking into global perspectives in health ethics. In these writers we find a dedication to consider the global impact and the biological commonalities that underlie health needs in the first place. There is an inverse ratio in health between economically rich countries and poor countries, between consumers and cheap suppliers of goods. The differential favours those in rich countries with kinds of health service that are easily accessed, and which reflect state of the art technology.

By contrast people in poorer countries experience worse conditions. For example illnesses associated with poverty and polluted living conditions lead to predictably shorter life expectancy and a lower level of well being. Transmittable diseases spread more easily and are more difficult to control because of lifestyle and social circumstances.

The horrendous scope and impact of AIDS in sub-Saharan African countries cries out for solution. Solution can only arise in a global willingness to act not because one knows and feels kinship with these particular people but because one can and should act. The ethical rationale is part of international justice (as distinct from local justice). This is mixed with political and economic arguments of undue enrichment of first world nations and impoverishment of countries that provide cheap labour and low cost goods for affluent consumer countries. At work here is the second Aristotelian account of justice, namely corrective justice, making up for a past wrong or correcting a wrong.

20.2.9   The Ethics Matrix

To help the reader understand how the different theories and approaches interact we will start with a chart of how the Belmont Principles relate in practice. The illustration below, the Ethics Matrix, is adapted from a schematic that Robert Veatch developed in his bioethics teaching. It consists of two horizontal rows and two vertical columns.

The top row captures the individual patient/health carer relationship. The bottom row captures the societal/system relationship. Personal consumer choice approaches and paternalism to individual health care tend to be reflected in the top row. Ethics of care, public health and solidarity approaches tend to be reflected in the bottom row.

The left column illustrates consequence-base approaches, the right column illustrates the deontological/rights based approaches. Patient and population outcomes tend to be reflected in the left column; patient preferences, patients as consumers and special interest group cultural or population considerations tend to be reflected in the right column.

What is not captured directly in the matrix is any virtue ethics approach. Possibly virtue approaches cannot be captured in such a schematic. This is because as Pellegrino says it refers to the character of the agent as a performer, not to the rationale for action or its consequences, virtue ethics is the link between the principles for action and the consequences. So a virtuous practitioner will always be one who considers the

---

21   James Dwyer, "Global Health and Justice" (2005) 83 *Bioethics* 875.

consequences, the preferences and the justice of any proposed course of action. In that sense the virtuous practitioner is not part of the matrix but may use the matrix as an aid to proper thinking and proper action.

The Ethics Matrix

	Consequentialist Principles (what are the likely effects)	**Duty-based Principles** (what are the duties)
INDIVIDUAL	**Hippocratic Utility** Beneficence/non-malfeasance (Patient's best interests, Medical Paternalism)	**Respect for Persons** Autonomy, Fidelity, Veracity (Patient's preferences)
SOCIAL	**Social Utility** Greatest happiness/greatest number (Public health programmes, preventive medicine)	**Justice** Fairness (Rare conditions, Special needs support services, Research)

20.3   Moral issues and problems

Talking about moral concepts and moral theories is all well and good, but it is vacuous if it is not applicable or not applied. So we turn now to ways in which health care practitioners can approach ethical issues that arise in the course of their work.

Possibly the biggest hurdle in health service ethics is getting the various parties to acknowledge the existence of ethical issues. The most important message to take from this chapter is the need for constant and conscientious monitoring of the entire situation. It requires constant awareness, consideration of, and attention to the circumstances. It also requires the same approach to different perceptions and different ways of life. A person should always be ready to ask, "Have I challenged my own values and beliefs? Are they consistent? Have I considered how others think and feel about this?" It is like learning to drive while constantly on the lookout for a child to run out from the footpath or for the drivers around you to behave erratically. In a phrase: heed others, challenge yourself.

One needs to recognise that different people subscribe to different moral theories, and sometimes switch from one theory to another. People may also act without reference to an overarching moral outlook. Various moral difficulties can arise in practice.

Problems may arise when someone is dogmatic in their approach. For example, they will use a cost-benefit analysis and fail to see that autonomy is an issue for others involved. Or a person may adhere so closely to a rule approach that they fail to see a different result would emerge from deviation from the rule — even if that same person believes a better result will arise from following rules. Or a person will hold another in such high regard that the flaw in the role model's proposed course of action will be overlooked. In these types of cases, the respective participants are blind to the existence of any moral conflict. For them, morality does not have a role in their decision-making.

A slightly different set of problems arise when a person recognises there might be an issue as far as others are concerned but is so convinced of their own position that contrary views are not considered. An example would be a practitioner who believes he knows the best interests of a sick child, and discounts the parents' wishes and beliefs. Readers are referred to the case of Liam Holloway (see 7.5.6) in which his parents took Liam into hiding rather than "surrender" him under a Court order so he might be "subjected to" or "treated with" (note the difference the vocabulary makes) further chemotherapy. This is more than a question of consent, which is addressed in chapter 7. In this chapter we are identifying the moral complexities, not just the legal complexities. Obviously, in practice, some decision will be made. It may not be the legally sanctioned one but the acknowledgement and recognition of the conflict of views are as important as the actual difference of views itself.

20.3.1   The Four Box Method

A useful tool that many multidisciplinary groups of health care providers find helpful when addressing particular clinical ethical issues is the "Four Box Method" — outlined below.[22] This helps us to think our way through issues about withdrawal of life sustaining interventions for particular patients or requests for a particular treatment. It does this by asking us to address and allocate specific salient items of information within four boxes that focus on different aspects of care planning for individual patients. Remember that a tool is only a tool; it must not take the place of communication and reflection or be thought of as an automatic decision procedure.

The four box method builds upon the recognition that even after reflection we can and do still disagree on which moral theory is ultimately correct. Yet even while acknowledging our uncertainties and philosophical disagreements we still agree that a health care decision has to be made. The alternative — not making a decision — is not morally neutral and is itself open to moral appraisal. Sheer practicality forces us to find a way through that will lead to a decision that we can agree is rational and ethical.

Four Box Method

MEDICAL INDICATIONS	PATIENT PREFERENCES
The Principles of Beneficence and Non-malfeasance	*The Principle of Respect for Autonomy*
What are the treatment options?	Is the patient competent?
	What would he/she want done?
	What is in his/her best interest?
QUALITY OF LIFE	**CONTEXTUAL FEATURES**
The Principles of Beneficence and Non- malfeasance and Respect for Autonomy	*The Principles of Loyalty and Fairness*
Prospects of survival with and without treatment?	How does this affect others: Family and Team?

22   Michael McDonald, Paddy Rodney and Rosalie Starzomski, *A Framework for Ethical Decision-Making: Version 6.0 Ethics Shareware* (adapted from A Jonsen, M Siegler and W Winslade, *Clinical Ethics* (3rd ed), New York, McGraw Hill, 1992). The McDonald Four Box Method is available online at www.ethics.ubc.ca.

Various effects on patient of treatment?	Cost to Central health system?
	Cultural/religious issues?
	Law and Policy?

Before we can use the Four Box Method as a tool we need a framework within which to work. There are five steps:

1.   Identify the issue(s).

2.   Specify feasible alternatives.

3.   Use ethical values and resources to evaluate alternatives.

4.   Propose and test possible solutions.

5.   Make the choice.

To understand better how the Four Box Method works it helps if we set it against the Ethics Matrix as a background schematic of the relationship among various moral theories. You need to recall the Ethics Matrix, above, and keep it in mind as we go through the Four Box Method approach to addressing clinical ethics dilemmas. Notice carefully that the boxes do not correspond exactly to the Ethics Matrix above. That is because we are turning our focus to application in a single case. In effect we are looking at an expanded version of the first row in the Ethics Matrix where we have built in the lessons from the Ethics of Care as social dynamic features in an individual's perspective. In other words, we have bolstered the patient-as-silo approach to include the significant others in the life of the patient.

Now, let us see how we can apply the Four Box Method to a real clinical care situation.

Some years ago there was public discussion about a well-loved toddler whose circumstances were heart-wrenching. We could give details because the circumstances were reported in the national press; details included the toddler's name, ethnicity and family circumstances but so as not to be too intrusive we will make some changes including the name. Bear in mind too that there would be strong feeling and lobbying by special interest groups and ethnic and cultural groups.

We will call this *TJ's story*.

Facts:

•   TJ is a 2 and a half-years -old, a boy who lives with mother and family in a warm and loving environment;

•   Hemophiliac — not recognized before birth;

•   Forceps delivery resulting in perinatal cerebral stroke;

•   Borehole to relieve pressure, partial paralysis;

•   Not expected by the clinical team to live but survives;

•   Pneumonia, second stroke at 1-year-old;

•   Not expected by the clinical team to live but again survives;

•   By age 2 and a half, TJ intensely dislikes doctors and hospitals;

•   Mum has heard that Factor VIII clotting agents form part of the treatment for hemophilia and wants Factor VIII clotting agents for TJ.

•   Doctors say "No, TJ isn't eligible."

- Mum fights through the media for TJ to get the intervention

Issues:

- Is it appropriate?
  - What would be?
- Is it ethical to (refuse to) administer a clotting agent?

Imagine yourself as involved in a clinical ethics consultation about TJ's care plan. How are we collectively to approach the resolution of the questions?

We start with Step 1 — Identifying the issue(s) and gathering the facts.

(1) *Step 1 — Identifying the issue(s) and gathering the facts*

We can begin by identifying some of the ways in which different people construe their common circumstances. First we need to marshall the facts, some of which are listed above. Assuming we have agreement at least on some of those facts, we now need to see how to apply ethical thinking to them. We will need to see how people construe those facts within their world views, their values and their goals for care. As we go along we will need to add other factual details and identify what significance people attach to them.

Now let us see what happens when we ask about Mum's reasons for seeking the clotting agents for TJ. The answer is straightforward: Mum wants to do what she can for TJ. She does not want TJ to bleed to death, so she wants what it will take instrumentally to stop bleeding. She wants the clotting agents for him because she believes it will help. When the doctors decline although they agree that clotting agents do stop bleeding, she hears it as saying that they think TJ's life isn't worth saving. She thinks they have moved from the clinical options box to the quality of life or justice box.

The doctors by contrast think that Mum has not listened to them when they say TJ is not eligible. They mean that as a matter of fact use of a clotting agent won't work given TJ's stroke history. It won't work not because clotting agents do not prevent bleeding but it won't work because blood clotting agents work only once spontaneous uncontrolled bleeding has started. That is, they are remedial, not preventive interventions. For TJ any uncontrolled bleeding would have already done the further damage to TJ's brain. So when they say TJ is not eligible, they mean the intervention can't work (instrumentally) for him. They mean the proposed course of action is instrumentally futile — bound to fail — not that TJ's life is worthless. So they construe Mum as not listening or refusing to accept an empirical truth. This can be seen to be a breakdown in communication, with Mum and clinicians not conversing on common ground. But more than that, even if both are conversing on common ground about matters of fact, we need to recognise the role of history: TJ has twice surprised medical people by surviving events they thought he would not survive. So compounding the communication failure, Mum does not think the doctors have got their facts right. They were wrong before, so why shouldn't they be wrong again?

In summary, if ethics is to help from the outset we must acknowledge that issue identification and even fact gathering and sorting are not value neutral. There may be contextual matters that a simple Consequentialist or Deontological theory is not sensitive to. We sometimes only recognise the divergence or the knowledge gaps when we try to fit our information into the four boxes. Learning that for one person a piece of information fits under clinical options while for another it fits under quality of life, sheds light on how to facilitate communication that will restructure the discussion.

The range of facts that will normally be covered include but are not necessarily limited to the following: presentation; diagnosis; prognosis; what the patient and/or supporting family have been told; what they have asked or indicated; what value sets and perspectives key people hold.

(2)   *Step 2 — Specifying the alternatives*

Once there is fairly broad consensus on the facts and where they fit, then it is possible to identify alternatives. Decision-makers need to take into account that the issues arose in most cases because there was no consensus. Someone is feeling moral distress that something wrong is about to happen or has happened. Depending on the fuller context this is often called moral distress or moral residue. Yet given the lack of unanimity people often realise they are all working towards a good outcome.

Here it might be that some of the decision-makers need to ask themselves whether they are so wedded to a particular value that they are unable to bend or cede on it. If they are inflexible then group deliberation is deadlocked and will be counterproductive. More often though, people come to see their values through a different lens when they see what effect their inflexibility would have on the lives and well-being of others. When this happens they accept the fact that although they do not like a proposed solution, they will address it as a matter of personal moral residue rather than as a matter of irresolvable moral distress.

To specify the alternatives we have to be able to say what the options are at each stage, what the likely outcomes would be for each and we need to identify levels of decision-making. Alternatives will be largely cause–effect approaches about what can be done. But even if they are right in principle they still might not be operable, not because someone has got a mistake in their reasoning but because some external factor, not under the control of the parties, makes it unrealistic. If the hospital, institution or health care system does not provide treatment X, it does not resolve the issue of what to do for TJ if the doctors and Mum agree that course of action X would be best for TJ. What would be best is ideal but not realistic in the circumstances.

(3)   *Step 3 — Use of ethical resources*

Here the decision-makers need to think about normative ethics such as utilitarian theories, respect for autonomy, the Belmont Principles and the ethics of care. A quick check-list survey of key concepts will help but may be incomplete. The list would include: beneficence, non-malfeasance, autonomy, justice, fidelity to trust, empathy.

In an actual consultation we should add to these some formal items covering official policy and law. While law and ethics are separate it is impossible fully to address a dilemma or a problem without considering both aspects. Examples of what might apply in any given circumstance include Codes of Ethics or Professional Conduct, Institutional Policies, applicable law and legal cases. These vary from profession to profession, place to place and time to time. It is therefore important that health practitioners try to keep current with items such as the Health and Disabilities Code, the nurses' and the doctors' Code of Ethics, Human Rights law and such like.

Sometimes codes of conduct of different professions conflict. This makes it especially important that decision-makers identify to themselves and others which, if any code, they are legally bound by. Then when legal obligations pull people in different directions, there needs to be an open acknowledgement that any ethical decision may nonetheless create legal difficulties for some of the people involved. This is a kind of distress experienced from time to time. It cannot be resolved by an algorithm or a framework. For some people it might be their stopping point, when as a result of what they see to be their moral duty or their legal obligation they are so conflicted they cannot participate further in the decision-making process. But recognising that there is a potential for legal tension and addressing it through consultation and seeking the help of one's professional mentors can ease the moral distress, even when it cannot remove it entirely.

(4)   *Step 4 — Proposing and testing possible alternatives*

The fourth step in applying the Four Box Method is to have the decision-makers state alternative solutions then consider what the impact of each might be on other people's ethical outlook and conduct. It requires the decision-makers to think through whether the proposed solution could be universalised for each of the alternatives proposed and whether it is something a good person would do. In other words this fourth step calls for clarification of possible solutions and examination of how they fit into the Ethics Matrix.

The testing can be done by a variety of means including investigating the experience elsewhere where the various alternatives have been adopted; reading literature case studies (paper cases) similar to the current situation or thinking hard and out loud about what the consequences might be.

Step 4 would be another opportunity for some introspection and reflection of one's own values. As mentioned above for step 2 one might find that what one had taken to be a firm principle or value with no exceptions is one that one had not previously probed so thoroughly as one is doing now and on reflection it is not as exceptionless as thought. This present situation makes one see there are exceptions, where none were expected, to one's expressed or internal value system.

The exceptions are acceptable because they fall under a different value that applies in the situation and that overrides in the circumstances. It might help if the reader thinks how we are prepared from time to time to disregard the refusal (autonomy) when the chances of maximising chances of survival with a fair prospect of an acceptable quality of life (doing good) will result. An example is a wounded person in an industrial accident who adamantly insists that he/she does not want a trapped, crushed limb removed yet whose survival depends on removing the limb. This example is strained, because it arises in an emergency setting where something like an ethics consultation is at best, an abbreviated telephone consultation, if it happens at all.

(5)   *Step 5 — Make a choice*

Clinical ethics must generate solutions. So the final step is that the decision-makers have to provide an operable answer.

20.4   Law and ethics

Much has been written on the relationship between law and ethics. It is never enough to stop at the level of finding out what the law says on any matter and doing that, whatever it is. That has been called the "Nazi defence" to the charges against medical professionals who performed or assisted in some of the outrageous activities in the 1930s and 40s. One can always say "That is the law", eg the compulsory sterilisation of communists — but is it a good law? That is to say the moral or ethical value is not exclusively and exhaustively determined by a statement of what the law is at any time. Remember, for example that hiding a runaway slave was a crime at a time when slave owning was allowed.

More recently the connection between law and codes of ethics was outlined in *Furniss v Fitchett*.[23] In that case a doctor disclosed details of a woman's mental condition for evidence in matrimonial proceedings in Court, under circumstances in which he ought to have known she would be physically harmed. The Court had to consider whether the ethical code was a relevant reference for determining a duty of care. The Chief Justice said:[24]

> "The British Medical Association's Code of Ethics is evidence of the general practitioner standards to which a reasonably careful, skilled and informed practitioner would conform. I think it was admissible for that purpose, and it, therefore, became necessary to decide whether the law, as distinct from the ethical code of the British Medical Association, permitted any departure from those standards."

Codes of ethics thus become not only ethical guides but, for the purposes of the law, standards by which "reasonably careful, skilled and informed" practice will be judged by the Courts, disciplinary bodies, and complaints units. Thus it will be up to the practitioner to provide a legally acceptable justification for any departure from the conduct required by a code of ethics.

20.5   Dealing with a decision-making dilemma

As discussed above, moral principles are not absolute rules — they guide one's actions rather than dictate them. They may conflict, for example the principle to maintain confidences and the principle to disclose information to prevent harm to others, giving rise to an ethical dilemma. This requires the weighing of values and determining which one will be given priority. The Four Box Method and its corollary five steps is a suggested guide.

It would not be enough to stop at this point. Resolving the issue does not mean everything is over and done with. Resolution of moral dilemmas often leaves people feeling morally uncomfortable. They may have been persuaded, more or less, that the best possible solution was found but they still feel as though they are not at peace with themselves over the matter. This is usually referred to as moral residue. What is required to address this moral residue is a respectful, empathetic, safe and caring environment where the individuals can voice their residual feelings and concerns in a manner where they will not feel belittled for their unease. It is helpful to remind oneself that unease is a healthy sign of moral sensitivity. Voicing and articulating the unease might lead to an overall heightened level of shared moral sensitivity. In itself that is a success.

---

23   *Furniss v Fitchett* [1958] NZLR 396.
24   *Furniss v Fitchett* [1958] NZLR 396, 405.

20.6   Conclusion

There are no perfect answers to these problems. Practicalities and politics may play a distorting role in decision-making and should be taken into account. Consequently, one cannot have an ethical programme that will solve all of the problems all of the time. However, all health practitioners need to develop a perception of themselves as principled practitioners who can be trusted to understand the legal, ethical, and social context in which they work. Discussion in an open and honest way on ethical issues affecting practice and standards of care should be encouraged, and all health practitioners should be comfortable about lobbying to change situations that are incompatible with good practice.

20.7   Further reading

T L Beauchamp and L Walters, *Contemporary Issues in Bioethics* (5th ed), Belmont, CA, Wadsworth, 1999.

Q Campbell, G Gillett, G Jones, *Medical Ethics* (3rd ed), Oxford, Oxford University Press, 2001.

M J Hanson and D Callahan, *The Goals of Medicine: The Forgotten Issues in Health Care Reform*, Hastings Center Studies in Ethics Series, Washington, Georgetown University Press, 1999.

D J Mason and J K Leavitt, *Policy and Politics in Nursing and Health Care* (3rd ed), Philadelphia, Saunders, 1998.

J K Mason, *Law and Medical Ethics* (7th ed), London, Butterworths, 2005.

O O'Neill, *Autonomy and Trust in Bioethics*, Cambridge University Press, 2002.

J Rachels, *The Elements of Moral Philosophy* (3rd ed), New York, McGraw-Hill College, 1999.

G Rumbold, *Ethics in Nursing Practice* (3rd ed), London, Harcourt Brace, 1999.

With the exception of Rachels' text, which is a general primer on moral philosophy, the above items are among many recent publications in bioethics and specialised nursing ethics texts. Any search of the web, by topic, author, or publishing house, will produce a lengthy current bibliography.

Appendix 1

ABBREVIATIONS OF LAW REPORTS

A guide to some abbreviations used in journal and law report citations.

A	Atlantic Reporter, first series: US commercial reporting service which covers State Supreme Court reports from the north-eastern States (1885-1938)
A 2d	Atlantic Reporter (US), second series (1938-present)
AC	Law Reports, Appeal Cases (England) (1891-present)
ACJ	Arbitration Court Judgments (New Zealand) (1978-1986)
ACTR	Australian Capital Territory Reports (1973-present)
ALJ	Australian Law Journal (1927-present)
ALJR	Australian Law Journal Reports (1958-present)
All ER	All England Law Reports (1936-present)
ALR	Australian Law Reports (1895-present)
AULR	Auckland University Law Review (New Zealand)
Aust Torts Reports	Australian Torts Reports (1984-present)
BCL	Butterworths Current Law (New Zealand)
Cal App 3d	California Appellate Reports (US), third series
Cal Rptr	Wests California Reporter (US) (1960-current
Ch	Law Reports, Chancery Division (England) (1891-present)
CHRR	Canadian Human Rights Reporter
CLR	Commonwealth Law Reports (Australia) (1903-present)
Co Rep	Cokes Reports (England) (1572-1616)
Cowp	Cowpers Reports (England), Kings Bench (1774-1778)
Cr App R	Criminal Appeal Reports (England) (1908-present)
CRNZ	Criminal Reports of New Zealand
DCR	District Court Reports (New Zealand)
DLR	Dominion Law Reports (Canada) (1912-1955)

ELB	Employment Law Bulletin (New Zealand)
EOC	Equal Opportunity Cases (Australia)
ER	English Reports (1220-1865)
ERNZ	Employment Reports of New Zealand
Ex D	Law Reports, Exchequer Division (England) (1875-1880)
Exch	Exchequer Reports (England) (1847-1856)
F	Federal Reporter (US) (1880-1924)
F 2d	Federal Reporter (US), second series (1924-present)
F & F	Foster and Finlaysons Reports (England) (1856-1867)
F Supp	Federal Supplement (US) (1932-present)
FLC	Australian Family Law Cases (1976-present)
FLR	Federal Law Reports (Australia) (1957-present)
	Family Law Reports (UK)
FRNZ	Family Reports of New Zealand
HLC	Clarks Reports, House of Lords (England) (1847-1866)
KB	Law Reports, Kings Bench Division (England) (1901-1952)
Ld Raym	Lord Raymonds Reports (England), Kings Bench and Common Pleas (1694-1732)
LJ Ch	Law Journal, Chancery (England) (1831-1946)
NE	North Eastern Reporter: US commercial reporting service which covers State Supreme Court reports from the north-eastern region (1885-1936)
NE 2d	North Eastern Reporter (US), second series (from 1936)
NJ	New Jersey Supreme Court Reports (US)
NSWLR	New South Wales Law Reports (Australia) (1971-present)
NW	North Western Reporter: US commercial reporting service which covers State Supreme Court reports from the north-western region (1879-1941)
NW 2d	North Western Reporter (US), second series (1941-present)
NYS 2d	New York Supplement, (US) second series (1938-present)
NZAR	New Zealand Administrative Reports (1976-present)
NZELC	New Zealand Employment Law Cases
NZFLR	New Zealand Family Law Reports (1981-present)

NZILR	New Zealand Intellectual Property Reports
NZLJ	New Zealand Law Journal (1925-present)
NZLR	New Zealand Law Reports (1883-present)
NZRL	New Zealand Recent Law
P	Law Reports, Probate, Divorce and Admiralty Division (England) (1891-1971)
	Pacific Reporter: US commercial reporting service which covers Supreme Court reports from the western seaboard States (1883-1931)
P 2d	Pacific Reporter (US), second series (1931-present)
PD	Law Reports, Probate, Divorce and Admiralty Division (England) (1875-1890)
PIQR	Personal Inquiries and Quantum Reports (England)
PRNZ	Procedure Reports of New Zealand (1983-present)
QB	Queens Bench Reports (England) (1841-1852, 1865-1875, 1891-1901, 1952-present)
QBD	Law Reports, Queens Bench Division (England) (1875-1890)
Qd R	Queensland Reports (1958-present)
QSR	Queensland State Reports (1902-1957)
SASR	South Australian State Reports (1921-present)
SC	Court of Session Cases (Scotland) (1907-present)
SCR	Supreme Court Reports (NSW) (1862-1876)
	Supreme Court Reports (Canada) (1876-present)
SE	South Eastern Reporter: US commercial reporting service which covers State Supreme Court Reports from the south-eastern region (1887-1939)
SLT	Scots Law Times (1893-present)
So 2d	Southern Reporter (US), second series (1941-present)
SR (NSW)	New South Wales State Reports (Australia) (1901-1970)
SR (WA)	State Reports, Western Australia (1980-present)
SW	South Western Reporter: US commercial reporting service which covers State Supreme Court reports from the south-western region (1886-1929)
SW 2d	South Western Reporter (US), second series (1928-present)
Tas LR	Tasmanian Law Reports (1905-1940)

Tas SR	Tasmanian State Reports (1941-1979
Tas R	Tasmanian Reports (1979-present)
TCL	The Capital Letter (New Zealand)
TLR	The Times Law Reports (England) (1884-1952)
	Tasmanian Law Reports (1905-1940)
VLR	Victorian Law Reports (Australia) (1875-1956)
VR	Victorian Reports (Australia) (1870-1872, 1957-present)
VUWLR	Victoria University of Wellington Law Review (1953-present)
WALR	West Australian Law Reports (1898-1959)
WAR	Western Australian Reports (1960-present)
WCR (NSW)	Workers Compensation Reports (New South Wales, Australia)
WLR	Weekly Law Reports (England) (1953-present)
WN (NSW)	Weekly Notes (New South Wales, Australia) (1884-1970)
WWR	Western Weekly Reports (Canada) (1971-present)

Health Information Privacy Code 1994 — Rule 11

Health Information Privacy Code 1994

Rule 11   Limits on Disclosure of Health Information

(1)   A health agency that holds health information must not disclose the information unless the agency believes, on reasonable grounds, that—

    (a)   the disclosure is to—

        (i)   the individual concerned; or

        (ii)   the individual's representative where the individual is dead or is unable to exercise his or her rights under these rules; or

    (b)   the disclosure is authorised by—

        (i)   the individual concerned; or

        (ii)   the individual's representative where the individual is dead or is unable to give his or her authority under this rule; or

    (c)   the disclosure of the information is one of the purposes in connection with which the information was obtained; or

    (d)   the source of the information is a publicly available publication; or

    (e)   the information is information in general terms concerning the presence, location, and condition and progress of the patient in a hospital, on the day on which the information is disclosed, and the disclosure is not contrary to the express request of the individual or his or her representative; or

    (f)   the information to be disclosed concerns only the fact of death and the disclosure is by a health practitioner or by a person authorised by a health agency, to a person nominated by the individual concerned, or the individual's representative, partner, spouse, principal caregiver, next of kin, whanau, close relative, or other person whom it is reasonable in the circumstances to inform; or

    (g)   the information to be disclosed concerns only the fact that an individual is to be, or has been, released from compulsory status under the Mental Health (Compulsory Assessment and Treatment) Act 1992 and the disclosure is to the individual's principal caregiver.

(2)   Compliance with subrule (1)(b) is not necessary if the health agency believes on reasonable grounds that it is either not desirable or not practicable to obtain authorisation from the individual concerned and that—

(a) the disclosure of the information is directly related to one of the purposes in connection with which the information was obtained; or

(b) the information is disclosed by a health practitioner to a person nominated by the individual concerned or to the principal caregiver or a near relative of the individual concerned in accordance with recognised professional practice and the disclosure is not contrary to the express request of the individual or his or her representative; or

(c) the information—

　(i) is to be used in a form in which the individual concerned is not identified; or

　(ii) is to be used for statistical purposes and will not be published in a form that could reasonably be expected to identify the individual concerned; or

　(iii) is to be used for research purposes (for which approval by an ethics committee, if required, has been given) and will not be published in a form that could reasonably be expected to identify the individual concerned; or

(d) the disclosure of the information is necessary to prevent or lessen a serious and imminent threat to—

　(i) public health or public safety; or

　(i) the life or health of the individual concerned or another individual; or

(e) the disclosure of the information is essential to facilitate the sale or other disposition of a business as a going concern; or

(f) the information to be disclosed briefly describes only the nature of injuries of an individual sustained in an accident and that individual's identity and the disclosure is—

　(i) by a person authorised by the person in charge of a hospital; or

　(ii) to a person authorised by the person in charge of a news medium—

for the purpose of publication or broadcast in connection with the news activities of that news medium and the disclosure is not contrary to the express request of the individual concerned or his or her representative; or

(g) the disclosure of the information—

　(i) is required for the purposes of identifying whether an individual is suitable to be involved in health education and so that individuals so identified may be able to be contacted to seek their authority in accordance with subrule (1)(b); and

　(ii) is by a person authorised by the health agency to a person authorised by a health training institution; or

(h)   the disclosure of the information is required—

    (i)   for the purpose of a professionally recognised accreditation of a health or disability service; or

    (ii)   for a professionally recognised external quality assurance programme; or

    (iii)   for risk management assessment and the disclosure is solely to a person engaged by the agency for the purpose of assessing the agency's risk—

and the information will not be published in a form which could reasonably be expected to identify any individual nor disclosed by the accreditation, quality assurance, or risk management organisation to third parties except as required by law; or

(i)   non-compliance is necessary—

    (i)   to avoid prejudice to the maintenance of the law by any public sector agency, including the prevention, detection, investigation, prosecution, and punishment of offences; or

    (ii)   for the conduct of proceedings before any court or tribunal (being proceedings that have been commenced or are reasonably in contemplation); or

(j)   the individual concerned is or is likely to become dependent upon a controlled drug, prescription medicine, or restricted medicine and the disclosure is by a health practitioner to a Medical Officer of Health for the purposes of section 20 of the Misuse of Drugs Act 1975 or section 49A of the Medicines Act 1981; or

(k)   the disclosure of the information is in accordance with an authority granted under section 54 of the Act.

(3)   Disclosure under subrule (2) is permitted only to the extent necessary for the particular purpose.

(4)   Where, under section 22F(1) of the Health Act 1956, the individual concerned or a representative of that individual requests the disclosure of health information to that individual or representative, a health agency—

(a)   must treat any request by that individual as if it were a health information privacy request made under rule 6; and

(b)   may refuse to disclose information to the representative if—

    (i)   the disclosure of the information would be contrary to the individual's interests; or

    (ii)   the agency has reasonable grounds for believing that the individual does not or would not wish the information to be disclosed; or

(iii)   there would be good grounds for withholding the information under Part 4 of the Act if the request had been made by the individual concerned.

(5)   This rule applies to health information about living or deceased persons obtained before or after the commencement of this code.

(6)   Despite subrule (5), a health agency is exempted from compliance with this rule in respect of health information about an identifiable deceased person who has been dead for not less than 20 years.

Note   Except as provided in subrule 11(6) nothing in this rule derogates from any provision in an enactment that authorises or requires information to be made available, prohibits or restricts the availability of health information, or regulates the manner in which health information may be obtained or made available: section 7 Privacy Act 1993. Note also that rule 11, unlike the other rules, applies not only to information about living individuals, but also about deceased persons: section 46(6) Privacy Act 1993.

Privacy Act 1993: Good Reasons for Refusing Access to Personal Information

Privacy Act 1993

1993 No 28

Contents

Part 4
Good reasons for refusing access to personal information

(s 27 to s 32)

27   Security, defence, international relations, etc

(1)   An agency may refuse to disclose any information requested pursuant to principle 6 if the disclosure of the information would be likely—

    (a)   To prejudice the security or defence of New Zealand or the international relations of the Government of New Zealand; or

    (b)   To prejudice the entrusting of information to the Government of New Zealand on a basis of confidence by—

        (i)   The government of any other country or any agency of such a government; or

        (ii)   Any international organisation; or

    (c)   To prejudice the maintenance of the law, including the prevention, investigation, and detection of offences, and the right to a fair trial; or

    (d)   To endanger the safety of any individual.

(2)   An agency may refuse to disclose any information requested pursuant to principle 6 if the disclosure of the information would be likely—

    (a)   To prejudice the security or defence of—

        (i)   The self-governing state of the Cook Islands; or

        (ii)   The self-governing state of Niue; or

        (iii)   Tokelau; or

(iv)   The Ross Dependency; or

(b)   To prejudice relations between any of the Governments of—

    (i)   New Zealand:

    (ii)   The self-governing state of the Cook Islands:

    (iii)   The self-governing state of Niue; or

(c)   To prejudice the international relations of the Governments of—

    (i)   The self-governing state of the Cook Islands; or

    (ii)   The self-governing state of Niue.

Compare: 1982 No 156 s 27(1)(a); 1987 No 8 s 4(2); 1987 No 174 s 26(1)(a)

28   Trade secrets

(1)   Subject to subsection (2) of this section, an agency may refuse to disclose any information requested pursuant to principle 6 if the withholding of the information is necessary to protect information where the making available of the information—

(a)   Would disclose a trade secret; or

(b)   Would be likely unreasonably to prejudice the commercial position of the person who supplied or who is the subject of the information.

(2)   Information may not be withheld under subsection (1) of this section if, in the circumstances of the particular case, the withholding of that information is outweighed by other considerations which render it desirable, in the public interest, to make the information available.

Compare: 1982 No 156 s 27(1)(a); 1987 No 8 s 4(2); 1987 No 174 s 26(1)(a)

29   Other reasons for refusal of requests

(1)   An agency may refuse to disclose any information requested pursuant to principle 6 if—

(a)   The disclosure of the information would involve the unwarranted disclosure of the affairs of another individual or of a deceased individual; or

(b)   The disclosure of the information or of information identifying the person who supplied it, being evaluative material, would breach an express or implied promise—

    (i)   Which was made to the person who supplied the information; and

    (ii)   Which was to the effect that the information or the identity of the person who supplied it or both would be held in confidence; or

(c)   After consultation undertaken (where practicable) by or on behalf of the agency with an individual's medical practitioner, the agency is satisfied that—

    (i)   The information relates to that individual; and

    (ii)   The disclosure of the information (being information that relates to the physical or mental health of the individual who requested it) would be likely to prejudice the physical or mental health of that individual; or

(d) In the case of an individual under the age of 16, the disclosure of that information would be contrary to that individual's interests; or

(e) The disclosure of that information (being information in respect of an individual who has been convicted of an offence or is or has been detained in custody) would be likely to prejudice the safe custody or the rehabilitation of that individual; or

(f) The disclosure of the information would breach legal professional privilege; or

(g) In the case of a request made to [Radio New Zealand Limited or] Television New Zealand Limited, the disclosure of the information would be likely to reveal the source of information of a bona fide news media journalist and either—

(i) The information is subject to an obligation of confidence; or

(ii) The disclosure of the information would be likely to prejudice the supply of similar information, or information from the same source; or

(h) The disclosure of the information, being information contained in material placed in any library or museum or archive, would breach a condition subject to which that material was so placed; or

(i) The disclosure of the information would constitute contempt of Court or of the House of Representatives; or

[(ia) the request is made by a defendant or a defendant's agent and is—

(i) for information that could be sought by the defendant under the Criminal Disclosure Act 2008; or

(ii) for information that could be sought by the defendant under that Act and that has been disclosed to, or withheld from, the defendant under that Act; or]

(j) The request is frivolous or vexatious, or the information requested is trivial.

(2) An agency may refuse a request made pursuant to principle 6 if—

(a) The information requested is not readily retrievable; or

(b) The information requested does not exist or cannot be found; or

(c) The information requested is not held by the agency and the person dealing with the request has no grounds for believing that the information is either—

(i) Held by another agency; or

(ii) Connected more closely with the functions or activities of another agency.

(3)   For the purposes of subsection (1)(b) of this section, the term **evaluative material** means evaluative or opinion material compiled solely—

    (a)   For the purpose of determining the suitability, eligibility, or qualifications of the individual to whom the material relates—

        (i)   For employment or for appointment to office; or

        (ii)   For promotion in employment or office or for continuance in employment or office; or

        (iii)   For removal from employment or office; or

        (iv)   For the awarding of contracts, awards, scholarships, honours, or other benefits; or

    (b)   For the purpose of determining whether any contract, award, scholarship, honour, or benefit should be continued, modified, or cancelled; or

    (c)   For the purpose of deciding whether to insure any individual or property or to continue or renew the insurance of any individual or property.

[(4)   In subsection (1)(c), **medical practitioner** means a health practitioner who is, or is deemed to be, registered with the Medical Council of New Zealand continued by section 114(1)(a) of the Health Practitioners Competence Assurance Act 2003 as a practitioner of the profession of medicine.]

Compare: 1982 No 156 ss 18(c)(ii), (e), (g), (h), 27(1)(b) to (h), (2); 1987 No 8 s 15(1); 1987 No 174 ss 17(c)(ii), (e), (g), (h), 26(1)(b) to (h), (2)

History

Subsection (1)(g) was amended, as from 1 December 1995, by s 20 Radio New Zealand Act 1995 (1995 No 52) by substituting the words "Radio New Zealand Limited, The Radio Company Limited, or" for the words "Radio New Zealand Limited or". See reg 2 Radio New Zealand Act Commencement Order 1995 (SR 1995/226).

Subsection (1)(g) was further amended, as from 5 July 1996, by s 2 Radio New Zealand Act (No 2) 1995 (1995 No 53) by substituting the words "Radio New Zealand Limited or" for the words "Radio New Zealand Limited, The Radio Company Limited, or". See cl 2 Radio New Zealand Act (No 2) Commencement Order 1996 (SR 1996/182).

Subsection (1)(ia) was inserted, as from 29 June 2009, by s 39(1) Criminal Disclosure Act 2008 (2008 No 38). See ss 41 and 42 of that Act for the transitional and savings provisions. See cl 2 Criminal Disclosure Act Commencement Order 2009 (SR 2009/130).

Subsection (4) was inserted, as from 18 September 2004, by s 175(1) Health Practitioners Competence Assurance Act 2003 (2003 No 48). See ss 178 to 227 of that Act as to the transitional provisions.

30   Refusal not permitted for any other reason

Subject to sections 7, 31, and 32 of this Act, no reasons other than one or more of the reasons set out in sections 27 to 29 of this Act justifies a refusal to disclose any information requested pursuant to principle 6.

Compare: 1982 No 156 s 27(1A); 1987 No 8 s 15(2); 1987 No 174 s 26(2)

31   Restriction where person sentenced to imprisonment (*Repealed*)

History

Section 31 was repealed, as from 29 June 2009, by s 39(2) Criminal Disclosure Act 2008 (2008 No 38). See ss 41 and 42 of that Act for the transitional and savings provisions. See cl 2 Criminal Disclosure Act Commencement Order 2009 (SR 2009/130).

32   Information concerning existence of certain information

Where a request made pursuant to principle 6 relates to information to which section 27 or section 28 of this Act applies, or would, if it existed, apply, the agency dealing with the request may, if it is satisfied that the interest protected by section 27 or section 28 of this Act would be likely to be prejudiced by the disclosure of the existence or non-existence of such information, give notice in writing to the applicant that it neither confirms nor denies the existence or non-existence of that information.

Compare: 1982 No 156 s 10; 1987 No 8 s 4(2); 1987 No 174 s 8

Appendix 4

CODE OF HEALTH AND DISABILITY SERVICES CONSUMERS' RIGHTS

Contents

REGULATIONS

Code of Health and Disability Services Consumers' Rights
(cl 1 to cl 6)

1   Consumers have rights and providers have duties

(1)   Every consumer has the rights in this Code.

(2)   Every provider is subject to the duties in this Code.

(3)   Every provider must take action to—

(a)   Inform consumers of their rights; and

(b)   Enable consumers to exercise their rights.

2   Rights of consumers and duties of providers

The rights of consumers and the duties of providers under this Code are as follows:

Right 1 Right to be Treated with Respect

(1)   Every consumer has the right to be treated with respect.

(2)   Every consumer has the right to have his or her privacy respected.

(3)   Every consumer has the right to be provided with services that take into account the needs, values, and beliefs of different cultural, religious, social, and ethnic groups, including the needs, values, and beliefs of Maori.

Right 2 Right to Freedom from Discrimination, Coercion, Harassment, and Exploitation

Every consumer has the right to be free from discrimination, coercion, harassment, and sexual, financial, or other exploitation.

Right 3 Right to Dignity and Independence

Every consumer has the right to have services provided in a manner that respects the dignity and independence of the individual.

Right 4 Right to Services of An Appropriate Standard

(1)   Every consumer has the right to have services provided with reasonable care and skill.

(2)   Every consumer has the right to have services provided that comply with legal, professional, ethical, and other relevant standards.

(3)   Every consumer has the right to have services provided in a manner consistent with his or her needs.

(4)   Every consumer has the right to have services provided in a manner that minimises the potential harm to, and optimises the quality of life of, that consumer.

(5)   Every consumer has the right to co-operation among providers to ensure quality and continuity of services.

Right 5 Right to Effective Communication

(1)   Every consumer has the right to effective communication in a form, language, and manner that enables the consumer to understand the information provided. Where necessary and reasonably practicable, this includes the right to a competent interpreter.

(2)   Every consumer has the right to an environment that enables both consumer and provider to communicate openly, honestly, and effectively.

Right 6 Right to be Fully Informed

(1)   Every consumer has the right to the information that a reasonable consumer, in that consumer's circumstances, would expect to receive, including—

(a)   An explanation of his or her condition; and

(b)   An explanation of the options available, including an assessment of the expected risks, side effects, benefits, and costs of each option; and

(c)   Advice of the estimated time within which the services will be provided; and

(d)   Notification of any proposed participation in teaching or research, including whether the research requires and has received ethical approval; and

(e)   Any other information required by legal, professional, ethical, and other relevant standards; and

(f)   The results of tests; and

(g)   The results of procedures.

(2)   Before making a choice or giving consent, every consumer has the right to the information that a reasonable consumer, in that consumer's circumstances, needs to make an informed choice or give informed consent.

(3)   Every consumer has the right to honest and accurate answers to questions relating to services, including questions about—

(a)   The identity and qualifications of the provider; and

(b)   The recommendation of the provider; and

(c)   How to obtain an opinion from another provider; and

(d)   The results of research.

(4)   Every consumer has the right to receive, on request, a written summary of information provided.

Right 7 Right to Make An Informed Choice and Give Informed Consent

(1)   Services may be provided to a consumer only if that consumer makes an informed choice and gives informed consent, except where any enactment, or the common law, or any other provision of this Code provides otherwise.

(2)   Every consumer must be presumed competent to make an informed choice and give informed consent, unless there are reasonable grounds for believing that the consumer is not competent.

(3)   Where a consumer has diminished competence, that consumer retains the right to make informed choices and give informed consent, to the extent appropriate to his or her level of competence.

(4)   Where a consumer is not competent to make an informed choice and give informed consent, and no person entitled to consent on behalf of the consumer is available, the provider may provide services where—

(a)   It is in the best interests of the consumer; and

(b)   Reasonable steps have been taken to ascertain the views of the consumer; and

(c)   Either,—

(i)   If the consumer's views have been ascertained, and having regard to those views, the provider believes, on reasonable grounds, that the provision of the services is consistent with the informed choice the consumer would make if he or she were competent; or

(ii)   If the consumer's views have not been ascertained, the provider takes into account the views of other suitable persons who are interested in the welfare of the consumer and available to advise the provider.

(5)   Every consumer may use an advance directive in accordance with the common law.

(6)   Where informed consent to a health care procedure is required, it must be in writing if—

(a)   The consumer is to participate in any research; or

(b)   The procedure is experimental; or

(c)   The consumer will be under general anaesthetic; or

(d)   There is a significant risk of adverse effects on the consumer.

(7)   Every consumer has the right to refuse services and to withdraw consent to services.

(8)   Every consumer has the right to express a preference as to who will provide services and have that preference met where practicable.

(9)   Every consumer has the right to make a decision about the return or disposal of any body parts or bodily substances removed or obtained in the course of a health care procedure.

[(10)   No body part or bodily substance removed or obtained in the course of a health care procedure may be stored, preserved, or used otherwise than—

    (a)   with the informed consent of the consumer; or

    (b)   for the purposes of research that has received the approval of an ethics committee; or

    (c)   for the purposes of 1 or more of the following activities, being activities that are each undertaken to assure or improve the quality of services:—

        (i)   a professionally recognised quality assurance programme:

        (ii)   an external audit of services:

        (iii)   an external evaluation of services.]

Right 8 Right to Support

Every consumer has the right to have one or more support persons of his or her choice present, except where safety may be compromised or another consumer's rights may be unreasonably infringed.

Right 9 Rights in respect of Teaching or Research

The rights in this Code extend to those occasions when a consumer is participating in, or it is proposed that a consumer participate in, teaching or research.

Right 10 Right to Complain

(1)   Every consumer has the right to complain about a provider in any form appropriate to the consumer.

(2)   Every consumer may make a complaint to—

    (a)   The individual or individuals who provided the services complained of; and

    (b)   Any person authorised to receive complaints about that provider; and

    (c)   Any other appropriate person, including—

        (i)   An independent advocate provided under the Health and Disability Commissioner Act 1994; and

        (ii)   The Health and Disability Commissioner.

(3)   Every provider must facilitate the fair, simple, speedy, and efficient resolution of complaints.

(4)   Every provider must inform a consumer about progress on the consumer's complaint at intervals of not more than 1 month.

(5)   Every provider must comply with all the other relevant rights in this Code when dealing with complaints.

(6)   Every provider, unless an employee of a provider, must have a complaints procedure that ensures that—

    (a)   The complaint is acknowledged in writing within 5 working days of receipt, unless it has been resolved to the satisfaction of the consumer within that period; and

    (b)   The consumer is informed of any relevant internal and external complaints procedures, including the availability of—

        (i)   Independent advocates provided under the Health and Disability Commissioner Act 1994; and

        (ii)   The Health and Disability Commissioner; and

    (c)   The consumer's complaint and the actions of the provider regarding that complaint are documented; and

    (d)   The consumer receives all information held by the provider that is or may be relevant to the complaint.

(7)   Within 10 working days of giving written acknowledgement of a complaint, the provider must,—

    (a)   Decide whether the provider—

        (i)   Accepts that the complaint is justified; or

        (ii)   Does not accept that the complaint is justified; or

    (b)   If it decides that more time is needed to investigate the complaint,—

        (i)   Determine how much additional time is needed; and

        (ii)   If that additional time is more than 20 working days, inform the consumer of that determination and of the reasons for it.

(8)   As soon as practicable after a provider decides whether or not it accepts that a complaint is justified, the provider must inform the consumer of—

    (a)   The reasons for the decision; and

    (b)   Any actions the provider proposes to take; and

    (c)   Any appeal procedure the provider has in place.

History

Right 7: subclause (10) was substituted, as from 10 June 2004, by reg 3(1) Health and Disability Commissioner (Code of Health and Disability Services Consumers' Rights) Amendment Regulations 2004 (SR 2004/116).

3   Provider compliance

(1)   A provider is not in breach of this Code if the provider has taken reasonable actions in the circumstances to give effect to the rights, and comply with the duties, in this Code.

(2)   The onus is on the provider to prove that it took reasonable actions.

(3)   For the purposes of this clause, **the circumstances** means all the relevant circumstances, including the consumer's clinical circumstances and the provider's resource constraints.

4   Definitions

In this Code, unless the context otherwise requires,—

Advance directive means a written or oral directive—

(a)   By which a consumer makes a choice about a possible future health care procedure; and

(b)   That is intended to be effective only when he or she is not competent:

Choice means a decision—

(a)   To receive services:

(b)   To refuse services:

(c)   To withdraw consent to services:

Consumer means a health consumer or a disability services consumer; and, for the purposes of rights 5, 6, 7(1), 7(7) to 7(10), and 10, includes a person entitled to give consent on behalf of that consumer:

Discrimination means discrimination that is unlawful by virtue of Part 2 of the Human Rights Act 1993:

Duties includes duties and obligations corresponding to the rights in this Code:

[ethics committee means an ethics committee—

(a)   established by, or appointed under, an enactment; or

(b)   approved by the Director-General of Health]

History

"ethics committee": this definition was inserted, as from 10 May 2004, by reg 3(2) Health and Disability Commissioner (Code of Health and Disability Services Consumers' Rights) Amendment Regulations 2004 (SR 2004/116).

Exploitation includes any abuse of a position of trust, breach of a fiduciary duty, or exercise of undue influence:

Optimise the quality of life means to take a holistic view of the needs of the consumer in order to achieve the best possible outcome in the circumstances:

Privacy means all matters of privacy in respect of a consumer, other than matters of privacy that may be the subject of a complaint under Part 7 or Part 8 of the Privacy Act 1993 or matters to which Part 10 of that Act relates:

Provider means a health care provider or a disability services provider:

Research means health research or disability research:

Rights includes rights corresponding to the duties in this Code:

Services means health services, or disability services, or both; and includes health care procedures:

Teaching includes training of providers.

5   Other enactments

Nothing in this Code requires a provider to act in breach of any duty or obligation imposed by any enactment or prevents a provider doing an act authorised by any enactment.

6   Other rights not affected

An existing right is not overridden or restricted simply because the right is not included in this Code or is included only in part.

TABLE OF STATUTES AND REGULATIONS

Abbreviations

D

E

N

O

TABLE OF CASES

Abbreviations

INDEX

Abbreviations

A

D

E

I

M

N

O

P

R

U

V

W

Y